DATE DUE

MAY 1 3 1993	
NOV 1 3 1994	
NOV 2 7 1994	
DEC 1 1 1994	

BRODART, INC.   Cat. No. 23-221

Bureaucrats and Beggars

The Marriage. Royal Beauvais tapestry. Cartoon attributed to François Casanova after sketches by Jean-Honoré Fragonard. The tapestry depicts the marriage of Antoinette, oldest daughter of Louis-Bénigne-François Bertier de Sauvigny, to the marquis de la Bourdonnaye de Blossac in 1782. Note the giving of manual alms to the beggar at the bottom of the stairs. Courtesy of the Cincinnati Art Museum, Gift of John J. Emery.

Bureaucrats and Beggars

French Social Policy
in the Age of the Enlightenment

THOMAS McSTAY ADAMS

New York   Oxford
OXFORD UNIVERSITY PRESS
1990

Oxford University Press

Oxford   New York   Toronto
Delhi   Bombay   Calcutta   Madras   Karachi
Petaling Jaya   Singapore   Hong Kong   Tokyo
Nairobi   Dar es Salaam   Cape Town
Melbourne   Auckland

and associated companies in
Berlin   Ibadan

Copyright © 1990 by Oxford University Press, Inc.

Published by Oxford University Press, Inc.,
200 Madison Avenue, New York, New York 10016

Oxford is a registered trademark of Oxford University Press

Library of Congress Cataloging-in-Publication Data
Adams, Thomas McStay.
Bureaucrats and beggars: French social policy in the Age of the
Enlightenment/ Thomas McStay Adams.
p. cm.   Bibliography: p.   Includes index.
ISBN 0-19-505168-8
1. Beggars—Government policy—France—History—18th century.
2. Almshouses—France—History—18th century.   I. Title.
HV4554.A33   1990
362.5'85'094409034—dc20   89-8819   CIP

2 4 6 8 9 7 5 3 1

Printed in the United States of America
on acid-free paper

To my mother and to the

memory of my father

Preface

This book began as an exploration of the social history of the French Enlightenment, as a study of that matrix of experience that nourished the eighteenth-century ambition to create a science of society. A Henry Vilas grant from the University of Wisconsin encouraged me to pursue this line of inquiry in French libraries and archives in the summer of 1968. There I came upon a rich source of social reflection in the policy debates and memoirs of Turgot's commission on mendicity (1774–1775). These debates pointed to an intriguing domain of administrative experience: the *dépôts de mendicité* where beggars were detained under the authority of royal intendants after arrest by the royal mounted police, the *maréchaussée*. The *dépôts* constituted a deliberate experiment in social policy, launched by royal fiat in the heyday of Physiocracy (1764–1767), only to become the target of intense criticism from a provincial elite.

A Fulbright Advanced Teaching Fellowship to the University of Nantes in 1969–1970 provided support for the initial project of relating Turgot's policy to the preceding experiments with the *dépôts*. After completing a dissertation on the subject for the University of Wisconsin in 1972, I extended my research, aided by a Younger Humanist Fellowship from the National Endowment for the Humanities in 1974. Some of the results of this research were presented in papers and articles.

The book that follows ranges over the history of the *dépôts de mendicité* from 1764 to the Revolution without claiming to exhaust the archives of a bureaucracy that accumulated correspondence in thirty-two *intendances* over three decades. Nonetheless, the comprehensive view taken here should obviate the most common errors that occur when a single institution in a larger network is studied in isolation. While sorting through directives from different archives, I found it relatively simple to distinguish the general circulars from the specific responses to local problems, and to identify real innovations amid the clutter of exhortation and self-advertisement.

If I can persuade the specialist that my subject is not too broad, I also hope to assure the reader in search of broader themes that this subject brings together in a single framework many of the most significant and fascinating problems of eighteenth-century history. Three themes especially deserve mention.

First, one of the commonplaces of eighteenth-century social policy debate was that the government "should not make men poor." Instead of assuming that the problem of low productivity could be solved by disciplining lazy workers, critics began to hold government responsible for correcting the conditions that failed to provide employment for willing workers or to guarantee their subsistence when employed. This line of reasoning obviously suggested a deterministic view of delinquent behavior and crime. More important, however, it provided a theoretical justification for treating economic, social, and criminal phenomena as an interlocking system to be observed empirically.

Second, the *dépôts* provided a clinical vantage point for the pursuit of new professional and scientific standards in the fields of public health and hygiene, just at the critical moment when the concept that medicine was to serve as a *science politique* took root and flourished. In the *dépôts,* medicine translated the scandal of inhumane treatment into systematic rules of observation and measurement, dissolving the moral hierarchy that originally determined the standards of inmates' treatment. Clinical observation in the *dépôts* gave urgency to policies that would improve the nutrition and sanitary condition of the common peasant and laborer.

Third, the demand that inmates be returned to society "better" than when they entered the *dépôts* forced an examination of old and new anthropological verities. While a form of behavior modification seemed to displace an older moralism, another development was at least as important: the emergence of a new civic credo that began to assert itself in discussion of how the alienated passions of the idler should be tamed. Amid discussion of techniques of correction, a new conviction took hold: that formerly abject victims could be transformed into autonomous citizens by a careful preservation of "the appearance of liberty."

These key developments in the history of the *dépôts* were embedded in a transformation of social values that has profoundly influenced the modern world. Eighteenth-century critics demanded that government intervene less in the decisions of each individual, while assigning to it an ever more inclusive responsibility for the well-being of all citizens. The state was expected to maintain a scrupulous respect for the rights of the citizen, while becoming a more effective educator and therapist of dependents and delinquents. It is hoped that this study will add to the understanding of contemporary social policy in connection with the past by presenting the eighteenth century as a period in which such issues were wrestled with as problems requiring not only good will but constant observation, thought, and adaptation.

I should like to acknowledge the generosity and thoughtfulness of fellow historians, librarians, and archivists who have discussed my research with me. None of the faults the reader may find in this book are theirs.

I owe much to my teachers at the University of Wisconsin: Henry B. Hill, whose seminar on the French Revolution spanned the decades before and after; John T. O'Connor, who promoted a broad cultural perspective on the early modern period; the late Harvey Goldberg, who shared his passion for working-class history with all who heard him; the late Hélène Monod-Cassidy, whose offerings on eighteenth-century French literature brought an age to life; and above all Edward

T. Gargan, who at every stage of my work shared his far-ranging knowledge and served as an enthusiastic, unstinting critic.

My dissertation research benefited from conversation with scholars whose interests touched on eighteenth-century social policy: Darline Levy, Steven Kaplan, Jeffry Kaplow, Philip Dawson, Robert Darnton, Keith Baker, and Bernard Lecuyer. I received generous advice on my research plans from the late Robert Mandrou of the University of Paris at Nanterre. Father Guillaume de Bertier de Sauvigny introduced me to the study of his ancestor, the last intendant of Paris; Yves Durand welcomed me as an auditor in his seminar on the Old Regime at Nantes; Jacques Depauw was most helpful, as were all my hosts at the Faculté des Lettres at Nantes. At Rennes, Jean Meyer and Roger Dupuy shared their Armorican expertise with me.

Of the many colleagues who have since influenced my work, I would especially like to acknowledge Louis Greenbaum, whose prodigious research on the reform of hospitals under the Old Regime broadened my perspective on institutional history, and Jean-Pierre Goubert, who spurred my efforts to understand the social history of medicine and public health. Olwen Hufton obligingly shared proofs of a key chapter of her work in press and offered research suggestions. Pierre Goubert gave me a stimulating forum for my work in progress at a meeting of his seminar in 1974.

I would also like to acknowledge others with whom I have discussed my work: Mary B. Anglim, Erica-Marie Bénabou, Serge Chassagne, André Corvisier, Cissie Fairchilds, Robert Forster, Toby Gelfand, Édouard Guéguen, Roger Hahn, Carolyn Hannaway, Henri Lozach'meur, Kathryn Norberg, Harold T. Parker, Jean-Claude Perrot, Jeremy Popkin, Ambrose Saricks, Donald Schier, Robert Schwartz, Howard Solomon, Jean-Pierre Surreault, Charles Warner, and Dora Weiner.

Archivists and librarians deserve a special bouquet. Staffs of the Archives Départementales made their resources available, responded to inquiries, and mailed cases of documents to the Archives of the Loire-Inférieure and to the Archives Nationales, where my loan requests were always handled promptly. I remember well the hospitable reception in many *salles de travail*—at Nantes, Rennes, Tours, Rouen, Caen, Besançon, and Laon, and in the libraries of Paris, especially the Bibliothèque de l'Assistance Publique à Paris, where Marcel Candille made available rare bibliographical guides and current memoirs and theses as well as eighteenth-century sources. I must also register my admiration for the patience and expertise of the staffs of the Bibliothèque Nationale and of the Archives Nationales, and to thank M. Marcel Baudot in particular.

The U.S. interlibrary loan network has served me well. I am grateful to the librarians of the University of Wisconsin, the University of Kansas, Ottawa University (Kansas), the University of Kentucky, and Transylvania University. Kenneth Carpenter kindly made special arrangements for my work at the Kress Library of Business and Economics at the Harvard Business School. Ronald Averyt and Hal Germer at Ottawa University helped me obtain a grant for research materials from the Kansas City Regional Council on Higher Education. Colleen Karimi typed some revisions at a crucial stage, by arrangement with Charles Holmes at Transylvania University. The librarian of the National Endowment for the Humanities, Enayet

Rahin, and the social science reference librarian of the University of Wisconsin, Erwin Welsch, kindly located a rare pamphlet needed at the last moment.

Nancy Lane at Oxford University Press has patiently encouraged my efforts to ready this book for publication. In its final stages, the manuscript benefited from the careful scrutiny of her associates, Marion Osmun and Henry Krawitz, and the copy editing of Clifford Browder.

I owe a special debt to my family: to my wife, Peggy, who has supported my work from first jottings to final page proofs in uncounted ways; to Sarah, Anne, and Jonathan, who have grown up with it; and to their grandparents, Frances and Wes, Ceil and Vin. I regret that my father, who never wanted to miss anything, died too soon to see these pages set in handsome type.

Arlington, Va.   T. M. A.
April 1990

A note on French monetary units: The standard unit of account, the *livre*, was equal to twenty *sous*. The *sou*, in turn, was equal to twelve *deniers*. The nomenclature corresponded to the Latin terms *libra*, *solidus*, and *denanus* (like the traditional English £.s.d.), and the *sou* was commonly written *sol*. The terms *sol* and *sous* are used interchangeably in the text. The French symbol for the *livre* was "$\#$". In this book amounts are presented in the form: 25 l. 3s. 4d.

Contents

Bureaucrats and Beggars

LOCATION OF DÉPÔTS DE MENDICITÉ BY INTENDANCE (1767–1789)

⊕ DÉPÔT AT SEAT OF INTENDANCE BOTH IN 1774 AND 1789.

★ DÉPÔT AT SEAT OF INTENDANCE IN 1774 BUT NOT IN 1789.

☆ DÉPÔT AT SEAT OF INTENDANCE CLOSED PRIOR TO 1774 (DATE OF CLOSING IN PARENTHESIS), AND OPEN IN 1789.

● DÉPÔT ESTABLISHED IN TOWN OTHER THAN SEAT OF INTENDANCE BUT CLOSED PRIOR TO 1789.

YEAR OF CLOSING DISPLAYED IF CLOSING OCCURRED PRIOR TO FEBRUARY 1774.

○ DÉPÔT IN TOWN OTHER THAN SEAT OF INTENDANCE, IN OPERATION IN 1774 AND 1789.

◉ DÉPÔT AT ENSISHEIM CLOSED DOWN IN 1774 BUT OPEN AGAIN IN 1789.

▲ DÉPÔT AT PAU IN 1774 AND AGAIN IN 1789. NOTE: PAU BECAME THE SEAT OF AN INTENDANCE IN 1784.

☐ SYMBOLS ENCLOSED IN SQUARES INDICATE DEPOTS THAT TURGOT PLANNED TO RETAIN (1776).

↘ ADMINISTRATIVELY LINKED.

NOTE: BOUNDARIES OF INTENDANCES ARE THOSE OF 1789.

Introduction

Sieur Vieuloup was an officer of the royal constabulary— a *cavalier de la maré-chaussée*—in a brigade headquartered at Rennes, the capital of France's western-most province of Brittany. With his wife, who sold tobacco, he lived over a shop in the Rue Vasselot, adjoining the Place de Toussaints and its bustling marketplace. The surrounding parish of Toussaints was a dreary, low-lying quarter subject to flooding by the meandering streams of the river Vilaine. It was one of the two parishes in which the poor of Rennes were most densely concentrated. A few of Vieuloup's neighbors were well-to-do merchants or judicial officials connected with the parlement of Brittany or other courts, but the majority were poorer than he. In the year 1777 Vieuloup and his wife paid a little more than the minimum assess-ment for the royal head tax, or capitation, contributing four livres.[1]

On a day early in September 1777, Vieuloup was patrolling the market square a few steps from his home, accompanied by the *cavalier* Pelicot. Whether he had chosen his prey deliberately or merely happened upon three men begging, Vieuloup apprehended Nicolas le Coz, Julien Buquet, and Guillaume Vary, none of whom could give a local address. After further questioning, he put all three under arrest, led them to the royal prisons, booked them, and wrote out the answers that they had given to his questions.[2]

On September 13 the three appeared before the provost of the *maréchaussée* for cross-examination, a procedure duly recorded by the provost's *greffier*. The royal prosecutor then reviewed the transcript together with the record of arrests and the prison register, countersigned the cross-examination, and formally ordered that the beggars be taken from the prisons "to the *maison de force* located at the *dépôt des mendiants,* situated in the Rue Saint Hélier, to be detained there until otherwise ordered." The building in question was a former seminary, converted for use as a jail and workhouse for beggars in 1771. It was located a few hundred yards from Vieuloup's residence, just outside the St. Hélier gate on the east side of the parish of Toussaints, facing a group of hovels that constituted the infamous Quartier de la Gripe and adjoining the St. Hélier mill on the Vilaine. Finally, Vieuloup conducted the prisoners to the concierge, or warden, of the *dépôt,* who in turn gave him a receipt for the prisoners and their papers. The prisoners' fate thereafter would be at

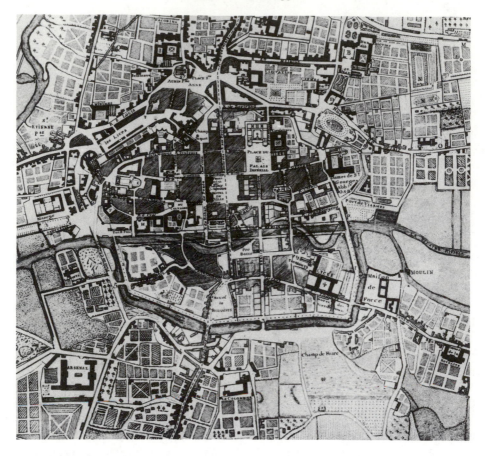

Map of the city of Rennes showing the *Marché de Toussaints* adjoining a branch of the river Vilaine on the south side of town and the *maison de force,* or *dépôt* to the east, adjoining a mill on the Vilaine. Based on a map originally dedicated to the intendant Caze de la Bove, this Napoleonic version shows a plan to straighten the channel of the Vilaine. (Musées de Rennes)

the disposition of the royal intendant, his subdelegates in Rennes, and the concierge of the *dépôt.*[3]

The arrest and confinement of beggars was a routine event in early modern Europe. But circumstances changed. The fact that each of the officials involved in the arrest of our three beggars acted as an agent of the king, independent of any municipal authority, departed from earlier practice. The institution on the Rue St. Hélier in Rennes represented an experiment conducted under royal auspices—a distinct novelty with an awkward name: the judge very reasonably translated the neologism *dépôt de mendicité* into a more concrete idiom, *dépôt des mendiants,* denoting a "jail for beggars" rather than a "jail for mendicity." In fact, the royal government fully intended to draw off mendicity into receptacles where enlightened administrators would transform the sum total of idle human substance into a useful, productive citizenry. The thirty-two royal provincial intendants who served the king throughout the realm were given undivided authority over the conduct of this experiment, initiated under the authority of two enactments, the Declaration of 1764 against vagabonds and the order in council of October 21, 1767. These were the work of a special commission named by the controller-general of finances, Laverdy, when he assumed office in 1764.

How the institution came into being, what institutional forms were given to it, and how it was run will be told in due course. A dramatic debate over the means and ends of social policy arises from this institutional narrative, a debate in which the ideas of the Enlightenment are tested and wrought into new forms. But to place narrative and debate in context, something must be said about the phenomenon of mendicity itself in the eighteenth century.

In the first chapter, the beggar will therefore occupy center stage—not mendicity in the abstract, but the individual beggars whom Sieur Vieuloup and his fellow constables apprehended on the highways and public places of their provincial capital and its environs in the year 1777. Of course these individuals cannot speak for all their fellow inmates throughout France over a thirty-year period. Studies done elsewhere for various periods will be used to supplement their testimony. But since our aim is to connect the experience of the incarcerated with policy debates about them, there is a positive value to becoming acquainted with this particular group of beggars who shared quarters in the converted Petit Séminaire at Rennes until they were released or died. Each captive justified his or her existence and intentions before a magistrate, who in turn listened long enough to write a statement that fit the accused into an existing category. The description of cases will thus help to reconstruct the judicial sociology of a particular place and moment and will illuminate the functioning of the *dépôts de mendicité* as an institution. It will then be easier to ask how the daily practice of bureaucrats related to policy and principle.

1

Mendicity—The Language of Poverty

All three of the men whom Vieuloup and Pelicot led away to the royal prisons at Rennes on that early September day in 1777 claimed to be searching for work. Like many others who gravitated to the market square of Toussaints, they were far from home. Nicolas le Coz (who went by the name of "Le Floc"), about forty-eight, said he was the son of a fisherman, Jan, and of Catherine Kersalle, and that he was born in the diocese of Quimper. The recorder could not spell the parish consistently, but it appears to have been the small community of Locronon, whose church tower looks out over an arm of the sea and the westernmost shores of Brittany, a hundred and fifty miles west of Rennes. Julien Buquet, aged seventy-four, came from the diocese of Dol on the northern coast, where he claimed to reside in the parish of La Boussac with his wife and children. At twenty years of age, Guillaume Vary was the youngest of the three. Born in Normandy, he gave the parish of Bazoges as his home. Gabliet was the name of his deceased father. His mother's name he could not recall.[1]

Under cross-examination by the provost, the three men insisted they were looking for work; only the youngest admitted begging, claiming ignorance of the declaration of the king. Vary, who called himself simply a *journalier* or day laborer, admitted freely that he had no fixed domicile and that he went from place to place looking for work. He only asked charity, he said, "because he was in need, having nothing to live on and finding no work, having come to this town however for the purpose of finding some."

In the eyes of the judge, Vary's story was no excuse for begging. The other two fared no better, although they responded differently. The aged Buquet denied that he had been begging at all. The judge then asked him if he had not come to Rennes for the purpose of begging. No, he had come to seek work. Had he then never asked for charity? What did he do when he could find no work? Julien, who called himself a *journalier laboureur* (farm laborer), answered, no doubt honestly, that he had sometimes asked for charity, but only as a last resort when he was without resources. The judge then asked him if he did not know that it was forbidden to beg. Julien replied that he had indeed heard that it was and that therefore he did it only, as he had said before, when he lacked money and work. Julien was sentenced to the *dépôt*.[2]

The middle one in age, Nicholas le Coz, was the most aggressive and consistent. He said he thought the reason for his arrest might have been that he lacked *passeports*. Asked what he did to subsist when he had no money and was on the road, Nicolas put up a brave front: he had never lacked money and never went on the road unless he had some. As soon as he lacked money, he worked wherever he could. Nicolas called himself a *domestique et journalier* (day laborer and servant). The judge found nothing in these replies to justify releasing him.

All three men were condemned by their situation. No one in the community where they were arrested could vouch for them. Since there was nothing in their stories to rule out the likelihood that they ordinarily resorted to begging at least as an expedient, there was no reason for the judge to doubt the word of the police officer.[3]

The Rural Setting

These three cases are the most typical of those recorded for the year 1777 in the *lieutenance* of Rennes. They involve ordinary day laborers born in rural parishes and arrested in the market square of Toussaints and its neighborhood. The men are typical also in having no fixed local address, although some of their fellows claimed to live "in the parish of Toussaints," or in a named street or parish of the town. In a broader sense, they represent a perennial social type, a fixture of the social landscape. The flight of poor rural laborers to towns in search of work or charity may be documented in the archives of almost any charitable or repressive agency in early modern Europe.[4]

The fact that males outnumber females two to one in our group of beggars locked up at Rennes in 1777, and that rural occupations are proportionally more frequently cited by males, may reflect a variety of factors, but the pattern of migration from country to city is probably an important one. In Brittany as elsewhere in France in this period, men commonly traveled the roads in search of seasonal work or charity in times of crisis, leaving families behind to tend small holdings or fend for themselves. Women also took to the roads with or without family. In the case of men and women alike, a spouse disabled or deceased might be cited as a reason for begging. Women particularly spoke of having been abandoned by their husbands, a circumstance suggesting that female migrants often represented a second contingent of dislocation.[5]

In describing the conditions that preceded the revolution of 1789, Hippolyte Taine pictured the French peasant standing in a pool of water up to his neck—one step further and he would go under.[6] Seeking to understand the economic background of the Revolution, several generations of historians since Taine have labored to collect information on wages, prices, population, and landholding, and to determine whether problems of subsistence and security were becoming more or less severe in the eighteenth century. In a broader chronological framework less strictly bound to the French Revolution, the past generation of historians has added to this core of research with studies of family structure, migration, popular mentalities and behavior, and the incidence of crime and mendicity.

The work of C. Ernest Labrousse, published half a century ago, established the broad contours of economic expansion from the 1740s to the Revolution, an expansion that was offset, however, by population growth. Although greater numbers of laborers were put to work, their wages did not keep pace with prices; smallholders found that the renegotiation of their seven-year leases usually ate up or even anticipated the gains hoped for from a steady rise in the price of grain. The result was that a large workforce of day laborers, landless or owning only small plots, were spared the agonies of recurring famine experienced the century before, only to suffer from hunger and insecurity whenever crops were poor or work slowed in the countryside. Labrousse spoke of them as being "under a suspended sentence of death." He also noted that certain sectors of the rural economy, the wine-growing areas in particular, suffered from periods of depression in the late eighteenth century, causing widespread distress in entire regions. The long cycle of expansion was also interrupted by periodic crises, including a prolonged one in the 1780s that set the stage for the Revolution.[7]

Labrousse's contemporary, Georges Lefebvre, showed how the majority of small landholders on the eve of the Revolution were excluded from the benefits of an expanding agricultural market. Complementing his own intensive regional study of of the Nord *département* with the findings of other researchers, Lefebvre concluded that the great majority of peasants throughout France on the eve of the Revolution could not support themselves on their own land and had to work for others in order to subsist. He estimated that in ordinary times some ten percent of the population might be described as *mendiant,* depending for at least part of its subsistence on begging. The proportion would rise dramatically in bad years when food prices soared. The prices of the poorer grains fluctuated the most, since the poorer consumers were in no position to retrench their consumption, delay purchases, or switch to other kinds of food. Work came to a standstill, supplementary occupations languished, and charitable resources were stretched beyond their feeble limits. Then, even the independent peasant might be forced to take to the road with a beggar's pack and staff.[8]

To the work of Labrousse and Lefebvre others have added light and shade. Pierre de Saint-Jacob revived Mathiez's theme of proletarianization in his study of the peasantry of Burgundy; Pierre Goubert, Emmanuel Le Roy Ladurie, and others accentuated the remission of the great famines that had afflicted peasants in the seventeenth century, in works enriched by the refinement of historical demography. Under the influence of Jean Meuvret, historians also tried to reach beyond the growing body of knowledge about the sedentary population in order to understand that "floating population" glimpsed in colorful but fragmentary evidence.[9]

The impulse for new research in economic and demographic history converged with studies on the political sociology of the Revolution. Georges Rudé renewed Marcel Rouff's critique of Taine, showing that the typical participant in the *journées* of the Revolution enjoyed established status in the settled working population of Paris. Such findings had to be balanced against growing evidence that the typical urban craftsman or day laborer was quite likely to be a seasonal migrant or a recent refugee from rural poverty.[10] Rude's interests also extended to rural riots under the

Old Regime, a topic illuminated by a growing body of research on popular disturbances, the regulation of trade in subsistance commodities, and the articulation of
collective mentalities. Again, the leaders of such actions were not beggars, vagrants, or criminals; they acted from a real fear of famine and destitution.[11]

Regular patterns of migration, long recognized as as general feature of economic life under the Old Regime, are now far better understood. In her broadly
based study, *The Poor of Eighteenth-Century France,* Olwen Hufton described "an
economy of makeshifts" that included migration as an option. Auvergnats left herds
to be tended by women and children and migrated regularly from their hilly plots
to work on the harvests of the valleys and flatlands of the Southwest, while Limousins trekked northward to work as stonemasons in Paris and other major cities.
Such travels spawned a lifestyle of marginal expedients; long journeys could not be
accomplished without taking work and alms as the opportunity arose. Raftsmen
who poled lumber down mountain streams had to walk back to their homes. Masons
who journeyed from the Massif Central to Paris would have spent all their earnings
on the way, had they not found other means of subsisting. A certain proportion, of
course, never returned. Some fell victim to accidents or illness; some tarried indefinitely where they had only meant to rest and replenish resources; some never ceased
their wanderings. Our dossier of beggars arrested in the *lieutenance* of Rennes includes young Bretons in search of a ship captain who would sign them on for a
voyage. Among wandering trades should also be counted traveling merchants and
those petty tradesmen who flourished along the borders of forests: woodcutters,
forgers of small hardware, knife-sharpeners, and menders of pots and pans.[12]

Royal edicts against vagrants usually made express provision for regular migrant
labor. One declared that "our good workers of Auvergne, Limousin, Dauphiné,
and Savoy" were not to be molested. On the other hand, the belief that begging
and vagrancy constituted "a school for crimes" pervaded the society from top to
bottom. Georges Lefebvre ably captured peasant attitudes toward the "wanderers"
in his study of the Great Fear of 1789. There was an element of paradox in peasant
fears of the outsider who lurked along the margins of rural communities. Peasants
were "afraid of themselves," he wrote, afraid of poor country people forced to
wander in search of daily bread. Precisely because the threshold between the "normal" peasantry and the uprooted wanderers was so easily crossed, the former felt
torn between feelings of sympathy and repugnance, between an impulse of mutual
aid and a fear of being "reduced to mendicity" by the depradations of the wanderers themselves.[13]

Research into criminal records of the period has shed light on the normal wanderings of the rural poor. A brilliant example of such work was Michel Vovelle's
study of the dossiers from the inquest into the activities of the Orgères gang in the
Orléanais, prompted by a remark of Lefebvre. What began as a study of organized
criminal behavior yielded profiles of the geographical and occupational mobility of
rural laborers.[14]

Typically, Vovelle discovered, a laborer from Normandy would travel in the
direction of Paris in search of work, alternating between work in the fields and
unskilled labor in Paris and neighboring towns. A worker who had gravitated to
Paris might return to the country when he could not find steady work in the capital,
attracted by the demand for labor in the grain-producing regions of the Beauce.

Such improvised wanderings would habituate the laborer to a variety of casual occupations and to begging as a natural alternative. While in the company of transients sleeping in farmers' barns, and at taverns with others of his own kind, the laborer might be recruited for illegal schemes, including the brigandage of the Orgères gang. The provocative implication of Vovelle's study was that the gang did not emerge from a peculiar, uniquely identifiable milieu, but from a broad, impoverished segment of society, people open to an endless variety of marginal expedients for earning a living.[15]

Studies devoted specifically to the records of beggars' arrests reveal similar patterns. A study of Versailles revealed that migrants were two to three times more likely to become beggars or delinquents than the indigenous population.[16] Another study based on burial records of inmates who died at the *dépôt de mendicité* of St. Denis, on the outskirts of Paris, reveals that nearly sixty percent of the males were originally from outside the diocese of Paris, while the female population (less than half the number of the men) was almost evenly divided between the diocese of Paris and the rest of the country.[17] Studies of Norman arrest records confirm the patterns of mobility among *journaliers* that Vovelle found in the Beauce. These *journaliers* included males of all ages, by contrast with those who confess having no trade or occupation at all, who are most frequently males in their teens and early twenties often lacking any ties with family, and occasionally mentioning the related fact that they were never taught any skill or trade. In addition to day laborers and the avowed shiftless *sans état* (without social station), there is a third category of petty trades that naturally complements the other two. These are the water-carriers and porters, the errand-runners *(commissionnaires),* the ragpickers, the wool carders, and the helpers of established tradesmen. Among the women, one finds spinners and seamstresses, hawkers of old clothes, and would-be servants. These petty trades often require no more skill, sometimes less, than that of rural hands.[18]

The list of occupations declared by those arrested for mendicity in the *lieutenance* of Rennes in 1777 (see table) provides another fairly typical example, representing arrests made in town and country by units of the *maréchaussée* residing at Rennes, Dol, Fougères, Vitré, La Guerche, Guer, Plélan, Montauban, and St. Servan. Apart from the large group of day laborers, most of the trades mentioned are exercised in town. However, most of them are only a step away from the country. The qualifiers that frequently accompany the mention of a trade (that of mason, in particular) reflect a marginal status. Certain trades are notoriously poor, if not marginal by definition (carders, spinners, and shoemakers, for example). With a few notable exceptions (baker, miller, carpenter, smith), most are relatively unskilled, and a few (the image seller, for example) are transparent cases of what Olwen Hufton refers to as "an economy of makeshifts."

In all categories, the breakdown of family ties and the debilitating effects of accidents or illness reflect the vulnerability of the laboring poor. Young men and women say their families have sent them to seek their fortune, having nothing to offer them at home. Men and women tell of incapacitating illness and disabling injuries; some are too old to work. The inability of those unfit for work to find aid reflects the inadequacy of those institutions intended to relieve the needy poor. Most of these institutions served the populations of towns only, and were quite inadequate to serve even the needs of their own poor. The rural poor had to throw

TABLE 1. List of Occupations Declared by Those Arrested for Mendicité in the *Lieutenance* of Rennes in 1777 [Source: A.D. Ille-et-Vilaine, BB70.]

Male	Female
1 boulanger (baker)	1 boulangère (baker or baker's wife)
3 charpentiers (timber-frame carpenter–joiner)	1 buandière (washerwoman)
1 cydevant commissionaire (former messenger, street porter; seller)	3 couturières (seamstress)
1 contrebandier (smuggler)	1 dévideuse de fils (reeler or winder of thread)
2 cordonniers (shoemaker)	1 domestique et fileuse (servant and spinster)
1 cydevant domestique (former servant)	1 auparavant domestique (former servant)
1 domestique et journalier (servant and day laborer)	1 faiseuse d'épluches (maker of combs for cleaning cloth)
3 écardeurs (carder; one of these may read, "carleur," i.e., cobbler)	11 fileuses (spinster)
1 faiseur d'eau de vie (distiller of spirits)	1 fileuse et brocheuse (spinster and stitcher)
1 faiseur de statues en cire (maker of wax statues)	2 laveuses (washerwoman or scullery maid)
1 fileur de laine (wool-spinner)	5 lingères (wardrobe-keeper)
1 fondeur d'étain et marchand de haquet (tin smelter and seller of ———)	1 fille lingère et tricoteuse (wardrobe maid and knitter)
2 forgerons (smith; including 1 *"garçon"*)	1 fille du monde et lingère (prostitute and wardrobe-keeper)
1 jardinier (gardener)	1 marchande (merchant)
5 maçons (mason; including 1 "cydevant," 1 "aprentif," 1 "manoeuvre," 1 "journalier," 1 "serveur de")	1 fille moulinière (silk-thrower)
4 marchands (nerchants; including 2 colporteurs, 1 mercier, 1 cydevant)	1 ravaudeuse (mender of clothes)
1 marchand d'images (image seller)	1 servante (servant)
1 maréchal (farrier)	4 tailleuses (tailoress)
3 matelots (sailor)	6 tricoteuses (knitter; stocking-knitter)
2 menuisiers (carpenter)	
1 mercier (haberdasher or peddlar of small wares)	8 journalières (day worker)
1 cydevant meunier (former miller)	
1 peigneur de laine (wool comber)	8 sans état ou sans profession (without a situation or without a calling—including one who does sewing and two who beg for a living)
1 pecheur (fisherman)	
2 portefaix (porter or carrier)	8 no response
1 porteur de peillots (ragpicker)	
1 peilletier (ragpicker)	
1 postillon (postilion)	
1 garçon tailleur (apprentice tailor)	
8 tisserands (weavers)	

Male	
1 travaillant à la terre	
9 laboureurs	
1 laboureur et manoeuvre	
1 autrefois fermier laboureur	(farm labor)
2 laboureurs journaliers	
4 journaliers laboureurs	
1 manoeuvre et journalier	
19 journaliers (day worker, town or country)	

1 mendiant de profession (beggar by trade)
1 sans éducation (without training)
23 sans état ou sans profession (without a situation or without a calling, including 6 who mention a former job or jobs: porter, schoolmaster, sailor, servant, stableboy, tripe-merchant; and 3 who beg for a living)
18 no response

SUMMARY

Male
54 with trades
38 at day labor
<u>43</u> without occupation or no response
135 Total

Female
44 with trades
8 at day labor
<u>16</u> without occupation or no response
68 Total

203 Grand Total

themselves upon the charity of their families and parishes; when all else failed, they went to town and begged in the market square, before churches, and at the doorways of the well-to-do.[19]

The results of a series of local studies in the Paris region, synthesized by Pierre Goubert, reflect as well as any others the typical categories to be found in the population of beggars arrested in the second half of the eighteenth century. About twenty to twenty-five percent might be described as confirmed idlers, a potentially dangerous group unsuited for any trade. The percentage is somewhat lower outside Paris itself. A slightly smaller group is incapacitated by accident, illness, or chronic infirmity, or left without family support. The remaining categories comprise over fifty percent even in Paris itself, and appreciably more as one moves away from the city. Goubert describes this majority as "unemployed occasional and seasonal laborers, from very unspecialized trades, a sort of reserve of cheap manpower and heavy labor, especially agricultural, but also including ditch digging and road work."[20]

Social historians have become increasingly sophisticated in their ability to explain cyclical adjustments of economy and population in terms of the actual life cycles of individual peasants. As the shared rhythms of ascent and impoverishment are recorded with more sensitive techniques, mendicity emerges as a background theme recurring in endless variations. Mendicity is an indicator of insecurity, just as ownership of a plot of land sufficient for one's subsistence is an indicator of security. The ordinary life of the rural poor fluctuates regularly between these markers as between high tide and low. Above this tidal region is a social terrain relatively protected from all but the most extraordinary flood tides of misery. The majority of the population, however, is normally subjected to a high degree of economic uncertainty in every form.

A recent demographic study has shown, for example, that the family structures of the poor were subject to sharper variation from one generation to the next than those of the small rural proprietors. The "autoregulating" mechanisms of age at marriage and intervals between births fluctuated more sharply among the households of day laborers than among proprietors as economic conditions improved or declined, just as the price of the cheaper grains consumed by the poor rose more suddenly in times of dearth than did the price of grains consumed by the well-to-do.[21] The same study shows how economic cycles affected households situated along the upper margin of poverty. The small independent farmer might see his son begin his working life as a day laborer, expecting that he too would establish himself as an independent farmer, only to find that the downward pressure on wages resulting from a previous population increase condemned the son instead to a lifetime as day laborer. As the son's ability to work diminished with age, he might become increasingly impoverished.

Although they lived with the prospect of being "reduced to mendicity," the majority of the common people vigorously denied being beggars. For them, to be a beggar meant not that one sought charity when all else failed—that was strictly normal—but that one had chosen begging as a station in life, literally as a profession. Hardly distinguishable from that profession was the status of being *sans état*. Mendicity thus stood in a temporary equivalence with all the other options facing those without property when they were unable to maintain their "station." Only those who enjoyed a station in life above that of the common tradesman or laborers were too proud to receive charity openly—these were the *pauvres honteux* who must be helped in secret.[22]

Of all the makeshifts of the humble poor, migration was the one most commonly allied with mendicity. Even those arrested for begging who had lived all their lives in town frequently declared a rural birthplace, underscoring the fact that rural migration fed the urban labor market of the Old Regime, as it does in many developing nations in the twentieth century. The towns were full of country folk, some of them recent arrivals, others domiciled over the years, few of them safely removed from mendicity.[23]

The Town Beggars

Vieuloup and his fellow officers at Rennes knew the urban "domiciled" beggars well; they were his neighbors in the parish of Toussaints and were concentrated in pockets throughout the provincial capital. The other great concentration of the poor outside Vieuloup's parish was in the parish of St. Germain, north of the Vilaine but east of the newer, well-to-do quarter of the city rebuilt in elegant style after the fire of 1720. The Estates of Brittany in 1786 heard a report estimating that in the two parishes of Toussaints and St. Germain alone there were six thousand inhabitants unable to subsist without alms—this in a city of about twenty thousand.[24]

The Rue Haute was particularly crowded with primitive wooden shanties, hidden from the street in chaotic inner courtyards back of the shops *(boutiques)* in which tradespeople lived and conducted their affairs. The tax rolls for the capitation of 1777 allow a glimpse into these courtyards. The royal assessor took a complete census at each address, enumerating the "poor" who were deemed lacking the means to pay the minimum assessment of one livre. As one moves along the street with the tax collector, one sees a repeated pattern of urban society, successive microcosms of those described as *"peuple,"* a great mass living in close contact yet divided between a handful whose relatively modest fortunes gave a modicum of security, and those whose petty trades gave only a provisional and intermittent income.[25]

The number 1442 Rue Haute included five shops at street level with rooms above, and a courtyard packed with shanties *(enbas)* and a bakery behind. The complex was dominated by the two shops of a baker, who formed a household with *compagnons* and a servant, and the baker's widowed mother-in-law. The baker paid a very substantial capitation tax—forty-five livres. A third shop housed an apprentice baker and his five children, paying but one livre. Above him lived a widowed laundress and a porter with his six children. She paid two livres, he paid one. In two presumably very small shops and the rooms above them lived a single woman who sold old clothes, a regrater (reselling food in small quantities), and another old-clothes seller and his wife, each of these three households paying but a livre. In a room above them, probably an attic, lived a carder with three children, "poor," paying no tax.

With the exception of the baker, these people living on the street were in modest circumstances. Some may even have stood in need of charity from time to time to make ends meet. Only one household, however, fell into the fiscal category of "poor." The inhabitants of the one- and two-story shanties built along the walls of the back courtyard offered a quite different picture. Of thirty fiscal entries, eight were assessed the one-livre minimum; only one paid at a higher rate, a weaver paying one and a half livres. Nineteen entries—a clear majority—were classed as "poor" and one was officially "invalid," while an *employé au tabac* appears to have been exempted. In this society of the courtyard, occupational status did not appear to be sharply distinguished. Unlike most of the inhabitants on the street, those in the courtyard all shared a relatively marginal existence, differentiated by personal luck and family situation. There was no marked distinction in occupation between those paying but one livre and those marked as "poor." The nine unspecialized laborers divided almost evenly into the two fiscal groups.[26] The lowly textile and clothing trades included a hatmaker *(chapellier)* who was "poor," and three who paid the minimum tax—a wool carder, a tailor whose wife sold clothes, and another clothes seller, a widow. Those paying the minimum tax included also a prison turnkey, while the "poor" included a coal seller, a miller's apprentice, a joiner *(charpentier)* and a student *(externe)*. The only petty trade that appeared more than once yet fell exclusively in one category was that of the three porters *(porte-faix),* who paid but one livre each. In this microcosm, all who declared no trade were "poor"—three men, two single women, and three widows.

In short, the occupants of the courtyard all hugged the threshold of destitution. The majority of the adults (predominantly male) lived alone. Of sixteen children, only five lived in households with two parents. Age, sickness, and death added to the burdens of poverty. Only one household with a child in it paid the tax, the other six households with one or more children were "poor."

In one case, two generations of the same family lived in adjoining shanties. A Julien Morel, *père,* and his wife lived with one child, next to another Morel, a coal seller, with two children. Both households were "poor."[27]

On November 4, 1777, the *cavalier* Bellet apprehended two men whom he had seen begging at the doors of houses in the Place du Bas des Lices and the Rue Neuve, near the location of the fabled lists where Du Guesclin once jousted. One was a sixty-nine-year-old man born in a rural parish near the northern seacoast town of St. Brieuc. For forty years he had lived in Rennes, he said, but for the past year he had been obliged to beg because he could no longer work, having been crippled in the right thigh. With him was Julien Morel, seventy-two years of age, living in the Rue Haute, parish of St. Germain. He was born in the parish of Acigné (spelled "Assigné" in the deposition), a few miles to the east of Rennes. He was, however, a resident of the capital, declaring himself to be a day laborer by trade. Although he knew it was forbidden to beg, he was obliged to do so every Monday, no longer being able to work because of a crippled right hip.[28]

This Julien Morel was undoubtedly the "Julien Morel, *père*" whom we just encountered living with his wife and one child in the courtyard of 1442 Rue Haute. If Morel, the coal seller, was his son, we know that he, like his father, was too poor to pay the capitation tax, and that he had to support two children from his petty trade. The grandfather would have had little alternative but to beg, and the fact that he spoke of doing so regularly on Mondays indicates that he followed a long-established custom of the city overruled by royal edict since 1767. A memoir of 1764 notes that the city had regulated begging in the past by allowing the domiciled poor to beg on Mondays only. The fact that Morel and his companion were apprehended going from door to door suggests that they may have had regular rounds, calling on charitable persons who knew them and would take pity on their infirmities.[29]

When Julien Morel exchanged his courtyard shanty for the men's dormitory of the *dépôt de mendicité* in the Rue St. Hélier, he no doubt recognized others whom he had encountered over many years in the streets of the town. On October 1 of the same year, only a month before Morel's arrest, the *maréchaussée* had picked up a seventy-year-old weaver named Ollivier Le Postel, whose home in the Rue St. Hélier was only a few steps away from the dépôt. Le Postel may have complained to Morel and other new arrivals about the circumstances of his arrest, if we are to judge from the expostulations dutifully recorded. He stated that he had been arrested "while at a shop speaking with a lady who had had the kindness to give him two liards in alms." The officers took him as he was returning from weighing some thread from Mlle Desgranges, which thread he intended to use in cloth. This protestation merely brought the question why Le Postel had asked for alms when he was able to earn a living by working. As the tax record showed, Le Postel was too poor to pay any tax assessment, and had a wife and two children at home. His age no doubt made him a natural object of charity. Le Postel must have known he could hope to gain release only by stressing his industriousness: he protested to the officer that "he works continuously at his loom, that he still has at home over sixty *aulnes* of cloth to do, and that he had ceased asking for any charity about six or eight months before." Whether he had asked for alms or not, the officers had seen him take it. One can only wonder whether Le Postel's skill as a weaver marked him as an attractive recruit, in spite of his age, for the workshops of the *dépôt.*[30]

Le Postel and Morel were in a sense typical of the domiciled beggar, men who had survived a bruising life of poverty and hard work, and who were no longer able to support themselves entirely by working. In Le Postel's case, an early tax survey shows him paying more than the minimum assessment of the capitation, illustrating the important fact that beggary could easily be the outcome of a "normal" life cycle for the working poor. These and other "Monday beggars" were also typical of the domiciled poor, in that the more secure or prosperous inhabitants of the city generally knew who they were and regularly gave them some alms, whether from compassion, ardor to do the Lord's will, or habit. The women arrested begging on Monday shared the same character. The day that Ollivier Le Postel was arrested, the officers also apprehended Marie Ruelle, whose age they estimated as being at least seventy. She said her father had brought her to Rennes as a small girl from a parish near Alençon and that she had worked as a *journalière.* She knew it was forbidden to beg, but being unable to work for the past ten years she was "obliged to ask for charity, which she did every Monday of each week only." Like many of the women, she was a widow. Arrested with her was Guillemette Duclos, an unmarried woman of forty-five, with her daughter. She was a spinster by trade, living in the parish of Toussaints, forced to beg because she found so little work.

While the pattern of begging by the aged suggests a common condition of the urban poor, so too does the pattern of arrests of young people. In the small sample collected in 1777 at Rennes, the young males were concentrated especially in the midteens, the young women in their midtwenties. David Mathurin of the parish of Toussaints, aged only thirteen, admitted to begging: his mother was dead, and his father, a *journalier*, was at the Hôpital St. Yves. Anne Aubrée, aged twenty-five, knitter, daughter of a *portefaix*, pleaded guilty to begging in the rue Vasselot, near her home, saying simply that she was not able to earn her living. Like a number of other young women, she had already been in the *dépôt*.[31]

Men and women in the prime of their working years were less likely to claim that they lacked a trade. In these age brackets, those who claimed to be unable to find work had most often come from other towns or the countryside to look for employment. Those who had resided in the city for some time were more likely to refer to some misfortune, especially an illness or an onerous family situation, that had forced them to resort to begging. A young woman twenty years old, born in the town of Vitré and living in the parish of St. Germain, pleaded guilty to begging in the Rue Vasselot. Her deceased father had been a wool carder, she was a knitter. "Recovering from a severe illness and finding no work, she was forced to beg in order to subsist, although she knew that it was forbidden to do so." A number of masons, carpenters, sailors, and others referred to injuries or illnesses that prevented them from working. A carpenter and his wife, a washerwoman, were arrested together for begging in the Rue Haute. Forty years old and a resident of the parish of Toussaints, born in a parish near Fougères, Pierre Lambert declared that he knew of the prohibition but, "lacking work and money, being worn out by illness" he begged. His wife told the police "that necessity constrains the laws, that she knew that it was forbidden to beg and that she did not ordinarily do it, and that she only did it because, lacking work and everything else, she was worn out by the lengthy sickness that her husband had had." If her language is a sign that people of some status could be reduced to begging by misfortune, the fact that a blacksmith arrested near St. Malo signed his deposition suggests a like conclusion. Aged sixty-two, he claimed that he had only recently been able to resume working after being ill and bothered by a hernia.[32]

Two parents in good health were lucky if they could provide children with subsistence and teach them useful skills. The death of a parent at a critical age made the child all the more vulnerable. One young boy complained that when his mother remarried, the step-father refused to support him. A thirty-eight-year-old woman begging at the doors of houses in the Rue Vasselot declared that she had to beg in order to keep her two children alive, since their father was insane. She had been in the *dépôt* before. Another woman, forty, arrested in the town of Vitré with her children five and six years old, said that she had been forced to beg in the ten years since her marriage, because her husband gave her and her children no support. She was a knitter and he was a wool spinner. She offered the proverbial opinion "that she preferred to ask for a living than to steal." She was several months pregnant.

The plight of some of those arrested seems so wretched that arrest must have come as a relief. At the other extreme, some were arrested without ever having begged, because their way of life was a "scandal" threatening to disrupt the moral economy of family and trades. The legal concept of mendicity could be stretched, in eighteenth-century practice, to cover both types of deviation from the norms of community life. It was a threat to the structures of social solidarity when a member of the community was unable to subsist by the options it normally offered; it was likewise a threat if someone succeeded in the quest for subsistance without loyally performing the duties of his estate. In either case, the person was considered *sans état,* without a social station, without a place in the world of trades; or *sans aveu,* without ties of responsibilities within the community. Such a person was associated even in legal texts with the vagabond, for he had lost or renounced the ties that subjected him to law and custom while assuring him their protection. Within this set of assumptions, family discipline functioned as an agent of law and order in the community as a whole. The role of family discipline is well known in cases of notable aristocratic families who had children locked up in royal prisons or *maisons de force*—Mirabeau at Vincennes, others at the Saint Lazare monastery in Paris— but the arrest of beggars cannot be understood in isolation from the legal sanction of family integrity and other notions of "police" operating at the lower fringes of society.[33]

The Two Faces of Police: Repression and Assistance

Dossiers on beggars arrested reveal that a substantial proportion of inmates were arrested on specific orders from the intendant. The largest category of such orders involves women charged with leading vagabond and debauched lives. At Rennes in 1777, the most common procedure was for one of the two subdelegates of the intendant to instruct the provost of the *maréchaussée* to imprison the individual in question after following the usual judicial procedures. The complaint, usually from a relative, would be the main evidence reviewed by the prosecutor, along with a pro forma cross-examination. The intendant Caze de la Bove himself signed a letter dated "Paris, May 9, 1777," to M. de la Glestière, stating that one Jean Marest, *portefaix,* of the Rue de la Magdelaine, parish of Toussaints, complained that his wife Sainte Toinette Martineau had given herself to vagabondage and all sorts of debauchery. The intendant noted that since the husband could not pay his wife's pension, it would be appropriate to have the woman confined in the *dépôt.* Thus the *dépôt* clearly served as a poor man's *maison de force,* and the intendant's letter was a poor man's *lettre de cachet.* The arresting officers reported that on receiving the order they went to find the woman at her home, but she was not there. Several neighbors told them to look for her at a farmhouse at Noyal-sur-Sèche. There, according to their report, they found her with a naval recruit. She told the judge that she was arrested in the Rue de la Magdelaine for a dispute that she had had with her husband, and not for begging. She was sentenced to the *dépôt.*[34]

The number of specific orders the intendant sent was small. How did he determine the cases to be considered? The fact that the attorney-general of the parlement of Brittany, La Chalotais, had a toothache led him to put in writing a recommendation that would otherwise have been made in a face-to-face meeting with the intendant. From this we may infer that the intendant normally collaborated with the highest judicial authority in the province to make use of the *dépôt* as an additional *maison de force* for the usual police purposes, charitable and repressive. The tone of the note is familiar and suggests the informal manner in which such business was usually conducted:

I only choose to write to you, Monsieur, because I am being held by the jaw for an abcess and because a confounded dentist keeps me from going out, otherwise I should go myself to ask that you be so good as to place in a house of confinement *[maison de force]* one Janne Debroize who gives a most decent family reason to fear even greater misfortune than her misconduct has already brought upon them. M. Elie who will present you my letter asks this as I do. I add to the interest that dictates my request that you do all you can to set at ease this decent and gallant man whom we all esteem greatly. *Vale Vale ama amantem.* De la Chalotais. M. Elie will give you a memorandum on the subject.[35]

The subdelegate Fresnais wrote on the intendant's behalf to the provost of the *maréchaussée* and asked him to have his *cavaliers* conduct Janne Marie Debroize to the *maison de force,* asking him "to fulfill the prescribed formalities to condemn her there." The memoir from the family declared that the woman had been living with a married man in the parish of Toussaints and that she had declared herself pregnant before the manager of the hospital, undoubtedly desiring to lie in there. The cross-examination reveals that she was twenty-five years old, the daughter of a country surgeon (both parents deceased), working as a *lingère,* and living in the Rue Vasselot. She declared that she believed her relatives had had her arrested: she had never begged and had always lived from her work.

The fact that two other "beggars" were arrested in the same batch by the officers of the *maréchaussée* suggests that they too might have been marked for arrest beforehand. The fourteen-year-old Jacques Clochon appears somewhat bewildered at his cross-examination, saying that he did not know why he was arrested, since he was not asking for his living at the time and did not ask for it except when there was no bread at his mother's home. Vieuloup declares that he was asked by the chaplain of the religious house of Le Colombier, called the "Visitation," to arrest the youth, who begged daily in the courtyard of the house. As the chaplain and the boy's father signed a certificate that the boy was a beggar and a *polisson,* it is possible they obtained his arrest from Vieuloup as a favor. As the boy was crippled in the right arm, he might not easily have found a trade. His father was a tiler; he himself was *"sans profession."*[36] At the same time, Vieuloup brought in a seventy-two-year-old native of Rennes, a *laboureur* who declared that he was not "asking for charity" at the time of his arrest but that he had been asking for it over the last two years, at least since he could no longer see.

These three cases were associated in the pattern of a day's work for Vieuloup. They were also representative of a cluster of ideas on the "police" of the poor, charitable and repressive. The association of these different types may emerge more clearly from a further examination of similar cases and the way they were handled.

The intendant ordered several other arrests of young women for debauched or libertine behavior on complaints from various sources, possibly with the recommendation of La Chalotais. In at least two cases, the *maréchaussée* responded to reports that women had returned to their evil ways after being released from the *dépôt.* In one of these, the subdelegate referred the officers to M. Ellie, *commissaire du parlement,* for information on the woman's whereabouts.[37] In the other case, mention of "the pox" indicates a concern for public health. This concern was reinforced by a special arrangement with the Ministry of War that had been made at the time the *dépôts* were established. In return for placing the *maréchaussée* at

the disposal of the intendants for the purpose of policing beggary, the *dépôts* were
to receive "women and girls of ill repute"—*femmes et filles de mauvaise vie*—
arrested by military authorities. In one case an officer stopped a woman with two
soldiers on the road to Châteaugiron, found the two soldiers' papers to be in order,
arrested the woman, and informed the comte de Guyan, the commander responsible
for military police in the province, from whom he received an order to have the
young woman taken to the *dépôt*. There was no cross-examination in her dossier.
In other cases the officers responded to unspecified complaints—one that a woman
was spreading venereal disease among soldiers of a garrison, another that a woman
in a parish a few miles northwest of Rennes "was causing scandal and debauching
the young men." In the latter case, the officers apprehended the seventeen-year-old
on the road to Bedée. She said at her cross-examination that her parents "were
reduced to the bread of the parish," and that she could live only by begging, "or
by engaging in *libertinage* with the first to pass by." She said she did not know
who the two young men were who had taken flight when the officers appeared, but
admitted that she was "living with" them.[38]

As if to recognize the fact that casual, episodic relationships of all sorts were
woven into the "economy of makeshifts" of the lower classes, the police did not
generally refer to prostitution as a profession, but spoke more inclusively of "women
and girls of ill repute" *(femmes et filles de mauvaise vie)*. Their bias in making
women bear the immediate responsibility for deviance from norms of sexual conduct, ingrained in social mores, was reinforced by the arrangement that the *dépôts*
would receive women arrested in the train of the armies. The military authorities
were particularly concerned with the spread of venereal disease; accordingly, they
paid for the medical treatment of the women they committed to the *dépôts*. In a
number of provincial centers, the *dépôts* were used to receive poor men and women
suffering from venereal disease. In this respect the *dépôts* functioned as a supplement to the *hôpitaux-généraux*.[39]

A comparison of the ages of males and females arrested in the group of beggars
at Rennes suggests that the police of morals affected males and females in different
ways. Young women whose families could not provide a dowry were obliged to
save money from their earnings, if they wished to find their place in a society of
families. Household work and petty textile trades performed in the house employed
many teenaged girls from poor families. While such work might preserve a young
woman from being *sans état*, it often paid so little that it gave no prospect of long-
term stability through marriage. Those branded as *libertines* in their twenties were
the victims in some cases of marriage promises, in others of coercion and violence.
Housekeeping trades such as *lingère* or wardrobe-keeper, *laveuse* or *buandière*, led
to casual relationships and exploitation. Popular perceptions of female domestics as
"kept women" alternated with sympathy for their vulnerable situation. While most
young women persisted in domestic service as a means of establishing themselves
with a small dowry, those who were less successful economically could hardly have
failed to perceive *libertinage* as an option in the struggle for survival.[40]

Young males, on the other hand, were expected to establish themselves in their
lifetime calling by their early teens, with the aim of establishing a family by their
late twenties. The crisis of moral character was thus likely to occur early for males.
Parents and relatives found their reputation besmirched by scandal when a male

youth failed to pursue an honest trade at an early age. He then acquired the status of *polisson* or rogue, in effect an apprentice to mischief and debauchery. Of the forty arrests of males in their teens in the *lieutenance* of Rennes in 1777, several explicitly involved family police. In addition to the case cited above, in which a boy was arrested on the complaint of a chaplain, several others were arrested without any charge that they actually begged. Several boys were aware that their families were unhappy with their behavior. One thought he had been arrested for "sleeping away from home." Another, it is known, was arrested on the complaint of his sister.[41]

One young male, completely nonplussed, had been tricked by his family. He said that he had been stopped in the Rue de l'Isle by his father, a spinner of wool and cotton living in the Rue St. Hélier, who said he would take him to a shop to work, where he would be well off; instead of taking him to the shop, however, he turned him over to Barbier, *cavalier* of the *maréchaussée*, who brought him to prison. He added that the reason for his detention was that he had left the *hôpital-général* where he had been before. Since this arrest was made at the order of the intendant, it may have been inspired by the judicial authorities, who kept under surveillance those released from institutions. In this case, an officer of the *hôpital-général* may have made an oral recommendation. In another case, a young boy was transferred from the Tower of Toussaints, the prison traditionally used by municipal police for confining dangerous or disorderly persons. Here again, the *dépôt* supplemented hospitals and prisons.

Although the judicial dossiers convey a sense of improvident debauchery among many of the poor, occasionally a touch of naive romance undercuts a disclaimer, as in the case of the nineteen-year-old peddlar from a village in the diocese of St. Malo who had come to Rennes two weeks before for his wares, but "having had the misfortune of associating himself with a girl of this town named Marguerite, he had not given a thought to leaving."

A modest number, perhaps five percent, of those arrested gave reasonably certain indications that they wished to be confined in the *dépôts*. The most typical case was the women who said she went begging in the Rue de Toussaints, "not knowing what will become of her" and hoping to be put in the *dépôt*. The *cavalier* Barbier, in another instance, found a thirteen-year-old girl begging, warned her of the declarations, and threatened her with confinement in the *dépôt*. She replied "that she desires with all her heart to go there." She said that she "knows how to make stockings with the needle" but could earn a living. Her father, a shoemaker, had left her mother two months back; her mother, being crippled, could not feed her.[42]

Several young women came from out of town with the intention of being locked up. Gabrielle Trevoyzant, native of Guingamp, twenty-six-years old, daughter of a deceased chair porter, said she had been begging for eight days in the city and "that she came on purpose to Rennes to have herself locked up in the *maison de force*." Several women had been in the *dépôt* before. The *cavalier* Pelicot arrested Marie Godio with a babe in arms. She said that she was a knitter, but was obliged to beg so as to feed her illegitimate child, to whom she had given birth at the *dépôt* of Rennes on February 23, 1776, and whom she called "Sainte."[43]

Other categories of the poor who might otherwise have been eligible for confinement in charitable institutions were confined to the *dépôt* by order of the inten-

dant. Families who could afford to pay a pension would generally have a dangerously insane relative confined to a religious house. The very poor could hope that
the *dépôt* might be available as a refuge of last resort, and that the intendant would
order the person received without payment of a pension. A rural laborer twenty-
seven years old was arrested in the parish of Bourgbarré on the order of the subdelegate Petiet, who referred to a *placet* by a Mme de Melesse. Her letter had said
the man's relatives were poor and "that he was very dangerous to the countryside
when he is in a mad rage and wants to kill everyone." In the case of a thirty-six-
year-old woman living in the parish of Toussaints, the subdelegate Fresnais appears
to have acted on a recommendation without waiting for the approval of the intendant. He assured the provost of the *maréchaussée* that the intendant would approve
the arrest of this "mad vagabond woman," and made the interesting general observation, "Although there is very little room in this house, the vagabond insane are
always received by preference." [44]

In many cases, the *maréchaussée* arrested poor wandering imbeciles and epilep-
tics on their own initiative or following up a report in a village. These cases suggest
an element of charitable intention, either desired or numbly accepted, in arrests that
appear to involve merely the repression of begging. In the case of a white-haired
former *lingère* with a sore on her cheek, begging before the cathedral at St. Malo,
the officer seems to have prompted her in the cross-examination. The record says
that she admitted begging, "which she only did because you were *[sic]* no longer
able to work and that she had no resource." In another case, one may wonder
whether the twenty-five-year-old carpenter disabled by a thumb injury was really a
"dangerous beggar," or whether the order of Petiet to arrest him was motivated by
the charitable dimension of "police."

If the *dépôt* was used in some instances to extend the resources of charitable
institutions, it was used with misgivings. One such instance of ambivalence came
from a request addressed to the intendant by Du Boistilleul, May 9, 1780, outlining
the case of a thatcher's daughter who, in spite of her parents' care, had been corrupted by soldiers. Her parents had put her in La Trinité, but since she was pregnant
and almost blind from "the pox," she could no longer be kept there. For the same
reasons, she could not be transferred to the tower of Toussaints. Noting that the
father was a decent man who could be spoken for by the rector of the parish of St.
Étienne and five other gentlemen named, the writer asked the intendant to grant
him the "sad favor" *(triste grâce),* "very sad indeed for a virtuous father and
mother," of having the girl put in the *maison de force.* The notion that the *dépôt*
was a humiliating alternative of last resort is confirmed by other instances in which
relatives beseeched the intendant to transfer an invalid from the *dépôt* to a regular
hospital.

Attacks on the police functions of the *dépôts* led the baron de Breteuil to issue
a directive, dated 1784, providing for stricter record-keeping. A bound register of
entries contains information on those detained "by order of the King" at the *dépôt
de mendicité* of Rennes from 1785 to 1787. Of eighty-three inmates in this category, thirty were confined for reason of insanity or mental disturbance. Six cases
involved violent behavior. Twenty-one cases involved *libertinage* or some form of
waywardness; five entries cited "excesses," perhaps referring to drunk and disorderly conduct. Ten cases involved accusations of theft or fraud, and twelve were

not specified. At Besançon, where the parlement overtly participated in the procedure of confinement, a register of those judicially confined in the *dépôt* lists numerous inmates interned for five years or more, and one confined for nine years or "until cured." Dated 1788, the register includes an entry for a "Mar^gte^ Senaillon," first confined on February 17, 1770.[45]

School for Crimes

Where the law treats begging as an offense, it must hold many individuals responsible for circumstances they cannot control. The significance of this contradiction cannot be understood, however, without speaking also of that small but identifiable minority of inmates who conformed to the ideological stereotype of mendicity as a "school for crimes." At the risk of confirming an all-too-vivid image of beggars as professional delinquents, some of these defiant or sullen reprobates must at least momentarily be thrust upon the stage.

The "dangerous" or "troublesome" beggar was generally arrested in rural areas on the complaint of local farmers and notables. A typical instance from Brittany is that of Jacques Besnard, sixty years old, originally from the parish of St. Vrand, living at Dinan, having no profession. He declared to the judge that he did not know that begging was forbidden and did so only because he was ailing and without resource. The account of his capture tells a different story. A declaration from the judges and notable persons of St. Malo states that this Besnard, also known as "le bondieu de pitié," was a beggar of the most dangerous sort. He had escaped from a hospital, "preferring to this place the profession of beggar, which he has exercised all his life." He had been recaptured, but eluded his captors and returned to begging, "making an appeal, by his assumed manner and gait, to pity and public charity, appearing to be unable to walk without difficulty." The constabulary found him soon after his escape begging openly on the main highway from Dol to St. Malo. He was chased away with a warning that he would be arrested, should he continue to beg, to which Besnard replied, "What's it to you?" (*"Quesque cela vous fait?"*). When the warning was renewed, "he threw himself at us like a madman [continues the report] . . . and finding some stones, he threw them at us, and one struck us and injured a leg. This resistance, this revolt against us, and his insolent replies, obliged the officer to get assistance in order to make an arrest." In case there were any doubt, the constable added a note for the lieutenant of the *maréchaussée* at Rennes, to the effect that special caution should be taken during the cross-examination of the said Jacques Besnard. In spite of his pitiable appearance, he was vigorous and fleet of foot: "he followed after me with a light step that astonished me." The man in question was a stock figure from the rogues' gallery, known in the argot as a *piètre,* feigning to be crippled.[46]

Another similar case was that of Louis Le Mohon, forty-six years old, with no permanent abode, claiming to be a weaver by trade and obliged to beg for lack of work. The report of arrest indicates that Le Mohon, "beggar and vagabond by profession, was found at the fair of Plancoët near Dinan, keeping one hand wrapped up to counterfeit a cripple with the intention of imposing on the public, although very strong and fit to work." The report details Le Mohon's reply at the time of arrest: "Seeing his imposture discovered, he declared that he had previously been detained for ten years at the *dépôt de mendicité* at Rennes, that from his youth onward he had gone begging and that he wanted to live as a beggar and die as a beggar, the which aforesaid Louis Le Moher [*sic*] we led away to the royal prisons of Dinan."[47]

The corresponding female stock figure is that of Marie Anne Le Goff, a *fille lingère* originally from Brittany. The rector and other notables of the parish of Baignon had notified the *maréchaussée* of Plélan that this libertine and vagabond woman living in a nearby village was staying in a cabaret on the highway leading to Ploermel, and that she exhibited scandalous conduct there. When the officers found her, they recognized her as a woman who had been in the *maison de force* and asked her for her *congé*, or certificate of release. She replied that she burned it at Rennes about a year before. When asked why she plied a beggar's trade, she said "because she wanted to" *(parce quel le voulet)*. She was consistent only in her defiance, for she also said that she never asked for alms and that she always lived from her estate of *lingère* and knitter. She had never been convicted of a crime and was only once put in the *"dépôt des mendians,"* from which she had been released.[48]

These three individuals may fairly be taken as cases of people who rejected the social norm of living by one's labor, but rather sought to impose on the charity of others. This leads one to inquire how many of those who rejected the norms of honest toil turned to criminal means of livelihood. Begging, after all, was commonly denounced as a school for crimes. If there was a high correlation between begging and crime, it should be accentuated in the population of the *dépôts de mendicité,* since the *maréchaussée* were more likely to arrest troublesome or suspect beggars. In spite of this, the level of criminality observed is low. In the few cases we have found in two hundred dossiers at Rennes, some are suspect merely because they are outsiders, lack a known means of livelihood, or have ties with others who are suspect.

It was routine to ask the arrested beggar whether he or she had been arrested previously, and to check the back, shoulders, and arms for marks branded into the flesh. In two hundred cases examined at Rennes, only seven had been "suspect of theft," most of them very young. Four had been whipped and branded under suspicion of crimes, two had only been detained and released, and one was suspect at the time of arrest because he had tried to sell a silver fork that he claimed to have found. One of the suspects was a seventeen-year-old mason's helper who was "recognized as a very bad character and as the son of Jean, presently detained in the prisons of Rennes on several charges." One man arrested after begging for shelter in a rural parish was found to have a large amount of money (127 livres) concealed in a belt pouch, together with several keys on a string. The man's explanation that he felt bound to save money for his old age did not remove the suspicion that he was a potentially dangerous beggar.[49]

Two of the crimes most frequently ascribed to beggars were arson and threats of violence against those who refused to give alms. In fact, very few fit this pattern. One homeless individual, forty years old, almost totally paralyzed, was picked up in a small village center *(bourg)* by the *maréchaussée* on a report that he was "making many threats against those who refused him charity, such as setting fires or causing the death of livestock, and especially when he found women alone.'' In another case, ''threats and violent behavior'' were cited. Although these two cases represent only one percent of a year's catch of beggars in the *lieutenance* of Rennes, they are not to be dismissed as insignificant. Repression was particularly sporadic in the countryside, where threats of arson were most feared; a few wanderers raving their threats could make peasants fearful of others seeking only a handout and a barn to sleep in.[50]

Another crime often associated with beggars was smuggling. The cases of two men arrested at Vitré fulfill, perhaps better than any other, the stereotype of the beggar as impostor, versed in many criminal arts. The report of arrest notes that Pierre and François Daligaut were found at the doors of parish churches, one pretending to be missing an arm and the other claiming to have fits of epilepsy. Pierre, aged thirty-seven, told the judge that he had come from Laval to invite his brother to his wedding, his intended bride being eight months pregnant. When asked whether any responsible citizens *(honnêtes gens)* might answer for him, he replied that ''he knew only people of a lower sort who might answer for his good behavior,'' including a butter merchant and an innkeeper. Under cross-examination he admitted that he had spent three months in the prisons of Laval for smuggling and had once been branded.

Examination of the two men's shoulders, a routine part of the judicial process, verified that both had the brand ''GLR'' to show that they had been condemned to the galleys. The older man, François, had been condemned by a judge at Le Mans for having smuggled salt—a lucrative trade, since the salt tax in Maine was much higher than it was over the provincial frontier in Brittany—and had been taken to Brest to serve five years in the galleys. The experience hardly chastened him: François avowed freely to his captors that he had come to Vitré to buy salt so that he might return to Maine and have money for his brother's wedding. Under questioning, he denied that he had begged, saying that he ''had always lived from his work and his industry, which was to engage in salt smuggling,'' which was why he had come to Vitré. Earlier in his statement, however, François had claimed to be a mason's laborer. An exchange of letters with the *maréchaussée* at Laval indicated that the masons in the area knew nothing of him. Nothing was to be learned, it appeared, but that these two were ''incorrigibles *[mauvais sujets]* who roamed from place to place plundering everything in reach.'' The elder had spent two terms in the galleys, one for theft. No one wished to vouch for them, and they were unknown to any ''qualified persons'' at Laval. They were known to the *maréchaussée,* however, and were involved in a case of theft in which the victim was unwilling to press charges.[51]

While the Daligaut brothers appear to convict themselves as arrant knaves, François Michel, about thirty-six, marked ''GAL,'' could have served as a prototype of Victor Hugo's Jean Valjean, the former *galérien* struggling against the weight of his past. In 1770 the parlement of Rennes had sentenced him to five years in the royal galleys for theft. By the conditions of his release, he had agreed to seek work in Nantes. Asked if he had ever begged, he said that he had never done so except in coming from Brest to Nantes, ''as all the former galley convicts do when they return home.'' Asked why he had left Nantes, he stated that in a month there he had not found enough work to clothe himself and eat. He had therefore come to his family in Rennes for that purpose. He had been living "chez Gateuil" in the Rue Haute, earning some money with Gateuil by cutting rushes in the country and selling them in town. The *maréchaussée* had arrested him on suspicion of being a deserter from the galleys. After an inspection of François Michel's certificates, the provost-general wrote for instructions to the minister of the navy, Sartine, and received the reply that the provost should decide at his discretion whether an individual violating the terms of his release, known as a man of bad character (a *mauvais sujet*), and leading a vagabond life, should be returned to the galleys. The provost's decision to lock up François Michel in the *dépôt* of Rennes was clearly a milder alternative to the "rigor" suggested to him.

Knowing no more than the dossier of arrests tells us, one cannot judge the character of the three galley convicts as neatly as the foregoing account suggests. François Michel may not have completely renounced his evil ways; the Daligaut brothers may have considered a life of honest labor. But from these and many other cases cited in studies of "criminality," there is little to suggest that the system of criminal justice made fine moral distinctions: circumstance was all.[52]

Taine said that the police system of the Old Regime was "Turkish" with respect to the people: "it flails at the entire heap, with a broom that does a great deal of damage but sweeps poorly."[53] The impression gleaned from reading the records of arrest and cross-examination confirms this view. The effort to separate wheat from chaff was but a crude, flailing technique. In two hundred cases examined closely, only two were released as a result of questioning. In one case, a young man was on the way to visit family, denied that he was begging or that he ever needed to, and gave names of respectable persons willing to vouch for him. In the other case, a wandering merchant *(colporteur)* had been denounced as a suspicious-looking character and had been arrested while reposing under a tree on the outskirts of town. He was able to give two pages of particulars concerning the merchandise he had sold, the places he had traveled, and his future plans.[54] But others in situations hardly different were marched off to the *dépôt*. The *maréchaussée* were loath to release their prey, once they had decided to make an exemplary arrest. They gave little heed to others who claimed to be petty salesmen. A woman purporting to travel in order to claim a bequest, a man seeking a hospital where he could find medical treatment, a woman trying to locate the husband who had left her, were all given short shrift. An Italian sailor, unable to explain himself in French, was given an opportunity to learn the language in the *dépôt*.

Plainly, not all the inmates of the *dépôt* were "beggars" or vagabonds" in a strict sense. The terms were stretched enormously to accommodate the needs of "police" as interpreted by the officers themselves, by peasants or local notables who brought complaints to them directly, and by higher authorities who channeled their requests through the office of the royal intendant. Some beggars, warned by officers to stop begging or be arrested, acted their delinquent part in order to be institutionalized. In other cases, there were grounds for believing that officers were bribed to make arrests. Thus the description of any given population of beggars arrested or incarcerated does not necessarily describe the actual social phenomenon of mendicity. The *maréchaussée* were perhaps more likely to arrest those who were suspected of criminal behavior or those who were especially irritating in their importunities. On the other hand, a few easy arrests may have been preferred to the pursuit of a troublesome and possibly dangerous character. Whatever the bias may be overall, it is remarkable how few hardened criminals left their traces in the records of arrests. There was, indeed, a sizable contingent of misfits and derelicts who annoyed or vaguely threatened the other members of the community, especially in isolated rural hamlets and farms. Nonetheless, the majority of those arrested were fit to work but could not find a regular way to earn a living.[55]

The repression of begging in these most ordinary cases can hardly be interpreted as punishment for a crime, but rather as a kind of social discipline or correction that drew an arbitrary line between the normal working population and the delinquent poor. The aim appears to have been to isolate the latter as one might clear a fire lane in the forest, or as one might quarantine healthy individuals suspected of being carriers of an epidemic disease. Such a policy of holding individuals responsible for circumstances beyond their control raised questions about the function of punishment and rehabilitation. How were the innocent to be "corrected"? What was the consequence of confining together in one building such diverse characters and conditions, united only by their poverty? Assuming that the state did not have the resources to support and house indefinitely those arrested, what expectation could there be as to their future conduct?

These apparently obvious questions were inherited, for the most part, from previous institutional experiments. Why did royal administrators expect their efforts to succeed where previous ones had failed? What were their initial goals and plans, and to what extent were they able to carry them out? How did policymakers respond to the results of their institutional experiments with the *dépôts de mendicité?* Such questions will be the focus of discussion in the next three chapters. Further chapters will deal with the outcome of a concerted impulse to reassess royal policy concerning mendicity, leading to the formalized bureaucratic strategy that dominated the prerevolutionary decade. It will be argued that while the royal bureaucrats were then swept away by revolutionary events, their policies and administrative strategies had a lasting impact, although a diverse and paradoxical one, on modern social policy.

2

The Impulse to Legislate

"Nam ista mendicorum frequentia arguit et in privatis malitiam ac inhumanitatem, et in magistratibus neglegentium boni publici," the humanist scholar Juan Luis Vives admonished the citizens of Bruges in 1526 in an unadorned Latin, exhorting them to provide for the poor in their midst. "For that throng of beggars," he was saying, "argues both the ill-will and inhumanity of private citizens and a neglect of the public good on the part of the magistrates." Whatever they thought of the medieval Christian tradition of sacred poverty, the reformers of the sixteenth century saw corruption—not beatitude—in the daily public jostling of beggars in the urban centers of an increasingly mercantile society. It was corruption of the human spirit, the reformers thought, in private citizens who lacked the good will to help their fellows extricate themselves from the degradation of a beggar's's life; it was corruption of the will in those magistrates who allowed such a state of affairs to persist, when it was in the interest of the community as a whole to turn idle hands to productive labor and to make true citizens of the outcast poor. Vives captures in a sentence the recurrent themes underlying the modern impulse to eliminate public begging.[1]

If the modern age in welfare policy begins in the sixteenth century, the reformers themselves drew heavily on tradition. Early modern definitions of the "true" and "false" poor are rooted in the debates of Church Fathers and canonists; the desire for efficacious, rational forms of municipal welfare predated the initiatives of a Luther, a Calvin, or a Vives.[2] But in the sixteenth century a new impulse of charitable reform swept across Europe, affecting almost every region regardless of its allegiance in the religious wars of the era. Throughout Europe, the impulse to organize public charity and the impulse to repress public begging went hand in hand. Both tasks were viewed as a responsibility of local leaders, municipal government, and above all the laity. Within the broader framework of the territorial state, efforts were made to coordinate and give form to local efforts through general legislation. Charles V set a pattern in Flanders; the Elizabethan Poor Law of 1601 in England imposed unity on measures of reform elaborated in preceding decades.[3]

Institutions

In France, the prohibition of begging accompanied measures to maintain a census of the poor and to provide for their aid, particularly in the form of work that could serve them as a permanent livelihood. The Grand Bureau des Pauvres in Paris (1544) and the *aumône-générale* in Lyons (1534) were the foremost examples of this dual impulse. As in England, the desire to provide a framework for local efforts inspired general legislation: the royal ordinances of Blois (1566) and Moulins (1572) spelled out a system of parish responsibility for poor relief. But the Civil Wars that only ended with the century prevented the effective implementation of these measures.[4]

For France, the seventeenth century was an especially important period for new initiatives touching on mendicity. From the revival of municipal institutions under Henri IV and his adviser Sully at the beginning of the century to the emergency decrees of Louis XIV in the disastrous later years of his reign, several key themes compete for attention. An overarching theme is the emphasis throughout the century on economic productivity based on a morally disciplined workforce. Mercantilist theory and legislation turned productivity into a system: all local institutional efforts had to fit together into a machine that could be mobilized at will by the head of the state. A second theme was religious: the manifold influence of the Counter-Reformation in France, affecting all classes but most markedly the aristocracy, generated a militant devotion to active works of charity and established institutions to perpetuate them. A third theme that overlapped the other two was the search for an all-encompassing rational order in the institutions of state and society. This commitment to rationality and order had to be imposed on a baroque universe of conflict and spontaneous energy.[5]

The most distinctive product of seventeenth-century thinking on social welfare in France was the creation of the *hôpital-général* of Paris in 1656, followed by a campaign to replicate its functions in provincial capitals by means of royal legislation of 1672 and a money-raising effort that took the form of a religious revival. The legislation of 1656 consolidated several existing Parisian charitable houses into a single institution that was therefore "general." Several important institutions were not included: the *hôtel-Dieu,* in particular, retained its separate identity as a place for the care of the sick. The *hôpital-général* served the disabled, the very young, the aged, the chronically ill, and those who needed to be forcibly confined. The consolidation of these functions served as the occasion for what Michel Foucault has called "the Great Confinement"—the peremptory order that all beggars and vagabonds should present themselves at the *hôpital-général* to be given work and support; those who failed to do so and continued to beg would be arrested by archers of the hospital and forcibly confined in the institution. Michel Foucault characterized this measure of 1656 as a new equation of reason with a hierarchical social order. Because the beggar shunned the rationality of work, he acquired the status of problematic marginality that European society had once assigned to the leper.[6]

The practice of confining beggars in workhouses certainly gained favor in the seventeenth century. But, as Jean-Pierre Gutton has shown, the practice stemmed from a variety of impulses and drew on long-standing institutional precedents in

France and elsewhere.[7] If Foucault's interpretation of the Great Confinement is too schematic, it is nonetheless true that debate over the *hôpitaux-généraux* generated new definitions of work as civic obligation. A late-seventeenth-century propagandist for confinement of the poor, Jean Guérin, upbraided those who argued that it deprived the poor of their rights:

> They were but the refuse and dregs of the world, and if one may put it thus, the excrement and the ordure. But now they are no longer as before useless burdens upon the face of the earth, nor gangrenous members that had to be cut off; rather, they have become by their work and by the exercise of the arts at which they are being occupied, necessary parts in the growth of towns, and they begin to merit the name of citizens.[8]

Later writers might not share Guérin's religious paternalism or his strictly urban outlook; but the ardor for productivity—an almost mystical belief that the secret of material wealth was linked with that of a spiritually fulfilling life as a citizen— would only gain force in the eighteenth century and beyond. Another related ambition would join forces with it, namely the desire to coordinate all dimensions of charitable finance and all provisions for the poor into a single uniform system, linked to an equally rational system of repression.[9]

A legislative summary prepared by Laverdy's commission in 1766 attests to the impression that Louis XIV's legislation made on royal magistrats in the 1760s. It described his edict of 1700 as "the most complete law on mendicity." Its repressive rigor was matched by a commitment to the relief of need. It required all ablebodied beggars to return to their places of birth or last residence. Men found begging would be beaten for the first offense: for a second offense, males under twenty years of age would be whipped and placed in stocks; those over twenty would be sent to the galleys for five years. Women were to be shut up in a hospital for the first offense; they were to be beaten and put in stocks for a second offense. The giving of alms would be punishable by a fine of fifty livres payable to the hospital.[10]

The king's provincial intendants were called to play a crucial role in implementing this law, as in many other areas where a uniform administration of royal policies was desired. They were to supervise the distribution of funds to aid those who obeyed the law, reimburse the cost of lodging and feeding beggars en route to their parishes of origin, and organize work projects *(ateliers)* during winter months. Reviewing earlier precedents, the memoir of 1766 noted that in 1693 the parlement had obliged parishes to raise an imposition to provide bread for the poor whom the king had ordered back to their parishes. In the edict of 1700 the king went further, offering to provide aid directly to those hospitals that might otherwise be obliged to release infirm beggars.[11]

The king's *lieutenant-général de police* in Paris, d'Argenson, enforced the law of 1700 for a time, but it remained a dead letter elsewhere. Emergency legislation invoked it anew in the disastrous year 1709. In the years of peace and recovery after the death of Louis XIV in 1715, another approach was touted: recruiting beggars for colonization. Initiatives launched in 1718 and 1720 were abandoned, however, in the face of a panic response in Paris at the arrest of beggars by archers who were referred to as *les Mississippiens.* The edict of 1720 set a precedent for making intendants directly responsible for detention centers: those arrested were "to be locked up in places designated for this, to be fed and provided for at the king's expense." In this context, of course, beggars would be held only temporarily, en route to the ports where they would take ship for the colonies.[12]

The main line of institutional experimentation promoted under Louis XIV entered a new phase with the enactment of the most ambitious effort to date to create a uniform general scheme for eradicating mendicity, the Declaration of July 18, 1724. The innovations contained in it were presented as remedies for specific shortcomings in previous legislation on the confinement of beggars in *hôpitaux-généraux*. The most important of these was the assignment of funds from the royal treasury to aid those hospitals unable to bear the cost of incarcerating beggars. This was needed especially because it was the intent of the minister, Dodun, to enlist a large number of hospitals in a dense network committed to this task.[13]

The technicalities of royal finance were not fully worked out for over a year. In effect, funding for mendicity was linked to the resolution of contradictions in the collection of excise taxes, some of which were levied for the payment of municipal officials whose offices had since been abolished. It was decided to cut these assessments in half and earmark the reduced levy for funding the execution of the Declaration of 1724 regarding beggars and vagabonds. While this arrangement affected the *pays d'états,* the *pays de généralité* were subjected to a new surtax on the *taille* assessed at a rate of three deniers per livre. Funds were also to be raised by consolidating charitable endowments, particularly those that funded general distributions of alms. The intendants were given inspection over these financial arrangements and disbursed the funds owed to the hospitals.[14]

Judging that the hospitals had failed in the past to set beggars to work, the framers of the new declaration enjoined all those who could not find work or parish aid to present themselves voluntarily to the hospitals, where they might indenture themselves in work companies and receive one-sixth of the amount paid for their labor, in addition to room and board. Those found begging in violation of the declaration would be treated more harshly, being fed on bread and water only and employed within the walls of the hospital. A second offense incurred a lengthier second detention and branding with the letter "M." A third offense entailed a galley sentence for men, and confinement for a term of five years to life for women. Separate provisions were made for invalids. In order to implement the penalties against recidivism, a central bureau was to be established in Paris for the collation of all records of arrest.[15]

The system elaborated in 1724 lasted for nine years. Then, in 1733, funds for mendicity were appropriated to the royal treasury. Some hospitals continued to receive beggars, under the supposition that funds would again be forthcoming. The special tax levies continued to be raised, and a royal *intendant des finances* retained the function of supervision over the funds in question at the *contrôle-général*. Since the immediate occasion for suspending payments was the outbreak of the War of Polish Succession, it is difficult to weigh the seriousness of royal bureaucrats' complaints that the Declaration of 1724 was not being executed effectively.[16] Later commentators alleged that hospital administrators had diverted royal funds in order to support the general upkeep of their establishments, and had failed to invest adequate funds and effort toward putting to work those beggars sent to them for rehabilitation. In his regional study of the Declaration of 1724 and its implementation, Jean-Pierre Gutton found evidence that some hospital administrators sheltered individual beggars from the harsh consequences of recidivism. He also found that efforts to employ beggars had mixed results. Daniel Trudaine, intendant of the Auvergne, inspired a sustained effort to produce cloth at Clermont, St. Flour, and Riom. Not all attempts were as well organized. Even the best-managed ones barely recovered the costs of production.[17]

The experiment of 1724 had a variety of results. Jean-Pierre Gutton suggests that the Declaration planted the seed for a notion that public assistance is a function of the state. Ironically, this may have contributed to a decline in religious enthusiasm for supporting the hospitals. Withdrawal of royal support, coupled with criticism of hospital administrations, may then have undermined confidence in them.[18] However, royal agents and a variety of critical observers had become intimately involved in the debate over the administration of poor relief and houses of correction. They commonly assumed that the Declaration of 1724 would be revived in some form. The chancellor put off an inquiry in 1738 with the assurance that the matter would be reviewed at a more propitious time. A subsistence crisis in 1740 led to a temporary but significant revival of the principle of parish relief. The parlement of Paris, citing emergency measures of 1693 and 1709 as precedents, authorized the collection of a local poor rate by churchwardens.[19]

Machault d'Arnouville, the controller-general from 1745 to 1754, attempted to revive the main provisions of the Declaration of 1724 by means of his Declaration of 1750. Renewing the prohibition on begging, this declaration promised royal funds for the maintenance of beggars in the *hôpitaux-généraux*, where they were to be interned. In the absence of an *hôpital-général* within four leagues of the place of arrest, beggars were to be jailed in royal prisons and transferred at royal expense to the nearest hospital. The repressive purpose of the declaration was underscored in the provision of penalties for beggars carrying arms or found guilty of unlawful assembly or *attroupement*, while migrant laborers were not to be molested as long as they were not begging. The preamble of Machault's declaration promised a forthcoming "general regulation that we have resolved to issue on this matter." He asked intendants to provide information on charitable resources and needs.[20]

Machault became embroiled with the Assembly of the Clergy over his effort to institute the *vingtième,* a five-percent personal income tax, as a regular peacetime levy. Since this tax would have fallen on the privileged orders as well as on *roturiers,* it provoked a political test of strength, prefiguring the fate of all later royal attempts to equalize the tax burden. In an atmosphere of intensifying jurisdictional rivalry, it became increasingly difficult to frame measures requiring regular collaboration between judicial authorities and the royal intendants. In this instance, the funds that Machault had promised to the *hôpitaux-généraux* in order to revive the Declaration of 1724 were not forthcoming, and the Declaration of 1750 joined the accumulation of ephemeral legislation in the archives. It was implemented primarily in Flanders and the *généralité* of Paris, with alternative sources of funding. The *dépôts de mendicité* were foreshadowed in the creation of supplemental *maisons de force* under the intendant's supervision in those places where *hôpitaux-généraux* lacked facilities for confinement. One such facility at Meaux in the *généralité* of Paris functioned until 1760. No more than a stopgap measure, the

Declaration of 1750 was nonetheless a significant "false start" midway between the collapse of royal funding for the Declaration of 1724 and the launching of a new scheme by Laverdy and his commission.[21]

Ideas

If the dream of an administratively uniform regulation of charitable functions drew inspiration from an agenda formulated under Louis XIV's reign, the ideological context for dealing with mendicity had also been reshaped by the debates of that period, in which Paul Hazard has located "the crisis of European consciousness." The abbé de Saint-Pierre best represents the paradoxical reformulation of Louis XIV's legacy, inspired as much by the critics of absolutism as by its defenders.[22]

Like the most radical of the *dévots,* the abbé de Saint-Pierre abhorred the cruel effects of war, but instead of denouncing the vanity of princes, he urged them to consider how their own interests dictated a compact of perpetual peace. Like Vauban and Boisguillebert, he was aware of the crippling impact of royal taxation upon the economy. But instead of proposing a radically new tax system, like Vauban's *dîme royale,* Saint-Pierre showed how much more efficiently the state might secure its revenue and encourage general prosperity by a modification of the existing *taille,* based on a careful assessment of all land in a systematic survey or *cadastre.* Instead of excoriating the despot who, in Fénelon's words, had turned all France into "a vast hospital, desolate and without provisions," Saint-Pierre suggested more effective means of using the *hôpitaux-généraux* to make useful citizens of the idle poor.[23]

Saint Pierre argued that the problem of mendicity could be solved by a careful distinction between voluntary and involuntary begging, and by a uniform system of confinement throughout the kingdom. A central bureau should coordinate all information and accounting, work should be planned for all inmates capable of it, and a reliable source of tax revenue should be provided. These proposals were related to an interlocking program of reform that was at once humanitarian and efficiency-minded. He pointed out to his readers that his objectives for hospitals would be more easily realized if mendicity were alleviated by a reform of the *taille.* Saint-Pierre's brochure on the begging poor appeared shortly before the Declaration of July 18, 1724, on beggars and vagabonds, and may well have had an influence on that major new initiative. But in a broader sense, Saint-Pierre's irenic program of improvement provides the link between the age of Louis XIV and the age of the *Encyclopédistes.*[24]

A generation later, Montesquieu brought into focus some of the key issues that underlay discussions about mendicity. In a brief chapter of his *Spirit of the Laws* devoted to *hôpitaux,* he articulated commonplace opinion on the subject and fortified it with a portentous challenge. Pious foundations, he noted, could nourish mendicity as a profession rather than extinguishing it: the city of Rome perpetuated a tribe of beggars with its too lavish charitable foundations. Deciding that the answer to general poverty was not to transfer wealth but to create employment, he framed a maxim that would be cited constantly in following decades: "A man is not poor because he has nothing, but because he is not working."[25]

But more startling than Montesquieu's critique of traditional charity was his formulation of new criteria of state responsibility. In a crucial sentence, he moved from a statement that a Vives or a Guérin might have understood and approved, to a modern concept of the welfare state: "A few alms given to a naked man in the streets do not fulfill the obligations of the state, which owes to all its citizens a secure subsistence, suitable food and clothing, and a manner of living that is not contrary to good health."[26]

The anecdote that follows in Montesquieu's text amplifies this radical conclusion. The great Mughal emperor, Aurangzeb, when asked why he built no hospitals, replied that he would make his kingdom so rich that there would be no need for any. He should have said, according to Montesquieu, "I will begin by making my empire rich, *and* I will build hospitals." Enlightened economic policy can alone diminish the general burden of poverty: all the hospitals in the world will not remedy a "general misery." But a rich society, a complex economic machine, can and must provide for the "particular accidents" that beset its citizens.

Montesquieu's criteria of obligation to the poor signal an emerging conceptual dichotomy between simple "poverty" and its wretched extreme, *misère*. Enlightened writers believed that the mass of the poor could be "happy" if they were not oppressed by *misère,* a condition equated with torture. Although such a view of happiness might indeed rationalize social inequality, it was essentially incompatible with the "utility of poverty" argument that frequently accompanied a mercantilist view of labor, subsistence, and production.[27] In the decades that followed, the "right" to well-being in this minimal sense would be translated into empirical standards. Expected to promote the aggregate accumulation of wealth and to police the harmony of a vast social organism, the state would now also be challenged to determine scientifically, with the help of experts, what the "rights" of its citizens were with respect to "happiness."[28]

Montesquieu's axioms reverberated in the opinions of the elite in the 1750s; on his death in 1755, d'Alembert published a eulogy at the head of the seventh volume of the *Encyclopédie.* He appended a summary of the *Spirit of the Laws,* including Montesquieu's thought that "one must begin by making the people rich, and then build hospitals." But d'Alembert did not relay the concluding challenge of the chapter and left a precariously balanced view of hospitals: they were needed as a momentary resource for pressing need, because the industry of a people was not always requited; all the same, hospitals and monasteries alike should not be allowed to multiply, lest all be at ease save those who work.[29]

Although d'Alembert's summary was not unfaithful to the author, it was tinged with the main preoccupation of the decade—the notion that the strength of the realm depended on an increase in productivity, and that such increase in turn required that a long habit of encouraging idleness and dependency be broken. That argument was most strikingly developed in the article that the young Turgot wrote for the *Encyclopédie* in 1757 entitled "Fondations" (endowments). Here, in the context of a discussion of charitable institutions, the term *laisser-faire* makes one of its earliest appearances as a description of public policy. Starting from the individualistic belief that people work most effectively when they respond to the needs they perceive, Turgot argued that perpetual endowments were ineffective instruments for achieving their goals. In charitably endowed hospitals, case-hardened attendants gave inadequate attention to inmates groaning in misery. Far better care would result from well-directed aid given to families of the sick and elderly. Turgot exhorted his compatriots to emulate the English in their private and municipal philanthropies. The accomplishments of the *bureau d'aumônes* of Bayeux were proof enough that the French could rival the English in displaying the true "spirit of the citizen."[30]

Soon after writing his article on endowments, Turgot took a post as intendant in the remote rural province of Limousin, where his ideas were to be tested and shaped by fifteen years of experience. He declined to contribute further articles to the *Encyclopédie;* it is said that he had agreed to furnish the entries for *"Hôpital"* and *"Mendiants."* Diderot supplied the article on hospitals, reflecting the view, recently expressed by Piarron de Chamousset, that the efforts of hospitals should be coordinated in a national network.[31] While this argument carried forward the theme of state responsibility for the needs of the poor, the article *"Mendiants,"* which did not appear until 1765, reflected a harsher view on the repression of mendicity and laid out the state's responsibility to set the idler on work.

The article *"Mendiants"* was the work of Jaucourt, a writer adept at ransacking the works of his contemporaries to produce articles for the *Encyclopédie.* In this case he drew upon a work published in 1758 by Véron de Forbonnais, a writer who became the chief economic adviser to the controller-general Silhouette in 1759. Véron de Forbonnais had criticized the mistakes of the past, reviving a mercantilist emphasis on work discipline fostered by state action. He noted that "the excessive poverty of the countryside and the luxury of the capital had drawn a crowd of beggars" to Paris at the beginning of the seventeenth century, yet the measures taken to confine beggars had resulted in waste worse than a plague. The error in Louis XIV's edicts on *hôpitaux-généraux* had been the omission of more specific provisions for the work to be done by inmates. The remedy was to use this army of cheap labor *(de bras à bon marché)* where it was most needed—in mines, for example, and in the colonies.[32]

In what could be taken as a pointed rejoinder to Montesquieu, Forbonnais wrote: "In a well-ordered society, men who are poor and without industry must not find themselves clothed, fed, and healthy: the others will soon imagine that there is greater happiness in doing nothing."[33] Turning from economics to crime, he added rhetorically: "How many offenses would society have been spared, had but the first unruliness been repressed by the fear of being shut away to work?" Treading lightly but decisively in the difficult matter of jurisprudence, Forbonnais concluded that there was no penalty between fines and corporal sentences but imprisonment. The cost of imposing this penalty would be borne not only by the prince and the public, but by the offender himself.

Forbonnais's view overlapped to some extent with that of the Physiocrats, whose *tableau économique* would not register a prosperous circulation if the "net product" of an agricultural kingdom were consumed in idleness by the very ones who should be adding to it. But Forbonnais, and a large body of opinion in the parlements and the royal bureaucracy, viewed "liberty" and "protection" as complementary, not contradictory, concepts. Removing some of the restraints on the marketplace might require redoubled activity on the part of the authorities, in order to regulate actions of all sorts that might disrupt its natural operation. The rational incentive to work, in particular, must be complemented by sanctions against idleness.[34]

Policy Debates at Midcentury

Early in 1759 an experienced royal councillor who would later play a crucial part
in establishing the *dépôts de mendicité* spelled out his ideas on the subject of mendicity and submitted them to the controller-general, Silhouette. The councillor was
Jean-François Joly de Fleury, the former intendant of Burgundy. Probably familiar
with Forbonnais's views on the subject, he had reason to think the minister might
be receptive. On April 4, Silhouette replied in a brief note stating his intention ''in
happier times and when I am less overwhelmed with business, to give special attention to these questions.'' In July the minister found a suitable moment and invited
de Fleury to dine with him at Bercy. ''I would like to discuss with you,'' he wrote,
''the means of deterring able-bodied beggars, and of deriving even some usefulness
from them for the state, by making them work.''[35] Silhouette referred in his letter
to the ideas that the intendant's father would have had on the subject. The minister
was referring to the *procureur-général* of the parlement of Paris, Guillaume-François
Joly de Fleury, who had been responsible for maintaining the central register of the
beggars arrested by virtue of the Declaration of 1724. The intendant of Burgundy
thus drew on administrative experience of several kinds. Like other intendants, he
had been obliged to deal with the breakdown of a previous royal policy on mendicity. He was familiar with the ideology of the parlements. The ideas contained in
his memoir harmonized with those of Véron de Forbonnais, while offering a more
specific blueprint for a new policy.

De Fleury's ''Memoir on the Means of Preventing Mendicity'' began on a dramatic note: ''Everyone knows that mendicity is the school for thieves and assassins:
that beggars have no religion or morals.'' Like Forbonnais, he stigmatized beggars
as the carriers of a moral ''contagion.'' By supporting themselves in idleness better
than many a farmer or artisan, they undermined the system of rewards that keep
society and the economy functioning. De Fleury may have been thinking of his own
experiences, particularly his encounter with the smuggler Mandrin, when he recited
the ''school for crimes'' argument, but the terms he used were time-worn formu-
las.[36]

Why had the Declaration of 1724 failed to eradicate the ''contagion'' of mendicity? The direct cause was a lack of funds, as it was again in 1750, according to
de Fleury. Overlapping jurisdictions paralyzed administration, and the effort to coordinate records of inmates in a central bureau had proven unworkable. At the local
level, the article of the Declaration requiring able-bodied beggars to be put to work
had not been enforced. Worst of all, hospital managers had not been held properly
accountable for funds disbursed to them under the terms of the Declaration. The
parlement of Paris had accused the controller-general of diverting funds intended
for the poor, but he ''had in fact taken back funds from hospitals whose administrators were abusing them to their profit.'' Any new effort would run into similar
problems, if it required the cooperation of hospital administrators. Few provinces
had true *hôpitaux-généraux,* and in most cases hospitals were already overloaded
and lacked funds.[37]

Prisons were no more suitable than hospitals for the purpose at hand, de Fleury
continued. The feeding and keeping of beggars would give rise to disputes between
intendants or subdelegates and the officers of each *baillage,* backed by the parle-

ment. The conclusion was inescapable: entirely distinct places were needed solely for beggars, "so that no one might claim to have jurisdiction over them except those to whom His Majesty sees fit to confide it." De Fleury recognized the difficulty that arose at this point. "This disposition will probably cause some difficulty with the gentlemen of the Parlement who will look upon these prisons where they have no jurisdiction as a *chartre privée*."[38] Procedures of arrest might also be a subject of dispute. De Fleury preferred a simple procedure that would minimize delay and expense: "people of the beggars' sort do not deserve to be treated with the same circumspection as useful citizens." He felt that the penalty of confinement should arouse no scruples. The aim was not to punish; it was merely a question of "forcing them to renounce a profession that is condemned by both religion and public order, and procuring work no more difficult than that done by farmers, which will become voluntary as soon as they have lost the habit of idleness."[39]

This confinement must be distinguished from prison in order to forestall objections from the parlements. "The courts," noted de Fleury, "will not fail to say that prison is not a penalty in France and that people cannot be condemned in their persons without a procedure *par récolement et confrontation*."[40] He would parry these objections by requiring certain formalities of the provosts of the *maréchaussée*. In any case, he observed, the scruples of the parlements were not to be taken seriously: "the courts can hardly have any objection to this sort of procedure, since they mete out sentences of a defamatory nature every day to individuals against whom they have no proof except being found with stolen goods not properly accounted for."[41]

De Fleury would appease the parlements on one important point. They would probably object to setting up a new system, as long as the special tax levied since 1724 for the subsistence of the poor remained diverted from its original purpose. This tax was the three deniers per livre of the *taille*, or a 1.25 percent surcharge on the *taille*. The best course would be "to return it to its original purpose, if one wants to avoid objections from the parlement that would be all the more difficult to answer, since they would have a quite legitimate foundation."[42] Politically, the essential point was to assure the complete jurisdiction of intendants over a new system of "special prisons" or "hospitals or buildings solely for beggars." Anticipating the ploy later used, de Fleury remarked, "Only by representing these special prisons as a purely provisional arrangement can the parlements be induced to consent."[43]

What buildings should be used to house beggars? From his experience as intendant of Burgundy, de Fleury observed that one religious house alone had twenty thousand livres of income and devoted itself entirely "to feeding travelers, which is to say, promoting beggary." The revenues of this single house would almost suffice to feed all the invalid beggars arrested in Burgundy, if it were taken over and "reformed." As precedent for such an action, de Fleury noted that beggars were locked up in the buildings of the order of the Holy Spirit at Dijon under the terms of the Declaration of 1724, and that the *hôtel-Dieu* of Besançon had been moved into buildings belonging to the same order. Convents of Jacobins, Cordeliers, and Capuchins were likely candidates for reform. The campaign to take over such properties should combine secrecy, prudence, and continual pressure from the controller-general. Individuals should be assigned to serve as liaison with each religious order. "There is nothing," added de Fleury with a flourish, "that cannot be brought about in this Kingdom when the will of His Majesty is well known and announced by a minister who is firm, wise, and enlightened."[44] If these suggestions evoke the age of Louis XIV, when "reunions" of pious foundations had been promoted by a commission of the royal council, de Fleury also resurrected the repressive legislation of *le grand siècle*. He advised beginning with a renewal of the Declaration of 1693, which condemned vagabonds to the galleys, as a means of bringing home the need for more efficient use of hospital foundations for the poor.[45]

De Fleury concluded his memoir with a list of practical suggestions reflecting his familiarity with the operations of the relevant administrative bureaus. First, the receiver-general responsible for the *caisse de pauvres,* M. Boutin, should be asked to provide an exact list of the numbers of poor arrested and fed from 1725 to 1727, with a statement of expenses for repairs and provisioning at that time. This would presumably allow new estimates to be made. Earlier in his memoir, de Fleury had estimated that there were some thirty thousand beggars in France, or about one thousand in each *généralité*. To keep the number of inmates in each location down to about two hundred, he projected four to six buildings in each *généralité*.[46]

Second, a circular letter should be sent to all intendants, asking them to suggest places where beggars might be locked up and to obtain estimates for repair and furnishing, along with estimates of the number of beggars in their jurisdictions. Third, M. Boullongne, *intendant des finances,* might be asked to furnish an exact list of hospitals, *généralité* by *généralité,* with a statement of their revenues, the purpose for which they were founded, the amount of their debts, and the state of their buildings. Finally, de Fleury suggested that the disposition of the case before the royal council involving the order of the Holy Spirit at Montpellier should be looked into as a possible answer to the problem of providing buildings for the new operation.[47]

Four months after meeting with de Fleury to discuss mendicity, Silhouette fell from office. Opinion turned against him when he proposed a "general subvention" along the lines proposed by Forbonnais. His successor, Henri Bertin, lasted longer than his immediate predecessors, serving through the last four years of the Seven Years' War. Defeats in those years provoked invidious comparison between British strengths and French weaknesses, a topic of learned debate before the war.[48] Efforts to tap the wealth of the privileged had failed repeatedly. But Bertin wanted to stimulate the production of wealth. If the resources of the entire country could be increased by a systematic reform of fiscal and economic policy, the burden of the royal fisc might be supported without crippling production, and privileged landowners might be more willing to pay taxes to a government that was actively promoting their prosperity.[49]

Such a strategy drew support from the new Physiocratic movement. The ideas of this group had first reached an influential public through the articles "Farmer" and "Grains" written by François Quesnay and published in volumes 6 and 7 of the *Encyclopédie,* appearing in 1756 and 1757. Although not a declared adherent to the doctrine, Bertin enacted some of its tenets. Notably, he adopted the policy of promoting free trade in grains, a move that required dismantling an elaborate institutional machinery for policing the market in subsistence commodities. Given the traditional dependence on such police measures, Bertin made some politic concessions to the fear of dearth and famine. When prices reached certain levels, protection would be reimposed; the provisioning of Paris would be treated as a special case. The edict freeing the internal trade in grain was registered by the parlement of Paris in 1763; the edict concerning the export of grain was not put into effect until Bertin had left office in 1764.

Free-trade ideas had been gaining support well before the Physiocrats made a doctrine of them. Landowners who had received only modest benefits from their years of good harvest at mid-century were easily persuaded to blame low prices on excessive prohibitions and regulations of trade.[50] Physiocracy buttressed free-trade arguments with a theoretical model of the economic system as a whole. The claim to have established a systematic social science appealed to readers recently inspired by Montesquieu's *Spirit of the Laws* and the "Preliminary Discourse" of the *Encyclopédie*. This "scientific" inspiration undoubtedly had an impact on leading figures in the royal administration, including to some degree Bertin himself.[51] Physiocracy also allied itself with a movement to promote agricultural improvement through scientific means. This movement coincided with a nostalgic reassertion of the claims of rural society as the truly productive element in a healthy state. The Physiocrats linked this theme to an economic critique of the mercantilist promotion of manufactures and their export. Bertin, as minister, promoted the scientific study of agricultural problems through the creation of royal *sociétés d'agriculture*, officially sponsored groups functioning as academies devoted entirely to agriculture and the problems of rural society.[52]

Early in 1763, Henri Bertin took a major step toward new legislation on mendicity in an inquiry addressed to the recently created *sociétés d'agriculture*. He invited them to give their opinions on the problem of mendicity and to suggest appropriate remedies. The fact that soldiers and sailors were about to be demobilized may have given urgency to his question. But Bertin displayed a consistent concern for the stability and security of rural society, launching inquiries into the enclosure of common lands and other matters affecting the poorer peasants. He was, of course, well acquainted with urban measures for combatting mendicity. His family was from Lyons, a city rich in charitable expedients. He had served as intendant of the *généralité* of Lyons from 1754 to 1757 and as *lieutenant-général de police* of the city of Paris for two years before being named controller-general.[53]

It is fitting that the most noteworthy reply to Bertin's inquiry came from the *société d'agriculture* of Orleans, situated in a grain-growing region with large-scale farming, the chosen terrain of Physiocratic *fermiers* on the one hand, and that of tramping day laborers and vagrants on the other. On March 18 the society sent to Parent, Bertin's chief clerk, a copy of a memoir read at a meeting of the society by the landowner, incipient Physiocrat, and local magistrate Guillaume François Le Trosne. A month later, Le Trosne agreed to publication of his memoir, although he expressed fear of reprisals by beggars if his name were printed. After consultations with other agricultural societies, including those of Paris, Rouen, and Soissons, the memoir was published. Le Trosne noted in its preface that the work "appeared to have merited the attention of the council." While Joly de Fleury's memoir of 1759 prepared the judicial and administrative apparatus to be used against beggars, Le Trosne supplied an economic and moral rationale for punishment. He established the harm done to agriculture by vagabonds and beggars, defined the responsibility of the state, and argued for new remedies more effective than the old. Overall, his message conformed to the reform program of Bertin.[54]

The responsibility of the state, Le Trosne argued, was to ensure "liberty for the sale of what is produced, and security for the farmer."[55] Vagabonds made the farmer fearful and insecure, discouraging him from producing. The economic damage inflicted by the plague of mendicity equaled the amount paid for the royal *taille* in poorer areas. Le Trosne alternated between agronomic metaphors—a plague of insects, for example—and images of a marauding troop to be opposed with disciplined force. In one instance—Le Trosne may have been referring to a misfortune of his own—arson perpetrated by vagabonds caused 1,800 livres' worth of damage to buildings and 3,000 to grain and straw. To be a vagabond, wrote Le Trosne, was to be at war with one's fellow citizens: "For isn't it waging war to attack personal safety and ownership of goods, to lay a country under contribution, to live only from booty, to eat no other bread but that which has been wrested by fear, to force compliance by threats only too often carried out?"[56]

Le Trosne proposed reviving the penalty of the galleys in perpetuity for convicted vagrants. Such had been the letter of Louis XIV's Declaration of 1687. He had prepared his reader for severity toward the vagabond by arguing, that "his estate is his crime, and a habitual crime that provides the ground for conviction." In the full flush of his indictment he had even asked why a government offering ten livres for the pelt of a wolf did not offer a bounty for the arrest of a vagabond: "A vagabond is infinitely more dangerous for society." A crude political arithmetic supported this reasoning. Severity would save lives in the long run, since some two hundred citizens were killed by vagabonds every year, and sixty to eighty vagabonds were executed for crimes they committed.[57]

If there were too many vagabonds to be pressed into service in the royal galleys, they might be used on land. He would have them branded as chattel slaves of the state. Desertion would be punishable by death. Once "confiscated," vagabonds would no longer be considered part of the civil order: "The laws no longer have anything to determine with regard to them; the King may dispose of them and use them in whatever manner seems most useful." If the soldier was subjected, even as a citizen, to absolute discipline, why, asked Le Trosne rhetorically, should not vagabonds be treated at least as harshly?[58] Discipline could produce economic benefits. Convict labor might be employed in mines or in the building of new ports "to stimulate circulation and life in certain provinces." Gangs might be hired out to contractors on public works; their employment on roads might lessen the burden of the *corvée*. Such ideas had been suggested before; some had been tried. For Le Trosne, they represented a systematic effort to restore movement in the Physiocratic *tableau économique*.[59]

Previous laws had been weakly executed because of compassion for the vagabond. But the criminal estate of the vagabond was truly "the effect of idleness consciously chosen by a man who has only his labor by which to subsist." Le Trosne appealed to his own experience and that of fellow landowners in the *société d'agriculture*: vagabonds made excuses for refusing work when it was offered to them.

It is assuredly not work which is lacking, but a willingness to work. In wartime any able-bodied man has the option of serving the King; in peacetime he has only to choose one of any kind of employment. Whoever has difficulty finding one, has only to offer himself for board, or even ask less than the ordinary rate; he is sure not to fail.[60]

Like de Fleury, Le Trosne presumed a radical separation between the status of vagabond and citizen, and therefore argued that the judicial conviction of a vagabond should not require a formal deposition *par récolement et confrontation*. By definition, a vagabond was not in a position to call witnesses. A simple cross-examination should suffice to determine whether a detainee fell within the definition set forth in article 2 of the Declaration of 1701: "Vagabonds are those who have no profession, no craft, no certain domicile, and no property in order to subsist, and who are not vouched for and cannot have their good behavior certified by trustworthy persons."[61]

Le Trosne insisted on sending convicted vagabonds to the galleys rather than to *hôpitaux*. Hospital administrators had undermined the execution of the Declaration of 1724 as well as the abortive measure of 1750. They welcomed royal subsidies for their houses, but failed to enforce the provision that recidivists were to be branded. As a result, the provision that a third offense was to be punished by a life sentence in the galleys was not strictly enforced. "People whose main occupation is not that of judging," Le Trosne observed, "will always be held back by compassion, and will never punish any faults but those that trouble the order of the house they govern."[62]

Since women convicted as vagabonds could not be sentenced to royal galleys, they would have to be put to work in special houses of correction. Until new buildings could be made ready, the old hospitals would need to function temporarily as *maisons de force* for this purpose. Le Trosne hoped that new facilities might succeed, with good management, in supporting themselves.[63]

It is difficult to reconcile Le Trosne's severe strictures on vagabonds with the case he presents for tolerating domiciled beggars in a concluding "plan for beggars." Speaking of the "great evil" of begging by children, he concedes that "it is an evil made necessary by the deplorable state of our countryside." Effectively contradicting his premise that all citizens could live by their work, he explains: "In the richest cantons, there are fathers and mothers unable to feed their family without this help."[64] He goes so far as to suggest that local judges might use their discretion to allow even able-bodied beggars to be tolerated on those rare occasions of dearth and unemployment for day laborers. The punishment for the domiciled poor who begged in other circumstances would also be less severe than that applied to vagabonds. The stocks, the lash, and even temporary banishment might be used for repeaters, while women could be confined in workhouses situated within hospitals.[65]

The fact that the domiciled beggars were more easily contained than vagabonds explains why Le Trosne did not regard them as a dangerous "foreign troop." However, there was some inconsistency in allowing the domiciled beggar to allege dearth or unemployment as an excuse for begging, while ruling out such mitigating circumstances in the case of vagabonds. Even more surprisingly, Le Trosne ended his

memoir by advocating a system of licensed begging by the infirm, who were traditionally the responsibility of the parish. Le Trosne conceded that voluntary alms
were inadequate, that the rich would object to forced alms, and that it would be
most difficult to find qualified persons willing to organize charitable contributions
and set up workshops for spinning or knitting. Le Trosne proposed therefore that
judges give out parchment certificates to the destitute entitling them to beg; those
who begged outside their parishes would be punished.[66]

Le Trosne's memoir served as a model for new measures on mendicity in some
important respects, confirming or supplementing the points made by de Fleury.
Vagabonds and some able-bodied beggars would become liable to a three-year sentence to the galleys for a first offense. Women would be shut up in *maisons de
force*. Ironically, the houses ''provisionally'' set aside for women and others unfit
for the galleys would later evolve into the *dépôts* used for the great majority of
beggars and vagabonds of both sexes.

Most important, royal policy would mirror the peculiar ambiguity that underlay
Le Trosne's awkward distinction between vagabonds and beggars. The secretary of
the *société d'agriculture* of Orleans forwarded the original memoir to Parent with
the note that the society felt bound to observe that two laws, distinct in nature,
were needed in order to deal with the distinctly different problems of vagrancy and
beggary. Obviously, the society welcomed Le Trosne's argument for treating vagabonds with severity. But a reading of his memoir may have raised doubts in their
minds as to whether the two categories of beggar and vagabond were so easily
distinguished. Unless new legislation were in place to guarantee assistance to the
poor in need, laws aimed at punishing vagabonds might strike unjustly at helpless
beggars. In the Place de Toussaints and the highways of Brittany, as in other market
squares and roads of France, the borderline between the two categories was not
easily drawn, since their existence stemmed from economic pressures affecting both
alike. The misgivings and afterthoughts expressed by Le Trosne and the society of
Orleans were to haunt royal policy on mendicity in the decades ahead.[67]

The controller-general, Bertin, followed his inquiries to the *sociétés d'agriculture* with others directed to his intendants. The letter received by the intendant at
Soissons, dated April 1, 1763, took note of complaints received concerning the toll
in produce and damage by fire inflicted by vagabonds and beggars: ''Farms are
being deserted and agriculture suffers most directly from these depradations.'' There
were laws on the books to deal with this problem, ''but perhaps some essential
point is lacking in their disposition.'' Bertin asked for details on the harm done by
vagabonds especially by those operating in bands; asked what sort of people these
were; and invited suggestions and remedies.[68]

Instructing his secretary in the orchestration of opinion, the intendant Méliand
at Soissons noted that the survey requested by the minister ''was meant less for
learning their opinion on the remedy to be applied than it was for determining the
necessity for it by instances, by the detail of evils they cause.'' Replies received
from subdelegates should be reduced to a summary that would advocate the necessity of the means proposed in the memoir by the society of Orleans, which he
forwarded. Méliand himself was an enthusiastic advocate of Physiocratic ideas and
had recently employed as his secretary the young Du Pont de Nemours, soon to
become a leading spokesman of the school.[69]

The desired summary was prepared in two columns: "Beggars: abuses and evils that they cause," and "Remedies for preventing beggary." It supports the main points of Le Trosne's memoir: parish obligation for maintaining the true poor; the need for repressive measures against the vagabond and the nondomiciled beggar (vagabonds must take up a domicile or suffer the lash and be banished); vagrant and nondomiciled beggars to be sent to the galleys for life. Instead of following the cumbersome procedures of the ordinance of 1689, cases should be handled by the provost of the *maréchaussée* or by the presidial courts established in the sixteenth century to provide a quicker procedure, civil and criminal, for relatively minor offenses and smaller claims than those handled by the established jurisdictions of the baillages. The Declaration of 1724, originally intended to remove any pretext for mendicity by obliging the beggars arrested to work in hospitals, broke down "because the places in hospitals were sought after and applied for, and as the number was always full, the excuse thus remained intact." The problem of putting beggars to work was noted also by the subdelegate of Guise in a letter upon which the summary drew: "It is always a major enterprise to maintain this human trash or to apply it to the work it abhors." He therefore proposed a measure similar to that of Le Trosne for galleys on land. If vagabonds were not sent to the colonies or to the galleys, they could be enrolled as state workers on the model of those employed by the Empress Maria Theresa on the repair of towns and bridges.

Laverdy's Commission

Like Machault and Silhouette, Bertin fell from office as a result of strong opposition to the tax measures with which he proposed to solve the state's chronic fiscal problems. Unlike his predecessors, Bertin bequeathed to his successors a clearly articulated policy of economic reform that was essentially unaffected by the change in ministry. Indeed, Bertin remained actively involved in policy as a *secrétaire d'état* and continued to supervise the *sociétés d'agriculture*. The new minister, Charles Clément-François de Laverdy, persuaded the parlements to register edicts freeing the foreign trade in grain—the companion piece to Bertin's edicts concerning the internal trade—and actively implemented the new legislation. In the area of mendicity, Laverdy confirmed Bertin's initiatives by establishing a commission of the royal council to draw up legislation. The first stage of its work, a strict law against vagabonds, was registered promptly by the parlement of Paris by August 1764.[70]

Laverdy's appointment as controller-general was intended to propitiate the parlementaires. He was one of them—a *conseiller* of the parlement of Paris. That he was no "mere slave of the parlements," as his detractors charged, is most clearly demonstrated in the series of "municipal reform" laws by which he hoped to create responsible administrative initiative at the local level. While Laverdy weighted the system heavily in favor of traditional elites, he gave the popular classes a voice. This innovation spurred objections in many provinces; the Estates of Languedoc won the right to preserve their own more conservative traditions of municipal representation. Rallying his fellow parlementaires to a scheme that would have curtailed the functions of the intendants, Laverdy also set in place a network of local consultation that might enhance local responsiveness to plans of institutional reform from the center, including, naturally, the reform of measures for local relief of the poor.[71]

Inheriting a broad Physiocratic perspective on economic development from Bertin, Laverdy was also concerned with matters of jurisprudence. In 1752 he had published an annotated summary of penal legislation entitled *Code pénal*. The chapter concerning beggars and vagabonds summarized the Declaration of 1724 but omitted the detail of it, "because the measures that it took against beggars have remained without execution, for the most part."[72] The commission Laverdy appointed was charged with the task of drafting three laws, one on vagabonds, one on beggars, and one on the organization of alms bureaus *(bureaux d'aumône)*.[73] Writing in 1791, a former inspector of the *dépôts de mendicité*, Bannefroy, lamented the failure of Laverdy to carry out his three-point program. Of the laws projected, he remarked:

> The one against vagabonds was the only one registered: it condemned men to the galleys, and women to be shut up in a hospital. Not long afterward, under the pretext that this law was not being executed, an order in council came down, ordering its execution and making it apply equally to beggars, in whose favor however the administration had drawn a just distinction; but the administration experienced difficulties registering the law that it proposed on beggary, and this because of the way it eluded the necessity of working with the parlement. With no less regret, one notes that the setting up of alms bureaus, solicited by humanity, was completely forgotten. It was thought sufficient to send a plan to the bishops by way of instruction and exhortation; the public workshops were likewise neglected; but in a moment there arose on every hand houses that could have been looked upon, in the beginnings especially, as vast tombs.[74]

It may be added that the three laws in question raised fears of new taxes and, like Laverdy's municipal reform, threatened to shift the locus of fiscal responsibility in ways that could affect the interests of the *parlementaires*. But, as Bannefroy suggested, the lords of the bench had good reason to mistrust the commission's insistence on increasing the intendants' control over the task of repression. Unmoved by arguments that those who might be arrested as beggars were entitled to the equal protection of the laws, the commission drew upon the arguments that the former intendant of Burgundy had composed in 1759, and fashioned a specious "provisional" response to a three-year stalemate.

Laverdy's agenda in the area of mendicity can be inferred from his selection of commissioners. Each of them represented the impulses of ideology and institutional experience. For administrative precedent and experience, for example, the commission would turn to the *conseiller d'état* Boullongne. As early as 1746 his father had been listed in the *Almanach royal* as the *intendant des finances* responsible for "the implementation of the Declaration concerning the beggars, and all that concerns the administration of hospitals." In 1756 the son held the father's title *en survivance:* his *département* included "the affairs of the hospitals and houses of charity of all the provinces of the kingdom that are under the department of finance." The father had become controller-general briefly in 1757 (between Machault and Silhouette), and the son assumed the title of *intendant des finances* previously held by the father, and retained it for nearly two more decades. Boullongne's signature appears as late as 1769 on letters to intendants concerning the finance of measures on begging and vagrancy, but there is little evidence that he initiated or accomplished anything worthy of note.[75]

The senior member of the commission, Feydeau de Marville, had two main qualifications. First, he had served as *lieutenant-général de police* for the city of Paris from 1740 to 1747. Any legislation on vagrants and beggars, any reform of hospital finance, would have to take into account the special problems of the capital and the legal precedents approved by the parlement of Paris. Marville's second qualification was political: he was a senior councillor trusted by the king in delicate matters. He was not a former intendant or an enemy of the parlements. The work of the commission came to a halt in the second half of 1765, when Marville traveled to Pau with the commission's *rapporteur,* Dupleix de Bacquencourt, on a special mission to put an end to remonstrances from the provincial parlement there.[76]

The most active members of the commission were probably the two former intendants of the neighboring provinces of Burgundy and Franche-Comté, de Fleury and de Boynes. Both men opposed the political claims of the parlements, favored an active role for royal intendants as agents of improvement, and believed that the state could turn the idle poor from a liability into an asset by means of institutional confinement, training, and discipline. De Fleury needs no further introduction. De Boynes was the son of a financier in the East India Company. He became *conseiller* in the parlement of Paris in 1739 and advanced to the rank of *président* in its Great Council in 1751. Meanwhile he had acquired the title of *maître des requetes* in royal councils, and broke with his colleagues in the parlement by serving in the so-called Royal Chamber, which took over the functions of the exiled parlement of Paris in 1753.[77]

De Boynes was named intendant of Franche-Comté in 1754. He tried to combine this role with that of leadership in the provincial parlement of Besançon, obtaining the title of *premier président* in 1757. The parlement criticized his administration of the province in the following year; he exiled members of the parlement in 1759. The struggle continued in the form of a pamphlet war; de Boynes was relieved of his post and promoted to *conseiller d'état* in 1761. An effective courtier and a personal friend of the king, de Boynes assumed the role of intermediary between the king and Chancellor Lamoignon, trying in vain to close the gap between them over the handling of political confrontations with the parlements. At a later date he worked closely with Chancellor Maupeou in staffing the new councils set up to replace the parlements disbanded in Maupeou's "coup d'état" of 1771. By 1764 de Boynes was well established as a legal expert in the king's councils, intimately familiar with the parlements and their proceedings, yet an uncompromising partisan of the *thèse royal*.[78]

De Boynes's activity as intendant of Besançon suggests that he shared the views of his confrere at Dijon. A garrison city, Besançon boasted an ample array of charitable institutions. De Boynes took a special interest in the hospital of Bellevaux, an annex of the *aumône-générale* used especially for the confinement of vagabonds and beggars ever since the Declaration of 1724. In July 1757 he selected a military surgeon, Sieur Bernier, to become the receiver and treasurer of the hospital of Bellevaux. Two years later the academy of Besançon offered a prize-essay contest "to indicate the best way to occupy the poor of Franche-Comté, with respect to the needs and resources of this province, especially the town of Besançon." The prize was awarded to a merchant named Puricelli, who based his entire memoir on his own experience managing the workshops established at Bellevaux.[79]

Another contributor to the Besançon prize-essay contest of 1759, a judge by the name of d'Auxiron, appears to have influenced de Boynes. Surveying in rich detail past legislation on mendicity and the reasons for its failure, d'Auxiron cited the continued toleration of public begging by the authorities, the fact that hospital endowments were insufficient for their tasks, the laxity of ordinances governing the poor (some merely offered admission to hospitals as an option), the failure to motivate those responsible for arresting beggars with precise penalties and rewards for their conduct, and finally the conflict of overlapping jurisdictions. D'Auxiron's voluminous memoir raised further issues pertinent to Laverdy's commission, such as the reactivation of parish responsibility for poor relief. D'Auxiron noted later that he had discussed with a member of Laverdy's commission the difficulty of enforcing a prohibition on begging, when religious orders were permitted to beg. Limitations on the right of religious to do so were written into the law on beggary that de Boynes would personally report to the Conseil des Depêches on June 14, 1765. But this runs ahead of the story.[80]

In addition to the four councillors, Marville, Boullongne, de Fleury, and de Boynes, a succession of young *maîtres de requêtes* served on the commission as *rapporteurs,* summing up the commission's discussion and reporting to the controller-general. As the work of the commission dragged on, each one received an assignment as intendant, Taboureaux de Réaux at Valenciennes in 1764, Dupleix de Bacquencourt at La Rochelle in 1765, and Thiroux de Crosne as *adjoint* to his father-in-law at Rouen in 1767.[81] The fourth and last of the *rapporteurs,* Louis-Bénigne-François Bertier de Sauvigny, was first associated with the commission as *adjoint* to de Crosne in 1766. He took part in the debates leading to the formal establishment of the *dépôts,* and the task of coordinating their management as a bureaucratic system fell into his lap in October 1767. Bertier had been assisting his father in his duties as intendant of Paris at least since 1764. He was formally appointed *adjoint* to his father in 1768. Then, in 1771, when the elder Bertier reluctantly accepted the task of presiding over the council set up by Maupeou to assume the functions of the disbanded parlement of Paris, the son became the de facto intendant of Paris, formally receiving the title in 1776.[82]

Laverdy's decision to narrow the scope of royal action in the face of opposition from the parlement would come at the very moment when public discussion of mendicity was broadening its scope. The literature in the two decades following the publication of the *Spirit of the Laws* had included a number of proposals for more effective measures of charity and welfare. In addition to the range of opinions reflected in the pages of the *Encyclopédie,* the *Journal oeconomique* and other periodicals published articles on matters of charitable administration, *hospitals,* and alms bureaus.[83] Among the works describing more effective forms of aid was a tract entitled *Philopénès* ("Friend of the Poor") that appeared in 1764, just as Laverdy's commission completed its law on vagabonds, and was reviewed in the *Journal oeconomique* in October 1764, along with Le Trosne's tract on mendicity and a commentary on the Declaration of 1764 on vagabonds, just promulgated.

The evolution of a critical public response toward the *dépôts* in later years is already foreshadowed in this lengthy review, which included a discussion of previous jurisprudence and ended up with a sharp questioning of legislative priorities. The author began by speculating that the commission that produced it might have been influenced by Le Trosne's memoir and by *Philopénès*. While the measure was mild by comparison with some of its precedents, it seemed to embody a middle course between the severity of Le Trosne and the leniency of Philopénès. As the reviewer noted, Philopénès said far more than Le Trosne about the legitimate reasons for begging, citing, for example, the case of *compagnons* who had completed their journeymen apprenticeships but were still subject to the authority of a master craftsman. They were frequently obliged to seek aid while completing their *tour de France,* traveling from city to city to work with a variety of masters, as they were required to do before they could be received as masters themselves. In spite of such differences of emphasis, both writings had emphasized the distinction between beggars and vagabonds. The new declaration, in spite of its title, seemed to be aimed at both indiscriminately. The reviewer conceded that the repression of the undeserving might reduce the total number of beggars, but those who remained would be so numerous that some form of licensed begging might be the only practical remedy for their need. Of course, obsolete endowments could also be reassigned. The reviewer concluded that the aim of ridding the kingdom of vagabonds would have to be linked to that of "procuring at the same time to the true poor a legitimate means of earning their living."[84]

The most articulate expression of the new, broader expectations, couched in a form that agreed with the agenda of Laverdy's commission, was a treatise by the abbé Nicolas Baudeau that appeared in 1765, *Idées d'un citoyen sur les besoins, les droits et les devoirs des vrais pauvres*. The reviewer of the *Journal oeconomique* found in Baudeau's work the argument that the harsh treatment of vagabonds should not be extended to others. In particular, able-bodied beggars should not be treated as criminals unless they obstinately refuse to work, in which case they could be "corrected." In discussing types of work to be arranged, Baudeau spoke of rehabilitating and training them for productive independence.[85]

At the heart of Baudeau's treatise, explains the reviewer, was his effort to state who were the appropriate ministers of the poor, and how their efforts were to be organized. Baudeau proposed a truly national hierarchy of administrative commissions, including a supreme commission of the royal council and special councils attached to each parlement, a further level of diocesan bureaus including officials of the royal judiciary, and a bureau in each parish composed of the judge, the *procureur fiscal,* the elected *syndic,* local notables, schoolmasters, and schoolmistresses. As the reviewer of the *Journal oeconomique* observed, the "fundamental principle" of Baudeau's proposal was that the supreme bureau would have ownership and control of all properties, funds, and income intended for the aid of the poor throughout the kingdom, and that it would be responsible for maintaining this fund and improving it. Baudeau thus supported the line of reasoning of Turgot and many others concerning the misappropriation of wealth originally intended for the poor. However, he emphasized the positive role of the state and specifically mentioned the need to recover for the relief of mendicity the three deniers per livre of the *taille* that had been appropriated to the royal treasury since 1733.[86]

The term "patriotic alms," as used by Baudeau, was an extension of the concept of a national obligation to provide public assistance, enunciated in barest out-

line by Montesquieu and foreshadowed in the Declaration of 1724. Obviously a
believer in administrative unity (and in this respect at odds with Montesquieu), he
spoke of making the kingdom "a simple machine." He argued that the main reason
for the great number of "false poor" to be found in the kingdom was "the lack of
a stable and permanent system of universal alms and patriotic philanthropy."[87]
Responding to the Declaration of 1764, Baudeau wrote that it should have been
supplemented by a system of "patriotic alms." The authorities should begin with
charity to the true poor, "reserving as a last operation the publication of prohibitive
laws."[88]

But we must return to the work of the commission, beginning in 1764, in order
to see how a new repressive apparatus was established, even as the broader impulse
to reform public assistance was deflected.

3

"Provisional Dépôts"

Laverdy's commission had moved quickly to frame a stiff law against vagabonds. The preamble of the "Declaration of the King concerning vagabonds and shiftless persons" of August 3, 1764, unmistakably echoes the words of the semiofficial propagandist Le Trosne. Banishment was deemed ineffective against those whose life was "a perpetual banishment." Therefore vagabonds were to be punished by a fixed sentence to the galleys in the case of able-bodied males, and confinement elsewhere for those excepted by reason of age, infirmity, or sex. The first article gave jurisdiction over the arrest of vagabonds to the *maréchaussée,* in conformity with the Declaration of February 5, 1731. The second article, modeled on the Declaration of 1724, defined as vagabonds "those who, for the previous six months, shall not have exercised any profession or trade, and who, having no position and no property for their subsistence, shall not be able to be vouched for or certified as to their upright conduct by persons worthy of trust." [1]

The third article provided penalties. Males between the ages of sixteen and seventy were to serve a three-year term in the galleys for a first offense. All others, male and female, were to be locked up in the nearest hospital for the same period of time; children were to be held until further order in hospitals, to be raised, boarded, and given instruction. Article 4 enjoined those released at the end of their terms to choose a domicile, preferably their birthplace, and to take up "some trade or work that will enable them to subsist," and not to settle in Paris or within ten leagues of a royal residence. A second offense (article 5) drew a nine-year term of the same penalty, and a third offense a life sentence. Article 6 allowed those over seventy the option of staying on voluntarily in the hospitals where they had been confined. Article 7 placed the financial burden of confinement on *hôpitaux-géné-raux* wherever these qualified as *maisons de force*. Elsewhere, according to article 8, vagabonds would be transferred to the nearest charity hospital or *maison de force* available in a neighboring province, and would be maintained at royal expense. The intendant would be responsible for ordering quarterly payments by the revenue farmers of the royal domain.

This enactment, duly registered by the parlements, was ostensibly only the first of a series of new measures governing charity, assistance, and the poor. However,

the Declaration of 1764 was cast in a form that gave intendants the broadest possible legal authority over *all* categories of beggar and vagabond. This intent may
be read in a quasi-official determination of policy on mendicity by Laverdy's commission, a *Résultat concernant la mendicité* that was sent to all intendants the day
before the Declaration on Vagabonds was issued.[2] Subject to further revision in the
light of intendants' comments, this working document contained a set of instructions that gave the first signal for establishing the *dépôts de mendicité*.

The definition of the first category of beggars in the *Résultat* included only
"able-bodied beggars," who "deserve no compassion" but need only severe penalties "to force them to work." No further advice was needed concerning them,
since the new law on vagabonds would purge the state of "this first class of beggars, which are undeniably the most to be feared, and the most deserving of punishment." Their punishment was provided by the Declaration of August 3, 1764.
At least one intendant remarked, however, that this text did not have anything to
say about able-bodied beggars as such. The answer, it would be noted in a memoir
of 1766, was that "they are assimilated with vagabonds."[3] In short, the commission was preparing a weapon for dealing with beggars while purporting to deal only
with a smaller category of vagabonds. The distinction later acquired importance,
especially when "domiciled' beggars were swept away into the *dépôts*.

The remaining three categories of beggars listed in the *Résultat* reflect the quan-
daries of charitable reform. The second category of beggars, "those invalid beggars
who need assistance, but who are still capable of some work," provoked the greatest divergence of views. The councillors agreed that "no person who is able to
work should be placed in hospitals; if this class of beggars were all admitted, the
expense would have no limits and could not be met." The principle of assistance
at home seemed to follow as a consequence. The councillor de Fleury, sharing Le
Trosne's doubts on the practicality of imposing local responsibility, had proposed
aiding the invalid by measures that would expand hospitals, bolster their revenues,
and add to their physical facilities through a sweeping reform of religious foundations. According to Bertier, de Fleury's colleagues decided nonetheless to promote
a system of poor relief based on parish alms bureaus:

> After having weighed the advantages and drawbacks of different plans proposed to
> attain this end, the simplest and most suitable means, in every way, has been felt
> to be that of engaging the Archbishops and Bishops of the kingdom to establish in
> each diocese a General Alms Bureau in the episcopal cathedral town and other
> towns and larger village centers. These individual bureaus will each have a certain
> *arrondissement* of country parishes, so that no parish will go without help.[4]

Noting the success of this approach in some dioceses, the commissioners stated
that such alms bureaus should be viewed "as a second indispensable prerequisite
to publishing a new law on beggary," a law on vagabonds, of course, being the
first prerequisite. Alms bureaus were needed, first of all, in order to keep beggary
from "reproducing itself." Second, a principle of justice was involved: it would be
unjust to order those invalids in need of help to return to their home parishes, or
parishes of birth, "without being assured that they would find help in proportion to
their needs." With this argument, the commission revived the principle of parish
responsibility invoked by the parlement of Paris as recently as 1740.[5]

The third class mentioned in the *Résultat,* "invalid beggars too old or too infirm to work," could be cared for only by confinement, voluntary or involuntary, in hospitals. Enunciating a principle of state responsibility, the commissioners argued that it would overload the system of parish relief to place this large category of dependents on the lists of the alms bureaus. The proper place for them was in the *hôpitaux-généraux.* The *Résultat* drew two logical consequences from this: it would be necessary to establish new *hôpitaux-généraux,* and those that existed would have to be enlarged or assured of more substantial revenues. Finally, the fourth class, "children under sixteen years," were to be returned home to their parents or guardians. If they had none, they were to be pensioned with farmers in the countryside at royal expense. They would then form a generation of industrious farmers rather than idlers trained to the routine of an *hôpital-général.*

This outline involved major policy decisions that Laverdy must have approved in person. The repression of dangerous vagabonds was presented as one phase of a reinvigorated French poor law based on the principle of parish support for outdoor relief, matched by a comprehensive role for hospitals. All phases of the new law would involve commitments of funding from the royal treasury. They also required the king's ministers and the parlements to collaborate more actively. The parlement of Paris was particularly anxious that royal aid for hospitals should be forthcoming; as it gave formal approval and registration to the Declaration of August 3, 1764, it published with the text of the law its request that aid be given to hospitals as provided in articles 7 and 8.[6]

Royal aid would be needed if the hospitals were to serve greater numbers. At the same time, Laverdy's *Résultat* implied that the hospitals would henceforth receive only certain types of inmate: the forcibly confined, those incapable of any kind of work, and finally the "invalids who are still capable of some work but have no known domicile to which they may be returned." The parlements would have to agree to some changes in the finance of poor relief, if the alms bureaus were to assume new responsibilities for those not received in hospitals. To supplement voluntary contributions, a new pattern of authority would have to be created: either the parishioners themselves would have to be given power to tax themselves, or the intendant would have to assume an active role.

Such understandings required a calm political climate. However, the year 1765 brought to a head conflicts between the king's ministers and the parlements, a duel that was temporarily resolved only to flare up again and again until Vice-Chancellor Maupeou, in his coup d'état of 1771, abolished all the parlements and dismissed their judges, who held their noble offices as a form of property. He then instituted a new system of superior courts whose magistrates officiated at the king's pleasure. The unwillingness of the king's ministers and the parlement of Paris to cooperate on the specific problems of mendicity derived from the political stalemate of the 1760s and contributed to it.

The deviousness of royal policy on hospital reform and finance stemmed in part, no doubt, from the desire, so clear in de Fleury's thinking, to set up a system of repression that would function independently of the hospitals. For de Fleury, it was a mere ruse to call the *dépôts* "provisional." It was necessary to mollify the parlements, who would not otherwise allow a new form of *maison de force* to be erected outside their control. It is therefore difficult to take at face value the instructions appended to the *Résultat:*

> While awaiting the establishment of *hôpitaux-généraux,* His Majesty desires that there be established in each *généralité* provisional *dépôts* for shutting up beggars as they are arrested, and that MM. the Intendants search out in their *départements* buildings satisfactory for this use.

This casual request was the first step in establishing the *dépôts.* The specifications given paralleled in almost every detail those spelled out in de Fleury's memoir of 1759. The *dépôts* were to contain from 150 to 200 people in low rooms for men and women, with a separate room for the infirm. They were to be located in towns where an *hôtel-Dieu* would be available to care for the sick, and where a seat of the *maréchaussée* could coordinate arrests.[7]

Correspondence with the Intendants

The intendants themselves were in many cases mystified by the apparent contradictions between the overall reform plan indicated by the *Résultat* and the series of instructions they received on setting up *dépôts.* Although it was later made to appear that the *dépôts* had become permanently established only because the hospitals had been unwilling or unable to cooperate in Laverdy's larger schemes, Laverdy in fact did everything possible to exclude hospitals from sharing the functions intended for the new *dépôts.* Moreover, the function of the *dépôts* was defined, approved, and funded even before there was any open conflict between Laverdy's commission and the parlement over the provisions of the draft edict on mendicity.

Superficially, the *Résultat* consisted with a view that the *dépôts* were indeed provisional. The limited capacity and facilities of the *dépôts* were justified on the grounds that they were meant to serve as a transit facility. The only group of beggars to remain interned permanently would be the beggars of the third class, those too infirm to do any work, "who will remain there until the establishment of the *hôpital-général* of the province, or until these *dépôts* can be converted into *hôpitaux-généraux* and united under administration of the customary form." The last alternative suggests the option of reabsorbing the *dépôts* into the system of *hôpitaux-généraux.* At any rate, the prospect of royal financial aid to *hôpitaux-généraux* was clearly tied to their utilization in the operation against beggary, under articles 7 and 8 of the Declaration of 1764, and by virtue of the paragraph concerning "the third class of beggars" in the *Résultat.*

Generally, intendants reacted favorably to the Declaration of 1764. Fontette at Caen was probably typical in desiring to apply the penalty of the galleys with discretion. Some intendants and their subdelegates, however, welcomed strict penalties.[8] In the *généralité* of Paris, for example, the subdelegate at Sens, Baudry, regretted only that the penalty had not been even more severe; a life sentence to the galleys had been suggested by "an author knowledgeable in these matters," by which he no doubt meant Le Trosne.[9] But there were also some unfavorable reactions. From the impoverished Auvergne came the intendant's reply that there was no need for stern repressive measures: Able-bodied beggars would respond by moving from town to countryside, where they would be more likely to form dangerous bands. Some intendants who favored a strict law on vagabonds strongly desired to maintain a clear distinction between them and able-bodied beggars.[10]

As to the second class of beggar mentioned in the *Résultat,* there were many who doubted that alms bureaus could cope with the needs of all the poor who were invalid but still capable of some work. The subdelegate Baudry distinctly echoed the doubts of Le Trosne and de Fleury on this score. The most recent precedent had been in 1740, when the citizens of Sens had been required by order of the parlement to establish an alms bureau. Once the peak of the crisis passed, the richer citizens refused to contribute voluntarily, fearing that a fixed rate would be established by precedent. A charitable donation could be converted into a tax; a tax could be diverted without notice. Pursuant to the Declaration of 1724, beggars had been confined in the *hôpital-général* of Sens by means of a levy on the municipal *octrois* (excises). These funds continued to be levied as late as 1764, but ever since 1734 they had been diverted into the royal treasury, and the finances of the *hôpital-général* had suffered.[11]

The intendant of Auvergne thought the infirm poor would be best provided for in hospitals. There, he argued, manufacturing tasks were already well chosen for these poor, "in keeping with their state of infirmity," unlike "those of the countryside, which require robust, healthy, and vigorous individuals."[12] The experience of the Auvergne was unusual, since the intendant Trudaine had been remarkably successful in promoting hospital workshops in the 1720s. Nonetheless, there were intendants elsewhere who also thought the *hôpitaux-généraux* were useful for keeping the infirm occupied.[13]

Another problem related to the second class of beggar was the absence of royal support for initiating alms bureaus, without which the mere prospect of new forms of parish relief in a forthcoming law on beggary was a weak complement to the *dépôts.* For the time, Laverdy contended himself with having the comte de St. Florentin address letters to the bishops and archbishops asking them to promote alms bureaus in their dioceses. The circular merely promised new burdens. The form of the bureaus was to be purely voluntary and conferred no form of precedence or privilege. Once the bureaus were known to be in operation in a given parish, beggars of the second class would be returned to their care. This would be done "without waiting for the establishment of *hôpitaux-généraux,* which will require more time and reflection."[14] In Brittany the intendant Le Bret requested help from the bishops but received no response. In a summary he left for d'Agay, who succeeded him as intendant in November 1767, he reached the obvious conclusion: "The fact that this plan lacked any commitment of funds for implementation is, one imagines, the reason that determined the bishops not to answer and not to give the orders asked on their part."[15]

Intendants generally received favorably the proposal to deal with the third category of beggars—those totally unable to work—by reinforcing the network of *hôpitaux-généraux* in every province. The intendant of the Auvergne, otherwise critical of the *Résultat,* argued strongly for building a new hospital in the populous region of the Haute-Auvergne. The subdelegate Baudry urged the ministry to aid the hospital at Sens. Its trustees had launched into building new facilities with the funds they received from executing the Declaration of 1724, but were then obliged to curtail their plans when royal funding ceased in 1734. The subdelegate of Nantes, Gellée de Prémion, on the other hand, was a severe critic of hospitals and cited the examples of Rome and England to argue, as Montesquieu had done, that charitable institutions could encourage idleness.[16]

Finally, intendants wrote of the need to care more effectively for the children included in the fourth class of beggars. The intendant of the Auvergne stated more sharply than others a common uneasiness with the practice of pensioning children with farmers: care was not always the best. The subdelegate at Rennes reported that facilities for children were cramped in an attic that was hot in summer and cold in winter. Lack of funds, there as elsewhere, had prevented the establishment of better facilities.[17]

Intendants and their subdelegates apparently understood the instruction for *dépôts provisoires* to be a short-term expedient, a stopgap substitute for correctional wings in *hôpitaux-généraux*. The Declaration of August 3, 1764, on vagabonds had, after all, promised that aid would be forthcoming for hospitals in order to provide detention centers for those not subject to galley sentences. It was therefore reasonable to assume that the "provisional *dépôts*" might best be located in a hospital, if such an arrangement could be made, following the precedent of 1724 and the aborted effort of 1750. This impression would have been reinforced when a further letter of September 5, 1764, instructed intendants to make alternative arrangements for the execution of the Declaration of August 3, wherever *hôpitaux-généraux* were not available.[18] Such was the assumption of the intendant of Tours, Lescalopier, who approached the administrators of the Hôpital-Général de la Charité on this matter.

The *hôpital-général* at Tours was, in the view of its administrators, a house of voluntary refuge. The function of a *maison de force* was "manifestly contrary to the letters patent accorded for its establishment in 1658, and confirmed in the month of August 1716." If the royal council insisted upon locking vagabonds and shiftless persons in the hospital, the administrators wanted to be sure that these sorts of people would "be cantoned off in the extremities of their buildings, with a separate entry, to avoid confusion with the good poor, and to prevent the enterprises that the officers of the *maréchaussée* and the royal judges might attempt in the rest of the house." They proposed establishing an isolated *quartier de force* or correction wing, for which the king would pay the inmates' upkeep. Above all, the *hôpital-général* "is unable to make any kind of advance in this regard." The administrators recounted the diversion of revenues, raised locally, for the Declaration of 1724, and the near ruin of the hospital that ensued when administrators had attempted to continue providing for the additional inmates from its own resources. The administrators now asked for a flat pension of six sols per inmate per day, sick or well, plus an itemized list of initial supplies for two hundred inmates.[19]

Passing the administrators' memoir on to Laverdy, the intendant argued strongly in favor of using the *hôpital-général* as a provisional *dépôt*. Initial outlays would be minimized, since it would be necessary only to close off parts of buildings and secure them from escape. Second, the cost of mounting guard would be reduced with help from hospital employees. Third, it would be almost impossible to bring together in a temporary *dépôt* all the special facilities available in a general hospital. Fourth, since the *dépôts* were only provisional, any expenditure in setting them up elsewhere would later have to be written off as pure loss, whereas the expense would be useful to the hospitals if applied there. Furthermore, "the hospitals will function provisionally as the *maisons de force* that are to be constructed, and it could be quite possible that the arrangement would remain definitive."[20]

Laverdy found the cost estimates high. In any case, "the choice of hospitals to serve as *dépôts* would have serious drawbacks." The intendant would no longer be master over the operation, if it were established in hospitals: his authority and that of the *maréchaussée* would be contested by hospital officials and ordinary judges. The issues of economy, convenience, and long-term planning raised by Lescalopier were not discussed at all. Laverdy's reply makes sense only if the provisional *dépôts* were intended to become permanent.[21]

The provisos and objections of hospital administrators in various towns vary in strength, but hardly amount to a blanket refusal to cooperate. At Sens, resistance was strong. The subdelegate there, Baudry, unwittingly fulfilled the ministry's intentions perfectly by suggesting the use of a decrepit barracks for a *dépôt*. Full of apologies, he wrote an eloquent plea on behalf of the administrators of the *hôpital-général* at Sens, who asked that the *dépôt* be situated elsewhere, and that funds be given to complete the charity workshop for unemployed youths that had been left unfinished when revenue for implementing the Declaration of 1724 was diverted. Such a plea gave some credibility to the official version of a "refusal" on the part of hospitals. It was, incidentally, the young Bertier, not yet associated with Laverdy's commission, who reported to the controller-general on arrangements at Sens on behalf of his father, the intendant of the *généralité* of Paris.[22]

In another case, hospital administrators were unabashedly anxious to cooperate. For the city of Rennes, in Brittany, a plan was drawn up for implementing the *Résultat* in every respect. Assuming that able-bodied beggars in the first class were to be kept in *maisons de force,* administrators proposed adding new quarters to the existing *hôpital-général* (the towers of the city gate of Toussaints would also serve, as in the past). Sisters of Charity were currently coping with some of the needs of beggars in the second class, the invalid and infirm who could still do some work. Since they badly needed a new building, it was suggested that the religious houses for women in the city be abolished and converted. Further, the previously existing relief organization for the parish of St. Aubin could be used as a model for other poorer and more populous parishes. The *hôpital-général* was prepared to receive beggars in the third and fourth categories, the aged and infirm unable to work and children under sixteen. The insane and the disfigured could be received in a special unit, and children could either be taught crafts in the hospital or be pensioned out to farmers. The memoir noted in closing that the administrators of charity at Rennes awaited a new law and instruction on beggary. They were open to suggestions for reorganizing their efforts in new ways and did not challenge the reasoning of the *Résultat*. They did of course mention that new funds would be needed in order to initiate these new measures.[23]

The intendant of Brittany, Le Bret, had assumed that the provisional *dépôts* were needed only where no *hôpitaux-généraux* existed. De Flesselles, who succeeded him, understood better. Laverdy noted that the manner in which he had provided for the *dépôts* in his previous *intendance,* Moulins, left no doubt "that you have grasped perfectly the intentions of the Council in this regard."[24] De

Flesselles instructed his subdelegate to see whether he could "find a large house to rent that would serve as a *dépôt*" in the faubourgs of Rennes. In his instructions to subdelegates of other towns, in April 1767, he noted, "Care must be taken not to choose [a site for] this establishment in any convent or charity hospital."[25]

In a few instances, the ministry yielded to political pressure. In a letter to the provincial administrators of Burgundy, the *élus,* Laverdy outlined his policy of parish support for the poor and the establishment of provisional *dépôts* for those who contravened the forthcoming law on beggary. "I must also observe," he wrote in a letter of December 18, 1764, "that it would perhaps be suitable to avoid using hospitals already established, or establishing any regular administration for the running of these *dépôts.*"[26] The *élus* ignored this advice and recommended using the Hôpital de la Sainte Reine, a foundation that received poor passing strangers. Although this choice appeared to accord well with the *Résultat* and with de Fleury's suggestion that religious houses—particularly in Burgundy—might be converted for use as provisional *dépôts,* Laverdy replied that arrangements had to be made promptly, whereas legal inspection of the titles of the hospital in question would take time. In any case, one *dépôt* would not be enough for Burgundy. Laverdy yielded slightly. Some of the six *dépôts* eventually established did utilize hospital buildings. Those that lasted longest, at Châlons-sur-Saône and at Bourg-en-Bresse, were strictly separate.[27]

The most significant exception to Laverdy's insistence on keeping provisional *dépôts* separate from hospitals occurred in Languedoc. In a letter of October 30, 1764, Laverdy spelled out his policy to the intendant, Guignard de Saint-Priest, and asked him to confer with the president of the provincial Estates, Arthur Richard de Dillon, archbishop of Narbonne, on a request for funds to operate the *dépôts.* On December 14 the intendant replied that it would be cheaper and safer to use existing hospitals at Toulouse and Montpellier; on this he was at one with the archbishops of Narbonne and Toulouse. Laverdy retorted with a sharp criticism of hospitals. Let not the errors of 1724 be repeated! Laverdy argued that if hospitals were used, beggars might multiply, "because the shiftless prefer to be fed in hospitals than to work." The hospitals of Paris already contained over twelve thousand inmates; there would be twice as many, if space and funds allowed.[28] Laverdy did not foreclose the intendant's options. If hospitals were indeed to be used, their administration must be kept entirely separate, and the *maréchaussée,* under the orders of the intendant, must be free to determine the status of beggars and to pass judgment on those arrested. Saint-Priest was still persisting in his views in May 1766, and Laverdy yielded. In the case of the Hôpital St. Jean de la Grave of Toulouse, hospital administrators agreed to renounce all jurisdiction over beggars interned.[29]

Special arrangements were also made for the cities of Paris and Lyons. Initially, no attempt was made to supplement the *hôpital-général* of Paris with a provisional *dépôt.* An arrangement was made, however, for beggars to be transferred by authority of the *lieutenant-général de police* of Paris to the *dépôt* of St. Denis, under the jurisdiction of the intendant Bertier.[30] At Lyons the administrators of La Charité had established a special "Bicêtre" for confining beggars and had operated it since 1759. They agreed to receive beggars arrested under the Declaration of 1764, but reserved the right to treat Lyons' beggars distinctly. In spite of the name "Bicêtre,'' which was used to frighten outsiders, the primary purpose of the work-house, they said, was as an adjunct to the city's manufactures.[31]

The royal intendant at Lyons decided to establish a separate facility, La Quarantaine, for the beggars arrested by the *maréchaussée;* the administrators of La Charité, in a deliberation of October 26, 1769, decided that thenceforth Bicêtre would be used solely for inhabitants of Lyons and its faubourgs. This division of responsibilities between the royal Hôpital de la Quarantaine and the municipally run Bicêtre was formalized in an instruction from the *secrétaire d'état* Henri Bertin to the intendant on November 3, 1769.[32]

There was evidently a scattering of instances in which arrangements were made with hospitals, particularly in the subsidiary *dépôts* outside the city of the intendant's residence. The municipal authorities of Strasbourg, in arguments that bore some resemblance to those of Lyons, asked to deal with the first class of beggars, the able-bodied, by putting them into a hospital where work would not be considered a penalty, but rather a means of advancement in a trade to which they could be admitted on their release. Apart from Strasbourg and Lyons, there appears to be little ground for the argument that hospital administrators "resisted" performing the tasks prescribed by the Declaration of 1764. Laverdy persisted firmly in creating a distinct network of *dépôts,* administered and controlled by the intendants alone, regardless of local opinion.[33]

Haggling over Draft Edicts

As Laverdy guided his intendants along the desired path, his commission prepared a draft law on beggary. Completed in December 1764, it was presented to him in January together with a draft regulation on alms bureaus. After minor changes, the drafts were shown confidentially to the *premier président* (chief justice) of the parlement of Paris and to the *gens du roi,* the king's official agents in the parlement. Of these men the *procureur-général* (attorney-general), Guillaume-François-Louis Joly de Fleury, played a particularly delicate role. As it happened, he was a brother of the de Fleury who played a leading role in the commission on beggary. A go-between for *parlementaires* on the one side and royal ministers on the other, he could easily find himself "between two fires," as his father Guillaume-François had remarked in 1740, when another sovereign court, the Cour des Aides, had disputed the jurisdiction of the parlement of Paris over the finance of an edict requiring parishes to provide for the subsistence of their own poor.[34] As a result of a first consultation, a few changes in the edict were agreed to. The councillor de Boynes then presented the draft for a royal decision in the Conseil des Dépêches on June 14, 1765. The function of the *maréchaussée* in arresting beggars was clarified following that meeting, and the king gave his approval in July.[35]

At this point, it would have been normal to submit the edict to the parlement to be registered. As a measure of caution, perhaps, Laverdy asked the *procureur-général* to sound out the opinions of select members of the parlement. The *procureur-général* sent back observations that, in Bertier's words, "tended mainly to entrust ordinary judges with the administration and operations concerning the de-

struction of beggary and in particular with the imposition and verification of rolls
to be drawn up for the subsistence of beggars.''[36] A long delay ensued. The objections
were withdrawn and a final revised version was presented to the parlement to be
registered in August 1766. In a deteriorating political climate, the parlement refused
even to deliberate on the content of the edict.[37] Before recounting how the *dépôts
de mendicité* emerged intact from this deadlock, one should consider the draft
edict itself. Its dispositions reveal what Laverdy's commission intended, or at
least what they projected as a scheme for reform. A decade later, Loménie de
Brienne reviewed these documents with the curiosity of an engineer examining
the building plans of a much altered and dilapidated structure. A quarter-century
later, a former inspector of the *dépôts* recollected that authorities had soon realized the defects of the operation, but ''did not have the courage to abolish the
law.''[38]

The commission attempted to frame a law that would leave no gaps in the
provision of assistance where needed, or in the apparatus for repressing public begging throughout the kingdom. Neither task could be performed efficiently without
the other. The first eleven articles provided a framework for assistance. Beggars
were ordered to stop begging and take a job, or to return to their homes. There,
local authorities would be obliged to lodge and feed them, ''as well as procuring
them the means to earn their living, by work proportioned to their age, and to their
force.'' Those who persisted in begging were subject to the penalties stipulated in
the remaining articles.[39]

Just as the beggar was offered a choice, so parishes were encouraged to discharge their duty to the poor voluntarily by establishing alms bureaus, as projected
in the *Résultat*. In order to facilitate the task, the commission drafted a model
regulation for these bureaus and agreed that they should receive certain tax incentives. Where parishes did not voluntarily institute alms bureaus, the draft edict
provided an obligatory mechanism. Two ''principal inhabitants'' were to join the
two *syndics* to determine needs and distribute funds.[40] The lists would be approved
by local assemblies of inhabitants and property owners, and the entire financial
operation would be reviewed by the intendant. Initial responsibility lay, nonetheless, with parish representatives. The collectors of the *taille* were to advance to
these agents sums sufficient to feed the poor two pounds of wheat bread *(pain bis)*
per day, or one and a half pounds for women and children. After verification, the
collector would be reimbursed by the receiver of the *taille*. Unlike the *taille,* however, this imposition would be assessed on ''all owners, ecclesiastical, noble and
privileged, domiciled or not domiciled, in the said community, without exception''
(article 9). Mindful of complaints about the diversion of the three deniers per livre
of the *taille* previously assessed for executing the Declaration of 1724, the commission proposed to discontinue that levy, in order ''to enable *taillables* to acquit themselves the more easily of the sums they will be assessed for the subsistence of the
said beggars or other domiciled poor.''[41]

Repression, like assistance, involved a system of parish initiative backed up by
an alternative procedure under the authority of the intendant. In towns and village
centers *(bourgs)* having their own police force for apprehending beggars, the accused would be placed in the local jail or the nearest royal prison. There they would
be cross-examined within twenty-four hours. Municipal officials and royal *juges de*

police might release those arrested for the first time for begging in their place of domicile. This concession to opinion was the only exception allowed in an otherwise absolute set of sanctions against begging under any circumstances. There were to be no exceptions for sex, age, health, or special permissions. Alms for those who had suffered calamity would have to be provided through special collections in church. Giving alms to a beggar was punishable by a fine of ten livres, and an even heavier fine of fifty livres was imposed on those who harbored beggars or allowed them to beg at their doors—farmers, innkeepers, tavern owners, and postmasters. All fines would go to the receiver of the *aumône-générale* or whoever disbursed payments for the subsistence of the poor.

Any domiciled beggar arrested a second time, and all other beggars, were to be transferred by officers of the royal *maréchaussée* "to *dépôts* that have been prepared by our orders for the provisional confinement of beggars" (article 22). In areas lacking a police force, the *maréchaussée* would make arrests. No formal interrogation would be required until the accused reached the *dépôt*. Thus a domiciled beggar might be removed some distance before he could be released. In all cases, where the *dépôt* was more than a day's journey from the place of arrest, beggars would be transferred from brigade to brigade of the *maréchaussée,* staying at night in "prisons of the places of passage."[42]

Jailed in the *dépôt* by request of the public prosecutor, beggars would be interrogated within twenty-four hours by the *prévôt, lieutenant,* or *assesseur* of the court of the *prévôt de la maréchaussée,* or provost's court." The details of the procedure to be followed reveal the commission's effort to enforce severe penalties and to forestall objections that might be raised against the summary procedure that was needed, if large-scale arrests were to be carried out promptly. Those with a fixed domicile who were arrested within four leagues of their home would be released without penalty for a first offense, but if arrested a second time, any such person would be branded on the shoulder with the letter "M" by the gatekeeper of the *dépôt* before being released (an exception was made for those under sixteen). Those begging farther from home would be branded even upon first arrest. This mark "would not bear a signification of infamy" and could be ordered by the summary procedure of the provost's courts, unless the judges themselves sought further testimony. Where an individual was to be branded, two officers of the royal *baillage* or *sénéchaussée* would have to be present, but no special writs were needed, and in all cases involving no "afflictive or infamous penalty," the provost's court would judge in last resort.

Severer penalties required a less summary procedure. Any able-bodied adult male arrested for begging who bore the mark of previous arrest for begging would be sent to the galleys for three years. Others so marked would, for a second offense, be locked away for three years in a *maison de force,* presumably in a *dépôt,* like vagabonds of the same sort. Such sentences required a writ of competent jurisdiction from the nearest royal *présidial.* In such cases, beggars would be held in the jails of the *baillage* or *sénéchaussée* before standing trial in the accustomed manner.[43] Five-year galley sentences, governed by the same procedure, were to be meted out to traditionally feared categories of adult male beggars, following the precedent of the Declaration of 1724: those asking alms "with insolence," or armed with guns, pistols, swords, metal-tipped sticks, or other arms; counterfeit cripples and soldiers; bearers of forged discharge papers; and those roaming in groups of more than three (not including women and children).

A brooding fear of the most dangerous beggars of all called forth the harshest penalty—a life sentence in the galleys, reserved for anyone branded with a mark of infamy, such as the letter "V" (*voleur,* or thief), and for anyone convicted of having threatened arson. The provost's court was required to surrender to the ordinary courts those beggars wanted on other charges.

These were the main provisions of this lengthy edict, which established a total prohibition on begging, created a system of parish responsibility for support of the poor, and deployed a network of arrest and repression, supervised by the intendants, with punishments ranging from detention in "provisional *dépôts*" to life sentences in the galleys. The commentary of the *procureur-général* of the parlement on these dispositions reflects the multiple preoccupations of the sovereign courts. While he seemed anxious to vindicate the rights of the individual citizen, he appeared to be at least as concerned with defending the corporate prerogatives of the parlement. These prerogatives included the right and obligation to define the legitimate application of judicial penalties, and, where state finance was concerned, to guard against illegal invasions of property rights. Frequently, as in the present case, the defense of corporate prerogative was an issue not easily disentangled from the cause of individual liberty.[44]

The *procureur-général* objected to the summary procedure of the first articles, especially those directed against almsgivers. To require payment of fines without right of appeal *(sans déport)* might provoke resistance. The phrase, "or whoever shall have been convicted of having begged," opened the way to convictions on vague suspicion: "actions taken in this matter other than *in flagrante delicto* will degenerate into vexations." Further on, he noted, "It appears quite severe to take away whatever money a poor man may have on him." He criticized the undue severity of various articles, denouncing especially the one providing that nondomiciled beggars be branded for a first offense. Such a penalty, "after all, is a corporal penalty"; the Declaration of 1724 had not carried severity so far. Penalties, he thought, should always have a fixed limit: the phrase "five years at least" left too much latitude in the determination of galley sentences. The *procureur-général* further objected to the irregularity of pronouncing sentence merely on the strength of the statements of the officer making the arrest (the *procès-verbal de capture*) and the cross-examination by the provost's court. Providing for subsequent inquest was of little use, since the beggar would already be subjected to penalty. This was not in keeping with precedent: article 7 of the Declaration of 1724 required an inquest and specified a procedure *par recollement et confrontation,* which allowed the accused to challenge the evidence given.[45]

From such procedural and humanitarian objections, the *procureur-général* turned to arguments against removal of the police of begging from the ordinary courts (whence appeal ran to the parlements). The role of the *maréchaussée* and the definition of the *dépôts* troubled him. Giving jurisdiction to the *prévôts de la maréchaussée* would confer upon them the powers of "ordinary judges":

> in truth, greater authority is conferred upon them than *présidiaux* and *baillage* have, since, with two officers of the *baillage,* they can inflict physical penalties, and since they do not have to have a *règlement à l'extraordinaire* or a judgement

of their competence in order to impose these penalties. Now, however important it may be to banish beggary, must one, in order to attain this, appear to take liberties with the rules that ordinances have established and custom has consecrated?[46]

The *procureur-général* recognized the need for some provisional supplement to the places of detention in ordinary hospitals and prisons. "But is it not to be feared," he continued, "lest the term *dépôt,* used and repeated in the bill with no provision for inspection by ordinary judges or hospital administrators, carry with it in the public mind the idea of a species of false imprisonment *(chartre privé)?"*[47] Finally, the *procureur-général* thought it unrealistic to expect the inhabitants of towns, *bourgs,* and villages to assume the functions of the *maréchaussée* in carrying out arrests. Lacking experience, it was likely that

> they would not bestir themselves to fulfill this against people who might be their relatives or whom they would at least regard as their fellow citizens. Would it not occasion them an expense perhaps more considerable than the imposition of the three deniers per livre upon the *taille* that was to be suppressed for their benefit?[48]

Councillor de Fleury had perfectly anticipated, in his memoir of 1759, the types of objections that might be raised against his plan for eradicating beggary. Perhaps his brother's observations were merely a rehearsal of earlier conversations. In any case, the reaction of the parlements should have come as no surprise. Chancellor d'Aguesseau had objected as early as 1738 to provisions for branding beggars, in commenting on a draft edict he had received.[49]

In reply to objections, Councillor de Fleury conceded a number of changes on behalf of the commission. Fines for almsgiving could be dropped, money found on a beggar's person need not be confiscated. The definition of a domiciled beggar could be relaxed by extending the radius to six leagues. De Fleury argued that at this distance from home, a beggar hardly differs from a vagabond. The commission would also accept a specified limit—five years—on the galley sentences provided in article 34. The commission was unwilling, however, to concede the substance of its provisions concerning the roles of the *maréchaussée* and the intendants. The provosts' courts had been established, argued the former intendant, in order to deal with certain types of offenses and a certain "quality" of person: "So that one may say that the provosts of the *maréchaussée* are veritably the ordinary judges in criminal matters where vagabonds, tramps, and beggars are concerned."[50] They were established precisely in order to police such people. De Fleury minimized the distinction between vagabond and professional beggar, but the commission, he noted, had not confused the two. Article 21 allowed ordinary judges to have jurisdiction over domiciled beggars arrested by local authorities. In any case, no infamous or afflictive penalty—by which he no doubt meant a sentence to the galleys—could be imposed without a writ of competence. The mark, he insisted, was but a "simple precaution."

The term *dépôt provisoire,* argued the councillor of state, had been chosen as least likely to give offense. Prisons were too small, and the *procureur-général* was surely aware that towns had complained of the extra burden on prisons resulting from the execution of the Declaration of August 3, 1764, on vagabonds. Hospitals, established to serve as *maisons de force,* "refuse every day to lend themselves to it and want to be houses of voluntary retreat only.'' The *dépôts* would remedy this situation, since they

> have been chosen in such a manner that they may become *maisons de force*, as a result of which there will be one in every *généralité*, which will be very advantageous for public order and will greatly relieve the general hospital of Paris, which is presently the only *maison de force* in the kingdom, or at least in the jurisdiction of the parlement of Paris.[51]

The nomenclature was not essential for de Fleury. The *dépôts* might be described in paraphrase as ''buildings that will serve provisionally to aid and assist hospitals or *maisons de force* that do not have sufficient lodgings or revenues to receive beggars.'' No more could be conceded in order to reconcile objections with ''the physical impossibility of doing without the *dépôts*.''[52]

In further exchanges the *procureur-général* again invoked the rights of the poor. Branding repeaters was objectionable, he argued, because it might ''confuse the true poor with those who are so only by lack of effort.'' He evoked the reality that even Le Trosne had recognized in his less frenzied moments: ''Whether by illness or other accident, one can find oneself one day in the position of being obliged to ask for one's bread, for a few months, either for oneself or for a child. Should such people be branded with a mark?'' Poverty, after all, ''is only humiliating when it is occasioned by idleness.'' Such echoes of canon law did not touch de Fleury's conscience. The responsibility for taking care of the true poor, said he, would lie with the community: the *syndics* would report those who refused to work and continued to beg. He merely brushed aside the objection that a summary procedure for beggars was likely to catch the deserving poor as well in its nets: ''Professional beggars have always been regarded as a peculiar class of citizens who merit no favor, and the severity of laws against them sets no precedent with respect to other citizens.''[53]

The *procureur-général* had raised a new objection to the penalties provided in the edict, pointing to the article that sentenced to the galleys in perpetuity all beggars found to be branded with marks of infamy. If this provision were enforced, begging could expose an individual to harsher penalties than he might endure for more serious crimes. Theft, for example, was punished only with banishment. Another consequence of the edict was that the penalty of banishment would automatically subject a convict to the likelihood of arrest and further punishment for vagrancy. De Fleury did not take his brother's last objections very seriously. He countered by suggesting stiffer penalties for theft. The king would give serious attention to whatever laws the *procureur-général* wished to propose with respect to the penalty of banishment: ''But it is not believed that one must wait for the publication of this law before publishing the edict on beggary, nor that in this edict the penalty of galleys in perpetuity should be reduced to a fixed term in cases of recidivism and beggary.''[54]

A few minor changes were made in the edict as finally resubmitted to the king in July 1766. Sanctions against almsgiving and the harboring of beggars were dropped, and there was no provision to confiscate money found on a beggar's person. Most important, the radius from a beggar's home within which he would be considered a domiciled beggar was extended to six leagues, and the severity of provisions for branding repeaters was somewhat relaxed. On other points, the *procureur-général* had withdrawn his objections. Bertier later summarized the objections presented by the *procureur-général* by saying they "tended mainly to entrust ordinary judges with the administration and operations concerning the destruction of beggary and in particular with the imposition and verification of rolls to be drawn up for the subsistence of beggars." From the commission's point of view, it may have seemed that the parlement's defense of the rights of the poor was a minor concern compared to the main business it entrusted to the *procureur-général*, namely, the defense of its corporate functions and prerogatives.[55]

The parlement, as noted earlier, refused to consider the edict approved by the king and revived their observations and objections. It was at this point that the younger Bertier de Sauvigny joined the commission as a deputy to the *rapporteur*, de Crosne. Since de Crosne was preparing to take over the duties of his father-in-law La Michodière as intendant at Rouen, the entire task of reporting soon fell to Bertier. In a later apologia, Bertier recalled what his first impressions had been upon joining the commission: "I was appalled to find myself in contradiction with them on the most important aspects of their opinions." The dispositions of their edict were, in his view, "oppressively severe, impossible to execute, and the means proposed subject to every sort of contradiction and harassment imaginable by the multiplicity of agents." In this later account, Bertier placed himself on the scene at a moment of impending doom:

> They were ready to resort to the fullest deployment of authority to obtain the execution of a system that I believed could not be executed. In spite of their enthusiasm, I dared to speak. I set forth my fears, and aided by the resistance of the courts, I managed to have the law suspended, and got them to be content with trial measures that could be consolidated by a law, if they succeeded.[56]

In 1766 Bertier reported to Laverdy on the commission's work and set forth six options for breaking the political deadlock with the parlement over the draft edict on mendicity. In explaining to Laverdy what the commissioners had intended to accomplish, Bertier stressed the principle of parish support for the poor. This had been determined, he wrote, by the need to avoid the pitfalls of the Declaration of 1724. Hospitals had proven unable to receive beggars of all types, able-bodied and infirm, in their great number, nor could they bear the enormous cost, which far outran the financial aid received from the king. Under the provisions of the draft edict, the apprehended beggar would be allowed to return to the place of most recent domicile, rather than to his birthplace, if he chose. The commission reasoned that he might be more familiar with employment opportunities where he had been living, and that it was equitable, "because the community that has for ten, fifteen, or twenty years benefited from the work and consumption of an individual has contracted a duty toward him."[57] In spelling out arrest procedures, the commissioners had taken care not to overburden the *maréchaussée* or to extend their range of activity to towns. However, they had enjoined communities to appoint special municipal officers to be responsible for arresting the poor. They had not wished to use the police officers of the *baillage*, for fear they would not work well with intendants. Indeed, the main purpose of the edict, wrote Bertier at the conclusion of his summary of it, "was above all to place the jurisdiction over beggars under

the authority of the *maréchaussée* and of the intendants, in order that its administration be easier, quicker, and less costly.''[58]

This statement clearly articulates what the councillor de Fleury had always desired. A further comment suggests that the provisional *dépôts* were expected to
establish themselves permanently as institutions performing a function complementary to that of *hôpitaux-généraux* in a new scheme of welfare and repression:

> They proposed subsequently by taking up the reform of hospitals to reduce all of
> them to two functions and two denominations. The general hospitals, which would
> be for the sick, the infirm, the invalids, and the aged of every sort, and the *maisons
> de force,* which would contain the able-bodied of both sexes who were to be shut
> up. The former were to remain in the hands of the ordinary administrators, but the
> latter were to be placed everywhere under the authority of the intendants.[59]

It is likely that Bertier understood the equivocation contained in this statement.
Since the *dépôts* were already defined as ''supplements'' to hospitals, performing a
function of confinement the latter were allegedly unable or unwilling to perform, it
is clear that the *dépôts* would become a new, permanent surrogate for the *hôpitaux-
généraux,* taking over their functions as *maisons de force.*

Bertier's summary completes the account of negotiations with the parlement of
Paris from the moment of their dramatic refusal to deliberate upon the commission's
draft edict in August 1766. The commissioners did reply with a memoir and two
alternative draft edicts. The latest objections of the parlement focused on the im-
practicality of the means proposed for enforcing parish support, and on the impro-
priety of giving jurisdiction to intendants. The burden of finding lodging and provisions, and of raising a forced imposition, would discourage agriculture. By the
report of Bertier, the *parlementaires* feared that the result of the new edict would
be ''that one half of a village would put itself on the charity of the other, and that
the new law would only extend and domesticate beggary.''[60] Thinking perhaps of
the debate over Laverdy's recent attempts at municipal reform, the *parlementaires*
believed it was dangerous to put royal monies in the hand of a *syndic,* ''of a peasant
who will make use of them for his profit or at least for his family.'' They objected
to the complexity of the draft, to its procedures, and to the disproportionate penalties. The counterproposal, wrote Bertier, would put ''directors of alms'' and ordinary judges in charge of a system that would rely on *maisons de force* to be built
in each *généralité* for confining all beggars arrested. The operation would be financed by the three deniers per livre of the *taille,* supplemented if necessary by a
local levy limited to a maximum of four sous per day for each beggar born in that
community. These, clearly, are some of the objections that Bertier later claimed to
have shared. No doubt, the nobles of the parlement were defending their own interests. They were chary of relinquishing too much of their traditional levers of
social control, as embodied in the manifold concept of ''police,'' and resisted any
measure that portended substantial new tax obligations for privileged landowners.[61]

Laverdy's commissioners rejected out of hand the proposals of the parlement.
They nonetheless drafted, apparently at Laverdy's order, an extreme compromise
version of the edict that, in their view, could only be executed lamely, if at all, by
means of supplemental administrative instructions.[62] On their own initiative, they

drafted an ordinance in eleven articles containing the essentials of their edict, in case Laverdy wished to impose a measure without the sanction of the parlement. Meanwhile Councillor d'Aguesseau asked Bertier to draft an *arrêt du conseil* that would accomplish the same effect by ordering the execution of prior regulations and laws.[63]

Bertier and the "Sixth Proposition"

It fell to Bertier, as *rapporteur* for the commission, to spell out the options for the controller-general. In so doing, he clarified the reasoning of the commissioners, analyzed the weakness of Laverdy's stance, and articulated his own preferences, following the course initiated by d'Aguesseau. The first option, strongly desired by the commission, was to send *lettres de jussion* from the king ordering the parlement of Paris to register the edict as conveyed to it in August, and to send it at the same time to all other parlements and *cours supérieures*. The commission was prepared, as Bertier later told Turgot and his associates, for "the fullest deployment of authority."[64] Public opinion, they argued, would favor the edict, which was the fruit of several years' work, approved by the king and the controller-general. It was in the public interest. It returned to the people a tax formerly imposed on them. The new levy relieved the burden upon the poorer *taillables*, since it fell equally on all. Changes in the edict would simply mar its intent.

Laverdy, unwilling to provoke such a confrontation, had apparently suggested a second option—having the edict registered first in the frontier jurisdictions, in the hope that others would follow suit rather than face a wave of beggars seeking a safe haven. The commission replied

> that with the knowledge one has of the correspondence that exists between the different parlements, it would appear difficult to have a law registered in a provincial parlement that had been refused by that of Paris; that besides, this approach could irritate the Parlement of Paris just as much as *lettres de jussion*.

In any case, the tax of three deniers per livre was not raised in most frontier provinces, removing an inducement to its passage there. The commissioners may also have remembered how previous efforts to play off one parlement against the other had backfired. Bertier added a doubt of his own. He reported a conference with the intendant of finances, d'Ormesson, who had raised some new objections to the financial mechanisms of the edict; it could not be effective without further modifications.[65]

The commissioners were equally opposed to a third option, which was to submit a compromise draft to the parlement. This, they thought, would produce an unworkable system, and in any case the parlements would not be appeased as long as the responsibility for the operation lay outside their purview.

> The gentlemen of the parlement of Paris have made their views known on this every time they have been consulted on the proposed law. They have complained that authority was being given to the intendants that they supposed belonged to them; their pretensions were revealed above all in the last proposed drafts that were

given to the controller-general and contain no essential changes but those dealing
with the supervision of the operation, which they gave entirely to the ordinary
judges and to the sovereign courts.

Are these de Fleury's accents? In more than one earlier memoir, the former intendant of Burgundy replied to such objections as Bertier did here, by arguing "that
the functions of administration would be separated from those of justice." The
essential point was that, in the past, laws against begging had failed because "execution had not been confided to active enough hands."[66]

Bertier's contribution as *rapporteur* may be inferred, to some degree, from the
manner in which he developed the last three options. The fourth proposition was a
purely administrative one: a "police ordinance" would be sent to the intendants
and to the *maréchaussée* containing the main provisions of the edict. The commission doubted whether effective new measures could be stitched together entirely
from old precedents. Bertier argued that a mere ordinance would not suffice to
authorize the innovations projected: "On the one hand, it is a question of disposing
of the liberties of a great number of men, and on the other of ordering a new
imposition in the greater number of parishes in the Kingdom." Although the objection might be countered (as de Fleury had done before) by insisting on "the quality
of persons on whom the law bears," the danger remained that the intendants and
the *maréchaussée* would be harassed in their new duties, presumably by the courts.[67]

The fifth option was a variant of the fourth: an *arrêt du conseil* (rather than a
mere police ordinance) would cite the legal precedents for the four major provisions
desired. Earlier prohibitions on begging abounded. The requirement that parishes
feed their own poor had been stated in the Declarations of 1724 and 1750, resting
on earlier precedents: the fundamental ones were the ordinance of Moulins and the
Declaration of 1586. Specific penalties for begging were authorized by the Declarations of 1724 and 1750. The same two precedents would serve, finally, to authorize the jurisdiction of the *maréchaussée*. Bertier may have contributed to the reservations expressed about this procedure: at one point he lapses into the first person.
The commission firmly intended to condemn recidivists to be branded or sent to the
galleys, but Bertier noted that if there were any drawbacks to imposing penalties
based on the harsh precedent of 1724, "I do not know whether the penalty imposed
by the Declaration of 1750 might not appear sufficient." That declaration had reduced the penalty to confinement in a hospital "during the time judged suitable by
the administrator." Bertier editorialized: "When beggary is the effect of waywardness and idleness, the penalty of being confined and the necessity of working are
penalties that make the greatest impression on beggars of this last sort." Were the
fifth option to prevail, Bertier spoke in favor of the milder penalties that had been
applied in his father's intendancy pursuant to the Declaration of 1750.[68] The commission felt that the fifth option was technically feasible but did not favor it. Bertier
concluded that past laws had not succeeded, "and that it would appear that new
ones would have to be found if success were to be hoped for."[69]

The final, sixth, option was to postpone any new legislation or ordinance for
the time being, but to put into effect a "literal and rigorous execution of the Declaration of August 3, 1764, on vagabonds," to encourage bishops to set up alms
bureaus, and to begin finding means to reform and expand the hospitals. The advantages of this course were political, fiscal, and administrative. Playing to Lav-

erdy, Bertier noted, "there may be good reasons for not wishing to antagonize or coerce the parlements, and they appear determined not to entertain any laws on beggary, unless the execution is confided to them." Second—and here Bertier appears to be critical of his colleagues' work—it might be unwise to abandon an assured revenue of 630,000 livres obtained annually from the three deniers per livre of the *taille,* while at the same time incurring costs that could not be estimated. The partial execution of the Declaration of 1724 had cost two million per year: "The lack of funds appears to have been at all times the reason for the failure to carry out laws on beggary—why begin today by depriving oneself of a certain fund?"[70]

Bertier's conclusion reflected an approach to administration that was at once cautious, pragmatic, and experimental. It fits with his later claim that he urged the commission "to be content with trial measures."

> It is thought that a strict and rigorous execution of the declaration on vagabonds can alone provide the government with the necessary information for making a definitive law on beggary, without compromising the government.
>
> This execution can give an idea of the number of beggars that exist in the kingdom, of their type, and of the funds needed in order to have success in preventing them from begging.
>
> It alone can procure the greater part of the effects desired from a law on beggars.
>
> It can be limited to the *dépôts* now in existence and the amount of funds that the controller wishes to sacrifice for this object.
>
> Finally, this law, since it has just been registered, will not encounter any difficulty in execution, and cannot in any way compromise those who are charged with it.[71]

Two further memoirs expanded upon the implications and advantages of the last option. The first, probably by Bertier, argued that most beggars could be arrested under a strict execution of the Declaration of August 3, 1764. "Strict execution" meant in fact a broad interpretation of the term "vagabond" contained in it. Anyone begging could be arrested on suspicion of vagrancy. Although the law required the release of those who could be vouched for, the cross-examination would provide data that could be used to measure the dimensions of mendicity. Relief measures and charity workshops could be organized in proportion to the number of "good poor" found begging. If voluntary alms bureaus were insufficient, one could impose the duty of relief on parishes with a fuller knowledge of the scope of the problem. In fact all beggars, even the domiciled, would probably be loath to subject themselves to the procedure of arrest and examination.[72]

No new authorization would be needed in order to use the provisional *dépôts* as places of confinement for beggars. A procedural subtlety would forestall any charge that beggars were being falsely imprisoned in a *chartre privé.* An *arrêt du conseil* would authorize the use of *dépôts* to "supplement" the hospitals designated as *maisons de force* in the Declaration of 1764. The sentences meted out by the *maréchaussée* would read: "to be locked up for three years in the nearest hospital or some other place designated for this purpose." Since the hospitals would be unable or unwilling to receive the convicts, the intendant would receive the list of those sentenced and would assign them to the *dépôts* under his supervision. The essential point was to ensure "the closest correspondence between the officers of the *maré-chaussée* and the intendants." The pace of arrests would have to be monitored with discretion according to space available in the *dépôts,* and in such a manner as to avoid touching off popular resistance.[73]

Another additional memoir, possibly by de Fleury, suggested that the jurisdiction of the *maréchaussée* as defined in the Declaration of 1731 would be sufficient to cover the "strict execution" of the Declaration of 1764. No new decree need be issued to revive legal precedents for repressing beggars. The parlement need not be offended, since it was to be presumed that a broader law on beggary would be forthcoming later. It might further be argued that the new operation relieved the hospitals of a burden, thus satisfying the request of the parlement to carry out articles 7 and 8 of the Declaration of 1764. As long as the *dépôts* were defined as supplements to hospitals, the intendants could exercise the functions of hospital administrators. Since the Declaration of 1750 allowed hospital administrators to determine the length of detention of beggars, the king could, "without compromising his authority," transfer this function to intendants.[74]

A few details rounded out this last memoir. Revealingly, the author distinguished between the role of the *prévôts* of the *maréchaussée* as mere "executors" and that of intendants as "administrators." "One cannot be as sure of the *prévôts,* as one may be of the intendants."[75] Therefore the instructions from the chancellor to the *prévôts* would not spell out the reasoning and motives in the same detail as those sent to intendants. It was also suggested that the procedure of "verifying" the statements of arrested beggars be eliminated; there was no need to exhume the ill-starred correspondence bureau that had compromised the Declaration of 1724. The memoir concluded with a key to the drafts of instructions needed for implementing an *arrêt du conseil.* By the time this memoir was written, Laverdy may already have agreed to the "sixth proposition." It was fitting, after all, that a "provisional" legal scaffold should cradle the "provisional *dépôts.*"

A Bureaucracy Is Born

The subtlety of the *arrêt du conseil* of October 21, 1767, concerning vagabonds and shiftless persons is illustrated by the fact that it provided the authority for locking beggars away in *dépôts de mendicité* without mentioning either beggars or *dépôts.* The preamble was based on a premeditated half-truth. It alleged that the Declaration of August 3, 1764,

> has not been executed completely and with the exactitude that its utility would require, under the pretext that in most provinces hospitals lack sufficient *rentes,* and that they have no secure enough place of confinement for receiving the vagabonds who, by the terms of the law, should be sentenced to be locked up.[76]

The first article of the order in council ordered that the Declaration of 1764 be executed. The second article, without naming the *dépôts,* authorized the establishment, in the different *généralités* of the kingdom, of houses sufficiently secure to detain vagabonds and shiftless persons *(gens sans aveu).* The third effectively placed these houses under the authority of the intendants, by providing that their inmates be fed and maintained at the king's expense, "as prescribed by article 8 of the said declaration, and this according to the special orders that will be given on this matter to the intendants and *commissaires départis.*" What a blow to hospitals! Having refused to entrust the management of provisional *dépôts* to hospitals, the minister turned around and gave each intendant buildings and funds to do the job, and the title of "hospital administrator"—all this allegedly because hospitals had been unwilling and unable to cooperate. He then rubbed salt in the wound by saying that this operation should satisfy the expectation of royal aid to hospitals!

Article 4 provided that a concierge in each house keep a register of inmates with an extract of their sentences, and that he also give a receipt to the officer or *cavalier* of the *maréchaussée* who brought each inmate in. The concluding article provided that a list of the "castles, houses, and other places" to be used be drawn up by the Council, and that the intendants and *prévôts* of the *maréchaussée* have extracts of this list. The intendants were formally enjoined to carry out this law. There is no hint of the fact that the provisional *dépôts* had already been selected in consultation with intendants over the past three years.

The younger Bertier was given responsibility for coordinating the overall administration of the newly formed "operation of mendicity." He drew up an estimate of expenses for the operation in an *Apperçu* dated October 31, 1767. Estimating that there would be one hundred *dépôts* and about ten thousand beggars locked up at any one time, he reckoned the cost of food and straw at nearly one million livres, and projected a total budget of 1,750,000. This was based on a modest estimate of five sous per person per day for a pound and a half of bread (2s. 6d.), four ounces of vegetables (1s.), rice (1s.), and straw (6d.). Accordingly, 125,000 livres per month should be budgeted from November 1, 1767, to the end of December 1768.

Some initial costs, such as original stocks of food, bedding, and utensils, should decline. Bertier assumed that the number of arrests would decline over time, and that work done by inmates, once organized, would bring in about 300,000 livres at a rate of 1s. 6d. per inmate per day. A budget of one million per year might therefore be expected after the first year. A general bureau under Bertier's orders might have expenses of 12,000 per year.[77]

This impressionistic budget outline was signed "approved," but it was later modified. The first year's expenses were limited to 1.5 million. A more gradual tapering of costs was allowed for, with a reduction of 100,000 in each successive year until 1774, from which point one million per year would be allotted. It is clear from these details that the provisional *dépôts* were expected to last five years and probably longer.[78]

Although Bertier took issue with Laverdy's commissioners, he objected primarily to the severity of the penalties they proposed for repeaters, and to the complexity of their system for parish support of the poor, not to their concept of a provisional *dépôt.* Bertier was undoubtedly influenced by the work he had done with his father in the *intendance* of Paris. Either the father or the son—the attribution to "the intendant of Paris" inscribed in 1775 is ambiguous—wrote a commentary on the draft edict that envisaged an even broader use for the *dépôts:* they might serve better than hospitals in providing for the subsistence of the poor who could not be cared for in their own parishes. The memoir argues that the intendant should be given sole control over the disbursement of funds for the arrest and confinement of beggars, as in the case of subsistence provided for prisoners. Arrest procedures themselves should be supervised by the intendant.

Under the heading "Article 22," which referred to the provisional *dépôts,* the "intendant of Paris" wrote: "No difficulty: this must and can be executed." Establishing the *dépôt* was a technical, administrative problem. The French conveys a "can-do" spirit: "On mettra au dépôt la main forte nécessaire; le local et les circonstances peuvent seuls en déterminer." It would merely be necessary that the subdelegate receive precise orders for ensuring that the beggars be well received and treated "with humanity." The articles following this one in the draft edict, the author notes, "are matters of legislation and indifferent. The great point is that one cannot beg without being arrested, wherever one goes."[79] If these enthusiastic views are penned by the elder Bertier, they no doubt influenced the son. The younger magistrate's initial enthusiasm for the *dépôts* needs to be seen in the context of a belief, perhaps somewhat idealistic, that they would function "provisionally" within a broad context of legislative reform concerning hospitals, the poor, and public relief.

Bertier was well suited to coordinate the new "operation of mendicity." He had already acquired a reputation in royal councils as a humanitarian reformer, and in his father's *intendance* as an indefatigable administrator. He had made arrangements for at least one of the *dépôts* in the *généralité* of Paris in an exemplary manner. The intendant of Paris, Laverdy knew, must play a crucial role in any set of measures to clamp down on beggars, since the city of Paris was a great magnet for them. With offices in the *intendance* of Paris, Bertier could easily keep in touch with the bureaus of the *contrôle-Général* and with other ministers, while carrying out his functions as *commissaire de la mendicité* unobtrusively. Bertier received an official appointment to be paid nine thousand livres, but care was taken not to create any visible concentration of authority in his hands. Most of the circulars to intendants concerning the *dépôts* continued to be signed by the controller-general, but certain accounting and record-keeping functions required Bertier to be in direct correspondence with intendants and the *maréchaussée.* A letter of December 15, 1769, to the provost of the *maréchaussée* at Rouen directed him to send records of arrest to Bertier, who was described as being "charged by the different ministers with everything concerning beggary." But in a letter of January 31, 1770, we find Bertier reassuring the intendant of Alençon that he did not have the function of *ordonnateur* for this administration. That is to say, he did not make decisions concerning allocation of funds, but merely gave advice and assistance to the controller-general, who made such decisions. Bertier took quickly to his role as "provisional bureaucrat."[80]

4

Running the Machine

I adopted the establishment of *dépôts,* but as *dépôts,* that is, as places less woeful than prisons, where beggars would be treated mildly, and only until investigations undertaken about them had made it possible to determine whether they should

Return to society purely and simply,

Be sent back to their families,

Be sent back in care of their parishes,

Be engaged for military service or for public works,

Be placed in hospitals,

Or finally, remain in the *dépôt.*[1]

Bertier is speaking energetically before Turgot and a group of his collaborators. They are assembled at the château of Montigny in October 1775, to review the report on mendicity prepared by Loménie de Brienne, archbishop of Toulouse. Having just recounted his initial misgivings on joining Laverdy's commission as *rapporteur* in 1766, Bertier launches into an earnest defense of the administration of the *dépôts* during their first eight years of operation. He knows that his audience is hostile to the *dépôts,* and that his own role as their chief overseer is under attack. He reaches into his portfolio, draws out a set of printed forms, and passes them around the table.

I strongly entreat the persons to whom I have the honor to report, to run their eyes over the model declarations, passports, and surety bonds that I drew up;

They will see that if I consented to arrest and confinement in the *dépôt,* my first preoccupation, as soon as the beggar had entered there, was to look for all the possible means to have him leave.

I also entreat them to note that, in this way, I found a means of relaxing considerably the rigor of the law of 1764 by condemning most of the vagabonds only to the *dépôt.*

In short, the purpose of the *dépôts de mendicité,* by Bertier's account, is to make the inmates useful to society as quickly as possible, not to inspire dread through lengthy, harsh imprisonment. If his audience accepts Bertier's version of events thus far, he must still account for the failure of so many good intentions. Why are there still so many beggars? Why have so many of them been kept locked away for long terms, often in idleness? Why have so many died? Bertier implies, as he continues his defense, that the *dépôts* would have functioned better had they been complemented by the other projects envisioned by Laverdy.

> But as it turned out, the change of ministry brought a change of principles, and no more was done to find ways of helping the poor in the parishes.
> There were long hesitations before setting up public works. Finally, there was not even any attempt to put hospitals into better order, and to have invalid beggars cared for there, with the result that we were obliged to keep in the *dépôts:*
> 1. All the infirm or invalid beggars, for whom infirmaries had to be set up costing considerable sums of money.
> 2. All the young healthy people whose waywardness had given cause to fear greater harm, if they were left to themselves.
> 3. An infinite number of good poor who preferred remaining in the *dépôts* to the uncertainty of being helped at home.

The questions that Bertier attempts to answer in this apologia can provide a framework for our inquiry. First, the actual policies of arrest and release of beggars are important indicators of the real purposes of the *dépôts,* and provide a key to evaluating their success or failure. Second, the treatment accorded inmates also reflects directly upon the motives and workings of royal policy. Finally, the role of the *dépôts* may be better understood when it is known how administrators viewed their functions with respect to other institutions and measures for relief, welfare, and charity.

Policies and Procedures for Arresting and Releasing Beggars

The correspondence detailing procedures of arrest is remarkably complete for the *généralité* of Tours. The young and eager intendant du Cluzel owned his appointment to the duc de Choiseul, whose estate at Chanteloup lay not far from the seat of the intendance. As minister of war, Choiseul had facilitated the operation of the *dépôts* by giving orders to the provosts of the *maréchaussée* to place their brigades at the disposal of the intendants for the purpose of arresting beggars.[2]

Two sets of instructions had to be prepared in order to set the *dépôts de mendicité* in motion. A first set instructed the intendant on the details of internal administration and on the implementation of arrest procedures. Another far more complex set of interlocking instructions was required in order to prescribe the activity of the *maréchaussée*. It may be assumed that all these instructions were drafted in a single batch by Laverdy's commission. Bertier undoubtedly had a hand in drafting them; certain provisions give a hint of de Fleury's role.[3]

Laverdy addressed general instructions on the administration of the *dépôts* to intendants two days after the *arrêt du conseil* of October 21, 1767.[4] He asked intendants to advise him when they expected their *dépôts* to be ready to receive inmates; an intendant who delayed risked having his *généralité* inundated with beggars and vagabonds from neighboring provinces where enforcement was under way.

Portrait of the intendant Pierre du Cluzel by Alexandre Roslin (1718–1793). (Tours, Musée des Beaux-Arts)

The instruction established one set of provisions for the vagabonds and shiftless who were to be interned by virtue of the Declaration of 1764 (if they were not fit for the galleys), and another for professional beggars, a distinct category interned by virtue of the Declaration of 1750. The term of detention for the first category would be determined by sentence. For those in the second category, the *maréchaussée* would not specify the term of detention; it would lie in the intendant's discretion. A "normal" correctional term would be three weeks to one month. Repeaters and certain others might be detained longer; in all such cases, a special order should be obtained from the *secrétaire d'état* having jurisdiction over the province. This provision highlights the importance attached to protecting the intendant against charges of false imprisonment.

Bertier's main concern, no doubt, was to control the scale of operations within a frame of uniform and universal enforcement. Repeating an earlier argument of his, the instruction advised intendants to keep terms of detention short in order to control expenses and keep places open for new inmates. In any case, long terms of detention were less effective as a deterrent than the assurance that any beggar leaving his home would be arrested. Domiciled beggars should not be sent to the *dé-pôts,* as a general rule.

On January 13, 1768, Laverdy informed du Cluzel that arrests had begun in the *généralités* of Paris, Soissons, Orleans, Rouen, Moulins, and Dijon, and warned him that vagabonds were likely to surge into the *généralité* of Tours unless arrests began there also. On the 16th the intendant advised the minister that his *dépôts* were ready and provisions contracted for. A packet of letters, all dated January 19, reached Tours soon afterward. It included a note from Bertier explaining that the orders of different ministers were all being dispatched to him as intendant, so that he would be the first to know their contents and could suspend them momentarily, if preparations were not complete.[5]

The cascade of orders concerning the *maréchaussée* began with a letter from the duc de Choiseul to the various *prévôts généraux des maréchaussées,* including a copy of the *arrêt du conseil* of October 21, 1767, "renewing," in Choiseul's words, "the provisions of the Declaration of August 3, 1764." The scope of execution was to include beggars, "who, not being deemed to have any profession, must be considered vagabonds unless they are vouched for by persons worthy of trust." As minister of war, Choiseul then spelled out the obligation of the officers of the *maréchaussée* to follow the orders of the vice-chancellor with respect to judicial procedure, and to follow the instructions of the intendant "to accelerate or slow the activity of the brigades, according to the state of the prisons and of the *dépôts* of your department." In a crucial sentence, Choiseul added that the provosts were to assure their companies that "gratifications" would be forthcoming to compensate the officers for their "zeal" in carrying out arrests. Accounts for the *dépôts* would regularly include a line for these officers and the court clerks, and for the cost of transferring detainees from the place of arrest to the *dépôt.* In an accompanying letter to the intendant, Choiseul asked to be informed of any complaints that might arise.[6]

The instruction sent by Vice-Chancellor Maupeou to the *prévôts-généraux* gives some hint of the difficulties that might arise. It states that convicted vagabonds should be taken to the galleys or locked in hospitals, "as you have done or should have done since 1764." A pointed reminder follows: "It appears to me needless to observe that all those arrested must be interrogated within twenty-four hours on the basis of the record of arrest." The officers were expected to make a difficult distinction between those individuals subject to the severe penalty for vagabonds, those identifiable as mere "professional beggars," and those not subject to any penalty, the "domiciled beggars." Although in fact such cases shaded into one another, a sharp, arbitrary line was drawn at two points. A "domiciled" beggar who took one step beyond two leagues from his home became subject to confinement in the *dépôt* as a "professional" beggar. If he had also been unemployed for over six months and could find no one to vouch for him, he was automatically a vagabond. In cases of doubt, Maupeou directed the provosts to refer to him, or the intendant, or the *prévôt-général,* or whatever authority "shall appear the most prompt, for obtaining the verification of the prisoner's replies and the papers or certificates he produces." This advice may slightly have diluted the strict accountability to the intendant underlined in the last phrases of the letter:

If any doubts should arise in your mind, you will address yourself to the intendant of your province, who will remove them, and to whom the King has confided the coordination of this operation and its details. The intention of the King is that in this matter you adhere to the instructions he gives you.[7]

The forms of procedure tended to discourage convictions to the galleys, since vagabonds were to be tried by the provost's court only after a writ of competence had been obtained from the judge of the *présidial*. No such writ was needed in the case of beggars: A cross-examination would serve as the basis for an order from the provost to transfer the accused to a *dépôt,* "without other form of procedure or inquest." This *ordonnance* could be cast as follows:

Having reviewed the record of arrest, of the cross-examination, and of the minutes of the verification of the prisoner's replies, the same having been communicated in full to the King's Attorney, we order that the aforenamed . . . shall be conducted to . . . (location of the *dépôt*), there to be detained until it shall be otherwise ordered.[8]

Properly certified copies of all proceedings against the inmate were to be handed over to the concierge of the *dépôt,* who would give in return a receipt for the beggar and his papers. The *maréchaussée* was also obliged, in accord with the purposes Bertier had outlined, to keep records on all domiciled beggars apprehended and released. In a separate letter the vice-chancellor instructed the *procureurs du roi* of the *maréchaussée* to transfer convicted beggars to the *dépôts* only after the intendant had designated the place and ordered the transfer. Those convicted by *jugement* as vagabonds should have a copy of the record of their conviction sent to the superior *procureur-général* of the *maréchaussée,* so that these records could be reported to the vice-chancellor.

Laverdy explained his intentions in fuller detail to the intendant.[9] His main concern was to prevent overcrowding of prisons or *dépôts*. After posting the Declaration of 1764 and the *arrêt du conseil* of October 1767, the intendant should allow two weeks for beggars and vagabonds to return home voluntarily. Then arrests should begin "with restraint." The most "dangerous" should be arrested first, in order to impress the others. The king's intention, however, was to proceed then against all beggars as well as vagabonds. All came under the terms of the Declaration of 1764, "as being at least suspect of vagrancy." It was "just," nonetheless, to make a distinction "according to their way of life." Those arrested over two leagues from home would be regarded as "professional beggars." Those arrested closer to home should be released, if they promised not to beg; records of their arrest should be kept.[10]

From the very beginning, there was a certain degree of confusion in categories of priority for arrest. There was, of course, no hesitancy in assigning first priority to bands of beggars extorting tribute from farmers. The domiciled beggar was obviously at the other end of the spectrum, although still liable to arrest. But Laverdy undermined Bertier's intention of obtaining an estimate of the number of domiciled beggars, by suggesting that the intendant might wish to await further orders before even troubling to have them arrested. An even more striking inconsistency was the suggestion that infirm beggars should be arrested before others, because it would be more difficult to stop them from begging than it would be to force the able-bodied to find work.

Laverdy explained the technicalities that gave intendants the authority to direct the "correction" of beggars. Previous declarations of 1724 and 1750 gave hospital administrators the authority to confine beggars in their institutions. Since the *dépôts* were established as "supplements to hospitals," the intendants responsible for them became provisional hospital administrators. This legal fiction was an important step in establishing the correctional function of the modern secular state.[11] In the immediate context, it created an extensive sphere for administrative detention. If the logic of "correction" extended on the one hand to the infirm beggar whose only need was, in Bertier's later phrase, to be "sent back in care of his parish," it also extended to any vagabond who seemed amenable to reform. Bertier had suggested to Laverdy in 1766 that confinement might be more effective than galley sentences. The circular to intendants as signed by Laverdy included the statement: "Since a course of mildness is always preferable, it will be proper for the *maréchaussée* to be very sparing of the penalty of the galleys." Tables accounting for the number of galley convictions throughout France from 1765 to 1777 show that the yearly average went from 150 vagabonds per year throughout the country in the period 1765–1768 to 59 per year for the nine years 1769–1777. The sharpest drop was from 161 in 1768 to 72 in 1769. These data, coupled with Laverdy's instruction to intendants, support Bertier's later contention that his adoption of a correctional approach to mendicity in effect reduced the severity of the law of 1764 against vagabonds. The practice of the provosts' courts tended also to leniency in the sentencing of vagabonds.[12]

Laverdy asked intendants to report on the first stage of operations, reminded them that payments would be made to the *maréchaussée* for their pains, and in a postscript asked that all correspondence on the subject be labeled "*mendicité*," presumably in order to channel the incoming flood of paper directly to Bertier's office. The packet contained one final instruction for the intendant from the *secrétaire d'état*, St.-Florentin, who wished to be kept generally informed. If any beggar was to be detained longer than three weeks, the intendant should request from St.-Florentin an order to that effect. Although the king did not intend that domiciled beggars be detained, St.-Florentin would also write particular orders to detain any who might be dangerous. The intendant thus commanded a further range of discretion in his correctional functions.[13]

Such was the basic procedure. Later instructions from Choiseul prescribed onerous reporting tasks. He wanted the commander of each brigade to keep two daily lists: one of domiciled beggars released, one of beggars and vagabonds imprisoned. Each month lists of convictions, divided into those by *jugement* and those by *ordonnance*, were to be sent to him and to the intendant. A daily record of domiciled beggars apprehended and released was to go to the lieutenant of the *maréchaussée*, who would compile them every two weeks and forward copies to Choiseul and to the intendant. This correspondence, dictated in part by Choiseul's desire to apprehend deserters from the army, was also designed to facilitate Bertier's effort to regulate the operation of the *dépôts* as a system with the aid of empirical data. Further letters from Choiseul, originating perhaps in Bertier's office, asked the *maréchaussée* to adhere to a specific format spelled out column by column. It was essential, for example, to have the date of capture in order to ensure that those arrested were promptly transferred to the prisons of the *prévôts*.[14]

Elaborate as these instructions were, the first weeks of arresting beggars prompted a major shift in general policy. In a letter of February 19, 1768, Laverdy abandoned the view that a short term of detention would serve to deter begging. Arguing that "it would be illusory to set free people likely to be recaptured a few days later," he ordered that no inmate should be released without giving a promise not to beg, declaring his resources, and indicating where he wished to live and why. The intendant would verify the inmate's claim to know a master or employer, to have lived in one place for a long time, or to have family support. If the intendant could not locate relatives of the inmate able to pay travel expenses, he could prescribe a route and assign three sols per league to be traveled, payable to the released inmate at each day's stage in his journey. The intendant had authority to release beggars on their own recognizance, but commonly inmates would have to post bond themselves or have relatives or another third party promise to pay their pension in the *dépôt*, if they were again caught begging.[15]

Few who satisfied these conditions of release would ever have found themselves in the *dépôt* in the first place. Laverdy ordered that the intendant obtain authorization from the *secrétaire d'état*—so that he would not be compromised—in any case in which an inmate was to be detained longer than a month. But such terms of detention became the rule, requiring intendants to give more thought to the care and rehabilitation of inmates who would not simply be passing through.

A second shift in policy emerged over a longer period in a series of decisions leading to the arrest of domiciled beggars. Before any general instruction had been issued, the intendant of Tours asked to be allowed to start arresting them. He was displeased that the *maréchaussée* had not been more active. He made allowance for the fact that the brigades were busy supervising the drawing for militia service in the villages, that they needed time to adapt to their duties and to realize that enforcement was expected to continue beyond an initial sweep. However, the *dépôts* were nearly empty. On July 1, 1768, du Cluzel reported that there were only twenty-one beggars in the *dépôt* installed in the château of Tours, eleven at Le Mans, fifteen at Angers, and twenty-one in a spacious former religious house at Baugé. He informed the subdelegates that he had received complaints from farmers about beggars who had apparently fled the towns at the publication of the new law. His subdelegate at Tours reported that "the *maréchaussée* has begun imprisoning domiciled beggars because it finds no others." Du Cluzel responded to the situation by asking permission to arrest domiciled beggars and imprison them, beginning with the insolent and the able-bodied.[16]

Shortly after du Cluzel's letter of July 1, Laverdy met with the king at Compiègne. The result of their discussion on mendicity was twofold. The first step was to ask intendants for statistics on the operation, and for observations concerning its effect on the public and the ways in which it might be improved. Laverdy asked them, in a letter of July 12, for up-to-date charts and accounts to be sent to him by the first week of August. The second step, formalized in a set of circulars dated July 20 from Laverdy, Choiseul, and Maupeou, was to redefine the term "domiciled beggar" to include only those arrested within a half-league of their domicile. Laverdy in effect erased the previous distinction between the "way of life" of domiciled beggars and others, telling intendants that beggars had been tolerated within two leagues of their homes only for fear of overcrowding the *dépôts*. Maupeou, in his instruction to the *procureurs-généraux* of the *maréchaussée*, likewise explained that there was ample space in the *dépôts* and that the number of domiciled beggars was on the increase. He also pointed out that it would be easier to verify statements of domiciled beggars within the new, smaller radius. Choiseul attempted to mobilize the brigades more effectively in a circular to the *prévôts-généraux*. He noted that high food prices and scarcity of employment during a hard winter had served as an excuse for begging and for some laxity on the part of the *maréchaussée*. His intention was, however, to have the declaration strictly enforced, especially since the resumption of work in the fields removed any excuse for idleness. He scolded the *maréchaussée* for failing to forward the forms as requested, and for not filling them out completely.[17]

A stroke of the pen, multiplied by scribbling clerks in neat stacks of formal circulars, turned many former "domiciled" beggars instantaneously into "outsiders" subject to incarceration without further question. A few days later, on July 25, 1768, du Cluzel received a specific response to his earlier request for authority to subject all domiciled beggars without distinction to arrest and confinement. St.-Florentin granted this blanket authorization, based on "the prudence and intelligence with which you have conducted this operation to date."[18] Du Cluzel issued orders for the arrest of domiciled beggars, but the *maréchaussée* dragged their feet, having received no order other than that of July 20 directly from the minister of war. Choiseul, who had already asked for du Cluzel's help in correcting the laxity of the brigades, wrote to the *prévôts* from Fontainebleau, reminding them that the king intended that the *maréchaussée* should follow the intendant's orders in this matter. The success of the operation to date, he told them, had persuaded him as well as St.-Florentin, the controller-general, and the chancellor of the need "to carry this operation to the degree of perfection that it is capable of, and that one could now arrest domiciled beggars."[19]

Choiseul did not minimize the difficulties the *maréchaussée* might encounter. In the first stages it would be essential to use great caution, in order that the arrest of domiciled beggars give rise to "no complaints and no stirrings among the people." He also asked that records of arrest be forwarded immediately. The *prévôt* at Tours replied by explaining some of the problems he faced in coordinating the records of his brigades, many of them far removed from his immediate supervision. Although ideally beggars should be transferred immediately upon arrest, his officers found it necessary to convoy them in groups. Records therefore had to be held up in order to include the date of transfer. Failure to include this information could lead to costly delays in the conviction or release of those apprehended. The *prévôt* then turned to a more general complaint about the complexity of the instructions that his men had to cope with. "This type of person," he noted, "having little skill at organization, is not capable of that precision which demands sustained attention." The *prévôt* explained that he had found it necessary to write out the word "number," because his men were not familiar with the abbreviation "n°" on the printed forms. The instructions themselves, he added, "give contrary meanings to the same expressions, so that they seem expressly designed to make the instruction unintelligible: and I often find in speaking to [the *maréchaussée*] that I cannot speak simple enough language to them to make them understand the simplest thing.''[20]

Laverdy's successor, Maynon d'Invau, continued most of his policies during a term of office that lasted from the end of 1768 to the end of 1769. Confirming Laverdy's retreat from a policy of uniformly short periods of detention, the new controller-general instructed intendants not to release beggars ''on the faith of their declarations and promises alone, nor with vague and lightly hazarded claims on their behalf.'' Bertier had no doubt composed the printed forms that were sent with this letter, forms for recording promises not to beg and surety bonds. All such documents were to be directed to the minister, with the results of the intendant's verifications. The degree of centralization of records was coming to resemble the abortive schemes of 1724. The minister conceded that the conditions imposed and the guarantees required were too onerous for many poor families to accept: ''and indeed I have decided on this only in order to render more circumspect those who stand surety, and to force those who undertake it to assume a genuine interest in seeing that the man released does not fall back into beggary.''[21] This concern again highlighted the problem of rehabilitating those who would be denied their freedom.

In the course of 1769, Bertier appears to have become persuaded that the *dépôts* were succeeding in their original purpose. Reviewing the statistics he had in hand, he decided it was time to close the bureaucratic net on beggars of every sort. At some time before August 1769, he wrote a memoir advocating the extension of arrest to all domiciled beggars as a general policy throughout the kingdom. Beginning with a summary of operations to January 1, 1769, he noted that some twelve thousand beggars and vagabonds had been sentenced throughout the land, and about the same number of domiciled beggars had been apprehended and released. Of these, some had been released on surety bonds from friends, protectors, or communities willing to pay their pension in the *dépôt,* should they be taken begging again. Some had enrolled in the army; some clearly intended to work and were released; some died; and others were sent to the galleys. Only five to six thousand remained in the *dépôts.* Far from being overcrowded, these facilities had ample room to receive ''all the beggars that remain, even the domiciled ones.''[22]

Bertier argued, with more than a touch of exaltation, that severity toward beggars had excited the zeal of charity: alms bureaus had sprung up in many places, and beggary had disappeared in several towns and parishes. Stricter proscription of beggary might stimulate charity even more. Arrests were becoming more difficult, as beggars took refuge in towns and mingled with the domiciled beggars not subject to confinement. To bring the operation to its perfection only required unleashing the zeal of the *maréchaussée;* such a move was all the more important because previous measures were never pushed far enough. Now, he wrote, the funds were assured and the buildings chosen, prepared, and arranged; furnishings, utensils, clothes had been purchased in sufficient number, provisions were stocked, employees instructed in their duties, and workshops of every kind were beginning to gather momentum. Bertier concluded this grand survey of his bureaucratic domain with a flourish: ''In sum, one might say that the machine is wound up, and it is only a question of releasing the last spring that will set it in motion.''[23]

Bertier's recommendation that all beggars be arrested without distinction was accepted. He had drafted a letter for the chancellor to send, which presumably supplied the text of Maupeou's circular sent from Compiègne on August 12, 1769. This order gave intendants latitude in delaying the arrest of domiciled beggars, if local conditions warranted.[24]

In advocating the arrest of domiciled beggars, Bertier aimed to discipline a much-needed workforce: "The labors of the countryside are about to begin, farmers have need of hands to gather in a harvest that all appearances give reason to hope will be abundant. It is important therefore to inspire fear in those who are of no service solely because of their slothfulness." But hardly a month later he received word from du Cluzel that the poor harvest in the *généralité* of Tours militated against enforcing the latest order, and that religious houses were flouting prohibitions on public begging by distributing alms at their doors. By the winter of 1769–1770 the *dépôt* at Tours was swamped with inmates of all categories. Schemes were afoot to extend the function of the workhouse at the *dépôt* to serve the needs of the "free poor" of the town as well as constraining arrested beggars. This crisis represented a swift reversal. At the beginning of the year, du Cluzel had been authorized to close the spacious facility at Baugé because the number of inmates remaining there was so small. Now, just as the government had moved to end toleration of domiciled beggars, a crisis of high food prices and unemployment erased the boundary between idle poor and working poor in a quite different sense.[25]

Deteriorating economic conditions in many parts of France created a general institutional crisis in the *dépôts*. The total number of inmates admitted to them rose from 8,875 in 1768 to 9,079 in the following year—a modest rise in view of the fact that the last few months reflected the influx of domiciled beggars whose arrest was universally ordered in August. Then the total number jumped sharply to 12,502 in 1770, reached a peak of 14,147 the following year, and maintained a similar level in 1772, falling gradually in 1773 and rapidly in 1774.[26] These increased numbers strained the facilities of the *dépôts* and imposed high costs in a time when foodstuffs were expensive. There could be no consistent policy toward any single category of beggars, least of all the domiciled, as long as such conditions lasted.

Maintaining a Standard: Between Hospital and Prison

Bertier's drive for bureaucratic uniformity affected the treatment of inmates in the *dépôts,* just as it shaped the procedures of their arrest. Here also, Bertier and his colleagues elaborated and modified their original instructions. Again, subsistence crises conspired to expose the latent contradictions that underlay the policies governing the treatment of beggars in captivity, just as they demolished the rationale for arresting domiciled beggars.

Laverdy's founding instructions, "On the internal management of the *dépôts,*" charted a course explicity bounded by the considerations of "economy" and "utility." A reading of the instruction reveals, however, that the chief function of bureaucratic control was to impose a uniform ceiling on expenditures. The instruction noted that cost overruns would certainly destroy the utility of the operation as a whole, since royal funding was strictly limited. The instruction also contained a bureaucratic presumption that a utilitarian standard had been calibrated in advance.

However, far be it from us to think that we have foreseen every object of expense that may naturally be entailed. His Majesty relies with the fullest confidence upon the prudence of MM. the Intendants, who should be aware that the engagements they might enter upon for this purpose will always be approved when they are founded upon reasons of utility.[27]

In effect, the minister would pursue economy with the ardor of a prosecutor; if he wished, the intendant might come before the bar as an advocate of utility.

The main provisions of the first general instruction emphasized the intended simplicity of the operation and the strict accountability for expenses. A rapidly mounting scaffold of particular instructions followed. Control was achieved, as Michel Foucault writes in another context, by a network of writing: the regular blanks on printed forms marshaled data for review by Bertier and his panoptic clerks. Galiani's notion that administration was a social science, "the science of details," could hardly have been more ardently embraced.[28]

By Laverdy's first general regulation, the majority of the inmates were to be detained only for short terms. The *ordonnances* committing them to correctional detention for three weeks to a month in the *dépôt* were to be kept in one register, while another contained the *jugements* by which vagabonds and others were sentenced to longer terms. A monthly extract of these registers would allow the minister to determine how many inmates were to be fed at the king's expense.

The instruction explained in detail the construction of beds, the sole "furnishing" that required mention. Beds in hospitals were large, curtained pieces of furniture where several patients slept together high off the ground. Shunning such useless expense, the minister recommended military-style *lits de corps de garde,* or guardhouse bunks, consisting of no more than a wooden platform with two or two and a half feet of clearance to allow for sweeping up refuse from the floor, and boxed in around the sides to hold in the straw used as bedding. Along the foot of this common bunk a single large blanket would be nailed the length of the frame, reinforced with a leather strip to prevent tearing. The infirm needing special treatment would enjoy a slightly superior but still military standard. Placed three by three in *lits de caserne,* they would be given a stuffed mattress, pillow, blanket, and sheets. In all these details, the administration turned decisively away from hospital practices to adopt a strictly utilitarian standard based on military practice.[29]

Subsistence was another area in which the "frills" of hospital care were to be snipped away. The measure of food was closer to a prison ration, allowing a pound and a half of wheat bread *(pain bis)* for men and women, and one pound for children, with a supplement of vegetables cooked in water and salt. Vegetables might be replaced with rice, which was to be cooked according to a forthcoming recipe, "as used in times of dearth." If the standard was at all above that of a prison, it thus derived from the meager allotment given for emergency relief, a minimal standard for keeping body and soul together.[30]

Care of sick inmates required a clear policy, especially since the *dépôts* were to be distinguished from hospitals. The intendant was to choose a doctor or surgeon whose chief function in the course of inspecting inmates was to distinguish between those whose passing infirmities might safely be tended in a separate room in the *dépôt* (with more comfortable bedding, as noted, and with a restorative diet of soup or broth), and those whose serious condition warranted transfer to the *hôtel-Dieu* of the town. Although royal policy maintained that charitable houses had an obligation to receive the sick gratuitously in such cases, the instruction conceded that intendants might pay pensions up to six or seven livres per day for inmates transferred to hospitals. Pregnant women should also be transferred to the *hôtel-Dieu,* but after giving birth they could return to the *dépôts* and nurse their infants there.

Stocks of clothing for inmates were to be kept to an absolute minimum. Assuming that some inmates would have adequate clothing, each *dépôt* could begin with a stock sufficient for twenty people or so. Three shirts of the coarsest material for every two inmates to be clothed was deemed to provide an adequate change. Trousers could be provided from the same material; a wool bonnet for the head, and stockings and *sabots,* would complete the men's outfits. Women would be clothed with corset and petticoat, and a coarse wool outer frock; two women would share three bonnets and three *cornettes.* This costume presumably represented a common peasant standard of decency. On the other hand, the instruction recommended an abnormal precaution: shaving the heads of all inmates, for the sake of cleanliness and for ease of recognition in case of escape.[31]

The final portion of the instruction moved from specific standards to general management. Intendants were asked to send their ideas on how to occupy inmates— a matter not yet decided—and they were to instruct their subdelegates to maintain "good order, discipline *(police),* cleanliness, and health, visiting the *dépôt* two or three times a week to receive complaints and verify the treatment of inmates. The provisioning of the *dépôt* was to be carried out by an annual letting of bids for food and straw at a fixed daily price per person. This was best done at the end of the year in order to fix the price of grains purchased. Copies of these contracts should be sent to the minister. The web of paperwork was to include monthly lists of prisoners' names (including a note on who arrested them), their age, sex, state of health or disability, and cause of arrest. Each quarter the intendant should send two lists of expenses, one of daily recurring expenses, the other of extraordinary outlays. The controller-general would authorize disbursements from the revenues of the crown lands *(la domaine)* after reviewing these statements.

Seen from Bertier's office, the stream of instructions that he coordinated over the next months flowed naturally from this highly utilitarian and reasonable general instruction. Supplemental circulars were based on questions that arose from experience, simply codified so that the best results obtained might be uniformly applied. Some were in the form of technical advice, others elaborated the basic principles of the instruction. A circular on food provisioning and the preparation of rice combined both of these functions. The instructions on cooking rice noted that this highly economical form of nourishment had been known to go to waste from mere ignorance of the proper method for preparing it. On the matter of bread, Laverdy belabored the point that beggars, the shame of their country, should not be given finer fare than the brave defenders of the fatherland. He prescribed a recipe for bread composed of an equal mixture of three grains: wheat, rye, and barley. The finer flour could be left out entirely. When wheat prices rose above 12 l. 10s. the quintal, the bread ration should be reduced by half a livre in any case, and two ounces of rice could be substituted. "With a pound and a half of bread and two ounces of rice," wrote Laverdy, "a man, whosoever he be, shall be perfectly nourished." Allowing four and a half deniers per two-ounce ration for cooking and seasoning, the rice serving could be kept to one sou. Vegetables ought to replace rice three or four times per week, at a maximum price of one sou. Under the rules, the food ration should never exceed three and a half sols per day, a figure that tallied with Bertier's reckoning in the budget submitted to the king and approved the month before. The circular reminded intendants to keep a strict accounting with contractors and to make them supply spoons and any other utensils needed.[32]

While Bertier undoubtedly helped frame the cost-containment strategy for the system, the search for more economic means of subsistence for the poor reflected Physiocratic influences. In September, Laverdy had advised intendants that he had allocated shipments of rice for their *dépôts,* and asked that they inform him if they had cheaper means of obtaining provisions. If not, he would send rice. Rice, wrote Laverdy, was "the healthiest and most economic" nourishment.[33]

"Economy" was the overriding theme of further circulars to intendants over Laverdy's signature. One of these informed them that it would not be necessary to construct beds at all on the upper stories of *dépôts,* since straw might be laid on floors; on ground level, where dampness was likely to be a problem, bed frames would still be needed. Two days later, on January 9, 1768, a circular providing for the spiritual needs of inmates reiterated the suggestion made in the general instruction that the intendant might arrange to have local priests and religious take turns saying Mass in the *dépôts,* a task he should persuade them to accept without remuneration. The original instruction had noted that "decent" provisions for setting up an altar should be made, but clearly there was no wish to make the *dépôt* an ostentatious "house of God," in the sense frequently elaborated in the architecture and decoration of *hôtels-Dieu.* Portable altars could be set up in rooms normally used for other purposes, following military practice.[34]

Who was the author of these many instructions? Bertier, who was paid nine thousand livres per annum for his services as commisioner of mendicity, undoubtedly drafted circulars and took note of problems reported by intendants. On the other hand, Laverdy conferred with Bertier, setting limits, authorizing new initiatives, perhaps raising questions or making changes. In some instances, Laverdy may have drafted an entire letter from start to finish; in others, he may have given blanket authorization to use his signature. Other councillors, bureaucrats, and technical experts may have spelled out the content of some letters. This is particularly true of financial instructions for drawing funds and reporting expenditures, many of which Bertier dispatched in his own name. A further uncertainty of authorship arises from the fact that Bertier himself certainly relied on his clerks and subdelegates to prepare some of his administrative correspondence. These caveats should be borne in mind hereafter. Administrative reality is best reflected by speaking of "Bertier" in a partially disembodied sense, as a bureaucratic locus animated by a flesh-and-blood figure acting in concert with his confreres and with numerous functionaries above and beneath him.[35]

In spite of such uncertainties, there are some obvious clues as to Bertier's direct involvement. The strongest clue is the recurring reference to the administrative experience derived from *dépôts* in the *généralité* of Paris. The most striking early circular of this kind amplifies the general view of the *dépôts* contained in the original instruction. Concerned with the hiring of concierges, the letter shares with intendants some ideas that seemed useful to the minister "in order to try to bring to this matter the spirit of economy that must reign in every part of an operation of which the details are immense." First, the concept of the *dépôt* itself should be distinguished from that of a prison. Since the two sorts of inmates confined in them were not very dangerous, the guard of the *dépôt* should be simple and cheap compared to that of prisons. Vagabonds were presumably those too weak to serve in the galleys, and beggars were only under correction, not being punished for a crime. If they escaped and resumed begging, they would be arrested. If they begged no more, there was no reason for further concern.[36]

For similar reasons, there should be no need to reinforce concierges with turnkeys *(guichetiers)*. The *maréchaussée* would have to be summoned if any revolt broke out, and it could be used routinely to make rounds of the *dépôt* twice a day. Nor should concierges need helpers for the housekeeping of the *dépôt,* since inmates could be employed at such tasks. The writer of the circular comments on the need to maintain strict cleanliness in the lodgings of the inmates, and to punish the derelict by short rations of bread and water or by confinement in a cell or in irons. Here, the subdelegate would play a general supervisory role, "in order to establish among these people, if possible, some slight subordination and rule, and to force them above all to maintain the greatest cleanliness." He would need to make frequent visits to the *dépôt* for this purpose, "and to ensure that the inmates are treated humanely and in a healthy fashion." Even the intendant might set an example of zeal by visiting the *dépôt* in person from time to time.

Returning to the main point, the minister noted that in the *généralités* of Soissons and Paris, where food costs were high, concierges were hired for 200 to 300 livres to manage *dépôts* that contained large numbers of inmates. Such economy was strongly recommended. Sober veterans retired on half pay might be considered ideal candidates. A letter of March 24, 1768, returned to the subject of the circular of December 29 with a request for detailed information on the guard of *dépôts*. A detailed questionnaire—a veritable personnel-management résumé—accompanied the circular, and the minister asked that the intendant forward (if he had not already done so) the contracts agreed to by concierges in the *dépôts* of his *généralité*.[37]

Bertier used the *dépôts* of his own *généralité* as a benchmark for economy in a number of areas besides the hiring of concierges. In a circular of February 15, 1768, Laverdy advised several intendants, including those of Besançon and Caen, that their estimates for the costs of clothing were higher than those of other intendants. The minister proposed sending complete sets of clothing from the *généralité* of Paris. The intendant should simply determine whether there would be a savings over the price that could be obtained locally, after reckoning transport costs from Paris. He also reminded the intendant that clothing should be provided only for those inmates who absolutely needed it, and that beggars should be released with the clothes they had on their backs when they entered. In a further housekeeping note, the minister observed that these clothes brought in by beggars should be cleaned in boiling water, a precaution "often necessary for cleanliness, which must be looked to with the greatest care." One of Bertier's secretaries, named Loir, followed through by dispatching shipments of clothing in a number of instances.[38]

The need to erect a framework of periodic accounting for the *dépôts* spurred Bertier to further rounds of letter-writing and provoked a further review of administrative policies. A circular of January 13, 1768, for example, reminded intendants of the minister's desire to have copies of all contracts relating to the *dépôts*. On March 8 Laverdy repeated an earlier request that intendants send drawings showing the physical layout of the *dépôts* in detail. He wanted these in order to judge the capacity of each *dépôt* according to a common standard. For accounting purposes, it was also essential for him to be able to evaluate whether costs for rental, repair, and alterations on buildings were justified.[39]

Soon after requesting these plans, Laverdy sent a major circular on the form to be observed in filing monthly reports for accounting purposes. The information on inmates was needed in order to regulate and evaluate the impact of arrests and to keep a running account of the costs of maintaining inmates. A model of the printed form proposed was based on one drawn up for the *dépôt* at Pontoise in the *généralité* of Paris. Laverdy suggested that intendants have such forms printed. One copy should be sent every month to him, and the intendant should retain one copy. Laverdy then stressed the need to distinguish clearly between three categories of inmates. The anticipated expense for each category differed. In the first were those willing to work: special arrangements—presumably incentives for industrious inmates—would be reviewed, once work had been set up for them. The second category included all those placed in the infirmary or transferred to an *hôtel-Dieu:* those who remained in the *dépôt* would be allocated a ration of bouillon or *tisane;* the others would be pensioned at an agreed-upon rate. The third group required less than an ordinary ration. It comprised those being punished by confinement in cells on bread and water only.[40]

This same circular detailed the information to be provided in each of fifteen columns. It began with the request that proper names of inmates be alphabetized "in order to facilitate inquiries and comparisons." The columns giving age, height, state of disability or health, date of entry, and formal grounds of detention were to be completed only in the cases of inmates who were new that month. The remaining columns were to be completed in order to record changes in the current month: work at which an inmate was employed and the date work was begun; date of entry into and return from the infirmary or *hôtel-Dieu;* entry into and release from *cachots* (or disciplinary status); and reason for leaving the *dépôt* and the date of leaving. The sample form gave ages from eighteen to sixty-nine; heights from four feet, nine inches to five feet, six inches; disabilities including a bad leg and epilepsy; and three titles of detention: one by judgment of the *maréchaussée,* one by *ordonnance,* and one "by order of M. de St.-Florentin." Two instances of work were given— spinning hemp and tailoring. Causes listed for leaving the *dépôt* were "by order of the King," by request of relatives, enlistment, and death. Such were the minister's conceptions of the typical operation of the *dépôt,* purportedly based on a report submitted January 31, 1768, at Pontoise.

As the majority of the *dépôts* became operational, the monthly reports were followed by quarterly summaries allowing the minister to evaluate the progress of the system as a whole. The circular of July 12, 1768, mentioned in an earlier context asked intendants to add their observations on the success of the system and on its problems to the packet containing their printed monthly situation reports *(états de situation)* and their quarterly accounts for the second quarter, the *trimestre d'avril.* These would be assembled with those of other intendants in order to follow through upon a general policy review that had just been conducted in the king's presence at Compiègne. In that meeting the council had decided to tighten the net on mendicity by restricting the tolerance of "domiciled" beggars, as noted earlier, to half a league from their homes rather than the two leagues previously stipulated. The response from intendants must have been relatively positive in general.[41] The near absence of new instructions and policy circulars indicated that Bertier had left the machine to run without further tinkering for an extended period of observation. It appears that the system operated in a relatively steady state through 1768 and most of 1769, and that the adjustment in the criteria for arrest yielded a manageable flow of inmates. By the end of the summer of 1769, as already seen, Bertier was confident that the machine was ready to execute a universal prohibition on begging, including even domiciled beggars.

Experiment and Expedient

From the point of view of the intendants and their subordinates who administered Bertier's grand design, the operation did not always seem so logical and coherent. The tensions within the system became more strikingly apparent in the fall of 1769, as the arrest of domiciled beggars coincided with a deepening economic crisis. Strain on the system brought to light contradictions that were latent everywhere. The situation in Brittany in 1769 was especially sensitive, because the *dépôts* had been established there with some delay and in a context of political controversy.

When the order of August 12, 1769, concerning the arrest of domiciled beggars reached the intendant of Brittany, the *dépôt* at Rennes was already bursting at the seams. After receiving reports from his subdelegates, the intendant d'Agay asked the controller-general for authority to defer the arrest of domiciled beggars until the *dépôt* had been expanded or moved to larger quarters. Terray approved the decision and authorized a search for the best means of expanding capacity. Fresnais, subdelegate at Rennes, had outlined the need for expansion. The capacity of the *dépôt* at Rennes would depend in part on the function it was to perform: "If you judge it sufficient to keep the inmates packed in as in a prison, the aim that His Majesty proposes will have been missed in an essential part."[42]

No work was possible without allocation of space for sleeping, for an exercise yard, and for a workshop. More space would be required if women were to be kept in completely separate quarters. If, as the intendant projected, the number of inmates were raised to two hundred twenty, there would be no work area except the dormitories, even with every possible expansion of the building. If the dormitories were the only room allocated for work, inmates would be restricted to a few simple tasks such as spinning and knitting, types of work suited to only a few inmates. A work program for all would require setting up a variety of occupations in well-equipped, unobstructed workshops. A further demand on space was the need for a small infirmary. Even if this were set aside, there would still be no separate place for inmates afflicted by venereal diseases.[43]

Fresnais observed that the rented building then in use could not be made suitable without major alterations. But renovations in a building not owned by the king would be pure loss. The only solution that reconciled utility and economy would be to establish permanently a much larger *dépôt*. The intendant d'Agay approached the famous architect from Nantes, Ceineray, and cajoled him into drawing up plans for two new wings to be added to the old buildings. Ceineray preferred a utilitarian, low-cost design, including a detailed drawing to show how waste from the latrines could be flushed away by channeling rain water from the roof.[44]

These plans were superseded by an arrangement negotiated with the bishop of Rennes, whereby the *dépôt* was moved to the spacious quarters of the Little Seminary, situated on low ground near the mill of St. Hélier, on the Vilaine River.[45] The new quarters, providing a capacity for about five hundred inmates, seemed to answer the needs expressed by the subdelegate. However, new problems arose, and the costs of acquiring, converting, and operating the new facility were high. Meanwhile, similar calls for more adequate facilities came to the intendant from subdelegates of Quimper, Vannes, and Nantes.[46]

The fiction that *dépôts* were "provisional" lent plausibility to de Fleury's mental image of rude quarters in old buildings. The *Résultat* of 1764 conformed to that image. But as soon as it became clear that the *dépôts* would serve for an indefinite period as places of detention for a large class of inmates for terms of several months, it became necessary for them to provide the security of a prison, the medical resources of an infirmary, and the industrial facilities of a diversified manufacturing establishment. When royal engineers were called in to advise the intendant on the necessity of repairs and improvements, they inspected the chosen sites and applied their professional notions of hygiene and architectural design to dormitories, work areas, kitchens, lavatories, and infirmaries. Occasionally they found themselves at odds with a penny-pinching minister of finance. The engineer at Tours, de Voglie, insisted that parts of the old castle were not habitable because of dampness, poor ventilation, and lack of usable space. He resisted the notion that a single exercise yard would suffice for male and female inmates. At Limoges, Trésaguet advised Turgot that drainage was inadequate and that a place was needed to hang laundry out to dry. Viallet at Caen collaborated closely with the intendant in designing a functional *dépôt*.[47]

In response to an early challenge, Bertier himself conceded that the proposed standards for the maintenance of inmates, "in between that of a prison and that of a soldier," might well "appear harsh to someone who had not well sounded the views of the minister." For this reason, he adamantly resisted demands for a right of inspection, as advanced by the parlement of Besançon.[48] The goal of uniformity must not be disrupted. In practice, nonetheless, a correctional standard was not so easily calibrated, and in fact three standards were recognized, including a harsher standard for disciplinary purposes and a more fastidious one for the sick. Furthermore, workers would be allowed to better their lot with a portion of their earnings. While an abstract notion of hierarchy placed the reprobate beggar on a lower step than the valiant soldier, military specifications for items such as bedding and infirmaries were frequently applied with little modification. They were conveniently close to a utilitarian minimum—the eighteenth-century French soldier was not cosseted in luxury. Intendants and their subdelegates were familiar with these standards, since they were in charge of the supply of armies passing through their provinces, and supervised military hospitals.[49]

In theory, the intendant was to transfer gravely ill beggars to hospitals, but this did not relieve *dépôts* of the need for maintaining regular infirmaries. There was some truth to Bertier's allegation that hospitals had forced this function upon the *dépôts* by refusing to accept inmates from them. Gelée de Prémion, subdelegate at Nantes, spluttered angrily in one such instance of refusal, expressing his view that hospital administrators were pious benighted hypocrites lacking any concern for humanity.[50] From the point of view of hospital trustees, on the other hand, the royal government had still not made good its promise to aid hospitals financially. If the *dépôts* were advertised as "supplements to hospitals," they offered no substantial relief—only new burdens.

Hospital boards were particularly unhappy with the prospect of receiving women from the *dépôts*. Laverdy and Choiseul had agreed that *dépôts* would receive women and girls of ill repute arrested by military police "in the train of the armies," with the understanding that costs of their maintenance and of medical treatment for venereal disease would be paid for by the Ministry of War from the fund called *l'extraordinaire des guerres*. This general arrangement appears to have developed from an earlier agreement that such women in the region of Brest could be transferred to the *dépôt de mendicité* at Quimper.[51] The presence of these women in the *dépôt* at Quimper created a scandal. They gathered at windows near the street and exchanged raucous greetings with passersby. There were rumors that some young men had gained illicit entry to their quarters. Under these circumstances, the hospital at Quimper refused to receive the influx of patients from outside the city. After visiting the town, Fresnais wrote to the intendant; "You, Monseigneur, will have to speak for your beggars; the bishop has expressly declared that he will not receive them."[52] At Angers, likewise, a priority traditionally granted to women of the town for places in the hospital's maternity ward was reinforced by a desire not to expose virtuous women to shameful diseases, the just desert of libertinism.[53]

In many instances—at Rouen and at Châlons-sur-Marne, for example—the hospitals were willing to receive patients from the *dépôts,* but the intendant and his subdelegate did not send them until their condition was critical. Laverdy had specifically warned intendants against sending any dangerous inmate to the hospital, except in very serious cases, lest he escape. A consideration of security thus reinforced the requirement that the *dépôt* function as a medical facility. The dual function actually required of the *dépôts* as prison and hospital was well illustrated by an incident at Rouen. In an audit of accounts, the controller-general asked the intendant of Rouen to verify the fate of twenty-eight inmates transferred to the *hôtel-Dieu* and pensioned there in 1770. The answer was that nineteen had died there and eight had escaped. The remaining one was presumably either expiring or preparing his escape![54]

The ministry gave ground slowly, eventually approving expenditures for fitting out infirmaries in most *dépôts,* complete with pharmacies and in some cases, as at Tours, with an herb garden. The subdelegate at Rennes may have touched a raw nerve in Bertier's office when he argued that, if infirmaries were provided, there would be no need to fear the spread of disease, "since then we would have all the resources of hospitals." Nonetheless, his recommendation was adopted. A general circular in 1770 further instructed intendants to provide separate cells for the insane. As *maisons de force* for the very poor, the *dépôts* naturally received the dangerous or unmanageable insane, but no thought had been given to their care. Another traditional charitable category included in the net that swept up beggars was that of young children. A circular of December 26, 1769, informed intendants that schemes to pension youthful inmates to peasant families had worked successfully in some *généralités,* and especially recommended the procedures adopted by the Hôpital de la Charité in Lyons.[55]

The same arguments that left the concierge almost singlehandedly in charge of guarding the inmates weighed against expensive prison architecture. Thoughtless improvisation of security measures contributed to poor conditions within the *dépôts.* In the cramped quarters first utilized at Rennes, for example, the isolation cell was simply an empty space in a dingy stairwell. Ad hoc measures to discourage escapes there included a decision to brick up the windows in the men's wing. Health conditions deteriorated soon afterward in quarters filled with the latest arrests, leading Fresnais to suggest that some windows be reopened and secured with bars.[56] In many of the old buildings converted for use as *dépôts,* security was difficult to maintain, in spite of repeated outlays for bricklaying and repair of loose bars, installation of locks, and purchase of leashes for guard dogs.[57]

The *dépôts* were supposed to be like *hôpitaux-généraux* in one key respect: they were to put as many as possible of their inmates to work. Lacking experience in such enterprises, those responsible for running the *dépôts* were tempted to employ persons experienced in running charitable work projects in hospitals. In any case, it was clear upon a moment's reflection that well-organized work projects required special facilities, or at least a separate workplace within the *dépôts.*

A typical complaint was that of the subdelegate at Nantes, de Prémion, who observed that cotton spinning was the only work that could be done in the squalid dormitory where the beggars lived. With a large open area, looms could be brought together and all the work could be supervised by a single overseer, "which would bring about more order and more emulation in the work done, and consequently more discipline, progress, and profit for the inmates." The cost of setting up workshops was estimated at 4,248 livres. De Prémion clearly envisioned the *dépôts* as an institution of a new type. "For establishments as useful as the *dépôts,*" he exclaimed, "there should be buildings designed especially."[58]

Bertier was intimately aware of these problems. He wrote a letter in his own hand, addressed from his estate at Sauvigny on June 1, 1770, to inquire into the state of affairs at Angers, the subject of a complaint relayed from the parlement of Paris to the chancellor. The subdelegate's reply, returned to Bertier by du Cluzel, was only partially reassuring. The inmates were not piled in heaps, although some preferred the floor to their mattresses. In warm weather, it was true, the beggars were afflicted by fleas—not lice or vermin, as alleged—and careful sweeping had not eliminated the problem. The beggars did not have much elbow room, but at three to a mattress they had more space than Laverdy's regulation allowed (four to a mattress, or a foot and a half apiece). The subdelegate took advantage of the occasion to press his request to acquire an adjacent structure, which could be added to the *dépôt* to provide a work area.[59]

As a result of the complaints about the *dépôt* at Angers, du Cluzel received some housekeeping advice from Terray. Economy, the minister noted, should not be carried to the point of compromising the health of the inmates. He noted further that loose straw had served well for bedding in some *dépôts.* Mattresses could be reserved for winter (before use they should be aired, of course). The intendant was authorized to expand the *dépôt* at Angers as requested, or to transfer those capable of working to the *dépôt* at Tours.

The problem of providing adequate facilities at many of the smaller *dépôts* led to a concentration in the network. In Brittany, for example, it was too much to expect that costly repairs could be made at Vannes and Quimper, and a new model *dépôt* built at Nantes, while major costs were being incurred for an ambitious project of converting the Little Seminary at Rennes to a *dépôt* and building new workshops there. A report of 1791 explained the action taken:

> At this time an *arrêt du conseil* of September 15, [1771] united all the establishments spread throughout the province into one. Greater economy and a surer and easier administration were the motives that determined this merger. The residence of the *commissaire départi* for Brittany at Rennes and the greater means of surveillance on his part, were decisive in the choice of this city as the site for a *dépôt de mendicité* common to the province.[60]

As a consequence of this decision, and the closing of the *dépôts* at Quimper, Vannes, and Nantes in July 1772, beggars throughout the province were transported by the *maréchaussée* to Rennes. For those in the West who spoke only Breton, Rennes was practically a foreign capital.[61]

A summary of annual expenses presented by Bertier to Turgot in 1774 reflected the trend toward concentration of investment in more adequate, less provisional facilities. After an initial outlay for buildings and rentals amounting to 502,000 livres by the end of 1768, expenditures fell to 183,000 in 1769, only to rise to 257,000 in 1770 and 276,000 in 1771. Expenses for furnishings, bedding, clothing, and religious ministrations all increased from 1769 to 1771. Outlays for care of the sick and for infirmaries rose steadily. Costs of provisions rose phenomenally in 1769, but were actually reduced in 1770 and 1771, a reflection of Terray's bulk-contracting methods and the use of rice shipped for relief distributions. There was substantial investment in projects to employ inmates in 1769, after an initial phase of neglect, but the level of investments was greatly curtailed in 1770. Given the need to contain generally rising expenditures, only a concentration of resources on fewer *dépôts* would permit further expansion of workshops. Unless the number of detainees dropped sharply, the remaining *dépôts* would also have to be larger.[62]

Beginning with some excess capacity, the *dépôts* were overcrowded by 1769. From 1768 to 1771, the number of inmates admitted per year climbed from a little under nine thousand to over fourteen thousand, while the cumulative growth in inmate population, reflected in end-of-the-year tallies, rose from 4,148 in 1768 to 9,164 in 1771. Although the number of inmates dwindled only slightly after 1771, twenty-four of the original eighty-eight *dépôts* were eliminated by 1773. Thus, on the eve of Turgot's ministry, the average population in a given *dépôt* was about 130 (or 8,615 in 64 *dépôts*), compared with an initial average population of about 45 per *dépôt* (4,148 in the original 88) at the end of 1768. Under recurring budgetary pressures, the same economic logic would dictate a further concentration of the network of *dépôts* to one per *généralité* in 1780.[63]

As Bertier tried to impose bureaucratic coherence on the competing claims of utility, he focused his attention on the search for a formula that would link the upkeep of inmates with the organization of work projects. The concentration of inmates and resources in fewer *dépôts* was but one consequence of this quest.

5

Deriving a Formula

Ambiguities in the mission of the *dépôts* nourished a corresponding set of uncertainties concerning their management and control. Utility and economy at first seemed to dictate a radically simple arrangement. A concierge would be responsible for all the day-to-day operations of the *dépôt,* with the assistance of inmates who would be paid minimal wages for performing menial tasks. Laverdy especially praised the intendant of Châlons for suggesting that the *maréchaussée* be quartered within the *dépôts* in order to simplify the task of guarding inmates. The work of the concierge would be overseen by the subdelegate of the intendant, who would review the concierge's records and reports, inspect the *dépôt* in person, and make recommendations to the intendant on all matters that required his authorization, including discipline, release of inmates, transfer to hospitals, and all business dealings, contracts, and payments. The intendant would simply review the subdelegate's reports, give the appropriate orders, regulate the pace of arrests, and serve as the essential link with Bertier and the controller-general.[1]

Management: Incentives and Controls

This chain of command and supervision was not adequate. The minister's description of the suitable type of person to be employed as concierge gives a hint of the vague and contradictory expectations governing the management of the *dépôts*. He was to be a man of intelligence and brawn, a man of scrupulous rectitude, and one with military experience who could impose discipline by his mere presence. Preferably he would have a wife able to assist him in his duties. Above all he should be willing to work for very modest remuneration. Anyone capable of discharging the concierge's diverse functions competently was likely to be enterprising and intelligent enough to find ways to compensate himself beyond his meager pittance.[2]

In arranging for food provisioning, the subdelegate was to let a contract for the daily bread supply. However, the diet supplements, especially the vegetables for the broth, could be provided by contract with the concierge, if his bid were the lowest. This arrangement seemed ''fair'' and would allow him to make a small profit. Laverdy asked merely that intendants be watchful, lest concierges make the condition of the inmates too hard "in order to procure themselves greater gains." The history of the *dépôts* from the point of view of the inmates was governed in large measure by the habits and personalities of these lowly jailers and their helpers.[3]

The subdelegate found himself in the position of executive director of the *dépôt* in his town, serving voluntarily, wielding little authority and next to no discretion over the use of funds. The first instruction to intendants indicated vaguely that further instructions would direct the subdelegate in one of his most important duties, that of devising work for the inmates. In fact, no such general instruction came, as the ministry prolonged its search for examples of how best to manage this essential correctional function. Each subdelegate was urged to devise some arrangements in a provisional manner. Use of hospital personnel for this task was discouraged. The subdelegate at Rouen, Alexandre, who avowed that he knew little about the details of manufacturers, first gave this duty to the concierge. As a consequence of repeated complaints against the concierge, the subdelegate brought in an outside contractor. The concierge, jealous of the contractor's new power, was suspected of having a part in the riot that broke out in April 1773, in which the inmates made weapons of the iron rods in the contractor's spinning wheels and used the knives imprudently left out in the workshops.[4]

A variety of earlier experiments elsewhere had failed to produce a general model. The proper amount to allow for incentives to working inmates was one of the points of difficulty, depending as it did upon a shifting rationale. In January 1768 Laverdy approved an arrangement proposed by the intendant of Champagne, Rouillé d'Orfeuil, to have inmates employed in a school for workers to be established in a wool manufactory under royal protection at Châlons-sur-Marne. The king would pay only the cost of their bread and straw; the inmates' earnings would provide for their clothing, vegetables, and bedding. Laverdy at first accepted the notion of a work incentive, "improving the lot of these people in order to incite their diligence the more." He had not realized, however, that the intendant planned to allow inmates to keep one half of the product of their labor to provide their amenities. The intendant observed that he was only trying to manage the king's funds as economically as possible. That was not the issue; the minister thought it better to allow only one or two sous per day, "inasmuch as if these people found that they were fed on the king's account and that they earned a decent amount besides, there would be reason to fear lest they be happier than the other inhabitants of the country, who apart from bestirring themselves to great effort must also take thought for the morrow." They must be made aware that they are under correction and must desire to return to "the work on the land, for which they are made."[5]

In January 1770 a letter from Terray to the intendant of Champagne indicated that the minister had found the model workshop. It advised the intendant of a forthcoming visit from a Sieur Bernier, inspector of military hospitals in Franche-Comté, who had achieved remarkable economies by the establishment of workshops in the *dépôt* at Besançon. Terray suggested that Bernier be allowed to make observations on the means used to employ inmates in the *dépôt* at Châlons, and to share with the intendant any suggestions he might have for improvement. The irony of this announcement was that an epidemic was raging in the *dépôt* at Besançon at the time Terray was writing, and that conditions there were blamed on Bernier's administration. A proud model of economy was in shambles. What had happened?[6]

When Bourgeois de Boynes's successor at Besançon, La Corée, was instructed to set up a *dépôt de mendicité,* he chose the Maison de Bellevaux, where Bernier had established workshops under the direction of a Sieur Puricelli. Puricelli had complained in 1761 that Bernier was feeding the inmates poorly, but the directors of the *aumône-générale* had stood behind Bernier. In August 1769, the ministry approved a contract with Bernier for the maintenance of inmates at Bellevaux in sickness or health at the unusually low rate of four sous per *journée* (i.e., per person per day). Bernier was allowed to profit from the inmates' labor, and was obliged only to set aside one-eighth of the profits "in order to encourage them and to excite their emulation." No cash would be paid to inmates until their release, but an agent of the intendant might use sums set aside for them "in order to procure for inmates the amenities that he may deem suitable."[7]

Less than a year later, the epidemic broke out. Massive outlays for medical care and increased food rations shattered cost estimates from July 1769 to July 1771, when a new contractor took over. In a year and a half, 193 shrouds were purchased. An arrangement to cover Bernier's actual costs led to mutual recriminations between Bernier, the intendant La Corée, and Bertier. The former intendant, de Boynes, intervened personally. In a letter to Terray, La Corée drew the lesson of false economy: "No doubt it was desired that his price stand as a rule and a model elsewhere; what was the result?" The actual amounts paid to bail out Bernier raised the average daily rate to 10s. 11d. per *journée,* whereas the contractors who took over in 1771 charged 7s. 9d.: "Here is what it comes down to—the advantage of a contract done at 4s. that was proportioned neither to the price of victuals nor to the other objects of expense."[8]

The Expanding Burdens of Utility

If Bernier's experiment at Besançon demonstrated the dangers of pressing economy too far, a series of experiments at Tours drew the ministry further than it wished into projects of general utility. The animator of the project was a local merchant and magistrate, Sieur Rattier, *syndic-receveur* of the town, who contracted for the provisions of the *dépôt* and had begun work projects on a very modest scale, installing twelve spinning wheels and hiring two men and a woman to teach inmates to card and spin wool.

Rattier had provided an additional incentive to inmates from the city of Tours, promising them work after their release in a place separate from the beggars. In this project Rattier was seconded by Sieur Le Comte, an expert *bonnetier* "highly esteemed at Tours and at Amboise," whose house adjoined the *dépôt.* Le Comte distributed raw wool in the morning and took in the spun product in the evening. Selling the wool at 1s. 6d. per pound, he paid a quarter of the product to those working as inmates of the *dépôt* and three-fourths of the product to "free workers." The balance he set aside for the purchase of looms, for his own payment and that of the instructors, and for supplies of wood for stoves and candles to work by (work progressed from six in the morning until nine in the evening).[9]

In devising plans for the inmates of the *dépôt,* Rattier and Le Comte worked closely with the subdelegate, Restru, a magistrate in the *baillage* of Tours. Restru was undoubtedly aware that the intendant had been directed in March to supply monthly reports on his *dépôts* listing the tasks at which individual beggars were employed.[10] In July Bertier had asked all intendants that these reports be summarized in quarterly statements for review in royal council. The zealous du Cluzel would not have wanted these columns left blank. Submitting a proposal to expand his project, Rattier explained to the intendant that he had provided a double envelope for his letter to the controller-general, "so that he will read it himself."[11]

Rattier's memoir of August 18, 1768, explained the plan that he had devised with Le Comte to set up two looms in the *dépôt* to work up the wool spun by beggars into blankets. Blankets made from the better quality of thread would be sold at the going price to bourgeois, whereas those made from the second grade of thread would be used in the *dépôt* and would be sold at a reduced price to hospitals and for charitable distribution to the parish poor. The project would require sending a bright young unemployed worker who was already familiar with looms for the manufacture of silk and wool to Orleans to learn the techniques of blanket-making. He would bring back a diligent journeyman, so that the two might set up looms for the employment of inmates of the *dépôts* and free workers.

To make the scheme work, it would be necessary, Rattier argued, to provide a cost-of-living subsidy for the free workers, who would otherwise not be able to subsist in the face of bread prices that had risen twenty-five percent (from ls. to ls. 3d. per ration) since 1762. He justified this request by analogy with the *"plus vallue"* paid to soldiers by *ordonnance* of the royal intendant. Rattier explained the involuntary character of mendicity at Tours: a depressed textile industry could not employ its qualified workforce; the few who worked were unable to subsist on their earnings. Rattier reported that many in this category had asked to be admitted voluntarily to his new workshop. Restru, he added, had encouraged him to find means of employing inmates of the *dépôt* on their release. Clearly, the prohibition on begging could not be enforced without a solution to the problem of unemployment and inflated food prices.

Rattier followed up his request with another letter to the intendant detailing the recent accomplishments of the *dépôt,* to which Restru, who had just visited there, might attest. He was especially proud of the productivity of an eighteen-year-old who was earning from 2s. 6d. to 3s. per day, although Rattier was paying only a quarter of the rate given by the clothiers in town. Such an example was encouraging to other inmates. At Restru's request, Rattier had provisionally admitted a twelve-year-old girl blind since birth and was able to report, "My good peasant woman has taught her to spin and she is handling it fairly well." Rattier estimated that he could procure bread for a good many under existing arrangements by accepting a loss on the sale of the wool produced; he speculated that with a greater number of beggars, he might be able to break even at the current daily rate provided for the subsistence of inmates.[12]

Restless and excited, Rattier had gone off to consult with the director of a middling-sized manufacture in the countryside, not knowing whether his memoir to the controller-general had been received and forwarded. His letter cited Restru's support for Rattier's project, even giving him credit for the idea. He need not have worried. Du Cluzel wrote a note to his secretary, Duval, across the bottom of Rattier's letter, "Reply to M. Rattier that I am as satisfied as I could be with the new establishment, and that I beg him to bring to it always the same zeal and the same economy." He added, "Make up an order to put the blind girl in the *dépôt.*" [13]

Rattier's project bore fruit as intended, under the benevolent protection of the subdelegate Restru and the intendant du Cluzel. The intendant helped by obtaining from his confrere at Orleans, Cypierre, responses to a list of questions on the trade of blanket-making.[14] Once Rattier established his looms, he apparently sold a good number of blankets of the better quality, stocked the *dépôt* with those of the second quality, and sold some of the latter for charitable distributions. Before long, however, he must have found he was producing more blankets than he could sell locally. Such was the impetus, presumably, for the formal request on his part to accord to his workshop a *privilège* as a royal manufacture, so that his blankets might be sold duty-free throughout the kingdom for use in the *dépôts de mendicité.* The request was routinely referred to the Bureau of Commerce. There, Trudaine referred the petition back to the intendant for his advice. The request was finally approved by *arrêt du conseil* of February 13, 1770, on the report of Terray, giving Rattier's establishment a privileged status as a *manufacture des pauvres.* Rattier was entitled to employ both the inmates of the *dépôt* and free workers from within and without the city of Tours. Without delay, the minister proceeded with the arrangement he had made with du Cluzel to dispatch bundles of blankets to *dépôts* throughout France. A printed order form advertised the full line of Rattier's wares, and Bertier's office advised intendants of a provisional allotment for their use.[15]

While Rattier's request for a *privilège* was under review, Bertier, assuming no doubt that it would be approved, submitted a new contract with Rattier for the approval of the new controller-general, Maynon d'Invau. The "observations" accompanying the minister's letter of approval of November 11, 1769, appear to reflect Bertier's search for a general contracting model. Praising the advantages of making a single person responsible for maintaining beggars and putting them to work, Bertier argued that the contractor could recoup his costs on the former only by the profit from the latter:

> This personal interest of the entrepreneur will make him industrious in seizing upon and using every means to establish different kinds of work proportioned to the age, the station in life, and aptitude of the inmates; all being occupied thereby will acquire the habit and capability of working and will lose that of an idle, mendicant life.[16]

According to Rattier's new contract at Tours, inmates were to receive only one-eighth of the product of their labor—a proportion later adjusted to one-fourth—but any payment was to be regarded purely as a favor and must be doled out in small amounts, in order to prevent inmates from procuring amenities that could be superfluous or even dangerous. The one-eyed and the lame were to partake of the prescribed correctional remedy—they would crank hand-mills provided for the grinding of grain. A model, or even a full-sized machine, could be sent on request from Paris or Orleans, where such mills had been used with success.[17]

Hardly two weeks after Rattier's workshop received its formal *privilège,* a thor-

ough medical inspection by the renowned local doctor Dupichard revealed a dis-
tressingly poor state of health among the inmates of the *dépôt*. The aim of the visit
was to discover the cause of the illness that regularly attacked new inmates a few
days after being confined. Dupichard examined the beggars themselves and their
food. He found that the living quarters were poorly lit and humid, and the air stuffy
and ill-smelling. The window openings were too small. The thick walls covered
with saltpeter were always damp, as were the flagstones laid at a level below that
of the courtyard.[18]

Food might be adequate, in view of the fact that inmates were inactive, but
Dupichard believed that inmates suffered from the sharp change they experienced
upon entering. He maintained that their diet before confinement included meat, and
that the money they begged allowed them to buy eau-de-vie in the morning and
wine in the evening.

> The regime of the *dépôt* is quite different. They are held in strict confinement
> against their will, reduced to a pound and a half of bread, a portion of vegetables
> cooked in water and salt, and drinking water. This sudden change makes them ill,
> as they are almost all weakened by infirmities or age.

Sick rations, including some meat and soup, were sufficient, although Dupichard
thought it desirable to have this supplement continue during convalescence. He
admitted that he had formed a negative impression of the beggars themselves. They
were slow, lazy, troublesome, and unclean enough to foul their own straw. However, he did not blame them entirely for their condition. The causes of their maladies, including dysentery, "bilious" disorders, catarrh, and respiratory infections,
lay in the poor state of the living quarters, the excessive economy in the food, and
the unclean condition of the beggars themselves. The air of the *dépôt,* in particular,
was infected by the cloud of inmates' breath mingling with the smoke from coal
braziers used for heating. Breathing was stifled and the asthmatics in the *dépôt* were
suffocating.[19]

Dupichard recommended several remedies. Cleanliness must be strictly enforced, while the old and infirm should be allowed some wine on first entering.
The quarters needed better air circulation and fires should be built in the fireplaces
rather than in open braziers. Inmates should be exercised outdoors, weather permit-
ting, and the "law of working" must be imposed universally. Dupichard suggested
that the supervision needed might best be carried out by the three *soeurs grises*—
Sisters of Charity—whom Rattier was waiting for. He cautioned that they would
need an established infirmary before they could adequately help the inmates. In any
case, there would be deaths. Among the forty-five currently detained, over half
were on their last legs, crushed by age and infirmities. Dupichard took a measure
of solace from the thought that mendicity would be wiped out if Rattier's manufacture succeeded in offering a resource to the poor, and in imposing on children the
love of work. He promised to repeat his visits to the *dépôt*.[20]

The timing of Dupichard's visit suggests that Rattier was only waiting for his
privilège to be officially confirmed before submitting a further request for royal aid.
The request was soon linked to proposals for a greater expansion of the workshops
and for the addition of new facilities for the medical care of inmates in the *dépôt*.

A detailed proposal for changes, including a botanical garden for growing herb remedies, was forwarded to du Cluzel at Chanteloup, Choiseul's residence, on May 25, 1770. The archbishop of Tours had agreed to assign three *soeurs grises* for the service of the *dépôt,* and the intendant concurred. They originally expected that the town of Tours would pay the cost of bringing the sisters to the *dépôt,* but the municipal alms bureau was already overburdened with the care of the disabled needy poor in the town. Would the royal treasury pay?[21]

Rattier argued that he needed the help of three *soeurs grises* in order to perform supervisory tasks. He found himself overburdened, even with the help of his two children. He must supervise workers directly, receive finished work, make payments, and attend to paperwork. He must buy provisions, prepare and distribute them in economic fashion, and maintain cleanliness, "which requires continual care because of the shameful habit in which idleness plunges the beggar—who allows himself to be covered with vermin." Minor illnesses required constant attention, for if not treated they led to grave ones. Those returning from hospital care must also be treated during convalescence. Finally, the need for religious training added a further reason for Rattier to request the three sisters. They would inspire the work of the beggars, he also believed, especially the children. Each sister would be paid 250 livres per year. By taking a part of the "alms of the clergy," a permanent foundation could be established for this purpose.[22]

The archbishop of Tours endorsed the utility and economy of Rattier's proposal, complimenting the intendant's "zeal for the public good." Du Cluzel had written Terray that the project represented "a very estimable object of utility and I am not surprised that M. the Archbishop favors it." Medical expertise was of little avail, "if there is no one present to ensure that prescriptions are observed by the sick and convalescent."[23] Terray approved the project on February 20, 1771, with changes that du Cluzel had discussed with his secretary, Duval. According to the terms of Rattier's contract, the sisters would have to treat the venereal diseases that were common in the *dépôt.* The introduction of a new method of treatment by the *dragées de Keyser* under a contract with Keyser's widow, which was recommended for use in all *dépôts,* should remove any repugnance on the sisters' part. Two sisters (not three) would be maintained by an annual payment from the royal treasury for the term of Rattier's contract, rather than being established in perpetuity by a costly endowment.[24]

Before this extraordinary request was approved, du Cluzel had proposed a substantial expansion of Rattier's operation and asked for increased funding for the cost-of-living supplement to Rattier's wages for "free" workers. He placed these requests in a broad economic context. Rattier could be expected to absorb the costs of the workshop up to a point, but as the numbers employed grew, the excess costs rose. These swollen numbers were the product of economic crisis—the collapse of Tours manufactures. Terray's reply of January 30, 1771, approved the request in principle, but asked that the intendant review the terms of Rattier's contract. If Rattier were entirely responsible for the feeding of one hundred poor, then the king might pay a subsidy of four sols per day to those beyond this number, or about two hundred additional poor in winter and one hundred in summer. This would entail increased royal outlays, but the dearth of provisions and the quantity of indigents whom the intendant was loath to treat harshly induced the minister to consent. Terray warned against the abuses to which such an arrangement was liable and urged du Cluzel to terminate it as soon as possible.[25]

Terry approved further expansion of the *dépôt* at Tours. Engineer's estimates sent to Terray on January 23, 1771, included 11,258 livres for Rattier's planned expansion of workshops and 4,500 livres for the construction of twenty-five cells for lodging the insane. These measures went forward. A *cabaretier* and his wife who lodged within the castle walls were evicted to make room for expanding the *dépôt,* and the royal engineer visited the castle again in June 1771 in order to expand living quarters for inmates and provide facilities for putting them to work in greater numbers. As a result, 150 men and seventy women could be kept securely, and 150 of these inmates could be put to work.[26]

Rattier's success reflected unanimous support from the authorities at Tours. Local merchants and curés were aware of the inadequacy of the alms bureau. The intendant and his subdelegate focused their attention on the economic dimension of mendicity; the archbishop seconded their support of Rattier's schemes. Rattier claimed, after all, to employ 400 workers through the winter, accepting those who could produce certificates from their employers specifying how long they had gone without work. Du Cluzel may also have invoked the discreet patronage of the duc de Choiseul at Chanteloup. As minister of war, Choiseul controlled the *maréchaussée* and was responsible for the castle of Tours, in which the *dépôt* was situated. Trudaine assured the intendant a friendly hearing in the Bureau of Commerce for his efforts to rescue the ailing textile industry. Bertier appears to have been interested in Rattier's workshop as a model whose success might be advertised to other intendants by the dispatch of blankets for their *dépôts.*[27]

This favorable conjunction of influences was only temporary. The employment of free workers could not be considered a routine function of the *dépôts de mendicité* under normal conditions of employment. As food prices returned to normal, there could be no question of a cost-of-living subsidy for these workers. The provision of *soeurs de charité,* accepted as an emergency measure, was a troublesome "charitable" precedent. Finally, Bertier must have been chagrined that Rattier's industrial accomplishments failed to supply the desired spur to emulation by the directors of other *dépôts.* Gêlée de Prémion, subdelegate at Nantes, was inspired by the example, but he was an exception. In any case, the *dépôt* at Nantes was shut down in order to save money. Subdelegates at Angers and Le Mans were more typical, arguing that, since they lacked Rattier's special resources, they could not achieve comparable results.[28]

Bertier did not move to dismantle the experiment at Tours until May 1773, when the controller-general let a consolidated "general" contract for the provisioning of *dépôts* in sixteen *généralités,* including Tours. Du Cluzel was displeased when the decision was announced, but Terray insisted. Vindicating his action at a later date, Terray noted that the new contractor successfully employed inmates of the *dépôt* whom Rattier had deemed unsuited for work, and reminded the intendant of the poor conditions of health that had marked Rattier's management of the operation.[29]

A New Equation Given

The general contract, signed May 1773 with the Paris company of Manié, Rimberge et Cie, reflected the early years of experience in operating the *dépôts*. The new contractors would receive a sum of six sols per *journée* during the first four years of the contract and five during the last six years. This price, more realistic than that of Bernier at Besançon, allowed substantial lead time to organize productive work-shops. The contractors were required to give inmates one-sixth of the product of their labor, "to encourage them and excite their emulation." This fraction was a shade more generous to the inmates than the one-eighth recommended earlier. The regulation of discipline emphasized punishment, but also provided for control by the intendant in order to prevent abuses that might provoke outbreaks, injury, or scandal. A prohibition on the use of tools that might be used as weapons reflected the experience of various revolts, such as the one that had occurred at Rouen just the month before.[30] The "general" contract was limited in fact to only seventeen of the thirty-three *généralités*. Local contractors continued to provision *dépôts* in other *généralités* not included in Manié's contract, but apparently there was at least one other general contractor, the company of Teissier et Engren, whose contract for the *dépôt* at Châlons was similar to that of Manié, but cheaper.[31] Both companies made use of subcontractors and agents.

Before deciding to combine provisioning and workshops in a general contract with Manié, Rimberge et Cie, the ministry had experimented with a variety of other arrangements. While original instructions had left the initiative for workshops to the subdelegate, they stated that the provisioning of food—or at least the main item, bread—would be contracted out. In 1769, Maynon d'Invau, the controller-general who served for a year between Laverdy and Terray, launched a new policy of direct provisioning by the subdelegates, a policy that was continued by Terray in 1770. D'Invau's circular of December 9, 1769, suggested that subdelegates purchase large stocks of grain at opportune times in order to ensure that inmates of *dépôts* would be fed and to avoid incurring the cost of sudden price increases.[32]

This measure was obviously a response to grain shortages and high prices. It also blended smoothly with the desire of d'Invau's successor, Terray, to manage subsistence commodities by a centralized bureaucratic network of data collection and control. This experiment was no more successful than the one making sub-delegates directly responsible for arranging workshops in the *dépôt*. The task re-quired specialized knowledge and imposed burdens on the subdelegate that were incompatible with his many other functions as agent of the provincial intendant. The subdelegate of Angers complained to du Cluzel at Tours, in a letter of June 30, 1770: "What it means is taking upon myself all the hassles of a grain mer-chant's agent."[33]

To become so directly involved in provisioning raised another sort of problem that would alone have discouraged subdelegates from touching it: they became sus-pect as profiteers or even as agents of an organized monopoly. When du Cluzel advised the subdelegate at Angers to manage his provisions so that he bought cheap and sold dear, the subdelegate reminded the intendant that the parlement, in an edict of May 29, 1770, had renewed former police regulations requiring the regis-tration of all buyers of grain for resale. To lay in stocks as a private citizen, especially in the position of subdelegate, would expose him inevitably to the charge of hoarding. The subdelegate at Le Mans raised similar objections against managing the stocks of the *dépôts*. Later in the year Turgot informed Terray that the mere delivery of grain by government order to his subdelegate Boisbedeuil at Angoulême had led to accusations from the common people *(peuple)* that he was engaging in commerce or monopoly, "and whoever says 'common people' at Angoulême is speaking of a great many. He has received letters threatening to assassinate him or burn him in his house, and I myself have received several letters of this sort." [34]

Problems such as these led to a return to former methods of contracting for rations with an entrepreneur at a set price per daily ration, a price that allowed for some anticipation of profit. Combining the two contracts in one and joining together sixteen *généralités* had the advantage of spreading some of the risks, and conferred some economies of scale, since shipments and purchases could be coordinated over a large area. If the price of the *journée* could be set realistically at a low level, the general contract would serve as a benchmark against which any remaining local contracts could be evaluated. [35]

In the evolution of contracting arrangements, the engineering of an effective set of incentives for managers and provisioners was as important as designing the proper incentives for inmates. The contractor must be encouraged to make the inmates productive by allowing him to profit from their labor, and this must be done in the most economical manner possible. One advantage of combining the contracts for subsistence and for workshops was that the contractor was thus encouraged to find some kind of work suited to the capacity of every inmate, since he had to support all of them. A further incentive was built in to encourage the contractor to keep the inmates in good health. By allowing a fixed *journée* for all inmates, in sickness and in health, a contract gave the entrepreneur an incentive to keep his workers healthy. [36]

This ideal mechanism had weak points. The contractor might find that he had an unspoken interest in allowing the chronically sick or infirm inmates to languish or die. Even a healthy, active worker might not be worth costly care and dainty feeding, if the entrepreneur could be sure that any gaps in the ranks of workers would be replaced by new arrests. In any case, it was simpler for a lazy or stupid agent to cut corners on provisions than to invest in ambitious plans for increasing the profitability of inmates' labor.

The intendants continued to play a direct role in dealing with complaints, enforcing contracts and regulations, and monitoring the finances of the *dépôts*. Each one turned to experts for advice as needed. Royal engineers continued to advise intendants on maintenance, hygiene, and repairs. Doctors and surgeons were enlisted to examine the sick and infirm, to authorize transfers to infirmary or hospital, and to enforce contract provisions concerning infirmaries within the *dépôts*. [37]

Laverdy had requested that intendants set an example of zeal by inspecting the *dépôts* in their provinces from time to time. Terray made a more specific request in a circular of June 26, 1771, asking that intendants personally inspect the bread given to inmates in order to still the "murmurs" that commonly arose in times of high grain prices. [38] Samples of bread were sent to Terray at his request. Presumably, royal experts examined the loaves in Bertier's office, perhaps taking some with them for a brief audience with the minister or a meeting of royal councillors. Like Laverdy, Terray promoted the use of rice. [39]

In a letter of January 7, 1772, addressed to the intendant at Châlons, Terray complained of incomplete forms. Each entry should include the age of the inmate, his ability to work *(état de validité),* and the date of his internment. Terray stated that this information was essential so as to evaluate the ability of the inmates to work inside the *dépôt* or after their release; the entry date was needed in order to review the propriety of the penalties being imposed.[40] In more than one circular, Terray clearly assigned the intendants an important discretionary role in regulating the release of inmates according to the demand for seasonal agricultural labor.[41] He also asked intendants to forward data on the release of beggars under surety bond, a procedure that was to be more uniformly required. This data could be compared with arrest data throughout the country in order to identify recidivists and hold the signers of bonds to their engagements.[42]

Terray thus expected the intendants to act in close cooperation with Bertier, who was in turn expected to monitor and regulate his vast "machine" from a bureau in Paris, at the ultimate direction of the minister and his master, the king. The direct day-to-day responsibility for managing the *dépôts* and keeping records remained, nonetheless, with the lowly concierges.

Assistance and Repression: The Conundrum Remains

An economic crisis had thrust forward the unstated assumption that the *dépôts* could be effective in deterring beggary only if the "true poor" could find work or relief when they needed it. Bertier later blamed the "imperfections" of his operation upon the failure to provide these "complements" to it, and upon the burdening of the *dépôts* with many who deserved special care elsewhere. Bertier himself had not forgotten the Laverdy commission's charge to promote alms bureaus; he cited progress in this area as an argument for beginning the detention of domiciled beggars. He even suggested that a policy of arresting them might spur their communities to organize alms bureaus where they did not already exist.[43]

Du Cluzel at Tours appears to have been willing to test Bertier's supposition that stricter arrests would promote the creation of alms bureaus. After giving notice to the chancellor of his belief that "the total suppression of beggary requires for the moment some accommodations," he wrote all parish priests to notify them that, pursuant to the king's intention that no one be allowed to beg anywhere, he would order the arrest of anyone in contravention of the law after a grace period of two weeks. The reaction to this missive was perhaps stronger than the intendant anticipated. The *procureur-général* of the parlement of Paris informed Chancellor Maupeou that he had received complaints that du Cluzel's orders were depriving the "good poor" of the alms available to them from religious endowments in many parishes. Maupeou advised the intendant to confer with religious authorities in order to make the best possible use of available alms. This episode, among others, elicited a circular to all intendants signed by the newly appointed controller-general, the abbé Terray, on December 26, 1769, on the need to make use of all available charitable resources. Each intendant was to conduct a survey of such resources. The intent of the king was not to suppress them, but rather to use them more effectively, especially through the organization of alms-bureaus.[44]

Tours already had such a bureau. Du Cluzel attempted to promote new ones at
Angers and Le Mans, but encountered mistrust of royal intentions. The bishop of
Angers submitted the survey of local charitable resources as requested, but advised
him that it was probably not reliable, since the people feared there would be a
forced contribution. He urged the intendant to take emergency measures for provisioning the markets, where prices were rising dangerously. Le Mans provided relief
to its inhabitants through an ad hoc bureau in the winter of 1769–1770, but reacted
unfavorably to outside efforts to formalize the bureau. Bertier, as commissioner of
mendicity, became directly involved in implementing Terray's directive. In November 1770 he sent du Cluzel a draft *arrêt du conseil* formally establishing an alms
bureau at Le Mans. As soon as the intendant had joined with the bishop and the
subdelegate of Angers in giving qualified approval to the text, Bertier obtained an
official *arrêt* giving the statute the force of law.[45]

Bertier's initiative was politically inept. The subdelegate there observed that few
parishes nominated treasurers following the reading of the *arrêt* in churches. The
statement in article 12 that assessments *(cotisations)* would be imposed where existing funds were insufficient "has caused alarm in naturally anxious minds: no one
envisages anything but a forced contribution or imposition." Furthermore, the dominant role accorded to the bishop and his grand vicar ruffled corporate self-esteem.
The royal council duly received the objections of the *présidial* and of the *hôtel de
ville*. The subdelegate at Le Mans, displaying perhaps his own municipal outlook,
voiced his opinion that "the operation appears to me to have missed the mark
entirely."[46] Still, the royal council turned down a formal petition to revoke the
arrêt. Terray explained in a letter to du Cluzel that a permanent bureau was needed
in order to respond quickly in time of need. As for the fear of an assessment, he
replied: "When the inhabitants have seen to it that their poor are aided and that the
spectacle of beggary, as upsetting as it is dangerous, is banished from their town,
they shall have no fear that more will be required on their part." This was hardly
reassuring.[47]

Even the best-organized alms bureau could not cope with a general economic
depression. In one of his memoirs, Rattier explained the effects of two bad winters
compounded by a more protracted decline in the textile industry of Tours.[48] The
alms bureau of Tours, presided over by the archbishop aided by sixteen parish
priests and sixteen notables named "commissioners of the poor," had three objects:
to aid those households where the head was sick, convalescent, aged, or infirm; to
provide work at home for women who could not leave their homes; and to give aid
to those whose work did not earn enough for their families to live on. The alms
bureau had been unable to deal with the last category at all. The going wage of
twenty to twenty-five sols per day—many earned less—would not provide a family
with food, firewood, care in time of sickness, and instruction of children in the
craft. For the last two years, bread prices had been such that the seven to nine
pounds of bread needed for a family with three children consumed the entire wage.
Night work led to debility and sickness, and many families were left destitute.
Occasional food distributions, a loaf of bread here and there, could not begin to
solve the problem of the families who required double their present cash income in
order to subsist. Meanwhile, high bread prices everywhere had curbed consumption
of the goods produced in the shops, leaving large numbers of workers unemployed.

The subsistence crisis produced insistent appeals for royal aid; intendants passed on requests from the bishops and the subdelegates. The royal government distributed food and medicine throughout the country but hardly touched the general shortage. In the winter of 1769–1770, Terray launched a special effort to promote use of rice in order to spread resources more quickly and cheaply. By the end of 1770, Terray had reviewed Laverdy's policies on the grain trade in correspondence with the intendants, and decided reluctantly that a large part of the former apparatus for policing the market would have to be restored. At the same time it would be brought up to date with a more centralized coordination of data and state-supervised systems for storing and distributing commodities.[49]

Terray could offer only miserly stocks of food at Tours. The archbishop noted, in a postcript to a letter to du Cluzel, "he is quite parsimonious." Du Cluzel resorted to a number of expedients, spent money of his own, and sold off some of the surplus stocks of the *dépôts de mendicité* to supply the market. Making ample use of large-scale public works, he was one of several intendants who initiated *ateliers de charité* before a general policy of encouraging them took shape under the direction of the *intendant de commerce,* Albert, and the *intendant des finances,* d'Ormesson. Du Cluzel had the royal engineer coordinate the choice of road projects in order to provide employment where needed most. Such *ateliers* were du Cluzel's preferred mode of relief, since they "gave the unfortunate the ability to procure their subsistence, maintained them in the habit of working, and even gave them the taste for it, since children were admitted."[50]

Rattier had argued that his "manufacture for the poor working freely" might not only be useful from a local perspective, but even "necessary in order to sustain the admirable harmony in the kingdom that the controller-general has just established in order to destroy mendicity and all the crimes that flow from it."[51] Rattier could not have read du Cluzel's mind any better. Once the workshop was fully operational, complementing the aid provided by the *ateliers de charité* in the country and by food distributions, du Cluzel confidently enforced the royal prohibition on begging. He expressed his firm belief that assistance and repression were essentially interdependent in a letter he wrote several years later to Turgot, in response to the new controller-general's inquiry on the subject of mendicity:

> I proved it on a small scale in the town of Tours, applying these two approaches
> for several years: then circumstances required the curtailment of the help we could
> grant to the poor who had a real need for relief, and I saw myself forced into
> indulgence for the others because of the difficulty of distinguishing those to whom
> it should be granted.[52]

Du Cluzel clearly believed that Terray's false economies had undermined the "utility" of the *dépôts:* repression could not be effective without a well-coordinated policy of public assistance.

Many other intendants adopted measures similar to those of du Cluzel during the subsistence crisis that reached its peak in 1770. The experience of Turgot in the economically backward *généralité* of Limoges set the stage for his actions as minister of finance. Du Pont de Nemours included a laudatory account of Turgot's method for setting up *ateliers de charité* in his journal, the *Éphémérides du citoyen.* Turgot's accomplishment in forming the administration of the *corvée* in his province received even wider acclaim. By finding a way to spread the fiscal burden over all landowners, Turgot relieved the farmers living along royal highways of an onerous and damaging obligation to supply labor, materials, carts, and draught animals. The wages for road work were then used to give employment to the needy.[53]

Turgot deferred implementing the order to arrest domiciled beggars in 1769 and intensified his efforts to provide emergency relief. In particular, he collaborated with his fellow Sorbonnien, the bishop of Limoges, in establishing a system of alms bureaus, to which he contributed. His instruction on their administration included safeguards against waste: only those who could not work were to receive food or money directly; the able-bodied were to be given useful work to do on public roads or in workshops. At the same time he suspended the collection of exorbitant rents in scarce grain, and required owners to provide subsistence for their sharecroppers, arguing that those who had worked to provide the wealth of the owner could not rightfully be abandoned in their need.[54]

The results of Turgot's campaign to set up alms bureaus were disappointing. In his article of 1756 on endowments for the *Encyclopédie,* Turgot cited the alms bureau of Bayeux as evidence that the French were no less capable than the English, when it came to displaying the "spirit of the citizen" through voluntary provisions for the relief of poverty and distress. In 1769 he conceded that experience had made him and the bishop of Limoges more pessimistic: "We see no small obstacle in the little liking shown by minds in this region for lending themselves to any arrangement that has the public good as its sole aim."[55] While remaining a staunch economic liberal on the benefits to be obtained from free trade in grain, Turgot believed that in a time of economic crisis there was no alternative but direct royal assistance: "the King is the father of all his subjects, and it is from him that they must expect the succor that none other can procure for them."[56] Accordingly he used royal funds to employ large numbers of people on work projects, arranged for large shipments of grain to be put on the local market, and used some of the stocks purchased for the *dépôts de mendicité* for the same purpose.

Turgot concentrated on the task of juggling resources, using institutional stocks as reserves for the marketplace. A letter of October 30, 1770, explained his arrangement with the hospital of Limoges to supply rye bread, broad beans *(fèves),* and potatoes to the inmates of the *dépôts.* Meanwhile he had sold off some of the rye and wheat grain stocks of the *dépôt* at Angoulême in order to provision the markets there. Accounts for the *dépôts* of Limoges and Angoulême in 1770 record a sum of 5,349l. 11s. 6d. in receipts for sale of grain. In a letter of December 16, 1769, Turgot noted that his experiments in the *dépôts* had shown that a person could be fed for less than one sol per day on a diet of rice. He asked permission to make a bulk purchase of about 25,000 livres worth of rice for the *dépôt,* for sale on the market, and for charitable distribution as needed.[57]

Turgot saw no reason to arrest beggars under such circumstances. In letters to his subdelegates on February 19, 1770, he advised great caution in the arrest of the domiciled, in order "not to risk confusing two things so different as real poverty and voluntary beggary occasioned by waywardness and a love of idleness." Then he suspended the order to arrest domiciled beggars until such time as "the diminution of grain prices shall have brought an end to the beggary forced by the misery at large in the countryside." No arrest for begging would be authorized unless the curé attested to the provision of subsistence to the poor in the parish of the accused. Even in these cases, domiciled beggars would not be locked up for a first offense. A domiciled beggar would be subject to arrest like the professional beggar only under special circumstances verified by inquiries addressed to local officials.[58]

Some found Turgot too lenient. His subdelegate at Angoulême, the agronomist Boisbedeuil, wrote early in 1771 to say that he was awaiting the intendant's orders to deal with beggars. Turgot demurred: "Since the dearness of subsistence multiplies the number of the poor and obliges peasants to go begging in the towns, I hesitate as to whether I should perhaps postpone for another time the instruction to give the the *maréchaussée* concerning professional beggars." This answer only agitated Boisbedeuil the more:

> Allow me to observe that it is only in order to ensure public tranquillity that *dépôts* for beggars have been established; the other consideration, which is that of proscribing idleness, tending toward the same end, since one would not have anything to fear from evildoers if everyone kept busy earning a living by working."[59]

Turgot resumed arrests eventually. Meanwhile he had formed a strong antipathy toward the *dépôts* and had come into conflict with Bertier over a number of matters relating to their administration.[60]

How did Bertier, grand administrator of the *dépôts*, respond to the problems of subsistence crises, by comparison with du Cluzel, Turgot, and his other confreres? His *intendance* was one of those most directly affected by these crises, since the uprooted poor swarmed toward Paris and combed the fields of the Île-de-France in search of work or alms. Bertier reminded Turgot and his commission on mendicity that he, Bertier, had never denied the imperfections of his operation, and that he had "urged the necessity of providing its complement." He added, confidently, that "one ought to find at the *contrôle-général* a pack of memoirs that will bear this out."[61]

Taking up the challenge, Turgot searched out a memoir on the administration of the *ateliers de charité* by Bertier dating from November 1770. In general, *ateliers* were funded through rebates on the *taille* allotted to distressed areas or to individuals. Instead of being granted as an exemption, the rebate took the form of wages and food distributed to workers in the *ateliers*. The basic mechanism had been established in Louis XIV's reign. D'Ormesson, who was the *intendant des finances* responsible for approving such adjustments in the *taille*, informed Bertier in a letter of December 21, 1770, that "it would not have been possible to grasp better the spirit of the letter that he [the controller-general] sent you November 5, nor to show more zeal in carrying out the wishes of the King." D'Ormesson personally committed six hundred livres of his own in matching funds for projects near his estates. Turgot, who welcomed arguments in favor of *ateliers*, showed Bertier's memoir to the king. In a letter of November 5, 1774, he told Bertier that the king had read the memoir and applauded its "wisdom, equity, and beneficence."[62]

Bertier, Turgot, and other intendants shared a commitment to several broader administrative reforms aimed at removing the causes of misery. The best known of Bertier's efforts, in the tradition of Vauban and the abbé de Saint-Pierre, was a reform of the *taille,* the main source of the king's revenue. The reform had been launched by the elder Bertier, but it was executed in large part by the younger, who consciously envisaged his efforts as a means of reducing the burden on the poorer producers. The key to the reform was the *cadastre* or land survey, from which the value of holdings could be fairly assessed.[63] In 1775 Turgot would assist Bertier in having the legal framework for his system of graduated assessments registered by the Cour des Aides. As intendant, Turgot had attempted to rectify abuses in the *taille*. In 1761 he had written that its oppressiveness was such that "the inhabitants who are accustomed to working part of the year outside the province will perhaps choose to abandon absolutely their native province and seek elsewhere, perhaps in beggary, the subsistence they will not be able to find at home."[64]

The younger Bertier also carried on the interests of his father in agricultural improvement, public health, and the promotion of charitable establishments, including alms bureaus.[65] One of his more original projects, the "companies of provincial workers," also known as the *corps des pionniers,* was clearly intended to complement the function of the *dépôts*. Bertier later recounted to Turgot and his colleagues that the tasks of administering relief projects and assessing impositions had revealed that "one of the principle effects of the dearness of grains had been to diminish the number of owners and to swell unduly the number of those in the class of common laborers." An unfortunate consequence of this was that many young men in their prime, fit to work, were confined in the *dépôts* for indefinite terms, whereas they should have been kept "in a momentary state of correction." Neither the offer of work in *ateliers de charité,* nor the sedentary discipline of workshops inside the *dépôts,* could contain these men, "whom misery had forced to leave their families." Bertier had proposed to offer such inmates of the *dépôts* the alternative of enlisting for nine-year terms with other volunteers in work companies organized under a quasi-military discipline by agreement with the minister of war. One company was formed in the Paris region in 1773, and Bertier hoped to extend the experiment to other *intendances*.[66]

These three intendants—du Cluzel, Turgot, and Bertier—represent distinct shades of "enlightened" administration. Some of their confreres no doubt conceived of the problem of mendicity in less systematic ways. It is noteworthy, however, that a pragmatic, traditionally oriented administrator like Depont at Moulins was inspired by the emergency measures of 1770 to speculate upon the positive effect that *ateliers de charité* might produce on the local economy, if used regularly over a period of ten years.[67] By 1773 there were few intendants who believed that the domiciled beggar could be transformed into a useful citizen simply by means of a short spell in the *dépôt*.

6

Attack on the *Dépôts*

Laverdy's commissioners had shrewdly anticipated the range of attacks that the courts would direct against the *dépôts*. Resistance from this quarter was effectively neutralized, not only by recourse to the planned defenses, but also by carefully calculated appeals to the interests and concerns of the *parlementaires*. In the long run, the tireless resistance on the part of the provincial Estates was to prove more significant in shaping the history of the institution. Whereas the arguments of the judges ran from technicalities of procedure and jurisprudence to the legitimacy of repression, those of the Estates met administrators on their own terrain of economy and utility.

If the creators of the *dépôts* had not thought to anticipate this resistance, they had also neglected entirely to foresee that intendants themselves might add to the difficulties of administering a uniform operation by raising objections and in some cases siding with critics. Turgot was one of these doubters. As controller-general of finance, he gave voice to a "provincial" point of view on certain questions of royal finance. The appointment of his friend Loménie de Brienne to direct an informal commission on mendicity was a case in point. As archbishop of Toulouse, Brienne had taken part in the debates of the Estates of Languedoc and helped to articulate their criticisms of the *dépôts de mendicité* as early as 1769. The political sources for Turgot's policy on mendicity must be taken together with the more familiar ideological dimensions of his reform strategy and the all-important lessons of his experience as intendant of Limoges.[1]

Judicial Resistance

Like the parlement of Paris, that of Besançon desired some clarifications concerning the Declaration of August 3, 1764. Exchanges with the controller-general and the chancellor led them to believe that they would continue to have a right of inspection in the Maison de Bellevaux, a dependency of the *aumône-générale*. An extended defense of the rights of the parlement, drafted by the *premier président* (chief justice) Chifflet, was apparently provoked by the creation of the *dépôt de mendicité* in

1767, and by the *arrêt du conseil* of the following year providing provincial financing for the operation.[2]

Chifflet argued that as long as the Maison de Bellevaux were merely a *maison de charité*, the magistrates of the parlement would leave its operation entirely in the hands of the directors, but that they had learned from letters addressed to the bishop that it would now be used as a *maison de force* at least for the homeless invalid poor and the insane. In these circumstances they claimed the right to send commissioners "to visit the same as ordinances and regulations so prescribe, be it in order to examine the registers of the jailer, or to receive the complaints of prisoners, and to ascertain whether they are suitably treated withal." Citing the usages of the Paris parlement in visiting the houses of St. Lazare and Charenton, Chifflet insisted most strongly on the obvious responsibility implied by the fact that the hospital in question was intended to receive those whom the parlement condemned to be confined there:

> Does it not follow as a necessary consequence that this court may assure itself of the execution of its decisions, by ascertaining whether prisoners are kept securely, whether they are kept only as long as they should be, whether they are not set at liberty before the time fixed by the decision of the court?[3]

Bertier was called upon to respond to this challenge, and to answer further charges that the new operation was being carried out as a "military operation devoid of judicial forms." Bertier noted first that the text registered by the parlement gave the intendant full authority to carry out harsher measures than those in question. The policy adopted had been to convict only as beggars many who might have been liable to a term in the galleys as vagabonds. He repeated the standard justification of the intendant's authority to administer *dépôts* inasmuch as they were supplements to hospitals. Special procedures had been adopted simply in order to avoid "severity" and to render "less uncertain the liberty of citizens."[4]

Bertier repeated the well-worn half-truth that hospital administrators had alleged a lack of funds and facilities for confining beggars. Instead of pushing inquiries further and forcing hospitals to confine beggars, the king had chosen to assume the burden of the task and confide its administration to his intendants. This argument seemed rather forced in the case of the Maison de Bellevaux, since the directors had agreed to using the house for that purpose, and in fact had even maintained the position that they were responsible to the intendant and not to the parlement, by virtue of the Declaration of 1724. If it was not clear in such circumstances why the Maison de Bellevaux must be labeled a "provisional *dépôt*," Bertier provided a clue by drawing a distinction between those hospitals and permanent foundations, which as public patrimony were subject to regulation by the parlements, and *dépôts*, which were by no means to be viewed as "perpetual establishments." Indeed, "the cessation of beggary or the better establishment of hospitals may render them unneeded or diminish their number."

Any inspection by the parlement would be "dangerous" and might lead to "confusion and anarchy," argued Bertier. The parlements, after all, were not the "ordinary overseers of the revenues of the king." Taking a leaf from Montesquieu, he added, "In general, these bodies are not well suited to administration." The right of inspection proposed would in effect make the ministers answerable to the parlements. Otherwise, what practical purpose would it serve to have a right of visit? Such a right "could only disturb the subalterns and discourage the superiors." The intendant, after all, would take less interest "in an establishment where he might fear that his arrangements would be obstructed." Even wisely used, the precedent would be harmful. In towns other than the seat of the parlement, ordinary judges would have to assume the right of visit: "the slightest animosity between a *conseiller* of a *baillage* and a subdelegate could provide the matter of a quarrel that could suspend or destroy the success of the operation." Locally inspired inspections would only interfere with an effort to set uniform standards throughout France. A new administration of this kind was particularly vulnerable to interference; remedies to whatever problems arose were best sought within the administration. Granting a right of visit to the parlement at Besançon would only revive claims by other parlements: the chancellor had refused similar rights to the parlements of Rouen and Metz. The principle must stand.[5]

In spite of this uncompromising reply, it appears that a purely formal right of visit with no power of enforcement was later conceded by the chancellor. The significant concession of substance was to allow the parlement to continue to condemn individuals to confinement at Bellevaux. This was done only with the understanding that this was a temporary expedient until a prison could be built; meanwhile the chancellor asked "great circumspection in view of the different employment to which the King had put this house." The *arrêt du conseil* of July 23, 1769, remained in force, giving the intendant the direction over the *dépôt* at Bellevaux and prescribing the collection and use of royal funds in the province for the upkeep of beggars and vagabonds. These circumstances, noted the chancellor, removed Bellevaux from any dependence upon the *aumône-générale*. He formally denied that the parlement was to have any right of *police* over the *dépôt*, then stated that the king did not mean to deny the parlement's right of *police* over establishments confided to it, and would "not disapprove" if the parlement sent commissioners to visit the house as it judged useful or necessary.[6]

In effect the chancellor granted a purely pro forma right of visit and allowed the parlement "temporarily" to commit certain types of individuals to the *dépôt*, with the understanding that the parlement would address any "representations" concerning the *dépôt* to the intendant. If the *dépôt* could serve as a provisional supplement to hospitals, why not also as a provisional supplement to prisons? Records of the *dépôt* at Besançon in 1788 indicate that the parlement of Besançon did make use of its right. One woman had been sentenced to Bellevaux by the parlement in 1770 for a term of twenty years and was still there in 1788.[7] A memoir of 1781 reviewing the history of the *aumône-générale* recalled that the directors had not expressed any objection to having the intendant assume responsibility for the Maison de Bellevaux. On the contrary, they may have been relieved to have the *maréchaussée* take over the functions of the archers of the hospital, and to have the royal treasury assume the cost of repairs and alterations in the building.[8]

Bertier's memoir mentioned that there had been another challenge from the parlement of Rouen. Responding to complaints that the water supply in the *dépôt* there was spreading contagion, the *procureur-général* of the parlement of Rouen, Belbeuf, inspired the high court to decree that the concierge of the *dépôt* must obtain his commission from the *procureur-général* and must take an oath before ordinary judges. Laverdy rebuked Belbeuf for crediting rumors of "contagion." Only two inmates had died in a population of 193, and those deaths were from "ordinary maladies." Belbeuf ackowledged that the rumors had been false. In reply, Chancellor Maupeou observed that further decrees by the parlement on the subject would be "dangerous," as they could only serve "to multiply the anxieties that the common people form so lightly." He further urged Belbeuf to report future abuses, if any, to the king. Laverdy advised the intendant de Crosne that royal finance must be based on undivided accountability, and could not work if other authorities were involved. Bertier had sent this letter for Belbeuf to de Crosne with his own cover letter of May 7, 1769. He appears to have been coordinating a political defense based on an appeal to the parlement's awareness of the risk of popular stirrings and their desire to have royal finance for the *dépôt* continue.[9]

Few other significant objections to the *dépôts* were raised by the parlements. In one isolated instance the parlement of Paris relayed to the chancellor an objection from religious houses in the *généralité* of Tours against the plan to prohibit begging even by the domiciled poor. Du Cluzel received a copy of the response to the chancellor prepared by "M. Fleury," presumably the *conseiller d'état* and former intendant of Burgundy who played a leading role on Laverdy's commission. De Fleury argued that the intendant had gone too far in ordering that all public distributions of alms were to cease. Those alms distributed by religious houses to the domiciled parish poor were to be allowed, even if the distributions were made at the gates of those houses. He noted, however, that the decrees of the parlement reuniting many endowments for almsgiving to the funds of hospitals had been motivated by the conviction that alms given indescriminately at the gates of religious houses merely promoted mendicity. Defending du Cluzel's order that beggars must return to their domiciles, de Fleury implied that they might be better cared for if the parlement had not held up new royal legislation on alms bureaus. The intendant's order, he observed, "is in keeping with the declarations of the King of 1724 and of 1750, both registered, and with the new plan drawn up for this purpose, although this new plan, as you know, Milord, has not been registered in the parlement."[10]

Any potential obstruction by the parlements was removed by the Maupeou coup d'état that abolished them in 1771. Judicial opposition was therefore limited to scattered local incidents of the sort that occurred at Orleans in 1772, when a local judge presumed to commit individuals to confinement in the *dépôt* without consulting the intendant. Bertier produced a crushing legal memorandum for the occasion.[11] After Turgot restored the parlements in 1774, they again responded to complaints about the *dépôts* and the disorders they caused. Turgot was favorable to their complaints, but his remedies did not include any plan to share authority over the *dépôts* with them.

Dunning the Provincial Estates

The distinction between *pays de généralité* and *pays d'états* was one of the determining features of eighteenth-century French administration. In the former, the intendant levied all major taxes in the name of the king. In the latter, depending on the circumstances that had brought ancient lands such as Brittany and Languedoc under the direct rule of the French king, the intendant functioned in some respects as a plenipotentiary of a foreign power. Provincial deputies chosen by order met in a periodic assembly to receive from the intendant and other commissioners of the king a detailed request to assume a share of the fiscal burden for the administration of the province and the kingdom. At the same time, the deputies would draw up a list of grievances and requests bearing upon items in the king's request. Commissioners of the estates would present these petitions in a carefully prescribed ceremony at the royal court.[12] Articles of the *cahiers* or grievance lists were then reviewed by appropriate ministers. Those relating to finance were sent to the bureau of the *pays d'états* at the *contrôle-général*, headed during most of our period by Ménard de Conichard. The final disposition of grievances and of each article of finance was reviewed at a council session of La Grande Direction in the king's presence, and the resulting instructions were then sent to the royal commissioners in the province, of whom the intendant was always one.[13]

The Estates of Burgundy did not meet in an assembly; there was simply a vestigial executive commission of *élus* who represented the interests of the province and those of the king, including the royal intendant. Laverdy had approached them in 1764 about initial preparations for provisional *dépôts*. They were the first to be approached with a request for finance, presumably because the negotiations seemed most likely to produce the desired precedent. Bertier drafted a memoir that was to serve as a pattern for requesting funds from each of the *pays d'états*. In a preamble he stated that previous attempts to solve the problem of beggary had failed because of "the exceptions that the general law had included." The king would suffer no exceptions in the execution of the new law. *Pays d'états* were expected to contribute to the finance of the operation in the same proportion as the twenty-one *pays de généralité*. The share to be paid would be computed by a three-part formula based on amounts paid by *pays de généralité* for the three-deniers-per-livre supplement to the *taille*, on past expenses, and on expected costs in the province.[14]

Bertier assured the *élus* of Burgundy that the sums requested would not even cover the expense anticipated: the king had already borne a substantial share of it. No immediate reduction in costs could be anticipated, since the imminent extension of arrests to domiciled beggars would soon swell the total number of inmates. "It is to be hoped," he added, "that perhaps in several years the number of inmates will be fewer." Bertier's computations produced a total figure of eighty thousand livres, but he confided to Ménard de Conichard that he would be happy to concede a figure of sixty thousand. The Estates should be reminded that by paying from the year 1769, they released themselves from obligation for all previous expenses. Ménard de Conichard embellished Bertier's budgetary forensics by inferring from incomplete figures that the actual annual expense for the first two years had been 104,000 livres, probably a high estimate.[15]

By tradition, the family of the prince de Condé held the office of royal "governor" of the province of Burgundy and, ex officio, the position of *élu*. The prince presented the objections raised by the province in a memoir to the comte de St.-Florentin. He remonstrated that the request was far higher than the sum spent annually for the repression of begging under the Declaration of 1724; that the assessment based on the formula of the three deniers per livre of the *taille* was far out of proportion with the *taille* actually paid in Burgundy; that furthermore, the province was suffering from a bad grain harvest and from three successive years of poor wine production. The *élus* had also observed that the new burden might render more difficult the collection of funds for the *milice*.[16]

The reply to the prince de Condé was prepared by Ménard de Conichard, presumably after consultation with Bertier. The counterarguments were that the operation of 1724 had failed, whereas the new one had met the test of experience; that the lack of proportion with respect to the *taille* merely reflected the light assessment with which the province was favored. Ménard offered to reduce the request to sixty thousand, and in a further interview with the prince de Condé was persuaded to accept fifty thousand. A revised request was then sent to the comte de St.-Florentin. In order to forestall further reductions, the instruction spelled out the amounts already granted in relief because of the winegrowers' distress, underlined the success achieved in eliminating vagrancy, and noted that further benefits were to be expected from "recent" orders to arrest domiciled beggars. The *élus* should be aware that the king could legitimately have demanded that the province reimburse initial costs since 1767.[17]

On November 11, 1769, immediately after the figure of fifty thousand was agreed upon as the contribution from Burgundy, the intendant of Languedoc, Saint-Priest, received an instruction allowing him to reduce the sum requested from the Estates of Languedoc to the same amount.[18] Ménard had noted on Bertier's memoir that the requests from the different *pays d'états* would have to be comparable, "since the deputies and *syndics* exchange information on their agreements." The reduction in Languedoc would also be allowed in view of harvest conditions. The commissioners must, however, insist on payment from 1769 onward.[19]

The Estates of Languedoc, presided over by Loménie de Brienne, archbishop of Toulouse, voted to ask that they be "excused from consenting," in the interest of a burdened people and in the name of the privileges of the province.[20] They objected to the fact that they had not been consulted in the establishment of the *dépôts,* although the Estates were in session at the time. They argued that the abolition of beggary was an object of general expense to be borne by the royal treasury. If the Estates were to contribute, because of an obligation to support the poor and in keeping with the practice of supporting other general measures, then they must know the details of past and future expenses.

The sum of fifty thousand was agreed to only after the controller-general promised to render an account to the treasurer of the Estates for all expenses to date. The Estates attached a further proviso that none of the funds voted were to be spent outside the province, and they instructed the archbishop of Narbonne and the other deputies at court to persuade the controller-general to allow the Estates to manage the expenditures for the *dépôts* of the province.[21] This extraordinary incursion into the intendant's function was approved. A later memoir, probably written in 1776 by Bertier or Ménard, noted that the administrators of the province had obtained budgetary control over the *dépôts* of Languedoc "by an extraordinary credit." The Estates had always held an aversion to allowing funds they voted to be deposited elsewhere, "and notably to having those for *mendicité* pass into the account which they have several times allowed themselves to refer to as that 'in the name of M. Bertier.' "[22] Bertier was not consulted until after the fact. Ménard had gone so far as to assure the archbishop of Narbonne that Bertier would not be informed of their negotiations until they were completed, suggesting, however, that Narbonne contact Bertier directly.[23]

Presented with a stinging fait accompli, Bertier pointed out that even if the Estates could assume the purely "economic" administration of the *dépôts* themselves, they would still have to be asked for ten thousand livres to cover the cost of arrests by the *maréchaussée,* inasmuch as this was an operation of general police. The Estates took financial responsibility for the *dépôts* on this basis from 1770.[24] The Estates discovered, to their chagrin, that actual expenses far exceeded the fifty thousand that would have been paid in compliance with the original request. Reviewing past arrangements in a report to the Estates on January 5, 1775, the archbishop of Toulouse noted that the Estates had asked the king in February 1774 to credit the Estates with the sums spent in excess of fifty thousand livres per year. They had also asked to halt arrests and eliminate the operation entirely. Terray had gone no further than to state a willingness to have the Estates contribute a lump sum of fifty thousand per year to the royal treasury. He explained that savings derived from a new general contract enabled royal administrators to operate the *dépôts* more cheaply.[25]

In the sessions of January 1775, the archbishop of Toulouse recommended on behalf of his committee that the Estates agree to continue the previous arrangements for another year, while awaiting the plans for reform entertained by the new controller-general, Turgot. "The change that occurred in the Ministry of Finances," he explained, "has also produced one in this part of the administration."[26] Indeed, the archbishop had accepted Turgot's invitation to preside over a review of legislation on mendicity. Instructions to the the royal commissioners in October had indicated a willingness to consider the objections of the Estates. A letter from Turgot to the archbishop of Narbonne, following Turgot's preliminary review of the matter, stated that the *dépôts* would be emptied gradually, and invited the opinions of the Estates on how the problem of mendicity should be approached.[27]

Although the Estates continued to argue that the *dépôts* had not curbed beggary at all, they followed the archbishop's advice and voted to continue financial support for them in order to smooth the task of reform, "and to avoid returning to society a crowd of unfortunates that, surging forth, might cause disorder." Expressing confidence in the intentions of the ministry, they observed merely that some new means had to be devised for assuring the subsistence "of beggars whose age or handicaps deprive them of any resource to subsist, and to give back to the state the too considerable number of able-bodied citizens."[28]

In yet another *pays d'états,* Brittany, royal policy prevailed without modification, after lengthy resistance. As early as 1764, Laverdy had prepared a request for the intendant Le Bret to present to the Estates. The timing was unpropitious. Le Bret, seconded by the governor of the province, the duc d'Aiguillon (excoriated by Bretons as an agent of despotism), advised the minister "that it would be time ill spent to make this proposition in a session so stormy, with minds agitated as they were, and that, besides, one would be unable to present any determined object of expenditures."[29] In October 1766 Laverdy advised Le Bret's successor, de Flesselles, that there was no time to wait for a vote of funds from the Estates that year, since an edict had been submitted to the parlement of Paris and would soon be sent to that of Brittany. No request was made in 1768, although the *dépôts* were in operation.[30]

In February 1770 Terray asked the intendant d'Agay for advice on the most suitable form of levy in Brittany to support the *dépôts,* and for details of any levy since 1724 designed to serve the same purpose as the three deniers per livre of the *taille*. D'Agay found no instance of such a tax. He suggested that an increase in the excises and indirect taxes, "which would be imperceptible to the peoples of the province, would be preferable to an increase in the capitation, the assessment of which is already too high in Brittany."[31] D'Agay went on to say that the four existing *dépôts* were ill suited to their function; according to plans he would soon submit, the expense might be expected to run to ninety thousand livres per year for the next two years.[32]

Terray disingenuously told d'Agay that the Estates of Burgundy and Languedoc had agreed to contribute, "without resistance, and even with the alacrity that [His Majesty] may rightly expect from their zeal and their fidelity." D'Agay said the examples would serve well; he expected the request would raise a lively debate. Knowing perhaps more than he revealed about events in Languedoc, he underscored his own view that the administration of the *dépôts* must remain exclusively in his hands. The Estates must be dissuaded from their desire to have accounts rendered to them for monies appropriated for the *dépôts*. His views on this matter contrasted sharply with those of Saint-Priest, intendant of Languedoc, who tended rather to adopt a "provincial" stance.[33] In June d'Agay reminded Terray about the item of finance for the *dépôts*. Bertier sent Ménard de Conichard a draft and suggested that Contaud, who was to draw up the final request, review what was done in Burgundy the year before.[34] To his standard memoir he added a reference to the fact that beggars were now being arrested "even in the very place of their domicile," and spoke of the fine precedents set by the Estates of Burgundy and Languedoc. He also attempted to head off questions about the funds raised for implementing the Declaration of 1724 by noting that contributions in the *pays de généralité* were not limited to the three deniers per livre. Municipal tolls *(octrois)* had also been levied.[35]

Bertier drew up a request, based on d'Agay's recommendation, for a contribution of ninety or one hundred thousand livres. With this, Bertier hoped to recoup some of the initial two years' costs, estimated at 70,000 livres per year, and to cover some of the projected operating costs after expansion of facilities, estimated at 124,000 livres per year. The figures were round, if not padded. Bertier added a note to the controller-general suggesting that seventy or even sixty thousand would be acceptable. The sum actually requested at the meeting of the Estates was eighty thousand, reduced in the course of the session to fifty thousand. The Estates nonetheless refused, arguing that there was no way to increase taxes sufficiently to raise the sums demanded.[36] The Estates' commission of finances argued, furthermore, that expenses of justice, including small crimes as well as large, should be borne by the king: the Declaration of 1764 and the *arrêt du conseil* of 1767 both gave assurances of royal financing. In response to Bertier's stock admonition that Brittany risked being inundated by beggars from neighboring provinces, the commission suggested it would be wise for the king to continue financing the *dépôts,* if he judged that their closing would result in harm to his province of Brittany.[37]

The Estates of Brittany assembled at Morlaix in 1772 finally agreed to pay for the *dépôts*. They raised objections, but royal policy, now in the hands of the trium-virate of Maupeou, d'Aiguillon, and Terray, was more peremptory than in 1770. The *cahier* presented by the Estates in 1772 requested that the administration of the *dépôts* be confided jointly to the intendant and the *commission intermédiaire* of the Estates, but met blank refusal. The royal commissioners stated that the king was willing to forgo any claim for the six hundred thousand livres spent in the first six years of operation of the *dépôts* in Brittany, but that he could not for any reason whatsoever drop the demand for a contribution of fifty thousand livres for each of the next two years.[38]

In case of refusal, levy of funds by *arrêt du conseil* was one option considered. It was decided instead to force a vote. On January 18, 1773, the Estates received a royal order to deliberate on this and on another request within twenty-four hours. The Estates couched their assent in a sarcastic expression of their desire to see the poor of Brittany gathered in one place, so that the king would be impressed with the state to which his subjects of Brittany were reduced. They also renewed their request to have the *dépôt* run with the participation of the *commission intermédiaire* of the Estates.[39]

The intendant who represented the king at Morlaix in 1772 was Dupleix de Bacquencourt, the same magistrate who had served as the second *rapporteur* for the Laverdy commission. He imposed royal authority in the province with a firm hand. At the beginning of Louis XVI's reign in 1774 he was replaced by a new intendant, Caze de la Bove. The Estates met that fall and renewed their demand for a share in the administration of the *dépôt* at Rennes. They argued that contribution of funds conferred such a right; furthermore, they asserted, the *dépôt* had been administered badly under the intendant.[40] The instructions to the royal commission-ers, on the other hand, specified that the intendant must retain full control of ex-penses for the *dépôts* and that the pretensions of the *commission intermédiaire* must be quashed. In debate, the finance commission of the Estates revived the question of previous levies contributed pursuant to the Declaration of 1724, and on January 31, 1775, the Estates voted their refusal. The order of the clergy concurred, but suggested that in order

> to prevent the disorder that would result from the release of vagabonds, shiftless persons, and beggars confined in the said *dépôts,* if provision were not made for them and their subsistence, the said order moves that there be allocated fifty thou-sand livres for this purpose, and an equivalent sum to be employed in charitable work projects in the nine bishoprics of the province, to be administered by the *commission intermédiaire* in each bishopric.[41]

The royal commissioners used a combination of threats and promises to induce the Estates to reverse their decision and vote funds on February 8, 1775. The king's grant of certain forms of tax relief was made contingent upon the Estates' decision on funds for the *dépôts* and for the coastal militia. The prospect of reform under Turgot's new ministry may also have softened resistance. The bishops, in particu-lar, knew that Turgot planned to review the problem of mendicity and its remedies, because he had addressed a circular to them on the subject dated November 18, 1774. Their opinion of January 31 regarding monies for the *dépôt* echoed Turgot's emphasis on public works projects in that circular.[42]

In spite of the bishops' demurral, the Estates of Brittany presented their case against the *dépôts* in a memoir read by the bishop of Léon on February 19. This document contained the germ of the most important criticisms to be developed in the remaining years of the Old Regime. Condemning the fiscal exactions of the Crown, the bishop and his committee complained that the state impoverished its subjects instead of encouraging local efforts to care for the needy. They rehearsed the familiar argument that the king should be responsible for the costs of justice. The *dépôts* at Rennes had served no purpose, in any case, they said, since "it does not rid Brittany of the thirtieth part of its beggars." Furthermore, confinement provides no remedy for the inmates' behavior. On the contrary, "the captivity of these wretches drives them to despair by the idleness and unproductiveness in which they are maintained." [43]

The Estates reinforced the parlements' objections against procedures employed in the arrest and detention of beggars. They spoke forcefully on behalf of domiciled citizens exposed to arrest and confinement in the *dépôt* by virtue of *lettres de cachet:*

> Be they obtained at the solicitation of families, it is no less true that the Estates, in contributing to the expense of this *dépôt,* did not think to set up in the capital a *maison de force* in which the inhabitants, perhaps even its own residents, removed from their administration and hidden from the inspection of the local authorities and the magistrates, could fall victim to orders filched from the King's justice by hatred and cupidity. [44]

In complaints conveyed to the new intendant, the commissioners of the Estates elaborated their indictment with a bill of particulars concerning unhealthy and indecent conditions within the *dépôt.* Caze de la Bove took these complaints seriously, and made a three-hour inspection of the *dépôt* at Rennes in person. Although he determined that some of the complaints were unfounded, he gave them a sympathetic hearing and contributed to a provincial groundswell of reform aspirations during Turgot's ministry. [45]

Provence was the last of the major *pays d'états* to be dunned for the operation of the *dépôts.* Ménard de Conichard received from Bertier a memoir in the same format as the others, with a few refinements. It incorporated, for example, d'Agay's argument in favor of indirect taxes as the best means of finance for the *dépôts.* Although the tally of costs through 1769 could not justify a demand of fifty thousand per year, Bertier argued that the projected acquisition of a new, large *dépôt,* and an increase in the number of beggars to be arrested, would bring costs for 1770 to ninety-nine thousand livres. He admitted to Ménard that he had forced the figures a little, but only in order to make the subsequent reduction to perhaps thirty thousand more fully appreciated. [46]

The assembly of the Estates of Provence rejected the request in 1771. Provence, they argued, had already enforced the principle that each community was obliged to provide for the subsistence of the poor, including beggars. Vagabonds, on the other hand, were subject to the police power of the officers of justice. In any case, the expense of public security was not to be borne by the province. [47] The demand was dropped and was not repeated in following years, although the operation continued with funding from the royal treasury. This apparent timidity requires some explanation. The answer appears to be that the Estates of Provence successfully demonstrated that they were already paying. Furthermore, they were prepared to press counterclaims.

In the 1720s, they argued, the king had created municipal offices as a fiscal expedient. In 1722 the province and local municipalities subscribed to buy out these offices and prevent their sale to individuals. The offices were abolished in 1724 with the agreement that the purchasers would be reimbursed. In the case of Provence, the Estates themselves were the creditors. Then in 1725 new offices were again created, and the Estates were allowed to buy out these offices on new terms. Half of the king's outstanding indebtedness to the Estates of Provence was liquidated. The remaining half was constituted as an annuity, with the agreement that the king would pay the proceeds of that annuity (forty thousand livres per year) into a fund for the support of hospitals, in connection with the confinement of beggars pursuant to the Declaration of 1724. In effect, Provence contributed four million livres of ready cash in return for a commitment of perpetual royal funding of hospitals for the purpose of maintaining arrested beggars and vagabonds. The royal treasury ceased payments for confinement of beggars in hospitals in 1733, but the payments continued to fall due in theory. In 1738 an *arrêt du conseil* diverted the annuity into the royal treasury retroactively to 1733. Accordingly, the Estates of Provence replied to royal requests for new sums for the *dépôts* in 1771 by advancing a claim for arrears amounting to 1,446,109 livres and 19 sols.[48]

The intendant Gallois de la Tour remarked that the claims seemed to be well founded. The observations drawn up at the *contrôle-général* tended likewise to affirm the position of the Estates. De Boullongne had sent his own dossier on the matter to another official, Le Clerc, without comment. Le Clerc observed that the claims would be difficult to deny, but that it would be dangerous to concede them, since they would set a precedent for other *pays d'états*. The author of the "final observations" on the *cahier* of the Estates noted that recognition of such a claim could even inspire claims from the *pays d'élections* concerning the three deniers per livre. On closer reflection, it was decided that the claims of Provence "were not at all founded." The king had directed the sums in question to be paid to the royal treasury—but not "to his profit." The royal treasury "was but the repository (*"dépôt"*) for these funds until a ripe examination of mendicity should enable him to give the most suitable order for achieving that end. Such is the spirit and indeed the disposition of the *arrêt* of December 23, 1738."[49] Even if one could accept the strained argument that the treasury was a provisional *dépôt* for impounding idle funds, no plausible ground was left for demanding an additional levy for the same purpose. The king's commissioners did their best to argue that the royal treasury was already bearing a burden for the new operation. Costs for the *dépôts* since 1767 had been absorbed, and even with a payment of thirty thousand livres from the Estates, the anticipated operating costs in future would not be covered. The amounts in question were negligible by comparison with the Estates' claims. The royal argument appears to have been no more than a smokescreen for evading the question of funds owed to the province and beating an orderly retreat. Since Bertier argued, on a later occasion, that all the *pays d'état* "had contributed with alacrity" to the expense of the *dépôts,* he may have meant to concede, tacitly, that Provence had paid.[50]

Opposition from the Estates of Provence did not end there. The archbishop of

Aix, the presiding officer of the Estates, reviewed subsequent events in a letter of
1776. Conditions in the *dépôt* at Aix had been a matter of public scandal. Inmates
were crowded in quarters where "a continual epidemic" prevailed. The contractor
received five and a half sous per day and spent only two, providing insufficient
food for subsistence, and making no provision for work in the *dépôt*. These facts
were verified under Turgot's ministry. A commission including members of the
parlement and the Estates inspected the *dépôt* and discovered that many inmates
had been arbitrarily arrested by special orders. Turgot subsequently approved the
suppression of the *dépôt* and the release of its inmates.[51]

Consent by the provincial estates for funding of the *dépôts* had appeared to
Bertier as an essential means of securing a uniform system for the repression of
begging throughout France. Fiscal objections from the Estates tended, however, to
focus and reinforce the scattered grievances against the *dépôts* and their administrators voiced by parlements, municipal officials, and charitable administrators. Their
objection to arrest procedures challenged the fundamental premise that beggars might
justly be arrested, in addition to underscoring the difficulty of separating out the
idle or "guilty" beggars from the true or "deserving" poor. Challenging the authority of intendants to administer houses of correction independently, the Estates
drew attention to abuses within the *dépôts,* and questioned the efficacy of rehabilitating beggars through confinement and coercion. Lamenting the penury of their
constituents, the Estates demanded that the royal treasury bear the burden of providing at least a measure of relief to the poor. The minister who had to defend the
administration of the *dépôts* before the royal council found that the Estates' complaints were being heard and seconded by influential court personages. Even the
intendants, including Saint-Priest, Caze de la Bove, and Gallois de la Tour, were
inclined on some occasions to support the objections raised by the Estates.

In promoting Turgot to the position of controller-general in August 1774, the
new king gave hope to those who desired a change in the administration of
the *dépôts*. Continuing complaints against them were fended off with promises
that the new ministry was contemplating a sweeping reform of policy. As an earnest
of this intention, and in a clear gesture of sympathy with the Estates, Turgot invited
Loménie de Brienne, who as archbishop of Toulouse presided over the Estates of
Languedoc, to coordinate an inquiry into all matters of policy and legislation relating to mendicity. Bertier reported on his bureaucratic "machine" at a meeting in
October. According to Brienne's report to the Estates of Languedoc on January 5,
1775, a change of policy concerning the *dépôts* was enunciated in a set of instructions to the royal commissioners to the Estates of Languedoc dated October 26,
1774. Thus the need to respond to the formal grievances of the Estates elicited
Turgot's first official statements on the subject of mendicity.[52]

Public Opinion, Popular "Stirrings"

The intendants shared with their critics among the judicial elite and with other
notables a well-articulated set of assumptions about the problem of "police" and
the irritability of public opinion. They knew that their actions would be judged by
a familiar language of signs, and that the popular reading of these signs would have

a significant impact on their effectiveness in carrying out royal policy. From this point of view, the "strict execution" of the Declaration of 1764 was a provocative act of rigor—no matter that Bertier justified it by saying that he had abated the severity of the measures intended for the punishment of vagabonds.

"Severity" toward beggars activated a set of counterpoised popular emotions. There was, on the one hand, a measure of satisfaction. Local reports confirm the impressions noted by Georges Lefebvre on the genuine fear of the wanderer experienced by the isolated rural tenant or proprietor.[53] Townspeople were less threatened. Their threshold of tolerance for harassment and insult by ragged, dirty, smelly, and noisy beggars was probably very high by modern standards. At a certain point, nonetheless, the voice of common tradespeople joined the moralistic chorus of the elite and condemned the "scandal" of idleness and depravity. They also realized, as had Juan Luis Vives long before, that these noisome throngs were a blot upon the civic pride of a community, parading the scandal of their city's inhumanity, lack of charity, and incompetence in the arts of government.

The popular perception of the beggar was as ambivalent as that expressed by Le Trosne and other members of the elite. The beggar loomed in popular imagination as a voracious, almost demonic stranger, yet once he became the ward of the authorities, he could be seen as the victim of oppression and accident, the brother whose misery had overwhelmed self-respect. In hard times, especially, those who felt the pinch of high food prices and unemployment naturally identified with the poor devils locked away in institutions, even if they continued to feel that such people should be kept under an austere regimen. Ballainvilliers, intendant of Languedoc, maintained that the *maréchaussée* were reluctant to arrest beggars in the towns of his province, "for the reason that, often, these beggars are related by ties of kinship to the people of these same towns and that the *cavaliers* fear the hot climate and the enterprises of the populace."[54]

As Ballainvilliers' remark indicates, the *maréchaussée,* like the archers of hospitals in the 1720s and before, laid hands on beggars only to find themselves, in many instances, jostled and threatened by an angry, vociferous crowd. Resistance to *chasse-gueux* was a popular tradition. Special edicts prescribed penalties for interference with officers arresting beggars.[55] In one spectacular instance, the mounted police offended cherished popular custom by dragging beggars away from a wedding feast near Vannes, in Brittany.[56] While a great number of "dangerous" or suspicious-looking beggars were arrested on popular complaint, public opinion supported others who protested that they acted only out of necessity, not from any choice of mendicancy as a profession. When the parlements or the Estates objected to the arrest of beggars receiving alms from religious houses, as in the case cited near Le Mans, or when they defended a local custom of allowing children to eke out their parents' income by begging, deep-rooted popular assumptions reinforced the critical perceptions of the magistrates.[57]

The lowly agents of police were commonly suspected of acting from base motives. Formal complaints addressed to the ministry reflected a popular concern that the *cavaliers* of the *maréchaussée* used their powers of arrest to settle old scores, to take bribes, and for other arbitrary reasons. One case involving a woman from Nantes who drank too much came to the attention of the intendant in 1775 as a result of the subdelegate's routine inquiries. When the husband, a gardener, was asked if he would sign a bond for her release from the *dépôt* he replied that he certainly would not, since he had paid good money to have her put there. Statements taken before a parish priest later revealed that four of the woman's relatives had jointly raised a bribe of thirty livres to have her arrested when she went to market with her vegetables. The subdelegate at Nantes went on to tell the newly installed intendant, Caze de la Bove, that the previous intendant had been advised "of the abuses that are committed daily in such circumstances." The provost-general of the *maréchaussée* took the side of his lieutenant, noting that the dossier showed the woman to be a drunkard and that she begged "in order to drink and to provide for her wandering life." Skirting the matter of the bribe, he defended the summary procedure employed, suggesting in effect that abuses were inevitable:

> According to the most recent instructions of the ministry concerning beggary, the lieutenants of the *maréchaussée* are supposed to rely on the testimony of the *cavaliers* and not on the denials of the beggars, who never fail to deny having begged and who afford no proof in their favor, and since the lieutenants are expected to sentence on the basis of the arrest record and the cross-examination, it is not possible for them to order inquiries, which would be too expensive and have never been prescribed.[58]

Once the beggars were in the *dépôt,* they became a mystery of state. Respectable townspeople felt some anxiety at the hidden concentration of wayward humanity in their midst, fearing both a moral and a physical contagion. The subdelegate Fresnais reported such a reaction in a letter to the intendant of Brittany about his tour of inspection at Quimper, where windows facing the street allowed passersby a glimpse of the inmates:

> [T]he provision of clothing is one of the most revolting aspects of the *dépôt* of Quimper. . . . the beggars are in their tattered garments, without linens, without any change of them since there are none in the *dépôt;* they poison the house as they poison themselves; this has the whole town in uproar. Twenty people have spoken to me about it.[59]

Most people expected that beggars would be given plain food and subjected to stern discipline, as justice required. But popular ambivalence toward beggars could express itself in a sudden outburst of sympathy for inmates and a sense of outrage directed against their jailers. "Police" was a double-edged sword.

Of all the scandals that could stir up popular feeling, death was the most powerful. A corpse bore incontrovertible witness. While administrative inquest might exonerate a concierge and his superiors of any blame, the collective judgment could be severe and swift. Like a crowd opposing the shipment of grain in time of shortage, a community incensed by the rumor of death would hear no explanations. The subdelegate Duhamel urged the intendant of Caen in July 1778 to adopt emergency measures of hygiene at the *dépôt,* citing the danger of popular stirrings: "It is high time, Monsieur, to remedy a great ill that can entail the most serious consequences, not only for the lives of these unfortunates, but also with respect to the poisoned discourse of the public, before whom they are daily borne to the cemetery of the parish of St. Nicholas."[60] While released inmates' ordinary conversations left no trace, some official documents reflect the secondhand observation of inmates' conditions and the report of their complaints, as conveyed to the authorities or to the public by those who had business in the *dépôts,* including contractors, concierges, subdelegates, clergy, and medical personnel.

Doctors, surgeons, and nurses who visited the sick in the *dépôts* undoubtedly provided the most authoritative statement of the inmates' conditions. That of Dupichard at Tours, cited earlier, is classic. In many cases these visits confirmed the apprehensions voiced by others, as at Tours and Besançon. In a sense, however, the function of the health professional was to still anxiety by specifying a dose of improvement. Scandal faded away in the light of a medical prescription addressed to a benevolent authority. Behind the scenes, perhaps, doctors may have influenced important officials and leaders in the community by the tone of their own observations and by the conclusions they drew. It is remarkable, for instance, how closely Dupichard and du Cluzel mirror each other's conviction that the operation of *ateliers de charité* would lessen the number of beggars liable to confinement.[61]

The clergy articulated the most strident critique of the *dépôts.* In the *pays d'états* where the clergy took part in provincial administration, bishops judged the charitable professions of the monarchy by the treatment of its wards in the *dépôts.* The responsibility to visit prisoners and the sick held high honor among the traditional Seven Mercies, and bishops performed such visits in person. Olwen Hufton reports such a visit to a *dépôt* by Champion de Cicé, bishop of Rodez, clothed in his pontifical robes. More often, no doubt, bishops learned of conditions within the *dépôts* from the reports of priests and religious who heard confession and celebrated Mass for the inmates. The bishops had been obliged to insist that the government recompense those curés who visited the *dépôts* by means of a suitable offering. Where they felt that the decency of the divine service was impaired, they complained. In specific instances at Châlons-sur-Marne and Tours, curés refused to descend into the putrid squalor of the *dépôts.* Such incidents were particularly embarrassing, since the visiting curés were expected to reinforce the moralizing function of the *dépôts.*[62]

The curés may have helped to shape a stereotyped vision of the *dépôts* as ''an image of hell,'' as reported by the prize essayists of Châlons. In these accounts, inmates are arranged in a poorly lit tableau. Housed in dank, crowded spaces, they are piled upon one another without enough air, clothed in rags, and covered with vermin. Lacking proper food, they barely stir except to moan or scream in their suffering; left in an appalling state of idleness, they are not properly cared for in sickness. Such charges, based on fact, were shaped to a model. If curés functioned as go-betweens carrying messages between some inmates and the outside world, they may also have helped to define those perceptions of the *dépôts* that were shared by beggars themselves, townsfolk, clergy, and the various elements of a provincial elite.[63]

In fact, the image of the *dépôts* seems to have been communicated in stereotyped forms. De Fleury foresaw this when he suggested in 1759 that *dépôts* should all be located near hospitals, so that inmates who were sick could easily be transferred there. ''The people,'' he noted, ''would not fail to say that the ill are poorly cared for.''[64] Authorities made a sustained effort to ensure that the stereotypes were not perpetuated by untoward glimpses of the inmates themselves. The sight of inmates in rags, the sight of corpses in winding sheets on their way to the cemetery, cries of agony or rage from within the *dépôt*—these sights and sounds shaped popular opinion toward the *dépôt* and served as recognizable signs that disposed people to react with sympathy toward the inmates on occasions of full-scale revolt.

The inmates themselves participated in the attack on the *dépôts* in various ways. Instructions on the regime of individual *dépôts* give hints of their resistance against the disciplinary ideal set by their captors. Work had to be carefully supervised, materials had to be guarded and counted. Petty regulations had to be enforced with sanctions such as solitary confinement. Expenses for irons and shackles came under a standard heading on the accounting form used by Bertier. The most common form of resistance was escape, whether through holes laboriously torn loose in masonry, payment of bribes, passage through unguarded doors—even through latrines—or violent breakouts.

Inmates' grievances could coalesce into revolt, given a suitable incident. At Rouen in 1775, a spectacular pitched battle resulted from an incident in which a soldier, Dumont, apparently insane, raged against the concierge for treating him as an ordinary beggar. He shouted out for all to hear that he had been feeding a child for a month before his arrest and that the child had been taken from him. After Dumont smashed a spinning wheel, the *gardien* went for help from the concierge, who advised Dumont that he would have to be put in a solitary cell. Dumont replied: "only scoundrels are put there and you would not dare put me there." The concierge went for reinforcements, who on their arrival were set upon by Dumont, wielding a spindle. In a rage, he bit the soldiers. The official deposition taken by the *procureur-général* of the parlement of Rouen says at this point simply that the other inmates, "animated by his lively entreaties," broke the soldiers' guns and forced them to retire.[65]

A recently admitted inmate then ran to the main workshop of the *dépôt* and spread word of the revolt. The spinning wheels there were smashed. Several other soldiers vainly attempted to enter. A company of grenadiers finally arrived, reinforced by a second company and a detachment of one hundred men. Meanwhile the inmates had improvised bayonets from the metal *broches* of their spinning wheels. They did not fall back until two of their number had fallen, and at that moment the *grand prévôt* and the lieutenant of the *maréchaussée* arrived with their brigades. The officer commanding the regiment de Penthièvre explained that the revolt had been extremely violent and had required using *"la dernière rigueur"* (extreme measures). After shooting blanks for fifteen minutes, the soldiers used live ammunition. Two beggars were seriously wounded, including one who died of his wounds.

There had been numerous revolts at the *dépôt* of Rouen. Obviously, they could not succeed against military force. However, they effectively drew attention to the *dépôts* and mobilized critical opinion. Any such breakdown of normal "police" provided the occasion for a judicial inquiry. The *procureur-général* of the parlement at Rouen, which had been reinstated along with its sister parlements at the beginning of Louis XVI's reign, demanded an investigation of the complaints he had heard during his inquest into the revolt in the *dépôt* at Rouen.[66]

Turgot and the Contradictions of Physiocracy

Neither the people nor the magistrates were willing to resolve their ambivalent feelings toward beggars into a simple impulse of repression. The new advocates of liberty shared this uncertainty, in spite of their shrill denunciations of idleness and their repeated warnings against misplaced charity. Although Le Trosne's essay of 1764 had provided legitimation for the *dépôts,* Physiocratic principles could also provide a foundation for denouncing them as futile. Quesnay, the father of Physiocracy, had suggested, after all, that "idleness" was an essentially economic phenomenon: a new psychology of abundance would promote regular, industrious habits. The elder Mirabeau, an early light of the Physiocratic movement, penned one of the first critiques of royal policy on the *dépôts* in an article for the *Éphémérides* written shortly after the *arrêt du conseil* of 1767. He derided the new decree as an instance of the belief that "paper is sufficient for governing everything." The government must instead cease providing pensions for beggars through its aid to hospitals.[67]

The abbé Baudeau, who edited the *Éphémérides* in collaboration with Mirabeau from 1765 to 1768, outlined a version of charitable reform that was in keeping with the spirit of Turgot's article on endowments. Like Turgot, he argued that alms for the helpless sick and the aged would be best administered by those who had an interest in the well-being of the needy. Resources would be adequate if managed effectively; the need would be more manageable under a regime of economic liberty. Only if these preconditions were met could voluntary idleness be repressed, and only then by means of a regularly funded police network uniform in its operations.[68]

In 1768 the editorship of the *Éphémérides* passed to Du Pont de Nemours. For the next three years severe grain shortages would subject the system of free trade to its severest trial. At a General Assembly of Police held in Paris in November 1768, representatives of the Paris parlement, chief administrators of hospitals, police officers of the Châtelet, and other local officials called for a review of the measures in place for policing the trade in subsistence commodities. The Physiocrats were cast on the defensive.[69] In April 1769 the abbé Roubaud launched a polemical treatise against the positions adopted by the General Assembly. He sent Voltaire a copy, hoping to enlist the master publicist in the Physiocratic ranks. Voltaire's reply, printed in the *Mercure de France,* supported free trade in principle, but took issue with several articles of Physiocratic doctrine. Voltaire pointedly urged Roubaud and his colleagues to address themselves more directly to the problem of mendicity.[70] Voltaire's satire of Physiocracy in *L'homme aux quarante écus* reinforced the reasoned doubts of Mably, the sprightly dialogues of Galiani, and the diatribes of Linguet. Enlightened opinion favored a revision of the free trade measures of Bertin and Laverdy.[71]

Embattled, Du Pont devoted the pages of the *Éphémérides* to reasoned calculations absolving free trade from any suspicion of contributing to the subsistence crisis, and fulminated against "brigandage," by which he meant any interference with free trade. Price ceilings he anathemetized, public granaries he denounced as folly. The merchants of Lyons who sold grain below cost exhibited a "misguided asceticism" and betrayed their families' welfare, acting as "madmen," not merchants. Any form of "forced alms" provoked Du Pont's ire. Reporting on a measure taken in Flanders obliging landowners to provide for the subsistence of their tenants, Du Pont decreed: "No question of political economy should be decided by charity."[72]

But the Physiocrats themselves promoted certain types of charitable measures that would complement their vision of free trade. In an article on food shortages in 1768, Baudeau had stated that alms were preferable to price-fixing. Responding to the call for renewed grain controls voiced by the General Assembly of Police, Du Pont found it useful to emphasize the importance of "royal alms" in relieving misery. In a later article he outlined the means of satisfying "the needs of fortuitous and involuntary indigence," including advice on cheaper methods of milling grain and baking bread, and a soup recipe for the poor using rice in place of bread.[73]

In a section of the *Éphémérides* that listed "praiseworthy actions" and "acts of public beneficence," Du Pont gave pride of place to public relief in the form of road work. Such labor would keep an agricultural work force in trim; laborers' expenditures on food would stimulate agricultural production. Work on side roads was especially valuable because it facilitated the circulation of produce to market and removed a material obstacle to the workings of the *tableau économique*. Road work could also contribute to the progress of liberty by replacing the obligatory royal *corvée*, a tax in kind that in the view of Physiocrats disrupted agricultural production.[74] In towns Du Pont favored temporary workshops for spinning and the putting out of domestic piecework. Praising Rattier's workshop for the "free" poor at Tours in particular, he obliquely disparaged the *dépôts* in general: "The more work it offers to free workers, the less will one consider it necessary to deprive people of their liberty, whom irresistable circumstances have already deprived of their fortunes."[75]

In 1771 Du Pont went so far as to set forth the principles of hospital reform, beginning with the axiom that the Physiocratic program for eliminating poverty was a precondition for reform. Second, he argued that work rather than alms should be offered wherever possible, so that the poor might retain their self-respect. Third, the disabled infirm who deserved total support should be aided at home, if possible, instead of being placed in wasteful establishments that constrained them to a monastic vocation. Finally, Du Pont conceded a need for gradual improvements in hospitals already established.[76]

Turgot's initiatives as minister conform in important respects to the principles enunciated by Du Pont—indeed, Du Pont had listened to Turgot in formulating them. However, Turgot broadened the Physiocratic prescription for mendicity in two major respects. First of all, he did not found his commitment to free trade on the sanctity of property, but rather on decisions of public utility to be determined by citizens acting as rational, virtuous, and free individuals. From practical administrative experience he drew a further conviction: a government committed to free trade would need to make provision for various categories of individuals who could not earn their subsistence either because of their disabilities or because of market dislocations.[77]

Autonomy was the key to Turgot's liberalism. He took acquisitiveness for granted, but did not sanctify it. As a young man accompanying Gournay in the inspection of manufactures, he absorbed the lesson that a regime of privilege and prohibition promoted greed and placed the poor at the mercy of the rich.[78] Many years later, writing to Terray by candlelight after long days spent in allocating local tax assessments in the hills of the Limousin, Turgot argued with reason and passion that free trade was the key to economic self-sufficiency for the people under his administration. Producers, protected against sagging prices by the stimulus of a wider market, would expand output and improve productivity. But even more important, the poor consumer would be protected against the most devastating threat to his survival, namely, the dread scourge of famine prices and the habitually wide swing of prices in markets confined to a small region.[79]

With self-sufficiency would come a rehabilitation of the "spirit of the citizen," a phrase that rang out from the text of his article on endowments, echoing the "virtue" of Montesquieu's republican ideal and anticipating Rousseau's "general will." Criticizing a system of education that depended on charitable endowments, Turgot expressed the concern for civic virtue that lay at the core of his liberalism: "Should men be accustomed to asking for everything, receiving everything, and owing nothing to themselves? This sort of mendicity that extends to all conditions degrades a people, and replaces lofty passions with a character of baseness and intrigue."[80]

By this yardstick, the Limousin proprietors who displayed an aversion for undertaking projects of public utility stood in need of civic rehabilitation at least as much as did the hapless beggars trudging over the land. Freed from the daily travail of assuring their own subsistence, such proprietors would constitute the natural support for projects like alms bureaus.[81]

If Turgot referred in jest to the abbé Baudeau as "Brother Paul," or asked Du Pont to send "missionaries" to his benighted Limousins, he pointedly referred to his own statement of economic principles as a "Confession of Augsburg" and resisted Du Pont's attempts to impose Physiocratic dogma on all those who supported free trade. He excoriated the term "legal despotism," introduced by Mercier de la Rivière.[82] He took Du Pont sharply to task for altering a phrase in the manuscript of his treatise *Réflexions sur la richesse,* before publishing it anonymously in the *Éphémérides* in 1770. The effect of Du Pont's revision was to found the right of property in the original "investment" by the first owner. Turgot held to an opposing view that property was a social institution founded on utility.[83] The disagreement was fundamental. In the very article where he launched the term "laisser-faire" on a broad career, Turgot had justified the community in setting aside the solemn legal stipulation of original property owners in order to meet its changed needs. Later, at the very moment when he was attacking the *corvée* as an infringement on property, he felt no compunction against issuing an ordinance requiring owners to aid their sharecroppers following a crop failure.[84]

The "system of liberty" as Turgot understood it rested essentially on three interlocking principles, each implying a humanitarian obligation to guarantee the poorest members of society a decent standard of well-being and security. The initial principle was to maximize the sphere of autonomy for the individual, even if this meant abolishing regulations that claimed to protect the economic order. Second, the free market must be enlarged as a utilitarian strategy for increasing productivity and total wealth. Finally, the functions of administration and law had to be judged by the yardstick of rational public utility. Strict bureaucratic accountability would abolish preserves of greed and parasitism. Definite service contracts of *régies* should take the place of *fermes* or speculative enterprises based on the delegation of public functions to private companies.[85]

Given this background, it remains to be shown how Turgot's determination to reform royal policy on mendicity fed upon his growing frustration as an administrator responsible for running a *dépôt de mendicité*. At the same time, Du Pont de Nemours, chastened by the failures of Physiocratic propaganda, drew closer to Turgot's perspective on mendicity. In essays composed on the eve of Turgot's ministry, he recognized, implicitly at least, that the operation of a free market economy required a new definition of the citizen's right to public assistance.

Turgot and the *Dépôts* of the *Intendance* of Limoges

The royal government recognized the need for relief measures on a sporadic, ad hoc manner, generally requiring intendants and other officials to speak as advocates attesting to the misery and distress of their charges. The task of repression was, by comparison, thoroughly institutionalized. Although Turgot focused his efforts on agricultural improvement and emergency relief, his duties as intendant required him to serve also as jailer of the poor. Since the motley crew of economic casualties and misfits confined in the *dépôts* at Limoges and Angoulême were in less than perfect health, he was also obliged to enter into the details of hospital administration, an ironic predicament for the critic of charitable foundations. Having to conform to Bertier's directives added to the frustrations of a disagreeable task. Although the documents concerning Turgot and the *dépôts* of his intendance are limited to a few exchanges over accounting matters, they provide evidence that the future minister's repugnance for the *dépôts* was founded in part on his experience as intendant.

Health problems plagued the *dépôt* at Limoges as they did elsewhere, in spite of precautions taken on the advice of the royal engineer. In the early months of 1772, an epidemic carried off about a third of the inmates at Limoges. Sieur Faye, the doctor, apparently fell ill and died; his widow received two hundred livres for his services from March 5 to April 20 of that year.[86] Another dossier relates to the violent insane incarcerated at the *dépôt* of Limoges. As they were causing damage to their cells, Turgot authorized the subdelegate to give them tobacco to chew, which seemed to pacify them. Bertier disallowed the expenditure, noting that it was not incurred in any other *dépôt*. Turgot later sent in statements for the repair of cells once again battered by the raging insane.[87]

The most significant sniping between Bertier and Turgot centered upon the question of work and rehabilitation. Bertier insisted on having standard entries under the chapter "work" filled in to indicate both receipts and expenditures. Turgot entered the work done by some of the inmates in the garden of the *dépôt*. Bertier expressed dissatisfaction, obviously expecting to see more tangible and marketable products of industry. He also objected to the fact that Turgot had placed the acquisition of spinning wheels and the setting up of a loom under the heading of "furnishings" for the *dépôt*. Was this obtuseness deliberate? Perhaps it reflected on Turgot's part the same wry humor that produced a library of whimsical titles embossed on the spines of dummy volumes. Seeing little to be gained from the industrial training of inmates, Turgot chose instead to give them substantial travel allowances to wherever they hoped to find employment. Bertier could not believe the sums Turgot had spent under this heading, and assumed that they must include some other object of expense. Turgot asked his subdelegate to supply the list for this item, "over which M. Bertier is exercised."[88]

Turgot probably found himself in agreement with Terray's seasonal release of inmates from *dépôts* during the planting season, a policy repeated from 1772 to 1774. On the other hand, he took no action on Terray's instruction to retain able-bodied young men for a national work project that was to be announced imminently, according to a circular of March 3, 1772. Turgot instructed his subdelegate to carry on as before: "It would be strange to keep in prison people who do not deserve to be there, pending receipt of instructions that can be delayed for any number of reasons."[89] The project in question was Bertier's *corps des pionniers,* a concept that Turgot later supported.

Turgot probably discussed his views on mendicity with Du Pont de Nemours. Meeting in Paris in 1773, the two discussed a series of letters Du Pont was composing at the request of the Duke of Baden, who desired a practical exposition of Physiocratic reform principles.[90] Turgot wrote to Condorcet to assemble their exchange of correspondence on criminal procedure for Du Pont's use. In the course of this exchange, Turgot spoke of the bias of the law in favor of the rich and against the poor.[91] His concern for individual liberties may have shaped the cast of Du Pont's letter to the Duke of Baden on the subject of mendicity:

> Under the pretext that among the crowds of quite involuntary poor, there are to be found some vagabonds who make of beggary an ignominious career, or who even steal when they are not given enough, it has been decided that all beggars of whatever sort should be arrested.[92]

Turgot's accents seem to make themselves heard especially in the sentences that follow an orthodox Physiocratic litany of the evils of administration that promote begging:

> As the case may be, there are a great many poor. A large number of them have begged their bread. It is a sad state to be in. It is not to be believed that people stay in it because they like it; and yet that has been assumed. An old proverb says that "Poverty is no vice." A new usage would have it that poverty be punished.

Observing that beggary still abounded, Du Pont alleged that the only beggars locked up were those who had not earned enough from alms to pay off the *maréchaussée.* Within the *dépôts* themselves, abuses arose. Tended carefully in some provinces, in others "they have appeared as a burden to the administrators, who have pretty much neglected them." The provision of spoiled grain by contractors had impaired the health of inmates. These contractors appeared to be linked into one large monopoly, especially around the capital, where they also contracted for the provisioning of Paris.[93]

Du Pont also criticized efforts to put inmates to work. In those rare instances of commercial success, the effect was to "take away work and wages from the free workers who, becoming poor in their turn, reduced to begging, and shut up in the

workhouses . . . will find themselves also metamorphosed into slaves.'' Workshops such as those at Lyons "appear good but are not." On the other hand, Du
Pont had some kind words for Bertier's *corps des pionniers* in the *généralité* of
Paris. These companies brought about an "improvement of the fate of beggars
previously locked up, and who benefit from open air and honest pay: the reduction
of *corvées* for the cultivator, or if nothing else, the multiplication of outlets for
commerce." Public opinion rightly favored these results. Still Du Pont noted some
reservations. The beggars are still assembled by force—a point that had concerned
Turgot more than Du Pont in the past. The utility of the original projects was
limited, and the operation was highly bureaucratic. Might it not be better to keep
army units fit for battle by means of regular outdoor exercise on works of public
utility, rather than trying to make soldiers out of beggars?[94]

Essentially, Du Pont adopts Turgot's stance in opposition to Bertier's machine.
Du Pont's concluding remarks anticipate the interlocking character of Turgot's later
economic and institutional reform proposals, encompassing, as they would, the reform of charity and repression. Invoking the fashionable dictum, *il ne faut point
faire des pauvres,* Du Pont underscored the economic benefits of laisser-faire and
the Physiocratic program. Indirect and arbitrary taxation, in particular, should be
replaced by a tax on the "net product" of the soil. This anticipates Turgot's plan
to replace the *corvée* with a universal tax on landowners, including the privileged.
Once the causes of general misery were attacked, the particular accidents that needed
relief would be limited to a manageable scope.[95]

Existing policies, noted Du Pont, lumped together the poor, vagabonds, and
criminals. But the needy poor were forced into leaving their homes because relief
was not provided on the local level. The fear that such poor would become criminals was self-fulfilling, especially if they were treated harshly for the "crime" of
vagabondage. A "paternal" policy of investigation, returning vagabonds with passports to their true domicile, and providing for their subsistence en route, would
reduce their number. This, of course, was what Turgot had tried to do as intendant.
Under a wise government, the number of poor would be small enough so that
families and communities could provide for them. Communities could employ their
own poor on public works of a local character during the off season, taking care
not to assign tasks in competition with other workers. The detail on the administration of such projects, as outlined by Du Pont, follows closely that which Turgot
had prescribed. Finally, those who were truly unable to work—the aged, the infirm,
the ill—could be provided for by methods discussed at greater length in an earlier
letter to the Duke of Baden concerning projects for reconstructing the *hôtel-Dieu* of
Paris. The main point was to distribute aid to individuals, in their homes if at all
possible, or in small establishments, rather than assembling them in large hospitals.[96]

If Turgot's opinions reverberated in the writings of Du Pont, they also provided
a rallying point for leading provincial notables who were demanding institutional
reforms. Two influential leaders of the provincial Estates, Loménie de Brienne and
Boisgelin de Cucé, archbishops of Toulouse and Aix respectively, were friends of
Turgot since their student days at the Sorbonne. Boisgelin, of a noble Breton family, became archbishop of Aix after serving as bishop of Lavaur in Languedoc. On
his way from Paris to Aix in 1770, his carriage overturned not far from Limoges,

where he recuperated as Turgot's guest. Boisgelin discussed with his host the causes of the current economic crisis and told him of the relief measures taken on the estates of his family, according to letters he had received from Brittany. The intendant persuaded the archbishop of the beneficent principles of free trade, according to Boisgelin's biographer, who also reports that Boisgelin visited Turgot on subsequent journeys between Paris and Aix. In his years at Aix, Boisgelin argued that local institutions would respond more effectively to problems of poor relief, if the oppressive fiscal demands of the Crown were reduced.[97]

Shortly after Turgot's appointment as controller-general in the first year of the new reign, Boisgelin made some casually unfavorable remarks about the younger Bertier in the company of the abbé Rousseau, who reported them to Madame de Sauvigny, the mother of the young magistrate. Boisgelin complained that Bertier had not returned a greeting (was he short-sighted?), and that he had made no reply to an inquiry regarding the tax assessment of one of Boisgelin's tenants in the *généralité* of Paris. The archbishop apparently implied that the intendant showed favoritism to his own friends—such as M. de Montyon, intendant of Aix—and had little concern for the unfortunate. The latter remark, of course, echoed acrimonious discussion of the *dépôt* at Aix.[98]

Through the good offices of the abbé Rousseau, Madame de Sauvigny conveyed her regret that any unfavorable impression had been given, and asked for information concerning the archbishop's complaint—could she have the location of the abbey as well as its name? Noting that small misunderstandings could lead to unfortunate enmities, she expressed the wish that the archbishop of Aix might be reconciled with "our friend, M. de Montyon." She asked the abbé to assure the archbishop that her son would never refuse a greeting, "and that whatever change occurs in the ministry there will be none in his conduct nor in the regards that a good education prescribes." She portrayed her son as a diligent public servant, occupied in his work in royal councils at Fontainebleau and in travels throughout the *intendance* (the yearly allocation of tax levies and adjustments was in progress), taking what time he could to return to the side of his wife, who was about to have a child. In addition to painting a picture of public and domestic solicitude to describe her son, Madame de Sauvigny insisted, "We have all our life given marked preferences to the unfortunate."

The archbishop assured the abbé Rousseau that he had never meant to complain seriously: "I have not been treated with injustice, but with neglect, and one can be annoyed at being neglected without being surprised." Having but slightly mollified the archbishop, Madame de Sauvigny reconciled herself to the fact that the appointment of Turgot by the young king signaled a clean break with the policies and personnel of the abbé Terray. The father of her son's bride, Foullon, was one of two *intendants des finances* from the old ministry repudiated in the new. She expressed the hope that Madame de Polignac would not visit, lest the husband of her visitor reproach his wife some day for the fact that their son had no bishopric or that their daughters went unmarried![99]

It was Boisgelin who preached the sermon at Louis XVI's ceremonial coronation, the *sacre* of June 11, 1775. Those who heard it remembered that the speaker emphasized the meaning of the ceremony as an act of consecration on the part of the king to serve the law and the nation; that he spoke of the plight of the poor in

tones that echoed Massillon; that he summoned the new king to reform his kingdom, in phrases that verged on indiscretion. The sermon was never published, although it was cited in Boisgelin's nomination to the Academy.[100]

By the time of the coronation, the new king had reigned for slightly over a year
and his minister of finance, Turgot, had laid the groundwork for sweeping reforms.
In the early months of his ministry, Turgot had confided to Loménie de Brienne,
archbishop of Toulouse, the task of coordinating a broad review of measures relating to mendicity.

Turgot's First Measures on Mendicity

Those who attended Turgot's first conference on mendicity in October 1774 represented the main sources of discontent with the *dépôts*. Loménie de Brienne, as
chairman, represented the objections of the *pays d'états* and shared Turgot's liberal
economic views. He asked to serve without any formal commission, in order to
work "with less éclat and more effect."[101] Boullongne had sat on the Laverdy
commission and continued to supervise the finance of hospitals, encompassing charitable foundations, privileges, and royal support for hospitals. Of all Turgot's collaborators, Trudaine de Montigny was perhaps the most closely attuned to his own
views of administration, justice, and economic policy. Turgot had dealt with his
father, Daniel Trudaine, concerning reform of the *corvées* in the Limousin, a matter
involving his department of *ponts et chaussées*. Under Turgot's ministry, the younger
Trudaine kept his dual responsibilities for *ponts et chaussées* and the bureau of
commerce. In the latter function, Trudaine had acquired familiarity with the economics of unemployment. Among other proposals he had reviewed and approved
was that of Rattier for the employment of the free poor of the city of Tours in a
workhouse attached to the *dépôt*.[102] Albert, like Trudaine, shared Turgot's economic views. He had played a role in promoting *ateliers de charité* in the crisis of
1769 and 1770, but Terray had removed him from his post on the *bureau des
subsistances* because of Albert's insistence on the merits of free trade in grains.
The tables were turned when Turgot's disagreements with the *lieutenant de police*
of Paris, Le Noir, over the police of subsistence led to Le Noir's dismissal. Albert
took his place.[103]

Bertier was not in friendly company. Loménie de Brienne wrote later that Laverdy's work on mendicity had produced only

> an uncertain, arbitrary, inadequate operation, one that did nothing but procure M.
> Bertier a sort of department where he did not do a great deal of harm, unless one
> deems harmful the expenditure of money without any effects being obtained. This
> is not the first time that useless tasks have been created and maintained by people
> who know how to take them over, and by the ineptitude and credulity of their
> superiors.[104]

The first conference on mendicity, according to its chairman, "was vague—M.
Bertier gave a report on the present status of his charge."[105]

Although there is no record of Brienne's first meeting with his working group,
the main lines of Bertier's presentation may be inferred from the summary he drew

up a little over a year later. He would then argue that he had joined efforts with members of the parlement to lessen the rigor of penalties and to broaden the range of measures taken to cope with mendicity. Public works were supposed to have been encouraged (a nod to Albert at this point), hospitals made ready to receive all invalid beggars (Boullongne was the expert on this), and alms bureaus established in every parish to help the domiciled poor (no need to cite Turgot).[106]

Bertier would maintain that these plans had been "neglected" owing to "changes in the ministry." Brienne later observed that d'Invault had been too preoccupied with the state of the royal treasury to concern himself with anything else. It was a matter of surprise to him that Terray had supported the *dépôts,* since they were not affairs of the heart and cost the treasury while bringing in nothing. Bertier hinted that he had not been responsible for the contracting arrangements that had brought disrepute upon the *dépôts.* "People were so well persuaded of the solidity of the operation," he wrote, "that companies aided by a superior credit obtained the general contract for the upkeep of beggars in the *dépôts.*" Brienne saw in this only a more pervasive corruption:

> Madame du Barry ended up turning it into a business deal for her protégés. Such is the evil, in a monarchy, of general operations, involving maintenance and expenditure—they end up always being taken over by credit and favor. Only local and particular administrations endure amid revolutions.[107]

Prejudged as a self-serving bureaucrat, Bertier tried to convince his listeners that the *dépôts* were redeemable as part of a broader attack on mendicity. He made the point that he himself had urged broader measures, and pointed to his own success in establishing "companies of workers in a military form whose work is succeeding fairly well." In terms of overall cost, Bertier asserted that the *dépôts* had been managed within the original projections for expenditure, declining to an annual level of one million livres. Approximately one million beggars had been interned in an eight-year period, while the number confined at any one time ranged generally from ten to fourteen thousand.[108] Turgot chose not to take any precipitous action with respect to the *dépôts* and asked Brienne to gather further information and advice. Meanwhile he signaled his intent to carry out major reforms. In a letter to the archbishop of Narbonne, noted earlier, he acknowledged that the complaints of the Estates of Languedoc were well founded: the *dépôts* had failed in their purpose. It was already decided, he wrote, "to take, at least in part, other measures than those employed to date."[109] The *dépôts,* he implied, might be retained for certain types of inmate, but they would be emptied "of those who should not have been confined in them." Inmates would be released gradually, and changes in arrest procedures would be made with caution. As a clear first step, Turgot ordered that by March 1775 arrests were to be limited strictly to vagabonds. Inmates not fitting that description would be released. The intendant of Languedoc received instructions, accordingly, that the pace of arrests should be "imperceptibly" diminished, "without halting them entirely in this season in which the number of beggars increases, and in which their importunity is felt more."[110]

The circular addressed to all intendants on November 16 spelled out a new policy. Turgot blamed the failure of past measures upon a fatal "reversal of priority between two complementary parts of a single plan." He referred here to Laverdy's intention of assuring subsistence and care for the invalid poor before ordering the confinement of vagabonds. Turgot noted that difficulties of execution and obstacles born of circumstance had prevented these measures of assistance from being implemented. The great error, in these circumstances, was to have proceeded willy-nilly with the repressive part of the operation,

> which should have been second in order of time, since it is impossible to destroy beggary and unjust to proscribe it as long as the beggar cannot be regarded as guilty, as long as misery can force him to beg in order to live, as long as measures have not been taken to assure relief for the invalid poor and suitable work for the able-bodied poor.[111]

The purpose of the letter, then, was to assert the priority of measures for providing "relief for the invalid poor and suitable work for the able-bodied poor." The *ateliers de charité* established in every *généralité* might be "extended and perfected according to the observations that experience may have suggested to you." Provision for the invalid poor involved more difficulties. Plans in this area could not be executed without full knowledge of existing charitable resources. Accordingly, Turgot launched yet another in a series of administrative inquiries into the revenues of hospitals and charitable endowments. This inquiry was to be directed

> parish by parish, into all the establishments of charity that exist in the different provinces of the kingdom, by whatever denomination, such as *hôpitaux, hôtels-Dieu,* houses of charity, endowments for food distributions, alms, and handouts, and generally into all that has been established for the solace of the ill and poor, and even of prisoners.[112]

Such an inquiry was similar to others that Boullongne had coordinated before. Previously, however, he had filed away the replies and nothing had been done with them. What would the celebrated author of the article on endowments do with such information? Turgot's instructions were suggestive in their specificity. For all endowments, he asked for details on "the charges with which they have been burdened by their original titles, on the manner in which they are presently implemented, and on the changes that may have occurred in the use that has been made of them and the successive dispositions that have governed them."[113] A sample table accompanied the inquiry.

This inquest received more emphasis in a circular Turgot sent to bishops explaining his review of measures taken to eliminate mendicity. Although he said nothing about the *dépôts,* he explained his intention of providing *ateliers* for the able-bodied and new resources for the infirm. The purpose of launching an inquiry into resources for the subsistence of the poor was to be able "to consecrate them entirely to their purpose and to supplement their insufficiency, if need be." As the bishops' cooperation was essential, Turgot explained to them,

> this various information is absolutely necessary in order to rescue the hospitals from the state of distress to which the greater number is reduced, to consecrate to the solace of the poor of each parish the property that the piety of the faithful has so designated, and finally, to prevent having the large establishments that may be helped by other means absorb all the particular relief that is never better employed than when it is most divided, and distributed in those places where misery is felt.[114]

Such an explanation could easily be construed as a prelude to a total overhaul of hospital revenues. Were large hospitals to be divested of charitable revenues assigned to them by previous royal measures of consolidation? If so, what administrative changes would be made? The letter from Turgot (composed by Brienne) strove to allay the anxiety that it raised, urging bishops to employ their good offices in persuading curés and hospital administrators to cooperate in the inquiry "with zeal and confidence, since [the information to be provided] contributes to the succor of the poor whose interests are confided to them, and whose misfortunes are of equal concern to religion and humanity." In closing, the letter invited bishops to submit their views, to evaluate present operations, and to present successful local examples or new solutions.[115]

Having established the logical priority of a general welfare reform, Turgot sent another circular to intendants on November 19, 1774, explaining his intention to limit further arrests and release certain categories of inmates, as indicated in his letter to the archbishop of Narbonne. He reminded them that this previous letter had explained his view on invalid beggars and on the need to expand *ateliers de charité* in order "to furnish a great resource for the subsistence of the poor whose misery is only momentary." The repressive function of the *dépôts* would be continued, but it would be applied only to the vagabonds specified in the Declaration of August 3, 1764. This directive effectively reduced the penalty for vagrancy from a term in the galleys to confinement in the *dépôt* (in keeping with actual practice), while nullifying the effect of the *arrêt du conseil* of 1767. This restriction would go into effect the following May. Meanwhile arrests were to be made "with the greatest possible restraint," and were to be suspended entirely in the case of domiciled beggars, barring exceptional circumstances. Reversing the policy enunciated on April 12, 1769, regarding domiciled beggars, Turgot in effect reinstated the initial instruction issued to the *maréchaussée* in 1767 and 1768, and prepared a return to a more strictly limited construction of the Declaration of 1764. Bertier's great machine was to be wound down.[116]

7

Philosophy and Bureaucracy

By 1774 the critics of the *dépôts* had undermined the schemes of Joly de Fleury, breached the defenses of the system confided to the energetic younger Bertier, and resurrected all the issues that Laverdy's commission had swept under the rug in 1767. The controller-general of finance, Turgot, had spoken with the voice of the *Encyclopédiste,* urging that citizens' energies be mobilized by means of more rational institutions. His close relationship with provincial spokesmen for "advanced" opinion—the archbishops of Aix and Toulouse—seemed to promise a new era of cooperation between the king's council and provincial elites in sharing the tasks of reform.

The grain shortages that developed in Turgot's first year as minister posed a challenge to the free-trade assumptions upon which his reforms all rested. In the preamble to the decrees of September 13, 1774, that reinstated free trade in grain, Turgot had stated bluntly that stockpiling and unobstructed transport "are the only means of communication that turn surpluses into a resource for need."[1] To think that controls can compensate for physical scarcity is an "illusion," he argued: they invariably raise the overall cost of subsistence and discourage production. The interest of the people dictated free trade, for "in the alternation between abundance and dearth, all would be exposed in turn to the last degree of misery, which they would be assured of avoiding by aiding each other mutually." Turgot had nonetheless reassured the vulnerable consumer: "If Providence allow that, during the course of [the present] reign, the King's provinces should be afflicted with dearth, he promises to neglect no means to procure the truly efficacious relief for the portion of his subjects that suffers the most from public calamities."[2]

As shortages worsened in the spring of 1775, public outbreaks intensified into movements known collectively as the *guerre des farines,* or the "flour war." In tracts disseminated through local curés, Turgot attempted to argue that there was no logical connection between these outbreaks and an "excess of misery." Prices had not approached previous highs, and royal measures of relief had included the establishment of *ateliers* in the provinces and the capital, providing the poor with "the means of earning wages and bringing the price of bread within their reach."[3] His instructions to intendants and local authorities revealed a preoccupation with providing the kinds of work that all those wage earners in need of employment might be able to perform—road projects, workshops, and cottage industry in particular.[4] He drew upon his experience at Limoges, experience that had once inspired him to remind Du Pont that free trade was of no avail if the people were too poor to trade.[5] The special circumstances that might require the authorities to "multiply wages" were evident enough:

> The sudden augmentation in the price of foodstuffs can give rise to a disproportion between wages and subsistence, between faculties and needs: the meagerness of harvests, the distance grains must travel, can raise them above the feeble resources that work procures for the most indigent class of consumers: an augmentation of work is the most natural means to remedy this.[6]

Differences arose between Turgot and Bertier over the measures taken to quell the outbreaks concentrated around Paris. The rumor passed that Bertier might be replaced in his *intendance*, just as Le Noir had been replaced by Albert as *lieutenant de police* for the city of Paris. But Bertier was formally vindicated by a letter from the king to Turgot expressing satisfaction with Bertier's response to the *guerre des farines*. Turgot would have to take account of Bertier's views on all matters that affected the region around the capital, including questions relating to mendicity.[7]

After the king's coronation at Reims in the summer of 1775, Turgot began to elaborate a package of reforms to complete the framework of free trade. These measures would eventually be presented to the parlement of Paris in the form of the Six Edicts in the spring of 1776. These edicts freed the labor market by abolishing the guilds, and replaced the royal *corvée* for the maintenance of royal highways with a tax to be raised on privileged and unprivileged alike, based on land value. The formulation of these measures was interwoven with discussions on mendicity. Trudaine and Albert, in particular, were involved in planning for the Six Edicts as they joined the general discussion of Brienne's memoir on mendicity in October 1775.[8]

Following the preliminary directives mentioned in the previous chapter, Brienne launched a full review of past legislation, current practice, and the best-informed opinion. Turgot referred to him all memoirs on the subject of mendicity and hospital reform. As a first step, Brienne asked Bertier to provide documents he had referred to in his initial report, including memoirs pertaining to the Laverdy commission, Bertier's report of 1766, draft edicts and objections, and letters sent to intendants and to the *maréchaussée*. Brienne asked for copies of figures given on the number of inmates in the *dépôts,* expenses of the operation, "and finally a notion of your companies of workers, which appear to me to be very important to retain, and even to extend." Brienne concluded with a compliment to Bertier and a genuflexion to empirical method: "I ask your pardon for requesting so much information, but you recognize how essential it is not to be content with simple speculations, but to join to principles the knowledge of what has been practiced—and concerning this you are more knowledgeable than anyone."[9]

Bertier replied on November 7, saying that his duties had taken him away from Paris, but that he had written to have copies made of those documents he did not have to prepare in person. On the 29th, back in Paris, Bertier forwarded a batch of documents, with apologies for the delay entailed in copying lengthy texts. He included a brief memoir on his *corps de pionniers,* suggesting however that he might better explain the details in conversation. He noted, finally, that the memoirs submitted to Laverdy were still in the keeping of the former controller-general.[10]

Brienne promptly followed up with a request to Laverdy for copies of the observations made by the parlement and of the two draft edicts considered. By gathering in what had been proposed, Brienne observed to Laverdy, it was thought new plans would be more certain of success, more likely "to unite opinions." Brienne went out of his way to voice an unalloyed "provincial" enthusiasm for broader participation in government in his letter to Laverdy. Perhaps he was already preparing in his mind the phrases he would use in reporting to the Estates of Languedoc in January as he wrote: "Behold a great and happy revolution that is taking great strides. We await it in the provinces with impatience. Never was a reign more happily announced. It is to be hoped that everyone will take part in the realization of such fond hopes."[11]

Brienne's Memoir: A Quest for the "Spirit of the Laws"

Brienne's enthusiasm went beyond the routine courtesies required in a letter to a former minister. The memoir he prepared for Turgot's commission on mendicity may be seen, indeed, as a supporting argument for the otherwise vaguely rhetorical statement that "a happy revolution . . . is taking great strides." Analysis of this text in the following pages will show how closely Brienne identified that "revolution" with the challenge of providing an effective set of remedies for the problem of mendicity.[12]

Divided into two parts, Brienne's memoir contained a fundamental distinction between the tasks of administration and those of justice. The law, he noted, is limited to prescribing what is just, whereas the scope of administration is infinite because it concerns all that may be "useful." Du Pont de Nemours had made a similar distinction in his letter of 1773 to the Duke of Baden, a letter that also contained the germ of many of Brienne's arguments on mendicity.[13] Some laws, Brienne argued, were unjust because they reached beyond their proper sphere of maintaining public order and repressing crimes. Administration, on the other hand, could obviate the need for some laws, by removing the conditions that corrupt the individual and promote crime. Progress depends, then, on the close coordination of justice and administration. The breakdown in royal policy on mendicity since 1764 resulted in part from the inability of the royal council to reach agreement with the parlements on an appropriate legislative framework. Defining the appropriate spheres of justice and administration was thus an important analytic task *and* a political precondition for enlightened reform. Law and administration needed to be "conciliated." Turgot's advice to Louis XVI to recall the parlements disbanded since the Maupeou coup d'état of 1771 should probably be understood in this context.[14]

To analyze the two parts of Brienne's lengthy memoir in terms of the experience of the *dépôts de mendicité* imposes a certain bias on the deliberately general sweep of the author's discourse, but that experience was more important as a guiding motive than it appears to be on the surface. The first part, on law, is a critique of the official rationale for the indiscriminate arrest of beggars; the second, on administration, insists on the need for a systematic policy of public assistance as a precondition for any successful legal sanctions against begging.

The laws of 1764 and 1767 were too obviously unjust and became unenforceable. They had failed because they did not distinguish begging as an act of necessity from begging as a chosen habitual profession. Unlike a true crime, begging was dangerous to public order only if it covered a reprehensible intent. Legislators had sought out various tests of that intent. The distinction between sturdy beggar and invalid was germane, obviously, but difficult to draw, since healthy individuals could be forced to beg. A further distinction between domiciled beggars and vagabonds was useful, but previous edicts had acknowledged that many workers needed to travel far from their homes in search of work. Brienne argued that the domiciled beggar was a negligible police problem, since it was rare for a beggar to make a profession of misery in his own community. Perhaps the law might require those forced to seek work or alms outside their parish to obtain certificates to that effect from the authorities in their own parish.[15]

Brienne argued that a system of certificates for the truly needy beggar would fulfill the intent of article 2 of the Declaration of 1764, punishing only those vagabonds whose good character and standing could not be vouched for. He thus shared the assumption that had led Le Trosne, in 1763, to soften his proposal for a harsh law against vagabonds with a lenient view of domiciled beggars. Like Le Trosne also, Brienne reasoned that the resources of organized charity were so far from meeting the need of the domiciled poor that the giving of small amounts in personal encounters probably served an essential function.[16] Brienne went somewhat further still, arguing that it was bad jurisprudence to prohibit a morally praiseworthy action. The harm done by undiscerning almsgivers was negligible, in his view; the policies of charitable institutions were liable to far more serious abuse.[17]

Brienne was willing to concede that the profession or status of begging constituted "a school for vice and crime and that those who pursue it always end up troubling public order," but he could only go so far as to treat begging as an act to be "corrected," not punished. The purpose of a sanction against begging was not to avenge society, but to preserve it. Brienne's proposed system of certificates was based on the assumption that vagrancy thrives on anonymity: "Surveillance, shedding light on it, must destroy it."[18] Government surveillance and public inspection play important parts throughout Brienne's memoir. In the context of "the law," he tends to support the paradox that a government devoted to the liberties of its citizens must also be vigilant in its surveillance of their behavior. Only then can it act swiftly against any breach of its mild laws.[19]

A poorly drawn law on begging had led to an indiscriminate policy of confinement, including even the blind, the mad, and the imbecile: "All have been led away to the *dépôts,* which have become, contrary to their intended purpose, hospitals as well as houses of detention, and in this dual role have truly fulfilled none at all."[20] Once the offense has been redefined, Brienne recommends forced labor as a suitable penalty. He rules out imprisonment as "the worst of all penalties; it gives a dispensation from working, it costs money and brings in nothing, it entertains idleness instead of destroying it."[21] The purpose of the penalty should be to correct the offender and render him "useful to others and to himself." The term of correction should be long enough to instill a habit of working—Brienne recommends three years. The offender should be given no food or amenities beyond the bare necessities, except for what he might earn by hard work. If sturdy beggars work in groups, they can surely earn much of their upkeep. Their expense would "certainly be less than that which [the government] has fruitlessly incurred in the last few years." [22]

A subsection on the "agents of the law" again relates to the experience of the *dépôts,* particularly in controlling abuses committed by the *maréchaussée.* Brienne would give concurrent jurisdiction to ordinary judges in order to compensate for the negligence of the provosts' courts, especially in pursuing investigations. Brienne accords equal importance to ensuring that none escape the net of the law and that no person be improperly arrested: "Liberty is the first property of citizens." [23] The complementary role of liberty and surveillance in Brienne's thinking develops more clearly in his comments on the rationale for a summary jurisdiction. The curtailment of procedural safeguards can be justified, he argues, only if the act to be repressed is simple and obvious, so that there is no room for discretion or error. Furthermore, the penalty must not be of a nature to cause any harm to the guilty. Beggars should therefore not be locked up with criminals; it was an abuse to detain them for long periods in prisons en route to the *dépôts.* Future legislation must in any case take care to avoid giving the occasion for grave abuses, as the procedures of arrest followed since 1768 had done. Those procedures had greatly exceeded in scope the original dispositions of 1764. Intendants may indeed have intervened to ward off abuses, "but it is for the law to answer for what it orders, and one must not rely on the wisdom of those who execute it." Beccaria had expressed himself in almost identical terms in *Dei delitti.* [24]

"To make laws useless: this is the aim of administration." This maxim, stated in the first part of Brienne's memoir, could serve as the motto for the second, concerning administration. [25] Citing the old saw that "the government should not make men paupers," Brienne touches upon several reforms undertaken by Turgot, examples of what can be done to prevent impoverishment:

> Modest taxes distributed and divided without the immense costs that absorb a part, the doors of justice opened to the poor as to the rich, the freedom allowed to each person to use his brawn and brain as he sees fit; all the means in fact that a wise government can employ for the benefit of its people. [26]

Brienne mentions several such reforms in the course of his memoir, including reform of the *corvée* and of municipal government. However, he is quick to note that "general measures" undertaken by the government would not eliminate the need for specific actions to "relieve" mendicity. In a deliberate extension of Montesquieu's dictum, Brienne argues that it is not enough for a man to have work, he must have work that pays him enough to feed himself and his family. If the government responds by employing the poor on large-scale *ateliers de charité,* preferably roads and public works, the general wage rate tends to rise—a desirable result in areas where food prices are high. Brienne drew on his own experience and that of Boisgelin to note that proprietors in Provence and Languedoc had complained of the *ateliers'* tendency to inflate wages. To work as a consistent means of public relief, such *ateliers* should be established in permanent form, "and this necessity is also (to say it in passing) one more reason for accelerating the suppression of the *corvées*."[27]

The economic well-being of society progresses as the government encourages useful behavior, punishes the criminal, and mildly "corrects" the citizen whose actions, while not criminal, burden the society unnecessarily. All such interventions are intended to release the natural springs of action and remove obstacles to freedom. Laisser-faire, as Brienne and Turgot understood it, requires the active surveillance of a national authority. This surveillance, based ideally on enlightened citizens' participation, is not limited to a transitional period, for even in an ideally functioning system of liberty, administration would fulfill essential tasks. Brienne's discussion of mendicity illuminates strikingly the intertwined role of repression and assistance that the state must provide. The two functions are fused in a uniquely edifying manner in Bertier's correctional companies, the *corps des pionniers*. Brienne seems to have caught Bertier's excitement over this scheme, an excitement akin to that of the alchemist who has found a new amalgam that will help purge the contradictions in base matter. Bertier had combined a body of freely enlisted workers with others who signed on as a means of winning release from the *dépôts*. Brienne thought the arrangements devised by Bertier for his recruits well suited to "animate and contain" them. A new "spirit" is breathed into carefully tended vessels.[28]

Brienne apologized for dwelling on the administration of *ateliers* and Bertier's companies, noting that some details of his memoir might seem unrelated to mendicity, "if there were not an essential connection between all the branches of administration."[29] Indeed, Bertier's companies seem to represent the apotheosis of the complementarity that Brienne wishes to establish between law and administration: "The law will punish only in order to turn over to administration those whom it had condemned; their common vigilance must at last return beggars to society, whether by inviting them to work or by forcing them to it."[30]

The remaining portions of Brienne's memoir deal with the reform of charitable administration, beginning with royal legislation on orphans and foundlings. Brienne argues that the policy of requiring unwed mothers to declare their pregnancies has the effect of promoting the very abuses—abortion and infanticide—that it aims to prevent. An enlightened policy, promoting the welfare of families, would act by "offering aid to weakness and misfortune," not by forcing women to chose "between infamy and crime." Brienne sketches the elements of a new policy, and suggests that children arrested for begging should be included in new measures for care of foundlings.[31]

Another category of the poor inappropriately deposited in the *dépôts* was the sick. In principle, sick and invalid beggars were to be cared for in hospitals, but neither hospitals nor *hôtels-Dieu* were equal to the task. The destruction of the *hôtel-Dieu* of Paris by fire in 1772 had provoked intense debate as to whether the old buildings should be rebuilt or whether the city would be better served by constructing facilities on a new plan, possibly in several dispersed sites, or at a healthier location. To this debate, Du Pont de Nemours had contributed a scheme based on principles of charitable administration enunciated in the *Éphémérides*.[32] Although Brienne did not adopt all of Du Pont's ideas, he shared his ideological preference for delivering health care to the indigent in their homes, rather than concentrating them in large establishments.

Turgot himself had argued that large endowed establishments, not accountable for the use of their funds, became self-perpetuating monuments to routine. Brienne articulated throughout his memoir an idea that all administration should be subject to public scrutiny: "Any management that remains secret cannot complain if it falls under suspicion."[33] Small operations and care at home were preferable from this point of view, being easily observed. The poor themselves become the ultimate "inspectors" of such arrangements, finding themselves well placed to judge and make known whether or not the care they receive is satisfactory.[34]

Brienne's attitude toward the proper function of a hospital was evidently affected by the progress of medical opinion, which Turgot brought into closer official consultation with the government.[35] If most cases of illness and the task of relieving the invalid poor could be taken care of in patients' homes, the medical functions that ought to be performed in hospitals could be organized more effectively. Surgery, in particular, should be isolated from the treatment of communicable diseases.[36] The insane likewise required their own therapeutic regimen. It was cruel to inflict the company of the insane on those confined to hospitals for correctional purposes. The remaining correctional functions of hospitals required separate administrative arrangements to be spelled out in a new criminal code.[37]

Brienne arrives finally at the broad question of determining the responsibilities and allocating resources for relief of all kinds. He proposes consolidating all such functions into a nationwide hierarchy of bureaus reaching from the parish to the diocesan level, in a scheme resembling the abbé Baudeau's plan for a "national" system of public assistance. In this context Brienne observed that it would be appropriate to incorporate these functions in a refurbished "municipal" framework for local administration. His proposed diocesan hierarchy was thus a transitional arrangement and a precedent for the type of responsibilities that municipal assemblies might eventually assume. The aspiration for a municipal reform, acknowledged by Turgot and referred to Du Pont de Nemours for study, represents an important dimension of that revolution eagerly awaited in the provinces, that great step forward that Brienne alluded to in writing to Laverdy. In his memoir Brienne writes:

> If there were in the Kingdom a municipal administration, if one could rely on that which already exists in the big cities, it would be no trouble to decide who should be the agents of public charity. But since one should not make one important objective depend on another that is yet more difficult and remote, it is best to set out from the present and make up for the lack of municipal administration with bureaus.[38]

Brienne's recommendations reflect a current of advanced opinion on public administration. Less obviously, perhaps, they indicate how the domain of public relief and charitable administration contributed to the formulation of these new ideas. Several persistent notions have been identified so far: the distinction between administration and justice as it applies to mendicity; a further distinction between measures of prevention and relief; and a concept of public inspection as a means of ensuring accountability and cost-effectiveness. Brienne elaborates another tenet of administration as he describes the functions of the bureaus in his plan. Charitable services, he argues, should be run by bureaus entirely separate from those that manage charitable revenues. The reason why hospitals are currently plagued with debt, he writes, is that "they have predetermined revenues for unpredictable expenses." Hospitals that have surpluses tend to expand their facilities rather than saving; then in years of deficit they must borrow, which leads to ruin.[39] Brienne would consolidate all revenues and convert investments into *rentes,* to protect against inflation. Hospitals would be forbidden to incur debts, and institutions would be financed by fixed formulae of pensions or fees for each inmate or patient according to the cost of services. In other areas of public administration, it should be noted, Turgot was converting *entreprises* contracted for fixed sums into *régies* based on payments for verified expenditures. Charitable administration, as analyzed by Brienne, sees to offer a paradigm for rational budgetary process on a national scale.[40]

Installing a network of bureaus should ensure "that there be established a natural level between their needs and their expenses." Individual bureaus could reallocate surpluses in one fund to serve another, and bureaus at higher levels could coordinate mutual relief between bureaus. The government would provide only a backup role in supplying a "temporary shortfall," although certain funds, including the three deniers per livre of the taille, would be included in the regular pool of charitable resources. In the final analysis, nonetheless, the only safeguard against deficit and indebtedness would lie in the power of these bureaus to recommend impositions to be approved by parlements and intendants. Of course the notorious abuses of the English system of poor rates must be avoided, but taxation must be viewed as "the last and unique resource for every type of public expense."[41]

Brienne unequivocally categorized assistance as a public service. He argued, for example, that recipients of aid should feel no shame in seeing their allotments publicly posted for inspection, since this aid was in no sense a work of "superogation" (in the vocabulary of traditional Christian charity), but rather the discharge of a public obligation that must be subject to public review. If the ultimate responsibility for public welfare imposed a substantial role on the state, Brienne wished to minimize long-term commitments of resources at the national level. Effective government required a consistent economy of effort obtained by coordinating well-informed citizen participation upon a municipal base. Thus the avowal of a state responsibility for public assistance was not inconsistent with the fundamental "economist" view that the primary role of government must be to reduce the scale of that task by enacting policies extinguishing misery rather than perpetuating it.[42]

Nowhere did government damage its credibility more seriously than when it promised to solve a problem and failed. That is what happened, wrote Brienne, when the government failed to resolve the objections originally raised against its orders on mendicity in 1768. If administration was to "march little by little to its perfection," then it must reconcile the recurring objectives of previous piecemeal legislation and distill a "spirit of the laws." Brienne believed that his own memoir was built upon five principles or recurrent practices of French government regarding public charity.[43]

The first of these principles was to proscribe mendicity as "a dangerous profession," a principle that must be coordinated with the others. The second principle was the use of work as a means of voluntary relief or as a forced penalty. The third principle was to assign to parishes and their charitable bureaus the responsibility for relieving the needs of those poor who could not provide for themselves by their work. The fourth was to treat foundlings as wards of the state. And the fifth was to employ bureaus in the administration of charitable ''works,'' by which Brienne meant all the various types of endowments that provided local relief—soup kitchens, nursing care, clothing for the poor, and so on. The last point, taken with the third, was the foundation for Brienne's call for a hierarchy of bureaus to be established as an interlocking national system.[44]

Was administrative reform feasible? Brienne felt that it could be achieved by proceeding on a broad front, not delaying implementation of isolated elements. The plan could work only as an integral whole. The reform of public charity, as far as Brienne was concerned, overlapped the entire range of administrative reform issues. ''All is bound together,'' he wrote, ''since poverty is a single object, one must treat as a whole everything that concerns it.'' Brienne's memoir was not only an appeal to Turgot's critical reason; it was also a challenge to his boldness as a reformer.[45]

Advice from the Provinces

Brienne did not include any sampling or synthesis of the opinions of royal intendants in the final compilation of his commission's working papers. Turgot presumably made available the replies he received to his circulars. Whether or not Brienne studied them in detail, they undoubtedly provided an important context for Turgot's decisions.

Intendants' opinions on the subject of mendicity at the time of Turgot's ministry reflected a generally shared reformist outlook. Turgot and Bertier represented opposite poles of this compact body of opinion. Even those who shared Turgot's belief in the beneficent effect of a free market were inclined to continue the arrest of some dangerous beggars, if only to encourage industrious behavior among the lower orders. Even those who interpreted broadly, as did Bertier, the police functions of the state supported economic and institutional reforms designed to remove the causes that impelled the poor to beg and wander. For most intendants, reform of the *corvée* was a concomitant of expanding the *ateliers de charité*. Most also concurred in the view that those beggars who were unable to work, particularly because of some illness or infirmity, deserved to be supported by their own communities or received in hospitals. They differed in the degree to which they thought these responsibilities could be enforced.[46]

Generally supporting a combination of measures to attack the problem of mendicity, some strongly supported the *dépôts* as an institution, while others were more or less critical. Esmangart at Caen believed that the *dépôt* at Beaulieu provided an essential function in reinforcing work discipline in his *généralité*. Continuing the efforts of Fontette, he invested considerable thought and energy in the design of the *dépôt* and the supervision of its operations. In contrast, his nearby confrere at Alençon, the intendant Jullien, thought that manufacturing workshops in *dépôts* were useless. Sturdy beggars would use the *dépôts* to rest for a spell before resuming their profligate ways, and would never give more than perfunctory and inept attention to the tasks set out for them.[47]

In the correspondence of Jullien, provision for the sick and infirm stands forth as another important issue. Having used the *dépôt* at Alençon as a stopgap refuge for some beggars in this category, Jullien was sensitive to Turgot's statement that it was improper to arrest and confine people who deserved aid rather than punishment. Writing to Turgot's successor in June 1776, Jullien recounted an earlier exchange: "Seeing, Sir, the abhorrence that M. Turgot had for taking away the liberty of people whom need alone obliged to beg, I proposed to him that parishes be forced to feed those deemed unfit to work."[48] The sturdy beggars remaining could be assigned to outdoor public works projects. These solutions, Jullien observed, would have required a new parish levy.

Local conditions shaped intendants' views. Caze de la Bove called for economic development and institutional reform in Brittany. With an impoverished countryside fresh in his mind's eye after a first tour of the province, he urged relief from feudal exactions and begged for *ateliers*. At the same time, he believed that the complaints addressed by the parlement and the Estates of Brittany against the *dépôt* at Rennes could be countered by thoughtful regulation and energetic inspection.[49]

Pleased with Turgot's initiatives of November 1774, the intendant Le Peletier de Mortefontaine at Soissons wrote the minister that there had been no dramatic increase in the number of beggars since the implementation of his order to limit arrests. The only areas showing an increase were those that were relatively rich, confirming the intendant's view that "misery ordinarily seeks out the wealth that can give it succor." With the renewal of free trade in grain, improvement could be expected. But he added as a proviso: "The remedy for mendicity can be expected, nonetheless, from the land alone." He went on to explain: "If the harvests of every kind are abundant, the poor who are in a position to subsist will renounce a profession that degrades them, and if the contrary occurs they will follow in spite of themselves the imperious law of necessity."[50]

Le Peletier shared the view of Turgot and Brienne that parish responsibility for the invalid and aged poor was just in principle. However, economic realities limited its application. Where towns and rich arable provided a surplus of wealth and ease to be taxed, it would work, but it was "absolutely impracticable in the winegrowing parishes, where the inhabitants, generally poor, are more numerous and in no position to aid one another." A general tax might answer the problem, but Le Peletier foresaw drawbacks and obstacles. It would make the common people mindful of their own misery; property owners would raise endless objections to any assessment on them; if the tax were raised as an adjunct to the *taille*, it would fall on the very same poor who were to be helped.[51]

Le Peletier believed, therefore, that an awkward transitional period was unavoidable before a new policy of liberty bore fruit in a prosperity shared by the people. *Ateliers*, a boon to commerce and agriculture, would provide some relief, but never enough to employ the multitude of farm hands when work was at a standstill. "It is therefore just," wrote the intendant, "to use indulgence toward the beggars since they cannot be helped, but at the same time it is wise not to give them a sense of security."[52]

The prudence of a Le Peletier was not far removed from the socially conservative reflexes of most intendants. After dealing with beggars for many years, intendants might be touched by the plight of the suffering poor, but they also became "case-hardened" and skeptical. Nowhere does this attitude emerge more clearly than in the apologia of the intendant of Rouen, Thiroux de Crosne, following the revolt of March 13, 1775, described earlier.[53]

The newly reinstated parlement of Rouen had responded immediately to the revolt, sending its officers to take depositions while the muskets of the local regiment sent in to quell the revolt were still smoking. The *procureur-général* of the parlement, Belbeuf, who had been a thorn in Bertier's side as early as 1768, was not content to lodge a protest in writing; he discussed the problem with Bertier in person when the two happened to meet at Châlons.[54]

In the course of defending his administration against Belbeuf's charges, de Crosne discounted most of them by maintaining Bertier's standard line of defense. Beggars were not confined without due process: none were received except by judgment of the *prévôt* or of a *cour de guerre*. The intendant had even in some cases refused to receive in the *dépôt* some individuals who were more appropriately treated as *mauvais sujets* than as beggars. As for internal discipline, de Crosne argued that the regulation was perhaps too leniently applied. Unlike a hospital, a *dépôt* had to contain dangerous individuals and prevent the escapes "that they plot unceasingly."[55]

Complaints about treatment in the *dépôts* were to be expected. Soup prepared for three hundred people was not for delicate tastes, but the inmates themselves preferred it to rice or to prisoners' rations of bread and water. Allegations about the contents of the soup, especially the reference to mice, could be dismissed out of hand. Linen and straw were changed every week, and the contractor extracted no more than eight or nine livres profit per month from the inmates' work. The chaplain performed the religious offices of the *dépôt,* an infirmary served even the rebellious inmates, and the seriously ill were transferred to the hospital. De Crosne accounted for the case of a raging maniac who died because his illness was not noticed soon enough. He further dismissed the complaint that children judged ipso facto with their parents were neglected and then dumped on local hospitals with atrocious cases of scabies and mange. It was thought to be more in the children's interest not to separate them from their parents, but to concentrate on instilling habits of work in the *dépôt*. In sum, de Crosne believed that complaints were inevitable in dealing with such riffraff: "They will always complain. The privation of liberty, the subjection to work and frugality are unhappy circumstances for a vagabond beggar, and it is impossible that he will find a house of confinement to his liking."

De Crosne also discounted the opinions of ignorant townspeople not far removed from the condition of inmates who shared their feelings. The revolt in the *dépôt* at Rouen occurred simply because the commotion caused by one deranged soldier raised a momentary hope among the men (not among the women) of a general breakout. It is in the nature of things, de Crosne explained, "that a hundred and fifty men in confinement should seek to escape when they think they can." Then he went back over his draft and changed "men" to "reprobates." Other revolts had occurred elsewhere, de Crosne reminded Turgot, including one where six hundred regular soldiers had been called in to restore order.[56]

Undoubtedly the intendants' habitual role as enforcers of royal police made it difficult for them to imagine an entirely new script in which beggars would be essentially free of their tutelage. Habits of authority reinforced habits of belief:

among the categories of the poor was a category of delinquent beggars subject to arrest and correction. As archbishop of Toulouse, Brienne shared this paternalistic reflex, accounting for the correction of beggars with reference to "the spirit of the laws." But he had also developed from his experience in Languedoc a commitment to reform more optimistic on balance than that espoused by many intendants. It most nearly resembled that of the intendant of Soissons.

How directly Brienne was associated with the opinion of the Estates of Languedoc becomes evident from a reading of two of the memoirs he included in the second volume of the *Recueil*. The first of these is an extract of the proceedings of the Estates of Languedoc for December 1, 1772, a session occupied with the report of the commissioners of the Estates to the whole body concerning the administration of the *dépôts de mendicité* since the Estates' last meeting.[57] Most of the problems concerned unforeseen costs arising from the opening of a new, expanded *dépôt* at Montpellier. A more complex permanent operation had entailed new expenses to secure and maintain the property, to feed inmates in a time of high food prices, to cover losses of clothing stolen by escaping inmates, and to raise the remuneration of the doctor, surgeon, and concierge.[58]

Following Brienne's recommendations, the Estates voted the funds requested for the *dépôts,* but urged that measures be taken to prevent further waste of resources on an object that would otherwise be "without limits and without effects."[59] Brienne had put his stamp on this resolution. His ideas on the matter had developed in the course of recurring debates on funding for the *dépôts* ever since the initial request approved with difficulty in 1769.[60] The session of 1772 seems to have sharpened Brienne's reflections, transforming them into a general proposal for reform. A further summation of the proceedings of December 1, 1772, contains key phrases that anticipate those of Brienne's later memoir to Turgot, drawing the outline that would be executed in detail on that canvas.[61] Several points in it suggest an inclination to place the entire problem of mendicity in a municipal framework. The problem of disciplining the *maréchaussée,* for example, leads to observations on the desirability of having a more effective *police des communautés.* The author sharpens the point that "forced" and "voluntary" beggars are being confused in a single operation, saying that *dépôts* are becoming "hospitals and asylums for mendicity rather than a remedy against it."[62]

Brienne's later proposals for a systematic, scientific hospital reform are also prefigured in the Estates' final memoir of 1772. "Hospitals," he declared, "should contain only those who cannot be helped separately." These proper functions, he added, need to be categorically guaranteed by public tax revenues raised in the province as necessary.[63] Equally important, efficient management required a rational determination of uniform rates for the services provided by hospitals. The phrases of the memoir explaining the problem of indebtedness would appear again in Brienne's report to Turgot: "A variable expense should have a variable revenue proportioned to it. The rich hospitals dissipate, the poor ones borrow and go to ruin."[64] Brienne's later argument that budget problems could be managed by setting uniform rates within the jurisdiction of a bureau probably drew inspiration from the experience of the Estates of Languedoc. For example, the Estates had responded to a request for a rate increase from the Hôpital St. Éloy at Montpellier by establishing a general *tarif* for sick beggars received anywhere in the province. This regional perspective also contributed, no doubt, to Brienne's view that the reform of the *dépôts* was interlocked with general problems of hospital reform. In the 1772 memoir, we find these assorted problems referred to more than once as an "ensemble" requiring a coordinated solution.[65]

The Estates' memoirs of 1772 seem to represent an important stage in Brienne's thinking about the the problem of work. The Estates complained that in the *dépôts* the inmates "stagnate in idleness, fall sick, perish in great number, and those who escape leave more beggarly and reprobate than they came in."[66] The solution, of course, was to employ inmates on public works, referred to in the proceedings as *galères de terre,* and in the ensuing memoir as *ateliers ambulants.* The only fair test of the "voluntary" beggar was to offer him work and to force him to it if he refused. Thus the *ateliers ambulants* would include beggars who had freely chosen to work. These workers would be rewarded by good maintenance and by pay that would secure them from the necessity of begging upon their release. A stricter regimen would be employed for those who initially refused to enroll or who deserted their tasks. Preventing escapes would be harder than within the walls of the *dépôts,* but well-organized supervisory brigades could answer this objection.[67]

Brienne's vision of the economic role of *ateliers* emerged as a model for national reform reinforcing Turgot's experiences in the Limousin. He noted specifically that the absence of the *corvée* in Languedoc made it practicable to employ work companies wherever road work and public works would otherwise be contracted for. At the same time, debates on penal reform—from Montesquieu to Beccaria—echoed most audibly in a remark on the possibility that the galleys might be reserved as a severer grade of punishment. It was probably not a useful approach, the author argued: mendicity, "which is the seed of all crimes, will be more effectively curbed, like crimes themselves, by police, vigilance, and gentle means employed consistently than by the severity of punishments."[68]

The response to "forced" beggars raised a host of hospital reform issues. In an aside that prefigures the broad hospital reform proposals of 1775, the memoir of 1772 alludes to the "great question" whether the *hôtels-Dieu* are necessary as is believed—"whether bringing together the sick is not itself the most dangerous of sicknesses."[69] As long as *hôtels-Dieu* are used in the care of the sick, beggars in need of their care should be sent there, finance must be provided, and royal authority must be used to enforce equitable rates. The memoir refers specifically to the inadequate palliatives used to treat the common lingering illnesses of beggars—scurvy, mange, and venereal disease. If beggars are to be deemed fit for work, they must be cured of such ailments. If beggars are not adequately treated, either in *hôtels-Dieu* or by expert care in the *dépôts,* then arresting them "tends only to make them perish." Here, a traditional sense of "scandal" has been brought up to date in terms of scientific medical observation and a concept of the rights of a citizen.[70]

If Brienne's memoir of 1775 owes its basic structure and essential concepts to his provincial lucubrations of 1772, the *Recueil* indicates some of the key points where Brienne's views received reinforcement and elaboration. The idea of transforming the *dépôts* into *ateliers ambulants* coincided with a vision based on a variety of local experiments, notably Bertier's own *corps des pionniers.* Bertier provided detailed memoirs on their administration, and Brienne, as noted, urged that they receive expanded government support as an alternative to incarcerating beggars in *dépôts*. In addition to Bertier's blueprint, several other memoirs recommended other variants of the same basic ideas as a remedy for mendicity.[71]

A further set of memoirs deals with welfare and hospital reform measures: reconstructing the *hôtel-Dieu* of Paris, providing new cadres of administration, dealing with the problems of orphans in new ways, and making better provision for convalescents so that they will not be arrested for begging.[72] Willing in 1772 to entertain the notion that *hôtels-Dieu* themselves might not be the ideal solution to all problems of "forced" mendicity, Brienne encountered a wealth of proposals that helped him spell out a commitment to sweeping institutional reform. Brienne's ideas converged with those of Du Pont de Nemours and others in support of a strictly medical rationale for hospitalization, complemented by nursing care and medical visits in patients' homes. This reorganization was part of a new approach to mendicity that would treat poverty as an "ensemble," as a "single object."

Some projects addressed to Turgot did not find their way into Brienne's *Recueil*. The municipal officers of Reims, encouraged by a verbal commitment at the time of the *sacre,* submitted a proposal that would have placed the police of beggars and the provision of assistance under municipal control, with a large place for the clergy. Turgot referred the proposal to the intendant of Châlons, and in December wrote in his own hand to rule out the use of the clergy's *don gratuit* for this local charitable purpose. Suggesting that other funds be identified, Turgot explained that the king did not intend to transfer responsibilities and funding for the police of beggars out of royal hands until a general review of police led to new dispositions. He asked nonetheless to see a copy of the regulation for the alms bureau at Reims.[73]

Some of the projects outlined in Brienne's *Recueil* were strictly local in scope but exemplary in concept. The bishop of Lyons, for example, had ordered existing confraternities in the city of Bourg to amalgamate their charitable functions exclusively under the aegis of the alms bureaus. The leading merchants of Carcassonne, dependent on a fluctuating trade with the Levant, decided to supplement the resources of the hospital with regular workshops for the unemployed. Financing their alms bureaus from monthly contributions rather than from fixed endowments, they could regularly provide for about a hundred poor.[74]

Of still broader significance were the measures devised in Toulouse, Brienne's diocesan seat and the second locus of the intendance of Languedoc, watched over by the intendant at Montpellier with the aid of the powerful subdelegate of Toulouse. The Toulousains had developed a system that was beginning to reach beyond the city walls to encompass an entire region.[75] *Bureaux de charité* offered "the double resource of charity and industry," and established "a discipline and oversight from which the beggar cannot escape or extricate himself." Since the receipt of aid was not to be viewed as an object for shame if it were truly needed, the magistrates of Toulouse abolished the category of *pauvres honteux,* a point that Brienne incorporated in his memoir for Turgot.[76]

The regulation that accompanied the memoir adumbrated a regional scheme for public assistance reaching throughout the provinces of Languedoc and Guyenne. The provision that local parishes outside the city could send patients whose need was duly certified to the hospital of Toulouse conferred an explicit regional function on this institution. Brienne included in the *Recueil* a complete set of the standardized forms used by the bureaus of Toulouse, a network of paper emanating from a municipality and serving as a model for the bureaucratic grid that would be required for a national system of public assistance.[77]

During the course of 1775 the subdelegate of Toulouse, Raynal, addressed a memoir to the intendant Saint-Priest at Montpellier in support of the Estates' call to put sturdy beggars to work on roads and other public works in the province. In this memoir of 1775, not included in Brienne's *Recueil*, Raynal also supported a proposal that provoked debate after Brienne incorporated it in his memoir, namely, the suggestion that local officials—in Languedoc, the "consuls"—give certificates to the old and infirm domiciled poor, allowing them to beg within two leagues of their homes. Saint-Priest forwarded Raynal's memoir to Turgot with further comments of his own. Turgot replied on September 25, 1775, that "he would keep his reflections in mind in the course of the work ordered by the King in this matter and which he is about to take up."[78]

Three weeks later, on October 17, Turgot was at Trudaine's château at Montigny discussing Brienne's memoir, and wrote the following note to the abbé de Véri:

> We have come to Montigny with M. de Malesherbes, M. Albert, and the archbishop of Toulouse in order to busy ourselves principally with plans for suppressing beggary and for relieving poverty, for one must not confine oneself, as M. de l'Averdy did, to suppressing the one without providing for the other.[79]

The abbé de Véri had been among those who read Brienne's memoir and submitted their reflections on it to Turgot. Summarizing his own memoir, Véri expresses the conviction, in line with that of Turgot, that pious foundations must be reorganized with the aid of the Church, if royal funds were to have any impact. He also thought that licensed begging would be a necessary palliative for the needs of domiciled beggars. The best law to imitate would be that of Charles-Emmanuel III of Piedmont, a law that allowed begging in the parish of birth or domicile. He foresaw the objection, however, that many who went in search of work far from home might also be forced to beg. Turgot complimented the abbé de Véri on his "excellent" observations, which, he said, "come close to our ideas."[80]

One might expect to find relatively little debate over issues prepared so thoroughly. But Turgot wished to go further than Brienne in dismantling repressive laws against beggars. Under pressure from Bertier and his allies, Turgot compromised on the need for repression, while he groped toward a strategy for initiating a system of public assistance that he had accepted in principle.

At the Château of Montigny, October 1775: Philosophers Confer

Trudaine, the host at Montigny and perhaps Turgot's closest confidant, set the terms of discussion. Praising highly Brienne's analysis of what fell within the purview of administration, he agreed that large establishments were generally impossible to administer and that relief in the home was preferable. He pointedly seconded Brienne on the need to provide "municipal administration" in the greater part of the kingdom. Agreeing with Brienne that welfare reform should not be made to depend on this even larger issue, he desired nonetheless that any new welfare scheme be based on civil units of jurisdiction, so that it would be compatible with later municipal reforms.[81]

Passing quickly from consensus to critique, Trudaine took issue with Brienne's proposals for what the law should prescribe. Carrying further the logic of Brienne's own argument on law and administration, he concluded that administrative prevention and remedy were the sole efficacious measures to be taken: "If the vices of administration produce a true poverty, then it is impossible for the law to pronounce a penalty against a forced crime, or rather against an act that, not being free, can in no case be a crime." A law without utility, he argued, was the most dangerous— laws on sorcery provided a case in point. In particular: "When someone wants to arrest a man or get rid of him, it will be said that he begs: and whether the thing be true or false, it is sufficient that it *can be,* for it to give rise to many injustices." Trudaine dismissed all past laws with a sweep of the hand. Abrogate them all: they had not been in effect at the time they were "renewed" in 1764.[82]

In practice, argued Trudaine, the distinction between the domiciled and non-domiciled beggars by means of certificates was not feasible. Those who would be obliged to keep them were poor, illiterate, and not accustomed to keeping papers they could not read and whose contents they could not remember. In a Voltairean phrase, Trudaine noted that such provisions were contrary to the requirement that laws should be simple and clear. Although Brienne had set store by the distinction between vagabond and beggar, Trudaine found neither guilty of any crime. The poor individual, he argued, "should be allowed to be a vagrant, for several professions require it; he should be allowed to beg, because he may not be able to find work, and then he is without resources." To speak of begging as a profession was absurd, because "beggary is never a profession by choice."[83]

Why keep any penalties for begging? Laws should be as few as possible and only for crimes committed against men as well as against the law. Calling for exclusively administrative remedies, Trudaine enthusiastically endorsed Brienne's arguments concerning *ateliers* and the abolition of the *corvées.* He praised Bertier's company of *pionniers,* but denied they might serve as a model for forced labor— they succeeded precisely because they obscured the stigma of compulsion.[84]

Trudaine's arguments were reinforced by the impetuous rhetoric of the arch-bishop of Aix, who could not attend the meeting but submitted his arguments in writing. The second part of Brienne's memoir, said Boisgelin, made the first part unnecessary. The fault for beggary lay with the administration and with the break-down of hospital institutions. Unjust and unequal taxation was the greatest single cause of mendicity: "Whoever follows the more or less obvious relations between the faults of the government and mendicity [sees] that it is the government that becomes guilty when beggars multiply, and that when it inflicts penalties upon them, it punishes them for its errors."[85] Was this perhaps the theme that had brought Boisgelin's powerful coronation sermon to the verge of indiscretion?

Wielding a philosophe's pen, Boisgelin unmasked the social bias of laws against beggary. To ask alms, to travel at will, and to keep one's plans to oneself were surely free acts: "In the classes of ease and wealth, reasonable citizens alter their plans and undertakings of all kinds unceasingly. Why should people made more inconsistent by a crude upbringing not have the liberty to fall into the same contradictions?''[86]

The legitimate reasons for begging could not be distinguished from the pretexts. The laws erred in punishing not acts committed, but acts feared: ''Why should a single class of men be governed by principles and by laws that all other classes would reject as the extreme degree of injustice and tyranny?'' Personally, Boisgelin recoiled at the repressive model of a society under constant surveillance: ''The police armed with the law resembles the head of Medusa that kills all those whom it looks upon.''[87]

Finally, Boisgelin objected to the *dépôts* as established, in remarks that followed closely what he said elsewhere about the *dépôt* at Aix. He spoke of ''these horrible *dépôts* where the poor are heaped together and breathe an infected air. The meager portion that is given to them does not suffice to feed them; their forces are consumed by hunger and contagion.'' Whatever work was provided in the *dépôts* was forced labor and thus tainted: ''The parlement, which constantly rejected the penalty of the galleys, will not wish to admit it under another denomination.''[88]

Brienne replied to Boisgelin. He maintained his position that some laws against begging were still needed, even if administration supplied the essential remedy for mendicity. Laws of police were required in order to regulate some acts that were not criminal in themselves. Certainly he could agree that police laws should be limited in scope and not arbitrary, but ultimately, ''the equity of police is measured by the necessity of the means that it employs to maintain good order and public tranquillity.''[89]

But if Brienne had reason to defend his position, it was Bertier who was directly under attack at Montigny.[90] Bertier had much to answer for: the condition of inmates in the *dépôts,* the charge of arbitrary arrest procedures, and Brienne's charge that the *dépôts* had ineffectively combined the functions of hospital and prison. Parts of Bertier's lively defense have been cited: his insistence that he had played a moderating role on Laverdy's commission, his protestation that he had favored the *dépôts* only as places of temporary detention from which every means would be sought to return beggars to their communities.[91]

Apologizing for the real shortcomings of the *dépôts,* Bertier noted that public works were long postponed, and that ''no attempt was even made to put hospitals in better order, and to have invalid beggars cared for there.'' In consequence, as Brienne rightly observed, the *dépôts* had been forced to serve as hospitals and prisons both. They would have functioned far better as simple *maisons de force.* lonetheless, Bertier defended his own role in correcting the worst shortcomings of the *dépôts,* in instituting the *corps de pionniers,* and in bringing budget within the limits originally prescribed.[92]

Agreeing that the problem of mendicity could only be solved by a broad range of administrative measures, Bertier argued that the need for repression would remain. Even if the principles and the ''wise views'' of the archbishop of Toulouse and of Trudaine were adopted, it would be difficult to dispense with the *dépôts.* ''There is but one *maison de force* in France for the people, which is Bicêtre,'' he noted, adding, ''Everyone knows it is always overflowing.'' Bertier was certainly aware that Malesherbes, present at Montigny, was involved in a review of the use of *lettres de cachet.* One of Malesherbes' concerns was the apparently haphazard nature of the grounds for imprisonment at Bicêtre.[93]

Passing to the offensive, Bertier asked his colleagues rhetorically, "What is to be done, then [if one destroys the *dépôts*], with the four hundred reprobates in the *dépôt* at Pontoise, and with the several thousand who are in the other *dépôts?*" Imperfect as they might be, the *dépôts* had served a purpose. Bands had previously taken their toll from farmers in the Brie, the Beauce, and the region of Chartres, "and," he remarked, "I have seen several farmers whom they cost seven to eight hundred livres a year." Venturing a reproof of Turgot, Bertier observed that the scourge had for a while abated, but that since the arrests of beggars had been relaxed, it had broken out anew.[94]

Hardly pausing to draw breath, Bertier crisply set forth his own recommendations in terse summary form:

> After these observations, which are rather my justification than an opinion, I will say:
>
> 1. That I adopt in their entirety the principles of the Archbishop of Toulouse,
> 2. That I fear the law like M. de Trudaine; that I fear it all the more because there is no need for it, because former laws provide sufficient titles for executing all that is proposed at this time.
> 3. That it is indispensable to keep the *dépôts* while reducing them to a single one per *généralité;*
> 4. But that an effort must be made to return to the hospitals, as promptly as possible, all the infirm who are contained there,
> 5. To force the parishes to feed the good poor who will be released,
> 6. To transfer to the corps of provincial workers the individuals who are fit to work,
> 7. To issue an ordinance or title of some kind to the corps in order to retain the officers and prevent desertion.
> 8. That one could establish forced labor as a penalty for desertion (then each company would have a certain number of convicts sentenced to hard labor whom it would have to guard, and who would serve: one could even add other criminals).
> 9. That I request that the number of provincial workers employed on the canal of Burgundy be raised to 2,000 men, so that I can establish there a complete corps of administration, the costs whereof can be paid by the extent of the works, and which can make known all the advantages that may be drawn from this establishment which, in my speculations, can change the military system in France, and bring savings of several millions. (In these 2,000 workers, I can accept 400 convicts who would cost nothing.)
> 10. That it will be necessary to continue some arrests and confinements in the *dépôts,* to continue the elimination of the vagabonds who are a vexation to farmers, and to halt the emigration of young people who seek to shake off family discipline, and finally, in order to restrain dangerous individuals: it would suffice to write to the intendants without changing the orders to the *maréchaussée.*
> 11. I would desire the establishment of a regular commission that would be empowered, at the summons of the *procureur-général,* to see to the collec-

tion of funds that have been taken away from hospitals, examine their pre-
. sent administration, and initiate the reunions, changes, and reforms needed.[95]

Thus Bertier fought to preserve the *dépôts,* while accepting a curtailment of
their number. He welcomed a restriction in the categories of inmates they would
receive, and a corresponding enlargement of the role given to his companies of
provincial workers (referred to also as *pionniers).* He supported the call for welfare
reform, although he emphasized the traditional principle of parish responsibility.
Any institutional reform of hospitals should be overseen by the parlement, the *procureur-général,* and a special commission of the royal council.

What Turgot himself contributed to the discussion at Montigny lay unnoticed
until recently in a text entitled, "Mendicité et autres objets relatifs de M. Ducroc."[96] The text offers the most direct evidence to date of Turgot's personal contribution to the debate over Brienne's memoir.

The minister-philosopher comes directly to the point in his opening words. "I
think that it is a waste of time to try to frame a law directly against beggary and
here is why." He follows Trudaine, but stops short of Boisgelin, in criticizing
Brienne's proposed system of licensed begging. His arguments are at once libertar-
ian and practical. A law, he notes, would have to be framed in such a way that
those who deliberately chose a vagabond life of habitual idleness could be posi-
tively identified. Such cases would have to be distinguished from the *cas fortuit,*
the act legally defined as being beyond the voluntary control of the individual. A
judge must be able to apply such criteria with certainty, "otherwise one would be
left in a vague and arbitrary situation as one is today."[97]

Certificates would be a license for professional begging, raising endless possi-
bilities for fraud. Turgot drew upon his knowledge of the rural poor to amplify the
objections of Boisgelin and Trudaine:

> The poor man when he travels has neither trunk nor portfolio; everything that he
> has on him is exposed like himself to all the onslaughts of the elements. When his
> certificate is ragged, worn, full of holes, covered with grease and grime, in a word,
> illegible, this cannot be held against him as a crime—whatever it pleases him to
> say it contains, he will have to be believed.[98]

Practised rogues would circumvent any precautions. Brienne had done well,
thought Turgot, to show how easy it was to err in making beggary a crime. Any
legal definition of habitual beggary "will always be too close to injustice in its
disposition, and to arbitrariness in its application, for one's sense of justice, if
healthy and precise, to be happy." Awkward in phrasing but forthright and un-
equivocal in substance, this is an important statement of liberal principle applied to
the rights of the poor.

Brienne believed that what was true and just could not always have eluded
previous efforts to formulate it. But for Turgot, the "spirit of the laws"—in this
case, at least—was a will-o'-the-wisp. There was no law to be found: "from the
fact that one has been sought in vain until now, I am all the more inclined to
conclude that there is none suitable, and the effort to find this law must be given
up."[99]

Turgot liked better Brienne's argument for a close surveillance of those considered likely to commit crimes. Since some beggars and vagabonds were quite

innocent and others harmful, police surveillance, as applied to any *"frippons"* or rogues, would have to take the place of any general law. Beggars could not be arrested unless they committed crimes, including threats, violence, carrying weapons, and unlawful assembly, against which there were laws that merely needed to be enforced.[100]

The tone of Turgot's remarks shifts from asperity to unalloyed praise as he turns to Brienne's discussion of administrative remedies:

> The more I reflected on it, the more enchanted I was with it. It consoles me completely for the emptiness in which my reflections on the first part had left me, and I quite certainly believe that by employing the means presented in this second part, all that is treated in the first part will prove to be unnecessary.[101]

Turgot accepted Brienne's proposed solution for the reform of hospitals and welfare administration: "everything set forth in this second part is excellent in theory and I see nothing that does not appear possible to execute in practice." Clearly excited by the prospect, Turgot shared a momentary effusion of confidence: "This is a quite encouraging point and one which shows that, with a constant desire to do good, one can accomplish anything by not forcing measures."[102]

"Not forcing measures" meant that the first steps would have to be modest. Turgot repeated, in the course of his remarks, Brienne's point that welfare reform should not be suspended while awaiting the creation of a new municipal administration. He shared with Brienne and Trudaine the belief that the two areas of reform were related. Shortly before meeting at Montigny, Turgot had written to Du Pont to acknowledge receipt of the latter's draft of a plan for municipal administration. In that draft Du Pont argued that local supervision of funds for public works could be most effectively coordinated with the *police des pauvres*.[103]

Mulling over Brienne's words, Turgot went on to suggest that the first order of business should be to proceed with those tasks presenting the fewest difficulties, make plans accordingly, begin executing them immediately, and follow them "with some vigor." First of all, the expansion of public *ateliers*, a requisite step once the *corvée* was abolished, could easily be coordinated through instructions to the intendants. The second point was to reorganize the *maréchaussée* so that it would depend entirely on the civil authority (that is, the intendant), rather than on the military administration. Here Turgot mentioned his own experience as intendant and digressed on the folly of trying to economize by having the tasks of the *maréchaussée* done by regular troops. Instead, the number of the *maréchaussée* should be increased, and their status restored to that which had been established in 1724.[104]

The third point was the easiest of all: it was a matter of introducing a new technique. The government could bring to France German women who could teach the method of raising foundlings without wet nurses by means of goats' milk. Malesherbes had proposed this innovation, and Turgot believed that it might lead in turn to further institutional reform in the care of orphans and foundlings.[105]

These three initiatives could be launched immediately. On these points, he added, "I see no reason not to apply a certain dose of resolution and even of stubbornness, which will not be lost." Clearly, Turgot stopped short of any official inauguration of Brienne's plan for institutional reform. Just as clearly, he was groping for a strategy that would overcome the inertia of existing charitable arrangements. In his concluding remarks, Turgot alluded to the difficulties to be expected, and called on Malesherbes to suggest some of the ways in which a general reform might be sparked:

> As for the rest—that is to say, the hospitals, the *hôtels-Dieu,* the particular works of charity that will diminish; the new agents who will on the one hand take in the amounts to be distributed and on the other provide for the disbursement of the revenue—that is where the greatest obstacles are to be surmounted, because that is where there is the greatest particular interest to be sacrificed. Eloquent examples that refute by the evidence of facts—reasonings against which reason alone can do nothing—are the unique means of getting through. Languedoc, Brittany, Artois, and Flanders present for this [purpose] quite good possibilities which I shall not enter into in detail, because M. de Malesherbes has appeared persuaded by them, and he can better than anyone set them forth and put them to good use.[106]

How the meeting went from this point is not entirely clear. Malesherbes' annotations on his copy of Brienne's memoir reflect the difficulties that occurred to him on a first reading, but his review of "eloquent examples" to be taken as models for reform does not appear to have been transcribed.[107] Among the difficulties to be anticipated, he noted first of all that the diocese was probably not the best administrative unit for a national system. It would create the impression that all was in the hands of the bishops, "and not all bishops are the archbishop of Toulouse or of Aix." Second, Malesherbes doubted the wisdom of a new imposition, which seemed liable to the notorious flaws of the English Poor Law. Charity was likely to diminish, and the control of expenses might grow lax. Turning to broad issues of correctional police, he expressed disquiet over the power of fathers to commit members of their families to detention for reasons not inspected by any court. Royal authority, in turn, was riddled with arbitrary principles of action stemming from a view of a father's rights that could no longer bear rational scrutiny. In spite of these doubts, he felt that Brienne went too far in attacking the legal concept of vagrancy. He doubted that mere surveillance could be as effective as Brienne hoped in policing an estimated hundred thousand vagrants throughout the kingdom.[108]

What, then, were the immediate consequences of the meeting at Montigny? Confirming the main lines of Turgot's memoir, Bertier reported that there had been general agreement on Brienne's treatment of administration. But so many objections had arisen in the discussion of law and the repression of begging that further meetings were planned. Of the three questions involved in the first part, only the one concerning the proper agents of the law produced accord. All agreed that the intendants and the *maréchaussée* were the proper agents, and that the *maréchaussée* should be placed more directly under the control of the intendant. The system for distinguishing legitimate from illegitimate beggars by issuing certificates gave rise to general criticism. Agreement was lacking whether begging should be considered a crime. Finally, some argued that public works should not be used as a penalty.[109]

Any new law on begging, it was agreed, should be delayed "until the new resources offered to present beggars and to the poor will have rendered them guilty in fact of whatever crime it was desired to prescribe." Pending a further meeting, several decisions were made: (1) all captures would be suspended or perhaps reduced; (2) the number of *dépôts* would be reduced in order to retain only the notoriously dangerous; (3) beggars with no particular mark against them would be sent home; (4) the beggar's parish or local hospitals would be requested to take the invalid beggars presently confined, or to pension them in the countryside; (5) the young people were to be signed on in the companies of provincial workers presently established, and their number raised to two thousand, if appropriate, for the canal of Burgundy; and finally (6) the decision was made to eliminate, as of January 1, 1776, the services of the company that had obtained the general contract for the feeding and upkeep of beggars in the *dépôts*.[110]

These decisions, relayed to intendants in November 1775, essentially reaffirmed the policy outlined in the provisional measures of the year before and carried them a step further. The *dépôts* were to be reduced immediately in number to one per *généralité*, a move that Bertier had agreed to. In a further step, Turgot announced on November 21 that all but five *dépôts,* those of Tours, St. Denis, Bourg-en-Bresse, Châlons, and Bordeaux, were to be closed by May 1776. By that time no merely "suspect" beggars were to be kept in confinement, and those judged truly "dangerous" were to be transferred under guard to the five remaining *dépôts.* Thus Turgot conceded that a certain number of royally funded *maisons de force* were needed outside the city of Paris.[111]

The function of correcting sturdy beggars was to be entirely reorganized in the form desired by Brienne and promoted by Bertier, namely, by means of companies of provincial workers. A large portion of Turgot's circular of November 21 was accordingly devoted to explaining the procedure of enrolling young men in these companies and sending them to the *caserne* at Roule, near the *dépôt* at St. Denis. Turgot paid close attention to these enlistments, observing in one instance that the youths in question need not be accompanied on their designated routes by the *maréchaussée,* "for they are destined to be free."[112]

Yielding to counsels of prudence, Turgot instructed intendants that they should continue to order the arrest of "able-bodied beggars openly exercising the profession of begging habitually and who are denounced by persons whose word is to be trusted." However, brigade commanders were to forward denunciations for verification by the intendant, after which the beggars could be freed or retained. Turgot gave a further incentive to empty the *dépôts* by ordering that all those currently detained who were not "dangerous" but were able to earn a living be sent home "with routes," that is, with a daily travel allowance to be disbursed at assigned checkpoints. Here Turgot in effect urged intendants to follow the example of liberality he had instituted at Limoges to the dismay of Bertier.[113]

Since the able-bodied beggar would be put to work outside the *dépôts,* Turgot announced in a circular of November 22 that the contract for the provisioning of the *dépôts* would be abrogated as of December 31, 1775. Inasmuch as the *dépôts* would henceforth contain only those inmates not suited for productive labor, one of the main conditions justifying the original contract no longer obtained. This decision reflected Turgot's long-standing conviction that beggars could not be transformed into willing or productive workers in the coercive setting of the *dépôts.*[114]

Of the points mentioned in the memorandum by Bertier, the only one not included in Turgot's instructions of November 21 and 22 was the assignment of sick beggars to hospitals. Turgot did however tell intendants that those inmates of *dépôts* who were unable to work and who could not draw on family resources might be assigned a pension of thirty to forty livres "to aid them in living the first year." Parishes would thus be relieved of the immediate burden of supporting infirm beggars released from the *dépôts*. This stopgap measure should perhaps be taken as a presage of further reform.[115]

The debates on mendicity at Montigny brought into sharper focus the interlocking consequences of economic and fiscal reform. Indeed, the legislative package that would come to be known a few months later as the Six Edicts was adumbrated in Brienne's memoir. Abolishing the guilds would free the market for labor and increase opportunities for employment. Abolishing the royal *corvée* would encourage agricultural production; the tax collected in its place from all proprietors of the land could be recirculated through public *ateliers*. Brienne's advocacy of projects to employ the able-bodied poor through a permanent system of *ateliers* and through Bertier's *pionniers* harmonized with the arguments in support of the Six Edicts. Abolition of the *corvée* would also entail administrative rationalization carrying over into the domain of poor relief. According to Du Pont de Nemours, Turgot intended to consolidate into a single fund the 18.5 million livres for public works, the 10 million assigned to replace the *corvée,* together with 800,000 added from the budgets of *ponts et chaussées* (public highways) and the entire 800,000 allotted for navigable canals.[116]

There is no reason to infer from Turgot's deferral of Brienne's blueprint of reform that his endorsement of it was insincere. If, as Camille Bloch argued, the elimination of mendicity was the touchstone of Turgot's policies as intendant and minister, it is also true that Turgot shared the strategic assumption of his fellow *économistes* that a government that no longer "made men poor" would be better able to sustain effective charitable institutions. Turgot apparently agreed with Brienne that the reform of these institutions was intertwined with questions of municipal reform, but he raised to a more general level Brienne's observation in this context, saying, "One should not make an important object depend on another that is more difficult and more distant." [117] The "spirit of the citizen," essential to a system of liberty, would have to be aroused in stages. In this connection it is noteworthy that Bertier composed a summary of Brienne's memoir, dated October 21, 1775, containing several revisions that may signal Turgot's plans for implementation. The most important revision was the replacement of the diocese by a civil unit of jurisdiction in the prescribed hierarchy of bureaus for the distribution of aid.[118]

Political considerations would have dictated a prudent deferral of hospital reform. The meeting at Montigny occurred in the midst of a series of new initiatives constituting what Edgar Faure described as the "second wind" in Turgot's reforming ministry. The appointment of Malesherbes as minister of the royal household in July signaled a curtailment in expenditures and enhanced the prospect for judicial reforms championed by him. Turgot wrote Du Pont on September 23 that he planned to take ten days at the end of October for "some truly useful projects." Turgot's retreat to Montigny followed immediately a private interview with the king in which the decision was made to appoint the reformer St. Germain to the post of minister of war, left vacant by the death of du Muy. If at this point Turgot wished to build a consensus in favor of major economic and fiscal reforms, it would have been impolitic to challenge the rights and prerogatives of hospital administrators and raise the specter of new tax levies for the poor. The protectors of the existing charitable order were to be found in the parlements, at court, and in municipal councils. This is probably what Turgot had in mind when he said that it was this part of Brienne's memoir that contained "the greatest obstacles to surmount, because that is where there is the greatest particular interest to be sacrificed."[119]

Turgot did not entirely ignore hospital reform after Montigny. A decree regulating the indebtedness of hospitals and municipalities attacked one of the major problems identified by Brienne.[120] Turgot's initiative in establishing the Société Royale de Médecine gave indirect support to the task of redefining the mission of ancient hospitals for the poor in more strictly medical terms, as Brienne urged. The urgent need to rebuild and reform the *hôtel-Dieu* of Paris made the capital a natural amphitheater for a strategy of reform by experts. In this context, Turgot's attention to Malesherbes project to feed goat's milk to foundlings seems less incongruous than it might otherwise.[121]

The drafting of the Six Edicts began in November, shortly after Montigny. Brought before the royal council in January, they were sent to the parlement of Paris for registration at the beginning of February. The ensuing debate in the parlement allied many of the magistrates with Turgot's opponents at court. Miromesnil, keeper of the seals and chief judicial official in royal councils, opposed the edicts. Formerly *premier président* of the parlement of Rouen, he had been exiled under Maupeou. When Louis XVI restored the parlements, Miromesnil took the disgraced Maupeou's place. It was especially damaging, therefore, when Miromesnil condemned Turgot's proposal to replace the *corvée* with a tax on proprietors as an attack on the constitution of the kingdom. The image of Turgot as purveyor of despotism was confirmed in a *lit de justice* of March 13, 1776: the young king overrode the objections of the parlement in person and ordered that the Six Edicts be registered. Less than two months later, on May 12, Turgot was dismissed.[122] His Six Edicts were rescinded.

Marked as the destroyer of ancient privileges in the matter of taxation, Turgot was also portrayed as the destroyer of wise police precautions. Bertier relates that the parlement opposed Turgot's closing of the majority of the *dépôts,* and that Turgot agreed, in a last meeting with him before leaving office, to reestablish eleven of the *dépôts* he had closed.[123] Perhaps the image of Don Quixote releasing the galley convicts had crossed Turgot's mind: at Montigny, he spoke wryly of the *maréchaussée* as "la Sainte Hermandad." The sense that he had loosed the forces of disorder by abandoning a prudent system of police found expression in a doggerel verse of the day entitled "Turgot's system":

> Flood the state with brigands,
> Multiply the beggars;
> Multiply misfortune's sum,
> And stir up all the peasants:
> These are the odious fruits
> This great man's system brings.[124]

Condorcet spoke for the defense in a biography published in 1786. Knowing Turgot's projects intimately, he waxed especially enthusiastic over the new municipal assemblies that Turgot would have promoted, had he stayed in office:

Educational establishments, houses of charity, the relief given to the poor, would have been administered by these assemblies, according to a general plan given by the government; a plan already prepared by M. Turgot and which, like all the others, would have borne the stamp of his genius. Thus establishments of charity would no longer have degraded or corrupted the human species, swallowing up future generations. Families would have been sustained and misfortune succored, without encouraging idleness and depravity.[125]

Not all partisans of enlightenment shared this enthusiasm. The abbé de Montlinot wrote in a pamphlet of 1789 that "a famous man" had wanted to establish "a ladder of *bureaux de charité* in France that would divide France into two parts: the poor, the vagabonds, and those who would have to administer them.[126]

Opinion could not easily be satisfied. A repressive policy elicited a sense of scandal; a more liberal provision for the poor and a respect for their rights evoked the specter of a costly administration and the fear of a spirit of license among the lower orders.

8

Old Medicine and New

Looking back in 1778, Bertier could allude to Turgot's ministry as an unfortunate episode that had only momentarily frustrated a lengthy campaign to eradicate mendicity: "the dearness of grains and the suspension ordered by M. Turgot arrested the complete success that had been expected." Since Turgot's departure, the *lieutenant de police* of Paris (the restored Lenoir) and Bertier had devised new measures. By the beginning of 1778, Bertier's machine was credited with having eliminated organized bands of vagabonds and greatly reduced the total number of beggars:

> the new generation no longer enters this profession, most of the former beggars have returned to work and to agriculture, some ten thousand young people have gone to the armed forces, either of France or of the colonies, the children without resource have been placed with farmers, or in manufactures established at Sassenage, Barcelonnette, Fontainebleau, etc.[1]

While Bertier's name does not appear on this memoir, it is almost certain he wrote it for the parlement of Paris. It states that the overall number of inmates had fallen from a peak of somewhere between twelve and fifteen thousand to a level of seven or eight thousand. Many were receiving help from alms bureaus, and the total expense had been reduced from 1.5 million livres in 1772 to 900,000 at the time of writing, a reduction of 100,000 per year.[2]

Turgot's ministry had left its mark nonetheless. While his measures provoked skepticism in some quarters, a current of opinion still ran strong in favor of his reforms. For such reasons, and above all because of the costs involved, Bertier did not insist on restoring every *dépôt*. And as he put his machine back together, he took the occasion to make improvements. In a broader sense, the challenge he had weathered sharpened his own conception of the function of the *dépôt* and spurred him to express and pursue it more aggressively.

Repairing the Defenses: The Provisional Revives

The general order reversing Turgot's policy on the arrest of beggars was sent out May 29, 1776, over the signature of the new controller-general, Clugny de Nuis,

who was to remain in office as a caretaker figure until he died the following October. The orders of 1768 issued by Choiseul, Vice-Chancellor Maupeou, and the
two *secrétaires d'état* Bertin and La Vrillière were reaffirmed. At the same time an
important assurance was renewed: the aid to be given to the true poor would receive
royal attention, and the instructions of 1768 were to be kept in force pending a new
règlement.[3]

On June 14 the new minister asked intendants to report on the method of contracting and subcontracting that had been in use in their *dépôts* before and after
Turgot's abrogation of the general contract, and to note any complaints or observations that might guide the choice of new arrangements.[4] Less than a month later
the minister announced a decision to revive the general contract with Manié's de-
signee. Inspection had shown that local contracting was more costly, and it was
essential to organize the work of inmates on a contractual basis. Manié had agreed
to waive damages arising from the abrogation of his contract by Turgot, provided
it were renewed in the name of a Sieur François Jacques Danger. Another circular
detailed instructions for pensioning children in the countryside.[5]

Bertier apparently intended to adopt the principles of Brienne's commission at
least insofar as he had assented to them at Montigny. The new instruction of July
29, sent over Clugny's signature, noted that the framers of the declaration on vagabonds had intended that distinct arrangements be made for invalid beggars; it was
essential that they not be confused with the vagabond and the shiftless. Accordingly, it would henceforth be royal policy to enforce the principle of parish responsibility for assistance, as embodied in the Ordinance of Moulins of 1566 and the
Declaration of 1586. Consequently, intendants were authorized to transfer the sick,
the aged, and the infirm from *dépôts* to hospitals. If hospitals lacked sufficient
revenues for receiving beggars, pensions could be paid from the funds allotted to
the contractors. This policy would entail promoting alms bureaus in every parish.[6]

De Crosne at Rouen was strongly skeptical that any attempt by the intendant to
enforce the principle of parish responsibility could be successfully launched on the
authority of a sixteenth-century ordinance; the ordinary courts having jurisdiction
over such matters would obstruct it. Moreover, the principle could not be applied
generally, because those parishes with the greatest number of poor were also those
least able to contribute to their subsistence. Likewise, the directive to send aged
and infirm beggars from *dépôts* to hospitals was liable to be undermined, just as
similar directives had been in the past. Information gathered on hospitals and endowments (presumably Turgot's survey) showed that the resistance was not entirely
unreasonable. Only one hospital in the *généralité* of Rouen had income exceeding
its obligations. Many were forced to turn away the poor of their own parishes.[7]

De Crosne warned that the order would be effective only if the king issued a
special declaration requiring administrators of hospitals to receive old and infirm
beggars from the *dépôts* at the order of intendants. Further, the intendants would
have to be empowered to assign pensions of at least a hundred livres per year for
the subsistence of each person transferred. Even such a measure might prove illusory. Since the hospitals of Rouen were not *maisons de force*, beggars could easily
escape from them. The experience of the *dépôt* at Rouen indicated that hospitals
would not long restrain sickly beggars from their wanderings. Believing that habit
had corrupted all beggars alike, de Crosne argued that relief and repression could

not be separated. Even the deserving poor had become, in a sense, professional. "And unfortunately," he argued, "those of this kind are so numerous that it will be very difficult to exhaust their source."

Jullien at Alençon, far more sympathetic to the views of Turgot, was also critical of Clugny's approach to parish responsibility. He observed that the intent of Turgot and his successor were at bottom the same: to use the *dépôts* only as houses of correction and confinement, and to assist the needy poor "without depriving them of their liberty." Jullien remarked dryly that he did not have the provisions of the Ordinance of Moulins before him as he wrote, but that any scheme for parish relief would require a new form of provincially based tax levy, duly authorized. Bertier responded personally from his home at Sainte-Geneviève on October 17, 1776, to assure Jullien that the laws had not fallen into desuetude, and to cite instances of their enforcement in the *généralités* of Limoges, Châlons, Orleans, and Paris by *arrêts* of 1769, 1770, and 1771. Establishing the principle in a few parishes would set an example to others.[8]

Some immediate efforts at implementation can be noted. At Tours, for example, the *hôtel-Dieu* contracted to receive sick patients from the *dépôt*. However, as such transfers proved costly, they remained limited to cases of grave illness. When serious epidemics broke out later, the hospital protested against the abuse of its contract.[9]

Shortly before Necker was officially placed in charge of finance with the special title of director-general, the king intervened personally to complain about the swarms of beggars that assailed him at Versailles and Paris. On June 8, 1777, Louis XVI wrote to Amelot, minister of the royal household, to find a remedy. With a genius for the commonplace, the king offered a formula: "Work for the able-bodied, hospitals for the invalid, and *maisons de force* for all those who resist the benefits of the law." The king asked Amelot to have the *lieutenant de police* of Paris and the intendant of Paris submit memoirs on the use of *ateliers* for the able-bodied poor, and on methods for supplying aid to parishes and hospitals.[10]

The immediate result of this instruction was a report by Le Noir and Bertier to the parlement, leading to the enactment of new ordinances against begging. One, dated July 27, 1777, provided for Paris, and the other, dated July 30, applied throughout the kingdom. The ordinances were essentially repressive in nature. The first clarified the authority of the *lieutenant de police* to arrest beggars, and the second reaffirmed the declarations of 1724 and 1764. The ordinance offered no new thinking. It contained a fatuous expression of royal "surprise" that beggars should still exist, in light of the provisions made for the able-bodied and the infirm, aid to hospitals, and help to individuals desiring to return home. The new text implied a stricter policy of incarceration, as it expressly prohibited all begging, "vagabond or domiciled."[11] The circular that accompanied the new ordinance in an August dispatch to intendants also linked repression to the principle of parish responsibility. Intendants should see to it that the invalid and those without resources either be placed in hospitals or be cared for by their parishes or communities.[12]

Named director-general in October 1777, Jacques Necker gave a new impulse to social welfare policy. He had already reaffirmed Turgot's commitment to hospital reform, appointing a commission to survey all hospitals and relief measures in the city of Paris in September 1777.[13] The prize-essay subject proposed by Academy of Châlons-sur-Marne in 1777—"How to make beggars useful to the state without making them unhappy?"—indicated that the *dépôts* would come under renewed public scrutiny. The need to draft a response to the *cahiers* of the Estates of Languedoc, bristling with all the objections that Brienne had carried with him into Turgot's ministry, provided the occasion for an extended consultation between Bertier and Necker in the fall of 1777 on all matters relating to the *dépôts*.[14]

By November, the Ordinances of July had already been translated into a new policy that made the *dépôts* the agency for transferring beggars back to their parishes of origin. Bertier himself signed the circular of October 20, 1777, in which this new policy was announced. By transferring beggars in convoys to the *dépôts* closest to their parishes of origin or residence, it would become more feasible to make communities and hospitals responsible for the care of the infirm and for the employment of the able-bodied. The *dépôts* would be restored to a short-term correctional function. With a continual turnover of inmates, there would be room for all those who might be arrested under a more systematic enforcement of the prohibition against begging. In keeping with the rationale for the new policy, Bertier urged the importance of establishing alms bureaus in every parish.[15]

Bertier's circular was not received with cries of joy. Intendants immediately realized that it would entail a cumbersome procedure of grouping and routing transfers of inmates under guard from one *dépôt* to another; also, the Paris region would disgorge itself of provincial captives who would then crowd the already strained provincial facilities. Bertier's friend Montyon, intendant of La Rochelle, was upset enough to solicit opposition to the measure from the intendants of Rennes, Poitiers, Tours, Orleans, and Caen. While he agreed that alms bureaus might relieve the pressure on provincial hospitals, Montyon doubted that this "superb establishment" would meet immediate needs. The policy of transfers would require a costly exchange of inmates to no purpose. Paris, he pointedly remarked, must have far more beggars from other provinces than any other region, since it was at the center and "offered more resources."[16]

The intendant of Brittany, Caze de la Bove, had already asked Bertier for clarification of the new policy. Bertier was not content with a dry recapitulation, but explained excitedly how the policy had been applied in the *intendance* of Paris. He admitted that there were pragmatic necessities involved. In particular, the police of begging in Paris required that increasing numbers be transferred to the *dépôt* at St. Denis. Meanwhile the *intendance* of Paris, which had four *dépôts* in 1776, as a result of Turgot's measures had but two in 1777. Facilitating higher turnover in the *dépôts* around Paris had thus been one consideration in the new policy.[17]

The rapid dispatch of beggars to their place of origin was justified nonetheless by a broader principle, namely, the obligation to provide for welfare needs on a local level. These local efforts were closely linked in Bertier's mind with administrative reforms that would improve the lot of the inhabitants and thereby remove the most serious causes of beggary. He enclosed a printed copy of a letter he had sent to his subdelegates, explaining the importance of setting up alms bureaus in every parish. He voiced enthusiastic hopes in a letter to Caze de la Bove:

> For the last few years I have been able to moderate the impositions of the lower classes *[bas peuple]* in such a way that they pay almost nothing. The charity work projects that I have been able to set up and the relief that I take from the diminu-

tions [of the *taille*] to aid family heads and the miserable have greatly diminished
the cause of mendicity. I am presently establishing alms bureaus in all the parishes
by means of which I hope that in a few years the poor will be completely provided
for.[18]

Obviously anxious to discuss such matters at greater length, Bertier urged Caze de
la Bove to visit him at Sainte-Geneviève on his next journey to Paris and gave him
directions to get there.

Letters preserved in the tax district of Sens corroborate Bertier's claim to have
promoted alms bureaus. Writing to his subdelegate Baudry at Sens, he made his
expectations clear. In reply to Baudry's complaint that beggars were more common
as a result of the removal of a brigade of the *maréchaussée* from one locality,
Bertier retorted that the problem would be solved if alms bureaus were in place.
These would be as effective as the *maréchaussée* in providing surveillance of beggars. He reminded Baudry that those parishes that failed to set up alms bureaus
should not expect favors in the form of tax rebates or relief. In a further letter
Bertier sent Baudry the names of beggars who were originally from the *élection* of
Sens and had appeared in the *dépôts* of St. Denis and Melun. The majority of the
parishes in the *élection* of Sens were eventually induced to form alms bureaus. The
standard form as written out generally specified that the community had formed the
bureaus after the intendant had threatened to withhold assistance and relief from
those that failed to comply.[19]

Following the initial rash of correspondence regarding Bertier's circular of October 20, 1777, Necker and Bertier held their working session on the means of
implanting the new policy and articulating it further. The intendants and the Estates
were not alone in raising objections to the July ordinances and subsequent instructions. The *premier président* of the parlement of Paris had referred to Bertier a
complaint arising from the fears expressed by religious houses in the region of
Alençon that traditional almsgiving and the begging of small children near their
homes might lead to unwarranted arrests. Bertier in turn had asked the intendant of
Alençon for a report, saying he would show it to Necker.[20]

Necker reaffirmed the directives of October in a circular to intendants dated
December 3, 1777. In it, he stated the expectation that regions of large-scale farming would be able to muster their own resources for providing relief, except in
extreme emergencies. Only certain poorer areas, where farms were small and population dense, might require royal aid in normal times. These assumptions had been
stated in almost identical terms by the intendant of Soissons in the letter on mendicity he wrote in reply to Turgot's inquiry. Since Necker conferred on various
matters with his friend Le Peletier de Mortefontaine, it is quite possible that he
used the intendant's letter in drafting his own circular. In any case, Necker went
on to give assurance that royal measures would be taken to avert crises. Intendants
were to adjust tax burdens and provide *ateliers de charité*. In case of emergencies,
intendants could also distribute medicine and rice.[21]

Royal aid would be contingent, however, on local initiative. Alms bureaus must
make effective use of local resources before royal aid would be forthcoming. Necker
suggested that intendants might threaten to withhold relief and tax rebates from
those communities that failed to establish alms bureaus. These agencies, once established, would become responsible for distributing all forms of aid. In this con-

text, the number of poor turning to begging should fall, and the repression of beggars might eventually become unnecessary, as the act came to be viewed in a more shameful light. For the time being, the ordinances were to be strictly executed.[22]

This policy reflects in many respects the main lines of "administrative" remedies for mendicity, as outlined by Brienne, but without the nationally restructured network of administrative bureaus that he proposed. The effort to reinvigorate alms bureaus in traditional form embodies a belief that welfare could be administered effectively only through a local, municipally based network. Necker advised intendants that they could obtain practical suggestions on their establishment from "M. the *lieutenant de police* and from M. the intendant of Paris, who have tried these establishments with some success." The intendant of Soissons had already asked Bertier for information on the measures he had taken, and had received a printed brochure of a regulation for the parish of Saint-Sulpice in Paris, signed November 4, 1777 "De Sauvigny" and "Le Noir."[23] It had been Brienne's suggestion to use a parish in the city of Paris as a model for the new form of bureaus he proposed.[24]

While Bertier and Necker refurbished the image of the *dépôts,* provincial resistance simmered and boiled over fitfully. In Provence the institution had received a death blow as a result of a commission of inquiry organized by the archbishop of Aix and authorized by Turgot. Inspection of the *dépôt* at Aix confirmed allegations that some inmates had been detained on flimsy charges and that the contractor had failed to maintain the conditions of his contract. Bertier conceded that the *dépôt* had not been well managed. In a request for funds from the Estates of Provence in 1777, he recommended the establishment of a large new *dépôt* in a healthy location near Marseilles, as approved by the intendant. He noted that "complaints of murders, thefts, and other excesses committed by beggars and vagabonds had increased so much that the government had been obliged to give new orders for arresting them and taking them to the *dépôts.*" Leading the opposition of the Estates of Provence against reinstatement, Boisgelin wrote: "it is a sorry thought that at bottom the contribution asked would not have for its object the needs of the province, and would serve only to sustain the enterprise of the intendant of Paris for the *dépôts* that he thinks he must establish at Paris and in his *généralité.*"[25]

According to the Estates of Provence, there existed a "municipal" form of relief sanctioned by the laws of the province; crime rates did not justify the need for *dépôts.* Bertier was unable to reestablish his system in Provence. Elsewhere he prevailed, but there were to be periodic expressions of discontent, particularly from the Estates of Languedoc and Brittany. These eruptions required Bertier to refine a systematic rationale for the *dépôts.* Again and again he parried charges of mismanagement and injustice, then turned to an aggressive vindication of the positive good to be derived from royal policy on mendicity.

Bertier drafted the most strenuously confident of his apologias for the *dépôt* as an institution in response to a remonstrance from the parlement of Brittany. In the fall of 1777 the magistrates of this sovereign court had objected to the implementation of the ordinance of July 30, 1777, as a blanket authorization for the intendant to direct the procedures of arrest and confinement of beggars in the *dépôt* at Rennes. These objections were particularly significant, as they threatened to repeat the pattern of events in Provence, where the Estates and the parlement combined against the *dépôt*. At Rennes, however, the intendant strongly supported Bertier and his system.[26]

Bertier's memoir prepared for the parlement of Rennes reminded the judges of the duly authorized functions of the *maréchaussée* under laws approved by the parlements themselves. The arrest of beggars was not cruel or arbitrary, coupled as it was with measures to aid the poor by means of tax relief, *ateliers*, and alms bureaus. In any case, repression had generally been relaxed in times of dearth. He went on to argue that the ordinance of 1777 had not been issued until a full study had been made of the numbers of the poor and resources of each province. Bertier thus implied that Turgot's successors had made use of the inquiry he had launched, and had come to the conclusion that parish relief was a workable principle, used in combination with royal aid to poorer parishes.[27]

Bertier placed on the Estates the onus of failing to provide *ateliers* and failing to equalize the burden of taxation. This was a sore point with the Estates, since they had understood both Turgot and Necker to have committed royal support to funding *ateliers*—support that had been delayed and stinted. Caze de la Bove supported this grievance in acrimonious letters to the minister. Bertier rubbed salt in the wound by explaining to the Estates that if Provence was indeed the sole exception to the network of *dépôts,* it was because Provence provided for its poor by a legal structure of municipal obligation. He suggested that the Estates might levy an excise tax to provide for the *dépôts*. Certainly neither Estates nor parlement would be in a position to direct the day-to-day administration of the *dépôts,* a function of administration rather than legislation.[28]

Bertier averred that administrators made every effort to remove inmates from the *dépôts* once they were confined. Inquiries were sent throughout Europe to enable administrators to send beggars home, and to place them in hospitals or in the care of their parish if they were sick. The *dépôt* as Bertier described it might be compared to a retort or alembic, in which each fraction of the poor population was distilled, drawn off, and restored to its purity. The unfortunate and the wayward were guided home, sturdy shiftless youths were enrolled in the army, those who were too short or otherwise unsuited were freely engaged in the work companies of the pioneers, and the underaged were pensioned to farmers. All that were left in the *dépôt* constituted a residue—what Bertier referred to as a *caput mortuum,* a term associated with wine-making and the distillation of liquors, with alchemy, and with the new science of chemistry.[29]

Nevertheless, Bertier insisted, the administration was far from being guilty of the inhumanity toward these unfortunates that critics charged. The treatment of inmates was humane, if severe, between that of a soldier and a prisoner—but in fact the bread was better than a soldier's.[30] Hospitals had cruelly refused to take the sick from the *dépôts,* but infirmaries established within the *dépôts* provided the care needed. Earlier problems of high mortality rates had been investigated by doctors and enlightened administrators, and had been found to arise not from negligence on the part of the jailers, but from the filthy habits of the inmates themselves. With better efforts to enforce hygiene, mortality had been reduced to a level lower than that of most hospitals. So he argued.

The consequence of distilling useful citizens from these receptacles of wayward humanity was that the *dépôts* retained only those dangerous persons or *mauvais sujets* whom parishes themselves wanted locked up. The argument here hardly differs from that of Turgot. As for measures of "administration," these too embodied a domain of consensus shared by Turgot, Brienne, and Bertier, not to mention Laverdy and earlier administrators. The intendants would promote alms bureaus in every parish, and distribute royal aid to those that were overburdened. This approach, Bertier insisted, had worked successfully in the town and *généralité* of Paris and in some neighboring *généralités*. The *dépôts* were functioning everywhere except for Provence, where laws of the province required every parish to take measures for the subsistence of the poor.

Bertier penned this defense at about the time he was explaining to intendants the scope of operation of the *dépôts* under the newly defined policies of the fall of 1777. No doubt he hoped that opponents would be won over or silenced by a vigorous, rational defense. The outcome of a further challenge from the parlement of Paris early in 1778 gave him reason to be confident. Although the parlement had attacked Turgot for curbing the arrest of beggars, there were younger members of that body, d'Espresménil in particular, who objected to the arbitrary arrest of some working citizens in the city of Paris. These citizens had been transferred outside the city's normal jurisdiction to the *dépôt* of St. Denis. The vehement objections of d'Espresménil were linked with an attack on the king's power to deprive citizens of their liberty by *lettres de cachet*. The protest was calmed by the arguments of the *conseiller* Louis Séguier, who assured the parlement that the specific cases in question had not involved any breach of procedures approved by the parlement. He reviewed the means adopted to transfer those arrested on the sole charge of begging or vagrancy to the *dépôt* at St. Denis, through the intermediate jurisdiction of the officers of the Châtelet. He reminded his colleagues of the "disorders" that had occurred when Turgot disturbed these arrangements.[31]

Bertier could rest assured that opposition from the parlement was neutralized for the time being. But the arbitrary power of arrest of beggars was quietly added to a lengthening bill of particulars to be brought forward in an ultimately revolutionary indictment of "royal despotism."

The broad claims for the success of the *dépôts* cited earlier in connection with the aftermath of Turgot's fall from office were probably composed in order to meet this challenge from the parlement in 1778. In the course of that same year, Bertier was involved in a personally embarrassing challenge from inhabitants of the *généralité* of Paris who also happened to be his tenants on vast properties he owned at L'Isle-sous-Montréal. The dispute concerned various seigneurial rights, such as the exclusive right to take fish from ponds. Bertier referred the matter to the royal council in order, he said, to avoid a conflict of interest. In a letter of September 7, 1778, addressed to Necker, Bertier noted, "As intendant I was their tutor; as their seigneur, I was their adverse party." Protesting perhaps too much, he insisted, "I am not a violent and unjust seigneur."[32]

Although the chronological sequence of texts must remain conjectural, it seems likely that the review of Bertier's role as seigneur and intendant required him to undertake the sweeping apologia, embattled in tone, that has been preserved in the private archives of the family. The year 1778 seems to be indicated for the composition of this undated draft in his own hand. Its main thrust is to refute the charge that Bertier had used his public position for private gain. As the memoir progresses, it becomes more personal and touches upon some of the details of his fortune. It begins, however, with a review of his career as administrator, a public existence that began with service as master of requests in royal council, where he claimed to have reported more than any of his peers in the four years from 1764 on. It then moves to a vindication of his role in supervising the "operation for the destruction of mendicity," for which he claimed to have found sources of funding whereby "it never cost anything." [33]

The operation of the *dépôts* was about to be perfected when Turgot came to office. "This minister," Bertier avers, "had the intention of destroying the operation and the operator." To no avail: "no one did me greater service than M. Turgot." Once reconstructed, the *dépôts* effectively abated the nuisance of begging in Paris and the *généralité*. Bertier assessed the benefits of the operation as a whole and assigned monetary value to those realized in his own intendance:

> Instead of 6,000 who were shut up in the *dépôts* of this province, there are no more than 400, [so] that the funds that had been set at 1,500,000 livres no longer amount to more than 900,000, [so] that the diminution of reprobates that this operation produces saves over 300,000 livres in costs of justice per year, [so] that it supplies the king's troops with more than ten thousand men who would otherwise perhaps have destroyed an equal quantity of their fellow men, and that finally these human rejects *[ce rebut de l'humanité]* not only provide defenders of the state but have accomplished some 2,500,000 livres worth of public works.

Such accomplishments in social alchemy were part of a larger scheme of regeneration. The *magnum opus* of Bertier's career, in his own view, was the system he had devised in his *généralité* for allocating the *taille* in a manner "at once the most just, the mildest, and the most favorable to agriculture and population." Other reforms complemented these. He had constructed barracks, built new prisons, opened new roads in order to improve the land, and had reformed the method of drawing for duty in the *milice*. Finally, he had eliminated the *corvée de bras* and reduced the *corvée de voitures*. [34]

Bertier weathered the challenge. At the same time, he seems to have been persuaded that a more expert and regular system for supervising the welfare and rehabilitation of inmates in the *dépôts* was indispensable.

The Inspectorate of Dr. Jean Colombier

Political and bureaucratic pressures gave urgency to the drive for regulation and uniform inspection of the *dépôts* after the fall of Turgot. Repairing the old defenses would not suffice. The predicament of the intendant of Brittany highlighted the nature of the problem. Caze de la Bove carried out a thorough personal inspection of the *dépôt* at Rennes and took prompt measures to correct abuses in its administration, only to find that the parlement and the Estates continued to demand a right of inspection or supervision over it. He then tried fending off these demands by printing the existing regulations in 1778. A regulation concerning "the feeding, clothing, bedding, and treatment, in health and in sickness, of all the inmates of the *dépôt*," dated October 18, 1776, was designed to carry out the provisions of the general provisioning contract reinstated after the fall of Turgot. Another regulation spelled out all the duties of the concierge as day-to-day inspector of the *dépôt*.[35]

The political function of a printed regulation emerges clearly in the correspondence between Caze de la Bove and Necker in 1780, when the Estates, in their repeated demand for inspection, went so far as to complain that "obscurity" reigned in the management of the *dépôt*. The intendant rejoined: "The alarums of the Estate concerning the administration of the *dépôt* are quite gratuitous; there is no 'obscurity' in its administration: the regulations that relate to it have been printed: everyone is cognizant of them." In fact, the intendant had written public accountability into the regulation, providing that the surgeon-major of the *dépôt* fix the rations and remedies of the sick, and inscribe them in a register that would be "at all times open and public in the pharmacy of the *dépôt*." It appears that Bertier came in person to see how the regulations were applied. "I dare flatter myself, Sir, that there are few more exact," Caze de la Bove wrote Necker. "Monsieur Bertier is due to arrive here presently; I shall be most gratified to have him give you an account of them himself upon his return."[36]

Political pressures eventually persuaded the intendant of Brittany that a local regulation was not sufficient. In 1782 a revolt at the *dépôt* in Rennes required military repression and led to one death. The parlement investigated the incident and renewed its demands for a right of inspection. In the wake of this incident, the intendant reported that his subdelegate, Fresnais, who had ably supervised the operation of the *dépôt* for many years, had become discouraged by the unending attacks on it, and that he would surely resign if any inspection over it were given to the parlement. The problem went beyond one incident; others were likely in a house containing five hundred inmates. The parlement had considered drawing up a criminal indictment on this occasion. In Fresnais' view, the legal authority of subdelegates and the jurisdiction of ordinary justice needed to be clarified. The claims of the parlement were seconded by those of the Estates, who respected Fresnais but still challenged his authority. The intendant wondered aloud whether the answers to such questions must not arise generally. There should be, he said, some "uniform and certain rules." Politically, the institution was vulnerable: "it is absolutely necessary to destroy these sorts of establishments, or to give them a solidity that may establish the confidence of their administrators."[36]

Apart from external political pressure, a variety of internal bureaucratic initiatives had been at work for some time. Administrators groped continually in search of new means for applying uniform standards. In particular, the role of the concierges had raised difficulties for their superiors, ever since Laverdy had suggested that it was just to permit these subalterns to eke out their meager wages by contracting for the provision of the miscellaneous supplements to inmates' bread rations. The administration had unreasonable expectations of such humble agents. Subdelegates had occasionally requested the appointment of more qualified individuals as supervisors, such as "charitable persons" familiar with the operation of workshops. The administration responded with lengthy questionnaires designed to screen out all but the most fully qualified concierges. Intendants drew up regulations for their concierges to follow. In spite of such efforts, problems continued. The introduction of a general contract in 1773 further weakened the effectiveness of the concierges, who were required to dispense the provisions stocked by the contractors and to verify that the terms of the contract were performed. The concierge was responsible to the contractor in the enforcement of discipline—in the workshops especially— but was also obliged to see that contractors paid the inmates the share due them for their labors. The conflict of interest became especially noticeable in cases where concierges continued to supply certain provisions, thus becoming the subcontractors as well as the inspectors of the provisioning company.[38]

When Turgot was replaced by Clugny de Nuis and the *dépôts* were reinstated, a number of administrative changes were made. As noted earlier, Clugny's request for information and suggestions on contracting procedures was overtaken by a decision to reinstate the general contract with Dangers, an associate of Manié, Rimberge et Cie. The latter agreed in this case to waive the penalties owed to them for Turgot's abrogation of their contract. However, the new controller-general signaled a desire for more effective bureaucratic control. In particular, he wrote intendants in a circular of July 29, 1776, that since the concierge was "the King's man," he could not "be at the same time the man or the subcontractor of the general contractor."[39]

Bertier seems to have thought it possible to promote uniform standards by extending the efforts of his own bureau, which carried out a constant paper supervision of accounts, building plans, and proposed measures of utility. In 1777 he went so far as to inform intendants that complete stocks of inmates' clothing could be shipped directly from the contractors who clothed inmates of the *généralité* of Paris, should prices or quality be less than satisfactory elsewhere. Bertier's secretary enclosed cloth samples.[40] In another case, probably at Bertier's instigation, Necker had personally approved the dismissal of three sisters in the community of Saint-Maurice for negligence in managing the provisions of the *dépôt* at Orleans. In the same year—1777—the *dépôt* at Orleans obtained a new "regulation for the governing of the infirmaries, the preparation and administration of remedies for the sick, the distribution of food, cleanliness, salubrity of the air, etc."[41]

Questions of economy and utility inspired Jacques Necker to experiment with various changes. Reviving the questions that Clugny had posed, he advised intendants in a circular of April 22, 1779, that "certain circumstances" might lead him to abrogate the general contract. In that case, he wished to know whether it was better "to administer [*régir*] the *dépôts* by salaried employees, or to entrust them to individual contractors?" In the latter case, "it would be necessary to know what rations they would be obliged to provide and what price should be set for each day's subsistance." The decision to reduce the overall number of *dépôts* for reasons of economy provided the occasion for a circular of December 10, 1780, inviting intendants' reflections and observations. The intendant Le Peletier at Soissons took advantage of the occasion to repeat an earlier request for a special inspector; other intendants, less insistent than he, shared his concern. Necker's decision to eliminate the cashiers who has previously prepared the quarterly accounts of each *dépôt* gave urgency to the issue of inspection. While Necker assigned this accounting task to the receivers-general, subdelegates and secretaries of intendants were obliged to take a larger part in maintaining the paper inspection of the *dépôts'* running accounts. With payments in arrears and expenditures subject to challenge, this was a nettlesome task.[42]

When Necker fell from office in 1781, he was succeeded by the same Joly de Fleury who had played a major part in establishing the *dépôts*. Soon after becoming controller-general, Joly de Fleury advised intendants of his decision to abrogate as of August 1, 1781, the general contract that was to have run until July 31, 1783. He asked intendants to negotiate new contracts locally based on revised terms, including additional servings of soup and vegetables to inmates, more ample provision of clothing, and an allowance of one-third rather than one-quarter of the product of workshop labor to the inmates themselves. An extensive correspondence ensued with the intendant of Tours concerning the general policy and the terms of agreement with the former subcontractor at Tours, the widow Chalmel.[43]

Du Cluzel expressed surprise at the ostensible reason for abrogating the general contract. Danger and his associates advanced no funds to the subcontractor, and merely took nine deniers per *journée* from the amount paid to her. Although he was not opposed to an improvement in standards, the intendant observed that it would be extremely difficult to revert to the prior standard, should the new one prove too burdensome for the royal treasury. This note of caution was based on the experience of Turgot's ministry. Chalmel had improved the lot of inmates in a contract that superseded the one with Manié that Turgot had abrogated in 1776. When Turgot's successor, Clugny, renegotiated the general contract and attempted to impose the old terms, the intendant had been forced to yield to an outcry "from the high clergy" at Tours and maintain the new standard by means of a regular indemnity to Chalmel, who became the subcontractor of the new company.[44]

The particular arrangements with the widow Chalmel were still being adjusted in 1783, the year when du Cluzel died at his post. Whatever combination of motives lay behind the decision to terminate the general contract, the company obtained relief from its creditors in 1784 and was still answering claims from its subcontractors as late as December 1789.[45] While abandoning the general contract, Joly de Fleury persisted in the view that contractual arrangements were preferable to procurement and management by agents of the king. Since the work of inmates would bring profit to the contractor, it was likely that the "principle cause" of mendicity—idleness—would be removed. The single rate for *journées* of healthy and sick inmates would make it in the contractors' interest "to contribute to the good health of the inmate by the good quality of the victuals."[46]

By 1780, then, a search for a new standard of maintenance had begun, giving an impetus to the formulation of a general regulation. The intendant of Châlons-sur-Marne, pressed by his subordinates for a new regulation, wrote Bertier twice in 1780 to ask whether there was a regulation for the *dépôts* of the *généralité* of Paris that might be used as a model. The draft of a local regulation that was completed while the intendant was waiting for a reply bears the marginal note, "There is already a general regulation planned."[47] It was at about this time—early in 1781— that the eminent doctor Jean Colombier began to leave traces of his activity in the records of the *dépôts*.

According to a memoir written in 1784, Jean Colombier had been chosen in 1777 to undertake improvements in the hospitals of Paris. In 1780 he gave up all other activities to work entirely for the government. The author of the memoir credits him "both with improvements in the *hôtel-Dieu* and the *hôpital-général,* to be carried out subsequently, and with the establishment of civil prisons in the Hôtel de la Force." Furthermore, he had executed "the most useful changes in other prisons of Paris; in the different *dépôts de mendicité:* notably in that of St. Denis under the orders of the Intendant of Paris." The memoir also touches on his work at the Hospice de Vaugirard under the orders of the *lieutenant de police,* and of his tours of inspection in different provinces, "particularly at Lyons, to arrange the hospitals of this town, which were in a most sorry state."[48]

When Necker drew him into a general consulting role in 1777, Colombier was well known for his outstanding treatises on military medicine and hygiene.[49] He probably became involved in the inspection of the *dépôts* as a result of reviewing conditions in the prisons of Paris. Colombier's report of January 26, 1780, to the Académie Royale des Sciences on the three principal prisons of Paris inspired an inquiry by Duhamel de Monceau, Montigny, Le Roy, Tenon, Tillet, and Lavoisier. Their report of March 17, 1780, recommended sanitary precautions of the sort that Colombier would later insist upon in his inspection of the *dépôts:* cleanliness of bedding, circulation of air, suitable food, and—particularly noteworthy—the need for bathing inmates and disinfecting their clothes on their arrival.[50] It was in January of 1781 that Colombier received the official title of "inspector of hospitals, prisons and *maisons de force* of the Kingdom."[51]

It is quite possible that Bertier enlisted Colombier's assistance as early as 1780, when it was decided to reduce the overall number of *dépôts.* The earliest mention of Colombier at the *dépôt* of St. Denis is in the accounts for 1781, which include payment of forty-five livres to him for bathrobes.[52] In the same year he is mentioned in correspondence relating to the *dépôt* at Soissons. Bertier was no doubt impressed with Dr. Colombier's medical and administrative skill. Colombier directed the *service des épidémies* in the *généralité* of Paris and published observations drawn from the memoirs of these public health doctors. In effect he reviewed the work of other doctors, as in the case of the doctor serving the *dépôt* of St. Denis, a Sieur Davan, who diagnosed and combatted an epidemic in the village of Groslay, two leagues from the *dépôt.* Colombier excused some faults in Davan's diagnosis in light of his rounds of visits, twice daily, at the infirmaries of the *dépôt* at St. Denis.[53] A letter of March 26, 1782, from Bertier to the intendant of Soissons allows a glimpse of Colombier reassuring the intendant that the inmates due to be transferred from St. Denis were fit to make the journey. All had been examined by the health officers of the *dépôt* and all were sufficiently clothed. Dr. Colombier preferred cold, clear weather—*un beau froid*—in any case.[54]

Responding to a sharp rise in the number of inmates dying in the *dépôt* at St. Denis, the authorities provided funds for the extermination of rats in 1782. Rats and bedbugs both were targeted in 1783. By 1783 the inspection of the *dépôt* at St. Denis appears to have been taken over by Bannefroy, and it seems that Colombier had helped establish a regime in which supervision was divided among several inspectors, including an "economic inspector" who applied a system of strict daily accounting for all supplies. In 1784 a mechanical ventilator was installed, and Bertier soon thereafter recommended to intendants that such machines be installed wherever the lack of circulating air caused a health problem. Three years later Dr.

François Doublet, Colombier's son-in-law and his assistant in the post of inspector-general, advertised the success of the ventilator and other reforms at St. Denis in an article for the *Encyclopédie méthodique*.[55]

Colombier's effort to extend the regime established at St. Denis to other *dépôts*, and to adapt it for the purpose of a general regulation, becomes evident from correspondence of 1783. In that year Colombier's official list of expenses includes travel to Rouen in March. The newly appointed controller-general, d'Ormesson, sent the intendant there a letter in April based on Colombier's report. Although the regime at Rouen was generally satisfactory, the minister noted that the negligence of some of the subaltern employees might have been avoided by the use of "a regulation similar to the one in use in the *dépôt* of St. Denis." Further correspondence from the intendant at Rouen indicates that improvements in standards of hygiene and diet were being generally implemented, apparently in response to Colombier's directives.[56]

From April to October 1783, in a hiatus between the strong ministries of Joly de Fleury and Calonne, the intendant of finances d'Ormesson held the position of controller-general. Soon after d'Ormesson's appointment, Bertier appears to have prevailed upon him to respond aggressively to challenges for the provincial Estates regarding the *dépôts*. In 1783 the *cahiers* of the Estates of Languedoc contained sharp objections that were seconded by the intendant, Saint-Priest. The intendant was particularly frustrated by his inability to control the *maréchaussée*, accused of lax enforcement and venality.[57] In a circular issued in May, d'Ormesson advised intendants that the king in his council had reviewed the operation of the *dépôts* after several *pays d'états* had objected to paying for them. The review had confirmed the utilty of the *dépôts:* intendants were told that a strict execution of the orders of 1768 was needed in order to proscribe begging entirely. The council ordered, however, that intendants should pay special attention to the standing instructions concerning procedures of arrest, and should release those falsely imprisoned. Stricter procedures went into effect for authorizing, recording, and reviewing the detention of inmates by "orders of the king." D'Ormesson concluded his circular of May 25 by inviting intendants to indicate whether "there existed any obstacle to the operations necessary for the entire extinction of mendicity, which the King has close to his heart."[58]

D'Ormesson's review would be cited two years later in the preamble to a general regulation. Colombier might have produced that regulation sooner, had he not been involved in a grueling round of visits to hospitals, prisons, and *dépôts* in 1783 and 1784. He was also committed to several extraordinary tasks. Early in January 1783 the controller-general, Joly de Fleury, had announced to the intendant of Lyons a forthcoming visit by Colombier to review the financial situation of the hospitals there. The minister credited Colombier with having made notable improvements in "the charitable establishments of the capital." On Colombier's recommendation and over the vocal opposition of the hospital administrators of Lyons, a royal decree of September 9 terminated the special arrangement whereby the royal operation of arresting beggars had been entrusted in part to a branch of the *aumône-générale*. With the closing of Lyons's "Bicêtre"—as this institution was called—its repressive functions were transferred entirely to the "dépôt royal de la Quarantaine," a distinct establishment operating strictly under the supervision of the intendant.[59]

The political need for a regulation at Lyons was obvious: administrators of the *aumône-générale* would be quick to denounce abuses in the royal *dépôt*. On December 4, 1783, Colombier was present—along with the administrators of the *dépôt* of La Quarantaine, the subdelegate, the doctors, and the intendant of the province, de Flesselles—for the reading of a new regulation. The preamble reflected a bureaucratic impulse in addition to the unstated political one. Although previous efforts had been made to reform "the abuses introduced in the said *dépôt,* under the direction of the general contract," new efforts were needed as a result of the elimination of the municipal *dépôt* and its merger with La Quarantaine.[60]

A reading of the regulation itself reveals a great number of provisions later incorporated in the general regulation of the *dépôts*. New arrivals were to be bathed and their clothes disinfected and washed. Latrines were to be flushed twice a day. Inmates with fevers were to be placed in separate beds. In the infirmaries, every two beds were to be provided with a sick robe, two pairs of sandals, two bowls for infusions, two ladles for bouillon, and two chamberpots. There would be a toilet seat for every four beds. Venereal-disease patients and those with mange would be kept separate from the others, and "the insane will be treated for their maladies, if recent, in conformity with a regulation of health agreed upon by the doctors."[61]

The regulation at Lyons (see illus., p. 181) prefigured the pattern of the general regulation in the authority of inspection it conferred upon doctors with respect to the entire population of inmates: "The doctors are the proper inspectors of the salubrity and of the health service in the infirmaries and in the dormitories." Colombier's bureaucratic role as inspector was reinforced by his function as a medical expert. Remedies were to be stocked in the pharmacy "in the quantity and quality prescribed according to a list to be drawn up by the health officers, and by the inspector-general of the *dépôts de mendicité.*" Colombier again appears in the article concerning the treatment of patients suffering from venereal disease and mange, and the insane. These treatments were to consist of "measures agreed upon and signed by the doctors, the surgeon, and the inspector-general of the *dépôts.*"[62]

Colombier was involved in tours of inspection throughout 1783, while continuing to supervise the corps of public health doctors in the *généralité* of Paris, an activity that inspired a further volume of observations on the nature of epidemics in the *généralité*. After his journeys to Lyons and Rouen, he concentrated on the Paris region for several months. He was at Senlis in May; June he devoted to inspection of the hospitals of the *généralité* of Paris; July found him at Provins and Melun; in August he visited Soissons; and in September he worked in the region of Fontainebleau. On his journey to Lyons from October through December, he visited Orleans, Gien, and the Bourbonnais, and returned to Paris through Burgundy. In January he was back at Mâcon and Bresse.[63]

In the early months of 1784, Colombier gave considerable time to the *dépôts*. Although his travel expenses are not recorded in as much detail for 1784 and 1785, the results of his activities are reflected in a letter from Bertier to Gojard, *premier commis* of the controller-general, dated July 10, 1784, requesting a supplement of 200,000 livres for current needs and past expenses, "for rebuilding and expansions that have to be approved." Bertier supported his request with the statement, "M. Colombier, who has just inspected seven or eight principal *dépôts,* has confirmed for me the nature of this expense."[64] Bertier noted that many expenses had been curtailed or deferred because of the American war, and expressed hope that, with peace, funds would be forthcoming. Although it is not certain which *dépôts* Bertier referred to, Rouen and Soissons were probably two of those intended, since Colombier left traces of his activity there. Lyons was another. The intendant de Flesselles wrote Calonne on April 3, 1784, to recommend adding space to the dépôt at Lyons for a venereal disease hospital and a workshop. In a letter of May 14 he explained that the administrators of the *dépôt* wished to construct a building where it would be possible "to occupy beggars in order to tear them away from idleness, and even to prevent the illnesses that beggars contract less often when they are not working in their sleeping rooms." [65]

In the later months of 1784, Colombier's attentions were drawn away from the *dépôts*. In a letter of October 15, he explained to the new intendant of Lyons, Terray, that he had been sick since a trip to Provins, and that he had been absorbed by "the great ills of our prisons of the Abbaye, the Conciergerie, and the Châtelet, which have obliged me to give myself over entirely to the dispositions that the parlement has prescribed in order to prevent new catastrophes." His letter also reflects his involvement in a new regulation for the *hôtel-Dieu* of Lyons, and plans for a visit to Cherbourg, followed by "a trip to Orleans, then to Grenoble, and on this route Lyons is my principal object." [66]

From such funds of accumulated experience, a regulation matured. Mention of an adopted regulation emerges from a welter of other business in a letter of March 4, 1785, from Colombier to Terray. Colombier refers to the affairs of the *hôtel-Dieu,* the combatting of epidemics—"Monsieur the Controller-general has charged me to make a new general plan for this operation"—and the *dépôt* of La Quarantaine at Lyons, where Bertier appears to have intervened in person: "I am not unaware of what happened in the course of M. Bertier's trip," he confides to the intendant:

> I think that the administration, such as it is, exists only on paper, and that the guard is poor. I have said so before. There is every reason to think that during your stay here, Sir, you will bring this matter to an end. In any case, there is a general regulation adopted—it will be presented to you. [67]

A complete draft of the regulation had been ready since the beginning of the year. The subdelegate at Caen had received a copy with a letter from the intendant dated January 6, 1785. Evidently Colombier valued the expert opinion of Chibourg and Amiel, the doctor and surgeon who served the *dépôt* of Beaulieu at Caen, as they were selected to comment on the draft regulation. The intendant asked them to comment particularly on those articles dealing with the infirmaries and the treatment of the sick. He had also asked the subdelegate to propose "all the additions and changes that you think suitable, in general as well as respecting the country and locale of the house of Beaulieu." [68]

The intendant of Picardy was less favored. He received a copy of the regulation with a letter form the controller-general, Calonne, March 20, 1785, containing Colombier's strictures on the poor condition of the *dépôt* at Amiens, the paltry rations (two pounds of butter and a few herbs for a broth serving ninety to ninety-four persons), and the lack of a stove in the dormitories. The intendant passed on the regulation to his subdelegate with an extract of the articles concerning subsistence.

"The Minister does not ask for an opinion," he notes, adding, "There is reason to believe that it is adopted." Aware that he was being given short shrift, the intendant was probably pleased to receive some further explanation in a letter of May 27. The regulation, he learned, would not appear in printed form "before the end of the year, in order to profit from the observations that might be made."[69]

According to the preamble of the general regulation, the text resulted from a report on the *dépôts* presented to the king, as a result of which "His Majesty has seen fit to confirm anew the orders he had given to assure their existence and usefulness, and to assemble in a general regulation the principles of their administration and of their regime." The body of the regulation is arranged under three titles: General Constitution (six articles), General Police (48 articles), and Administration and Internal Regime (81 articles). Articles relating to hygiene and to the disposition of infirmaries bear a close resemblance to those of the regulation for the *dépôt* at Lyons (December 1783). The regulation of 1785 specifies in more detail the beddings and linen to be used, the rations of the sick, and the stuffs from which clothes are to be made. The Lyons text forbids the use of cooking scales made of copper; the regulation of 1785 provides that "the kitchen pots shall be of cast or wrought iron and there shall be allowed no copper vessels." Both regulations prescribe traditional fumigations with vinegar (omitting the older practice of burning juniper), the bathing of new inmates, and the steaming of their clothes.[70]

The Regulation of 1785 and Its Impact

Further examination of the provisions of the regulation shows how Jean Colombier synthesized prevailing medical expertise and redefined conditions of hygiene and levels of provisioning according to a strictly biological standard. New administrative machinery was devised in order to ensure that the new standards were actually applied. These developments raise a further question that can be treated only in grossest terms here, namely, whether the changes prescribed by the regulation were in fact translated into improved and better regulated conditions systemwide in the *dépôts*.

It is clear that the regulation of 1785 represented a distinct elevation of the general standard of maintenance by comparison with earlier standing orders. The change lay as much in the attention to quantifying the standard in terms easily inspected as in the ration itself. Adult inmates would continue to receive 1½ pounds of bread *(poids du marc)*, but the quality of flour was now specified as "third and fourth grades of flour" for three-fourths of the total; the remaining fourth would be rye with the bran removed.[71] The daily addition of a vegetable broth or *pitance*, mentioned in earlier instructions, was now specified as a twelve-ounce portion per inmate to be served from ladles of the prescribed measure. Rice would be the main ingredient three weekdays (9½ pounds per hundred inmates), and peas, lentils, or green beans (12 pounds per hundred inmates) the other three. On all six days, 10 pounds of white bread made from pure white flour would be added to each batch, 2 pounds of grease and 2 pounds of salt. On the seventh day, Sunday, a serving of beef would be added to the morning pot, specified as a *quarteron* for each inmate, to be served up in equal portions.[72]

In these provisions, a scientific standard for the maintenance of health supersedes the goal of maintaining a status hierarchy. Under the initial instructions approved by Laverdy, the diet prescribed was deemed adequate for maintaining health, but in fact reflected the prevailing deficiencies in the bread-dominated diet of the people at large. Animal protein had been almost entirely lacking, vitamin deficiencies were inevitable, and the total quantity of calories available would have been insufficient to maintain an adult male involved in active labor. But even this standard, if regularly provided, was superior to the diet of many working peasants.[73]

The effect of the regulation of 1785 in this domain was to codify supplements that had been allowed in certain *dépôts*. More animal proteins were specified, mirroring a trend that was beginning in parts of France at about the same time. While some deficiencies remained, the new regulation promoted a more balanced diet, especially by requiring an accounting record of vegetables used in the daily broth. By requiring that working inmates be allowed to receive a share of the earnings from their labor, the regulation also generalized the practice of allowing workers to supplement their basic rations, thus fulfilling a physiological need while providing a moralizing incentive.[74]

Measures of preventive hygiene tended also to augment the prevailing standard of well-being. The installation of baths and ovens established a routine of cleansing new inmates on their arrival and of steam-baking their clothing.[75] The stocking of spare clothing for summer and winter, and items of bedding (including sheets for women), taken together with instructions for upkeep and laundering of bedding, entailed further expenditure in an area in which contractors had cut corners notoriously.[76]

As one might expect, the regulation departed most sharply from a hierarchical or punitive standard in its articles concerning the care of sick inmates. The regime for infirmaries required the allocation of resources for a separate space containing double beds divided by a partition (with separate bedding), individual robes and urinary vessels, semiprivate chamberpots, regular medical supervision, and a standard pharmacy. Uniform medical standards determined diet. According to cases, the diet might include beef, mutton, or veal. Eggs or rice might be prescribed. The convalescent would ordinarily receive wine, beer, or cider.[77]

The new administrative armature provided by the regulation was at least as significant as the new standards themselves. A pamphlet of 1791 penned by Bannefroy, a former inspector of the *dépôts,* highlights in retrospect the importance of the new arrangements. He echoes the common litany of complaints against the *dépôts,* but argues nonetheless that the regulation of 1785 improved matters, particularly by instituting administrative accountability: "In these establishments, the life of hapless inmates has long been calculated by bidding and contracting. Companies had made speculations on the bread of these wretches; and it was but recently that the administration at last established, in the *dépôts,* an overseer accountable to the King."[78]

The role of this official was especially important, since the regulation prescribed a standard of maintenance superior to the one currently contracted for. Colombier undoubtedly pressed for this innovation. He had argued the merits of a *régie* and denounced the abuses of general contracts in his writings on military hospitals ten years earlier.[79]

The wording of the third article of the first title of the regulation gave the overseer sweeping powers: "The police, the subsistance, and the regime of the interior of the *dépôt* will be confided to an overseer, having a commission from the Council, and the said overseer will alone command in the *dépôt* under the orders of M. the Intendant, as far as concerns the duties that he will be charged with." The overseer *(régisseur)* supervised personnel and managed funds. He coordinated the activities of an inspector of police (who would be the lieutenant of the *maréchaussée* in the town in which the *dépôt* was situated) and several officers: "one or two almoners, a doctor, a surgeon-in-chief, one or several surgeon's aides, as needed, an apothecary in case one of the surgeons cannot perform his functions, and an overseer-clerk, who will all be chosen and named by M. the Intendant." This miniature bureaucracy appears to have been modeled on that of St. Denis.[80]

While the concierge was still responsible for keeping detailed registers on the status of inmates, the overseer was to extract a daily report to the intendant from these records (Regulation, 2:28). Taking over the role of treasurer *(caissier),* the overseer was also responsible for all financial transactions, bookkeeping, and inventory, including the rendering of quarterly accounts. These accounts would be reviewed by the subdelegate charged with "the inspection of all objects of administration, housekeeping *(économie),* and internal regulation *(régime intérieur)*" and presented to the intendant (3:1–4).[81]

The overseer himself was obliged to defer to a professionalized code of observation and action that superseded his own. Not medically trained, he was expected to apply faithfully the rules of hygiene codified in the regulation, and to facilitate the work of medical professionals. Although the overseer stocked and inspected the infirmary's provisions, a *maîtresse infirmière* directed its nursing functions under the authority of doctors and surgeons (3:44).[82] The doctor himself was to taste the *bouillon* served to the sick following his morning visit (3:48). Doctors and surgeons were to record their observations and prescriptions on patients in a *cahier de visite,* and, as if to buffer potentially conflicting authority roles, the overseer's clerk was to relay to him the dietary prescriptions that the overseer would then have administered (3:55). The apothecary or surgeon would be responsible for administering medicines (3:59).[83]

Although the overseer acted at the orders of the intendant, his commission implied that his primary responsibility was to implement the general regulation subject to centralized inspection. The control of subsistence, in particular, was to be maintained by a newly standardized procedure. The printed form labeled *régie économique* set forth the formula into which local variables were to be substituted. A single chart presented a daily reckoning of the number of inmates by category, from which should be derived in parallel columns the number of daily rations of bread of each quality and weight, according to the categories of ration for male and female in sickness or in health. A recapitulation on a facing page totaled the rations served of each type and the unit price and total cost of the two types of bread.[84]

Similar tables listed the nature of each food commodity consumed each day for a given assortment of inmates, paired with a monthly summary of amounts on hand, purchased, consumed, and remaining at the end of the month. The accompanying illustration conveys a sense of the detail and order expected. The printed entries served undoubtedly as a reminder of the standards of provisioning to be maintained.

ÉTAT Journalier du nombre des Mendians, tant bien portans que malades, renfermés dans le Dépôt de *Bourges* & de la consommation du Pain servant à leur nourriture, pendant le mois de *Janvier* 1786.

NOMBRE DE RENFERMÉS.								PAIN BIS.				PAIN BLANC.						
Dates du Mois.	HOMMES			FEMMES				TOTAL des Renfermés.	HOMMES.		FEMMES.		VALIDES.	MALADES.					restans.
	Bien Portans.	Malades.	Infirmes.	Bien Portantes.	Malades.	Infirmes.	Enfans.		Ration à la Ration z. 4.	Employés à la Ration de 2 e.	Ration à la Ration z. 4.	Employés à la Ration de 2 e.	Soupe des Renfermés 20 onces.	Portion de 20 onces.	Portion de 12½ onces.	Portion de 10 onces.	Portion de 5 onces.	à la Diète.	Portion de 20 onces.
1.	68	2	..	48	5	..	.	123	68	.	48	.	.	.	7	.	.	.	.
2.	67	2	.	48	5	..	.	122	67	.	48	.	.	.	7	.	.	.	.
3.	58	5	6	43	6	4	.	122	64	.	47	.	22. 10	.	10	1	.	.	.
4.	59	5	6	43	6	4	.	123	65	.	47	.	22.	.	10	1	.	.	.
5.	59	5	6	41	8	4	.	123	65	.	45	.	22	.	11	1	1	1	.
6.	59	5	6	41	8	4	.	123	65	.	45	.	22	.	11	1	1	1	.
7.	59	5	6	43	6	4	.	123	65	.	47	.	22. 4	.	10	1	.	.	.
8.	59	5	6	43	6	4	.	123	65	.	47	.	11.	.	10	1	.	.	.
9.	59	4	6	43	6	4	.	122	65	.	47	.	22. 4	.	9	1	.	.	.
10.	59	4	6	43	6	4	.	122	65	.	47	.	22. 4	.	9	1	.	.	.
11.	58	5	6	42	7	4	.	122	64	.	46	.	22.	.	11	1	.	.	.
12.	58	5	6	42	7	4	.	122	64	.	46	.	22	.	11	1	.	.	.
13.	58	5	6	42	7	4	.	122	64	.	46	.	22	.	11.	1	.	.	.
14.	58	5	6	42	7	4	.	122	64	.	46	.	22	.	11	1	.	.	.
15.	58	5	6	42	7	4	.	122	64	.	46	.	11.	.	11	1	.	.	.
16.	60	5	6	42	7	4	.	124	66	.	46	.	22	.	11	1	.	.	.
17.	61	5	6	42	7	4	.	125	67	.	46	.	22. 8	.	11	1	.	.	.
18.	61	5	6	42	7	4	.	125	67	.	46	.	22. 8	.	11	1	.	.	.
19.	61	5	5	42	7	4	.	124	66	.	46	.	22. 4	.	11	1	.	.	.
20.	63	5	5	42	7	4	.	126	68	.	46	.	22. 4	.	11.	1	.	.	.
21.	60	8	5	44	6	4	.	127	65	.	48	.	22. 4	.	12	2	.	.	.
22.	60	8	5	44	6	4	.	127	65	.	48	.	11. 4	.	12	2	.	.	.
23.	60	8	5	44	6	4	.	127	65	.	48	.	22. 8	.	12.	2	.	.	.
24.	60	8	5	44	6	4	.	127	65	.	47	.	22. 8	.	13	1	.	.	.
25.	61	7	5	43	7	4	.	127	66	.	47	.	22. 8	.	13	1	.	.	.
26.	61	7	5	43	7	4	.	127	66	.	47	.	22. 8	.	13	1	.	.	.
27.	61	7	5	43	7	4	.	127	66	.	47	.	22. 8	.	13	1	.	.	.
28.	61	7	5	44	7	4	.	128	66	.	48	.	22. 8	.	13	1	.	.	.
29.	61	7	5	44	7	4	.	128	66	.	48	.	11. 12	.	14	.	.	.	.
30.	61	7	5	44	7	4	.	128	66	.	48	.	22. 8	.	14	.	.	.	.
31.	60	9	5	44	7	4	.	129	65	.	48	.	22. 8	.	14	2	.	.	.
	1861	175	161	1337	205	116	.	3862	2029	.	1453	.	601. 8	.	346	32	.	2	.

Standard pages from an early printed version of the *Régie économique* from the *dépôt* at Bourges for the month of January 1786. (A.D. Cher, C.96)

First page: Daily reckoning of bread rations for inmates.

DÉNOMINATION des DENRÉES	EXISTANTES au 1.er Janvier 1786	ACHATS pendant CE MOIS.	TOTAL.	CONSOMMÉES pendant CE MOIS.	RESTANTES au 1.er Février 1786
Pain bis......		5223	5223	5223	
Pain blanc.....		877	877	877	
Haricots......	617 8	208	825 2	330 4	494 14
Bœuf		33 4	33 4	33 4	
...en Fricot	146		146	77	69
...de terre		100	100	74	26
Riz.........	306 8	463	769 8	306 8	463
Graisse........	45	45	90	55 4	34 12
Sel..........	25 8	119	144 8	134 8	10
Viande.......		399 4	399 4	399 4	
Lait........		45	45	45	
Œufs........					
Vin Rouge....	189 1/2		189 1/2	28 1/2	161
Vin Blanc....	364		364		364
Vinaigre.......	246		246		246
Huile à brûler...	7 1/2	17	24 1/2	17	7 1/2
Balais.........	150	84	234	72	162
Bois de corde	6 1/4		6 1/4	4 3/4	1 1/2
Bois de charbon		1 1/2	1 1/2	1 1/2	
Sabots........		38	38	15	23
Cuillers de bois...		96	96	33	63
Bouteilles	1864		1864	243	1621
Savon........		8	8	4	4
Chandelle......	8	12	20	20	
Charbon.....	18 1/2		18 1/2	2 1/2	16
Baume de genièvre	9	90	99	18	81
Toile à ensevelir	12		12	3	9

376

Fourth page: Monthly accounting for stocks of victuals and supplies. Note *"toiles à ensevelir—12 aunes"* (winding sheets for the dead) and the use of juniper sprigs, traditionally burned as a means of purifying air, although no longer recommended in the 1785 regulation.

The standardized printed *régie* must have facilitated a panoptic sense of regularity and discipline that was to be conveyed throughout the establishment by the actions of trained civil servants.[85]

The training of overseers was not mentioned in the regulation, but official correspondence contains several references to a school for overseers at the *dépôt* of St. Denis. The principle that all overseers should pass through it was still recognized in 1791. The minister of the interior wrote to the administrators of the *département* of the Orne on April 30 of that year concerning the commissions bestowed on overseers:

> The administration had imposed upon itself the obligation of conferring them only upon persons who, after having performed a prerequisite training period *[surnumérariat]* at the *dépôt* of St. Denis (it being the largest establishment in the Kingdom), were recognized as being capable of exercising them. This rule had been established in order to maintain a necessary uniformity, be it in the interior regimen, be it in the use of funds, be it in the keeping of records and accounts.[86]

A Sieur Bence, overseer at the *dépôt* of Bourges, requested payment of emoluments that were due to him "for the time that I oversaw *ad interim* the *dépôt* of St. Denis in 1787 and 1788"; he mentions having had responsibility for a school for *surnuméraires* there.[87]

Colombier's regulation was not printed at the end of 1785 as he had projected. Perhaps he wanted to modify the text in the light of further experience. Perhaps there was some reluctance to publish it before it could be fully applied everywhere. In fact, introduction of the regulation was coordinated with the adoption of the *régie* as conditions permitted in each *généralité*. This process was well advanced by 1789, when the Revolution suspended all but routine decisions in many *départements*. By then, twenty-three of the thirty-four *dépôts* were governed by *régie*. Colombier himself died at a most dramatic moment, on a tour of inspection in Alsace, on August 4, 1789.[88]

Two supplements to the regulation of 1785 were distributed in printed form almost immediately. They reflected a process of medical codification that did not depend on the full implementation of the regulation in every *généralité*. Writing to the intendant of Rouen on July 26, 1785, Bertier announced the intention of the minister to apply a "uniform method of treatment" in the *dépôts*. He sent a ninety-page printed booklet entitled *Matière medicale des dépôts de mendicité du Royaume*. Each *dépôt*, said Bertier, had to have "an established pharmacy, suitably provisioned."[89] The regulation had also promised an instruction on the manner of governing the insane. The abbé de Montlinot had referred to a plan by Colombier for the treatment of the insane in his *Compte-rendu* of the *dépôt* at Soissons for 1782, and the Lyons regulation had also mentioned it. The instruction drawn up by Colombier with the collaboration of Doublet was printed in 1785. The fact that the accounts of the *dépôt* of St. Denis included payment to Mauduyt for "an electric machine" may offer a clue to medical experimentation with the insane in the *dépôts*, especially since the official instruction on the insane included a reference to *commotions électriques* as a form of treatment.[90]

In a much later move that still reflected the impulse of the general regulation, the controller-general sent with a circular of February 13, 1788, an "Instruction on

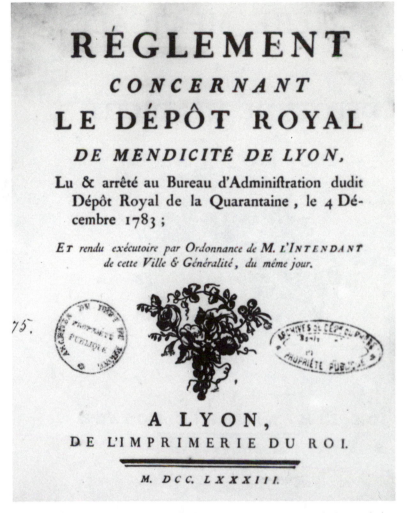

RÉGLEMENT

CONCERNANT

LE DÉPÔT ROYAL

DE MENDICITÉ DE LYON,

Lu & arrêté au Bureau d'Adminiſtration dudit Dépôt Royal de la Quarantaine, le 4 Décembre 1783 ;

ET rendu exécutoire par Ordonnance de M. L'INTENDANT de cette Ville & Généralité, du même jour.

A LYON,
DE L'IMPRIMERIE DU ROI.

M. DCC. LXXXIII.

Regulation of the *dépôt* at Lyons (1783), precursor of Colombier's regulation of 1785. (A.D. Rhone, C.175)

the correspondence of doctors and surgeons attached to the *dépôts de mendicité.''* The inspector-general wished to receive information on the disposition of each *dépôt,* on the state of its infirmaries, on the illnesses of the inmates, and on the ''medical topography'' of the *dépôt* itself. This information would be assembled into a monthly summary of the illnesses in all the *dépôts.* This initiative no doubt reflected Colombier's work in combatting epidemics. Much earlier, however, he had made a proposal that similar information be assembled from military hospitals.[91] The procedures and intent would already be familiar to those health officers of the *dépôts* involved in the work of the Société Royale de Médecine and the campaign against epidemics—men such as La Hardrouyère at Rennes, Dupichard at Tours, and Davan at St. Denis.[92] In 1787 Doublet had already included reports from *dépôts* in his published collection of medical observations. One that involved

MATIÈRE MÉDICALE

DES

DÉPÔTS DE MENDICITÉ

DU ROYAUME.

C.1035

A PARIS,

DE L'IMPRIMERIE ROYALE.

M. DCCLXXXV.

Medicines to be stocked in the pharmacies of the *dépôts* were listed in this ninety-page brochure. (A.D. Seine-Maritime, C.1035)

well-known figures in the profession was entitled, ''Observations made in the *dépôt de mendicité* of Rouen on uncommon maladies and on venereal diseases by M. Marc, surgeon of this *dépôt,* under the direction of M. Le Pecq de La Clôture.''[93]

From 1785 until his death, Colombier pressed relentlessly to implement his regulation. Two sorts of obstacles commonly arose: the preference felt by some administrators for working with general contractors rather than managing operations directly under a bureaucratic *régie;* and the alleged difficulty of applying specific articles of the regulation in local circumstances. Against these obstacles, Colombier was able to marshal the authority of the minister and to overcome local objections by exercising a direct chain of verification. His own frequent and ubiquitous inspections enabled him to make expert judgment on local requests, to rebut local objections, and to evaluate the competence of individuals. His authority was that of a bureaucrat, reinforced by that of an expert.

Colombier's method of implementation is illustrated in the instruction that the minister, Calonne, sent to the intendant of Riom on December 11, 1785. He sent a copy of the regulation and stated that the king had ordered "that it be executed as soon as possible in all the *dépôts.*" He also sent a commission for a Sieur Henrion de Bussy as *régisseur-caissier* (cashier-overseer) of the *dépôt* at Riom, noting that de Bussy "is perfectly acquainted with the *régie* prescribed by the regulation." In fact, de Bussy had previously served at the *dépôt* of St. Denis. The written instructions for de Bussy, signed by both Colombier and Bertier on December 12, 1785, provided that he was to draw up an inventory of the effects within the *dépôt,* keep records of the price of victuals and provisions for the *dépôt* over two months, and to consult with the intendant upon the choice of employees, so as to apply the new system from April 1 on. It is noteworthy that the signature of the doctor-clerk Colombier, routinely countersigned by Bertier, authorized decisions that were merely to be executed by a royal provincial intendant.[94]

But what happens in Riom? The intendant, Chazerat, attempts to assert his own authority by putting forward arguments based on his special knowledge of local conditions. A "system" must yield to empirical observation! The regulation was "most wise," he wrote, "but one is appalled by the expense entailed in constructing the prodigious number of apartments that must compose each *dépôt.*" According to his estimate, the costs of administration, given the number of employees listed, would exceed the total expense of the *dépôt* at Riom in 1784, at 6s. 9d. per day for each of 140 inmates. Although the *dépôt* presently lacked infirmaries, the sick were being received at the *hôtel-Dieu* for 5s. per day, and the surgeon ministered to minor illnesses. The controller-general, normally dependent upon the intendant for such observation, here gave credence to the report of Colombier, based on a recent visit at Riom. "It is necessary," he admonished the intendant, to establish "greater order and salubrity" in the *dépôt.* His conclusion was categorical: "The remedy lies in the general regulation." The minister observed, as if the buildings were before his eyes, that the *dépôt* was clearly unsuited to its rehabilitative function. Since no workrooms or infirmaries could fit within existing quarters, "the inmates are in a state of inaction and one cannot prevent the mingling of the sexes." It might therefore be necessary either to enlarge the *dépôt* at Riom or to rent space from the *hôpital-général.* In a separate report on the *hôpital-général,* Colombier had noted that the manufacture in that hospital was losing money, adding that such efforts were generally not suited to hospital establishments. The broad purview of Colombier's inspectorate, coupled with his mastery of local detail, gave special force to his recommendations.[95]

The high cost of bringing physical facilities up to the standards required by the regulation may have been one reason for spreading out the implementation over a number of years. First estimates at Soissons, based on the need to build a metal

oven for disinfecting, two or three bathing pools, water conduits, and other improvements amounted to two thousand livres. Intendants who desired to make improvements in their *dépôts* were pleased to have Colombier's support. The intendant
of Picardy wrote to Calonne on July 11, 1785, to say that "M. Colombier, a man
of great sense and talent, has seen the place." He had approved an expense of
1,202 l. 10s. for changes in the *dépôt* at Amiens. In some cases, expenses mounted
as work proceeded. In the case of Tours, where the entire *dépôt* was moved to a
healthier location, contamination from the latrines, compartmentalized at the new
site to serve each category of inmate, caused severe health problems. As a result of
visits by Bannefroy and Colombier, the latrines were completely rearranged.[96]

Colombier and the minister turned a deaf ear to all objections against the *régie*
as opposed to a contractual agreement. Shortly before his death, Colombier commented on a report concerning the *dépôt* at Alençon: "The reasons given by M. the
Intendant for keeping the contract are each one feebler than the next. One would
reply to them in this report, if it did not seem best to wait for the end of the
agreement before establishing the *régie*. The regulation must at least be executed
in all the applicable sections."[97]

The work of Colombier and his subinspectors undoubtedly had some effect. In
some cases, inspection reports reflected a spirit of parsimony, as when Colombier
advised that worn garments should be used to repair newer ones. More commonly,
they recorded objections to unhealthy foods, soup prepared without enough meat,
lack of heat in the dormitories or disorder there, improper accounting procedures,
and above all, failure to observe proper order in the care of the sick.[98]

Whether the inmates of a particular *dépôt* benefited from the provisions of the
regulation depended on a variety of factors. Much depended on the thoroughness
and scruples of the overseers and those they supervised. The regulation that soup
be ladled out in precisely measured portions could be verified only by daily oversight on the spot. The quality of meats and vegetables depended on the quality
purchased from the butcher and the greengrocer, whatever notation was made on
the pages of the *régie économique*. Even when this task was performed conscien-
tiously, the inmates themselves could foil efforts made on their behalf. Some at
Rennes reportedly gambled away their rations; Bertier reported to his confrere at
Soissons that inmates transferred by convoy from St. Denis had managed to sell the
serviceable garments in which they set out in exchange for tatters and a jolt of *eau-
de-vie*.[99]

In order to vindicate the *régie*, much of Colombier's effort was directed to
supervision and evaluation of personnel. At Châlons, where the princesse de Ber-
gues and the comtesse de la Tour d'Auvergne were protecting an incompetent *régisseur*, Colombier reminded the intendant of their discussions during his inspection
visit, and reported bluntly to the minister that the intendant had assured him that
the individual in question "was not suited in this regard except to bungle the simplest matters." Colombier's report on another matter, a fire at the *dépôt* at Amiens,
seethed at the concierge, who allowed an insane inmate to follow him with a lit
taper into the bedding stores in the attic. Although firing him would not remedy the
problem, "it is an example to have posted in all the *dépôts*." The buildings would
have to be repaired and an estimate asked for.[100]

A newly emerging pattern of collaboration between administrators and scientists

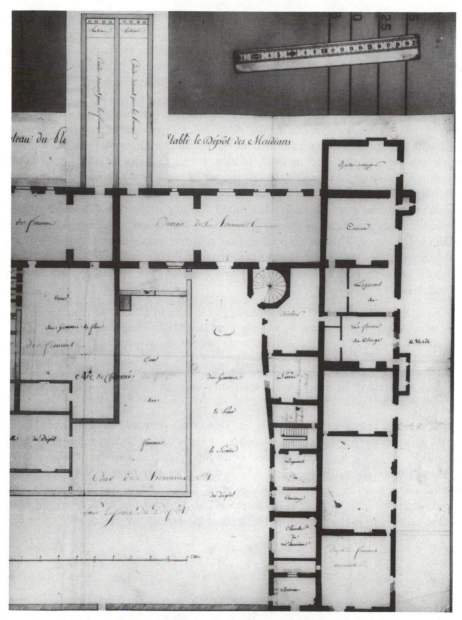

Ground plan of a *dépôt* established in the Château du Plessis at Tours. Note removal of latrines to enclosed location outside the walls of the *dépôt,* following the advice of medical inspectors in 1788. (A.D. Indre-et-Loire, C.314)

provided an intellectual and political context for Colombier's dual role as expert and bureaucrat. Turgot's promotion of the Société Royale de Médecine and Necker's campaign for hospital reform both served to strengthen the partnership between royal authority and the scientific community in the pursuit of public welfare.[101] The political optimism that could be engendered by this partnership found expression in the context of Colombier's efforts to improve conditions of hygiene in the *dépôts*. François Doublet, Colombier's son-in-law and closest collaborator in the inspectorate of prisons, hospitals, and *dépôts de mendicité,* voiced such a feeling in an article he wrote on "Air" for the volume of the medical dictionary of the *Encyclopédie méthodique* published in 1787. Ideally, he argued, the renewal of air within a hospital was assured by architectural design. But where it was necessary to remedy unhealthy conditions, mechanical ventilators had proven effective. Doublet referred to Duhamel's reports on Hales's initial design published in 1759, and praised the refinements in efficiency obtained by Sieur Weurlersse, a mechanical engineer in the king's navy. This, of course, was the machine that Bertier had touted to his confreres after its successful introduction at the *dépôt* of St. Denis. Doublet's testimonial to the art of the engineer turns into a song of praise for learned intervention of many kinds:

> to have astonishing proofs of the effect of preservative measures, one must see the marvelous change that can be wrought in places where contagion in most to be feared. At the *dépôt* of St. Denis, the dormitories are low-ceilinged and poorly aired; an epidemic uncleanliness of the deadliest sort formerly reigned in this place; cleanliness, good food, and discipline were established there; the contagious malady disappeared; mortality there has greatly abated; and this place of horror has become more salubrious than half the hospitals of France.[102]

The actual record of the *dépôt* at St. Denis was probably more mixed. It suffered as a dumping ground for the police of Paris and reflected the poor general conditions of public health during the deepening economic crisis of the late 1780s. The evils that persisted were enough to sustain a sinister image. Nonetheless, the record shows that the number of deaths at St. Denis, while appalling in absolute terms, declined after a surge in the early 1780s, and did not flare up to the same peaks again even in the most difficult years at the end of the decade.[103]

9

Laboratory of Virtue

Not long after Turgot's fall from office, the academy of Châlons-sur-Marne announced a prize-essay contest on the subject, "How to make beggars useful to the state without making them unhappy?" There was nothing extraordinary about the academy's desire to serve as critic and counsellor of authority. The provincial academies were, in Daniel Roche's phrase, "daughters of administration" in several senses: they were promoted by royal authority and protected by royal intendants; they counted among their members a high proportion of officials and consultants in royal bureaucracies; and when they addressed policy issues, they cast themselves in the role of experts whose critical diagnosis of a problem would reflect credit both on the civic zeal of a local elite and on the beneficent intentions of the king and his ministers.[1]

In announcing its approach to the stock subject of eradicating mendicity, the academy of Châlons-sur-Marne reflected nonetheless the more intensely humanitarian and more impatiently reformist spirit of Jacques Necker's first ministry. The notion that beggars should be made useful was a cliché: to imply that the solution must not make beggars "unhappy" had a certain air of paradox and novelty. The academy chose not to publish the winning entry, but instead assembled a topically ordered compendium of all the memoirs, creating a text that was qualitatively as well as quantitatively different from a memoir by a single author. In effect, it was a pocket encyclopedia of social and legislative reform, focused on the problem of mendicity.

The Compound Eye of the Academy of Châlons-sur-Marne

The winner of the prize accorded in 1777 was a M. Clouet, squire, counsellor, *médecin ordinaire du Roi,* doctor of the military hospital and the charity hospitals of Verdun. Clouet appears to have won favor with the judges particularly because he cast his suggestions in the form of a general regulation. Thus the articles of the *règlement* that rounds off the compilation were mostly his.[2]

Squarely in the reformist tradition of the age, the composite *règlement* would have pleased Laverdy or Loménie de Brienne. Its first section prescribed a machine-like *police* that operated with uniform precision in every part of the kingdom and detected every infraction of the law. The offender was to be put to work, of course. The remaining three sections of the *règlement* dealt with the constitution of *bureaux de charité,* the designation of their agents, and the provision of their funds. The call for a revived system of parish responsibility based on such bureaus was a feature of practically every memoir, according to the abbé Malvaux, compiler and editor of the compendium.[3]

If Clouet soft-pedaled the use of royal authority in his scheme, it was in order to promote the civic virtue and voluntary responsibility of the citizen. Other essayists joined in resuscitating this civic theme of Turgot's article on endowments. Voluntary civic initiative flowed from a broader sensitivity to the need for liberty and "moderation" in the laws relating to mendicity. A system of laws that respected the liberty of the poor themselves would constrain the delinquent idle by reason, encouraging them to choose the occupations best suited to them. It would use fear and constraint only when that other, too-often-neglected motive, hope, had lost the power to inspire virtue.[4]

The bland voice of Clouet provides a foil for more astringent tones. Tirades against greed, despotism, and injustice, revelations of mismanagement and waste, and flights of utopian fervor offer variations on a reformist theme. Certain accents of rebellion were, of course, admissible by the conventions of academic rhetoric, just as *parlementaires* donned their robes and imagined themselves Roman tribunes, or as churchmen chastised the mighty form their pulpits. One thinks of a Belbeuf at Rouen, or of a Boisgelin at Louis XVI's coronation. Academic essayists had latitude to dramatize the seriousness of a problem or decry an injustice before specifying the terms upon which harmony could be restored.

The most frequently cited memoir appears in fact to have been that of the abbé Leclerc de Montlinot, "honorary canon at the church of St. Pierre at Lille." The runner-up in the Châlons contest, he resubmitted his essay two years later for a prize on a similar subject offered by the Agricultural Society of Soissons. As Malvaux noted in an appreciative footnote, Montlinot won the first prize there. The manuscript retained in the archives of the Society of Soissons shows that Montlinot did not even recopy his memoir; he simply scratched out the word "Academy" and wrote in "Society" where applicable. In awarding their prize, the judges at Soissons advised that extracts be chosen with care for a public reading, so that offense might not be given "to any order of citizen." In recognizing the memoir, they added, they "did not intend either to adopt all the principles contained in it, nor even to consecrate by [their] approbation its generally very vehement and often epigrammatic style."[5]

Who was this Montlinot? Born at Crépy-en-Valois in 1732, he obtained doctorates in theology and medicine at Paris in the 1750s, then pursued literary and philosophical interests while functioning as a librarian for the collegial chapter of the church of St. Pierre at Lille. Meanwhile, he leagued himself with Charles-Joseph Panckoucke, son of a self-made bookseller, would-be *polytechnicien,* future publishing baron of European renown. Montlinot served as editor of a provincial review published by Panckoucke and wrote controversial brochures. He defended the *Encyclopédie* against censure on religious grounds, wrote an irreverent, anticlerical history of Lille, composed extracts of La Mothe Vayer and the abbé de Saint-Pierre, and praised Rousseau's *Émile* (then under royal censure) as a work that explained how men could be trained to virtue and happiness.[6]

Incurring the wrath of local authorities, Montlinot resigned his prebend as canon in the chapter of St. Pierre in 1766. Accounts of the next decade in his life are sketchy and conflicting. He undoubtedly maintained his connection with Panckoucke, who had established his bookstore, Au Parnasse, near the Comédie in Paris in 1762. He was also associated for a time with the *Journal encyclopédique* and maintained contacts in Lille. He also appears to have cultivated his old quarrels or started new ones, for in 1779 he was directed by *lettre de cachet* to go to Soissons and not set foot outside the town until further notice. In that year he managed to have the full text of his prize-winning essay printed at both Soissons and Lille.[7]

Malvaux remarks that he used almost all of Montlinot's memoir in his compilation. At the beginning, he cites Montlinot in connection with the indictment of the dissembling idle beggar. Soon thereafter, Malvaux deploys quotation marks for a verbatim transcription of Montlinot's classic description of the system used in French Flanders to provide for the poor. The method involved an auction in which the idle youths of the parish were indentured to the person willing to accept the lowest "pension" for their upkeep. The community provided the youths with spending money and clothes, and sent a visitor to inspect their condition. Communities financed this arrangement by collections and by a voluntary assessment that fell on every owner in the community. The entire operation was conducted by village officials, who also expelled vagabonds from the community and conducted the insane to suitable *maisons de force* in the towns. There were no hospitals or special bureaus involved. Montlinot offered this regional instance as proof that the legal principle of parish responsibility for the poor could be enforced even in poorer rural parishes.[8]

By such means, the poor person who received aid was attached to his own community and was truly settled on the land. He was thus "useful" in the terms set by the academy, and "happy" even if the auction procedure seemed degrading: "He breathes a pure air, he keeps his health and strength, he lives with others like himself, he is happy because he feels the necessity of working." Malvaux drew from Montlinot's account a lesson in social policy, continuing to excerpt the author's language, but without quotation marks, thus contriving an illusion of dialogue between author and compiler:

> In general, the fault of those in power is to complicate too much the machinery by which they would move men. They are like those older physicists who multiplied circles and *tourbillons,* not being able to conceive the majestic simplicity of the laws that rule the Universe. System-mongers, Deep Politicians, do not always have such a poor opinion of the human species, let men do as they will, and believe that they will almost always do well.[9]

By contrast, the cities that Montlinot knew provided only object lessons of failure. Montlinot brought his medical training to bear on the description of urban hospitals. Malvaux took up his expostulation, "Enter a hospital, political calculator," and his medical description of the conditions to be observed there: youths with rickets, anemic young women, endemic cases of mange, not to mention "hospital fever'' (typhus). Montlinot went on to describe the psychological syndrome of dependence and apathy, and the breakdown of a sense of family identity or responsibility. With an image of the patient as ''automaton'' responding only to the impulse of a hospital administrator, Montlinot provided the argument for Malvaux's chapter heading, ''Hospitals stifle the sentiments''—an elaboration of a theme from Turgot.[10]

To Malvaux's chapter on ''Dépôts publics des Mendians ou Renfermeries,'' Montlinot contributed phrases that were even more highly charged. While the magistrates cited in Malvaux's footnotes undoubtedly contributed a grievous bill of particulars and probably referred to the deaths of thousands in these ''tombs,'' it was Montlinot who wrote, ''I have felt a dread chill for humanity as I compared these dens to the kennels of our great lords. There man received fewer attentions than the animal raised for pleasure.''[11] This vehement expression set an emotional context for a chorus of further objections to the *dépôts,* including charges of injustice and venality in the arrest of the innocent, and of profiteering by contractors.The essayist Romans de Coppier added some imagery no less inflammatory than Montlinot's, speaking of ''these new adjudicators of the food and sweat of the unfortunate,'' whom he compared to vampires feeding on the substance of the poor.[12]

In a further section on workhouses for the poor, Montlinot argued that measures taken at great expense in Lille and other large cities had done little to secure the lot of the poor. The urban worker—especially in the luxury trades—was inherently vulnerable to waves of unemployment from shifts in demand. Further, the type of work chosen for a workhouse always had to be an object of great care, so as not to harm the livelihood of independent tradesmen and yet make the work itself profitable and well-suited to the inmates.[13]

In common with other essayists, Montlinot articulated a belief that the poor themselves must be vouchsafed a sphere of autonomy. ''In general,'' Montlinot wrote and Malvaux copied, ''there is too little attention paid in Europe to the education of the people.'' Scholarships and foundations provided classical literary training, whereas ordinary workers could benefit from free instruction in useful trades.[14] If education would remove a cause of mendicity, by making men fit for trades that were in demand, the distribution of relief could be made more effective by involving common tradespeople in its administration. In the model proposed by Montlinot, two honest workers would serve with a respectable bourgeois on each committee as caseworkers interviewing households to determine need and dispense aid. Those in need would obtain certificates from master artisans attesting their previous employment, and guild masters would have a seat on the general assembly of a town's *bureau de charité.*[15]

Montlinot and his fellow essayists did not generally equate liberty with Physiocratic orthodoxy. His appreciative view of the guilds as a voice for sentiments of autonomy among working people was at odds with the laissez-faire creed. His strongly worded argument against the concentration of landed property also deviated from the new economic science. One essayist, a law professor at Caen, mildly but firmly reproved the Physiocrats for excluding manufacture as a source of wealth, and advocated a healthy balance between agriculture and manufacture. The essayists as a group heeded Galiani's doubts raised against the new economic science. They were sensitive to the precarious situation of the working poor in the face of fluctuating markets for labor and foodstuffs. Clearly, they were a receptive audience for Necker's philanthropic perspectives.[16]

The first half of the Châlons compendium is strongly shaped by Montlinot's leading ideas; it appears as if Malvaux arranged other texts around the core of Montlinot's memoir until it was spent. But Malvaux marshaled the ideas of all the contributors and focused their diverse lights, as if by some compound lens designed to illuminate the course of writers and administrators dealing with the problems of mendicity.

Like Loménie de Brienne's report to Turgot, the Châlons compendium of 1777 divides the question of mendicity into prevention and relief, and gives administration a much larger task than "law" in both spheres. The sections on legal repression emphasize the Beccarian themes of moderation, rational proportion, and public utility. By such standards, the current repression of begging was unjust and inhumane. According to the new dispensation, even a serious offender was to be treated as a fit subject for moral reform; *a fortiori,* thoughtless idlers should be offered positive inducements in order to nourish their self-esteem and their desire to function as useful citizens.[17]

Like Brienne, Malvaux linked the entire agenda of late eighteenth-century administrative reform to the attack on mendicity. Thus reform of the *corvée* was strongly urged by the essayists, who feared that the suspension of Turgot's edict might be permanent. They also urged more productive use of commons and waste lands, not by consolidation in large farms as the Physiocrats desired, but by the creation of a greater number of self-sufficient holdings. They called for a variety of police measures to reform the manifold abuses that promoted mendicity: usury and monopoly, the excessive number of domestic servants, the distraction of working people from productive activity by cabarets, gambling, and prostitution.[18]

Malvaux's compendium sounds a distinctive note, nonetheless. Announcing the aspirations and accents of a generation that would soon find itself engaged on a path of revolution, it called for a national regeneration at once individual and social. It was not enough to reform abuses or to give the individual citizen his rights: the decay of civic virtue and the sense of oppression and misery within the community were interrelated. The feelings of the citizen would revive as the community was once more made whole. The rehabilitation of the criminal and the retraining of the idler were to be accomplished as part of a larger task of reawakening the citizen. The fullest expression of this new aspiration was to be found in the revaluation of work—of each man and woman's proper activity within the community.[19]

The revaluation of work was a theme that coalesced from various milieux. Writers who had experience in managing the poor, such as Puricelli at Besançon or Lambert at the *hôpital-général* of Paris, dealt with the problem of motivating inmates to be productive. Officers of police offered their opinions on correctional procedures and institutions: de la Balme, lieutenant of the *maréchaussée* at Senlis in the *généralité* of Paris, urged large installations in port cities (an idea inspired by the *bagnes* and later taken up by Montlinot). Engineers and specialists in manufacture advanced promising new techniques: Duperron at Caen insisted that new processes of silk-weaving promised new markets and a perfect project for employing beggars—an idea implemented already at the *dépôt* of Moulins. But most important of all was the point urged by the curé de Monques, namely that an increase in the standard of living of ordinary people was the most promising remedy for mendicity. The distillation of the phrase, "une aisance générale répandue parmi le peuple," was thus not Montlinot's doing. The Châlons chapter heading may well have caught his attention; by 1781 he was to incorporate the idea as an essential working assumption in his strategy of rehabilitating beggars.[20]

The original character of Montlinot's entire memoir of 1777 was fully revealed to the public when it was published two years later after winning the first prize of the Agricultural Society at Soissons. Speaking as vindicator of the rights of the poor, Montlinot begins his memoir by attacking the "cruel codes" that the rich have imposed. Enveloped in the ample cloak of virtue, this admirer of *Émile* apostrophizes his judges:

> If I had to plead the cause of the poor before a troop of sybarites, I would perhaps content myself with soliciting some help while promising to remove from their eyes the spectacle of misery, but I speak before an august tribunal, composed of virtuous men of feeling—may I prove worthy of them and of my subject, reconciling all at once the gentleness of the Gospel, the severity of the laws, and the honor of humanity.[21]

Louis David should have painted a picture entitled, "Prize-essay judges of the Society of Agriculture of Soissons reading Montlinot's essay (originally written for the Academy of Châlons-sur-Marne)." He would no doubt have caught them severely pondering Montlinot's adjuration to abolish alms and hospitals and to institute those measures that will respect the poor person, letting him "dispose of his own existence in the pure air of liberty."[22]

Speeches about human happiness were too often made from a bed of roses, Montlinot insisted. All recent writings on happiness, he observed, had still not formulated a method of determining what the population of France ought to be, in order to serve the happiness of the individual, let alone decide what should be done with some nine hundred thousand persons languishing in prisons, *maisons de force,* or hospitals. "The whole fracas of our political principles reduced to the fewest possible terms," he declared, "hardly touches upon anything but the art of employing men at little cost in the service of the rich—thus softness and idleness have been regarded as the ultimate happiness."[23]

While a cult of *bienfaisance* had flourished, Montlinot charged that nothing had been done for the "hardworking indigent," for the "decent woman overburdened with her own fertility," or for the "artisan without work." Attention given to those immured in institutions allowed the well-to-do to ignore the fundamental reality: inequality "seems to have divided all the individuals of Europe into two classes: that which has too much and that which has nothing." Europeans were becoming less sensitive to the needs of their fellows, even as they made a cult of beneficent feeling.[24] The tableau of European society that Montlinot offered here recalls that which the flamboyant journalist Simon-Nicolas-Henri Linguet had just drawn in the opening number of the *Annales politiques, civiles et littéraires* in April 1777. Linguet argued that the progress of social change was leading inexorably to the creation of a rich exploiting class and a mass of propertyless workers bound to a "free" marketplace. A great civil war might be expected to engulf the enlightened nations of Europe unless they guaranteed the economic security of this new slave class by carefully engineered social institutions.[25]

An exile from both France and Belgium, Linguet edited his journal in London. He seemed to draw, as Montlinot did, upon a Flemish tradition of paternalistic social police coexisting with working-class revolt, in a region where agriculture was becoming intensely commercialized and the evolution of an old industrial tradition offered glimpses of a new age of mechanization. In Malvaux's footnotes Montlinot finds himself more than once in the company of two other Lillois, the abbé Blanchard and the publisher "Pankouke."[26] Attuned to Brussels and London as well as Paris, Montlinot seems to have derived the materials for an ideological position resembling that of Linguet.[27] Montlinot was ultimately more successful in managing the duality of his roles as rebel and grand administrator. Adept at distilling critical insight to the most caustic permissible concentration, he accomplished the unusual feat of carving out a position for himself as inspector of the *dépôt de mendicité* of Soissons in 1781. In published accounts of that *dépôt,* he diagnosed the sociological symptoms of mendicity as if he were a doctor of the Société Royale de Médecine publishing clinical observations. The Revolution drew him into the work of the Comité de Mendicité of the Constituent Assembly, and he would end his career as a bureaucrat in the Department of the Interior.[28]

"The Best of All Possible *Dépôts*"

The intendant of Soissons wrote to his subdelegate at Laon on April 21, 1781, to advise him that the *dépôt* in that town was to be shut down by May 1. The inmates were to be transferred to Soissons, he explained, "where M. Necker proposes to establish a more economical administration, and which might serve as a rule and example in the other provinces." The new plan was to be carried out by the abbé de Montlinot, whose appointment as inspector of the *dépôt* at Soissons was confirmed by a letter from Necker to the intendant March 13.[29]

Recounting later his move to initiate improvements in the regime of the *dépôts,* Necker wrote that he looked to the *généralité* of Soissons, near Paris, "where I could be seconded by an intendant full of zeal and love of the good, and by the intelligence and methodical spirit of an ecclesiastic who had already displayed his special aptitude for this sort of administration." Official correspondence attests to the reality of collaboration between minister, intendant, and inspector. Louis Le Peletier de Mortefontaine, intendant of Soissons since 1765, had voiced hope that Turgot's program of liberalization would bring about the well-being of the people. Writing in 1777, he argued that the campaign against mendicity had to take account of regional patterns of landholding. Necker, Le Peletier, and Montlinot shared the view that royal policy should especially concern itself with augmenting the class of small owners and farmers, supporting their security and well-being.[30]

The appointment of Montlinot fulfilled a long-deferred wish of the intendant. On several occasions he had asked for funds to employ an inspector of the *dépôt.* In December 1780 Necker had circularized the intendants to announce an economy measure—a reduction in the number of *dépôts* to one per *généralité*. Royal finances were strained more than usual by support for the American colonists. Expenses were being curtailed and deferred everywhere. The intendants were asked to submit plans for effecting the reduction in question so as to use the remaining facilities to the best effect. The intendant of Soissons consulted with Montlinot on a proposal that promised minor savings on such items as clothing repair, food preparation, and medicine, but also called for some new initial funding in order to make the operation at Soissons more effective, particularly by the establishment of workshops.[31]

The intendant would probably have had little success in cracking the uniformity of Bertier's bureaucratic model, had not Necker been predisposed to experiment with ways of improving the *dépôts,* and had not the idea taken shape in direct consultation between intendant and minister. Encountering resistance from Bertier's bureau, Le Peletier reminded Necker in May of the arrangement "agreed upon verbally between you and me" that 28,000 livres would be put at the disposition of the abbé de Montlinot for the current year. Le Peletier enlisted further aid in cutting through the red tape of Bertier's bureau from Dr. Colombier, whom Necker had appointed in January to the new position of inspector over hospitals, prisons, and *dépôts de mendicité.*[32]

Necker's fall from office at the end of May 1781 could have raised uncertainty about Montlinot's position, but Le Peletier apparently won the support of the new minister, Joly de Fleury, for continuing the experiment. One of Joly de Fleury's first acts in office was to grant the request of the general contractors for the *dépôts* to abrogate their contract, which was to have run until July 31, 1783. He asked intendants to take new bids, preferably from the subcontractors of the old provisioning company. Bertier, already consultating with Colombier, may have encouraged a move to reexamine the standards of provisioning in the *dépôts.* The minister sent out a model contract with a common *journée* for inmates in sickness and in health. In the context of such consultation, it may have seemed fitting to allow the experiment at Soissons to continue.[33]

In order to document his experiment in workhouse reform, Montlinot kept unusually complete records. Thus it is possible to trace general developments in the bureaucratic history of the *dépôts* in the 1780s with special ease at Soissons. But Montlinot's records are of special interest for other reasons. Most obviously, his installation at Soissons presented Bertier with a challenge. This challenge, and Bertier's response to it, is one of the major threads in the history of the *dépôts* in the last decade of the Old Regime. As an unexpected bonus, the study of these archives uncovers a trail of unusually frank and sprightly letters between Montlinot and the first secretary of the intendant, Favier, who was Montlinot's link with Le Peletier during those extensive periods when the business of the *Généralité* was conducted from Paris. Favier, like Montlinot, was a man of letters. The two of them vied with each other in trading allusions and *bons mots.* In their correspondence, as in the memoirs of the academies, bureaucratic and literary modes of consciousness converge.[34]

Finally, Montlinot's work was documented in yet another fashion by means of a series of published accounts. Jacques Necker set an example of public accountability by outlining the state of royal finance in his *Compte Rendu au Roi* of January 1781. In the section of that account entitled "Hospitals and Prisons," Necker referred to the two annual published accounts for the hospital of the parish of St. Sulpice in Paris. Hospital boards were wont to give out more or less detailed statements of their financial condition as a means of justifying their appeal for further donations. The accounts for St. Sulpice represented a departure, however, in purporting to be experimental in nature. They had served to demonstrate empirically the health benefits and the economic feasibility of placing hospital patients in single beds. The sick bed at the new hospital had cost 17s. per day, well below the 24 to 25s. estimated for the large Paris hospitals. Necker also reported on attempts to reform the treatment of foundlings, including the use of cow's milk in the artificial feeding of infants.[35]

Montlinot was to publish annual accounts of the *dépôt de mendicité* at Soissons in the same spirit. The first one covered the last eight months of 1781, the second 1782, the third 1783. Accounts for 1784 and 1785 were published together, following the appearance of an article on the *dépôts* by Montlinot in the *Encyclopédie méthodique*. An account for 1786 accompanied the essay on mendicity that Montlinot published in 1789.[36]

The First Two Years: From *Dépôt de Mendicité* to *Maison de Travail*

Le Peletier wrote directly to Bertier on July 10, 1781, to request the funds agreed upon by the minister and to report on Montlinot's efforts. He claimed to have produced some savings in the *journée* of inmates by simplifications of regime; record-keeping had also been simplified. Mattress covers filled with moss (dried out, presumably) proved cheaper than straw bedding, and healthier—troops camping in the *généralité* had been so provided. Montlinot had added a touch of gadgetry by using foldaway platforms for bedding, leaving space in which to work during the day. Inspection had demonstrated the need for some extraordinary expenditures, however. Disinfection was a major problem, as the mange was endemic. Outlays for new clothes and linen were urgently needed, especially for pregnant and nursing women. Montlinot's concept of hygiene was clearly conveyed in the intendant's letter: "There can be no health without cleanliness, and these two things naturally bring about order and work."[37]

As the months passed, Montlinot grew frustrated with petty obstacles. In a progress report to the intendant in August, he wrote bluntly, "M. Bertier sends us many beggars and no money—I have written to M. Colombier to look into this matter." He also drafted an urgent request to require the board of the hospital at Soissons to reverse their decision not to receive children of *filles mendiantes,* and to ask that, if the children remained in the *dépôt,* they receive an allotment from royal funds for the support of foundlings. The intendant forwarded the request to the *intendant des finances,* Chaumont de la Millière, whom Necker had put in charge of hospitals (at last replacing Boullongne), but advised Montlinot "not to protest the decision of the minister contrary to your desires, which are also mine in this regard." The occasion could be exploited by pointing out that the problem of crowding in the *dépôt* might be eased, if the hospital would agree to cede a patch of garden in order to build a workshop for the *dépôt.* The intendant was inclined to think, in any case, that it was better to keep the children with their mothers.[38]

In November the intendant thanked Dr. Colombier for taking up money matters and these other subjects with Bertier, and suggested they meet to discuss such matters further on the intendant's return to Paris. If Montlinot's combativeness was well harnessed by Le Peletier's counsels of prudence, his efforts to renovate the regime at Soissons were also well served by Le Peletier's active bureaucratic diplomacy.

"Air" and "work" were the magic words of Montlinot's first account, printed as a brochure early in 1782 and distributed in April by the intendant to subdelegates, officers of the *maréchaussée*, and other interested parties, with a request for suggestions as to how the experiment might be improved. Cleaning out the old building, once used as an inn, required a concentrated effort and some special outlays to be repaid in long-run improvements in efficiency. Montlinot claimed that his immediate attention to hygiene, building repairs, furnishings, and medical treatment had met with gratifying results: the high morbidity rates of the previous year had fallen, "as if by enchantment."[39]

The essential function of the *dépôt* ought to be educational. For that reason, Montlinot had taken down the old sign of the *dépôt* and put up the new inscription, *"Maison de travail."* In his essay of 1779, Montlinot had observed that it was important for those in power to understand that honor was important even to the poorest members of society. Once the odium of idle squalor was removed, rehabilitation could begin: "[A]ir and work were given to individuals who had huddled in filth and inaction, and it was attempted, if I may so express myself, to wind up again the springs of these machines that had been crushed down in this asylum of misery."[40]

Montlinot's preaching on the subject of work dramatically intensifies common enlightened precepts. In particular, he reshaped the accepted notion, expressed by Brienne, that work was to be administered both as reward and penalty, as a means to "animate and contain" the idler. Montlinot gives a new emphasis to the positive term of this duality, to make of it the bedrock assumption of his strategy of rehabilitation:

> It has already been said, but cannot be repeated too often, that the whole secret of the new administration consists in making work the recompense of the unfortunate and the penalty of the idler: it is in this double relationship that the *dépôts* must be envisaged, if one wishes to destroy mendicity. Nothing must be spared to keep the poor in health and to engender in them the desire for work that brings a wage, the sole patrimony of the obscure and propertyless.[41]

The vision that Montlinot puts before the reader is not necessarily that of the consumer basking in security, but rather of a poor person who is no longer content to endure a miserably poor and dirty standard of living, and who will therefore make extraordinary efforts to work his way out of the pit of indigence. "Emulation," a key word in many writings on the rehabilitation of idlers as useful citizens, now means not only pride in achievement, but confidence in its rewards. While cleaning the Augean stables of the converted inn that served as the *dépôt* at Soissons, Montlinot experienced an annunciation of sorts as to the redemptive function of cleanliness in a new social order. "Cleanliness," he noted, "is, physically speaking, one of the first bodily needs." But a further perspective was equally important:

> "Besides, as the goal of the Administration is to seek to destroy mendicity, one must be sensible that he who has tasted the pleasure of lying in a bed is far less tempted to ask basely for permission to sprawl out on the dungheap of a farm."

At this point Montlinot is struck by an irresistible paradox and an equally irresistible image, which he records in the breathless style of *La Nouvelle Héloïse*:

If the point is not to perpetuate the race of beggars, then accustom them to the luxury of ease. . . . The luxury of the *dépôts*! . . . This appears strange at first glance, but nonetheless we are persuaded that if one could train all the women of the workhouse to the point of desiring gloves, these women would be regenerated for society, hard-working, and worthy of being mothers. . . . In short, one may say in conclusion that cleanliness gives rise to demands, demands to work, work to thought, thought to the desire for those enjoyments that sustain and augment emulation in all the classes of society.[42]

Montlinot admitted that the savings he had obtained in the first eight months were more modest than might have been expected, because a considerable investment had been made in securing the inmates' well-being. He argued that healthier inmates would be more productive workers: rehabilitation and economy were not in conflict. He did not describe the training process in detail, saying only that it involved "indescribable nuances." He was able to report that the intendant had secured a plot of ground from the adjoining hospital garden, on which workshops could be erected to provide more space for the men.[43]

Commenting on Montlinot's first account, Le Peletier pointed to the savings that had already been made. Further savings could be realized as the arrangements for putting inmates to work were perfected. Montlinot had this task firmly in hand, and the intendant was fully confident that the annual appointments of 1,500 livres paid to him would be well returned.[44]

A year later, Montlinot reported on the progress made in 1782. The initial housecleaning done, he brought the inmates out of the shadows. He had made some observations on their generally small stature in the first account; now he followed them through each stage of life in the *dépôt*. He commented on their origins, their declared professions, their state of health, their treatment in the *dépôt*. Restating the bedrock assumptions of his first account, he drew new conclusions from the data accumulated. In simplest terms, *misère* and *pauvreté* were more important than *débauche* and *fainéantise*. At Soissons the especially vulnerable status of winegrowers and herdsmen was etched in the registers of the *dépôt*. The theme of exploitation developed in his essay of 1777 became more specific. Noting that the aged were particularly likely to be without resources after a lifetime of serving society, Montlinot called for a state system of old-age pensions. Surely it would be simple justice to establish *prébendes* for these worthy servants.[45] Montlinot closed his review of occupational data from the *dépôt* with a suggestion that such information be collected and analyzed on a national scale.[46]

The catalog of inmates' maladies gave a further insight into the empirical conditions of life of the poor. As inspector of the *dépôt*, Montlinot was primarily interested in finding cheap efficacious remedies. Quinine was the only expensive drug in the pharmacy of the *dépôt*. On the other hand, no scruple of moral hierarchy interfered with the provision of meat to the convalescent, nor with the routine provision to healthy inmates of small beer brewed in the establishment. Clothing was washed regularly, and cotton had been substituted for wool for sanitary reasons. In a glimpse ahead, Montlinot warned that the account for 1783 would show a jump in mortality attributable to conditions beyond control.[47]

The organization of work in the *dépôt* had advanced with the installation of provisional workshops for the polishing of mirrors, sponsored by the St. Gobain manufacture. The results of this hard, demanding labor promised to improve, as more inmates were employed in the permanent building still under construction. More textile production was also envisaged. Montlinot noted that the modest results to date should be viewed in light of the fact that initial costs, especially for tools, were high; having inmates repair clothing and materials offset these costs to some degree.[48]

Under the heading "Police," Montlinot announced that no harshly punitive actions had been necessary. The women who refused to work at their tasks were simply marked for the ostracism of their fellow inmates by being placed in a separate cell with an open grill, in a costume of two colors. The most effective punishment for men had proven to be that of forbidding them to work in the *ateliers*. The effectiveness of this strategy furnished proof, if any were needed, that Montlinot had succeeded in orienting the "dual aspect" of work toward the pole of positive reinforcement. The conclusion of his essay returns to this essential point:

> Nothing therefore is more simple than the rules of the house; mendicity is attacked by the hopes that are fixed on those rewards that are born of labor.
>
> . . . . . .
>
> Inmates are paid more or less as if they were free; they consume while saving as they wish. Work is always shown as the route of happiness; it is the image of every social institution, where work has as its end the pleasure of consuming, and where the pleasure of consuming in turn brings a general abundance.[49]

But Montlinot does not end quite there. He appears to stumble upon a conundrum: was his artificial schedule of reinforcement a true mirror of the expectations that the inmate ought to have of society at large? The very process of impoverishment that Montlinot had documented earlier in his essay suggested that the problem of mendicity could be solved only by correcting the failure of society to reward honest labor. Montlinot made one of his most radically critical statements—albeit far from the most vehement—on this point:

> It would be a cruel and ineffective policy to wish to destroy beggars: to destroy mendicity entirely is a recognized impossibility: therefore one must go back to the source of an evil that stems from the inequality of conditions, to seek out all the means of preventing the poverty that is but the consequence of arduous and poorly paid labor: there lies perhaps the solution to the great problem of mendicity.[50]

Was "the pleasure of consumption" the philosophe's version of the *fraude pieuse?* Was it valid only as a projection of a future that might at best be hastened by belief in it?

The Chastening of an Inspector: A Matter of Language

The evolution of Montlinot's thoughts, or at least his public expression of them, was deflected by a sharply defensive reaction of the ministry in 1784. If Bertier was irritated by Montlinot's writings, he bided his time in 1782 and 1783. During Joly de Fleury's ministry, the fiscal strain of the American struggle sharply limited expenditures on the *dépôts*. Taking a constructive approach, Bertier harnessed the talents of Dr. Colombier to solving the most pressing health problems in the various institutions of his own *généralité,* including especially the *dépôt* of St. Denis.[51]

Then, in 1783, Joly de Fleury was succeeded for a period of only about eight months by Bertier's friend and colleague d'Ormesson, who also happened to be the son-in-law of the intendant of Soissons. Choosing the moment of d'Ormesson's arrival in power to bring before the royal council the complaints raised against the *dépôts,* Bertier obtained a renewed mandate for them and turned to the task of framing a new general regulation. Montlinot's model *dépôt* could be enveloped in the general reform described in the last chapter.[52]

When d'Ormesson was succeeded in office by Charles-Alexandre de Calonne at the end of 1783, many reforming impulses were suspended or reversed. Undoing the efforts of his predecessors to establish a modern treasury system on a bureau-cratic model, Calonne reinstated various financial offices, including the *caissiers de la mendicité* that Necker had abolished. He did this in February, after four months in office. The following month he addressed a letter to the intendant of Soissons sharply criticizing Montlinot's second published account. Bertier may have inspired Calonne's letter, but Calonne would have had his own reasons. Before serving as intendant at Metz and then at Lille, he had served as attorney-general in the parle-ment of Flanders. It was he who, in 1762, obtained a court order against Rous-seau's *Émile* and complained to the intendant about the "ridiculous and impertinent eulogy" of that work that had appeared in Pankoucke's *Annonces.* He knew his man.[53]

Calonne ended his letter of March 31, 1784, to Le Peletier by suggesting that "your subdelegate of Soissons should have, under your orders, the supervision of this house." In other words, Montlinot should be fired from his anomalous post as inspector. The minister praised the "order and economy" detailed in the account, but offered the ironic observation, "I do not doubt that all those who are shut up there enjoy a more pleasant lot than that in most of the other *dépôts* of the king-dom." Calonne went on to say that it was precisely in the treatment prescribed for the inmates that the *dépôt* at Soissons departed from the mission of the institution, particularly as the distinctive use of the term *maison de travail* was intended "to diminish the fear that these sorts of asylums inspire." In a somewhat forced argu-ment, Calonne then reasoned that the softening of "a necessary rigor" resulted in the overcrowding of the *dépôt* at Soissons by individuals other than the beggars and vagabonds for whom the *dépôt* was intended. This argument seems to be aimed at silencing the intendant's complaints about overcrowding with ragged convoys from St. Denis. It may also be interpreted in the light of d'Ormesson's circular of the year before on the "total execution" of laws against mendicity, in response to which the intendant had said that some sick beggars had to be kept at the *dépôt* because the hospital consistently refused to take them.[54]

Calonne returned to the heart of Montlinot's argument by saying that the king had not intended to establish hospitals or houses of charity, but simply *dépôts* for beggars. The inmates of the *dépôts* should receive no more than "exact necessity." Confronting Montlinot's social hypothesis, he pointedly observed: "Any other treatment, and such as it would be pleasing to procure for all the indigent subjects of the king, can only make the inmates desire to settle themselves in an asylum where they should be recalled to the taste for work, and where they must be given a desire to get out and apply themselves to it once more.''[55] There must be no voluntary admissions to the *dépôt*, and the name of the institution must be maintained as a *dépôt de mendicité*. The minister was displeased with Montlinot's account and with Montlinot.

Le Peletier de Mortefontaine had no intention of abandoning the experiment that he had established under Necker's aegis. He left Calonne's letter unanswered for over a month. In his reply of May 20, 1784, he began: ''It was with the most studied reflection that I decided to endow the *maison de travail* of Soissons with the rule and regime that exists there now in all its dimensions.'' Three years' experience had convinced him that his efforts were approaching the government's aims as closely as possible (the science of administration not being subject to mathematical perfection). Consistently recorded observations on the inmates had provided the rationale for establishing nuances in their treatment. ''And I think besides,'' he wrote, ''that there [are] no men even in the class of those whom the law cuts off entirely from society, to whom humanitarian care is not due until the very moment of execution of a sentence.''[56]

If Le Peletier was extraordinarily outspoken, his boldness no doubt had something to do with the fact that he was a senior intendant recently appointed by the king to the chief municipal office of the city of Paris. He was used to thinking of Calonne as a *confrere* administering a neighboring intendance. Few other letters to the minister from intendants include such assertive phrases as Le Peletier's remark, ''The success [of my administration of the *dépôt*] would have encouraged me, if my principles had not sufficed.'' He accordingly asked to be allowed to continue his methods in the little time remaining to his administration of the province. He humbly allowed that his successor, in collaboration with Bertier, would possibly do better, ''but I would give you surely a poor account of myself, if I were to destroy or diminish my own work.''[57]

Following this general defense, Le Peletier narrowed his attention to the particular charge that he had denatured the purpose of the *dépôts* and that the *maison de travail* resembled a hospital. He had merely wished to obtain savings for the king by putting the inmates to work and economizing on their maintenance and care; the result profited the king further ''by returning beggars and vagabonds to society corrected and consequently better.'' The charge that the workhouse was too much like a hospital could be refuted by a reading of the accounts themselves:

> All the inmates are clothed uniformly in the coarse cloth manufactured in the house—which is not like a hospital. The inmates are given only bread, soup, and water; all that they consume beyond this is the product of their labor alone—which is not like a hospital. The men sleep without sheets, without bed curtains, with a simple blanket made of sackcloth and wool—this rule is not like that of a hospital. The mirror-polishers have a quarter of the product of their labor deducted, the weavers and the women one half—this is not like a hospital.[58]

Calonne's response does not appear in the files, but Montlinot's position and his regime were suffered to remain. When Le Peletier retired later in the year he was replaced as intendant of Soissons by Paul Esprit Marie de la Bourdonnaye de Blossac, former intendant of Poitiers. It is tempting to attach some significance to the fact that Blossac had recently married the eldest daughter of Bertier. Was it assumed that this personal connection would ensure a better understanding between Soissons and Paris on matters of mendicity and the *dépôts?*[59]

In any case, Montlinot adapted his public stance in response to official criticism. Several passages in his account for 1783, delayed in its publication well into 1784, replied directly to the objections stated in Calonne's letter of March. Disclaiming any pretention to have established a general model for all *dépôts* to follow, Montlinot avowed that "the administration alone can carry out this great operation, applying in common to all the *dépôts* of the realm, the small number of wise regulations that will, in a fixed manner, establish uniformity in overall direction." At the same time, he claimed a distinct role for local inspectors: "The shape of secondary details, the art of guiding opinion and producing results, should be left to the well-intentioned citizen who is willing to assume the task of overseeing the poor. He alone, perceiving relationships and local differences, can take advantage of circumstances."[60]

Montlinot reiterated his disclaimer in a letter to the intendant d'Agay at Amiens, who wished to reform the regulation of his *dépôt* and was favorably impressed by the review of Montlinot's published accounts in the *Mercure de France.*[61]

The other point where Montlinot's defensive posture is most evident is in the conclusion, which reads like a rhetorical variation on the final portion of Le Peletier's letter to Calonne. Where the intendant's litany was built on the phrase, "not like a hospital," Montlinot used the formula, "They are punished." Deleting a phrase in which he had spoken of the exceptional humanity and gentleness of the method of rehabilitation adopted at Soissons, Montlinot wrote this year that other *dépôts* might be supervised as strictly, but nowhere were men treated with greater rigor. The shift in rhetoric was undoubtedly intended to mollify superiors who felt that Montlinot had been flaunting the exceptionally humane regime of his *dépôt*. In fact, the treatment of his charges probably changed little, if at all. He had been strict from the outset, imposing a constant discipline on the inmates, manipulating them by relative deprivations and by encouraging inmates to police one another for their common profit. He still continued to emphasize care for the biological health of the worker and the importance of instilling hope and self-esteem. The "harsh necessity" of working was not harsh, if rewarded by decent conditions and some freedom to consume. Food that was "healthy and very common" might be a punishment for a well-to-do sybarite, but not for an undernourished day laborer.[62]

Montlinot's sociology does not lose its radical edge in 1784. He repeats his suggestion that the state should establish "prebends" for the aged workers who have spent themselves in the service of society. Simplifying a phrase that he had used the year before, he writes, "Agriculture devours men, as the crafts enervate them." If there is any retreat toward acceptance of the status quo, it is in Montlinot's brief references to education. Whereas he had mentioned in his second account the teaching of rudimentary literacy and the reading of moral lessons on the virtues of Henry IV and Louis XV, in 1784 he argues that the most suitable education is on a model farm. The brief sketch he offers for such a project prefigures the reform colonies established for youths in the midnineteenth century. Perhaps Montlinot also means to bow to the spirit of "rigor" by dwelling somewhat longer in his third account on the *mendiants de race*. If so, he clearly implies that the *dépôts,* however strict in their intent, have little impact on these miscreants. The hardened delinquent drifter views a term in the *dépôt* as "an accident of the profession, as a farmer views hail," and forms new associations in the *dépôt* for the conduct of questionable activities upon release. The true utility of the *dépôt* remains, as in 1781, the rehabilitation of the worker's self-esteem by establishing an association between self-discipline and "the pleasure of consuming."[63]

In the account for 1783, the external demand for "rigor" thus elicits from Montlinot a rather severe "disciplinary" model of rehabilitation. In its vision of man, institutions, and society, it conforms closely to the model of a "disciplinary society" that Foucault sees emerging in the first half of the nineteenth century. Nowhere is the duality of Montlinot's role as "rebel" and "grand administrator" more sharply defined than in this account, in which he again declaims against the unjust exploitation of the worker only to propose a surer method for keeping him docile and content.[64]

Details on the method of motivating workers appear for the first time in the account for 1783. The work discipline in the *ateliers* for mirror-polishing and cloth-making derives its effectiveness from a schedule of reinforcement that is both positive and negative, combining material and social incentives. Payment for work done enables the inmate to supplement the rations in the canteen of the *dépôt;* without that wage he eats only bread and water. The tasks are organized by "master" workers who are allowed to pick their own *compagnons,* a system that rewards cooperation and stigmatizes the less productive worker in the eyes of his fellow inmates: "Want and the reprimands of his comrades are far more liable to excite [the worker's] energy than any other sort of punishment." The selection of apprentices by "masters," Montlinot goes on to explain, coupled as it is with the expectation of reward, "takes away from inmates that anxious and dissatisfied air that one encounters in forced-labor workshops."[65]

Explaining thus the "inexplicable nuances" that he had alluded to in his first account, Montlinot now describes the hierarchy that binds workers and their supervisors to the inspector. "Let the inspector never be thought absent!" he exclaims. His description of supervisory relationships as "an invisible chain [connected] to a single point, as in a center of force," anticipates Bentham's panoptic vision, while evoking at the same time a Newtonian analogy of natural forces of attraction operating at a distance. Montlinot remarks, in an earlier context, that the police of the *dépôt* as a whole has been organized in a manner that simply enlarges upon the discipline of the workshops. Instead of concierges and their helpers who, under the "old regime" of the *dépôt,* were "more or less intelligent but always predatory," Montlinot hired supernumeraries of the *maréchaussée* who imposed their authority in a military manner. These authority figures supervise the distribution of food and administer punishments, mainly by assigning latrine duty or clean-up details. They are assisted by *prévots de chambrée,* or room monitors, chosen from among inmates without criminal records.[66]

The inmate who is the object of the inspector's gaze is in more than one sense a model for Everyman in a society subject to the *magnum opus* of reform. It is the desire to have one's level of material existence transmuted to a higher plane that animates the activity of the baser souls in society. The sense of "liberty" that releases the potential creative force within them is to some extent an illusion. The inspector himself is free to do good only so long as he agrees not to step beyond his sphere. Above him, an inspector applies the more general laws of the kingdom, delimiting in his wisdom the sphere of freedom that will be most beneficial at each lower level of contingency. "The worker," writes Montlinot, "seems to keep an appearance of liberty in the employment of his forces—an error always dear to man, in whatever station he finds himself." [67]

Struggling in his web of contingency at Soissons, Montlinot had little time in the early months of 1785 to publish an account for 1784. In any case, he may have wished to take the measure of his new superior, Bertier's son-in-law, before hazarding new observations in print. Inundated with new forms of paperwork, he was coping with difficult conditions within the *dépôt*, again related to massive transfers from St. Denis. Preparing to close his accounts for 1784, he wrote Favier to say he would agree to any honorable solution for the shortage of funds, "so long as the house be governed and the work not cease." Some 14,000 livres were owing. An accounting of all obligations outstanding for the year was requested by January 10—an impossible task, Montlinot lamented, since new debts would be incurred and accounts could not be closed and tallied until the end of the year. [68]

Montlinot found it necessary to borrow 1,200 livres on his personal credit in order to keep operations going: some amounts owing for expenses in 1783 had not been paid. Montlinot complained to Favier that Bertier was citing an annual budget of 28,000 livres as if it had been a contractual agreement. At the time that the figure had been set, he noted, "M. Necker never intended to place the administration at the mercy of multiple convoys, the dearth of wheat, the inclemency of the heavens, and unforeseen repairs—and it was well understood that in certain cases the house would receive further aid." A little later, Montlinot thanked Favier for explaining the situation to the intendant de Blossac, and braced him for problems arising from yet another convoy. [69]

Although the matter of transfers to Soissons from St. Denis elicits a stream of complaints year after year, there are few moments when it exasperates Montlinot more than in the early months of 1785. In a letter of February 26, Montlinot rails at the senseless peregrination of a madman from St. Denis to Champagne and back: "Eighty leagues for the *menus plaisirs*. There are so many general inspectors, lieutenant generals, and individuals who govern the poor world at St. Denis, that one should not fail to accomplish some good. Good God! What a hard job it is being *contrôleur-général* and having so many crowns to distribute!" It was particularly exasperating to Montlinot to realize that Bertier and his underlings, with their well-financed inspectorate, were taking the luster off his experiment at Soissons while forcing him to take surplus inmates from St. Denis, which was being elevated as a model for Colombier's regulation. [70]

In the midst of this travail, as he was writing a note to Favier concerning some accounting ledgers, he idly inquired—in confidence, of course—"if they have read the latest work by M. Necker on the Rue de Vendosme [where the hôtel of the intendant of Paris was situated]. Given the stature this former minister has achieved, it is a feather in our cap to have received some praise on account of our poor little *dépôt*, volume III, p. 117." The compliment Necker paid Le Peletier and Montlinot in his three-volume treatise *De l'administration des finances* has already been cited; a full twelve pages were devoted to a general discussion of *dépôts de mendicité*. [71]

Pressing the Limits of Reform

Necker praised Montlinot for publishing his accounts of the _dépôt_ at Soissons, a practice that gave "general instruction" and spurred other administrators' efforts at no cost to the state. What Necker went on to say about mendicity and the _dépôts_ furnished elements of a political agenda. In the course of his discussion, Necker reached into the academic wardrobe for the toga of the tribune and the insignia of the consul. With the ardor of the Gracchi, he improvised the speech of a beggar justifying the necessity of begging after serving the state and bearing its exactions. Then he evoked consular dignity and the rods of authority to pronounce the most effective means of administering the _dépôts de mendicité._[72]

Necker expressed the view that poverty would always exist in a state where some citizens were born without fortunes or lacked the education that could give them marketable talents. Those who depended on the force of their muscles alone to earn a living were at the mercy of employers and harvests, a point reinforced in the current French case by the subdivision of small property and the concentration of large estates. These effects were products of human legislation, not of natural law. Where Turgot merely deviated from his Physiocratic colleagues on this point, Necker made a sharp break. The poor, Necker believed, must bend to the yoke of social institutions, but government had an essential role as "interpreter and depository of social harmony."[73]

Necker recounted briefly how the good intentions that had inspired the measures of 1767 were undermined. The underlying problem, as he saw it, was that the government acted spasmodically. A more constant reflection on the nature of the problem would take into account the inevitable effects of taxes, trade cycles, and "the rigorous exercise of the rights of property." Reviewing the system of the _dépôts_ as it existed at the end of his ministry, he claimed some progress in the care of their six to seven thousand inmates. Some of the thirty-three _dépôts_ were still in need of great improvements; others were fairly decent. More thought had been given to putting inmates to work, and those who had begged for "accidental reasons" or who could find help in their parishes were released. The lesson of the _dépôt_ established at Soissons, like that of the Parisian _grand hospice de charité_ for the sick, was that humanitarian measures could be carried out with good results at reasonable cost. Order and economy were not inconsistent with "indulgence and commiseration."[74]

Necker went on to recommend stricter controls over arbitrary action by the _maréchaussée._ If France lacked the constitutional safeguards that protected the poor in England, she should be guided toward the same end by her national spirit of gentleness and humanity. Hopeful that in time of peace the state might be able to meet all the most urgent welfare needs with the aid of private charity, Necker cautioned against blaming the government for inaction. He outlined the measures taken—public works, aid to the sick, tax rebates to disaster victims, and a variety of local relief measures. Writers on the subject of mendicity too often treated _ateliers_ as a cure-all, without recognizing the limits of their effectiveness. Workers without skill or education were not easily employed, and if they produced for the market, they invariably competed with free industry. The complexity of this problem, like that of apportioning tax burdens, was too great to be managed from a central administration. A coordinated network of provincial assemblies would manage welfare measures and taxation more effectively. Both tasks required data collection and coordination at several levels.[75]

This conclusion to Necker's chapter on the *dépôts* thus brought the reader back to the overarching thesis of his book, namely, that administrative reform could best be realized through the creation of provincial assemblies. Articulating a state responsibility for poor relief within that framework, Necker distanced himself carefully from Montlinot's bold assumption that a general prosperity might prevail among the people. The idea had been portrayed with ardor in a chapter of the memoirs of the academy of Châlons in 1777, and Montlinot had woven it into his model of rehabilitation, conceived as a microcosm of society at large. If the provincial assemblies realized their aims, according to Necker, "I would see them finally become the guarantors, not of a general *aisance*—this is a chimerical idea—but of being exempt from those evils that wise precautions can prevent." As they assumed increasing responsibility for management of royal funds, their activity would form, in effect, a *faisceau de bienfaisance,* a "sheaf" of welfare measures ensuring that no inhabitant could complain of neglect under their "economic tutelage."[76]

The attention warmed Montlinot's spirits. His letters to Favier in the early months of 1785 bespeak a jaunty spirit, even if they are larded with dark allusions and sarcastic thrusts at Bertier and his minions at St. Denis. On March 21, following a note on the total lack of funds, Montlinot told Favier in a Hippocratic vein that the cold winds were inauspicious: "This breeze that we are receiving from the states of the Emperor will do little to improve the health of our sick." In a postscript to accounts for February, Montlinot dramatized the problem of illness in the vein of Voltaire's *Candide:* "We are dying here thick as flies since the beginning of the month—not that there is any epidemic of note. I will talk with you about all this, for like Pangloss, I want to explain the origin of moral evil and physical evil and still prove that all is for the best in the best of all possible *dépôts.*"[77]

In another letter he spoke of the problem of maintaining workshops as the fitter inmates were released, to be replaced by unskilled weaklings. Many inmates were plagued by colds and minor indispositions. "We are still in great disorder, many sick, a convoy, new dinner guests," Montlinot wrote Favier on April 27. "Without our bandits who are working, we would have the honor of being a poor hospital." Waxing literary on yet another occasion, Montlinot vented his feelings of exasperation at the Panglossian doctors, experts, and assistants whom Bertier had assigned to the task of making St. Denis the model for a new regulation:

> If I held by the chignon the medico-chemico-bureaucracy of St. Denis, I would put them in the way of their patron, so wroth am I. . . . I know no one so badly served as M. B[ertier], with his great and little inspectors: I for one know of six of them who *belabor* St. Denis, may the Good Lord keep them:
> "O wisdom of the gods, I trust thou art most deep,
> But to such shallow sirs thou giv'st the world to keep!"[78]

If Montlinot's notes to Favier assume a more literary tone in these months, it may have been because the good abbé was sharpening his pen for new jousts in the world of letters. His old associate at Lille and Paris, Panckoucke, had moved from a successful venture in publishing a quarto edition of the *Encyclopédie* to a new and vaster project for an entirely new "methodical encyclopedia," a collection of topical dictionaries that would bring up to date the state of learning in all fields and organize it in a more sophisticated manner, as befit the increased scientific expertise of the French intellectual community thirty years after Diderot and d'Alembert launched their prospectus. Montlinot had collaborated in editing the first volume of the *Dictionnaire d'économie politique et diplomatique,* which appeared in May 1784. The second volume, containing an extensive article on the *dépôts de mendicité* by Montlinot, was published at Liège in 1786. Montlinot probably wrote it in the spring of 1785, about the time that he was alluding to Candide and Pangloss in his letters to Favier. The article includes an exposition of the accounting system in use at Soissons, with instances drawn from the account for 1783. The general discussion of the *dépôts* reflects a further stage in the evolution of Montlinot's experience and perception, influenced most recently by a harrowing winter at the mercy of sickness, a rough batch of inmates, accounting problems with Bertier, and a voice as if from the clouds of his patron and former protector, Jacques Necker.[79]

Montlinot's encyclopedia article provides a bridge between Necker's general account and Montlinot's own earlier writings on the *dépôt* at Soissons. Unlike Necker, Montlinot harshly criticized the management of the *dépôts* in their early years. In less than three years, he states, the execution of the laws of 1764 and 1767 on vagabonds caused the deaths of twenty-five thousand men in cells and more than six thousand in the galleys. The rigor of branding was relaxed, but the poor were left to "the brutality of concierges and the voracity of the *régisseurs.*" In a truly vehement public denunciation, Montlinot depicts the ravages of greed organized at the expense of the *dépôt's* inmates:

> . . . then companies ran about the country, and efforts were made to drag out profits from the thirty-three cesspits where all that the *maréchaussée* could round up was deposited: contracts were made at five sous, at six sous a head; pestilence established itself in several *dépôts,* and death devoured those whom hunger, filth, and misery had spared.[80]

Montlinot was scarcely kinder to Turgot, portrayed as a Don Quixote of liberalism releasing beggars without a thought as to what would become of them; the disorders that inevitably ensued led to a restoration of the system in its full rigor. In a transparent reference to the essay contest in which he had participated, Montlinot made light of the prizes academies proposed to those who would find the means for destroying mendicity. "This was," he said, "to ask, in other terms, how one might establish the primitive equality of conditions; thus the question was hardly touched, and all we have from these literary exercises are a few vague projects, or plans that would be difficult to carry out." A ray of light falls across the dark chronicles of the poor with the initiatives of Necker, particularly the establishment of a model *dépôt* at Soissons following the success of the hospital experiment at Vaugirard. Montlinot does not hesitate to observe that his printed accounts of the *dépôt* had earned an "honorable mention" from M. Necker "in a work too well known to give the title here."

Montlinot then sketches a general reform of the *dépôts* as a national system. He does this hypothetically without too brashly touting his own achievements. In his scheme there would still be in Paris a main administrator, a secretary, and a cashier.

However, in place of Colombier's highly centralized role as inspector, Montlinot suggests five general inspectors residing at Le Havre, Orleans, Amiens, Soissons, and Bordeaux. Each would receive appointments of 1,500 livres and expenses of 500 livres to make inspections in their bailiwicks. They would make annual reports in person during a month's residence in Paris in December. Such a position, one imagines, would have suited Montlinot. Other inspectors would be chosen for each *dépôt*, but since they would not be obliged to travel, their appointments would be set at 1,500 livres altogether. Implicitly critical of the corps of *régisseurs* being trained at St. Denis under the eye of Colombier, Montlinot devotes an entire paragraph to arguing that the inspectors should be of a certain social class "above the bourgeoisie." He would prefer taking them from the *chevaliers de St. Louis,* in order to have "a rampart of decent people against all kinds of rapacity and vexation." Men of higher social status and assured public spirit would be forward in presenting projects to intendants "for ameliorating the establishments confided to their care."

Montlinot then went on to suggest nuances in the placement and function of *dépôts*. They should be established in port cities, not in garrison towns: the *dépôt* at Lille should be transferred to Dunkerque. The regional inspectors should help in the placement of youths so that young boys find positions in the navy, and that young girls be brought up in manufacturing regions. In order to match inmates with appropriate employment, Montlinot suggests that the initial cross-examination of a beggar on entering the *dépôt* should have less the character of a judicial inquest and more that of a placement-counseling session. Those who had suffered misfortunes would be more willing to cooperate, if they perceived that their captors were interested in their well-being. A voluntary placement process was certainly more effective than the arbitrary forced transfer of beggars to their places of origin. In general, he felt that the stigma (*flétrissure*) of the *dépôt* should be effaced: "Honor must be counted for something, even among the lowest classes of the people."[81] Transfers ought to be arranged with decency if still necessary, but Montlinot preferred sending inmates with an allowance to a destination. In cases known to him, the fruitless peregrinations of wandering ménages had cost two thousand crowns to the state, without producing any result but the death of some from the pestilential infections contracted en route.

Montlinot recommended a sharper separation between the merely unfortunate and those hardened recidivists who might be regrouped in the *dépôts principaux*. Those in the first category could have any number of good reasons for begging— here Montlinot rendered another justificatory diatribe in the vein of Necker's imaginary beggar. A term in the *dépôt* might not help such an unfortunate find a position or work. Lest such sympathy for the struggling poor be dismissed as mere sentimentality, Montlinot let fly an apostrophe incongruously compounded of the elements of baroque piety and clinical observation:

> Let no one accuse me of exaggerating here; I have too often seen these unfortunates; I have too many times put my hand on their wounds, not to affirm that the only means of diminishing the number of indigent families, and to make them quit the base occupation of beggary, when they are not entirely corrupted, consists in giving honor back to them, in giving them charity and not alms, and finally in setting them back more or less where they were when they began begging.

Accordingly, Montlinot suggested establishing a network of a dozen hospices, or rather pioneer colonies, for the tilling of uncultivated lands in Champagne, Lorraine, Sologne, Berry, and Corsica—perhaps even in Africa. Each year, the most promising families in the *dépôts* would be established in such colonies. Within three years, Montlinot estimated that the cost of the operation would be about forty thousand livres, but the benefit would be to restore these families to the land and increase agricultural output. If such a policy had been observed since 1764, Montlinot calculated, "there would be in the kingdom today two thousand four hundred more owners of land, untilled land brought under cultivation, and a mass of population that cannot be estimated." From this hypothetical observation Montlinot moved to another, based on the enormous concentration of landownership he had calculated. Villages that he knew had lost one-fifth of their properties under the value of 400 livres in the past ten years. In another century, if this "frightening progression" continued, there would be left only "the possessors of vast domains, and instead of a people *[au lieu de peuple]*, wretched day laborers." In the light of such developments, agricultural hospices could produce benefits far outweighing those of the massive establishments of the capital—La Salpêtrière, Bicêtre, La Pitié, and others. His further remark that in these large establishments "intriguers . . . impress the most decent administrators with the idea that they are doing the greatest good, because they desire it," seems to take aim at St. Denis as well as the hospitals named.

The article's treatment of the *dépôt* at Soissons is adapted primarily from Montlinot's most recent published account, that of 1783. In keeping with the defensive posture imposed by Calonne, Montlinot emphasizes the severity of the regime and the simple mechanism of reinforcement for work done by inmates. Work is always available, and the product of the labor performed can be spent in a canteen where vegetables, fruit, meat, and bread are available—small beer as well, but no strong spirits. The owner of the canteen makes a profit from the sale of his wares at a set price, but from these profits he is also obliged to serve free portions to the insane. The workers thus come to feel that they have a part in supporting a work of *bienfaisance* jointly with the *cantinier*.[82] The standard of treatment in the *dépôt* is spelled out; the typical cost of an outfit is itemized.

A description of the workshops provides further detail on their social dynamic, reproducing in microcosm a free labor market. The better workers are allowed to set terms for their apprentices, and the idlers soon find themselves wandering in the courtyard, reduced to bread and water (unless the inspector identifies the individual as physically weak, in which case he is set to more suitable tasks). Montlinot's theory of motivation subsists in chastened phrases. A stress on the word "need" camouflages the concept of a "desire to consume" beyond bare necessities: "A newcomer cannot stay long without working, because the administration leaves him to struggle alone with his needs, which become all the more pressing when he sees the others consume the fruits of their labor."

The entire paragraph concerning "the appearance of liberty" is retained as in the 1783 account, with a further remark that the heavy labor of polishing mirrors becomes lighter as it is shared. Should there be any doubt as to the positive incentive Montlinot wishes to emphasize, he estimates that the good worker can earn fifteen livres per month and even more in the *dépôt*. The section on work ends with model printed wage receipts, and the discussion turns to the related matter of the internal police of the *dépôt*. The reader of previous accounts learns more about the *prévôts de chambre* who serve under the *surnuméraires de la maréchaussée* and keep order among their fellow inmates. While they are never chosen from the *flé-tris,* or former criminals, they do often include inmates chosen from the class of vagabonds who are the most imposing physically. They are given their freedom after six months' service and receive other minor privileges. They police rules of behavior and hygiene, supervise the workshops, distribute linens, and relay requests for attention from inmate to inspector.[83]

A section on the remedies used in the *dépôts* emphasizes their economy and simplicity. Montlinot shares the learned opinion that the simpler remedies used for the poor are as effective as the more costly ones favored by the rich. "It has been thought just, in treating the inmates of the *dépôts,* as with the crew of a ship, to dispense with the apparatus of a doctor and with a too costly or nicely provided pharmacy." The theme of economic management leads, finally, to a listing of the accounting categories for the *dépôt*, a system designed for ease in monitoring expenses at a glance.

Taken as a whole, Montlinot's article for the *Méthodique* refines the defensive formulation of his strategy for rehabilitation, while adding some general observations critical of the new, highly centralized system of inspectors headquartered at St. Denis and of the bourgeois skinflints recruited for training as *régisseurs.*

In the course of 1785 Montlinot became increasingly confident of his relationship with Blossac, mediated by Favier, who continued in his post as first secretary of the new intendant. Late in 1785 Montlinot published an accounting of the two years 1784 and 1785, beginning with the triumphant assertion that the preceding year had seen a change in the heads of administration, but that the regime of the *dépôt* had continued. He made a point of noting that the intendant himself had taken an interest in the cross-examination of inmates for the purpose of finding them work. He referred his readers to his article in the "new *Encyclopédie*" and developed some of the ideas he had broached there.[84]

A sense that mendicity is above all the result of the exploitation of the poor by the rich is nowhere more clearly or more simply stated than in this "fourth account" by Montlinot. Four and a half years of observing inmates closely have sharpened his descriptions of them. While overtly he accepts the premise that society must protect itself against the dangerous *mendiant de race* and must deflect others from joining their ranks, he gives priority to the accidental causes that force a poor person to beg, and identifies these accidents as an inevitable product of the social system. While the cause and remedy of mendicity must vary from province to province, he argues that everywhere there are to be found

> more unfortunates than guilty ones, more inconvenient beggars than dangerous folk, more women abandoned and helpless children, more women debauched in garrisons than marked women and beggars from father to son: therefore some indulgence must be used toward the one, and a greater severity toward the other.

While this statement perpetuates the traditional distinction between "true" and "false" poor (the "true" he would attach to village parishes), the main point is that the problem of mendicity is primarily a welfare problem, not one of delinquency. Even in speaking of the able-bodied, he emphasizes the need to rehabilitate those not totally depraved. The government should follow the example of England and find places for such people. Transportation appealed to Montlinot as a means of correcting those not easily reintegrated into normal society. He takes the occasion to praise Bertier's use of *pionniers* drawn from the *dépôts* for use in Corsica, an idea that had been bruited in the Châlons memoirs: "It was a measure well taken by an administrator whom I cannot name to have established a work colony *[atelier]* in Corsica. This project, executed on a large scale, followed with perseverance, directed with order, will in twenty years add a new province to the kingdom."[85]

If this remark was meant to placate Bertier, Montlinot's indictment of the policy of transfers barely stopped short of a personal attack on him. Offering an analysis of data on the 704 beggars transferred in the previous two years from the *dépôt* of St. Denis, he referred to "the results obtained by the new combination of men and women sacrificed to the security of Paris and the repulsive delicacy of the rich." But it was the attraction of work in urban trades that produced the great concentration of potentially dangerous unemployed in Paris. By contrast with the beggars arrested in the *généralité* of Soissons, where all but a fifth were in the class of day laborers, about three-fourths of those transferred from St. Denis were tradespeople "who counted on their talent to live" in coming to Paris: tailors, shoemakers, wigmakers, weavers, cooks, masons, mercers, and a variety of miscellaneous trades, including domestics.[86]

Montlinot suggested the need for a government policy on trades, including support for workers' associations. But intelligent action would require more knowledge: the types of data collected at Soissons would be more useful if they were available for the rest of the kingdom. In a bid to establish an empirical social science serving a public purpose, Montlinot argued:

> If the Government included in these lists the number, the profession, the place of birth of people confined in prisons, *dépôts,* and hospitals, in the space of ten years one would have a series of observations that would perhaps change a part of our ideas on penalties to be inflicted and on public welfare *[la bienfaisance].*

A number of the new suggestions carried over from Montlinot's encyclopedia article were designed to deal separately with the police problem caused by the potentially delinquent beggar. He proposed ringing Paris with four *dépôts* designed to police the more dangerous inmate and to hold repeaters. Apparently he did not assume that these inmates were beyond rehabilitation, but envisioned a stricter regime and the option of transportation.[87]

Montlinot's vision, shaped by his experience close to the rejects of provincial society, was of a complex, corrupt society in crisis. "Agriculture devours men," he announced; "the rich consume the youth of the poor like a commodity." With a prophetic image of injustice, he went on, "The bread that we eat is thus stained with the sweat of the unfortunate being, as sugar is dyed with the blood of Negroes."[88] Only in the theater did one see the celebration of harvest with song and dance. In reality, he argued, workers in the August heat "are almost all attacked with intermittent fevers that wear down the last of their energies." He repeated his advocacy of government-supported old-age pensions after twenty years of labor, and suggested meanwhile using hospitals and *dépôts* to fill the present need for relief.[89]

Like many of his contemporaries, Montlinot feels that the corruption of the common people—physical and moral—is related to a crisis of social institutions. He sees a convergence in social and medical indicators: while the incidence of venereal disease in the *dépôt* has risen from one to twenty individuals, the number of properties renting for less than one hundred livres has dropped by half. He presents these developments as two sources of mendicity, wretchedness, depopulation, and degeneration. He reinforces this vivid but tenuous parallel with a reference to a study carried out by de Montver, commander of the Volontaires de Bourbon, in 1752, showing that the children of farm owners are most likely to stay to the end of their enlistment term and less likely to suffer sickness or to desert. The conclusion is obvious: "Everything is therefore in favor of agriculture exercised by owners: it is here that we must seek a vigorous population and the force of the nation." He reiterates once again his view that the government has a special obligation to aid those poor who have "sacrificed their youth to the arduous service of the well-to-do farmers."[90]

While Montlinot is careful to shun paradoxical phrases such as "luxury of the *dépôt*," he clearly believes that the poor peasant inside and outside the *dépôt* should receive support, compensation, and respect as a simple matter of justice, reinforced by utility and humane compassion. He does not speak here, as he did in his encyclopedia article, of having placed his hands on the wounds of the poor, but his medical nosology demonstrates his knowledge of their physical condition. While he says nothing about the injustice of depriving the poor of their liberty for the offense of begging, he urges dropping the judicial assumption of guilt from the moment of interrogation in order to help the poor recover independence and self-esteem. Finally, he simply assumes that the desire to consume is to be encouraged as a model for society at large. He speaks of the need to make the society at large conform to that model in order to overcome a moral and material crisis. His assumption emerges clearly in a statement of principle and utility concerning workshops: "It appears to us that the product of the labor a worker does should belong to him outright—this is the only way to encourage him; the profit the government makes on the handiwork of inmates is inconsequential, if one is persuaded that the *dépôts* are set up to correct idlers."[91]

As Montlinot sent to the printer his most polished diagnosis of the causes of mendicity and prescribed a set of remedies and changes in regime, Bertier was lending his authority to a new regulation elaborated by the inspector of hospitals, prisons, and *dépôts de mendicité*, Dr. Jean Colombier. This general approach involved rules of hygiene and accounting that were more technically circumscribed, more ideologically sanitized, than those of the abbé de Montlinot. But there was a significant common ground underlying the two approaches.

10

Reform and Revolution

Keeping Montlinot as inspector of the *dépôt de mendicité* at Soissons against his better judgment was not the last concession Calonne would be obliged to make to enlightened opinion. Historians date the "prerevolution" in France from Calonne's decision to convoke an Assembly of Notables in February 1787. He calculated that by this extraordinary measure he might circumvent the obstruction that the parlement would certainly raise against his plan for a general land tax—a tax to be collected without exemptions for the privileged and with the aid of consultative assemblies in each province. The strategy backfired. The Assembly of Notables called for a wholesale redress of grievances. Calonne turned over the reins of finance to his most outspoken critic in the Assembly, the archbishop of Toulouse, Loménie de Brienne.[1]

Brienne was ultimately no more successful than Calonne in solving the political impasse. But he carried out a number of administrative reforms, many of them inspired by the program of Turgot. Following Necker's example, he also published an account of royal expenditures in March 1788, pointing out the savings he had obtained and those he expected to realize. These accounts show that Brienne carried out, in effect, an administrative prerevolution in the operation of the *dépôts*.

Under the heading "mendicity," Brienne enumerated savings of 92,150 livres from a total budget of 1,322,003 livres. The most dramatic item was the saving of 13,000 livres "for the payment of the magistrate formerly charged with this department, which payment is eliminated entirely." Bertier would no longer oversee the *dépôts*. The administrative expenses of the *dépôts* were further curtailed by cutting 16,650 livres in salaries for clerks and office costs. Colombier's burden of inspection was greatly increased by the elimination of 6,500 livres allotted for the positions of under-inspectors-general" and their travel expenses. Finally, Brienne sliced away 56,000 livres in "expenses for the *pionniers,*" which Bertier had continued to carry on the budget of the *dépôts*. Brienne, once favorable to these work companies, now observed that "the retrenchment of these *pionniers,* whose utility is at least doubtful, will add further to savings."[2]

Brienne foresaw further reductions in administrative costs for individual *dépôts*. Aiming again at Bertier, Brienne noted that the expense for the *dépôt* of St. Denis, particularly in the area of salaries and office expenses, could be curtailed, as well as the emoluments for the *caissier de mendicité* of the Île-de-France. Finally, he called into question the policy of transferring beggars from one *dépôt* to another, an expensive procedure not as useful as first believed and seeming "even to have some drawbacks."[3]

Brienne's accounting provides a clear distillation of the prerevolutionary agenda for the administration of the *dépôts*. The removal of Bertier from supervision of the *dépôts* expressed the feelings of resentment in the Assembly of Notables against the "despotism" of certain royal agents, the intendants in particular. In criticizing the use of special funds available to Bertier, Brienne carried out the intention of the Notables, who had explicitly criticized the use of *caisses intermédiaires*. Brienne himself had helped to formulate the grievances of the Estates of Languedoc with respect to this issue on the eve of Turgot's ministry, as noted earlier. In 1783, when Bertier had proposed transferring 15,000 livres from the treasury of the Estates of Languedoc to the *caissier de la mendicité générale*, the intendant Saint-Priest had reminded the minister, Joly de Fleury, that the Estates had agreed to the most recent funding of the *dépôts* only on condition that all funds raised in the province remain in the hands of the treasurer of the Estates, and that all payments be certified as to their object. Any proposed exception, the intendant notes, should be concerted "with M. the archbishop of Toulouse, representative of the Estates of Languedoc." A marginal note on the dossier indicates that the effort to transfer funds was abandoned.[4]

Brienne reinforced a trend toward bureaucratic rationalization by placing the general management of the *dépôts* directly under the intendant of finances, Chaumont de la Millière. Unfortunately for La Millière, the rhetoric of reform and the exigency of deficit cut his staff down to a mere skeleton. The printed instruction of March 29, 1788, concerning a network of correspondence between doctors and surgeons serving the *dépôts* may have been envisioned as a means of supplementing a diminished inspectorate.[5]

A highly competent administrator who had declined an invitation to serve as controller-general, La Milliére carried out the initiatives Brienne had announced. In an early circular dated August 23, 1787, La Millière called on intendants to enforce strictly article 36 of the general regulation, in order to remedy "the mortality that results from the manner in which these beggars and vagabonds are fed and bedded."[6] In December the intendant, Meulan d'Ablois, broached the issue of transfers in the context of reviewing the parlous state of accounts payable for the *dépôt* at Limoges. A strong advocate of ending the costly practice of transferring inmates, he buttressed his opinion with a guarded reference to Montlinot's latest published account. Asking if La Millière had read it, he wrote:

> I do not speak of the content of the account. I found in it the charlatanry too common in this moment of those who rush into print on matters of administration— and not everything to be sure is so beautiful in execution as on paper—but what I noticed with pleasure was that an administrator under the orders of M. Berthier's son-in-law thinks as I do on the practical difficulties with transfers.[7]

Colombier's icy observations on the intendant's letter suggest that the administration was under conflicting pressures:

One will say nothing here of the opinion of Monsieur l'Intendant on the *compte-rendu* of the *dépôt* of Soissons, which he does not find good except for the article on transfers. One awaits with impatience the memoir of M. Montlinot which will probably induce M. de La Millière to eliminate transfers. It is to be presumed that measures will then be taken to relieve crowding in several *dépôts* that stand in need of such action.

A further effort to regulate transfers came on April 26 of the year following. La Millière addressed to intendants a copy of a printed circular to the *maréchaussée* from the comte de Brienne (the archbishop's brother), expressly ordering that transfers of arrested beggars be carried out weekly. A single beggar could walk, if fit. A horse would otherwise be provided, or a horse-drawn cart if more than two were to be transported. The preamble of the instruction made it clear that lengthy stays in prisons en route constituted a "prolongation of a penalty that the law has not pronounced." Maladies ensued from such abuses; costs of maintenance were often incurred without deriving useful labor from the detainees.[8]

La Millière made an apparently deliberate effort to mobilize the opinion of intendants against the policy of transfers. His letter of May 16, 1788, to the intendant of Caen invited the intendant's observations on the subject. La Millière prefaced his request by taking note of Brienne's comment on transfers in his published account of the state of royal finances. He went on to explain that he, La Millière, had given special thought to the subject since being put in charge of the department of mendicity. He then gave his own reasons for thinking it might be wise to terminate these transfers. The transfer time was excessive in the case of first offenders who would not be confined longer than three months. In the case of repeaters, some purpose might be served, except for women, who would have difficulty finding work, if returned to a locality where their reputation would have suffered because of their arrest (children should therefore not be transferred either). In the case of habitual offenders, transfer was not likely to bring about rehabilitation; lengthy detention in the place of arrest would appear to be the logical remedy.[9]

La Millière's desire to rationalize the functions of the *dépôts* in a more economical manner was not limited to the matter of transfers. In his early circular of August 23, 1787, he notified intendants that debauched women were to be incarcerated only at the expense of the Ministry of War. In the following months the lists of inmates were closely scrutinized, and instructions were issued to release those not duly detained. On August 31, 1787, for example, La Millière objected to the detention of beggars at Caen by sentence of municipal police authorities. He reminded the intendant that only three sorts of judgments for beggars and vagabonds were legal: (1) orders of the king; (2) ordinances of the provosts or lieutenants of the *maréchaussée*; (3) military ordinances concerning debauched women arrested in the train of royal regiments.[10]

Economic distress, which set the stage for the political crisis of 1789, put strains on the *dépôts* like those experienced in previous crises. Intendants again tended to use the *dépôts* to shelter some of the victims as well as to confine the "dangerous" beggar. La Millière would instruct intendants not to retain the indigent infirm on a voluntary basis, notwithstanding the provisions of title 1, article 15, of the general regulation. Only those who could earn their keep could stay as voluntary inmates;

others would have to be maintained in hospitals.[11] In Paris, where hungry provincials swelled the ranks of the urban poor, La Millière and Colombier repeatedly reminded the *lieutenant-général de police,* de Crosne, that random house searches at night to arrest beggars were unauthorized and were more likely to provoke disquiet than maintain order.[12]

The prerevolutionary impulse for institutional reform collided with the need to use the *dépôts* as a makeshift supplement to the police of the Paris region. But that impulse was also engulfed in a general challenge to the authority exercised by the king's agents. Although Bertier had been relieved of the general oversight of the *dépôts,* the fact that he was still master of the *dépôt* at St. Denis linked him with that institution in the public mind. The difficulties he experienced in defending his reputation as a reforming intendant reflect the general predicament of all the king's intendants in the period of the prerevolution. In his case, an insistence that the *dépôt* was an element in a beneficent strategy of reform became a personal liability to him, highlighting the ambiguous Old Regime legacy of that institution.

In 1784 Bertier had been the unnamed subject of a laudatory "Portrait of an Intendant" in the *Mercure de France.* With a transparent reference to the projects of Bertier the elder, carried on by a devoted son, the poet wrapped a resplendent mantle of *bienfaisance* around the two of them and praised their deeds: reforming taxation, maintaining order, championing the unfortunate, promoting virtue and the arts, and serving the "children of Ceres, Neptune, and Mars." But by 1787, what some of the notables described as "a system of reasoned insubordination" challenged even the best-intentioned acts of the king and his agents. Bertier found it increasingly difficult to cling to the mantle of *bienfaisance.* The provincial assembly of the Île-de-France that met in August 1787 at Melun wanted to claim that mantle for themselves.[13]

Following Calonne's advice, the king had invited his subjects to assemble in each province in 1787 to give their advice in matters of local administration and taxation. Committees of these assemblies would soon begin thinking and acting like those of the established provincial estates, rapidly adding new demands on behalf of the nation. Bertier's opening speech to the provincial assembly of the Île-de-France on Saturday, August 11, mixed paternalistic and republican rhetoric. "The nation has called you," he began, only to turn then to the image of the king as father of the people calling his family to share in the task of ruling. "He has confided his interests to you," he continued, "or, better said, he is persuaded that his interests are only those of his peoples." Moving to less abstract and more comfortable ground, Bertier spoke of his own early realization that taxes could be apportioned effectively only with the help of the taxpayer, an observation that introduced a lengthy review of his own career as reformer.[14]

In a gracious gesture, Bertier assured the provincial representatives, "I will rejoice in the good that you will do, and that I would have wished to do." However, his official role required him to communicate royal demands for heavier taxes, and for his own part he voiced some misgivings about the new levy. The tax, a renewal of the old *vingtième,* was a bitter necessity. The state of the royal treasury would further depend on a strict collection procedure to cut down on tax evasion. He confessed that it pained him—as one who took special pride in the title *tuteur des communautés*—to press these demands. He volunteered to provide any data that might be useful to the assembly in making a case for relieving the province of its disproportionate share in the burden of the *taille*.[15]

Turning to the future, Bertier focused his audience's attention on three main concerns: the poor *taillables,* the promotion of agricultural improvement, and the fate of his collaborators. His *magnum opus,* indeed, was the reform of the *taille,* a burden upon the poor that must make one weep. "I have, however, given him relief, and I have been reproached for it." Here Bertier's paternalistic fear was perhaps well founded. An assembly in which property owners held sway might not be disposed to assess themselves more in order to relieve the poorest. But in his appeal to acknowledge the loyal services of his collaborators, a cadre that he had taken pains to "purify," he seemed to be engaged in a futile effort to ward off growing demands for public accountability.[16]

In referring to the promotion of agriculture, Bertier had occasion to speak of all his efforts at "improvement" seconded by expert knowledge. Besides restoring the Society of Agriculture and instituting *comices agricoles* (fairs to promote agriculture), Bertier had seen to the distribution of new seed types and gifts of livestock to the poor. The committees of the assembly proceeded to explore the practices of the public works department and the disposition of aid of all kinds, including promotion of agriculture and aid to the indigent. While recognizing Bertier's initiatives, the assembly seemed anxious to take its own. Was there perhaps a determination to reshape Bertier's highly personalized fiefdom of improvement? It was noted that the contract for the largest of six royal nurseries was about to expire and should perhaps be left open to competitive bidding. It was situated at l'Isle-sous-Montréal, Bertier's largest estate.[17]

A memoir on mendicity read to the assembly by the abbé de la Bintinaye, a canon of the church of Paris, contained a similar prerevolutionary dissonance. The author gave credit to Bertier's reforming intentions, while calling for a new dispensation. The abbé praised the general regulation for the operation of the *dépôts,* and entered a copy of it into the official record of the assembly. At the same time, he reminded his hearers that beggars remained. "You will think it necessary to establish a new order of things," he told them. He reported the information he had received on the work performed by inmates at the *dépôt* of St. Denis, including the polishing of mirrors, the spinning of wool, and the making of clothes for inmates; yet, in an apparent non sequitur, he also suggested that it would be better to fix poor in their parishes "than to crowd them into *maisons de force* where they huddle in idleness."[18]

While Bertier's initiatives in establishing *ateliers de charité* were reviewed in another report to the assembly, the abbé de la Bintinaye argued that the provincial assembly could do far more by exercising the authority vested in it by the regulation of July 8 to apportion funds designated for remissions of the *taille.* The municipal assemblies might be empowered to organize relief works on secondary roads, augmenting the funds available with the sum of 84,063 livres levied on the *taillables* of the province for the purpose of combatting mendicity. While the abbé did not call for the abolition of the *dépôt* of St. Denis, he argued that it was a national institution that should not be supported by the province. A part of the provincial fund for mendicity might still be used to pay the pensions of those beggars interned at St. Denis who originated from the Île-de-France.[19]

The abbé's observations implied a broader dissatisfaction with the current approach to the problem of mendicity. He cited "just complaints" against venal officers who arrested poor citizens in order to gain a monetary reward. Many of the poor who fell into begging needed only the assistance of their communities to tide them over a temporary emergency; others were disabled by age or illness. The ideas that were to be articulated fully in the reports of the revolutionary Comité de Mendicité were already abroad in the form of statements akin to those of the abbé Baudeau or the archbishop of Toulouse. "In a word," the abbé de la Bintinaye told the assembly, "society owes assistance and protection to all its members: it must procure to all the indigent suitable work and wages." Even vagabonds would prefer free labor to the chain gang. The incorrigible few should be sent to the *dépôt* of the *généralité,* to remain under the inspection of the magistrate and to be released on evidence of good behavior.[20]

Finally, the abbé voiced a fervent prerevolutionary hope "that the renovation and education of the poor" would remove the scourge of mendicity and "recall to virtue those not reduced to an abject state." Accordingly, he urged the assembly to create the prerequisite mechanism of parish support. Bertier, it should be noted, had used his taxing authority to prod communities into establishing *bureaux d'aumône.* The assembly was not yet willing to promote such a network in the name of the province, nor did it act on the other proposals of the Committee on Public Welfare, except to adopt the abbé's arguments that funds raised for "mendicity" should pay only for objects of expense incurred for the benefit of its citizens. This principle of accountability on the provincial level implied another: a national accountability for taxes to be spent for purposes "common to the whole kingdom," such as the general operation of the *dépôt* at St. Denis.[21]

Similar demands concerning the administration of welfare and the repression of mendicity arose in other provincial assemblies. It was widely believed that charitable measures would be more effectively managed at the provincial level, whence, in turn, municipal support and participation could be mobilized. Antoine Lavoisier, who had served regularly as a royal consultant in matters of hygiene in prisons and hospitals, spoke in the assembly of the Orléanais to request that *ateliers de charité, dépôts de mendicité,* and other measures of public assistance be placed in the hands of the provincial assembly.[22]

A report to the provincial assembly of the Auvergne in December 1787 pointed out the difficulty of setting up new projects for employing the idle when 30,000 of the 52,000 livres raised in the province for the eradication of mendicity each year went to the *dépôt* at Riom alone. It would be better to return these funds to their "original purpose." If funds for relief were consolidated at the provincial level, a new system could be devised to combine "all the advantages of a general disposition, a particular surveillance, and a local execution."[23]

The call for an Estates-General, issued in the summer of 1788, established an official channel for grievances reaching from the meanest rural parish assembly to the "general" meeting of the three orders at Versailles. Few of these assemblies were so strident on the subject of the *dépôts* as the regular assembly of the Estates of Brittany in 1788, which approved a memoir denouncing them as "Bastilles for the people." [24] Such highly charged attacks on despotism from traditionally constituted bodies provided a backdrop for the more prosaic complaints and requests generally consigned to the *cahiers*. Throughout France, references to mendicity were colored by a desire to put provincial and municipal assemblies in charge of work projects, alms bureaus, and other measures of relief and repression. [25]

The *cahiers* of the Beauvaisis are of some interest because they reflect the participation of the duc de la Rochefoucauld-Liancourt, a deputy of the nobles, later to be chairman of the Comité de Mendicité. In an earlier brochure on royal finances, he had denounced the exploitation of beggars in *dépôts* by subalterns "who gnaw at their pittance and their meager wages." The *cahier* of his order called for the establishment of "one or two houses of correction or workhouses for each province, taking in the shiftless and the nondomiciled beggars who, in case of a repeated offense, will be transported overseas." These suggestions seem to indicate familiarity with Montlinot's writings. The duke had experimented with various charitable enterprises on his own estate at Liancourt and was in touch with Montlinot, at least indirectly. [26] The duke's *baillage* lay within the *généralité* of Paris; he had participated in the work of the Royal Agricultural Society of Paris at Bertier's invitation. [27]

The *cahiers* of the Paris region as a whole reflect an ambivalent response to Bertier's reform efforts. His most systematic reform, that of the *taille,* had antagonized those whose assessments were raised; the arbitrary power of Bertier's agents was particularly resented. A number of *cahiers* demanded the outright abolition of the office of intendant and of the subdelegates under him. There were a few scattered complaints against the *dépôts,* especially from the town of St. Denis and neighboring Villetaneuse. The latter tersely called for the abolition of the "dépôt de mendicité et de fainéants." Citizens of St. Denis wished to have the *dépôt* moved out of town. They were concerned about local property values and the disturbances that resulted when guards entered homes in pursuit of inmates who had escaped over rooftops. Other references to *dépôts* and prisons generally demanded that workshops and manufactures be established in them. [28]

Of the brochures on politics and administration that inundated France on the eve of the Estates-General, a number dealt entirely with the problem of mendicity and many others touched on it. Most writers reiterated the common desire for greater local responsibility for poor relief; many spoke of the oppression of the poor as a result of abuses and despotism; almost all touched on the need to make productive, happy citizens of the abject poor. One of the most significant series of pamphlets was written by the inspector of apprentices of the different houses of the *hôpital-général* of Paris, Jean-François Lambert. His writings from January 1789 to January 1790 refer back to the Châlons essay contest of 1777 and look forward to the Comité de Mendicité. Lambert, like the abbé de Montlinot, participated in both discussions. Both were employed in the interval in the institutional rehabilitation of the idle poor. [29]

In a brief *Précis de vues générales* written in January 1789, Lambert called on the forthcoming Estates-General to place the poor in the constitution by establishing a national system of public assistance. He exhorted citizens to repudiate the errors of the past and to recognize that hospitals and *dépôts* were not remedies, but symptoms. The concentration of property and the greed displayed in every order had been turning France into a great *manufacture des pauvres*. Soon France would be nothing but "a great hospital." The fundamental remedy was to restore the solidarity of citizens at the local level. Once responsibility was freely accepted there, poor relief could be coordinated.[30]

The *Précis* reverberates with the language of Linguet, Montlinot, and Necker on the debt society owes to the useful laborer. At the opening of the last session of the Assembly of Notables, observed Lambert, the keeper of the seals had emphasized the solidarity of the nation as if it were a family. But in reality, there is an unwitting conspiracy between the royal treasury, proprietors, and their agents to make money count for everything and men for nothing. Perhaps it would be wise, Lambert concludes, to heed the words with which the director-general closed the session: "Sooner or later everything bends, everything bows before the spirit of justice."[31]

Having urged deputies to include his points in their *cahiers,* Lambert went on to publish his own "Cahier of the Poor." No purpose would be served, he insisted, if a constitution only regulated the power of the state to impinge on liberty and property, while leaving the poor to the discretion of the rich. A just regard for useful labor required a constitutional guarantee that the laboring man would not be uncertain of his subsistence anywhere in the country. All the poor of the kingdom should be included in "a common regime of care and surveillance" designed to preserve them from corruption and disorder. Parishes should be responsible for bringing up foundlings as citizens.[32]

Turning to the problem of beggars, Lambert declared, "The indigence of the poor should no longer be a just cause for confinement." The *dépôts* should henceforth serve only for detaining "dangerous" men. The incorrigible idlers and vagabonds and prostitutes should be sent to a colony of the sort proposed by Montlinot. All these and other public establishments should be under the protection of the Estates-General, and under the immediate jurisdiction of the provincial estates to be established. Finally, Lambert's *"cahier"* touched on specific ways of improving the lot of the poor, giving a foretaste of Jacobin preoccupations and the Jacobin rhetoric of virtue. He called for public food sales to protect the poor from being gouged by small retailers; for a better system to finance public works of local utility and to employ the poor on them; for a reversal of the Physiocratic policy of turning pasture into arable.[33]

When the deputies met at Versailles, their political struggles focused on the relative rights of the three orders. Lambert argued, however—in a further "Supplication"—that in elections and *cahiers* alike, "the poor have neither been assembled nor heard."[34] Since the interests of the poor could not be represented by the body of deputies assembled, Lambert audaciously proposed that he and the abbé de Montlinot be added as voting members of the assembly to serve with the appellation "representative of the poor." He gave Montlinot a stirring encomium, mentioning his contribution to the contest of the Châlons academy on the suppression of mendicity, his work as inspector of the *dépôt* at Soissons, and "five years of continuous observations already published, on the class of men reputed the most abject and most vile, the vagabond beggars, etc."

It is particularly interesting that Lambert linked his own ideas of welfare reform with Montlinot's writings, with the legacy of the Châlons contest, and with Necker's patronage. Lambert suggested that Necker had been inspired by the same spirit that informed his own *Précis* in that section of his opening address to the Estates-General where he had spoke of a "second class of ameliorations that can be passed to the particular administration of each province." Lambert expressed confidence that if he were named representative of the poor, he could make use of information "already to be found in the bureaus of the Government." In his *Précis* he had suggested that many of his ideas were already in preparation in the bureaus of Chaumont de la Millière. Montlinot would provide a further source of expertise to the Estates-General. Lambert told his readers where to buy Montlinot's latest account of the *dépôt* at Soissons, and freely confessed that articles 10, 11, and 12 of his own *cahier* (relating to the dépôts) merely gave the bare bones of Montlinot's work.[35]

At the beginning of July 1789, it appeared briefly that the king was prepared to consecrate the initiatives of a truly National Assembly. Then, abruptly, he dismissed Jacques Necker on Saturday, July 11, amid rumors of reaction. Dismayed Parisians took up the cry radiating from the Palais Royal on the next day: "Aux armes!" Crowds formed to organize a defense against an expected attack by royal armies. Waxen busts of Necker and the duc d'Orléans, obtained from a gallery located in the Palais Royal, were paraded in the streets. The rumor circulated at the Palais Royal that Foullon had been named successor to Necker. His name and that of his son-in-law Bertier, with other would-be agents of oppression—twenty in all—were listed in a proscription posted in the Palais Royal on the 13th.[36]

Of those proscribed, de Launay and Flesselles were slaughtered in the immediate aftermath of the popular assault on the Bastille the next day. A week later, on July 22, Bertier and Foullon were both brought to Paris and slaughtered before the Hôtel de Ville. These two murders occurred *after* the king had reinstated Necker and had reassured Paris with a personal visit to the Hôtel de Ville on the 17th. Both the symbolism and the reality of Bertier's death need to be understood in terms of the underlying psychology of the Great Fear, a mass stirring that reached a peak in July. Revolutionary attitudes towards the *dépôts de mendicité* find a place in this revolutionary mass psychology and its political exploitation.[37]

Following the report of Foullon's death, the *Pennsylvania Gazette* told American readers that he had been a member of the "obnoxious ministry" formed after Necker's dismissal, adding that the intendant of Paris, Bertier, "was accused of having entered into the designs of the same ministry." Although no such ministry was formed, it is not surprising that the two men should have been cast in the role of replacements for Necker. Bertier's functions entailed a loyalty to the queen, if not to all the policies of her party. By 1788, if not before, Bertier was preoccupied with the defense of royal authority and the maintenance of public order.[38]

The fear that royal armies would be used to crush the people of Paris and cut them off from the deputies of the nation at Versailles joined with the fear that starvation would be used to force the people into submission. Involved in provisioning both the population of Paris and the royal armies, Bertier stood at the intersection of these fears. Later historians have discounted Michelet's picture of him scurrying in panic around his *intendance* after the fall of the Bastille, "not knowing where to lay his head." He was coordinating the logistical support for a withdrawal of royal troops from the capital, a move he had urged on the king in order to calm popular fears and relieve pressure on food supplies in the immediate area of Paris. He paid a visit to his daughter and son-in-law at Soissons on July 18, before going on to Compiègne. There he was detained by members of a local watch committee as he left a meeting with the subdelegate. His captors wished to have him answer for the charges brought against him, and persuaded the reluctant electors of Paris to have one of their number escort him to the Hôtel de Ville. Bertier objected that all his actions were based on royal orders that could be verified from his portfolio.[39]

As Bertier entered the city from the North on July 22, he found the streets lined with a taunting crowd. The signs they held read: "He has robbed the King and France"; "He has devoured the substance of the people"; "He has been the slave of the rich and the tyrant of the poor. He has deceived the King. He has betrayed the country." Suddenly the severed head of his father-in-law, Foullon, was thrust before him, a head with hay dangling from the mouth. The symbolism of the famine-plot mentality was fully realized in this hideous mockery of a man who was said to have remarked, at the time of Terray, "I will reduce them to eating bread at five sols the pound or feeding themselves with hay."[40]

At the Place de Grève the electors attempted to delay matters by ordering that all those arrested under suspicion of *lèse-nation* be taken to the prisons of the Abbaye de St. Germain pending an inquest. The crowd would hear of no delay. In the lynching that ensued, Bertier's heart was torn out and brought into the Hôtel de Ville. In the National Assembly, Barnave dismissed the event as part of "the storms inseparable from the movements of a revolution." Order would be restored as soon as a new constitutional authority was organized, with *gardes bourgeois,* municipal councils, and "a legal justice for crimes of state." He expressed the callous mood of those who had lived in the fear of powerful men such as Bertier. "Was this blood then so pure?" Mirabeau remarked, according to the *Moniteur* of July 23: "Ah! If the anger of the people is terrible, the coldbloodedness of despotism is atrocious; its systematic cruelties make more unfortunates in a day than popular insurrections slaughter as victims over years." Babeuf meanwhile reflected on the degradation of the masses under the monarchy.[41]

The deaths of Bertier and Foullon entailed the usual police formalities. The mutilated heads and torsos of the two men were officially identified by three of Bertier's servants: his private secretary, a porter, and a seventy-two-year-old *valet de chambre*. Bertier left behind him a fabulous myth of power and wealth: in 1793, when prisons teemed with a variety of illicit counterfeits and frauds, authorities at Bicêtre uncovered the practice of selling "letters of St. John of Jerusalem," purporting to disclose the treasure and correspondence of Bertier hidden after his death by one of his servants.[42]

Bertier's real estate holdings were eventually valued at over three million livres. The seals were placed on the Hôtel de Vendôme, although an exception was made for the office in which he worked, so that papers might be transferred. The furnishings, and the immediate claims against the estate, reveal a style of life befitting a councillor of state and wealthy aristocrat. A glance at the inventory takes in an ottoman, two *bergères* and six armchairs covered in embroidered white fabric, twelve armchairs covered in velvet, a *lustre* of crystal, and old damask of crimson color. Amid velvet and marble, there appear also to have been some of the fine wallpapers manufactured by Sieur Réveillon, whose house and factory had been pillaged in a wage-related disturbance on the eve of the Estates-General.[43]

On the desk in Bertier's office lay two reports "relating to the present state of provisions of the town and *généralité* and neighborhood of Paris." These documents, sent immediately to the Bureau of Provisioning, would have nourished the belief that Bertier was involved in a famine plot. Such was the purport of a pamphlet that claimed to publish documents found in Bertier's portfolio at the time of his capture, including plans for a camp at St. Denis, accompanied by an order to cut down crops while still green, with a promise of later compensation to owners. Although it is possible that some grain was harvested before it was fully ripened as a desperate expedient to provision the army, the charge against Bertier was part of a more general panic, reinforced in turn by Bertier's arrest.[44] A report from the Clermontais, not far from Compiègne, on July 26 told of parishoners "who, like everyone else in the countryside, have got it firmly in their heads that people are going to come and cut down their grain."[45]

Requests addressed to Bertier for cartridges to be supplied to military units also fit the pattern of fear, yet were of a piece with his official duties. Nor is the letter of July 12 from Bertier's daughter, urging him to flee a dangerous situation, a surprise in light of his public proscription. What is perhaps more surprising is that Bertier's role as jailer of the poor figures prominently in the attacks upon his reputation. Coincidentally, the first of over fifty claims made immediately upon Bertier's estate was that of a Jean Binbaule on behalf of his illiterate brother Pierre, a mercer, who claimed 1600 livres owed to him by the concierge of the *dépôt* at St. Denis according to a note given to him on his release.[46] Bertier's conduct of the *dépôt* is used as a theme giving sinister coherence to the other charges against him in the spate of pamphlets that followed his assassination. In some, he was linked with de Launay and Flesselles; in almost all, with Foullon. The legendary decapitation of St. Denis figures in one imaginary dialogue among the four unrepentent victims. When Foullon tells of his part in the famine plot, Bertier protests:

> And I, who had never had the idea of such a stratagem, who believed myself to be as white as snow—has this kept them from making a St. Denis of me?

De Launay enlightens him:

> Ill-intentioned persons have told us, however, that for a number of years you have doubled the impositions of the poor inhabitants of your *généralité;* that without pity for the unfortunate situation in which they find themselves, you have them seized and reduce them to mendicity; which means that, by your efforts, the *dépôts* for beggars are always full.

Bertier objects that starving five or six thousand people should be no cause for ignominious treatment of him: "Should people like us have consideration for those who have not ten or twenty thousand francs in *rentes?*"[47] Another pamphlet mentions that Foullon's arrest at Vitry was not far from Ste-Geneviève-des-Bois, "where Berthier has a superb château, purchased at the expense of the misery of the people of the capital, and of the unfortunates detained at St. Denis, and so many others." This pamphlet alleged that Bertier offered several millions to his captors for his release. Commenting on the mutilation of Bertier's corpse, the author reflects upon the fact that his body had been exquisitely pampered, "and that what revolts nature has so often pronounced acts of authority, humiliated so many decent people, and made so many unfortunate suffer. What a lesson for those in power!"[48]

Not content with such "lessons," the author of another pamphlet conjured up further torments in the underworld. After providing for Foullon, he writes:

> Let his most worthy son-in-law be immediately laden with chains and shut up in the blackest cells of Tartarus; let there be assembled with care all the unfortunate who have died by his cupidity in the infamous *dépôt* of St. Denis, whether by hunger or by spoiled and poisoned victuals. I [Pluto] give him over to their vengeance and to all the outrages they can devise for his punishment.[49]

The rhetoric of the famine plot drew strength from infernal images of the imprisoned poor. Apart from the intended harshness of the workhouse regime, the *dépôt* of St. Denis had several claims to notoriety. Bitter-tasting bread at St. Denis had prompted the expert survey by Cadet de Vaux of all the bread provided to prisoners in Paris. A further provisioning scandal was uncovered after Bertier's death, leading to the replacement of the overseer. The rumor that Bertier profited personally from such abuses is not easily tested. It is evident that he made discretionary use of funds assigned to St. Denis for a variety of purposes, including the *pionniers*. Some payments to Bertier or his wife were included in records for the *dépôts;* the claims at his death suggest that some obligations were incurred in his own name. Aribitrary accounting and the mixing of personal and public accounts would not in themselves be proof of profiteering. But Bertier's name was already attached to the specter of a famine plot. It was enough that the *dépôt* of St. Denis was in his province and that the provisions there were suspect; rumors converged.[50]

If Bertier was a fit target for popular rage, how was the attack on him orchestrated? Bailly declared Bertier a victim of a plot. The abbé Grégoire, in the National Assembly debate of July 23, was particularly disturbed by the premeditated character of the proscription. One pamphlet that describes in a more detached manner than the others the scene at the Hôtel de Ville states that Lafayette spoke for half an hour on the need for a fair trial, and that a well-dressed man in the hall said afterward, "What need is there for judgment, with a man judged for the past thirty years?" The connection with the Palais Royal is confirmed by the mention, in the list of items contained in Bertier's portfolio, of a report dated July 11 "of the number of soldiers of the sects of the Palais-Royal, and of the names of the orators." The pamphleteers' conception of political alignments emerges from an excited dialogue of the dead. Du Pujet, an officer at the Bastille, tells of a plan to blow up underground magazines, speaks of the machinations of the "Jesuitical Archbishop," and the *race calotine* of Artois and Polignac. Foullon declares that he served Bourbon, Condé, Conti, Artois, and the monarch, "closely allied with the second person of the Kingdom." But now the people is master. Noailles and Liancourt opened the king's eyes. The king had written a letter recalling Necker, but a conspiracy still vows his death. The pamphlet names further associates in the crimes of the deceased, clearly with the intention of neutralizing any further attempt at reaction against Necker and the Estates-General.[51]

One of the pamphlets written after Bertier's death is remarkable in its emphasis on the *dépôt* and its suggestion that that connection was broadcast at the Palais

Royal at the very moment when crowds were being mobilized for the physical attack. "It suffices," the author writes, "in order to print an indelible stain on his reputation, to bring out in broader view what was posted yesterday on a tree of the Palais Royal, a few instants before his death:

> M. Foulon, also known as "heart of bronze," has embezzled and stolen from the state twenty millions: it was he who wanted a general bankruptcy. M. Berthier de Sauvigny, his son-in-law, also stole sixteen million: this wretch has starved six thousand persons to death in the *dépôts de mendicité*.

The author reports that this statement was applauded, and that the following inscription was added at the bottom:

> Ci gît Foulon, ci gît Berthier:
> Ils sont morts sans Bénitier.[52]

It is remarkable that this compressed indictment fuses the middle-class fear of bankruptcy with the popular fear of being reduced to mendicity, imprisoned and starved. It is also remarkable that the number of deaths by starvation coincide with the actual number of burials recorded at the *dépôt* of St. Denis from its inception to 1789. The exact number, according to recent study of the registers, was 6,108. The pamphlet was entitled "Epitaphs of Messrs. Foulon and Berthier, posted and published at the Palais Royal: or Funeral Oration, followed by a historical account of their death by M. l'abbé A.L.L." It would be in keeping with the gallows humor of these pamphlets to ascribe the authorship to "M. l'abbé À La Lanterne!" The question we cannot refrain from asking is whether the abbé de Montlinot had anything to do with Bertier's death.[53]

Whether Montlinot had any direct part in a plot, it is well established that he was part of a journalistic network critical of existing authority, and that he had openly criticized Bertier's management of the *dépôts*. It may never be possible to prove a conspiracy. However, it may add to an understanding of the revolutionary climate in July 1789 to probe the motives that could have led Montlinot to act the part of a conspirator.

In his encyclopedia article published in 1786, Montlinot had passionately denounced Bertier's convoys of beggars from St. Denis as a sacrifice to the squeamishness of the rich. In the same article he had baldly stated in cold print that the *dépôts* were reinstated *sans ordre, sans principes* after the fall of Turgot. In a letter to the first secretary of the *intendance*, Favier, he spoke of putting the bureaucrats of St. Denis in the way of their patron, in other words, decapitating them. Finding that a doctor at St. Denis, Davan, had culled out sixteen inmates from a list of thirty to be transferred and ordered them to the infirmary, Montlinot inferred the worst from the infirmities of those deemed "fit" who tumbled off the carts at Soissons. In another letter he claimed to know the "secret" of the inmates' poor health at St. Denis. In jaunty chronicles from "the best of all possible *dépôts*," Montlinot personalized his struggles on behalf of his charges at Soissons as a constant duel with Bertier. One letter of June 1785 refers to a "victory" won with the help of the "aide-de-camp Blossac." At the same time, Montlinot alluded to an effort by Bertier to kick him upstairs with the offer of an appointment to the veterinary school. Having refused, he alleges that Bertier had been trying to place him "in mendicity." Hearing that Bertier might offer him a place in the bureau of Le Monier (a secretary of the intendance of Paris), Montlinot fantasized that he would ask ten thousand livres in salary for the job.[54]

These comments are contained in a letter that Montlinot wrote from Paris to Favier at Soissons. Most of his letters to Favier, naturally, were written from Soissons to Paris, when the intendant de Blossac was residing there in his father-in-law's spacious Hôtel de Vendôme. On this occasion, Montlinot enjoys the irony of the situation, reporting on the gossip of the capital. Apparently he takes a detached view of the Diamond Necklace Affair, in which Bertier would be a staunch defender of the queen:

All of us here are for the cardinal, only you folks in the province regard the affairs of the necklace and of the famous Caliostro detained at La Force as serious matters—matter for variety entertainment. What will not be entertaining is that there is talk of war, of treaties. Farewell, I am politicking.[55]

It is quite possible that Montlinot was in Paris in connection with his work for Panckoucke on the *Dictionnaire méthodique*. He vented his frustrations in an article highly critical of the *dépôts,* mentioning in particular the number of those who had died throughout the system. In his fourth account, written in the next year, he was preoccupied with various proposals for reform and seemed to have some hope for gradual improvement, especially with the support of Blossac himself at Soissons.[56]

In 1787, however, all Montlinot's old problems with Bertier surfaced again, worse than ever. In a letter to Favier he had expressed polite regret that Bertier had "lost out" under Brienne, but he was undoubtedly pleased by the indication from La Millière shortly afterward that the policy of transfers was under review and that the regulations concerning them were to be strictly observed. In November, Montlinot asked Blossac to take measures to help some of those transferred in the latest convoy from St. Denis. Remarking that he would show him a work he had prepared on the matter of transfers, he noted that the cases at hand "reinforce what was said in the printed account and prove the necessity of changing the present administrative dispositions." The discussion takes on a political overtone in a further letter of December 23 in which Montlinot reminds Blossac that he had noted on previous occasions that M. Bertier should be reminded that the prisons of Villers-Cotterets were placed in the courtyard of the castle, "and that there would be some difficulty in transferring beggars from the *dépôt* of St. Denis during the sojourn of M. the duc d'Orléans." Remarks in the same vein recur in 1788. The duc d'Orléans may have been aware of the convoys of beggars passing beneath his windows; he resided at Villers-Cotterets following his exile in 1787 for having supported the remonstrances of the parlement of Paris.[57]

On July 13, 1788, Montlinot complained to Blossac that the convoy of the 11th from St. Denis had been sent without sufficient notice and that the inmates included a mixture of first offenders, recidivists, and a great number who should have been routed elsewhere to reach their domicile. He asked that he be allowed to release them for work in the fields, with the exception of the five insane bound for Châlons. He ventured a judgment that must seem "prerevolutionary" in retrospect:

No justice, no goodness has entered into the dispatch of some individuals. I know that the *dépôt* of St. Denis is overcrowded, but it will always be overcrowded as long as nothing is done for the wretches it contains. The administration of the *dépôts* will always be a thoroughly vicious administration, if it is not approached with zeal, patience, and humanity.

Bertier replied on July 24 to each point that his son-in-law had forwarded to him on the 14th. Setting aside the complaint that insufficient notice had been given, he explained that full documentation had not been sent because it was not certain whether some would be fit to travel until the last moment. He denied that inmates were misrouted, but asked that documentation be sent with any complaints. He invoked circumstances beyond his control. Waves of arrests in the capital and its environs necessitated the dispatch of convoys without the full twelve-to-fifteen-day notice. On July 9, for instance, there were 729 inmates at St. Denis and the *lieutenant de police* was urgently asking him to relieve the prisons of the Hôtel de la Force by taking eight batches of fifteen beggars each. The details presented should demonstrate, Bertier concluded, "that the inconveniences that have affected you derive from a principle of necessity to which I myself have been obliged to subscribe, before making its effects felt upon you." [58]

Rising to Bertier's challenge, Montlinot documented the cases in question for Blossac, who sent a very firm letter to his father-in-law, a letter resting on the assumption that both were serving an enlightened government. The worst instance Blossac found in the transfer record was that of a man eighty-two years old who was lowered into the grave within twenty-four hours of his arrival, "after having given along the route the spectacle of a wretched, dying old man dragged in spite of his infirmities from one *dépôt* to another." The control number was cited. "You will find," he continued, "a blameworthy carelessness likewise in the lack of investigation with regard to numbers 4-5-6-8-9-11-12-22." The roll call continued: "a perfect futility in the transfer to Lorraine and elsewhere of numbers 7-13-14-15-16-17-18-19-20-24-25." [59]

From these particulars, Blossac drew the lesson of enlightened bureaucracy:

> I know that the underlings of the police are liable to committing involuntary and perhaps even voluntary errors; but would it not be unpardonable for those who can bring remedy to disdain or neglect doing anything to repair them, especially in circumstances where all parts of the administration are enlightened [éclairés].
>
> This reproach is meant less for you than for another. No one is unaware of that vigilance with which you supervise all those parts of administration that are in your province. That is why I doubt not that you will give the most precise orders to the employees of the *dépôt* of St. Denis to use greater attention and humanity.

Submitting some of his original lists as documentation in support of Blossac's letter, Montlinot commented to Favier, "The son-in-law has put a bit of honey in the letter to the father-in-law—there is even a compliment. It's Bertier's answer that I would like to see." Using a double-edged sense of *éclairer* that may have been implicit in Blossac's letter, he added, "We are going to shed light on him again with the report on the last convoy. . . . I am going to the *dépôt* for the whole day Sunday to attend to the business of these gentlemen." [60]

Bertier wrote a stiff reply to Blossac on September 1, obviously aware that Montlinot would read it. "I have given the most precise order," he wrote, "that greater attention be given and that one should watch with particular care that no

transfers be made except directly toward their destination." However, he acknowledged only two cases being out of order in the tables he had reviewed. Montlinot
was disgusted. In a further note to Favier, accompanying another list, he wrote:

> You have received today, my good friend, the law and the prophets: that is to say,
> the transfers. You can say what you think best to M. de Blossac based on my
> letter. His [Bertier's] reply is that of a man who knows not what to answer, of a
> child who after a thrashing says he will not do it again. This trial will definitely
> have to be judged by a minister, if he continues to assail us with beggars. I cannot
> squander my health or my purse to repair all the foolishness of such a badly orga-
> nized bureau. I am keeping all the evidence for the trial.
> Farewell, my friend. With a heartfelt embrace.

Brienne's ministry had recently collapsed. Necker was "the minister." Symbol
and mouthpiece of reform in the year of the Estates-General, Necker was particularly important to men like Montlinot and Lambert who were concerned with questions of poor relief and public welfare. Montlinot himself participated in the public
discussion of these questions in the early months of 1789 with a new account of
the *dépôt de mendicité* at Soissons, preceded by an essay on mendicity. The account
he used was that of 1786, resuming the sequence where he had left off. Although
he avoided reference to the political crisis, his essay took on a revolutionary significance when read as a call to the nation under Necker's leadership to judge the
injustices and errors of the Old Regime in the open court of the Estates-General.[61]

Montlinot introduced his tract with a comment on the current flood of writings
on mendicity, crammed with promises and plans. By contrast, he offered the reader
"observation and experience." Characterizing past legislation on mendicity as "a
conspiracy of the property owners against the propertyless," he explained how difficult it was to conceive of a genuinely new approach to the problem. Summarizing
an insider's knowledge of the working documents of Laverdy's and Turgot's commissions, he traced a legacy of futility: Laverdy's reform stymied by a parlement
fearing a coercive local poor rate; an administration of the *dépôt* scarred by incompetence and greed; Turgot's Quixotic impulse to extend the universal benefits of
liberty to a class of miserable beggars who had nowhere to turn upon their release;
a fatuous ordinance of 1777 that simply reiterated that of 1767, as if the mere
snapping of fingers in a declaration could make work available to all who desired
it; the declamatory exercises of the academies; and the continuing mindless incarceration of those who wanted nothing more than to earn an honest living, together
with those who had turned their backs on such virtuous hopes and scorned the
dépôts.[62]

Searching for a point of Cartesian simplicity amid a legacy of error, Montlinot
enunciated a maxim that Lambert was to seize upon shortly afterward in his *cahier*
of the poor. The simple act of begging could not be considered a crime in itself.
Anyone in France who was poor was ipso facto a beggar—that is, in a radical state
of insecurity: "It is absurd to multiply laws against mendicity in a country where a
fifth of the Nation is always on the verge of asking for alms from one day to the
next." A law against begging as such was bound "to pronounce indiscriminately
the privation of liberty against every individual who begs."[63]

Evidence drawn from the dossiers of inmates at Soissons was adduced in support of this general pronouncement. Whereas in his accounts for 1784 and 1785 Montlinot had contrasted the predominance of urban trades among the inmates transferred from St. Denis with the preponderance of rural day laborers among those arrested in the *généralité* of Soissons, he used the total population of 854 inmates on the registers at Soissons in the course of 1786 to illustrate "the sad truth, so often repeated, that the man without employment, or who, through disability, stops working, necessarily gives himself over to mendicity, especially if he reaches the age of 45." He explained that there were so many errors in the declarations of the 273 men and 59 women transferred from St. Denis in 1786 that he did not deem it useful to analyze their trades separately. In his general breakdown of adult male inmates (excluding the insane), he noted that there were 294 day laborers with no means of subsistence, and 256 who mentioned a trade. Commenting on this list (see table), he noted the presence of certain trades that had appeared in previous accounts—the tailors, the shoemakers, the wigmakers, and the weavers—who were "the most vagabond, and were often liable to lack work." Workers in the wool trade, he added, appeared to have suffered in that year from an interruption in production.

These observations on the the economic causes of mendicity did not lead Montlinot to deny the existence of a class of delinquent beggars. He merely denied that the *dépôt* had any effect upon this class. Indeed, he devoted a large part of his tract to a proposal for a penal colony off the coast of Africa as a more effective means of rehabilitation. Montlinot was also reluctant to argue that the state should minister directly to all the needs of the poor. He thought that a single comprehensive administrative structure such as Brienne had proposed in 1775 was chimerical, and he feared that a parish poor rate might extinguish local charity. Not content with long-range structural reforms of the legal and economic system that ignored the immediate needs of the poor, he echoed Lambert's fear that greed and self-interest would prevail in an unimaginative policy of repression: "If we cannot keep the government from making beggars, at least let us keep it from making France into an *hôpital-général.*"[64]

What then was the remedy? Unlike those who called for local control of the *dépôts,* Montlinot would retain correctional establishments in a centralized bureaucratic framework. However, the provision of relief to the poor and the disabled, to the young and the aged, required promotion and leadership on the national level combined with local initiative and support. Cities might effectively cope with their welfare needs by a reform of their traditional institutions. In the countryside, however, parish alms bureaus lacked the resources to support the needy. Montlinot took the example of the *généralité* of Soissons, a primarily agricultural region, to outline a proposal for a centrally funded system of pensions for agricultural laborers. This proposal, which Montlinot had sketched as early as his account of 1782, was his most important contribution to that national *cahier* of the poor that Lambert had solicited in January.[65]

Montlinot's proposal, echoed in a number of the official *cahiers,* was his way of throwing down a challenge to the society and government of the Old Regime. Society, he contended in a vigorous demonstration, owed a debt to the laborer who was consumed physically by a lifetime of labor. The government could give weighty support to the ideal of public utility by recognizing this debt. The public hospice

List of Trades Declared by Adult Male Inmates of the *Dépôt de Mendicité* of Soissons in 1786, According to Leclerc de Montlinot

chapeliers (hatmakers)	5
bourreliers (leatherworkers)	4
tailleurs (tailors)	14
cordonniers (shoemakers)	35
merciers (mercers)	20
pèlerins (pilgrims)	15
matelots (sailors)	8
cuisiniers (cooks)	3
charrons (carters)	4
menuisiers (carpenters)	8
tonneliers (coopers)	10
perruquiers (wigmakers)	13
maçons (masons)	6
couvreurs (thatchers or roofers)	7
cardeurs et fileurs de laine (carders and wool spinners)	31
tisserands (weavers)	10
boulangers (bakers)	9
bonnetiers (bonnetmakers)	6
paveurs (paving workers)	5
bouchers (butchers)	4
imprimeurs en étoffes (print makers)	3
jardiniers (gardeners and small vegetable growers)	9
drapiers (drapers)	4
maréchaux (farriers)	3
cloutiers (nailmakers)	2
selliers (harness makers)	2
serruriers (locksmiths)	2
ciseleurs (chiselers)	1
doreur (gilder)	1
salpêtrier (saltpeter mkr)	1
charpentier (joiner)	1
herboristes (herb sellers)	3
gaziers (lawn gardener)	3
notaire (notary)	1
TOTAL	25[3]

Note: Montlinot's subtotals contain errors. In his table, the number of adult males who list a trade totals 253, but he enters a total of 256. He also states in his text that there are 204 women, children, and insane inmates of both sexes, but the numbers he provides in these categories total 304 (including women convoyed from St. Denis). An additional 294 inmates Montlinot describes as "journaliers sans état et sans ressource, dès que les travaux de la campagne ont été interrompues, ou qui, par des causes particulières, ont été obligés de mendier leur subsistance."

Assuming that three adult males were omitted from the tally of trades, the corrected total agrees with the 854 in Montlinot's initial tally of all admissions to the *dépôt*.

Source: Leclerc de Montlinot, *Etat actuel du dépôt de Soissons, précédé d'un essai sur la mendicité. V. Compte. Année 1786* (Soissons, 1789), 57–59.

for the *cultivateurs invalides* would be run by the same authority as the *dépôts*, linking the public repression of idleness with an equally public reward for labor. Local charitable initiatives would be encouraged thereby; the honor of agriculture would be restored.[66]

The idea of pensions for day laborers implied a critique of the prevailing distribution of royal pensions; Montlinot attacked the hypocrisy that condoned an inversion of rewards. He attacked the notion that the poor were careless in providing for the future, contrasting the vulnerability of the poor with the provision made for the security of the rich at every stage in life. How thoughtless, likewise, to blame the poor for inconveniencing the rich by asking for alms, when it was the poor who spent their lives in serving the convenience of the rich! How inconsistent to blame the poor for their drunkenness, when the poor had none of the options for social activity or entertainment enjoyed by the rich! If the rich enjoyed castigating the poor for enjoying "the gaiety of their equals," it also helped to salve their conscience. Did they not in fact encourage their helots to deprave themselves in order the better to despise them? Above all, Montlinot insisted, the common association of the word "idleness" with the beggar merely served to mask the exploitation of lives exhausted in labor. How could the poor be expected to step lively, when their bodies were exhausted by hard work, poor diet, and unhealthy working conditions?[67]

In short, Montlinot's final essay on mendicity called for a revolutionary consciousness of society's obligations to its poorer members, based not merely on a collective humanitarian obligation to improve conditions, but on a personal right of the poor citizen, founded on a utilitarian social compact. In attempting to unmask the linguistic tools of class oppression, Montlinot evoked a powerful prerevolutionary equation, one that had already been transposed from the writings of Rousseau to the context of the Châlons essay on mendicity twelve years earlier. In the conclusion to the published compendium of those essays, the lessons of academic inquiry were linked to a citation from *Émile,* that treatise on the natural education of man and citizen:

> He who eats in idleness what he has not himself earned, steals it; and a *rentier* whom the state pays to do nothing, hardly differs in my eyes, from the brigand who lives at the expense of passers-by. Outside of society, an isolated man owes nothing to anyone, he has the right to do what he pleases. But in society where he lives necessarily at others' expense, he owes them in labor the cost of his upkeep; to work is an indispensable duty for social man; rich or poor, powerful or weak, every idle citizen is a ne'er-do-well.[68]

The editor, the abbé Malvaux, had gone on to speak of "a great revolution that is being prepared." The revolution that he spoke of was a radical change in public spirit, a change signaled above all by a devotion to the "social virtues" of *bienfaisance.* "Never have the dignity and the rights of man been better known," he wrote. With this change in public spirit would come a "regeneration" of the ways of the common people, a new spirit in their labors. Malvaux gave much of the credit for this transformation to the new initiatives taken in the capital—that is to say, under Necker's aegis.[69]

After the disappointments of the 1780s, Montlinot and others who ardently hoped for the regeneration spoken of in the Châlons compendium again looked to Necker to lead the nation to a new level of civic consciousness. Necker's return in 1788 had given Montlinot the patience to have his grievances adjudged in the ripeness of time. With the news of Necker's dismissal on July 11, Montlinot, like others, must have feared not only a period without hope, but a period of retribution against all who had spoken out their hopes and condemned the injustices of the past. If Necker represented the hope of regeneration, Bertier, for Montlinot, represented the broken promises of the Old Regime.

The abbé de Montlinot may actually have played no active part in bringing Bertier to his fate on the Place de Grève on July 22, 1789. There were others capable of translating their fears and grievances into support for a proscription. Nonetheless, it is illustrative of the nature of revolutionary politics that a Montlinot had marked the intendant as an enemy of reform. His grievances against Bertier, personal and ideological, were of long standing. He had worked on a variety of publishing enterprises and could easily have drafted a bill of particulars against Bertier. His correspondence reveals the rapier wit of a prosecutor; the judges of the academy at Soissons in 1779 did not fail to recognize an incendiary streak in this tribune of the poor. If eight years of service as inspector of the *dépôt de mendicité* at Soissons gave direction to the hopes and fears of Montlinot—alienated cleric, admirer of *Émile,* protégé of Necker—they also provided him with a wealth of administrative experience and an experimental outlook that prepared him to play a leading role as consultant to Liancourt's Comité de Mendicité.

11

Founding a New Regime

One result of the growth of clinical medicine in the eighteenth century, according to Michel Foucault, was that doctors began to lift their gaze from the individual case history to the environment in which the phenomena of disease and health were constituted. Foucault's interpretation applies particularly well to the *dépôts,* which functioned in the narrow sense as medical clinics, but which also provided amphitheaters for observing social pathology case by case. The revolutionary Comité de Mendicité carried this panoptic impulse to its logical conclusion, subjecting an entire society to diagnostic scrutiny. Two sets of issues linked the work of the Comité de Mendicité of the Constituent Assembly with the experience of the *dépôts* under the Old Regime. The problem of maintaining standards of hygiene within an institution became linked with an effort to monitor the welfare of the population at large. Likewise, the challenge of rehabilitating inmates through work came to be predicated on a broader social question: could every citizen expect to attain well-being through work? Work, well-being, and citizenship could no longer be defined in isolation from each other.[1]

Observation and Well-Being

A lyrically enthusiastic review of Montlinot's reports on the *dépôts de mendicité* appeared in the *Mercure de France* in two installments in 1784. "What a source of information useful to society society itself could be, if every class of individual belonging to it were observed with this ingenious sagacity and these beneficent intentions!"[2] The author of these words, Dominique-Joseph Garat, recently arrived from the provinces, saw in Montlinot's method of observation an example of that "science of man" that he was hearing about at the salon of Mme Helvétius at Autueil. Modeled on current medical canons, the method depended on the refinement of "conjecture" by the accumulation of empirical data. With sufficient data on the stature of male inmates, for example, the cause determining whether a man became a highwayman or beggar might become evident. But such investigations required a national system for collecting data, so that constant patterns could be disentangled from local circumstances. Garat saw the royal government as patron of such efforts: "A government such as ours easily carries its full powers to the most removed points of the Empire; this is the advantage of monarchies."[3]

Garat here reformulated the key virtue that Voltaire had praised in the monarchy of Louis XIV, and that the abbé de Saint-Pierre had translated into an agenda for eighteenth-century reformers. Intendants were instructed to carry out surveys of all sorts to be plotted on a single map for the guidance of the king's ministers. The controller-general Orry's map of the relative well-being of the provinces could be seen as a schema that would invite Montlinot and others to articulate the information-gathering potential of the *dépôts* at a much later date.[4] The notion that charitable needs ought to be evaluated and supported on a national level was kept alive by the abbé Baudeau and others, even as the Physiocrats protested against the bureaucratic direction of economic life. Operating on the presumption that new measures would replace those suspended in 1733, de Boullongne brought his statistics on charitable resources up to date on more than one occasion.[5]

Likewise, the idea of endowing the police of the realm with a universal system of surveillance persisted, even though the apparatus for maintaining information on all individuals arrested under the Declaration of 1724 had failed. A memoir addressed to Laverdy in 1768 by the president of the Third Estate of Brittany, de Coniac, expressed the view that free trade could be protected against the depradations of an expanding population of indigents only through an ambitious network of police surveillance.[6]

Set in charge of the "operation of mendicity," Bertier established procedures for collecting information to serve a variety of purposes. As chief warden and taskmaster of the disreputable poor, he and his staff scrutinized records of the daily operations of the *dépôts* in order to verify whether policies concerning terms of detention and procedures for release were being adhered to. It was his responsibility to forestall any challenge from the courts on the grounds that inmates were unjustly treated. His data also served as a tool for day-to-day management and for the fine-tuning of routine procedures. At a higher level, the data served an experimental purpose: to evaluate the success of various policies adopted with respect to the *dépôts,* and for the long term to formulate more effective solutions to the problem of mendicity viewed as a whole. In practice, Bertier's concerns seem most often to have been those of a quartermaster. *Dépôts* were to be managed very much like the *casernes* that Bertier was constructing in the *généralité* of Paris to separate soldiers from the people at large. When his troop of beggars fell sick, he called in surgeons and, if necessary, doctors. When faced with complaints about unhealthy quarters, he would defer to the advice of royal engineers, after reminding them to shun the nonfunctional amenities of hospitals.

The economic crisis of 1769–1771 focused attention on problems of subsistence. Terray pressed the *dépôts* into service as one agency among many in support of an interventionist police of work and subsistence. He worked closely with Bertier in coordinating the grain supplies of Paris and its region, and consulted with him on the *dépôts*. Agreeing with Bertier that contractors would respond to incentives to put inmates to work, Terray approved the general contract of 1773. But he did not leave the contractors to inspect themselves. He had Bertier obtain data on inmates from intendants in order to form an independent estimate of the income de-

rived from their labor, monitoring expenditures against their social outcomes. Charitable administrators were no strangers to such calculations. Terray, Fénelon might
have said, treated France as a hospital.[7]

Terray marshaled information to anticipate crises of subsistence and police the
hungry. Turgot, like Bertin and Laverdy before him, gathered data in preparation
for major structural changes. Brienne avowed a cautiously empirical approach to
matters of law and administration, but his remark in a letter to Laverdy about an
imminent "revolution" impatiently awaited in the provinces provides a context for
his method. Inspecting every phase of administration, he insisted that poverty could
be regarded only "as a whole." The tactics of Turgot's administration were incremental, the objectives revolutionary.[8]

Adding a new installment to the series of data that Boullongne had collected on
charitable resources, Turgot brought to them the liberal assumptions he had enunciated in the *Encyclopédie.* In the case of the *dépôts,* he dismissed certain types of
information as superfluous or turned them to new purposes. After the meeting at
Montigny, Turgot asked for complete reporting on inmates, not to monitor their
labor more closely, but to determine whether their release would present an immediate threat to society. There could be no other just cause for detention. In the long
term, mendicity could be eradicated only by a policy of economic growth coupled
with public assistance for those unable to support themselves.[9]

In recovering his bureaucratic domain from the onslaught of Turgot, Bertier
articulated and promoted his own version of what it meant to view poverty as a
whole, advancing those measures that he construed as a necessary "complement"
to the *dépôts.* In this broader framework, reminiscent of the schemes of the abbé
de Saint-Pierre, Bertier reckoned the benefits shared by the people and the costs
saved by the king as a consequence of the operations of the *dépôts* and the related
corps des pionniers.

Responding to the advice of savants in the 1780s, Bertier turned the *dépôts* into
observation posts for social medicine. The learned elite of the capital, men such as
Cadet de Vaux and Mauduyt, responded to the challenge of maintaining hygiene at
the *dépôt* of St. Denis. In concert with an official corps of inspectors, they gleaned
clinical data from the infirmaries there. The presence of *surnuméraires* training for
positions as overseers in other *dépôts* underscored the role of the institution as a
testing ground for procedures and regulations. The contribution of the *dépôt* to
clinical medicine was exemplified in the case of experiments involving rabies victims, who were ordered sent to the infirmary of the *dépôt* at St. Denis. The search
for simple, cheap remedies also led to the establishment of ties between the *dépôt*
at St. Denis and the veterinary school of Alfort, with which Colombier was also
associated. In this clinical atmosphere, social experiments were also in order. Bertier entertained a proposal to set up a special quarter at St. Denis for delinquent
youths too young to serve in the *pionniers.*[10]

On a more modest scale, other *dépôts* served similar functions. In cases of
venereal disease and insanity, in particular, they served as the poor person's clinic.
As agencies of royal *bienfaisance,* all the *dépôts,* but especially that of St. Denis,
were themselves subject to scrutiny. The incidence of mortality was carefully measured at Caen, Tours, and elsewhere and correlated with possible causes of illness

located within the *dépôt* or in its environs. While such information gave insight into disease and its cures, it also provided arguments for good stewardship or neglect on the part of administrators.[11]

The *dépôt* at Soissons under Montlinot's tutelage rivaled St. Denis in its claim to provide a model of humane and cost-effective rehabilitation. It also reflected the reform hopes crystallized around the person of Jacques Necker in the 1780s. In the case of public health and medical reporting, Necker consolidated the process that Turgot had set in motion with the establishment of the Société Royale de Médecine. Creation of an inspectorate of hospitals and prisons brought the *dépôts* together with these other institutions under a common regime of observation and reform.

In his use of information on the *dépôts* and their inmates, Necker refined the political arithmetic of *bienfaisance* and addressed it to the nation. His program had much in common with that of Bertier, but he turned his exemplary experiments into arguments in favor of provincial administration and public accountability. Lacking Turgot's vision of systematic change, he nonetheless encouraged expectations that Bertier and many of his confreres could only view as demagogic. Although he rejected Montlinot's bid to assure the common people a "general ease," he nonetheless stimulated revolutionary hopes for improvement.

In the compendium of essays on mendicity submitted to the academy of Châlons, Malvaux had included Montlinot's apostrophe, "Enter a hospital, political calculator!" The facts to be observed would testify not only to the medical incapacity of these institutions, but to conditions in the society at large that needed to be attacked directly. Later, at Soissons, Montlinot drew upon the cases he observed and laid bare the "constitution" of society's chronic maladies. "I have too often felt their wounds," he testified. While his observations included medical symptoms, his rhetoric castigated an elite that invoked the authority of the Church but daily abandoned the poor of whom Christ said, according to Matthew 25, "Inasmuch as ye have done it unto the least of one of these my brethren, ye have done it unto me." In one letter he referred ironically to the list of inmates to be transferred from St. Denis as "the law and the prophets"; in another he described the symptoms and listed the age of those transferred. Empirical description and statistics blended in his rhetoric with a republican sense of civic virtue. A vision of Lazarus at the rich man's door dwelled in the interstices. Of science and prophecy Montlinot concocted a corrosive mixture, an ideological *aqua regia*.[12]

Linguet, Mercier, and others blended the denunciatory passion of the moralist with the savant's commitment to empirical observation. It is remarkable, however, to find a similar rhetorical tension in places where one might expect unalloyed confidence in the ability of the authorities to carry out enlightened reform. In the same volume of the *Encyclopédie méthodique* where François Doublet's article on "Air" cast the progress of institutional hygiene in a favorable light, Jean-Noël Hallé, writing on "Agriculture," voiced pessimistic reflections on the debilitated peasant constitution observed by public health doctors. The typical village, he wrote, sat on humid terrain amid piles of manure and standing water, with families crowded together, "breathing a corrupted air." The germ of epidemic would spread in such an environment, sometimes claiming an entire village: "That is what one saw in the Autumn of 1776, in several villages of Brittany depopulated by dysentery."

The sick peasant was too weak to undergo traditional methods of therapy; blood-letting was especially dangerous. A fundamental change of environment was indispensable:

> Afflicted by such an appalling tableau, and one that is sometimes all too true, what advice can the doctor give to these unfortunates? He can only form hopes, often impotent ones, that a change in their lot may allow them to make a living from their work, to draw strength from their food, to live in homes that preserve their health. Then one can draw up wise laws on the proportions to be established, in the countryside, between the nature of tasks and the age of workers, and to see to it that youth is not blasted in its flower, and that age does not succumb under the burden of works and days. Then the day laborer will regain in his life in the fields all the goods that nature generally endows him with, and which too often the injustice of men dissipates or takes from him.[13]

The reference to "impotent" hopes verges on a confession of despair. The author seems to imply that "wise laws" to aid the tillers of the soil may need to await some more general "change in their lot." The phrase "injustice of men" almost certainly implies a reference to privilege and arbitrary authority. In urban and institutional settings, medical observation also heightened an awareness of the unequal incidence of disease among the poor and the common people as compared with the rich and the privileged.[14]

Other voices mixed the rhetoric of science and prophecy. The Estates of Brittany borrowed demographic concepts from Deparcieux in denouncing the high rate of mortality at the *dépôt* at Rennes, but went on to speak of each of the dead as witnesses against the administration. They objurgated Cabanes for requiring that inmates produce a fixed amount of cloth before their release from the *dépôt* and mocked his hypocrisy with a scientific image: "Behold the thermometer of liberty!" Let not the government send released beggars to the colonies, lest they teach the slaves there to revolt! Let not their sovereign misread the signs of misery: "In order to help the poor, we must know who he is, and beggary is his language; it is the sign that announces his claims and often his most justly founded rights." They would observe the phenomenon of mendicity with a diagnostic eye, without abandoning the traditional posture of tribunes appealing to a candid world.[15]

The diagnostic metaphor that informed social criticism in the late eighteenth century drew strength from a widespread interest in the Hippocratic writings as a model for useful social inquiry. The ideal of *bienfaisance* drew upon this corpus both for its strong emphasis on the environment in which health and sickness were defined, and its concern for a therapeutic relationship between patient and doctor. Montlinot had praised the intendant of Soissons for establishing a form of interview that departed from the former pattern of judicial interrogation and attempted primarily to counsel the inmate along the path to self-sufficiency. Garat had been impressed by Montlinot's ability to obtain extensive information from inmates by gaining their confidence: "In how many places a similar talent would be even more necessary, and would produce insights yet more useful to society! One governs men without knowing about them and one does nothing to know them better."[16]

The fusion, sometimes self-consciously ironic, of prophetic denunciation and scientific observation recurred in the debates of the Revolution. Before the Revolutionary assembly Barère spoke of mendicity as "the leprosy of monarchies"; a pamphleteer spoke of it as "the thermometer of states." Bannefroy, a former inspector of the *dépôts*, prefaced his revolutionary pamphlet on mendicity with an image drawn from geology. These *dépôts*, he said, were like the congealed lava flows in certain countries that announce the presence of a destructive volcano.[17]

The work of the Comité de Mendicité of the Constituent Assembly, tinged with prophecy, nonetheless exhibits a coherence and depth of observation that draws upon the experience of the Old Regime. The vision of the committee and of its chairman, La Rochefoucauld-Liancourt, could hardly have been articulated so strongly, had not observers with extensive knowledge of the *dépôts* contributed their expertise. Montlinot was given leave from his post as inspector at Soissons to work as consultant to the committee. Thouret, who succeeded Colombier as general inspector of hospitals, prisons, and *dépôts*, was an active member, and so was their bureaucratic superior, Chaumont de la Millière. These experts and their circle of academic and administrative colleagues shared convergent observations on the need for reform. Montlinot and Thouret were particularly suited to transmit this consensus: both were trained in medicine, both were bureaucrats, both linked medical statistics to the social environment.[18]

The revolutionary lessons that the Comité de Mendicité drew from observation of the *dépôts* appeared in several reports. The fourth report, in particular, categorized all those needs that the individual might be unable to provide for himself. Painting a somber picture of the short-term emergencies in welfare precipitated by the Revolution, Liancourt projected a long-run diminution of need as the new constitution worked its balm. Alluding to conversations with the commission on nationalized domains, Liancourt urged the Assembly to seize the opportunity for "augmenting the number of landholders." Some fifteen to twenty million *arpents*, he reckoned, "languish unused because of the aridity of the moors or the slime of the marsh, or because of the tyranny of feudal rights." The hope of bringing new land under cultivation, of removing the burden of feudal privilege, and of "augmenting the number of landholders" had figured in the discussions of mendicity under the Old Regime. Among numerous reports from intendants that spoke of such matters, that of Caze de la Bove in 1775 had especially castigated feudal privileges in Brittany as a cause of that province's impoverishment, and Necker had agreed with Le Peletier, intendant at Soissons, on the need to preserve the small landholder.[19]

The monarchy had promoted the idea that no point in the realm would be deprived of the sovereign's justice or of his sollicitude. Liancourt translated this ideal into a revolutionary national mode and lay bare the defects in existing public charities. He called for the new constitution to replace "this incomplete system by an enlightened and farsighted system that, embracing all *départements* and all parts of *départements*, . . . [will], in the distribution of aid, know no proportion but that of the unfortunate."[20] Implicitly in tune with Hippocratic principles of observation, Liancourt indicated that general regulations would be framed at the national level, but that initiative ought to lie with the *départements*. They can act in more useful fashion with their knowledge "of their climate, of their commerce, of their customs, of their needs." Civic pride and self-interest would be harnessed to prosperity. Such ideas were in keeping with Brienne's pyramidal model for administering welfare needs, and with Montlinot's definition of the complementary role of central direction and local initiative.[21]

Liancourt articulated a new view of *bienfaisance* as a political science based on justice, not charity. The organization of this science is modeled in part on the corps of medical officers mobilized by the monarchy in the 1780s. This network would be permanently established to ascertain and minister to the needs of the sick poor in the most efficient manner possible—by home care where feasible, in a network of local hospitals as needed. Each *département* would have its own more specialized hospital for treating serious and difficult cases. The need for some network of this sort had come into sharp focus in debates concerning mendicity from the time of Laverdy. Once in place, such a network would remove the sick poor from the purview of the *dépôts*.[22]

Analysis of the assorted population of the *dépôts* contributed to Liancourt's discussion of other categories to be aided. The notion that different ages and conditions of life require specific forms of aid emerges especially in the call for treatment of the insane, and in the formulation of mechanisms for ensuring that children—the largest category of aid recipients—receive assistance in accordance with their needs. Recognizing the needs of the aged, Liancourt suggested that their inability to work beyond a certain age could be predicted and that pension schemes could be designed accordingly. The committee had drawn up proposals based on Duvillard's actuarial tables and had them approved by a special committee of the Academy of Sciences including Condorcet, Vandermonde, and Laplace, before reporting them back to the Assembly.

There were many sources for this approach. Condorcet believed that annuities could be used as a system of social security, an instance of the application of probabilities to human affairs. But the *dépôts* provided further observations and a sense of urgency. A policy of providing "prebends" for the laboring poor in their old age, as proposed by Montlinot, might have spared the agony and shame of some of the aged beggars brought to the *dépôts*. Likewise, Montlinot's statistical inquiries on foundlings, commissioned by Necker, grew out of his observations in the *dépôts*. Concern for the condition of children was prominent in the literature on mendicity and in memoirs submitted within administrative channels. This concern was spurred on by scandalous reports from the *dépôts*.[23]

Finally, Liancourt proposed that the Old Regime principle of parish responsibility be modified to take account of conditions of employment in a national market economy. The divisive squabbles between parishes that characterized the British system could be averted by defining a *domicile de secours,* or residency for relief purposes, that would reflect a choice on the part of the individual after a set period of working in one locality. It would allow one under most conditions to claim one's birthplace as domicile, and would include rules for establishment of domicile by newly married couples. These formulations reflected a concern that had been expressed within Laverdy's commission and commented on by Bertier. Bertier had argued that a parish benefiting from a resident's labors ought to become responsible for him, if he fell into mendicity. Lacking a clear resolution of this issue, Bertier had embroiled himself in conflicts with his confreres as he attempted to disgorge the beggars of Paris and its region back to their provinces of origin.[24]

In the fifth report, Liancourt took a quantitative measure of the phenomenon of mendicity—that is, of all welfare needs including beggars and the sick poor—in a report prepared in large part by Thouret. Thouret had taken over the inspection of hospitals, prisons, and *dépôts de mendicité* following the death of Colombier. Drawing upon documentation from his own bureau, he undoubtedly consulted also with La Millière and Montlinot.

The form of inquiry employed by Thouret and his collaborators reflected a new sophistication in the method of social statistics. Not willing to wait until a definitive census of the poor could be tallied from the standard forms that Montlinot had helped prepare, these students of poverty attempted to extrapolate from a known sample by devising a rough index of the incidence of poverty, just as early demographers multiplied numbers of households by an average size of household in order to estimate total population. Thouret and his collaborators also attempted to define the range of error in their estimates, bracketing the upper and lower bounds within which the phenomena seemed to be contained.[25]

Montlinot contributed some indices. He had put together a survey of the households of inmates of the *dépôts de mendicité* of Soissons which indicated that there was one "poor" household in sixty in the *généralité,* an estimate that tallied with some results from Lille. Finding the estimate low, he offered another estimate based on an apparent rule of thumb that said that a roughly equal proportion existed between the number of poor not receiving relief in a community and those formally aided or incarcerated as beggars. A further index derived by Thouret would suggest that the maximum extent of hard-core indigence was one-tenth, and that the sick poor constituted one-tenth of that number at most. The minimum proportion in both cases was one-twentieth. A table listing the proportion of hospital beds to population indicated that Thouret had probably drawn up these figures from files in his bureau.[26]

These conservative indices of poverty were set against the still incomplete reports from intendants and the new departmental authorities. Of the seven *intendances* reporting, the lowest proportion of poor was observed in that of Auch, where subsistence agriculture by proprietors and a pattern of migratory labor predominated. The highest proportion was in the Soissonnais, where hail and a hard winter had swelled the ranks of the poor to a sixth. Montauban reported a similarly high proportion, correlated with bad harvests and vine cultivation. These data from intendants, from the hospital inspectorate, and from Montlinot's research, were supplemented by various other sources, including a study of the *bureau de charité* of Le Mans (an agency promoted by du Cluzel with urging from Terray and Bertier) by the abbé de Moncé, and from a random survey of parishes in the newly formed department of Seine-et-Marne recently conducted by Trembley de Rubelles, confirming a proportion of one-tenth. Finally, for comparative purposes, the committee made use of the abundant data available on the administration of the English Poor Law, establishing an index of five percent for England.[27]

Putting together estimates for each category of the poor, and using experiences such as those of the Hospice of St. Sulpice to estimate the cost of supporting the sick, the children, and the aged, Liancourt set forth a national budget estimate for all public assistance needs, and purported to demonstrate that the nationalization of existing charitable resources would provide operating income roughly comparable to these needs. This conclusion was similar to that of Brienne fifteen years earlier, both in its assurance that a nationalized system would bring gains in efficiency, and in its premise that any shortfall in funds to cover duly recognized needs at the local level would have to be regarded as a national obligation.[28]

If Liancourt's estimate was too optimistic, it was not for any lack of attention to empirical social realities. The threshold of need reflected in the surveys used by the committee may have been drawn too low by local authorities anxious not to overcommit resources, and the committee may have counted too much on a surge of economic prosperity once the canker of privilege was excised. The uncertainties of revolution disposed the assemblies against the sweeping commitments proposed by Liancourt's committee. When the Jacobins finally took steps in that direction at the height of the Terror, resources were preempted by the costs of war; the class of citizens in dire need had meanwhile swelled far beyond the worst estimates of the Comité of Mendicité.[29]

Work and Rehabilitation

"The philosopher's stone, so long sought after, has been found—it is work."[30] Of the phrases the abbé Malvaux culled from the essays submitted for the prize of the academy of Châlons in 1777, few went so directly to the heart of eighteenth-century thinking on mendicity. The question to be answered seemed to call for arcane arts: "How to make beggars useful to the state without making them unhappy?" This was truly the *magnum opus,* the transformation of a base metal into gold, redeeming the material and spiritual dross of idleness. The "puffers" of social alchemy in the eighteenth-century promised formulae that would, in Dostoevsky's phrase, "instantly reorganize humanity . . . without the aid of living historical development."[31] Commenting on a project to aid the poor of a large city in 1786, Du Pont de Nemours advanced a more sober claim to do "more good . . . at less expense." The results he certified were incremental: "More individuals find a means to satisfy their needs, more virtues are unfolded, vices have less occasion to develop; the human race improves and becomes less unfortunate." It was a visionary hope, nonetheless, that inspired Du Pont and others like him to promote ways to employ the poor in the improvement of their own lot: "This is an advance in morals and in civilization that should be noted with no less interest perhaps than an advance in what has been called—sometimes too exclusively—science."[32]

Bertier, following Joly de Fleury, had assumed that a universal penalty for begging would quickly drive the idle to seek work outside the *dépôts.* When experience demonstrated the need to train inmates and provide tools, materials, and a place of work for them, administrators of the *dépôts* rediscovered all the difficulties encountered in the management of the *hôpitaux-généraux.*[33] Would it be best to train inmates with a skill that assured their livelihood on release, or should profitability take priority? In either case, workshops that gained too large a share of local markets with their products would threaten the livelihood of independent artisans—unless, of course, the workshop served as a seed plot for new industries. For good or ill, a successful workshop would generally project the force of inmates' productivity beyond the walls. That force could be contained only if inmates confined themselves to housekeeping or make-work, or if their products were sold only for use in other *dépôts,* as in the case of Rattier's blankets manufactured at Tours.[34]

By its provision that the contractors retain two-thirds of the product of inmates' labor, the general contract of 1773 promoted new schemes for profitable workshops. Bertier reported to Turgot that the contractors had introduced cotton-spinning into many *dépôts.*[35] Mobilizing unskilled labor in a concentrated fashion, these enterprises may appear in retrospect to have been harbingers of a new industrial order, continuing a mercantilist tradition of industrial experiment with the labor of the idle or incarcerated poor.[36] Reports on economic crises in Rouen and Tours a few years before had shown how royal and municipal charities might palliate the cycles of urban unemployment by establishing textile workshops and putting out the spinning of thread. But by tracing the link between the fall in demand for textiles and the fall in rural employment, the writers of these reports reaffirmed the paramount importance of agricultural production and employment. Administrators agreed on the need to sustain habits of outdoor labor and to encourage field-workers through hard times by offering wages on public outdoor projects. A further argument was that field-workers adapted with difficulty to work that called only for manual dexterity.[37]

Terray's directives on *ateliers de charité* and on the release of inmates for spring planting presupposed that the mere availability of employment would effectively draw those idlers who had abandoned the vain search for work. But Terray wanted to adapt work to the force and ability of every inmate in the *dépôts.* Traditionally, charitable administrators had used work as a remedy to be prescribed according to the moral and physical constitution of the individual. Terray urged intendants to pay special attention to children, recommending the practice of the authorities at Lyons, who pensioned young inmates out to farmers. He also promoted an alternative scheme to gather young children into special workshops at Barcelonnette, until this plan encountered suspicion and resistance. Unruly adolescents were marked as another specific category. Some were recruited into military service; others were inducted into Bertier's corps of *pionniers.*[38]

Since work was a universal tonic, Terray was at pains to measure it in due proportion to the needs of the disabled, who were in danger of deteriorating mentally and physically in confinement. Hand mills for grinding grain were suitable for them and for others unwilling or unable to apply themselves to more complex manual tasks. In spite of such arrangements, the central problem remained: how could the generality of the inmates in the *dépôts* be made productive, when they were so recalcitrant to any regular work discipline? Condorcet articulated the view of a learned elite when he spoke of the idle as "cripples of a sort" who required a special therapeutic regimen.[39] For the good of the patient, it was commonly argued, some measure of compulsion might be required. But it was precisely at this point that the qualms of the eighteenth-century liberal were stirred. The dilemma in question may best be illuminated by returning to the debates of Turgot's commission in order to reexamine the issue of forced labor. It is particularly instructive for this purpose to see how Turgot came to adopt Bertier's proposal to expand his quasi-military *pionniers,* an experiment that had emerged in direct response to the conundrum of work in the *dépôts.*

Turgot shared to a greater or lesser degree with his collaborators the conviction that liberty was an anthropological verity as well as an axiom of the marketplace. He shared Montesquieu's belief, expressed with a certain trepidation in the *Spirit of the Laws,* that there is no necessary labor that cannot be performed by free men. Montesquieu had found this axiom of equity confirmed historically on the borderland between Hapsburg lands and those of the Turk, where mines operated under similar natural conditions were exploited by slaves on one side and by free men on the other. Although Montesquieu had raised this issue under the heading of slavery, the lesson for those who wished to correct idlers could not have been clearer: "Because laws were ill made, men were found to be lazy; because men were lazy, they were enslaved." A key proviso in Montesquieu's belief in free labor was that reason, not avarice, must direct it. Machines, he added, might ease the difficulty of proportioning work to the force of those who perform it.[40]

Turgot's reaction to correctional labor in the *dépôt* was in keeping with Montesquieu's principles. Workhouse labor was unlikely to be productive, because it was executed under conditions of servitude. The only meaningful "correction" would consist in freely offered opportunities for work, as provided by the network of *ateliers de charité* that Turgot had supported and developed.[41] Trudaine, host to Turgot and his commission at Montigny, expressed the objection to forced labor with great clarity. As a penalty for begging, it was "severe," he explained, because "it tends to deprive a man of his liberty. It becomes more so if one reflects that a man can be forced to work only by chains and blows. This sort of penalty will differ little from that of the galleys."[42]

Brienne himself had hesitated to adopt the term *galères de terre,* as suggested in one of the memoirs he had received, because it was too closely associated with the punishment of major crimes and with a costly and complex administration. Boisgelin de Cucé was still more categorical in condemning the harshness of forced labor: "These penalties would be regarded as more rigorous, if the criminal code were more humane."[43]

In spite of a shared aversion for slavery, Turgot and his collaborators could not entirely resolve their differences on the matter of correctional labor. Even the harshest critics of the repressive features of the law were ambivalent in their attitude toward work. Boisgelin had argued in another context that to be a prisoner was to be a slave. As the penalty of imprisonment became more common, the ill effects of constraint might be attenuated by employing prisoners in some form of *colonie de défrichement* or work farm. Boisgelin here conceded that "everyone agrees that the only practical remedy is to have prisoners work," since it made them happier, gave them a habit of working, and saved costs. Malesherbes had argued that an isolated labor colony might serve in place of existing penalties of banishment and death, and added that such a colony might also be used in the policing "of beggars and of vagabonds, once a decision has been made about this important part of the general police of the Realm."[44]

Not wishing to make beggars slaves, Brienne was intrigued with Bertier's *pionniers.* With grudging approval from military authorities, Bertier had concocted these "companies for provincial workers" in 1773 in order to gather and contain those youths who were suited only to general labor but, lacking any experience of work discipline, were easily tempted by libertinage and a life of idleness. The elements of positive and negative reinforcement were carefully contrived. By choosing to enlist, *pionniers* subjected themselves to a strict discipline "that contained them by the fear of penalties." Bertier argued that this side of the equation needed to be augmented by a formal statute of military discipline including harsh corporal punishment for insubordination and death for acts of physical rebellion.[45]

The positive incentives for the *pionniers* included three livres paid at the time of enlistment for a nine-year term, a daily wage *(solde)* of ten sous, plus one-fifth of the product of their labors. In the first companies, one-third were experienced workers who could set an example, one-third were veterans of guard regiments and other corps, and one-third were youths taken from the *dépôts* around Paris. A total of six companies was formed. "This mixture," Brienne observed, "may be necessary in order to animate and contain at once those who are working only by constraint." In alchemist's terms, the use of an amalgam within a closed vessel allowed a baser substance to receive a new spirit and be animated by it. One may also conjure up a series of retorts in which distillation and condensation were used to purify and transform substances. Bertier described a hierarchy of units subject to discrete forms of discipline within the *pionniers,* including a punitive chain gang for those who had violated discipline. Those who did not work would receive only bread and water; those who attempted to escape suffered harsher penalties. The rules rewarded those who worked by allowing them "to earn all that they can, and by turning their gain to their profit and to their ease."[46]

Such schemes were not entirely new. The elder Trudaine had supported a project in 1749 for employing beggars to perform *corvée* labor in the *généralité* of Paris.[47] The younger Trudaine now offered an appealing explanation for the success of Bertier's *pionniers.* Essentially, he argued, they were not forced labor gangs. He had inspected them at work and had asked the commander of a company to point out the recruits who were foundlings or had come from a *dépôt.* The commander told Trudaine that he did not know and that it was essential to avoid such distinctions within the company. Trudaine found that the companies offered a new identity and the rewards of free labor: "The certainty of finding an assured subsistence in regular work renders the lives of these soldiers of a sort fairly mild, and although they are looked down upon by the soldiers of the regiments, they take pride in affecting a sort of superiority over peasants, in the way the soldiery so commonly do."[48]

Montesquieu would surely have recognized the monarchical principle of honor at work! Bertier himself had emphasized the positive motivation of the recruits from the *dépôts* when he had originally defended his project against military critics. Monteynard had argued, on behalf of the army, that beggars would perform "shoddy work, and always too costly." It would be better to use workhouses to inspire honor in the beggars, and then to let them enroll in the army: "Must one debase the sinew of the state in assimilating them to it?"[49] Bertier emphasized the positive inducements that could be applied once a man had freely enlisted: "There has been no reluctance to incur the necessary expense to clothe them well, lodge them safely, and assure them a fortifying and agreeable existence, and this state, far from being a punishment, has become a school for work."[50]

The positive incentives for an inmate of a *dépôt* to enlist in the *pionniers* were essentially similar to those that drew peasants into the army: a degree of material security and status superior to what they might expect otherwise, particularly in times of famine or unemployment.[51]

Turgot was persuaded to expand Bertier's companies. However, he rejected the institution of a harsh code of discipline for the *pionniers*, agreeing with Trudaine that nothing was to be accomplished by "chains and blows." His instructions to intendants emphasized the prospect of economic independence after a voluntary nine-year period of enlistment.[52]

In the memoirs presented to the academy of Châlons in 1777, the problem of devising a humane workhouse was related to the challenge of turning criminals into virtuous citizens. The abbé Malvaux noted the contradiction inherent in the attempt to improve men by enslaving them, but asked rhetorically: "Why could not policy draw good from evil? Chemistry has indeed found the secret of converting a poison into a remedy." But the *dépôts* had manifestly failed to perform this transformation: "instead of making work appealing in the eyes of the poor, they have made him abhor it more and more, and far from relieving his misery they only make it worse."[53]

It was this failing above all that drew the charge that *dépôts* were "the image of hell." Having noted in an earlier context that prisoners should not be driven to despair by devising for them an anticipation of hell, they offered the suggestion that the ideal house of correction would serve as a kind of "civil purgatory" where inmates would receive favors in proportion to their merits. The term "purgatory" suggests spiritual alchemy—a purification by fire. Transposed into a secular context, it implies that the freedom of the citizen is heaven. The inmate would advance in stages, receiving one-fourth of the product of his labor: he would assume increased responsibilities until he reached the point of rehabilitation as a member of his community.[54] The Châlons essayist portrayed the ideal house of correction as a *prison graduelle*. Just as wards of a hospital required careful differentiation, and a manufacture had to be planned according to the work to be performed in each location, so a prison had to be conceived as an apparatus in which successive operations were performed in a regulated sequence.[55]

But the most skilled distillation and decanting of cast-off humanity in the *dépôts* would still leave a relatively unpromising residue, a "*caput mortuum* of humanity," as Bertier himself described it in a memoir to the Estates of Brittany. Could these lowly dregs be found worthy? The Châlons memoirs included a variety of proposals for work colonies on roads, on uncultivated land, on islands, or on distant shores— proposals with a long ancestry. A proposal of 1775 to receive able-bodied inmates of Bicêtre in a work colony to be established on the Isle de Groix resembled a variety of earlier projects. Belle-Isle had also been mentioned. Objections of residents and military authorities ruled out these modest options, which failed in any case to conform to the original blueprint for the *dépôts*. The advantage of an island colony was obvious, however, in the case of the more recalcitrant fraction of inmates: a natural isolation eased the problem of constraint and supervision. Projectors turned their gaze upon Corsica, French since 1768. Apparently inspired by Catherine the Great's penal colonies, the Châlons essayists suggested, "Corsica is well suited to become the Siberia of our kingdom."[56]

Bertier's *pionniers* fulfilled the essayists' prescription for the recalcitrant. Montlinot noted approvingly the arrangement to send companies of them to build roads in Corsica. More routinely, the *pionniers* were dispatched from their headquarters at the *caserne* at Roule to carry out public works in the Paris region, and formed work camps along the route of the Canal of Burgundy.[57] As a new component of the police apparatus of the capital, the *pionniers* served an assortment of functions that reflected both their liminal status and the amalgam of recruits their ranks contained. A regular company of grenadiers maintained discipline in the company and guarded the nearby *dépôt* of St. Denis, quelling a revolt there in 1779. They would also be used in searches for inmates escaped from the *dépôt*. Refractory members of the *Gardes françaises* could be demoted to the *pionniers,* and a model *pionnier* could advance to the *gardes.* The commander of the *pionniers,* du Puget, served also as inspector of security at the *dépôt* of St. Denis, until he was transferred to the garrison at the Bastille.[58] A memoir preserved in his papers reveals that he thought work companies like the *pionniers* might be adapted to the rehabilitation of criminals, in place of the death penalty.[59]

While the *pionniers* drew off a certain number of sturdy young men from the *dépôts,* new projects went forward to organize work more effectively within them. Bertier offered a judgment on the comparative success of some of these projects in the course of a dialogue he conducted in the margin of the official *cahier* of the Estates of Languedoc at about the time that Montlinot was named to his new post at Soissons. Responding to complaints from the Estates, the intendant of Languedoc had proposed to establish new workshops in the *dépôt* at Montpellier by adopting the one at Orleans as a model. Bertier replied by praising the humanity of the intendant of Orleans, but with the observation that the *dépôt* under his care too closely resembled a hospital: "One has only to go to the *dépôt* at Rennes—one will see that the inmates, while producing by their labor great profits for the contractor, have more of an air of health and contentment than at Orleans."[60]

Bertier took a personal interest in the *dépôt* at Rennes and particularly in the achievements of Sieur Cabanes, who first appeared on the scene as a subcontractor of Manié, Rimberge et Cie. Cabanes took over after the general contract was abrogated, expanding his operation continually thereafter. Bertier needed effective direction of the workshops at Rennes in order to stave off the barrage of attacks from the Estates and the parlement of Brittany against the *dépôt*. When he came to Rennes in person to inspect the *dépôt,* he undoubtedly hoped to find his confrere vindicated. Pleased with what he saw, Bertier encouraged Cabanes to add a special workshop for workers recently released from the *dépôt*. The Estates of Brittany continued to concentrate their hostile fire on article 12 of Cabanes's contract, which ensured that no worker in the dépôt would be released until he had woven a set length of cloth. While the Estates denounced this provision as a false gauge of freedom, Bertier was satisfied that Cabanes was in fact training beggars as workers and that the inmates were in better health and spirits at Rennes than at Orleans and elsewhere.[61]

Under Colombier's inspectorate, the provision of work received attention from the point of view of both physical hygiene and occupational rehabilitation. The regulation of 1785 specified that "the overseer will never allow any inmate to remain in a state of inaction, and will be authorized to punish whoever refuses to work." But in following articles it was further provided that only the overseer could inflict penalties, and that any other employee, including the concierge, who struck or mistreated an inmate would be subject to imprisonment for twenty-four hours at the first offense, and to greater penalties if the offense were repeated. The overseer was required to report all penalties to the intendant.[62]

The appearance of liberty would accomplish what chains and blows could not.[63] Colombier reported instances of brutality on the part of concierges, and insisted that the municipally run *maison de force* at Strasbourg dismantle its *machine fustigatoire,* used primarily to strike terror into the hearts of inmates.[64] The main incentive to work was to be that provided in the regulation, namely the promise to pay the able-bodied inmate who worked an amount one-half to two-thirds of the going rate for his labor, depending on the nature of the work and its product. Those who refused to perform the regular work provided were to be employed in emptying and cleaning of wastes, "until they ask to work in the shops." The daily schedule included regular periods of "recreation," preferably in outdoor courtyards.[65]

The introduction of Colombier's regulation no doubt accentuated a tendency to limit royal support for workshops to those that were strictly administered within the *dépôts*. Colombier had played a key role in withdrawing royal support for the municipally run Bicêtre at Lyons and reorganizing the royal *dépôt* at La Quarantaine. In a later inspection at Riom he urged shutting down the workshop at the hospital and improving the one in the *dépôt*.[66] At Grenoble, where a Sieur Ducoin had managed a workshop at Sassenage as an adjunct to the *dépôt,* receiving young women and employing them on their release from the *dépôt,* Colombier curtailed the funding that was provided from the budget of the *dépôt.* Ducoin argued, in much the same vein as Rattier had done at Tours, that providing work for free workers would keep them from falling into mendicity and would allow the *dépôt* to be used exclusively for rehabilitating those who were unwilling to work or lacked the most elementary skills and discipline required for it.[67] The one major concession in this direction was a provision in the regulation that allowed intendants to keep on some working inmates in the *dépôts* as *volontaires,* if they claimed that they would otherwise be unable to support themselves if released when no work was available.[68]

The degree of administrative consensus on the rehabilitative virtue of work in the decade before the Revolution should not be obscured by the account of conflicts between Montlinot and Bertier. These conflicts were not about the wisdom of establishing "schools for work": Bertier and Montlinot both subscribed to this charitable ideal. The inspector Bannefroy, writing about the *dépôts* on 1791, remarked that the two *dépôts* that had achieved notable results in establishing workshops were those at Soissons and St. Denis.[69] These two workshops were alike in that they employed able-bodied male inmates at the grueling physical toil of polishing mirrors, while providing a range of tasks suited to the force and ability of other inmates.

Where Bertier and Montlinot disagreed was in defining how society at large should reinforce or validate the mission of the *dépôts*. Even here, the two agreed that a strong appeal must be made to an inmate's desire for future ease and security. They further agreed that the eradication of mendicity ultimately required an improvement in the lot of the common agricultural laborer—Bertier's *pauvre taillable.* But Bertier would not follow Montlinot in extrapolating the moral economy of rehabilitation in such a way as to constitute a model of society. To promise that the industrious inmate would receive a decent sufficiency if he continued to work upon his release either raised false hopes or exposed the existing regime to attack.

As Garat had sensed in reading Montlinot, the *dépôt* at Soissons was not only a clinical observatory of society's ills, but a laboratory for experimental social design. By allowing master workers to choose their apprentices and guide their labors, Montlinot obviated the need for regulations and prohibitions. "Rights violated in many great societies," Garat declared, "are respected in this sort of prison." The freedom allowed inmates to spend their earnings "makes one forget that one is in a *dépôt,* and makes one believe one is in a village, in a hamlet."[70] Such language would have struck Bertier as extravagant and as a potential source of great mischief. He undoubtedly took umbrage at Montlinot's implied premise that an ordinary *dépôt de mendicité* could not also be a *maison de travail.*

Necker guided the National Assembly toward adoption of Montlinot's theses, with a crucial reservation. Few actions taken under the Constituent Assembly carried clearer ideological significance than Necker's decision, closely concerted with La Millière, Le Chapelier, and Bertrand de Molleville, to abrogate article 12 of Cabanes' contract at Rennes. This amounted to an affirmation of Montesquieu's precept that "reason, not avarice" must direct the work of free men.[71] The Estates of Brittany were vindicated, as were the scandalized almoners of the *dépôt* at Rennes. The notion that an inmate's term of civil purgatory in the *dépôt* could be measured by the length of cloth he wove for the contractor was in its enormity akin to the notion that a state of spiritual grace could be bought or sold. The denunciation of privilege here gained strength from a sense that the state's moral tutelage over the idle had been perverted under the Old Regime: a truly national and patriotic ministry would remove the taint of avarice from the care of poor and wayward citizens.

Yet Necker also set limits on the promises of revolution. He served notice on the National Assembly that it would be dangerous—fiscally and morally—to guarantee work to every poor citizen who asked for it. Setting full employment as a goal of policy was a different matter from treating work as an individual right to be demanded from the state. There is a continuous line of ideological development connecting this position with Necker's earlier objection to Montlinot's "chimerical" vision, and again with his later decision to disband the large work projects surrounding Paris, returning those workers not native to Paris and its region back to the provinces.[72]

The opening statement of principles in the sixth report of the Comité de Mendicité—the report that focused on the problem of repression—consecrated the view of work that Montlinot had formulated at Soissons. Montlinot, Thouret, and Liancourt had been working together on the area defined laconically as "beggars, repression" since September 3, 1790, and Montlinot prepared a draft memoir to the committee on January 19, 1791. Entire phrases and sequences from Montlinot's earlier memoirs echo in the report that Liancourt finally read to the Assembly on January 31.[73]

Liancourt placed the problem of work within the framework of a new constitution. Society, he said, rests on a contract providing that no person will work without recompense to support others who lack the means to subsist. By this formula the committee distinguished between owners of property or *rentes* from the beggar who not only "impoverishes society by his idleness" but disturbs it "by the uncertainty that he will be able to satisfy his own needs."[74] Montlinot had admitted in earlier writings that some injustice was unavoidable in protecting society from the dangerous beggar; Liancourt argued in effect that the beggar must be forced to be free. If Liancourt seemed to ignore the prophetic admonitions of Montlinot, he was fully expecting, as he spoke, that the Assembly would ratify a great principle of justice that he took to be the "cornerstone" of his committee's work: that the nation owed every citizen either the opportunity to work or support for those unable to sustain themselves thus.[75]

The portion of the sixth report devoted to houses of correction began with an invocation of the "immortal work of Beccaria," who had established the responsibility of government to remove and prevent the conditions that give rise to crime. In accordance with this principle, the issues raised in the committee's earlier reports would have to be resolved, before repressive measures could be put into effect. The distinction between the domiciled poor and the stranger, for example, would have greater meaning "once the aid provided under the Constitution is guaranteed."[76] Turgot and Necker had argued along similar lines; Bertier had always insisted that repression could not do the work of alms bureaus.

In a further statement of principle, the report argued that the distinction between deserving and false poor did not dispense society from strict obligations toward the reprobate. Citing another Beccarian principle that had figured in the Châlons memoirs, the author of the report argued that the legislator must hate the crime but no the criminal. Even within a code that contained "severe" provisions, there must be "gentleness" toward the criminal, so that he never be deemed beyond hope of amendment. The new houses of correction to be provided in the penal code for various categories of offender would receive obdurate beggars with the aim of rehabilitating them. In this they must shun the example of the *dépôts*.[77]

The terms of the indictment against the old *dépôts* as reported to the Assembly were brutally simple. After a brief statistical review drawn from Necker's *Administration des finances,* the report asserted that 46,000 inmates had died in the *dépôts* in the course of three decades, or approximately one-fifth of those admitted. The cost of running them had totaled 29,700,000 livres. This appalling balance sheet of "mortality and expense" constituted Montlinot's final reckoning with the shade of Bertier.[78]

What remedy could a new constitution provide for such ills? Liancourt reported that the committee had undertaken a search for model houses of correction and had found none completely suitable anywhere in Europe. France would therefore take the initiative, with a regime that incorporated many features of the workhouse at Soissons and many of the suggestions Montlinot had advanced in the *Encyclopédie méthodique* and his last two accounts. As at Soissons, the organization of work would be crucial. An utterly Spartan regimen would provide only the inmate's strict subsistence. On the other hand, ample opportunities for work would, in Montlinot's cherished phrase, "make his well-being depend upon himself." Workhouse products would have to be chosen carefully so as to avoid throwing free workers into mendicity; wage incentives would be used to persuade the inmate that he could indeed improve his own fate.[79]

In applying a "moral remedy" to the beggar's idleness, it was essential to respect his dignity and reason and to observe justice in every rule applied to him. "Political necessity" imposed a system of restraint, but this restraint must be applied with absolute fairness. Even the most wild and ferocious individuals had been tamed by a combination of quiet severity and firmness—a silent look could produce better results than blows and threats. For Montlinot, these lines would conjure up many images of his ruffians at Soissons. He might, for example, see them laboring mightily under his direction at the Herculean task of cleaning out the cesspool under the *dépôt*. The spirit of the discipline proposed in the sixth report also bespoke the gentle firmness that would later be associated with Pinel's treatment of the insane.[80]

A draft decree on houses of correction incorporated several details of Montlinot's earlier tracts, including the suggestion that such institutions be established in port cities. Several standing policies of the *dépôts* were reaffirmed. The directors of the new houses were not to be involved in any contractual arrangements from which they might benefit. Controls on the setting of fair wages for inmates were accompanied by a provision that corporal punishment could be administered only by a judicial order—two key safeguards against the abuse of arbitrary authority by the director of a house or by his subalterns. Finally, details on food rations, bedding, medical care, and standards of maintenance were left to a forthcoming regulation, presumably to be based on that of Colombier.[81]

Having found that the workhouse failed to rehabilitate certain dangerous vagabonds and *mendiants de race,* Montlinot had proposed as early as 1785 a project for transporting them to a penal colony. One of his tasks on Liancourt's committee was to investigate the suitability of various sites, such as Madagascar and Boulam, and to report on the use of *pionniers* in Corsica. In the sixth report Liancourt repeated Montlinot's argument. The constitution, he added, had no place for the punishments of slaves, by which he ruled out the former option of sentencing vagabonds to the galleys. The advantage of transportation, he continued, was that it offered the convict "the attraction of a better existence" through hard work, giving him the hope that his efforts might lead to "the enjoyments of liberty." He spoke then of unsuccessful schemes in Corsica, and dismissed Bertier's use of *pionniers* there as a project brought to naught by greed. A new attempt should be made to plant a colony of French beggars who would redeem themselves and cultivate a hitherto neglected land. This would be a fitting gift of the Revolution to Corsica. A draft decree on transportation provided a fitting utopian pendant to the sixth report.[82]

The principles that Liancourt's committee distilled from experience reinforced and sharpened revolutionary debate on the means to regenerate civic life. There is a striking convergence between the terms of Liancourt's sixth report and those of the report presented to the Assembly on the reform of the criminal law by Le Peletier de Saint-Fargeau on May 23, 1791, less than four months later. Le Peletier began by attacking the abuses that were foremost in the *cahiers* and in revolutionary consciousness—the disproportionately harsh penalties imposed, the use of torture and forced confession, the lack of any just proportion between crimes and penalties, and the wide latitude for arbitrary discretion by judges. In prescribing remedies, Le Peletier drew upon the interlocking discussion of mendicity, penal reform, and productivity that the abbé de Saint-Pierre had launched early in the century. Every penal law must be humane; moderate penalties could be effective if they were "justly graduated.'' The penalty for each infraction must be uniformly determined; the working of the law must be undeviating and public, with the purpose of preventing crimes.[83]

In the spirit of the Châlons discussions of mendicity, Le Peletier went further and asked, ''Could not one conceive of a penal system that would produce the double effect of punishing the guilty person and making him better?'' In practical terms, the most common source of crimes was idleness and want. ''The system of penalties must therefore be settled principally on the basis of work.'' Le Peletier's reflection on the nature of that work was consonant with the concern expressed in the Châlons text that the convicts not be treated as unregenerate slaves. The work done should not be a ''torment,'' otherwise ''it augments further [the convict's] natural aversion.'' The method of conditioning proposed was in fact precisely that argued for by Montlinot: ''The feeling of need must be brought into it; work must become for him the passage to a less painful state; he must find inducements [*adoucissements*] precisely in proportion to the zeal with which he gives himself.''[84]

The image of a gentle taming of unsocial passion by a process of reasoning and by a finely graduated chain of reinforcement is like that found in discussions of beggars and the insane. It was important, Le Peletier observed, that the rigor of penalties be scaled in such a way that the bitter feelings of the inmate be worked out and changed to ''gentler and more social affections'' by the time of release, when the inmate must return ''to society and to himself.'' The formal reintegration of the former convict into society would be marked by a ceremony that Le Peletier did not hesitate to call ''civic baptism.''[85]

Rehabilitation was, in the last analysis, a corrective intervention by experts in moral health, a minor miracle of individual regeneration. The regeneration of the body politic as a whole would have a much more substantial impact on the incidence of crime. ''In politics as in physick, the art that prevents evil is a thousand times more certain and more salutary than that which heals it.'' This essentially Hippocratic perspective was strongly rooted in eighteenth-century academic culture. Lavoisier formulated it in terms of hygiene; Loménie de Brienne emphasized the role of administration in preventing mendicity.[86] Here, Le Peletier praised the Assembly for adopting a broad range of ''complementary'' measures that would lessen the incidence of crime. Above all, he echoed the program of the Comité de Mendicité, praising its efforts to provide work, support old age and indigent infirmity, and destroy ''that condition so widespread in France of vagabond and unknown.'' So much for the generation at hand. For the future, Le Peletier, like Montlinot, envisioned a day when there would be ''more generally and more uniformly spread over all classes of citizens the well-being of a happy sufficiency.''

Economic regeneration and moral regeneration would be reinforced by a truly ''national education.'' Le Peletier looked forward to the fruits of Condorcet's proposals and to Liancourt's later efforts to establish and promote a national vocational school. By training all the *enfants de la patrie* with a useful and virtuous education, the state would form citizens who were free and good, ''and will tear away from crime even the seduction of need.''[87]

The Constituent Assembly deferred action on the decrees offered by its Comité de Mendicité, including those attached to the sixth report. The deputies responded to certain immediate problems and called upon Liancourt and his committee for advice, but they were unwilling to enact a general code of public assistance comparable to the penal code that they appended to the Constitution of September 1791. Nor would they ratify the principles that Liancourt had urged them to adopt as a "cornerstone" of reform. Provisionally, they authorized the continued arrest of beggars under the provisions of a "decree relating to the organization of a municipal and correctional police" in July 1791. Title 2 of the decree spelled out "general dispositions on the penalties of correctional police and houses of correction" but left open the details of sentencing, which were to be determined "in conformity with the laws on the repression of mendicity."[88] The deputies of the Constituent Assembly ordered that the reports of Liancourt's committee be published. They left to their successors the task of deliberating upon these reports and enacting new laws.

Epilogue and Conclusion

"What extraordinary things have happened, my friend, since we last saw each other," wrote Desbrières, *régisseur* of the *dépôt* at Rouen, to Boismaigre, whom he addressed as "head of the department of mendicity," on October 9, 1789, "and what will be the end of all this?"[1] As far as the *dépôts* were concerned, the sequel at Rouen was fairly typical of what lay in store.

The departmental administrators of the Seine-Inférieure, responsible for the *dépôt* at Rouen, wrote to the Legislative Assembly in May and July of 1792 for clarification of recent decrees on mendicity. Since local support for new measures would require a general reorganization of charitable resources, they asked that the renewed prohibition on begging be suspended for the time being. The minister replied bluntly that articles 23 and 24 of the law of July 23, 1791, on "correctional police" were to be enforced and that alms were not to be given or received in public. Again after Thermidor, the departmental administrators raised questions of revolutionary principle in calling for the abolition of the *dépôt* as a distinct institution. They noted that the Code of Crimes and Punishments specified only three kinds of prisons under the administration of departments. Furthermore, article 18 of the code provided sanctions against jailers who detained persons except by virtue of the forms prescribed in articles 222 and 223 of the constitution. Finally, they argued that the new designation of prisons superseded the "particular laws" governing the *dépôts*.[2]

The positions taken by the minister seemed to echo Old Regime arguments in support of the "provisional" *dépôts*. While new laws might alter the "definitive organization" of these establishments, no major change should be introduced in the interim. A similar message of provisional continuity echoed in replies to queries and challenges from Lille, Alençon, and elsewhere. But it proved easier to maintain old administrative forms than to create new principles of authority. At Rouen, Desbrières prudently resigned his post as *régisseur-caissier* in July 1793, when he learned that he could not obtain a *certificat de civisme*. The surgeon who had served the *dépôts* since 1783, Constantin Marc, testified later that only the fear of "public assassination" had silenced him in turn when "a member of the popular club, raised up by intrigues to the rank of administrator of the department," had taken his place. Similar challenges to *régisseurs* occurred elsewhere during the Terror, notably at Riom, Nancy, and Bourges.[3]

Another perspective on the *dépôts* in revolution emerges if we ask what became of Boismaigre, head of the department of mendicity, to whom Desbrières addressed his musings of October 1789. This seasoned bureaucrat would step into the post of *régisseur* of the *dépôt* of St. Denis on May 31, 1790, in place of a Sieur Douchet who was found to have paid inflated prices for old stocks of wine, vinegar, and eau-de-vie. Taking account of Boismaigre's twenty-two years of service and the burdens of a numerous family, La Millière assured him of a pension in case the new departmental administration should decide to eliminate his post. In the first draft of a memorandum, La Millière noted that "M. Bertier gave him the finest recommendations when he passed into my bureaus." He then crossed out Bertier's name and substituted an impersonal reference to Boismaigre's service in the bureaus of the *intendance* of Paris.[4]

A letter from the "citoyenne veuve Boismaigre" on February 8, 1793, reveals that she had taken over running the *dépôt* upon the death of her husband in March 1792; he had been *régisseur* a little less than a year. She was having difficulty closing the accounts for 1791 in the absence of both de Hauteclaire, the subdelegate-general of the old *intendance,* who had left for his estate at Alençon, and Duteil, the former secretary of the *intendance,* who had gone to Burgundy. The fragments of documentation that remain for the *dépôt* of St. Denis during the Revolutionary period indicate that it suffered from indecision as to its proper function and that it lacked funds to provide for those inmates it continued to house. Lafayette had used the *dépôt* as a center for interrogating rebellious members of the National Guard under the close watch of the *gardes françaises.* The administrators of the department of the Seine later reminded the minister that the *dépôt* had been used in February 1793 to lodge soldiers at no extra cost and appealed to him not to cut its funds.[5]

The widow Boismaigre continued to manage the *dépôt* through the penury of the Terror and the penury of Thermidor. At one moment there was a suggestion that the *dépôt* be sold off for commercial use. Revolutionary complaints against the *cydevant dépôt* suggested that it was being abusively run as a *maison de secours.* The minister of the interior, Garat, and his successor, Paré, ordered changes but maintained the institution, primarily as a resource for the indigent and for the insane. The files of the pre-Napoleonic period end with a plaintive letter from the District of Franciade to the Commission des Secours Publics, 13 Vendémiaire, Year III, relaying the substance of a long letter of the 9th from "La Citoyenne Boismaigre, Econome de la maison de secours de Franciade," reporting that the *dépôt* lacked funds to procure the objects of subsistence necessary for the consumption of the *dépôt.*[6]

Under the Directory and Napoleon, the *dépôt* at St. Denis detained inmates in numbers comparable to those of the Old Regime. Napoleon's decision to expand its operation and to supplement it with a new establishment at Villers-Cotterets laid the foundation for the sweeping directive of 1808 that called for a universal network of *dépôts* throughout the nation, from the Ain to Zuydersee. Article 274 of Napoleon's penal code had established mendicity as a punishable offense, but the network of institutions fit to receive beggars had suffered attrition since 1789. Thus the *dépôts* came to be identified as a Napoleonic initiative in the minds of some critics of the institution, when it survived the Bourbons' return.[7]

Restoration prefects—including a son of the last intendant of Paris, who served at Grenoble and Caen—attempted to revive the *dépôts* of the *départements* as the reforming agencies envisaged by Bertier under the Old Regime. But the same old doubts returned about the best means of repression and rehabilitation. Louis XVIII's minister of justice, Laîné, reported to the Chamber of Deputies in 1818 that the *dépôts* had proven in their latest incarnation to be lacking in utility. In spite of this verdict, the institution dragged out a fitful half-life for the rest of the century.[8]

Continuity of nomenclature conferred a deceptive illusion of coherence on a vestigial institution. The emergence of a national prison system overshadowed both the promise and the problems of the *dépôts*. Welfare advocates concerned themselves with the protection of the very young, wayward women, and the insane. The condition of the new industrial working poor also drew the attention of reformers, but for the greater part of the nineteenth century the *entrepreneur* was entrusted with regulating the conditions of labor *en bon père de famille*. Turgot, duly glossed and corrected by his new editors, was canonized as patron saint of *laisser-faire*.[9]

A new awareness of the social thought of the Enlightenment began to emerge in the last decades of the nineteenth century, amid a reappraisal of republican ideology and its origins. While social scientists described the alienation of whole classes of society from the values of an industrial civilization, a new concept of *solidarisme* took root. This sober variant of republican fraternity nourished the extremely modest legislative beginnings of social security in France from 1893 to 1905.[10] In connection with these proposals, the idea of the *dépôt de mendicité* was revived seriously for the last time. But a Dr. Joseph Viple, in a thesis of 1905 on "The Penal Repression of Mendicity," relayed the view of Granier, inspector of prisons, "that the noxiousness of vagrancy is rather contested."[11] While vagrancy could still lead to arrest and detention under the criminal code, residual enthusiasm for the *dépôt de mendicité* as an institution faded away.[12]

At the same time, historians recovered an eighteenth-century legacy. Ferdinand-Dreyfus published a scholarly biography of La Rochefoucauld-Liancourt in 1903. He then offered a series of lectures on the topic of "Assistance under the Legislative and the Convention," in which he echoed the debates of the 1890s on social security and cited Jean Jaurès's history of the French Revolution.[13] In 1908 Christian Paultre rummaged through archives in search of documentation on the repression of vagrancy and mendicity under the Old Regime. In 1911 Camille Bloch followed with his masterly, painstaking synthesis of the topic "Assistance and the State on the Eve of the Revolution." Reclaiming Turgot from his nineteenth-century editors, Bloch credited him with being the first to articulate a modern concept of assistance as a national public service. In the same year, an edition of the reports of the Comité de Mendicité appeared, edited by Bloch in collaboration with Alexandre Tuetey.[14]

If the broader lessons of the eighteenth-century debate on mendicity lay dormant until the first timid steps were taken toward a system of social security, the *dépôts* attracted limited interest even then, since they were regarded as an institutional failure. But this study has attempted to show that that particular institutional experience, for all its negative results, had a broad impact on the eighteenth-century debate on mendicity: in particular, the *dépôts* provided a laboratory for the empirical study of poverty, for the evolution of standards of institutional care and public health, and for the refinement of the psychology and jurisprudence of rehabilitation.

It is particularly striking to observe how many of the "original" features of the French prison system as it emerged in the early nineteenth century were anticipated in the practice of the *dépôts de mendicité*. If the nineteenth-century prison functioned as a "total institution" regulating every aspect of the internal regime and daily schedule followed in the institution, it differed little in that respect from an eighteenth-century *dépôt de mendicité*. Taking a longer view, it is true, of course, that the notion of disciplining the inmates of a house to an exemplary rule influenced all institutions designed to receive the poor since the Middle Ages. But a more specific modern transformation of this institutional model emerges in the governance of the *dépôts* and carries over into nineteenth-century penal institutions. The features of this modern penology included a clinical-therapeutic technique for changing inmates' behavior, and a new set of assumptions about the broader social context toward which the inmates' aspirations and responses were to be directed. Long before Cabanis suggested that prisons might serve as "hospitals for vice," the *dépôts* had been called to perform that function.[15]

The concept of work as rehabilitation, a key element in nineteenth-century prison reform, was at the heart of discussions about the function of the *dépôts*. Earlier charitable institutions mounted work projects in order to make idlers into virtuous, self-supporting citizens. But in the *dépôts* the notion of giving inmates a "taste for work" was transformed from a problem of spiritual redemption—a *metanoia* on the part of the abject sinner—into a problem of healing the inmate's defective rationality by appeal to sense experience. Overseers of the poor in more traditional institutions may have chosen a path of *douceur* or gentleness as being more Christian and more effective; the new approach was founded on a hedonistic assumption concerning the nature of the social contract. The inmate was led to discover empirically that the effort of disciplined labor was associated with the material and psychic rewards of "ease."[16]

The elaboration of a clinical-therapeutic model for the rehabilitation of delinquents was closely related to the definition of standards of treatment in the *dépôts*. As codified in Colombier's regulation, these were raised to a level rarely surpassed in nineteenth-century prisons. While the application of standards in practice is not easily evaluated, then or now, it would appear that nineteenth-century prisons were no more closely supervised from the center than were the *dépôts* on the eve of the Revolution.[17]

Eager to elaborate a new science of man, eighteenth-century observers of conditions within the *dépôts* anticipated the inquiries of the leading hygienists of the early nineteenth century, Villermé and Quetelet. Contributing in 1830 to one of the final volumes of Panckoucke's medical encyclopedia—thus sharing in a common enterprise with the official prison inspectors of the Old Régime—Villermé noted that the government had improved the record of many of its prisons, but that it had failed in others because of its ignorance of the ordinary conditions of life among the poor. Ranking institutions by the measure of mortality, he found the *dépôts* by far the worst. Villermé had been observing data on the *dépôt* at St. Denis since the early years of the Restoration. Statistics on mortality had also been used to assess conditions in the *dépôts* under the Old Régime—at St. Denis, of course, at Caen, at Rennes, at Tours, at La Rochelle, at Soissons—almost everywhere, in fact.[18]

Other statistics that Villermé and Quételet collected included the tally of inmates' heights—data that had fascinated Montlinot.[19] The incidence of epidemics and other diseases, a major topic of Villermé's research, had been studied by the Société Royale de Médicine. Observations from the *dépôts* had been integrated into the field of medical observation, as in the case of Le Pecq de la Clôture's reports of clinical studies at Rouen, and Colombier's accounts of epidemics in the *généralité* of Paris. Economic conditions had figured in case histories and medical topographies relating to the *dépôts*.[20] Villermé's special concern for the problems of women and children had been anticipated in the work of Montlinot, Colombier, and others. The concern for venereal disease and prostitution—an obsession with Parent-Duchâtelet in the nineteenth-century—had occupied medical officers and bureaucrats in the day-to-day operations of the *dépôts*.[21]

Institutional hygiene in the age of Villermé drew its scientific inspiration from the work of Lavoisier, Tenon, Colombier, and their fellow savants of the 1780s. The essential conditions for maintaining health, they had shown, depended on a given individual's metabolism and activity, not on his social status. Lavoisier published calculations on the volume of air required by normal respiration and on the specific gravity of various types of broth. In a similar vein, Tenon subjected the hospital bed to scientific study and argued that the problem of the spread of disease was identical, "whether it occurs in a hospital, in a prison, in a *dépôt de mendicité*, or in a workshop—in a word, in an establishment that contains a great number of people."[22]

Perhaps the most truly remarkable shift of consciousness that occurred during the Revolution was the abandonment of a conviction that bureaucrats and savants of the Old Regime had shared with the most ardent of Jacobins: the conviction that observation of conditions harmful to health should lead to action by public authority to change those conditions. Lavoisier had simply taken that responsibility for granted in the sober estimate he offered in a committee report of 1780: "it is better to preserve men in health than to spend money on curing them."[23] As the Revolution unfolded, men like Breteuil, Bertier, and Brienne fell from grace, but their collaborators in *bienfaisance*—La Millière, Thouret, Doublet, Tenon, Montlinot, Hallé—recast their Old Regime knowledge, experience, and commitment into a revolutionary nationalist mode.[24] As early as the Constituent Assembly, however, a countercurrent set in. After Thermidor, the specter of the duc de la Rochefoucauld-Liancourt was regularly exorcised along with Saint-Just and Robespierre. Did not one perhaps lead to the others?[25] Had not Barère, minister of the Terror, sat on Liancourt's committee? Cabanis and the Idéologues attempted to revive a cautiously activist model of social medicine as part of a new science of man; but nineteenth-century political econony would condemn all interventionist welfare schemes as misguided, dangerous, and utopian.[26]

The ghost of rebellion was not so easily exorcised from the sociological jurisprudence of the eighteenth century, a jurisprudence leavened by the dualities of Montesquieu's *Spirit of the Laws*. In his search for a method of social inquiry that was rational and empirical, Montesquieu also sought a natural vindication of justice and equity. Slavery and despotism might arise in certain conditions, but he argued that both did violence to human nature. "Moderation" prevailed even in his counsel that a regime survived by maintaining its "principle": admiration of liberty and the spirit of the citizen seemed at times to burst the honor-bound frame of a great monarchy.[27] At all levels, Montesquieu wrestled with the duality of freedom and constraint. Solution of the conundrum seemed to require either a preestablished harmony between individual desires and social virtue—the paradox seized by Rousseau—or the ultimate refinement of the "pious fraud": a government that controlled the actions of individuals while persuading them that they were free. In a "well-regulated monarchy," Montesquieu wrote in his journal, the people are like fish swimming in a widely deployed net: "they believe themselves free, yet they are taken fast."[28]

Eighteenth-century "police" applied increasingly sophisticated methods of observation to society. The repressive function of such observation blended with an economic mode of inquiry, especially under the Physiocratic impetus of the 1760s. But if this inquiry served an apparatus of control, it also subjected traditional jurisprudence to a new test of social observation. On the eve of the Revolution, an enlightened public eager for reform was consuming data on all forms of social behavior—demographic, medical, economic, and criminal. Although the magistrates of the parlements resisted reform on some levels, they articulated a critique of despotism that cherished the liberties of individuals. Crime and mendicity could be laid at despotism's door.[29]

Turgot drew directly from current jurisprudence as he attempted to winnow wheat from chaff in Brienne's memoir on mendicity. It could never be just to convict someone of an act that was a *cas fortuit,* that is, the consequence of a situation beyond his control. This judicial term could be transposed upon the collective study of all those individuals detained and incarcerated for mendicity. Inquiry into the forces of necessity that impelled a hapless citizen to beg led by an empirical route to the creation of a national system of public assistance. Defining the right to public assistance would remove mendicity from the realm of contingency to that of freedom.[30]

Once this was done, the "crime" of mendicity had to be rethought. Sharing Turgot's belief that it was a will-o'-the-wisp, Boisgelin de Cucé attacked the practice of arresting beggars and denounced the proposal to require passports of the poor traveling in search of work. Trudaine suspected that a psychological contradiction lay at the heart of the problem: mendicity was an abject expedient, not a free act. The economists' dream of a state "that would not make men poor" merged with the vision of one that would not make them vicious. A prerevolutionary pamphlet cited the telling epigraph to Voltaire's *Commentary on Beccaria:* "Take away mendicity, and you remove the source of the greatest number of crimes."[31]

But to "take away mendicity" would eventually mean redoubling the search for a science of production that would unite man's physical and moral nature. Such a science would unite the empirical impulse of mercantilist and Physiocrat with the quest for a spiritually and emotionally satisfying organization of labor. By attaching the startling proviso "without making them unhappy" to the challenge of making idlers productive, the academy of Châlons in 1777 had focused issues that would generate an explosive ferment of ideas in the early nineteenth century, renewing hopes that a humanely productive age was imminent. That possibility was framed anew and tested in the dreary practical experience of the *dépôts*.

In the broadest sense, the work of Liancourt's Comité de Mendicité distilled the vital legacy—direct and indirect—of eighteenth-century experiments with the *dépôts*. Guiding a systematic effort to analyze the environmental causes of mendicity, Liancourt wished to put this knowledge at the service of a broader conception of political community. Bound in many ways by the contingencies of the moment, the committee nonetheless succeeded in articulating a genuinely universal ideal as important as the Declaration of the Rights of Man. In an unusually coherent moment of modern consciousness, it defined a "political science" of *bienfaisance* that would serve the needs of all citizens.[32] It did not promise to achieve greater power for the state at less cost, or to pacify and regiment those classes of the population who might otherwise turn to revolt or despair. It used the harsh lessons of the *dépôts* to affirm a relationship between citizen and nation based on security and freedom, a relationship that today in the late twentieth century is still being constructed.

Abbreviations

Note: The titles of the following journals have been abbreviated in the notes and bibliography:

ADH   *Annales de démographie historique*

AESC   *Annales. Économies, sociétés, civilisations*

AHRF   *Annales historiques de la Révolution française*

BHM   *Bulletin of the History of Medicine*

FHS   *French Historical Studies*

RH   *Revue historique*

RHES   *Revue d'histoire économique et sociale*

RHMC   *Revue d'histoire moderne et contemporaine*

SVEC   *Studies on Voltaire and the Eighteenth Century*

''CNSS'' designates the proceedings of the Congrès national des sociétés savantes: Section d'histoire moderne et contemporaine (year and place of meeting).

Notes

Introduction

1. Archives Départementales (hereafter A.D.) of the *département* of Ille-et-Vilaine, C.4043. For further discussion of these tax records, see Chapter 1, note 25.

2. A.D. Ille-et-Vilaine, BB70. For explanation of the documents contained in the records of arrest, see Chapter 1, notes 1 and 2.

3. Ibid. On the topography of Rennes, see Claude Nières, *La réconstruction d'une ville au XVIIIe siècle. Rennes, 1720–1760* (Paris, 1972), especially 89 and 328 on *la ville basse*.

Chapter 1

1. The following discussion is centered upon the dossiers of those arrested for begging by the *maréchaussée* of the *lieutenance* of Rennes in the year 1777. Except for the special cases indicated, all dossiers are to be found in A.D. Ille-et-Vilaine, BB70. The year 1777 is of interest because it was the first full year of arrests following the suspension ordered by Turgot. An unusually complete tax survery at Rennes in 1777 affords complementary information on residents too poor to pay the capitation.

A growing literature on beggars and the poor provides a rich context for comparison with the microcosm examined here. Among scholars who marked out this terrain were François Furet, "Pour une définition des classes inférieures à l'épôque moderne," *AESC* 18 (1963): 459–474, and Robert Mandrou, *La France aux xviie et xviiie siècles* (Paris, 1967), 256. Jean-Claude Perrot called attention to the types of information available in the archives of the *dépôts de mendicité* in a comment appended to P. Massé, "Disette et mendicité en Poitou (xviii–xix siècles)," *L'actualité de l'histoire*, no. 27 (1959): 1–11, and again in "Rapports sociaux et villes au xviiie siècle," *AESC* 23:2 (1968): 255. He has drawn upon such sources in his published thesis, *Genèse d'une ville moderne: Caen au XVIIIe siècle* (Paris, 1975).

2. This information comes from the *interrogatoire*, or cross-examination, in the provost's court. In addition to this document, which contains the charge against the accused and the sentence of the court, the judicial dossier includes the statement of the arresting officer (the *procès-verbal de capture*), the copy of any jail records from places where the beggar may have been detained en route to trial (extract from a *registre d'écrou*), and, after sentencing, the receipt from the warden *(concierge)* of the *dépôt*. The *interrogatoire* generally

supplies the following information: name, sex, marital status and number of children (or names of parents), age, present residence, birthplace or place of origin, residence of parents (occasionally), profession or status, profession of parents or spouse, answer to charge, reason for begging, previous criminal record, and supplementary information (papers and other items found in the possession of the accused).

Further information on detained beggars comes from the papers of the *intendance*. At Rennes, A.D. Ille-et-Vilaine, C.1300 is a register of those detained "by order of the king" from 1785 to 1787. C.1304 contains bonds that had to be signed by each inmate before release, indicating where the inmate planned to go and how he or she would earn a living (*soumission de ne plus mendier*). Early release could sometimes be obtained, if an outsider would post bail that would be forfeited if the inmate were again caught begging. C.1304–1308 contain dossiers referred to the intendant concerning transfers of inmates to other *dépôts*, and requests to arrest or set free given individuals.

3. The best treatment of the procedures of the *maréchaussée* is in Iain A. Cameron, *Crime and Repression in the Auvergne and the Guyenne, 1720–1790* (New York, 1981), especially 101–115 and 133–175. Nicole Castan, "La justice expéditive," *AESC* 31 (1976): 331–361, analyzes over twelve thousand cases from central records of the *cours prévôtales* from 1758 to 1790. These include proceedings against vagabonds and those charged with crimes, but not those involving confinement of beggars in *dépôts*. She finds (p. 348) that the *cours prévôtales* released only six to seven percent of those they tried, as opposed to the parlement of Toulouse, which released twenty per cent of its accused. The still more summary procedure of confining beggars was presumably all but automatic. Of our two hundred cases, two peddlers were the only ones released. On the point that denials by the accused weighed little, see Cameron, *Crime and Repression,* 114.

4. See especially Jean-Pierre Gutton, *La société et les pauvres: l'exemple de la généralité de Lyon, 1534–1789* (Paris, 1971), 159; Olwen Hufton, *The Poor of Eighteenth-Century France, 1750–1789* (Oxford, 1974); Jeffry Kaplow, *The Names of Kings: The Parisian Laboring Poor in the Eighteenth Century* (New York, 1972), 30; and Cissie C. Fairchilds, *Poverty and Charity in Aix-en-Provence, 1640–1789,* (Baltimore, 1976), 103. Rennes and Brittany provided the focus for some of the earliest empirical research on the history of the urban poor and their rural ties. See Henri Sée, "Remarques sur la misère, la mendicité et l'assistance en Bretagne à la fin de l'ancien régime," *Mémoires de la Société d'histoire de Bretagne* 7 (1926): 103–132, and other articles of his cited below. The richness of a current generation of research on these topics is especially evident in Colin Jones, *Charity and Bienfaisance: The Treatment of the Poor in the Montpellier Region, 1740–1815* (Cambridge, 1982); Kathryn Norberg, *Rich and Poor in Grenoble, 1600–1814* (Berkeley, 1985); and Robert M. Schwartz, *Policing the Poor in Eighteenth-Century France* (Chapel Hill, 1988).

5. See especially Jean-Pierre Poussou, *Bordeaux et le Sud-Ouest au xviiiᵉ siècle: croissance économique et attraction urbaine* (Paris, 1983), 104–114, and the finely documented descriptions in Hufton, *The Poor,* 26–31, 69–106, and 114–117.

6. Hippolyte Adolphe Taine, *The Origins of Contemporary France* (abridged), ed. Edward T. Gargan (Chicago, 1974), 17.

7. C.-E. Labrousse, *La crise de l'économie française à la fin de l'ancien régime et au début de la Révolution,* 2 vols. (Paris, 1944), 1:xxiv and xxix, and his survey, *Le paysan français des physiocrates à nos jours* (Paris, 1962), 90.

8. Georges Lefebvre, *The Coming of the French Revolution* trans. R. R. Palmer (1939; Princeton, 1947), 115–116; Lefebvre, *Les paysans du Nord pendant la révolution française* (Paris, 1924), 1:46, 59, 279, 290–291, and 304. On the social impact of price fluctuations, see Fernand Braudel and Ernest Labrousse, eds., *Histoire économique et sociale de la France,* vol. 2: *Des derniers temps de l'âge seigneurial aux préludes de l'âge industriel (1660–1789)* (Paris, 1970), 412.

9. Albert Mathiez, "Notes sur l'importance du prolétariat," *AHRF* 7 (1930): 479–524, especially 523; Pierre de Saint-Jacob, *Les paysans de la Bourgogne du Nord au dernier siècle de l'Ancien Régime* (Paris, 1960), 547 and 552; Jean Meuvret, "Les crises de subsistances et la démographie de la France d'Ancien Régime," *Population*, 1:4 (1946); François Lebrun, "Les crises démographiques en France aux XVIIᵉ et XVIIIᵉ siècles," *AESC*, 35:2 (1980): 205–233.

10. Marcel Rouff, "Le personnel des premières émeutes de 1789," *La révolution française* 57 (1909): 213–238; George Rudé, *The Crowd in the French Revolution* (1959; Oxford, 1972). Albert Soboul promoted interest in related issues with his *Les sans-culottes parisiens en l'an II: mouvement populaire et gouvernement révolutionnaire, 2 juin 1798–9 Thermidor, an II* (Paris, 1958). See especially in Marc Bouloiseau, ed., *Contributions à l'histoire démographique de la Révolution française* (Paris, 1962), the articles by Jean Ibanès, "La population de la place des Vosges et de ses environs en 1791," 71–97, and Yves Le Moigne, "Population et subsistances à Strasbourg au XVIIIᵉ siècle," 13–44. From this era see also Jeffry Kaplow, "Sur la population flottante de Paris à la fin de l'ancien régime," *AHRF* 39 (1967): 1–14; and Michel Vovelle, "Le prolétariat flottant à Marseille sous la Révolution française,"' *ADH*, 1968, 111–138.

11. George Rudé, "La taxation populaire de mai 1775 à Paris et dans la région parisienne," *AHRF* 143 (1956): 139–179, and "La taxation populaire de mai 1775 en Picardie, en Normandie et dans le Beauvaisis," *AHRF* 165 (1961), 305–326; Guy Lemarchand, "Les troubles de subsistance dans la généralité de Rouen (2ᵉ moitié du XVIIIᵉ siècle)," *AHRF* 174 (1963): 401–427; Louise Tilly, "La révolte frumentaire, forme de conflit politique en France," *AESC* 27 (1972), 731–757.

12. Hufton, *The Poor*, 69–106. See also her essay "The Rise of the People: Life and Death among the Very Poor," in *The Eighteenth Century: Europe in the Age of the Enlightenment*, ed. Alfred Cobban (London, 1969), 279–310. Pierre Poussou introduced a volume devoted to the subject of migrations with his "Les mouvements migratoires en France et à partir de la France de la fin du XVᵉ siècle au début du XIXᵉ siècles: approches pour une synthèse," *ADH*, 1970, 11–78. Poussou incorporated data on beggars in his *Bordeaux et le sud-ouest au xviiiᵉ siècle: croissance économique et attraction urbaine* (Paris, 1983), 172–181. On the crucial region of the Auvergne, see Robert Liris, "Mendicité et vagabondage en Basse-Auvergne à la fin du XVIIIᵉ siècle," *Revue d'Auvergne*, 79:2 (1965): Abel Poitrineau, "Aspects de l'émigration temporaire et saisonnière en Auvergne à la fin du XVIIIᵉ siècle et au début du XIXᵉ siècle," *RHMC*, 1962, 5–50; and the same author's published thesis, *La vie rurale en Basse-Auvergne au XVIIIᵉ siècle (1726–1789)* (Paris, 1965).

13. Georges Lefebvre, *La grande peur de 1789* (Paris, 1932), 38. The draft edict on mendicity presented to the parlement of Paris in 1766 (B.N. f.f. 8129, fol. 118v.), included the passage:

> N'entendons néanmoins qu'il puisse être apporté aucun trouble ni obstacle aux habitans de nos pays de Normandie, Limousin, Auvergne, Dauphiné, et autres, même des pays étrangers qui ont été accoutumé de venir, soit pour la récolte des foins ou des moissons, ou pour travailler ou faire commerce dans nos villes et autres lieux.

For an interesting enumeration of all the forms of mobility within a relatively sedentary population, see Micheline Baulant, "Groupes mobiles dans une société sédentaire: une société rurale autour de Meaux au xviiᵉ et xviiiᵉ siècles," in *Les marginaux et les exclus dans l'histoire* (Paris, 1979), 78–121. See also the excellent analysis of geographical mobility based on the patterns of arrest of beggars in Schwartz, *Policing the Poor*, 167.

14. Michel Vovelle, "De la mendicité au brigandage. Les errants en Beauce sous la Révolution française," *Actes du 86ᵉ Congrès national des sociétés savantes (Montpellier, 1961, Section d'histoire moderne et contemporaine* (Paris, 1962), 483–512.

15. Hufton, *The Poor,* develops a similar point that crime and delinquency represented further variations on "an economy of makeshifts" (355). Part 3 of her book, "The Crimes of the Poor," synthesizes primary and secondary sources from several regions of France in support of this view. See also Hufton's "Le paysan et la loi en France au XVIIIᵉ siècle," *AESC* 38 (May–June 1983): 679–701, especially 692. According to the geographical analysis of Nicole Castan, in "Justice expéditive," 340 and 344, Brittany is part of "la France moyennement criminalisée," by contrast with the Paris basin and other areas with a higher crime rate. Castan also sees a long-term shift of criminality in the 1750s following the migration of troublesome elements from country to city: *Les criminels de Languedoc. Les exigences d'ordre et les voies de ressentiment dans une société pré-révolutionnaire (1750–1790)* (Toulouse, 1980), 21.

16. Janine Combes-Monier, "Population mouvante et criminalité à Versailles à la fin de l'ancien régime," in *Hommage à Marcel Reinhard: sur la population française au xviiiᵉ et au xixᵉ siècles* (Paris, 1973), 135–159 (especially 159). An article of broad general significance by Christian Roman, "Le monde des pauvres à Paris au xviiiᵉ siècle," *AESC* 37 (1982): 729–763, documents the preponderance of immigrants in search of work in a tally of arrests for begging by the officers of the Châtelet (734). The decline in admission of beggars at Bicêtre, as they began to be transferred to the *dépôts* of the *généralité*, is documented from the registers of Bicêtre in Cathérine Carillion, "À Bicêtre: mendiants 1755–1770, et bons pauvres 1746–1789," Mémoire de maîtrise, University of Paris I, 1973, 55, 112, 138, and 142.

17. J. Béaud et G. Bouchart, "Le dépôt des pauvres de Saint-Denis (1768–1792)," *ADH,* 1974, 127–143 and table on 135.

18. Paul Crépillon, "Un 'gibier des prévôts': mendiants et vagabonds au xviiiᵉ siècle entre la Vire et la Dives (1720–1789)," *Annales de Normandie* 17:3 (October 1967): 223–252; Véronique Boucheron, "La montée du flot des errants de 1760 à 1789 dans la généralité d'Alençon," *Annales de Normandie* 21:1 (March 1971): 55–86.

19. Hufton, *The Poor,* 173–176. Cissie Fairchilds, *Poverty and Charity in Aix-en-Provence, 1640–1789* (Baltimore, 1976), 113, stresses the importance of "unemployability," whether from sickness, injury, age, or lack of family support, in the cases of beggars arrested at Aix pursuant to the Declaration of 1724.

20. Pierre Goubert, "Le monde des errants, mendiants et vagabonds à Paris et autour de Paris au 18ᵉ siècle," in *Clio parmi les hommes: recueil d'articles* (Paris, 1976). The breakdown of support networks available to an individual through family, trade, or neighborhood is cited as a general factor in Daniel Roche, "A Pauper Capital: Some Reflections on the Parisian Poor in the Seventeenth and Eighteenth Centuries," *French History,* 1:2 (October 1987), 182–209, especially 206. It should be noted that the declaration of "profession" on court records was subject to distortion. The terms used were often accompanied by qualifications indicating that the individual had been only marginally or intermittently involved in a trade: *apprentif, serveur de,* or *cy-devant.* Migrants often combined geographic and professional mobility. See Kaplow, *The Names of Kings,* 132–133.

21. Bernard Dérouet, "Une démographie sociale différentielle: clés pour un système auto-régulateur des populations rurales d'ancien régime," *AESC* 35:1 (January–February 1980): 3–41.

22. Gutton, *La société et les pauvres . . . Lyon,* 23–29; Hufton, *The Poor,* 107–127; Giovanni Ricci, "Naissance du pauvre honteux: entre l'histoire des idées et l'histoire sociale," *AESC* 38:1 (January–February, 1983): 158–177.

23. See for example Poussou, *Bordeaux et le Sud-Ouest,* 143.

24. A.D. Ille-et-Vilaine, C.3796; Jean Meyer et al., *Histoire de Rennes* (Toulouse, 1972), 274–275; Paul Banéat, *Le vieux Rennes* (Rennes, 1926). I am grateful to Prof. Roger Dupuy of the University of Rennes for lending me his copy of a *diplôme de maîtrise* by M. Le

Pennec, *Aspects de la misère à Rennes au début de la Révolution* (Rennes, 1970), including a mapping of the list of indigents drawn up in the year II of the Revolution. Claude Nières, *La réconstruction d'une ville au xviiiᵉ siècle: Rennes 1720–1760* (Paris, 1972), 299–306, explains how shanties *(barraques)* were tolerated as temporary housing after the fire of 1720. They remained in use as tenements for the poor crowded in courtyards back from the streets, in open spaces near the center of town—the grimly named Quartier de la Grippe, for example—and on the outskirts.

25. Capitation rolls for 1777, A.D. Ille-et-Vilaine, C.4043. Henri Sée, who used the capitation rolls for 1758 as the basis for his article, "La population et la vie économique de Rennes vers le milieu du xviiiᵉ siècle d'après les rôles de la capitation," *Mémoires de la Société d'histoire de Bretagne* 4 (1923): 89–136, refers to these rolls as veritable *terriers urbains.* He noted that the roll for 1777 is one of the few including a notation for everyone who did not pay the tax, as well as those who did. About twenty percent of those inscribed on the rolls for 1777 are listed as *pauvres* according to Sée, "Statistique des pauvres de Rennes d'après les rôles de la capitation à la fin du 18ᵉ siècle," *Annales de Bretagne* 41 (1934): 474–477. The rolls also contain entries of *mendiant,* but this presumably means that the individual has no means of support besides begging and charity. Sée notes that some of those listed as *pauvre* are presumably able to live from their work.

26. Three *journaliers* are "poor," two pay at the minimum rate of one livre; one navvy *(terasseur)* is "poor," one pays; one *manoeuvre* is "poor," one pays.

27. In the courtyard, there are 14 single males living alone, 5 single women ("widow" mentioned in two cases) alone; 2 childless couples (both paying a tax); a male weaver living with his *compagnon;* two male porters living with children (4 with one, 3 with the other); and a widow with 2 children. The single parents are all *pauvre.* Presumably the two single males with children are widowers, but if so, the fact is not indicated, as it is in the case of the widows. Apart from the extended Morel *ménage* (the younger Morel, apparently a widower, lives with his two children and a carpenter in a shanty adjoining that of his parents and one child), there are two "complete" families—a hatmaker, his wife, and three children (poor), and a *journalier* with wife and child, paying a one-livre tax.

28. Of the two hundred dossiers for beggers arrested in 1777, seventy-five contain reference to Rennes as the declared place of residence. Some of these do not give specific street names, and eighteen avow being "without fixed abode." Only nine names of the accused could be matched tentatively with names on the tax rolls by street address, indicating that most of the beggars were transient, even if they considered themselves domiciled within a neighborhood. Julien Morel thus may represent the most highly integrated element among the beggars liable to arrest. Henry Sée, "La population . . . d'après les rôles," 129–130, comments on the types of professions and living quarters to be found in the poorer popular neighborhoods at Rennes. Julien Morel's neighbors, taken as a group, are similar to groupings Sée reports in the Rue St. Melaine and the Rue Bénoît.

29. The traditional practice of allowing beggars to make the rounds of merchants on Mondays is mentioned disapprovingly by the subdelegate Fresnais in a memoir to the intendant, September 6, 1769, A.D. Ille-et-Vilaine, C.1298.

30. The fact that Ollivier Le Postel appeared as a weaver on the capitation rolls for 1751 was kindly supplied to me by Henri Lozach'meur, who studied the parish of St. Hélier for a *diplôme de maîtrise* at the University of Rennes. Jean-Pierre Gutton was able to document downward social mobility in a number of cases of beggars confined pursuant to the Declaration of 1724 at St. Étienne, by checking earlier property records: see his *L'état et la mendicité dans la première moitié du xviiiᵉ siècle: Auvergne, Beaujolais, Forez, Lyonnais* (Lyons, 1973), 210.

31. The comments of Jean-Pierre Gutton on "La mendicité juvénile" in *L'état et la*

mendicité, 204–208, apply as well to Rennes in the 1770s as to Lyons and Saint-Étienne in the 1720s.

32. On the nature and extent of disease in eighteenth-century Brittany, see Jean-Pierre Goubert, *Malades et médecins en Bretagne, 1770–1790* (Paris, 1974), 255–348.

33. On the notion of *état* and its connection with work and community, see William H. Sewell, Jr., *Work and Revolution in France: The Language of Labor from the Old Régime to 1848* (Cambridge, 1980), 32–37.

34. While the facts of this case are open to interpretation, it is clear that the authorities made a point of invoking the husband's request as grounds for enforcing the authority of the family and halting public "scandal." There is no evidence in the dossier that formal *ordres du Roi* were obtained by the intendant from the minister responsible. In the case of a porter and his wife, the intendant's authority was apparently sufficient.

35. Presumably the "De la Chalotais" in question was the son of the famous protagonist of the Brittany Affair of the 1760s. The son held the position of attorney general in survivorship from his father, Caradeuc de la Chalotais, according to the *Almanach royal* of 1776, cited by John Rothney, ed., *The Brittany Affair and the Crisis of the Ancien Régime* (Oxford, 1969), page following p. x; it is noteworthy that the members of the restored parlement made use of the intendant's power to commit individuals by *ordre du Roi,* in spite of the fact that they renewed their efforts to curtail the intendant's judicial functions. See Henri Fréville, *L'intendance de Bretagne,* 3 vols. (Rennes, 1953), 3:67–83 (Caze de la Bove and the parlement). In one case, it should be noted, a wayward husband was confined.

36. The *Nouveau petit Larousse* (1970) defines *polisson* as "enfant malpropre et vagabond: *les polissons de la rue,*" or as "enfant espiègle." "Street urchin" has similar connotations in English.

37. The role of the *commissaire du parlement* Ellie (also written "Elie" in La Chalotais' note on page 19) appears to have been to coordinate the police function of the hospital authorities and those of the *dépôt.*

38. A letter from the duc de Choiseul to the controller-general dated August 21, 1768, indicates that women arrested by military authorities at Brest had been transferred, pursuant to a "previous request," to the *dépôt* at Quimper. Choiseul argued that *dépôts* might generally serve this function, "these girls falling exactly into the category of vagabonds, libertines, and shiftless" (A.N. F^{15} 2811). Records in the same dossier indicate that the number of *journées* paid by the minister of war for such women in the *généralité* of Rennes (in the last six months of the previous year, 1767) was 18,676, a number exceeded only by that for Metz (28,148) and followed closely by Nancy (17,816). In at least one case the *dépôt* at Rennes received the children of such women. A child abandoned in the barracks was received on the grounds that "the public is the father of this child": A.D. Ille-et-Vilaine, C.1305.

39. Treatment of women afflicted with venereal disease by means of *"dragées de Keyser"* was regularly provided, according to A.N. F^{15} 2811 documents. Dossiers in A.D. Ille-et-Vilaine, C.1305, indicate that indigent medical care rather than repression of begging was the motive for the arrest of some poor women suffering from venereal disease. In a batch of eight such women transferred from Vannes in 1780, one denied having begged but freely confessed to having led a dissolute life for the previous six years. In another case a woman suffering from venereal disease was transferred temporarily from the prison of the parlement at the request of the prison commissioner.

40. A.D. Ille-et-Vilaine, C.1305 (dossier on arrest of servant). For a well-documented discussion of the vulnerability of female servants to sexual coercion, their lack of legal recourse, and their exposure to popular calumny, see Sara C. Maza, *Servants and Masters in Eighteenth-Century France: The Uses of Loyalty* (Princeton, 1983), especially chapter 2,

"Love and Money," and 129–132. A dossier in A.D. Ille-et-Vilaine, C.1305, tells of a girl sixteen arrested at St. Brieuc who claimed that she had come to town looking for a position: she was taken in by a woman who offered to find her one, but when she went to see her, she was seduced by a soldier who led her off to the barracks without her having anything to say about it.

41. In an unusual case in 1780, the *premier président* of the parlement, Nouvel, wanted his wife's nephew locked up. He explained that he accepted wardship when the boy lost his parents at the age of thirteen. Failing to have the boy apprenticed, Nouvel had him equipped to take ship at St. Malo, giving him six livres and provisions. The boy returned saying he had been robbed by a soldier, but later confessed "that it had been with a miserable creature that he spent his money and lost his passports on the highway." He had a record of thefts on previous jobs. A.D. Ille-et-Vilaine, C.1305.

42. Compare Olwen Hufton's account of women beating on the door of the *dépôt* at Riom in Auvergne in the cold winter of 1786, demanding to be let in: "Women and the Family Economy in Eighteenth-Century France," *FHS* 9:1 (Spring 1975): 22.

43. In 1786 the intendant Bertrand de Molleville observed that most women released from the *dépôt* returned, since they could not find employment except in a life of debauchery. He accordingly asked the minister, Calonne, for funds to have young girls taken out of the *dépôt* between the ages of five and sixteen and taught lace-making. A.D. Ille-et-Vilaine, C.1302.

44. Fresnais's letter to de la Glestière accompanied the dossier of Marie Nicolle, dated September 6, 1777. Although in principle the intendant could require those requesting to have someone confined to pay a pension for upkeep in the *dépôt,* it appears that the *dépôt* was used as a place of confinement precisely for those who were too poor to pay. Mme de Melesse's request is in a dossier dated May 5, 1777. The presence of several other dossiers of this sort in May perhaps indicates that the release of inmates for work in the fields may have opened some "places" in the *dépôt.*

45. A.D. Ille-et-Vilaine, C.1300 (register); A.D. Doubs, C.1528, "État nominatif des personnes qui ont été renfermées dans le *dépôt* de mendicité de Besançon, en vertu d'Arrêt du Parlement et jugemens de Police de la même ville et des autres juridictions." See reference to the *dépôt de mendicité* of Beaulieu at Caen in Claude Quétel, "Lettres de cachet et correctionnaires dans la généralité de Caen au XVIIIe siècle," *Annales de Normandie,* 28:2 (1978): 127–159. Quétel includes the text of Breteuil's circular of 1784 in an appendix, 157–159. See also cases of *libertinage,* male and female, in Marie-Odile Deschamps, "Le dépôt de mendicité de Rouen (1768–1820)," *Bulletin d'histoire économique et sociale de la Révolution française,* 1977, 81–93, especially 88.

46. On the *piètre* and other stock figures of the false beggar, see Roger Chartier, "La 'monarchie d'argot': entre le mythe et l'histoire," in *Les marginaux et les exclus dans l'histoire* (Paris, 1979), 275–311, especially 284, and the case cited in Alan Williams, *The Police of Paris, 1718–1789* (Baton Rouge, 1979), 190.

47. While feigned illness or disability is charged in only two cases in the 1777 dossiers of the *lieutenance* of Rennes, thirty-six of the two hundred refer to illness or disability without being challenged in the cross-examination.

48. The suggestion of writers such as Hufton and Gutton that debauchery presented itself as an economic makeshift on a par with equally marginal trades is neatly represented in the case of Marie Anne Le Goffe. The two trades she declared are the two most commonly cited in our sample of women and girls arrested (excluding *journalières* and those who are *sans état*). Henri Sée cites the *lingères* as a group remarkable for their poverty in a generally impoverished textile trade in "Les métiers urbains dans la seconde moitié du xviiie siècle," *RHES* 13 (1925): 414.

49. The median age of the seven suspected of theft was fifteen. Hufton, *The Poor,* 253,

cites instances of women being sentenced to the *dépôt* (at Montpellier, in particular) in the absence of other penalties applicable to women besides hanging. In such cases, it is not the beggar who proves to be a criminal, but the criminal who is assimilated with beggars by the judicial authorities.

50. Instances of strange outsiders who spread anxiety are documented from the files of beggars confined at the *dépôt* of Tours in the study by Georges Surreault, "La mendicité en Touraine à la fin du dix-huitième siècle (1768–1790): étude sociale" (diplôme de maîtrise, Tours, 1971), 122–124. André Abbiateci, "Les incendiaires dans la France du XVIIIᵉ siècle: essai de typologie criminelle," *AESC* 25:1 (January–February 1970): 229–248, finds a common pattern of marginal employment among the beggars tried for arson (237).

51. André Zysberg's analysis of galley convicts by crime and by socioeconomic category, from records of 1748, finds that the preeminent peasant crime was smuggling (especially of salt). See his "Galley Rowers in the Mid-Eighteenth Century," translated from *AESC* 30 (1975): 43–65, in Robert Forster and Orest Ranum, eds., *Deviants and the Abandoned in French Society: Selections from the Annales. Economies, Sociétés, Civilisations,* vol. 4 (Baltimore, 1978), 91 and 105–107.

52. Another case in which incarceration in the *dépôt* was a lenient alternative to the galleys was that of Jean Cottereau, in trouble for salt smuggling and desertion, and later known to history as Jean Chouan. A protector paid his pension in 1787, 1788, and 1789, according to Fr. Le Bour'his, "Jean Chouan au dépôt de mendicité de Rennes," *Bulletin et mémoires de la société archéologique d'Ille-et-Vilaine* 67 (1944): 143.

53. Hippolyte Taine, *Les origines de la France contemporaine—l'ancien régime,* vol. 2 (Paris, 1910), 290.

54. See Véronique Boucheron, "La montée du flot des errants de 1760 à 1789 dans la généralité d'Alençon," *Annales de Normandie* 21:1 (March 1971): 55–86. Of 994 professional activities mentioned in the dossiers she studied, 119 fell into the category of "colporteurs, marchands forains, vendeurs de chansons, vanniers, musiciens, etc." (66).

55. Olwen Hufton suggests, in "Le paysan et la loi," 692–694, that there was a sharp social division between the ordinary peasant and the uprooted bands of brigands recruited from the ranks of vagabonds. The evidence noted in this chapter suggests that the beggar population of the *dépôts* tends more nearly to resemble the ordinary population on its broad margins of impoverishment and mobility. J.-P. Poussou, *Bordeaux et le Sud-Ouest,* 178, finds that patterns of immigration are very similar for beggars in the *dépôts* and for the immigrant population at large, while the pattern for those convicted of crimes is markedly different.

Chapter 2

1. J. L. Vives, "De Subventione Pauperum, sive de humanis necessitatibus," in *Opera omnia,* 9 vols. (London, 1964), vol. 4, 420–494, especially 492. See also M. Bataillon, "J. L. Vives, réformateur de la bienfaisance," *Bibliothèque d'humanisme et Renaissance* (1952), 141–158.

2. On the traditions themselves, see Brian Tiernay, *Medieval Poor Law, a Sketch of Canonical Theory and its Application in England* (Berkeley, 1959), 60, and Demetrios J. Constantelos, *Byzantine Philanthropy and Social Welfare* (New Brunswick, N.J., 1968), 71. On the use of St. Ambrose's precepts in redefining the charitable functions of the bishop, see Brian Pullan, *Rich and Poor in Renaissance Venice: The Social Institutions of a Catholic State to 1620* (Cambridge, Mass., 1971), 200 and 227. On the medieval search for accountability and more rational utilization of charities, see especially Michel Rouche, "La matricule des pauvres: Évolution d'une institution de charité du Bas Empire jusqu'à la fin du Haut

Moyen Âge,'' in Michel Mollat, ed., *Études sur l'histoire de la pauvreté,* 2 vols. (Paris, 1974), 1:83–110.

3. See the classic survey at the beginning of Sidney and Beatrice Webb, *English Local Government: English Poor Law History: Part I. The Old Poor Law* (New York, 1927), and Catherina Lis and Hugo Soly, *Poverty and Capitalism in Pre-Industrial Europe* (Atlantic Highlands, N.J., 1979), especially chapter 3, "Economic Growth, Impoverishment and Social Policy," 53–96. For three confessional perspectives, see Pierre Bonenfant, "Les origines et le caractère de la réforme de la bienfaisance publique aux Pays-Bas sous le règne de Charles-Quint," *Revue belge de philologie et d'histoire* 5 (1926): 887–904, and 6 (1927), 209–230; H. J. Grimm, "Luther's Contribution to Sixteenth-Century Organization of Poor Relief," *Archiv für Reformationsgeschichte* 61 (1970): 22–34; and Robert A. Kingdon, "Social Welfare in Calvin's Geneva," *American Historical Review* 76:1 (February 1971): 50–69.

4. Jean-Pierre Gutton, *La société et les pauvres: l'exemple de la généralité de Lyon, 1534–1789* (Paris, 1971), 215–287 ("L'apport du xvie siècle"); Natalie Z. Davis, "Poor Relief, Humanism and Heresy," in her *Society and Culture in Early Modern France* (Stanford, Calif., 1975), 17–64; and Louis Parturier, *L'assistance à Paris sous l'ancien régime et pendant la Révolution: étude sur les diverses institutions dont la réunion a formé l'Administration Générale de l'Assistance Publique à Paris* (Paris, 1897), 16–18.

5. On mercantilism, see the essays in D. C. Coleman, ed., *Revisions in Mercantilism* (London, 1969), especially Charles Wilson, "The Other Face of Mercantilism," 118–139; Joseph J. Spengler, "Mercantilist and Physiocratic Growth Theory," in Bert F. Hoselitz, ed., *Theories of Economic Growth* (New York, 1960), 3–64; Joyce Appleby, *Economic Thought and Ideology in Seventeenth-Century England* (Princeton, 1978), 155; and C. W. Cole, *French Mercantilist Doctrines before Colbert* (New York, 1931), 172. On the religious impulse to employ the poor, see Alfred Rébelliau, "Un épisode de l'histoire religieuse du XVIIe siècle," *Revue des deux mondes* 16 (1903), part 1: "La compagnie du Saint-Sacrement," 65; Emmanuel Chill, "Religion and Mendicity in Seventeenth-Century France," *International Review of Social History* 7 (1962): 415; and Henri Daniel-Rops, *Monsieur Vincent: The Story of St. Vincent de Paul,* trans. Julie Kernan (New York, 1961), 72–77. On the long-range influence of the Council of Trent, see Olwen Hufton, "The Rise of the People: Life and Death among the Very Poor," in *The Eighteenth Century—Europe in the Age of the Enlightenment,* ed. Alfred Cobban (London, 1969), 304–306.

6. Léon Lallemand, *Histoire de la Charité* (Paris, 1910), vol. 4, part 2, 377ff.; Olwen Hufton, *The Poor of Eighteenth-Century France, 1750–1789* (Oxford, 1974), 139ff.; Camille Bloch, *Assistance et l'état à la veille de la Révolution* (Paris, 1908), 48. Christian Paultre, *La répression de la mendicite et du vagabondage en France sous l'ancien régime* (Paris, 1906), 219–221, notes that the edict of 1662 reaffirmed the provisions of the edicts of Moulins and Blois and states that the establishment of *hôpitaux-généraux* would serve to carry out local obligations to the poor, urgent in that year of famine. Michel Foucault focuses on the edict of 1656, establishing the *hôpital-général* of Paris, in his chapter on "Le grand renfermement" in *Histoire de la folie à l'âge classique* (Paris, 1972), 60.

7. Gutton, *La société et les pauvres,* 326–349. See also Hufton, *The Poor,* 143ff.

8. Jean-Baptiste Guérin, *Discours sur le renfermement des pauvres* (Soissons, 1662), 50. This passage may be interpreted in the light of Norman O. Brown, *Life against Death: The Psychoanalytic Meaning of History* (Middletown, Conn., 1969), 234ff. See especially p. 299 on the alchemist's procedure of "cohabation," which returns spirits to their feces.

9. Karl Polanyi, *The Great Transformation: The Political and Economic Origins of Our Time* (Boston, 1957), 121 and 141; Mircea Eliade, *The Forge and the Crucible: The Origins and Structures of Alchemy* (New York, 1971), 172–178.

10. B.N. f.f. 8129, fol. 123; see fol. 54–57v. for the text of the "Déclaration du Roy,

concernant les Mandians & Vagabonds. Donnée à Versailles le 25 juillet 1700. Registré en Parlement.'' A series of edicts in 1693 (fol. 40–49v.) provided forced service in the galleys as a penalty for vagabonds. The demand for galley-rowers in the royal navy had led to the empressment of beggars at this time, according to Rouaud, ''Quelques mots sur la répression de la mendicité à Nantes avant la Révolution,'' *Annales de la Société académique de Nantes,* 6ᵉ série, 3 (1882): 256. See also Paul W. Bamford, *Fighting Ships and Prisons: The Mediterranean Galleys of France in the Age of Louis XIV* (Minneapolis, 1973), 180.

11. B.N. f.f. 8129, fol. 123v.; Gutton, *La société et les pauvres,* 439.

12. B.N. f.f. 8129, fol. 123v.; text of 1720 ordinance at fol. 76; Paultre, *Répression,* 322–323. Vagabonds who had been gathered at the château of Belle-Isle for transportation to Louisiana were released when the plan was abandoned; the comte d'Estrée gave an order from Ancenis, October 17, 1720, for them to return to their provinces of origin (A.D. Loire-Atlantique, C.633).

13. Jean-Pierre Gutton, *L'état et la mendicité dans la première moitié du XVIIIᵉ siècle: Auvergne, Beaujolais, Forez, Lyonnais* (Lyons, 1973), 35–40 and 225–230 (text of the declaration).

14. Ibid., 72–73. The English term *hospital* will be used hereafter as the equivalent of the French *hôpital*. The term will generally refer to *hôpitaux-généraux,* unless the context indicates a more inclusive usage.

15. Ibid., 37–38.

16. Circular of Orry to intendants, October 24, 1733, A.D. Ille-et-Vilaine, C.1288.

17. Gutton, *L'état et la mendicité,* 148–155, 165–166; softness toward offenders is documented on 108–126. Bertier cited inflated food costs in 1725, lack of space to lock up all beggars, cumbersome efforts to centralize arrest records, soaring costs to the royal treasury, and lack of cooperation on the part of hospital administrators as reasons for the failure of the Declaration of 1724, in his report to Laverdy in 1766: B.N. f.f. 8129, fol. 124 and 131. Gutton also argues, in ''Mendiants dans la société parisienne au début du xviiiᵉ siècle,'' *Cahiers d'histoire* 17 (1968): 141, that administrators had difficulty distinguishing sturdy beggars from deserving poor by the terms of the law.

18. Gutton, *L'état et la mendicité,* 166; Michel Vovelle, *Piété baroque et déchristianisation en Provence au xviiiᵉ siècle,* abridged edition (Paris, 1978), 240, 257, and 270–271. See also the evidence presented in Cissie C. Fairchilds, *Poverty and Charity in Aix-en-Provence, 1640–1789* (Baltimore, 1976), 133–136. Hufton, *Poor,* 153, suggests that loss of hospital investments in the schemes of John Law dealt hospitals a blow, and that even bishops shifted their charitable priorities after an initial surge of enthusiasm. Colin Jones, *Charity and bienfaisance: The Treatment of the Poor in the Montpellier Region, 1740–1815* (New York, 1983), 76–94, argues that the spirit of charity was alive and well, but found new objects, including specialized hospitals, refuges, and *confréries.*

19. Henri François d'Aguesseau, *Oeuvres complètes* (Paris, 1819), 10:184. The texts of the ''Arrest du Cour du Parlement, pour la subsistance des Pauvres, du 30 décembre 1740,'' and the ''Déclaration du Roy, concernant les Mendiants,'' of October 20, 1750, are in B.N. f.f. 8129, fol. 98–99 and 101–102. See also M. Bricourt, M. Lachiver, and J. Quérel, ''La crise de subsistances des années 1740 dans le ressort du parlement de Paris,'' *Annales de démographie historique,* 1974, 281–333.

20. B.N. f.f. 8129, fol. 101. Paultre, *Répression,* 365–379, treats the Declaration primarily as a temporary effort to cope with demobilized soldiers, noting however that the concept of a *maison de force* specifically for beggars was discussed.

21. B.N. f.f. 8129, fol. 126; Marcel Marion, *Histoire financière de la France depuis 1715, tome 1 (1715–1789)* (Paris, 1914), 178.

22. Paul Hazard, *The European Mind, 1680–1715* (New York, 1963), 281; John Rule, ''Royal Ministers and Government Reform during the Last Decades of Louis XIV's Reign,''

in Claude C. Sturgill, ed., *The Consortium on Revolutionary Europe, 1750–1850* (Gaines-ville, Fla., 1973), 1–13. On Saint-Pierre, see Nannerl O. Keohane, *Philosophy and the State in France: The Renaissance to the Enlightenment* (Princeton, 1980), 361–369; and Thomas E. Kaiser, ''The Abbé de Saint-Pierre, Public Opinion, and the Reconstitution of the French Monarchy,'' *Journal of Modern History* 55 (December 1983), 618–643. See Gutton, *Société et les pauvres,* 419–437, on the emergence of an ideology of *bienfaisance* between 1680 and 1730.

23. Fénelon's remark is cited in Lionel Rothkrug, *Opposition to Louis XIV: The Political and Social Origins of the French Enlightenment* (Princeton, 1965), 458. The continued ap-peal of Saint-Pierre's ideas later in the century is reflected in the collection, *Les rêves d'un homme de bien, qui peuvent être réalisés, ou les vues utiles et pratiques de M. l'abbé de Saint-Pierre, choisies dans ce grand nombre de projects singuliers, dont le bien public étoit le principe,* ed. Alletz (Paris, 1775). In his ''Projet pour renfermer les mendians,'' ibid., 255–265, Saint-Pierre claimed to have seen children sent out to beg as a consequence of the ruinous exactions of the *''taille arbitraire.''* Reform of the *taille* and funding of hospitals from city tolls and excises *(octrois)* would remove beggars from the streets. He made a similar observation in his ''Projet de taille tarifée,'' ibid., 98.

24. ''Projet pour renfermer les mendiants,'' cited in preceding note. Jean-Pierre Gutton summarizes the text, originally entitled *Sur les pauvres mendiants,* and assesses its possible influence on the Declaration of 1724 in *L'état et la mendicité,* 31. The brochure appeared in March 1724, three months before the Declaration.

25. Montesquieu, *Esprit des lois,* book 22, chapter 29, in *Oeuvres complètes,* ed. Cail-lois (Paris, 1958), 2:712–713. See Marcel Candille, ''Commentaire autour du chapitre de l'*Esprit des lois* relatif aux hôpitaux,'' *Revue de l'Assistance publique à Paris,* no. 22 (1953): 316–323.

26. Ibid. In a memoir prepared for Turgot in 1775, Brienne wrote: ''Un homme peut être pauvre, non seulement parce qu'il manque de travail, mais encore par ce que ce travail ne suffit pas a son besoin'' (B.N. f.f. 8129, fol. 257v.). See Chapter 7 for further discussion of the memoir.

27. Harry C. Payne, *''Pauvreté, misère,* and the Aims of Enlightened Economics,'' *SVEC* 154 (1976): 1581–1592. See also Robert Mauzi, *L'idée du bonheur dans la littérature et la pensée françaises au XVIIIe siècle* (Paris, 1960), 177: ''La notion de l'aisance tend à résoudre l'opposition traditionnelle, fondée sur la théologie, entre les riches et les pauvres.'' Montesquieu speaks of the need to give cultivators ''the desire of having a superfluity,'' in discussing the relationships between population, agriculture, production, and manufacturing (*Esprit des lois,* book 23, chapter 15).

28. Some of the implications of this challenge are explored in Harvey Mitchell, ''Politics in the Service of Knowledge: The Debate over the Administration of Medicine and Welfare in Late Eighteenth-Century France,'' *Social History* 6 (1981): 185–207. See also chapter 8.

29. Testifying to the influence that Montesquieu had on the generation of the *Ency-clopédistes,* Du Pont de Nemours wrote that the *Spirit of the Laws* had ''shown our nation, still so frivolous, that the study of the interest of men gathered in society could be preferable to researches into abstract metaphysics, and even more agreeable than the reading of little novels.'' See his ''Notice abrégé des différents écrits modernes qui ont concouru en France à former la science de l'économie politique,'' *Ephémérides du citoyen, ou Bibliothèque rai-sonnée des sciences morales et politiques,* 1769, 1:xii.

30. *Oeuvres de Turgot et documents le concernant, avec biographie et notes par Gustave Schelle,* 5 vols. (Paris, 1912–1923), 1:584–593, from the *Encyclopédie,* vol. 7 (1757). Hereafter cited as ''Schelle.''

31. Schelle, 1:59–60 (articles that Turgot was to have written); Roland Mortier, ''Di-derot et l'assistance publique, ou la source et les variations de l'article 'Hôpital' de

l'*Encyclopédie*," in *Enlightenment Studies in Honour of Lester G. Crocker,* ed. Alfred J. Bingham and Virgil W. Topazio (Oxford, 1979), 175–185. See Piarron de Chamousset's "Plan général pour l'administration des hôpitaux du royaume et pour le banissement de la mendicité," in *Vues d'un citoyen,* 2 vols. (Paris, 1757).

32. On Véron de Forbonnais, see Michel Marion, *Histoire financière de la France depuis 1715,* vol. 1, *1715–1789* (Paris, 1914), 195. Jaucourt's article *"Mendiants"* in the *Encyclopédie,* vol. 10 (1765), draws from François Véron de Forbonnais, *Recherches et considérations sur les finances de France, depuis 1595 jusqu'en 1721,* 6 vols. (Liège, 1758), 1:255. The late Robert Shackleton kindly guided me to this source.

33. For a review of similar doctrines, see Edgar S. Furniss, *The Position of the Laborer in a System of Nationalism* (Boston, 1920).

34. On these issues, see Steven L. Kaplan, *Bread, Politics and Political Economy in the Reign of Louis XV,* 2 vols. (The Hague, 1976), especially 1:228 and 249, and 2:435.

35. B.N. Joly de Fleury 1309, fol. 137–138. In his first letter Silhouette paid a compliment to the former intendant's father, "who knew how important it is to public order that such begging not be allowed by those able to earn their subsistence." On the Joly de Fleury dynasty, see the introduction to Auguste Molinier, *Inventaire sommaire de la collection Joly de Fleury* (Paris, 1881). On Jean-Francois' role as a councillor, see Michel Antoine, *Le conseil du roi sous le règne de Louis XV* (Paris, 1970), 10, 15, 17, 19, and 22. On his role as controller-general following Necker in 1781, see J. F. Bosher, *French Finances, 1770–1795: From Business to Bureaucracy* (Cambridge, 1970), 166–182. See also the negative anecdotes in Douglas Dakin, *Turgot and the Ancien Regime in France* (New York, 1965), 241, and *Journal et mémoires du marquis d'Argenson,* ed. J. B. Rathéry, vol. 6 (Paris, 1864), 437.

36. B.N. Joly de Fleury 1309, fol. 139. On the theme of "moral contagion," see Steven Kaplan, "Réflexions sur la police du monde du travail, 1700–1815," *RH* 529 (1979): 53. See also Michel Foucault, *Surveiller et punir: naissance de la prison* (Paris, 1975), 197–201. For an account of the intendant of Burgundy's discomfiture at the hands of Mandrin and his band at Bourg-en-Bresse on October 5, 1754, see René Fonvieille, *Mandrin* (Grenoble, 1975), 95–96.

37. B.N. Joly de Fleury 1309, fol. 144 and 147. For further detail on these points, de Fleury refers to "M. Boullongne, intendant des finances." Boullongne's inquiries of 1746 and 1753 are mentioned in the undated "Réflexions sur les lettres et mémoires concernant les mendiants relativement à la ville de Rennes," A.D. Ille-et-Vilaine, C.1288. Correspondence of 1749 and 1750 from Boullongne relating to reports on hospitals are in A.D. Indre-et-Loire, C.305.

38. B.N. Joly de Fleury 1309, fol. 148. The significance of the term *chartre privée* is explained in the *Encyclopédie méthodique par ordre de matières: dictionnaire de jurisprudence,* vol. 2 (Paris, 1783), article "CHARTRE ou prison." Once used to denote a prison, the term *chartre* was no longer used in that sense: "however, the term *chartre privée* is still applied to a place other than a public prison, where someone is detained by force without the authority of justice." It is essentially a concept of false imprisonment. The article adds, "The ordinance of 1670, title 2, article 10, forbids the *prévôts de maréchaux* to establish a *chartre privée* in their house or elsewhere on pain of removal from office; and requires that upon being apprehended the accused shall be taken to the prisons of that place, if there be any, or otherwise to those nearest, within twenty-four hours at the latest." De Fleury's remark concerning *chartre privée* is on fol. 148 of his memoir.

39. Fol. 155.

40. Ibid. Marcel Marion, *Dictionnaire des institutions de la France aux xviie et xviiie siècles* (1923; Paris, 1968), article "récolement," 173: "En matière criminelle, récoler un temoin, c'était lui faire lecture de sa déposition et lui demander s'il y persistait et s'il avait

quelque modification à y faire.'' It was in effect a check upon self-incrimination and altered testimony.

41. Fol. 159.

42. Fol. 172.

43. Fol. 148 and 163.

44. Fol. 168–170.

45. Fol. 169.

46. Fol. 151 and 172ff.

47. Fol. 169 and 172ff. He also suggested that Boutin be asked for a list of the sums deposited with him in the *caisse des pauvres,* and a statement of the number of poor arrested and fed from 1725 to 1727, and of expenses for provisions and maintenance.

48. Marion, *Histoire financière,* 195–198. For an example of the literature comparing English and French economic strengths, see Plumart de Dangeul (pseud. John Nickolls), *Remarques sur les avantages et les désavantages de la France et de la Grande-Bretagne, par rapport au commerce et aux autres sources de la puissance des états* (Leyden, 1754).

49. On the ''liberty lobby,'' see Steven Kaplan, *Bread, Politics, and Political Economy, in the Reign of Louis XV* (The Hague, 1976), 120–125. For an early discussion of mendicity in an economic context, see Claude Dupin, ''Sur les mendians et les enfans trouvés,'' in *Oeconomiques,* 2 vols. (1745; Paris, 1913), 177–191. Dupin excerpts *règlements* drawn up by ''two magistrates who have served in various *intendances.''*

50. Kaplan, *Bread, Politics and Political Economy,* 1:123; Georges Weulersse, *Le mouvement physiocratique en France (de 1756 à 1770),* 2 vols. (Paris, 1910), 1:83.

51. See Guy Caire, ''Bertin, ministre physiocrate,'' *Revue d'histoire économique et sociale* 38:3 (1960): 257–284; Michel Antoine, ''Le secrétariat d'état de Bertin (1763–1780),'' *Positions des thèses soutenues par les élèves de la promotion de 1948 pour obtenir le diplôme d'archiviste paléographe—école nationale des chartes* (Paris, 1948); and Marcel Marion, *Histoire financière,* vol. 1, 199–204.

52. Weulersse, *Mouvement physiocratique,* 1:80. In 1760, Daniel Trudaine persuaded Bertin to set up the agricultural societies and coordinate their activities by means of a committee of the royal council; the intendant of Paris, de Sauvigny, was on the first committee. For these details, see Michel Antoine, ''Les comités des ministres sous le règne de Louis XV,'' *Revue historique de droit français et étranger,* 1951, 196–228, especially 214–215. The fullest documentation on Bertin's activities is to be found in André Bourde, *Agronomie et agronomes en France au XVIIIᵉ siècle,* 3 vols. (Paris, 1967).

53. Weulersse, *Mouvement physiocratique,* 1:422 (Bertin to agricultural society of Paris, April 1, 1763); Henri Sée, *Vie économique et classes sociales au 18ᵉ siècle* (Paris, 1924), 11 (citing letter to society of Caen).

54. A.N. H.1502. The intendant of Orleans, Cypierre, probably encouraged Le Trosne. Émile Justin, *Les sociétés royales d'agriculture au dix-huitième siècle (1757–1793)* (Saint-Lô, 1935), 374, cites the archives of the *intendance,* since destroyed in World War II, in connection with Le Trosne's memoir. The memoir was printed immediately: Guillaume François Le Trosne, *Mémoire sur les vagabonds et sur les mendiants* (Soissons and Paris, 1764). See also Jérôme Mille, *Un physiocrate oublié: G.-F. Le Trosne (1728–1780)* (1905; New York, 1971).

55. Le Trosne, *Mémoire sur les vagabonds,* 14.

56. Ibid., 9.

57. Ibid., 39.

58. Ibid., 55.

59. Ibid., 56.

60. Ibid., 26.

61. Ibid., 37 and 61.

62. Ibid., 32.

63. Ibid., 58.

64. Ibid., 70.

65. Ibid., 65.

66. Ibid., 67–70.

67. Letter from Michel to Parent, February 28, 1763, A.N. H.1502. For the hesitations of royal policy, see Jacques Depauw, "Pauvres, pauvres mendiants, mendiants valides ou vagabonds? Les hésitations de la législation royale," *RHMC* 21 (July–September 1974), 401–418.

68. A.D. Aisne, C.701.

69. Weulersse, *Mouvement physiocratique,* 1:88. The reply of the subdelegate of Guise, also in A.D. Aisne, C.701, was dated July 20, 1763.

70. Antoine, "Secrétariat d'état de Bertin," 12; Kaplan, *Bread, Politics and Political Economy,* 1:140. On Laverdy's commission, see the standard works of Camille Bloch, *Assistance et l'état,* 157–178; and Christian Paultre, *Répression,* 381–405. In setting up a special commission to prepare legislation on mendicity, Laverdy followed a practice commonly used in organizing the work of royal councils; on this, see Antoine, "Les comités des ministres" (note 52 above), 221.

71. Maurice Bordes, "La réforme municipale du contrôleur général Laverdy et son application dans certaines provinces," *RHMC* 12 (October–December 1965): 241–270. The phrase "esclave des parlements" is applied to Laverdy in the context of Turgot's review of mendicity, B.N. f.f. 8129, fol. 119.

72. Charles Clément-François de l'Averdy, *Code pénal,* 2 parts bound in a single volume (Paris, 1752), 1:39 and 42; 2:123 and 125. We have followed the spelling common in modern French scholarship, "Laverdy."

73. B.N. f.f. 8129, fol. 127–129.

74. Bannefroy, *Mémoire sur la mendicité par M. Bannefroy, ancien inspecteur des maisons de force et des dépôts de mendicité du royaume* (Paris, 1791), 22. Brienne would later refer to the work of Laverdy's commission as "une besogne tronquée" (B.N. f.f. 8129, fol. 119).

75. See, in addition to the *Almanach royal,* Caix de Saint-Aymour, *Les Boullongne, une famille d'artistes et de financiers aux xviie et xviiie siècles* (Paris, 1919), especially 117ff. and 147. This work tells almost nothing about the official duties of the father and son, but amply conveys their ambition and taste for sumptuous expenditure. A document of August 21, 1769, relating to the *dépôt* at Rennes, refers to "fonds ordonné par lettre de M. de Boullongne et de M. Le Clerc, d'après des ordres particuliers de M. le Controlleur-général": A.D. Ille-et-Vilaine, C.1297. See also Joly de Fleury's memoir of 1759, cited on p. 38.

76. See the introduction to *Lettres de M. de Marville, lieutenant-général de police, au ministre Maurepas (1742–1747),* ed. A. de Boislisle, 2 vols. (Paris, 1896), which contains a few scattered references to the police of beggars (1:lxxvii; 2:39 and 119). See also the entry for Feydeau de Marville in François Bluche, *Les magistrats du grand conseil au xviiie siècle, 1680–1791* (Paris, 1966), and Antoine, *Conseil du Roi,* 625. Following Marville's report of December 27, 1765, on his six-month mission to Pau, the king rewarded him with a place on the *conseil royal des finances* and increased appointments (Antoine, *Conseil du Roi,* 133 and 185).

77. *Dictionnarie de biographie française,* ed. Prévost and Roman d'Amat, vol. 6 (Paris, 1954), s.v. "Bourgeois de Boynes, Pierre-Étienne." See also Alexandre Estignard, *Le parlement de Franche-Comté, de son installation à Besançon à sa suppression, 1674–1790* (Paris, 1892), 1:295.

78. Jules Flammermont, *Le chancelier Maupeou et les parlements* (Paris, 1895), 346–349. See also Edgar Faure, *La disgrâce de Turgot* (Paris, 1961), 29. Maupeou helped promote

de Boynes to the position of *secrétaire d'état* and is said to have recommended him to the king as the best man to succeed to the post of chancellor in the event of his own death.

79. Archives hospitaliers de Besançon, Aumône-Générale, XIX, fol. 142v. (deliberations of July 1, 1757) and fol. 214v., "Mémoire sur l'état actuel de l'hôpital Royal des mendians dit de Bellevaux établi à Besançon," dated July 15, 1762. On the regime of Bellevaux in 1759, see the winning entry for the prize offered by the academy of Besançon in that year, "Essai sur la question proposée pour indiquer les meilleures manières d'occuper les pauvres en Franche-Comté relativement aux besoins et aux ressources de cette province et principalement de la ville de Besançon, par Mr Puricelli négotiant en la même ville," Bibliothèque Municipale de Besançon, MS 1781 (d'Auxiron collection), fol. 442–470.

80. Jean-Baptiste d'Auxiron elaborated his ideas and promoted them for over thirty years; his memoirs and related papers are contained in Bibliothèque Municipale de Besançon, MS 1781, beginning chronologically with fol. 399–440, "Ouvrage fait par M. d'Auxiron juge gouverneur de la justice de vicomté et ancienne mairie de Besançon sur la meilleure manière d'occuper les pauvres en Franche-Comté." An expanded memoir appears to have been sent in response to Bertin's inquiries in 1763 (loose page at fol. 370).

81. Louis Gabriel Taboureau des Réaux was intendant at Valenciennes from 1764 to 1775 (Vivian Gruder, *The Royal Provincial Intendants: A Governing Elite in Eighteenth-Century France* [Ithaca, N.Y. 1968], 252); he served as a figurehead controller-general after de Clugny's death late in 1776, allowing Necker to serve as de facto minister. Taboureau's role on the commission must have been limited to the very early stages of its work. His successor, Dupleix de Bacquencourt, cannot have contributed actively beyond June 1764, since he accompanied Marville on a mission to Pau. On their return in December, de Bacquencourt was rewarded with a pension and the intendancy of La Rochelle, where he served for a year before being named intendant at Amiens (1767–1771), from which he went to Rennes. See Henri Fréville, *L'intendance de Bretagne (1689–1790),* 3 vols. (Rennes, 1953), 2:347. On de Crosne, see Gruder, *Intendants,* 252. According to Gruder, the Thiroux and Dupleix families were both "new," having risen through local offices, finance, and robe titles. Both men had been involved in bringing about a review in royal council in 1765 of Jean Calas's condemnation by the parlement of Toulouse, winning the praise of Voltaire (Grunder, 85 and 88n.; Fréville, 2:348n.). Thiroux de Crosne was *lieutenant-général de police* of Paris in 1789.

82. B.N. f.f. 8129, fol. 126v., states specifically that Bertier was *adjoint* to de Crosne in July 1766. See the articles on Louis-Jean Bertier de Sauvigny and his son Louis-Bénigne-François in Prévost and Amat, eds., *Dictionnaire de biographie française,* vol. 6 (Paris, 1954).

83. In an article concerning the hospital of La Charité at Lyons, the editors of the *Journal oeconomique* articulated the view that it was "an important service to the country *[patrie]* and to one's fellow citizens, to teach them a sure method for augmenting the resources of hospitals, or diminishing their burdens, without retrenching what is required for the charitable care of the poor" (November 1753). See also Harry Payne, *Philosophes and the People,* 126.

84. *Journal oeconomique,* October 1764, 442–448.

85. *Journal oeconomique,* February 1765, 49–56; Abbé Nicolas Baudeau, *Idées d'un citoyen sur les besoins, les droits et les devoirs des vrais pauvres,* 2 parts in one volume (Amsterdam and Paris, 1765). See also Camille Bloch, *Assistance et l'état,* 141n., 148, and passim; and the "Notice sur la vie et les travaux de l'abbé Baudeau," in *Physiocrates. Quesnay, Dupont de Nemours, Mercier de la Rivière, l'abbé Baudeau, Le Trosne, avec une introduction sur la doctrine des physiocrates, des commentaires et des notices historiques par M. Eugène Daire* (1846; Osnabruck, 1966), 1:645–654.

86. *Journal oeconomique,* February 1765, 49–56.

87. Baudeau, *Idées d'un citoyen,* 1:4, 156, 177, 191; 2:4, 98.

88. Ibid., 2:4. Cf. Weulersse, *Mouvement physiocratique,* 1:104. Baudeau went so far as to defend a right to beg where the needy were not provided for (*Éphémérides du citoyen,* 1767, 9:218). His brief note follows the second installment of Mirabeau's reflections on mendicity, which embody the dominant themes of the Physiocratic polemic.

Chapter 3

1. "Déclaration du Roi, concernant les vagabonds, et gens sans aveu, donnée à Compiègne le 3 août 1764," printed *affiche* in A.D. Ille-et-Vilaine, C.1295, and other departmental archives; also in B.N. f.f. 8129, fol. 103–104v.

2. B.N. f.f. 8129, fol. 225. Copies of the *Résultat* accompany the Declaration in the files of the *intendances,* as at A.D. Ille-et-Vilaine, C.1295, and A.D. Yonne, C.196.

3. B.N. f.f. 8129, fol. 127 (memoir by Bertier de Sauvigny).

4. Ibid., fol. 225v.–226.

5. Ibid., fol. 226.

6. A.D. Ille-et-Vilaine, C.1295. The parlement of Paris registered the Declaration August 21, with the petition "sera le Roi très-humblement supplié de venir au secours des hôpitaux, mentionnés en l'article VII de ladite Déclaration, dans le cas de l'insuffisance de leurs revenus, & d'y pourvoir en la forme portée par l'article VIII."

7. See especially B.N. Joly de Fleury 1309, fol. 149–153, and compare the *Résultat.* Specifically, de Fleury argued for keeping establishments small and simple. Reckoning there were thirty thousand beggars to be arrested in all of France or about one thousand per *généralité,* de Fleury suggested four, five, or six houses in each *généralité,* so that there would be no more than two hundred beggars in each. Each house would include separate rooms for healthy and ill, men and women, with "salles et chambres hautes pour les invalides, estropiés et enfants de l'un et l'autre sexe."

8. Fontette to Laverdy, March 29, 1765, A.D. Calvados, C.648.

9. Writing on September 1, Baudry claimed that the Declaration of August 3 had already dispersed many beggars; A.D. Yonne, C.196, "Mémoire sur les moyens d'empescher la mendicité publique."

10. Ballainvilliers, October 11, 1764, A.D. Puy-de-Dôme, C.1085. Baudry at Sens, in the memoir cited, argued that very few of the domiciled beggars were able to work. Baudry, who claimed to base his remarks on empirical data, seemed to contradict some of his harsh strictures against the idle in what he said about the needy poor.

11. According to Baudry, *arrêts du conseil* of October 2, 1755, and February 14, 1758, had farmed out the municipal *octrois* of 8s. 6d. per *muid* of wine set aside for this purpose to one François Haquin through 1767.

12. A.D. Puy-de-Dôme, C.1085; letter of October 11, 1764.

13. See for example the recommendation of the intendant of Châlons-sur-Marne in a letter to Laverdy of September 30, 1764, in A.D. Marne, C.2000.

14. A.D. Ille-et-Vilaine, C.1295. The text of the "Lettre écrite par ordre de Sa Majesté, aux Archeveques et Eveques du Royaume, concernant les mandians," is identified as St. Florentin's letter in Laverdy's circular to intendants dated August 2, 1764.

15. Ibid., "Mémoire sur ce qui s'est passé en 1764 en Bretagne au sujet de la mendicité."

16. A.D. Yonne, C.196 (memoir cited above, note 9); A.D. Puy-de-Dôme, C.1085 (letter cited above, note 12); A.D. Ille-et-Vilaine, C.1288, letter of de Prémion from Nantes, October 21, 1766.

17. A.D. Ille-et-Vilaine, C.1288, "Réflexions sur les lettres et mémoires concernant les

mendiants, relativement à la ville de Rennes.'' As an indicator of the scope of the problem of child abandonment, Olwen Hufton notes that when Rennes was rebuilt after the fire of 1720, a disused drain was found to contain over eighty small skeletons. See Hufton, ''The Rise of the People: Life and Death among the Very Poor,'' in *The Eighteenth Century—Europe in the Age of Enlightenment,* ed. Alfred Cobban (London, 1969), 302.

18. Laverdy to intendants, September 5, 1764, A.D. Marne, C.2000, and A.D. Ille-et-Vilaine, C.1295: ''la publication de cette loy vous fait connoître combien il est instant, s'il n'y a pas d'établissement d'hôpitaux et maisons de force dans votre généralité, de prendre des mesures pour y suppléer, à l'effet d'y renfermer ceux qui seront dans le cas d'y être détenus aux termes de cette déclaration.''

19. A.D. Indre-et-Loire, C.302; minutes of letters of August 11 and September 8, 1764, to Laverdy, and ''Mémoire du Bureau de l'hôpital général de Tours, 21 septembre, 1764.'' The estimates included beds and bedding (4,000 l.), sheets and shirts (6,000 l.), provisional repairs (3,000 l.), and clothing (2,000 l.) The memoir observed that article 3 of the hospital's letters patent forbade entry of the *maréchaussée.*

20. Ibid., letter of Lescalopier to Laverdy, November 19, 1764.

21. Ibid., Laverdy to Lescalopier, December 10, 1764. The letter warns against confusing the Declaration of August 3 with the forthcoming measure on beggary. The *dépôts* would not be used for the able-bodied convicts destined for the galleys, who were to be kept in secure prisons. Hospitals should be able to house the small number expected in the category of vagabonds unsuited for the galleys by age, sex, or infirmity. However, an overflow was anticipated when the forthcoming law went into effect against beggars.

22. A.D. Yonne, C.196; Bertier to de Baudry, Paris, September 1, 1764 (signed ''Bertier pour mon père''); reply of Baudry November 13 with accompanying memoir, ''Observations sur le inconvéniens qu'il y aurait de proposer l'hôpital général de Sens pour servir de maison de force et sur le Bureau de correspondence et d'aumône générale que l'on a dessein d'établir pour bannir la mendicité.''

23. A.D. Ille-et-Vilaine, C.1288, ''Réflexions sur les lettres et mémoires concernant les mendiants, relativement à la ville de Rennes.''

24. A.D. Ille-et-Vilaine, C.1295. Laverdy's letter of October 30 to Le Bret merely asked the intendant to look for *anciens bâtiments* suitable as *dépôts;* Le Bret's questionnaire to his subdelegates asked for a survey of hospital facilities, and followed this with questions pertaining to the establishment of a provisional *dépôt* to be used until a new hospital could be built, if none existed. Laverdy praised de Flesselles in a letter of October 19, 1766.

25. A.D. Ille-et-Vilaine, C.1288.

26. A.N. K683; ''Copie de la lettre de M.^r le Controlleur-Général écrite à MM. les Elus le 18 décembre, 1764.''

27. Ibid.; Laverdy to *élus* of Burgundy, April 30, 1766. See also Marcel Bolotte, *Les hôpitaux et l'assistance dans la province de Bourgogne au dernier siècle de l'ancien regime* (Dijon, 1968), 21–22. Laverdy referred to a forthcoming edict to be registered by the parlement in his correspondence with the *élus* (cf. correspondence with de Flesselles in Brittany, A.D. Ille-et-Vilaine, C.1295).

28. Josseline Guyader, ''La répression de la mendicité et du vagabondage dans la ville de Toulouse depuis la déclaration de 1724 jusqu'à la Révolution de 1789,'' D.E.S. en droit, Toulouse, 1966, 205–212. The influential subdelegate of Toulouse, Raynal, reported that the hospital had a capacity of 2,500, with separate facilities for the insane and a *quartier de la force* for women of ill repute. Six large vacant rooms could be converted to house 450 inmates under the new law proposed. Laverdy explained that the king intended to return the poor to their parishes, as had been done in Lorraine and Flanders, ''où il n'y a pas de pauvres.'' The *dépôts* would be used only as *''prisons provisoires'';* ''on y retiendra les mendiants le temps nécessaire pour prendre les renseignements sur leur naissance et sur leur

conduite." Laverdy also stigmatized hospitals as being "bien plus capables d'entretenir et favoriser l'oisiveté que de la prévenir," in a letter of February 1, 1765, to the intendant of Roussillon, cited by Pierre Lunel, "Les intendants de Roussillon et les questions sociales dans la seconde moitié du XVIIIᵉ siécle," D.E.S., Faculté des Lettres, Toulouse, 1970, 33.

29. Guyader, "Répression de la mendicité," 215–218, letters from Laverdy to Saint-Priest (intendant of Languedoc), April and October 1766. Laverdy's letter of October 19, 1766, agreed to using the Hôpital de la Grave, "a condition que les administrateurs des hôpitaux n'inspectent pas les mendiants, que les maréchaussées aient un libre accès dans les bâtiments où ils seront enfermés et qu'enfin l'intendant ait l'entière administration."

30. H. Monin, *L'état de Paris en 1788, études et documents sur l'ancien régime à Paris* (Paris, 1889), 259–260, citing the account given to the parlement by Séguier on July 31, 1778, in A.N. X¹ᴮ 8971.

31. Gutton, *Société et les pauvres,* 459.

32. La Charité, Lyons, E 74 (archival inventory); B.N. f.f. 8129, fol. 107 and 158.

33. A.N. F¹⁵ 232, "Règlement général de police pour la suppression de la mendicité dans la ville de Strasbourg."

34. B.N. f.f. 8129, fol. 129v. See background on Joly de Fleury in chapter 2. The father's remark on being "between two fires" occurs in a letter to d'Aguesseau, January 13, 1741, B.N. Joly de Fleury 1307, fol. 253.

35. See Michel Antoine, *Le Conseil du roi sous Louis XV* (Paris, 1970), 486 and note, based on the manuscript journal of de Boynes. The journal entry for May 18, 1765, states: "À l'occasion du projet de déclaration pour bannir la mendicité, il a été question au Comité de peu de service de la maréchaussée et des inconvénients qui résultant de la dernière ordonnance de M. de Belle-Isle [du 19 avril 1760—Antoine's note], qui ne laisse aux intendants aucune autorité sur la maréchaussée. M. de Choiseul a paru très disposé à revenir sur cet objet, pourvu que cela puisse se concilier avec MM. les maréchaux de France."

36. B.N. f.f. 8129, fol. 129v.

37. Ibid. See Paolo Alatri, "Parlements et lutte politique en France au xviiiᵉ siècle," *SVEC* 151 (1976): 77–108, for a review of issues; see p. 93 on the *lit de justice* of March 3, 1766, in which the king denounced the claim of the parlements to act in unison.

38. B.N. f.f. 8129, fol. 1v.; Bannefroy, *Mémoire sur la mendicité,* 22–23.

39. B.N. f.f. 8129, fol. 133. The draft *règlement* on alms bureaus and commentary on it is found in Ibid., fol. 217–224.

40. On the role of *syndics* in the village community, see Jean-Pierre Gutton, *La sociabilité villageoise dans l'ancienne France* (Paris, 1979), 69ff.

41. B.N. f.f. 8129, fol. 188v. (article 10 of the draft edict); see also fol. 130v. For Joly de Fleury's view, see p. 37.

42. En route to the *dépôt*, beggars were to be kept in "prisons des lieux de passage comme prisons empruntées." The legal meaning of the word *dépôt* appears to be associated with that of a *prison empruntée*. A circular from the controller-general Dodun, December 20, 1724, drew attention to the fact that many prisons were not sufficiently secure to "mettre en dépost" the beggars arrested by the *maréchaussée* under the Declaration of 1724 (A.D. Ille-et-Vilaine, C.1288). At that time, of course, the beggars were en route to confinement in *hôpitaux-généraux*.

43. Since objection was raised against branding, the text of article 29 is of special interest: "Lad. marque n'apportera pas note d'infamie, et pourra être prononcée sans recollement ou confrontation sur le vu du procès-verbal de capture, de l'interrogatoire de l'accusé et des conclusions de nos Procureurs, sans qu'il soit besoin de plus amples procédures et instructions. Sauf aux Juges à prendre tels éclaircissements qu'il appartiendra, même à ordonner qu'il sera entendu des témoins, si la preuve de la mendicité ne leur paroissoit pas suffisamment acquise." Article 27 exempted those under sixteen from branding.

44. Bertier's summary, B.N. f.f. 8129, fol. 129–140, has been used as a guide to identify the texts collected in the *Recueil*. The basic working draft of the edict approved by the
king in June, after unofficial consultations with the premier president of the parlement and
the *gens du roy,* is the text copied on fol. 187–193. The critical observations of the *procureur-général* following his consultations with members of the parlement are the "Observations sur le Projet d'édit," fol. 181–184.

45. Ibid., fol. 183. See p. 37 and note 40 on the procedure in question. A concern for the niceties of due process was also evident in the remark, "On ne peut pas dire
qu'un homme qui sera convaincu sera emprisonné, car pour le convaincre il faut l'avoir
emprisonné."

46. Ibid., fol. 182–183.

47. For a definition of *chartre privé,* see above, Chapter 2, note 38. These and the points
preceding illustrate a coherent if paternalistic defense of the rights and interests of the poorer
ranks of the Third Estate. On this theme, see the nuanced discussion in Bailey Stone, *The
French Parlements and the Crisis of the Old Regime* (Durham, N.C., 1986), especially 106,
113, and 209.

48. B.N. f.f. 8129, fol. 184. This brief passage touches on three key issues: (1) skepticism concerning the capacity for administrative responsibility at the local level, even as
Laverdy was implementing a municipal reform that would increase that responsibility; (2)
awareness of the degree to which ordinary citizens might identify with beggars; and (3)
awareness of the likelihood that any modification in fiscal burdens would be regarded in the
most suspicious light at the local level.

49. Letter of d'Aguesseau to the *procureur-général,* March 29, 1733, B.N. Joly de Fleury
1307, fol. 37. See above, note 43.

50. B.N. f.f. 8129, fol. 205. Bertier's summary, fol. 129v.–130, corresponds to the
memoir identified in the margin with the notation "M. de Fleury, c^{eiller} d'état" and entitled,
"Réponses aux observations envoyées par M. le Procureur Général sur le projet d'Edit concernant les mendiants," fol. 205–208.

51. Ibid., fol. 207.

52. Ibid., fol. 207. This position is anticipated in de Fleury's memoir of 1759; see p. 37
and note 43.

53. Ibid., fol. 209–210, "Dernières observations, auxquelles on s'est réduit, d'après les
réponses aux premières observations," and fol. 211–212v., "Réponses aux nouvelles observations," with the note in the margin, "de Fleury, Consllr."

54. Ibid., fol. 212v. ("Dernières observations").

55. Ibid., fol. 129v.–130 (Bertier's summary).

56. Bertier's memoir, written in the first person, is not identified and appears not to have
been previously attributed to him; B.N. no. acq. 943, fol. 270–273v. The B.N. catalogs
identify the volume in which the manuscript is bound as part of the collection of a *conseiller*
of the parlement of Paris, Lefebvre d'Ammécourt. Other documents in this collection are
copies of memoirs by Bertier, including his summary on mendicity presented to Laverdy in
1766, fol. 196–269v. (cf. B.N. f.f. 8129, fol. 119–140). The dates of the documents and
their range suggest that the collection may have been assembled in connection with a review
of the *dépôts* undertaken in 1783 by the controller-general Lefebvre d'Ormesson. This memoir appears to be a transcription of Bertier's report to Turgot's commission meeting at Montigny in October 1775; see the beginning of Chapter 4, and Chapter 7, note 91.

57. B.N. f.f. 8129, fol. 131, in "Mémoire expositif de ce qui s'est fait depuis 1764 et
années suivantes," fol. 119–140 (with marginal note: "Ce compte a été rendu en 1766 par
M. Bertier à M. de Laverdy").

58. Ibid., fol. 133. The reference to the *maréchaussée* is omitted (presumably a mere
copying error) in the version in B.N. n. acq. fr. 943, fol. 244.

59. Ibid., fol. 133.

60. Ibid., fol. 133v. The mechanism whereby local communities were to support their own poor was spelled out in a "Projet de Règlement concernant les Bureaux d'Aumône" (fol. 217–220v.); as Bertier notes (fol. 133), this was not proposed as a law, but rather as an "exhortation."

61. Bertier's summary, fol. 133v.–134, is apparently the only source for this final round of objections; the *Recueil* documents do not include the final counterproposal of the parlement in thirty-two articles, mentioned by Bertier, nor the version of the same length drafted by an unnamed individual and passed on to the commission by Laverdy. An indication of the *parlementaires'* concerns as urban residents holding properties in rural parishes may be inferred from their objection to the procedure for representing nonresidents in the assemblies of the *bureaux d'aumône,* in "Observations sur le Règlement pour les Bureaux d'aumône," fol. 221; the "Réponse aux observations sur le projet de Règlement d'aumône Géneral," fol. 222–223v., may be read as an effort to reassure nonresidents *"possédant fonds."*

62. Ibid., fol. 134. The "gutted" version of the declaration is the "Projet de déclaration redigée par MM. les Commissaires pour se conformer en partie aux observations contenues dans des mémoires remis par M. le Controlleur général au mois d'avril 1767," fol. 116–119. This version omitted the mandatory local provisions for assistance to the poor, stating merely that a local *bureau d'aumône* might receive funds for the poor, and that a tax would be levied, presumably under the authority of the intendant, on all residents and owners of land in a community, in the form used for repair of churches and parsonages, or other common charges. The provision that collectors and receivers of the *taille* would advance the sums needed (article 5) was left out, as was much of the detail on procedures of arrest. Bertier noted that the commissioners felt that these omissions might be compensated for by more detailed instructions to the *maréchaussée,* and by an alternative mode of payment, but that overall the measure should be seen as "une execution très imparfaite de leurs idées et comme une loi sèche et qui étant dépouillée des détails qui pouvaient en faire sentir la sagesse ne seroit pas reçue par le public avec le même succès qu'ils avoient espéré de la première."

63. "Projet d'ordonnance du Roi redigé par MM. les Commissaires dans le cas où on ne voudroit point envoyer de loix aux Parlem^{ts}," fol. 146–147 (in eleven articles, as Bertier notes), and the "Projet d'arrêt du Conseil redigé par M. d'Aguesseau," fol. 145 (also in B.N. n. acq. fr. 943, fol. 250).

64. See above, p. 000, and B.N. f.f. 8129, fol. 135.

65. Ibid., fol. 135v.–136. D'Ormesson stated that the three deniers per livre of the *taille* was raised in twenty *généralités* and in the departments of Metz, Franche-Comté, and Roussillon, producing 629,300l. 8s. annually. D'Ormesson raised two objections: (1) although the tax was in no case alienated, it was included in the *bail des octrois* farmed out for ten years; (2) a peasant *syndic* might abuse the power relating to an imposition, so that the accounts of the receivers-general would be thrown into uncertainty.

66. Ibid., fol. 137.

67. Ibid., fol. 137. In slanting the options in favor of the sixth, Bertier perhaps revealed his own sympathy for some of the scruples of the parlement. The language is important:

> D'ailleurs il est peu de matières sur laquelle il soit plus nécessaire de donner une loi authentique. Il est question d'un côté de disposer des libertés d'un grand nombre d'hommes, et d'un autre d'ordonner une imposition nouvelle dans peut être la plus grande partie des paroisses du Royaume.
>
> Si ce motif peut être écarté par la qualité des personnes sur lesquelles la loi porte, au moins il peut servir de prétexte pour mettre des entraves à l'execution de l'opération, il peut compromettre les Intendans, les maréchaussées que les cours ne verront pas tranquillement exécuter sans leur concours une loi qu'ils ont rejettée.

The phrasing of the last sentence suggests that Bertier differed with de Fleury on the potential prejudice to the "libertés d'un grand nombre d'hommes."

68. This fifth option was embodied in the "Projet d'arrêt de conseil redigé par M. d'Aguesseau," fol. 145. Bertier's objection (fol. 138) to harsh penalties in the context of this option leads to a general statement that prefigures the systematic critique by Turgot's commission:

> En effet la mendicité par elle même n'est point un crime, elle peut n'être que la suite de malheurs et l'effet de la nécessité; dans ce cas il est bien dur peut être même cruel de leur infliger des epines graves et afflictives.
>
> Quand la mendicité est l'effet du libertinage et de la fainéantise, la peine d'être renfermé, et la nécessité du travail sont les peines qui font la plus d'impression aux mendiants de cette dernière espèce.

69. Ibid., fol. 139. Bertier also raised some technical difficulties involved in the jurisdiction of the *maréchaussée* according to the Declaration of 1731, a text that de Fleury had relied upon since writing his memoir of 1759 (B.N. Joly de Fleury 1309, fol. 156). Articles 4 and 10 placed limits on their competence and gave precedence to ordinary judges even in cases of mendicity under prescribed circumstances. On the history of jurisdiction over beggars, see Christian Paultre, *Répression de la mendicité,* 515–550, especially 548 on the Declaration of February 5, 1731.

70. Ibid., fol. 139v. In the light of his later administrative role, it is noteworthy that Bertier stressed the difficulty of controlling costs under the proposed laws:

> ce qu'il y a de sûr c'est qu'elles sont ruineuses pour le Roy; elles le dépouillent d'un revenu certain d'environ 630,000 tandis qu'elles le chargent de la nourriture et renferme-ment de tous les mendians et étrangers, des invalides, des femmes, des mendians repris une seconde fois, de tous les vagabonds, de la nourriture de ces gens pendant toute l'instruction de leurs procès, de la translation de ceux des mendians qui sortiront des dépôts pour s'en retourner chez eux et enfin de la construction et entretien de tous les dépôts; rien de fixe sur l'objet de ces dépenses, elles peuvent être immenses.

71. Ibid., fol. 140. Cf. p. 63.

72. Ibid., fol. 140–142, "Mémoire sur l'exécution de la déclaration du mois d'aoust 1764 concernant les vagabonds et sur les moyens de la faire suppléer pour le moment à une loi sur la mendicité," also in B.N. n. acq. fr. 943, fol. 162–169. The memoir mentions a brief term of confinement for beggars, from three weeks to one month.

73. Ibid., fol. 142.

74. Ibid., fol. 142–144v. The untitled memoir begins with the words, "Le premier plan adopté par M. le Contrôleur général avoit pour base de faire une opération qui ne peut être barrée sous aucune prétexte par les Parlements." It went on to note that the word *mendiant* would be avoided in the *arrêt du conseil,* since all the laws on mendicity placed beggars under the jurisdiction of the ordinary judges, by contrast with vagabonds, who were placed entirely under the *maréchaussée.*

This memoir, unlike the preceding one, was not included with Bertier's other memoirs in B.N. n. acq. fr. 943. Apparently composed at de Fleury's direction or from his draft, it revived his transparent fiction that the new measures could be construed as fulfilling the promise of assistance to hospitals.

75. Ibid., fol. 144. The description of the markings on the various letters implementing the new policy may be checked against the originals in A.N. F[15] 138.

76. Ibid., fol. 104v.–105, "Arrêt du Conseil du Roi, concernant les vagabonds et gens sans aveu," dated Fontainebleau, October 21, 1767.

77. A.N. 80 AP 12: "31 oct. 1767—Apperçu de la dépense que pourra occasioner le renfermement des mendians à compter du 1er novembre 1767 à l'effet de faire les fonds qui

seront necessaires à cette opération.'' This document and others from the same series are drawn from the private archives of the Bertier family deposited at the Archives Nationales, consulted with the kind permission of Comte Henry de Bertier de Sauvigny.

78. Ibid. The revisions noted appear in a *Mémoire* beginning: ''M. Bertier à été chargé des détails de l'opération de la Mendicité à compter des deux derniers mois de l'année 1767.'' Further details are from a document entitled ''Bureau du conseil—gages, pensions, attributions et traitements.'' As intendant, according to this later document, Bertier received a yearly pension of 12,000 livres, appointments of 6,000, and clerical expenses *(gages du commis)* of 1,500.

79. B.N. f.f. 8129, fol. 185–186, ''Notes sur le projet de Règlement concernant les mendiants,'' with marginal notation, ''Intendant de Paris.'' The reference could be to either father or son, especially since the marginal notations date from Turgot's ministry. Several points in the intendant's commentary appear to fit best with the numbering of articles in the earlier version of the draft edict, fol. 187–192v (article 3 on work, articles 5 and 6 involving *collecteurs,* article 16 on *chasse-pauvres,* and a reference to the *dépôt* in article 22).

80. A.D. Seine-Maritime, C.1008; Bloch, *Assistance,* 318. Letters in A.D. Indre-et-Loire, C.302, indicate that Boullongne was reponsible for coordinating financial arrangements for establishing the *dépôts,* before Bertier was put in charge at the end of 1767: Laverdy to intendant of Tours, July 15, 1765; Boullongne to intendant, July 30, 1766; memoir from intendant to controller-general, November 27, 1767, with reference to Boullongne and de Crosne.

Chapter 4

1. B.N., n. acq. fr. 943, fol. 271. The source is described above, chapter 3, note 56. The remainder of Bertier's argument is discussed on p. 150.

2. Documents on arrest procedures are in A.D. Indre-et-Loire, C.303. For general background, see F. Dumas, *La généralité de Tours au XVIIIe siècle, administration de l'intendant du Cluzel (1766–1783)* (Tours, 1894). In the documentation that follows, a reference to a second departmental archive will commonly be used to substantiate the assumption that a letter from the minister is indeed a circular. In a few cases, the general nature of the letter has been taken as an adequate indication.

3. Traces of the commissioners' work in drawing up instructions and covering letters are to be found in a *Mémoire* contained in B.N. f.f. 8129, fol. 142–145v.; the key letters implementing the arrest of beggars are transcribed from fol. 147v.–160.

4. B.N. f.f. 8129, fol. 149v.–153v., ''Instruction sur l'administration intérieure des dépôts et l'entretien et subsistence de ceux qui y seront renfermés,'' accompanied by the ''copie de la lettre de M. le Contrôleur général à MM. les Intendans,'' fol. 147v.–149. The copy of the letter in A.D. Seine-Maritime, C.1008, is dated ''le—octobre, 1767, reçu le 25.''

5. A.D. Indre-et-Loire, C.303. Bertier's cover letter in the packet of January 19 noted that the minister was aware of the burden of paperwork imposed by the new operation and advised the intendant that he would entertain requests for gratifications to be paid to the clerk responsible for it in the intendant's bureau.

6. Ibid. Choiseul's letter is not in B.N. f.f. 8129. A.N. F[15] 965 contains correspondence from the late 1780s that reflects La Millière's efforts to make the payment of a gratification contingent upon a strict adherence to general policies on arrest. In a letter of July 19, 1787, to a de Trimond, La Millière rejects a claim for higher gratifications, demands stricter execution, and restates the standard allotment: 1 l. 5s. for the lieutenant, 1 l. for the *greffier,* and 3 l. for the *cavalier* making the arrest, for a total of 5 l. 5s. The bonus of 3 l. to the arresting officers was the amount initially established under Laverdy, according to Colin Jones, *Char-*

ity and Bienfaisance: The Treatment of the Poor in the Montpellier Region, 1740–1815 (New York, 1983), 173 and Iain Cameron, *Crime and Repression in the Auvergne and the Guyenne, 1720–1790* (New York, 1981), 107.

7. B.N. f.f. 8129, fol. 154–155; A.D. Indre-et-Loire, C.303.

8. The original language of this paragraph and the preceding one reads as follows:

> Sur l'interrogatoire que vous communiquerez au Procureur du Roi, vous rendrez une ordonnance sans autre forme de procédure ni d'instruction, laquelle portera que l'interrogé sera conduit au dépôt. Cette ordonnance peut être conçue en ces termes.
>
> Et vu ce qui résulte du procès-verbal de capture, de l'interrogatoire et du procès-verbal de la vérification des réponses du Prisonier, après le tout a été communiqué au Procureur du Roi, nous ordonnons que le dit . . . sera conduit à . . . (lieu du dépôt) pour y être détenu jusqu'à ce qu'autrement il en ait été ordonné.

9. Laverdy to du Cluzel, January 19, 1768, A.D. Indre-et-Loire, C.303; text the same as B.N. f.f. 8129, fol. 147v.–149, "Copie de la lettre de M. le Contrôleur général à MM. les Intendans." The fact that intendants received a fuller explanation of the motive for policy than the *maréchaussée* may reflect the distinction between "executors" and "administrators" mentioned on p. 68.

10. Although the domiciled are here favored on grounds of equity, it was later argued that the distinction had been a matter of administrative convenience only (see p. 78).

11. Tocqueville pointed to the portentous use of the term "administrative correction" in correspondence relating to the *dépôt de mendicité* at Rouen, in *L'ancien régime et la Révolution*, ed. J.-P. Mayer (Paris, 1951–1964), vol. 2, part 1:307 ("Exemple de la manière dont on procédait souvent à l'égard des paysans").

12. B.N. f.f. 8129, fol. 335, and B.N. Joly de Fleury 1309, fol. 186, reproduced in Christian Paultre, *Dé la répression de la mendicité et du vagabondage* (Paris, 1906), 603–604, and in Olwen Hufton, *The Poor of Eighteenth-Century France 1750–1789* (Oxford, 1974), 389. See Cameron, *Crime and Repression* 159, on the leniency of the courts.

13. An earlier memoir to Laverdy (see p. 68), bearing some marks of de Fleury's thinking, recommended three *year* terms of detention and argued that the Declaration of 1750 gave intendants, as substitute hospital administrators, the right to set terms of detention. The short terms and procedural safeguards first adopted may reflect Bertier's initial ideal of making the *dépôt* a simple way station, and a desire on his part to satisfy any scruples on the point of false imprisonment.

14. Choiseul sent du Cluzel the original of his letter of February 8, 1768, so that the intendant might forward it to the *prévôt* with a covering letter of his own. The paperwork Choiseul required was almost as onerous as that imposed by the ill-fated correspondence bureau of 1724.

15. Laverdy to intendant of Tours, February 19, 1768, A.D. Indre-et-Loire, C.303; the same circular is in A.D. Seine-Maritime, C.1008.

16. Du Cluzel had first complained of the slow pace of arrests in a letter of March 29, 1768, shortly after Laverdy had sent instructions on record-keeping within the *dépôt* (March 16), A.D. Indre-et-Loire, C.303.

17. Ibid.; the circulars are all dated July 20. A copy of the vice-chancellor's letter is in B.N. f.f. 8129, fol. 156.

18. Ibid. The response to du Cluzel's request—perhaps echoed by others of the same kind—prompted a circular from St.-Florentin allowing intendants to arrest domiciled beggars at their discretion, if they were "dangerous": B.N. f.f. 8129, fol. 157.

19. A.D. Indre-et-Loire, C.303, Choiseul to *prévôt-général de la maréchaussée* at Tours, October 15, 1768.

20. Ibid., letter from Moulon de la Chenaye, *prévôt-général* at Tours, December 18, 1768.

21. Ibid.; Maynon d'Invau to intendant of Tours, January 4, 1769, including the further instruction: "il est essentiel pour jetter plus d'ordre et de clarté dans cette opération, que toutes les déclarations faites dans les différents dépôts soient réunis dans un seul dépôt pour y avoir recours au besoin. Vous voudrez bien m'envoyer exactement celles que vous aurez fait vérifier avec le résultat des vérifications." Cf. A.D. Marne, C.2026.

22. A.N. F¹⁶ 936. The memoir in question is tied on a string with several others, to which a label "Bertier" is attached. On this set of memoirs, see also below, Chapter 6, note 4.

23. Bertier's use of the word "machine" in this context, combined with the image of releasing a "spring," suggested the title of this chapter. The notion that bureaucratic administration is a powerful machine, especially if regulated according to masses of data organized at the center, appears in other contemporary contexts. Terray's view of the police of provisioning was a break with the past in this respect, according to Steven Kaplan, *Bread, Politics and Political Economy in the Reign of Louis XV,* 2 vols. (The Hague, 1976), 546–554.

24. Copies of the circular of August 12, 1769, are in A.D. Indre-et-Loire, C.303, and A.D. Ille-et-Vilaine, C.1298. The letter authorized the arrest of all beggars, including those "qui mendient même dans le lieu de leur domicile et à ne pas faire distinction entre les mendians domiciliés at les autres, ni dans leurs punitions, ni dans la manière de procéder contr'eux."

25. Baugé had been a place for keeping those condemned to long terms and those who could not be vouched for, but du Cluzel noted that only six inmates were being held there when he asked d'Invau's permission to close it down on January 16, 1769. D'Invau assented in February 23. On the poor harvest of 1769 and du Cluzel's administrative response to it, see Shelby T. McCloy, *Government Assistance in Eighteenth-Century France* (Durham, N.C., 1946), 26–27, and Dumas, *La généralité de Tours,* 345–346.

26. The numbers remaining in the *dépôts* at the end of the year provide another indicator: 4,148 (1768), 5,851 (1769), 7,842 (1770), 9,464 (1771), and 8,838 (1772). These figures are cited in Paultre, *Répression de la mendicité,* 605, from B.N. Joly de Fleury 1309, fol. 187. See also Hufton, *Poor of Eighteenth-Century France,* 389–390.

27. "Instruction sur l'administration intérieure des dépôts et l'entretien et subsistence de ceux qui y seront renfermés," B.N. f.f. 8129, fol. 149–153. Copies in A.D. Indre-et-Loire, C.306, A.D. Marne, C.2026, and elsewhere; copy as modified for use by subdelegate, signed by intendant of Brittany, in A.N. K.911.

28. For Galiani's view that political economy was a "science of administration" based on "precise knowledge of circumstances," see Kaplan, *Bread, Politics, and Political Economy,* 596; Michel Foucault speaks of the *réseau d'écritures* in *Surveiller et punir: naissance de la prison* (Paris, 1975), 191. See also Elizabeth Eisenstein, "Some Conjectures about the Impact of Printing on Western Society and Thought: A Preliminary Report," *Journal of Modern History* 40 (March 1968): 1–56, especially 45. For a discussion of standardized paperwork imposed by the declaration of 1724, see Jean-Pierre Gutton, *L'état et la mendicité dans la première moitié du XVIIIᵉ siècle: Auvergne, Beaujolais, Forez, Lyonnais* (Lyons, 1973), 114.

29. See Michel Marion, *Dictionnaire des institutions de la France aux xviiᵉ et xviiiᵉ siècles* (1923; Paris, 1968), s.v. "casernement." Bertier enlarged the barracks of the *généralité* of Paris, according to the *Notice biographique sur M. Bertier, intendant de Paris* (Paris, 1847), 4. De Fleury, in his memoir of 1759, had referred to *lits de caserne* and *lits de corps de garde,* B.N. Joly de Fleury 1309, fol. 153–154. A retrospective memoir composed shortly after the fall of Turgot included the marginal comment, "traitement dans les dépôts au dessus de la prison au dessous de soldats," ibid., fol. 180.

30. An annotated version of the instruction at Rennes (A.D. Ille-et-Vilaine, C.1295) provides a fixed standard that apparently reflects the availability of local grains and "im-

proves'' the standard by sifting out the coarser bran: "il doit entrer dans le pain dont le gros son doit être seulement soustrait un tiers de froment et deux tiers de seigle." Although this copy of the instruction is undated, the copy in A.N. K.911 is dated April 13, 1768.

31. The women's clothes were described in the instruction as follows: "Aux femmes un corset, un cotillon, un juste de bure à chaume, et trois bonnets piqués et trois cornettes pour deux."

32. Letter from Laverdy, Versailles, December 25, 1767, A.D. Puy-de-Dôme, C.1290; reference to a similar letter in A.D. Marne, C.2026. Francois Lebrun compares the ration prescribed for the *dépôt* at Angers with other standards (the local *hôtel-Dieu*, a poor household, and a soldier) in *Les hommes et la mort en Anjou aux 17e et 18e siècles: essai de démographie et de psychologie historiques* (Paris, 1971), 273–274, and places it at the low end of the range. For other institutional comparisons, see Marie José Villemon, "À partir des sources hospitalières, l'alimentation du pauvre de l'Hôpital-général de Caen au début du XVIIIe siècle," *Annales de Normandie* 21:3 (1971): 235–260; and Yves Pottier, "La population de l'hôpital Saint-Yves de Rennes dans la 1ère moitié du 18e siècle (1710–1750)" (mémoire de maîtrise, University of Haute-Bretagne, Rennes, 1974).

For a guide to food consumption and nutritional standards in the eighteenth century, see especially Jean-Jacques Hémardinquer, *Pour une histoire de l'alimentation* (Paris, 1971); Huges Neveux, "L'alimentation du XIVe au XVIIIe siècle: essai d mise au point," *RHES* 51:3 (1973): 336–379; and Michel Morineau, "Budgets populaires en France au XVIIIe siècle—I," *RHES* 50:2 (1972): 203–237. Data from a poor region are provided in Michel C. Kiener and Jean-Claude Peyronnet, *Quand Turgot régnait en Limousin: un tremplin vers le pouvoir* (Paris, 1979), 121–130.

33. Laverdy to Monthyon, September 4, 1767, A.D. Puy-de-Dôme, C.290.

34. The instruction on bedding also suggested that mattresses stuffed with straw *(paille piquée)* might be cheaper than loose straw, and gave calculations to support the suggestion: circular from Laverdy to intendant of Champagne, January 7, 1768, A.D. Marne, C.2026; Laverdy to intendant at Caen, January 5, 1768, A.D. Calvados, C.648. For the instruction on *secours spirituels,* see Laverdy to intendant of Besançon, January 9, 1768, A.D. Doubs, C.1673 (carton 1186), and letter to intendant of Tours in A.D. Indre-et-Loire, C.303.

35. Bertier was occasionally obliged to confer with the minister of war and with the chancellor or vice-chancellor, with *intendants des finances* (especially his friend d'Ormesson), intendants de commerce (Trudaine's name appears) and various councillors of state. As *intendant des finances,* Boullongne appears to have maintained a tenuous responsibility for some financial matters pertaining to the *dépôts* in his *département.* The two most active members of Laverdy's commission, de Fleury and de Boynes, appear to have maintained an informal interest in the workings of the *dépôts.* De Boynes's name appears in a later controversy (chapter 5); de Fleury is never mentioned, but his influence may be surmised.

36. Laverdy to intendant of Tours, December 29, 1767, A.D. Indre-et-Loire, C.302; to intendant of Caen, December 25, 1767, A.D. Calvados, C.647.

37. Laverdy's follow-up questionnaire, accompanying a circular of March 24, is to be found in A.D. Calvados, C.647, and in A.D. Marne, C.2026. The answer to the questionnaire provided by the intendant at Châlons-sur-Marne provides an interesting profile of a concierge. Rémy Chauvet was at least forty years old, five feet six inches tall, and had served in artillery crews in the campaigns of 1744 and 1745. He had served for twelve years leading customs brigades against smugglers along the frontier. Married, he had daughters aged ten and three. His wife and older daughter helped him in his duties; without their help he could not discharge all the functions of his position. A single turnkey aided him. In addition to annual wages of 300 livres (plus 100 for the turnkey), the concierge received two rations of bread and the turnkey one, since the *dépôt,* being very large, required three large dogs to

guard it. Two *cavaliers* of the *maréchaussée* made rounds twice a day, and one was supposed to sleep there.

38. A.D. Doubs, C.1673; A.D. Dalvados, C.6776 (texts differ slightly).

39. A.D. Indre-et-Loire, C.303 (typical reminder on sending contracts, January 13, 1768); A.D. Marne, C.2026 (reminder on the need for building plans, March 8, 1768; intendant replied that he had sent them earlier).

40. Laverdy circular, Versailles, March 16, 1768, A.D. Indre-et-Loire, C.303, and A.D. Marne, C.2026.

41. For a positive response to this general inquiry, reflecting satisfaction with the further decision to restrict the radius within which beggars would be considered "domiciled," see the intendant of Champagne to Laverdy, August 3, 1768, A.D. Marne, C.2026.

42. Memoir from Fresnais to intendant, September 6, 1769, in A.D. Ille-et-Vilaine, C. 1298. A document of August 1, 1769 (appointment of a new concierge), gives Fresnais' official titles: "René Marie Bonaventure Fresnais, avocat au Parlement, subdélégué de l'intendant de Bretagne au Département de Rennes, chargé de la police du dépôt des mendiants établi en cette ville." He was still subdelegate and *commissaire du dépôt* in the mid-1780s. Earlier, the *dépôt* was surpervised by Jean-Baptistie François Raudin, "commissaire ordonnateur des guerres, subdélégué de l'Intendance de Bretagne," according to documents from 1767 through January 1769 (A.D. Ille-et-Vilaine, C.1298).

43. This complaint was typical. See for example that of the intendant of Champagne, June 30, 1768, to Laverdy, commenting on the drawings of the *dépôt* (A.D. Marne, C.2026). There were no workplaces except for a small one in the women's courtyard in a shed or passageway (*hangard* or *galerie*) that had been intended as a walkway (*promenoir*). A separate place could be built, perhaps with materials from the old rampart, instead of continuing to have inmates work in their rooms or on beds.

44. A.D. Ille-et-Vilaine, C.1298. The intendant told the subdelegate of Nantes in a letter of March 20, 1770, that he had desired "simplicity, security, and economy," but that the royal engineer had strayed from these criteria in the drawings he had provided. There should be no "ostentation" in the design of such buildings, and Ceineray's work at Nantes was a good example of the "economy" desired. He asked, however, that Ceineray not sign the drawings, so that they might appear to come "from the Court." Such subterfuge must have made Ceineray uncomfortable, and he stalled for various reasons before submitting the drawings to the subdelegates, who sent them on to d'Agay on March 20, 1770.

45. The new bishop of Rennes arranged to keep the old convent of the Cathérinettes outside of town, which d'Agay had wanted to purchase for a *dépôt*, and sold instead the Little Seminary. The seminarians returned to claim plants, bushes, ornamental locks, an expensive new altar in the chapel, doorways, paneling, and other objects too rich for the new occupants. The superior agreed to provide some older locks from the Cathérinettes and to repair damage after Fresnais protested (memo of October 30, 1771, A.D. Ille-et-Vilaine, C.1299).

46. Information on the *dépôts* at Quimper, Vannes, and Nantes is to be found in A.D. Ille-et-Vilaine, C.1309, 1310, and 1311, respectively. Fresnais inspected the *dépôts* at Quimper and Vannes in 1770 (see below, note 52).

47. Correspondence related to repair of château of Tours, including letter of August 20, 1766, A.D. Indre-et-Loire, C.302; letter of engineer Trésaguet to *caissier de la mendicité* at Limoges, October 3, 1768, A.D. Haute-Vienne, C.362; Viallet to intendant of Caen on overcrowding, September 28, 1767, A.D. Calvados, C.648. On Viallet's plans for the *dépôts*, see Jean-Claude Perrot, *Cartes, plans, dessins, et vues de Caen antérieurs à 1789—inventaire des collections,* offprint from *Bulletin de la Société des antiquaires de Normandie* 56 (1961–1962): 172–184.

48. A.N. F^{16} 936 (see pp. 107–109).

49. The intendant was also responsible for the surveillance of discharged soldiers and for hunting down deserters. He in turn used soldiers in some civil operations. In frontier areas, intendants were appointed by the minister of war; in Brittany the subdelegates and the *commissaires des guerres* were the same persons. See André Corvisier, *L'armée francaise de la fin du XVIIe siècle au minisère Choiseul: le soldat,* 2 vols. (Paris, 1964), 1:89–91 (intendants); 2:654 (sanitary conditions) and 2:821–847 (conditions of life). See also Col. Henri-Joseph de Buttet, ''La dépense du soldat en 1772,'' *Actes du 90e Congrès national des sociétés savantes, Nice, 1965. Section d'histoire moderne et contemporaine,* vol. 1, *Sources et méthodes: Ancien Régime* (Paris, 1966), 140–149.

50. ''Si ce n'est par l'intérêt, si ce n'est pas la charité écclésiastique toujours dominante dans ces maisons, qui les détournent d'un arrangement si conforme à la vraie charité, je ne puis attribuer leur répugnance qu'à l'habitude qui l'emporte toujours sur la raison, dans la plupart des hommes.'' Letter of March 16, 1771, A.D. Ille-et-Vilaine, C.1295.

51. Duc de Choiseul to the controller-general, August 21, 1768 (includes reference to ''previous request'' to use *dépôt* at Quimper for women arrested by military authorities at Brest (A.N. F^{15} 2811).

52. Fresnais to intendant, March 4, 1770, A.D. Ille-et-Vilaine, C.1309.

53. The complaint from the sisters of the *hôtel-Dieu,* presented by the *grand vicaire* of Angers, and the intendant's negative reply of February 22, 1774, are in A.D. Indre-et-Lloire, C.307.

54. Terray's query December 26, 1770, and intendant's reply January 16, 1771, A.D. Seine-Maritime, C.1009.

55. Fresnais to intendant, July 17, 1770, A.D. Ille-et-Vilaine, C.1298. The instruction of April 10, 1770, from Terray on providing *loges* for the insane and for those with ''incurable diseases'' cited the lack of hospital facilities in many provinces (A.D. Indre-et-Loire, C.307, and A.D. Ille-et-Vilaine, C.1296). The circular addressed by Terray to the intendant of Rouen on the pensioning out of children was dated December 26, 1769, A.D. Seine-Maritime, C.1009; the same circular is in A.D. Indre-et-Loire, C.306. In correspondence with the intendant of Tours, the subdelegate of Angers inquired about a successful system for pensioning children adopted by Cypierre at Orleans (de la Marsaulaye, Angers, May 5, 1770, A.D. Indre-et-Loire, C.307). De Fleury, the former intendant of Burgundy, had commented in his memoir of 1759 on the need to provide for children and the insane (B.N. Joly de Fleury 1309, fol. 152–153 and 171).

56. The placement of the *cachot* is mentioned in a list of alterations to be made in the *dépôt,* accompanying drawings and other documents sent (presumably to the intendant de Flesselles in Paris) on January 7, 1767. Fresnais discussed windows in a letter of July 17, 1770, A.D. Ille-et-Vilaine, C.1298.

57. At Alençon, records mention an escape by means of blankets tied to a bar in the window, and another by way of the latrines (A.D. Orne, C.283).

58. Gellée de Prémion at Nantes, August 27, 1769, A.D. Ille-et-Vilaine, C.1298.

59. Draft of du Cluzel's report to Bertier, June 18, 1770, and Terray's reply to intendant, July 5, 1770, both in A.D. Indre-et-Loire, C.304.

60. A.D. Ille-et-Vilaine, L. 1157, ''Rapport sur le dépôt de mendicité établi à Rennes.'' Camille Bloch provides similar documentation on the elimination of other *dépôts* in *Assistance et l'état,* 169n.

61. ''État de tous les dépôts destinés et servant au renfermement des mendiants vagabonds et gens sans aveu dans toutes les provinces du Royaume,'' with dates of closings, B.N. f.f. 8129, fol. 330v.–331.

62. ''Relevé général des dépenses faites pour l'opération de la destruction du vagabondage, 1768–1771,'' ibid., fol. 330.

63. Paultre, *Répression,* 605, reproduces data on the number of inmates per year from tables in B.N. Joly de Fleury 1309, fol. 187. This data probably accompanied a report to the parlement of Paris in 1778, since data runs from 1768 to the end of December 1777. See the beginning of Chapter 8.

Chapter 5

1. This model is derived from the general instruction and the later directives described in the previous chapter. Laverdy's praise for the intendant of Champagne is in a letter of December 21, 1767, A.D. Marne, C.2026; the minister notes: "je compte même faire usage de votre idée à cet égard pour les autres provinces du Royaume." The "idea" appears in the text of the instruction copied into the B.N. *Receuil.* Either that text was not the earliest version of the instruction or the minister was encouraging zeal with flattery.

2. See Chapter 4, note 37.

3. Laverdy approved Montyon's proposal of making the concierge of the *dépôt* at Clermont responsible for the purchase of all provisions, in a letter of February 1, 1768; he warned against exploitation in this context. He was also skeptical that rye bread could not be had for less than 2s. 6½d. the pound (A.D. Puy-de-Dôme, C.1090).

4. Letter of June 12, 1773, from intendant of Rouen, A.D. Seine-Maritime, C.1040. The complaints of the subdelegate Alexandre are in a letter of August 16, 1768, A.D. Seine-Maritime, C.1008.

5. Letter of intendant, December 4, 1767, and Laverdy's reply, January 13, 1768, both in A.D. Marne, C.2026.

6. Terray announced Bernier's visit in a letter of January 6, 1770, A.D. Marne, C.2026. There is no further correspondence on the subject at Châlons, it appears.

7. On de Boynes and the Maison de Bellevaux, see above, Chapter 2. Bernier's management was approved after Puricelli's challenge, according to the Archives Hospitalières de Besançon, Aumône-Générale, XIXm fol. 198v. (June 5, 1761). The contract for the *dépôt* is in A.D. Doubs, C.1582 (carton 1115).

8. La Corée detailed his negotiations involving Bernier, de Boynes, and Bertier in a letter to Terray of December 23, 1771, A.D. Doubs, C. 1673 (carton 1186).

9. A.D. Indre-et-Loire, C.306; Rattier and Le Comte provide a retrospective summary of their project in the *requête* approved in council February 13, 1770. See also the brief mention in F. Dumas, *La généralité de Tours au XIIIᵉ siècle. L'administration de l'intendant du Cluzel (1766–1783)* (Paris, 1894), 329.

10. Ibid. Laverdy's circulars of March 16 and July 12 are in A.D. Indre-et-Loire, C.303. Restru's title is included in the adjudication of a bid of May 21, 1765, A.D. Indre-et-Loire, C.302.

11. A.D. Indre-et-Loire, C.303: memoir entitled, "Moyens proposés pour faire travailler les mendiants renfermés au dépôt de Tours, pendant leur détention, et lorsque la liberté leur sera rendue," with letters of August 18 and 20 of Rattier to du Cluzel and of August 23 to Duval.

12. Ibid., Rattier to du Cluzel, August 20, 1768.

13. Ibid., Rattier to Duval, August 23, 1768.

14. Letter from Cypierre at Orleans to du Cluzel at Montpipeau, September 14, 1768, ibid.

15. Rattier's *requête* is in A.D. Indre-et-Loire, C.306, with a copy of the circular from Terray of February 10, 1770, promoting Rattier's blankets. The printed order form, from A.D. Haute-Vienne, C.365, touts the new workshop:

On y fabrique et on y vend des couvertures de laine de toutes grandeurs, couleurs et qualités; on y fabrique exprès celles qui sont commandées; on y fabrique aussi des étoffes de laines, comme molletons, pluches, ratines, flannelles, sergettes, tricots, frocs, tour-angelles et mazamets imitant ceux de Languedoc: le tout de differentes [laises?], cou-leurs, qualités etc., à juste prix—s'adresser à M. RATTIER, sindic-receveur de la ville, ou à M. Lecomte, négociant, directeur de ladite manufacture.

A letter of February 10, 1700, to du Cluzel from Terray (A.D. Indre-et-Loire, C.306) asks that the intendant's secretary inspect, label, and seal the packets of blankets to be sent, a total of 340. This total includes sixty for Paris and Tours, and twenty for Bordeaux, Bourges, Clermont, La Rochelle, Limoges, Lyons, Montauban, Montpellier, Orleans, Po-itiers, and Rennes. Each blanket would cost 14l. 10s. and its quality was to be "à quatre points de 2 aulnes 1/4 de longeur sur 2 aulnes de largeur."

16. A.D. Indre-et-Loire, C.306. The "Observations sur quelques articles du projet de marché cy joint pour la nourriture et entretien des renfermés dans le dépôt de Tours" are unsigned, but the suggestion that a mill for grinding grain might be sent, if the intendant so desired, is likely to have come only from the office of Bertier.

17. For the comments of Lenoir, later *lieutenant-général de police* of Paris, on the use of such mills at Bicêtre and in the Paris region, and Bertier's desire to deploy them in order to assure the provisioning of Paris, see Robert Darnton, "Le lieutenant de police J. P. Lenoir, la guerre des farines et l'approvisionnement de Paris à la veille de la Revolution," *RHMC* 16 (October–December 1969): 620.

18. Letter to Duval from Dupichard, February 26, 1770, A.D. Indre-et-Loire, C.306. Dupichard was dean of the college of medicine at Tours and was recommended by du Cluzel as the correspondent for the service of epidemics. See Paul Delaunay, *Études sur l'hygiène, l'assistance et les secours publics dans le Maine sous l'ancien régime* (Le Mans, 1922), 270.

19. On the social and cultural bias of doctors toward lower-class patients in the eigh-teenth century, see Jean-Pierre Peter, "Les mots et les objets de la maladie. Remarques sur les épidémies et la médecine dans la societé française de la fin du XVIIIᵉ siècle," *RH* 499 (July–September 1971): 13–38, especially 34 and 37.

20. One dimension of doctors' concern with hygiene, especially in the case of idle youths, is treated in Samuel Tissot, *L'onanisme, dissertation sur les maladies produites par la mas-turbation,* 5th ed. (Lausanne, 1772). Dupichard refers to "ordures," Tissot to a young watchmaker "uniquement livré à ses méditations ordurières" (p. 82 of 1805 edition). On Dupichard, see Raoul Mercier, *Le monde médical de Touraine pendant la Révolution* (Tours, 1936), 12–13. On his colleague Origet, who was the model for the doctor in Balzac's *Le lys dans la vallée* and who also served the *dépôt,* see ibid., 26–32.

21. A.D. Indre-et-Loire, C.307. The copy of Rattier's seven-page memoir contained in this bundle was the one prepared for the intendant. In a covering note to Duval, Rattier noted that he had included a digression on the *bureau d'aumône,* as requested. If the request was du Cluzel's, the copy for Bertier might omit that portion of the memoir. The note illustrates the mediating role of the secretary of the intendant.

22. The reference by Rattier to "alms of the clergy" is specified in a memo of December 1, 1770 to the intendant, probably from Duval, stating that annual upkeep of 750l. would be provided by an endowment of 18,000l. "taken from the 300,000 which the Clergy has given for the suppression of mendicity." Presumably this amount was voted by the Assembly of the Clergy that met in 1770.

23. Draft of du Cluzel's reply to Terray, December 1, 1770, A.D. Indre-et-Loire, C.307.

24. Ibid. Details of Keyser's remedy were published in Richard de Hautesierck, *Recueil d'observations de médecine des hôpitaux militaires,* vol. 2 (1772), 778. See also David M. Vess, *Medical Revolution in France, 1789–1796* (Gainesville, Fla., 1975), 25; and O. Temkin, "Therapeutic Trends and Treatment of Syphilis before 1900," *BHM* 29 (1955): 309–316.

25. A.D. Indre-et-Loire, C.307.

26. Ibid. The draft of the letter to Terray in January refers to Rattier as "animé de zèle pour ce qui peut contribuer à la conservation de ces misérables."

27. On du Cluzel and Choiseul, see Dumas, *La généralité de Tours*, 16. The archbishop supported the campaign against idleness, while maintaining a spirit of active charity. In a letter of April 12, 1771, for example (A.D. Indre-et-Loire, C.307), he intervened on behalf of a woman active in local charities who had been harshly treated by the subdelegate Restru after asking for the release of a young woman from the *dépôt*. St. Martin and St. Gregory of Tours were looking over the bishop's shoulder. See Kathleen Mitchell, "Saints and Public Christianity in the *Historiae* of Gregory of Tours," in *Religion, Culture, and Society in the Early Middle Ages: Studies in Honor of Richard E. Sullivan*, ed. Thomas F. X. Noble and John J. Contreni (Kalamazoo, 1987), 77–94.

28. Laverdy had refused a request to use *soeurs grises* in the *dépôt* at Châlons, in a letter of October 4, 1767, A.D. Marne, C.2026. De Prémion's enthusiasm for Rattier's model is expressed in a letter of February 10, 1771, A.D. Ille-et-Valaine, C.1311. De la Marsaulaye at Angers stressed the difference between the quality of work done by free workers and inmates in captivity in a letter of April 24, 1770. Prudhomme de la Boussinière at Le Mans, writing April 26, noted that funds and facilities were not available to him, and "we have here no one so well-to-do and well inclined as M. Rattier": A.D. Indre-et-Loire, C.307.

29. Terray to du Cluzel, February 9, 1774, A.D. Indre-et-Loire, C.307.

30. Copies of Manié's contract of May 15, 1773, in A.D. Indre-et-Loire, C.307; A.D. Calvados, C.677; and elsewhere. The signatures on it are the following:

> Jean Manié, négociant à Paris, rue de Touraine au marais.
>
> Pierre-Jacques Reculés de Basmarein, secrétaire du roi et receveur des tailles de l'élection de Sens, demeurant Paris, rue Meslé.
>
> Antoine Basile Pierre de Rimberg, et Cie, banquier à Paris, rue du Temple.
>
> André Marie Gruel, négociant à Paris, rue de Roulle.
>
> Jacques Bernard Le Roy, ancient lieutenant de l'amirauté de Saintonge. Rue de Puis à Paris.
>
> Pierre de Versen, négociant à Paris, rue St. Germain l'Auxerrois.

The revolt in the *dépôt* at Rouen in April 1773 is discussed in a letter of June 12, 1773, from the intendant to the controller-general, A.D. Seine-Maritime, C.1040.

31. The version of the contract cited provides for the *dépôts* of the *généralité* of Tours. From a list of work projects "established in the various *dépôts* entrusted to the compagnie générale" (B.N. f.f. 8129, fol. 332), it appears that Manié, Rimberge, et Cie contracted for provisioning of the *dépôts* in the *généralités* of Paris, Tours, Rennes, La Rochelle, Bordeaux, Limoges, Auch, Montauban, Roussillon, Aix, Grenoble, Lyons, Bourgogne, Moulins, Bourges, Alençon, and Caen. A letter of the controller-general at a later date addressed to Châlons-sur-Marne states that a contract of October 1773 obliged the contractors Teissier and Engren to provide for inmates at 5s. 6d. per *journée* in the first four years and at 4s. 6d. for the last six (A.D. Marne, C.2026). Teissier and Engren also held a contract dated July 17, 1773, for provisioning the *dépôt* at Besançon (A.D. Doubs, C.1673, carton 1186).

32. A.D. Haute-Vienne, C.364; A.d. Indre-et-Loire, C.306. Terray followed up with a circular of January 8, 1770, on the same subject.

33. Letters from de la Marsaulaye, subdelegate at Angers, June 30, 1770 ("c'est alors me donner tous les embarras d'un commissionaire d'un marchand de bled, c'est ce qui vient de m'arriver") and through late summer of 1770; letter of subdelegate of Le Mans, June 12, 1770. Terray's desire to create a body of accurate, uniform data on provisioning is evident

in his letter of September 20, 1770, asking that information on provisioning of grains for the *dépôts,* and on the sale of surpluses, be converted to Paris measures (A.D. Indre-et-Loire, C.307). See Steven Kaplan, *Bread, Politics and Political Economy in the Reign of Louis XV,* 2 vols. (The Hague, 1976), 545ff., on Terray's view of managing national provisions.

34. Turgot's letter of October 30, 1770, is in A.D. Haute-Vienne, C.364.

35. A request from the intendant of Caen to maintain a higher standard of provisioning on some items was refused by Bertier, on the grounds that the contractors would use it as an argument for demanding the same elsewhere and an increase in their rates, according to a letter excerpted in the inventory for A.D. Calvados, C.614 (1773–1776).

36. Article 3 spelled out the obligation to provide special care for the sick; article 5 made the contractor explicitly responsible for maintaining an infirmary, while keeping doctors, concierges, and other overseers in the pay and under the direction of the intendant; article 6 provided for a uniform *journée* in sickness and in health; article 7 authorized use of inmates' labor; article 8 specified that one-sixth of the product of their labor would be given to them and also provided for work discipline and penalties. Contract of May 15, 1773, in A.D. Indre-et-Loire, C.307.

37. The professionalization of bureaucratic routines is discussed in chapter 8 (Dr. Colombier's role as inspector).

38. A.D. Ille-et-Vilaine, C.1296, and A.D. Seine-Maritime, C.1009.

39. Terray argued that rice maintained good health at low cost in his letter of February 10, 1773 (probably a circular), to Turgot, A.D. Haute-Vienne, C.366; article 10 of Manié's contract in May of the same year required him to deduct the cost of royal rice shipments at 25 livres the quintal, *poids de marc,* from amounts owed him for *journées* of inmates.

40. A.D. Marne, C.2026.

41. See for example letters of June 24, 1772, and May 10, 1774, in A.D. Marne, C.2026.

42. Terray to intendant of Châlons, December 5, 1771, ibid.

43. See p. 79.

44. A.D. Indre-et-Loire, C.303: du Cluzel to chancellor, September 22, 1769. Complaint from parlement of Paris relayed in letter from chancellor to du Cluzel, December 14, 1769, with the observation that "vos deffenses trop généralement prises peuvent avoir des inconvéniens" (A.D. Indre-et-Loire, C.306). Terray's circular of December 26, 1769, opens with the following challenge: "Il pourroit être fâcheux de tarir cette partie abondante des charités publiques. Mais n'y auroit-il pas des moyens en changeant la forme, de les rendre plus utiles?": A.D. Ille-et-Vilaine, C.1288, and A.D. Indre-et-Loire, C.306. Muriel Jeorger mentions Terray's inquiry into charitable resources in "Les enquêtes hospitalières au XVIIIᵉ siècle," *Bulletin de la Société française d'histoire des hôpitaux* 31 (1975): 51–60, at p. 55.

45. Letter from Bertier to du Cluzel, November 19, 1770, and text of *arrêt du conseil* of December 18, 1770, containing the statute for the alms bureau, in A.D. Indre-et-Loire, C.307. See also Dumas, *Généralité de Tours,* 345.

46. Letters from subdelegate of Le Mans, March 8 and April 7, 1771; from subdelegate of Angers, April 28, 1770, and from bishop of Angers, April 25, 1770. Acting on a suggestion by one of his aides in a memo of May 3, 1771, du Cluzel obtained a copy of a pastoral letter sent by the bishop of Orleans on the establishment of the alms bureau. All in A.D. Indre-et-Loire, C.307.

47. Letter from Terray, June 19, 1771, A.D. Indre-et-Loire, C.307.

48. Memoir accompanying letter from Rattier to Duval, secretary of the intendant of Tours, November 29, 1770 (A.D. Indre-et-Loire, C.307). An indication of the depth of the crisis at Tours at this time is to be found in a letter of August 1, 1770, in which Terray relays to du Cluzel the request of Sartine, *lieutenant-général de police* of Paris, that beggars from Tours arrested in Paris be transferred to the *dépôt* at Tours from Bicêtre and La Salpêtrière, which were both overcrowded.

49. On Terray's grain legislation, made public in December 1770 and submitted to the parlement in January 1771, see Kaplan, *Bread, Politics and Political Economy,* 532ff.

50. The archbishop's comment is in a letter of April 12, 1771 (A.D. Indre-et-Loire, C.307). Du Cluzel's views on *ateliers de charité* (letter of May 19, 1770) are cited from A.D. Indre-et-Loire, C.96 and C.322, by Dumas, *Généralité de Tours,* 346. On similar measures by other intendants, and on Albert's role as coordinator, see Camille Bloch, *L'assistance et l'état en France à la veille de la Révolution: généralités de Paris, Rouen, Alençon, Orléans, Soissons, Amiens, (1764–1790)* (Paris, 1908), 201–203; Paul Ardascheff, *Les intendants de province sous Louis XVI* (Paris, 1909), 230–233; and Shelby T. McCloy, *Government Assistance in Eighteenth-Century France* (Durham, N.C., 1946), 26ff. Olwen Hufton argues that *ateliers* had little impact (*Poor of Eighteenth-Century France,* 182–193).

51. Letter of Rattier to intendant of Tours, August 18, 1768, with accompanying memoir, A.D. Indre-et-Loire, C.303. Terray later argued, in a circular to intendants on November 28, 1770 (A.D. Indre-et-Loire, C.304), that the establishment of *ateliers* should "vous mettre plus que jamais à portée de distinguer les bons pauvres et qui méritent la protection de l'état, de ceux qu'une indolence criminelle lui rend à charge."

52. Du Cluzel to Torgut, December 20, 1774, A.D. Indre-et-Loire, C.307. Du Cluzel's economic interpretation of mendicity at Tours is most clearly elaborated in a letter to Trudaine of January 21, 1771 (A.D. Indre-et-Loire, C.307). He recalled that, since his arrival in October 1766, the number of looms had fallen by over a third, and measures of local encouragement had failed: "I have judged and you, Sir, think the same, that we are only experiencing the general tremor." Three causes were to blame: the collapse in the sale of textiles, the high food prices ("which make it impossible for the worker to live on rates that the *fabriquants* do not wish to raise, lest prices of their textiles also rise"), and finally the prohibitions of the German courts.

53. See especially Douglas Dakin, *Turgot and the Ancien Régime in France* (New York, 1965), 63ff. (all of chapter 5). Du Pont published Turgot's official circular, "Police établie pour les atteliers de charité dans la Généralité de Limoges," in *Éphémérides du citoyen* 6 (1772), 2:195–205. Du Pont's comments are cited, with the instruction of February 11, 1770, on *ateliers,* in Gustave Schelle, ed., *Oeuvres de Turgot et documents le concernant avec biographie et notes par Gustave Schelle,* 5 vols. (Paris, 1912–1923), 3:205 (cited hereafter as "Schelle").

54. Schelle, 3:205–250, especially "Instruction lue à l'Assemblé de charité de Limoges," February 11, 1770 (205–219), and "Ordonnance imposant aux propriétaires de nourrir leurs métayers jusqu'à la récolte," February 28, 1770 (243–244). See also Schelle's narrative, 2:59–60.

55. Turgot to the controller-general, December 16, 1769 (Terray received it, since he replaced Mayon d'Invau on the 22nd): Schelle, 3:125–126.

56. Same letter. He went on to argue for a clear distinction of aid recipients into two classes: "ceux que l'âge, le sexe et les maladies mettent hors d'état de gagner leur vie par eux-mêmes et ceux qui sont en état de travailler. Les premiers doivent seuls recevoir des secours purement gratuits: les autres ont besoin de salaires et l'aumône la mieux placée, et la plus utile, consiste à leur procurer les moyens d'en gagner." The aid provided to the *généralité* in 1739 provided a precedent for this distinction, Turgot noted.

57. A.D. Haute-Vienne, C.364; Schelle, 3:433 (provisioning operations in 1770).

58. Instruction of February 19, 1770, Schelle, 3:250–253. See also the instruction to subdelegates of February 16, in which Turgot refers to the circulars of the previous autumn from Choiseul and Maupeou on the arrest of domiciled beggars:

Comme j'étais autorisé à suspendre l'envoi de ces ordres, j'avais différé cet envoi à cause de la misère générale; mais, dès qu'il aura été pourvu dans chaque paroisse à la subsistance des pauvres du lieu, et que les pauvres étrangers auront été renvoyés chacun chez eux, il n'y aura plus aucun prétexte pour mendier, et ce moment est la plus favorable qu'on puisse prendre pour exécuter complètement les vues du Conseil.''

59. Boisbedeuil to Turgot, January 4, 1771, and Turgot's reply of January 12, A.D. Haute-Vienne, C.364. Boisbedeuil was especially disturbed by the number of beggars from town who scoured the countryside, ''dont les pauvres s'estimeroient fort heureux si les charités qui se font journellement n'étoient en grande partie consommées par des essaims de frelons qui sortent tous les matins des villes ou ils reviennent ensuite chargés de bonnes provisions.'' Observation, or echo of Plato's *Republic*? Turgot also countered Boisbedeuil's complaint about the danger of insane beggars by noting that the *dépôt* at Angoulême lacked cells; once the *loges* at Limoges were expanded, there would be a place to put such individuals.

60. These conflicts are discussed in Chapter 6.

61. B.N. f.f. 8129, fol. 338v–339; same text in B.N. n. acq. fr. 943, fol. 271v.

62. D'Ormesson to Bertier, December 21, 1771, and Turgot to Bertier, November 5, 1774, in A.N. H.2105 (carton labeled ''Bureau de la Ville de Paris—Travaux de Charité, 1770–1780'').

63. For a general view of Bertier's reform, see Michel Marion, *Histoire financière de la France depuis 1715,* vol. 1 (1715–1789) (Paris, 1927), 284. The subject is treated in great detail in J. Guérout, ''La taille dans la région parisienne au xviiie siècle, d'après les fonds de l'élection de Paris aux Archives Nationales,'' *Mémoires publiés par la Fédération des sociétés historiques et archéologiques de Paris et de l'Île-de-France* 13 (1962): 145–360, especially 260. Bertier's ideas on this reform are set forth in a memoir strung with others in a set labeled ''Bertier'' in A.N. F[15] 936. He notes that a general *cadastre* was ordered in 1764 but not carried out because of the cost involved. Work began on it in 1771, after a formula was elaborated to apply both to poor areas like Vézelay and rich areas like Meaux. The private archives of the Bertier family contain a bound notebook entitled ''Classement des terres de la généralité de Paris,'' A.N. 80 AP 12.

64. The letters patent registered by the Cour des Aides on January 25, 1776, are in Schelle, 3:334–338. For Turgot's comment of 1761, see Schelle, 2:93. See also Edgar Faure, *La disgrâce de Turgot* (Paris, 1961), 106–107.

65. Bertier's career and reputation as a reformer are discussed further in chapters 8 and 10.

66. Detail on the establishment of the *pioniers* is in B.N. f.f. 8130, fol. 91–96.

67. Robert Forster, *Merchants, Landlords, Magistrates: The Depont Family in Eighteenth-Century France* (Baltimore, 1980), 139.

Chapter 6

1. The interpretation given in this chapter and the next builds upon the well-documented chapter in Camille Bloch, *L'assistance et l'état en France à la veille de la Révolution: Généralités de Paris, Rouen, Alençon, Orléans, Soissens, Amiens (1764–1790)* (Paris, 1908), 179–210: ''Turgot (1774–1776).''

2. Bibliothèque Municipale, Besançon, Collection Droz, vol. 68, fol. 68–70, ''2e mémoire pour ledit hôpital,'' in collection of ''Remontrances du parlement.''

3. Ibid. Chifflet cited ordinances of 1549 and 1558, and the criminal ordinance of Louis XIV, 1670, title 13, article 35. He also cited the letters patent of the *aumône-générale,* granted in 1712, and the usages of the parlement of Paris.

4. A.N. F[16] 936: second of eight memoirs on a string with a tag marked ''Bertier.'' The memoir notes that the *dépôts* have been established recently.

5. Bertier's argument follows de Fleury's memoir of 1759, discussed in Chapter 2.

6. Letter of December 15, 1769, read to parlement of Besançon January 2, 1770, in B.M. Besançon, Collection Droz, vol. 65, fol. 248–249.

7. A.D. Doubs, C.1582 (carton 1115), "État nominatif des personnes qui ont été renfermées dans le dépôt de mendicité de Besançon, en vertu d'arrêt du Parlement, juges de police de la même ville et des autres juridictions," January 1788.

8. "Mémoire historique sur l'aumône-générale et établissements annexes faits en 1781 par l'avocat Ignace Joseph Bichat, l'un des directeurs de l'aumône," in manuscripts of the Centre Régional Hospitalier et Universitaire of Besançon, box 99. According to this memoir, a specific *arrêt du conseil* of July 23, 1769, gave the intendant of Besançon exclusive authority over the Maison de Bellevaux. The directors of the *aumône-générale* asked to be allowed to continue using the house for confining some *"scandaleux"* and children; their request was granted.

9. A.D. Seine-Maritime, C.1040: Laverdy to de Crosne, March 4, 1768; controller-general Maynon d'Invau to Belbeuf, April 15, 1769; chancellor to *procureur-général* of the parlement of Rouen, May 6, 1769 (copy with cover letter from Bertier to de Crosne, May 7, 1769). Bertier had originally served on the Laverdy commission as *adjoint* to do Crosne.

10. A.D. Indre-et-Loire, C.306, "Copie de la lettre à Mr le Chancelier écritte par M. Fleury le 25 octobre 1769." See other correspondence in the same bundle and in A.D. Indre-et-Loire, C.303.

11. A.N. F15 2795, "Copie de la lettre écrite par M. Bertier à M. Paris avocat du Roy à Orléans le 14 octobre 1772."

12. See Roland E. Mousnier, *The Institutions of France under the Absolute Monarchy, 1598–1789: Society and the State* (Chicago, 1974), 606–627.

13. Ibid., 620. Cf. Marcel Marion, *Dictionnaire des institutions de la France aux xviie et xviiie siècles* (Paris, 1968, reprint), s.v. "Direction (Grande) des Finances," 179.

14. A.N. H. 1417, "Le Roi, pénétré des maux que causoient en France le vagabondage et la mendicité . . ." (piece 66). *Pays d'états* and *pays conquis* together were reckoned as one-third of the kingdom. Since the *pays de généralité* paid eight hundred thousand livres for the tax of three deniers per livre of the *taille,* four hundred thousand livres were to be levied on the other provinces. Two-thirds of this amount was assessed in the larger *pays d'états*: Languedoc, one-fifth (A.N., H.892); Brittany, one-fifth (H.374); Provence, one-eighth; Burgundy, one-sixth (H.1417). Some of the foregoing details are presented in Paultre, *De la répression de la mendicité et du vagabondage* (Paris, 1906), 474ff.

15. A.N. H.1417, piece 65.

16. Ibid., piece 57. Condé dealt directly with the minister of the royal household, St.-Florentin. On Condé's role, see Marion, *Dictionnaire*, s.v. "Gouverneur."

17. Ibid., memoir addressed to Ménard containing final instructions, November 8, 1769. Bertier's argument that further benefits were to be expected from the imminent arrest of domiciled beggars appears in piece 57, and in A.N. H.892, piece 53. Further objections arose over accounting for the enclaves of Bugey, Bresse, and Gex, and there were requests to reduce the original levy when the number of *dépôts* was reduced (A.N. H.135).

18. A.N. H.892, pieces 54–58. The general formula for finance is contained in a general memoir in which "Burgundy" is crossed out and replaced first by "Languedoc," then by "Provence."

19. Ibid., letter of controller-general to archbishop of Narbonne, November 18, 1769, and extract of letter to prince de Beauveau, November 19, 1769. In further exchanges, Ménard noted that Burgundy might appear favored, since it had six *dépôts* to Languedoc's three. Bertier proposed that seventy or eighty thousand would be sufficient, if payments began with the year 1769.

20. Ibid., request based on arguments reported from the commission on extraordinary affairs by the bishop of Uzès.

21. Ibid., "extrait du registre des délibérations," January 2, 1770; letter of controller-general to archbishop of Toulouse, December 20, 1769; letter of Ménard to archbishop of Narbonne, December 30, 1769.

22. A.N. H.910, piece 40, "Languedoc—assemblée de 1776, 28 novembre—points à décider pour l'assemblée des états de Languedoc convoqué au 28 ce mois et sur lesquels il paroitroit convenable que M. le controlleur général voulût bien se concerter avec M. l'archevèque de Narbonne."

23. A.N. H.892, piece 92, minute of letter from Ménard de Conichard to the archbishop of Narbonne, December 30, 1769. Ménard writes that he has replied directly to the Estates:

> par cette raison M. Berthier de Sauvigny chargé de l'administration de la mendicité n'a pas été prévenu non plus de ce qui se passoit ny de la réponse, et je differeray de luy en parler jusqu'à ce que vous vous soyez expliqués sur les arrangements à prendre pour donner une juste satisfaction aux états touchant cet objet conformément à l'intention de M. le contrôleur général. Vous jugerez peut-être à propos d'en parler vous même à M. Berthier.

24. A.N. H.910, piece 38. This document is cited in Josseline Guyader, "La répression de la mendicité et du vagabondage dans la ville de Toulouse depuis la Déclaration de 1724 jusqu'à la Révolution de 1789" (memoir for diplôme d'études supérieures, Toulouse, 1966), 258 and 280. Bertier's commentary is in an undated memoir, A.N. H.892, piece 76. He implies that he had faced a fait accompli in his letter of February 18, 1771, to Ménard (piece 72, ibid.). Piece 70 indicates that the intendant Saint-Priest had supported the Estates (letter to the controller-general, January 18, 1771).

25. A.N. H.910, piece 40 (unsigned memoir, perhaps by Bertier or Ménard), estimates that the Estates of Languedoc incurred a cost of 100,000 livres per year. A report to the Estates for the period November 1773 to November 1774 gives a total cost of 75,039l. 4s. 6d. for that year. A figure of 78,460 livres for the preceding year may be calculated from the same document (piece 38).

26. Ibid., piece 38, containing a report by the archbishop of Toulouse on behalf of the Commission des Affaires Extraordinaires, in an extract from the deliberations of the Estates-General of Languedoc, January 5, 1775, presided over by the archbishop of Narbonne.

27. The circular of November 18, 1774, to all bishops is in B.N. f.f. 8129, fol. 343v. (The copy received by the bishop of Fréjus is reproduced in Schelle, 4:264.) The letter especially to Narbonne (undated, but from context sent between November 18, 1774, and the session of the Estates of Languedoc, January 5, 1775) is in B.N. f.f. 8129, fol. 343.

28. A.N. H.910, piece 38. The reply of the Estates echoes the language of Turgot's circular to bishops.

29. A.D. Ille-et-Vilaine, C.1295: "Mémoire sur ce qui s'est passé en 1764 au sujet des mendiants." A note in the margin indicates that a copy was sent to d'Agay in Paris, presumably by his predecessor de Flesselles. Le Bret's reply to Laverdy was dated November 15, 1764; Laverdy's inquiry, October 1764.

30. Ibid., letter dated from Paris, October 27, 1766, probably from de Flesselles to his subdelegate-general, Raudin, enclosing a letter from Laverdy dated Versailles, October 19, 1766. In this letter, Laverdy referred to a forthcoming edict. In a similar letter to the *élus* of Burgundy of April 30, 1766, he announced: "Sa Majesté enverra incessament au Parlement l'édit qui doit bannir la mendicité" (A.N., K.683). The fact that no request was made in 1768 provides grounds for an objection by the Estates' commission on finances in 1770, A.D. Ille-et-Vilaine, C.3796.

31. A.D. Ille-et-Vilaine, C.1288; Terray to d'Agay, February 8, 1770; reply of intendant

to controller-general from Rennes, February 22, 1770. D'Agay's argument for indirect taxation echoes that of Montesquieu, *Esprit des lois*, book 13, chapter 7. Physiocrats disagreed.

32. D'Agay noted, in his letter of February 22, "les quatre dépôts établis en Bretagne sont peu vastes, très incommodes et qu'en général ils furent très mal choisie par l'ancien subdélegué-général que mon prédecesseur chargea de ce soin dans des momens critiques et orageux où il lui était absolumment impossible de s'en occuper.'' The subdelegate-general Raudin became an ordinary subdelegate after the departure of de Flesselles. The special title was not used again until Bertrand de Molleville conferred it upon Petiet (Fréville, *Intendance de Bretagne*, 2:308–309).

33. In his letter of February 22, 1770, d'Agay wrote: "Je n'ai pas besoin, M., de mettre sous vos yeux tous les inconvéniens qui résulteroient de confier cette administration à la commission intermédiaire qui d'ailleurs n'a point et ne doit point avoir de juridiction contentieuse dans la Province.''

34. A.N. H.374, letter of d'Agay to controller-general, June 22, 1770. D'Agay's letter was passed to Bertier July 3, and Bertier's draft instruction was sent to Ménard July 12.

35. Ibid. The abridged version of Bertier's memorandum actually presented to the Estates of Brittany is recorded in a bound register of proceedings, A.D. Loire-Atlantique, C.450, fol. 67v. (Thursday, October 25, 1770). I am grateful to Prof. Jean Meyer of the University of Rennes for guiding me to these indexed registers.

36. A.N. H.374; A.D. Loire-Atlantique, C.450, fol. 205. The Estates' refusal of this request was symptomatic of d'Agay's weakness, according to Fréville, *Intendance de Bretagne*, 2:322.

37. A.D. Ille-et-Vilaine, C.3796. The memoir of the commission of finance also argued that the request should not exceed the level of expenditure incurred to date. It cited articles 3, 7, and 8 of the Declaration of 1764 and articles 2 and 3 of the *arrêt du conseil* of 1767 as promises of royal finance.

38. A.N. H.373, piece 69, memoir entitled "Pour obtenir que l'administration du dépôt soit fait concurrement avec la commission intermédiaire.'' Terray opposed the request but asked that a further report be made to him on the matter at the time the Estates met. Bertier sent a draft of instructions for the royal commissioners with a cover letter to the controller-general on July 11, 1772; it was forwarded to Ménard two days later (A.N. H.374, pieces 193 and 194; pieces 186 and 167 are earlier versions of Bertier's draft). According to Bertier's final memoir, expenses in Brittany had amounted to 91,000 livres in 1770 and 102,000 in 1771; 106,000 were projected for 1772. Operation of the new, larger *dépôt* at Rennes was expected to cost 139,000 per year. Bertier set a firm tone: "Le refus que les Etats se sont permis sur la première demande qui leur a été faite à ce sujet, ne doit pas les affranchir de ce qu'ils doivent, ni opérer une surcharge aussi considérable pour sa majesté.'' The Estates' motion to refuse, November 3, 1772, is in A.D. Loire-Atlantique, C.451, fol. 32.

39. A.N. H.374, piece 189, and A.D. Loire-Atlantique, C.451, fol. 170.

40. Fréville, *Intendance de Bretagne*, 3:14 and 34. Caze de la Bove, having just arrived in the province, did not serve as a commissioner to the Estates in 1774. The memoir of the deputies of the Estates of Brittany at court is in A.D. Ille-et-Vilaine, C.3796.

41. A.N. H.374, piece 264, article 36 of commissioners' instructions for the sessions of the Estates in 1774, new articles proposed; A.D. Ille-et-Vilaine, C.3796, "1774, Rapport de la commission des finances''; A.D. Loire-Atlantique, C.452, fol. 252v.

42. A.D. Loire-Atlantique, C.452, fol. 279. Turgot had stated in his letter to the bishops, B.N. f.f. 8129, fol. 344, that subsistence of beggars would be provided for, "soit par des salaires offerts à ceux qui sont en état de travailler, soit par des fonds assurés à ceux dont l'âge ou les infirmités ne leur permettent pas de subsister du travail de leurs moiens.''

43. A.D. Loire-Atlantique, C.452, fol. 356. The memoir itself is in A.D. Ille-et-Vilaine, C.3796.

44. A.D. Ille-et-Vilaine, C.3796.

45. A.N. H.556, piece 16. Fréville, *Intendance de Bretagne,* 3:34–5, gives excerpts from Caze de la Bove's letter of February 15, 1775, based on his inspection.

46. A.N. H.1417, piece 19. An accompanying note (piece 18) by Bertier is dated September 15, 1770.

47. The arguments of the Estates of Provence are reviewed retrospectively in A.N. H.1417, pieces 6 (1777) and 17 (1776).

48. A.N. H.1235, piece 145, article 7 of *cahier de Provence,* 1771. Hypothetically, if the annuity of 39,000 were added to the contribution of 30,000 livres requested, an annual deficit of 30,000 would be borne by the royal treasury, if the estimated expenditure were reckoned accurately at 90,000. It would take forty-five years to pay off the arrears owed to the province! Bertier had also mentioned that royal funding had indeed supported hospitals in Provence, but the argument was not pressed.

On charitable legislation in Provence, see G. Valran, *Misère et charité en Provence au XVIIIe siècle* (Paris, 1889), 316 ff., and the narrower but more rigorous and critical article of Nicole Arnaud-Duc, ''L'entretien des enfants abandonnés en Provence sous l'ancien régime,'' *Revue historique de droit français et à l'étranger,* 4th series, 47(1969):29–65, especially 52ff.

On the imbroglio concerning finance of the Declaration of 1724 and the redemption of municipal offices, see Monique Etchepare, *L'hôpital de la Charité de Marseille et la répression de la mendicité et du vagabondage (1641–1750)* (Aix-en-Provence, 1962), 182; Gutton, *État et mendicité,* 72–73; and p. 31.

Further background on the unique financial institutions of Provence is to be found in René Pillorget, *Les mouvements insurrectionnels de Provence entre 1596 et 1715* (Paris, 1975), 885–889. I am grateful to James Collins for this reference and for explaining to me some of the more puzzling features of provincial finances at the end of Louis XIV's reign and the early eighteenth century.

49. A.N. H.1235, article 7 of cahier of 1771. The intendant Gallois de la Tour served simultaneously as *premier président* of the parlement of Aix. At the time of the Maupeou coup d'état, he was replaced by Auget de Montyon, who quarreled with the Estates and was replaced for a brief period by Sénac de Meilhan. With the return of the parlements under Turgot's ministry, Gallois de la Tour also returned as intendant at Aix. See Lavaquery, *Le cardinal de Boisgelin,* 2 vols. (Paris, 1920), 1:115–116.

50. A.D. Loire-Atlantique, C. 454 (Estates of Brittany, 1778), fol. 205.

51. A.N. H.1417, piece 13, letter from archbishop of Aix, December 12, 1776. The breadth of opposition to royal policy in establishing the *dépôts* is elaborated in Cissie C. Fairchilds, *Poverty and Charity in Aix-en-Provence, 1640–1789* (Baltimore, 1976), 150–154.

52. A.N. H.910, piece 38. See p. 113.

53. See p. 10 and note 13; p. 25 and note 50.

54. Ballainvilliers, ''Mémoire sur le dépôt de mendicité,'' in ''Mémoires sur les Hôpitaux,'' MS volume in the library of the Archives de l'Assistance Publique à Paris, fol. 246v. See also the comment of de Crosne, intendant of Rouen, on popular sympathy with inmates in the context of a revolt in the *dépôt* in 1775: he said one should pay no heed to ''people who do not know what is going on inside and who, tied by interest with the inmates because their estate puts them close to their condition, are naturally inclined to adopt their sentiments.'' Letter to Bertier, November 24, 1775, A.D. Seine-Maritime, C.1040.

55. On the problem of mentalities involved in resistance to the archers who executed the edict of 1724, see Jean-Pierre Gutton, ''Les mendiants dans la société parisienne au début du xviiie siècle,'' *Cahiers d'histoire* 13 (1968):139–140. See also Arlette Farge, ''Le mendiant, un marginal? (les résistances aux archers de l'hôpital dans le Paris du xviiie siècle),''

in *Les marginaux et les exclus dans l'histoire,* introduction by Bernard Vincent, Cahiers Jussieu (University of Paris VII), no. 5, 312–329 (Paris, 1979).

56. This instance was cited in a paper kindly communicated to me by the author, P.-E. Guéguen, "La mendicité au pays de Vannes dans la 2e moitié du xviiie siècle," subsequently published in the *Bulletin de la Société polymathique du Morbihan, 1970* (1969), 105–134.

57. See p. 101. A detailed defense of the custom of allowing young children to seek alms and earn petty sums tending flocks before they had the strength to earn regular wages is contained in a memoir addressed to the parlement of Paris by the province of Perche in 1777, A.D. Orne, C.285.

58. Letter of La Glestière, defending his officers and including a copy of the *interrogatoire,* March 12, 1775. The complaint of the subdelegate of Nantes, Bellay, in response to the intendant's request to verify the declaration of "Barbe Mariot, fe Briand, arrêtée moyennant 30#," is dated February 19, 1775. Both letters in A.D. Ille-et-Vilaine, C.1305.

59. Fresnais to intendant of Brittany, March 4, 1770, A.D. Ille-et-Vilaine, C.1309. See also p. 88. Turgot had to negotiate for closing of a road that passed near the *dépôt* at Limoges, because it allowed access by "mischievous persons who were dismantling the walls and allowing the girls and women of ill repute who were shut up there to escape" (A.D. Haute-Vienne, C.365).

60. Duhamel, subdelegate at Caen, to intendant, July 1, 1778, A.D. Calvados, C.6774. Edward Thompson's concept of the "moral economy" of the poor might be applied to the hygiene of inmates, just as Louise Tilly applies it to the policing of the grain trade in "La révolte frumentaire, forme de conflit politique en France," *AESC* 27 (1972):731–757, especially 748.

61. See p. 96 (Dupichard's advice). The role of doctors as official consultants is treated especially well in Jean-Pierre Goubert, *Malades et médecins en Bretagne, 1770–1790* (Paris, 1974), especially "Les pauvres malades," 182–254.

62. A.N. H.1417 (archbishop of Aix); Olwen Hufton, *The Poor of Eighteenth-Century France, 1750–1789* (Oxford, 1974), 235 (also mentions bishops at Bayeux and Rennes); circulars from Laverdy of January 5 and 9, 1768, A.D. Marne, C.2026, and A.D. Indre-et-Loire, C.303. A note to the intendant of Tours, presumably from the subdelegate, contained in correspondence files dated from 1770, observes: "La mauvais odeur, la malpropreté, les dégoûtent [les écclésiastiques] à un point, que les vicaires des paroisses de la ville de Tours, qui doivent la dire [la messe] alternativement, ont commencé et aujourd'hui ils refusent. Je viens d'apprendre que les Capucins assistoient avec beaucoup de répugnance à y dire seulement la messe." The intendant agreed to allot 300 livres for an *aumônier.*

63. See especially the composite description in *Les moyens de détruire la mendicité en France en rendant les mendians utiles à l'état sans les rendre malheureux. Tirés des mémoires qui ont concouru pour le prix accordé en l'année 1777, par l'Académie des Sciences, Arts et Belles Lettres de Châlons-sur-Marne,* ed. Malvaux (Châlons-sur-Marne, 1780), 51; also Louis-Sébastien Mercier, *Tableau de Paris* (Hamburg, 1781), 2:69. On the role of curés as "defenders of the poor" and as pillars of social and political order, see Timothy Tackett, *Priest and Parish in Eighteenth-Century France: A Social and Political Study of the Curés in a Diocese of Dauphiné, 1750–1791* (Princeton, 1977), 157–162 especially.

64. Joly de Fleury's comment, from the memoir of 1759 analyzed in chapter 2, is in B.N. Joly de Fleury 1309, fol. 148.

65. Deposition taken March 13, 1775, in A.D. Seine-Maritime, C.1040. This file and A.D. Orne, C.283, give typical material on escapes and revolts.

66. The *procureur-général* of the parlement of Rouen, Belbeuf, refers to his own visit to the *dépôt* and the results of depositions taken by a *commissaire* Javin concerning abuses in the *hôpital des pauvres* in his letter of June 14, 1775, also in A.D. Seine-Maritime, C.1040.

67. *Éphémérides*, 1767, 7:169–191, "Lettre de M. B. à l'auteur des Éphémérides, contenant des réflexions sur la manière d'exercer la Bienfaisance envers les pauvres," especially
175. Quesnay's view of the relationship between investment, productivity, and population is
expressed in his article "Fermiers," written for the *Encyclopédie* in 1756, republished in
François Quesnay et la physiocratie, 2 vols. (Paris, 1958), 2:427–458: "Les fermiers riches
occupent les paysans, que l'attrait de l'argent détermine au travail: ils deviennent laborieux,
leur gain leur procure une aisance qui les fixe dans les provinces, et qui les met en état
d'alimenter leurs enfants, de les retenir auprès d'eux, et de les établir dans leur province"
(p. 453). The ideal landowner who gives no manual alms but promotes productivity and
independence is portrayed in *Éphémérides*, 1767, 9:183–216 (second installment of an article
by "B," identified as Mirabeau by Georges Weulersse, *Le mouvement physiocratique en
France [de 1756 à 1770]*, 2 vols. [Paris, 1910], 1:xxiv). A contrasting portrayal of the well-
meaning curés who amass charitable endowments for their parishioners and reduce them
unwittingly to misery is found in *Éphémérides*, 1768, 12:193.

68. Baudeau's commentary follows Mirabeau's article cited above, *Éphémérides*, 1767,
7:192–194.

69. The ideological vulnerability of the Physiocrats has been explored in the classic study
by Weulersse, *Le mouvement physiocratique*, especially in chapter 5, "L'intérêt du peuple,"
2:434–683. Du Pont's role as propagandist for Laverdy's free-trade measures is described
by Steven L. Kaplan, *Bread, Politics and Political Economy in The Reign of Louis XV*, 2
vols. (The Hague, 1976), 220. On the Assembly of Police and the reversal of Laverdy's
edicts, see, in the same work, chapters 9 and 10, both titled "The Government, the Parlements, and the Battle over Liberty," 408–490, especially 424–436.

70. Voltaire to Roubaud, letter published in the *Mercure de France* in August 1769,
Voltaire's Correspondence, ed. Theodore Besterman, 104 vols. (Geneva, 1953–1965), *Best.*
#14740. On Roubaud's *Représentations aux magistrats*, see Kaplan, *Bread*, 481.

71. Kaplan, *Bread*, 590–611. See also Darline Gay Levy, *The Ideas and Careers of
Simon-Nicolas-Henri Linguet: A Study in Eighteenth-Century French Politics* (Urbana, Ill.,
1980), especially chapter 3, *"Travaux Pratiques:* The Politics of Subsistence," 84–136.

72. *Éphémérides*, 1771, 12:217; also cited by Weulersse, *La Physiocratie à la fin du
règne de Louis XV (1770–1774)* (Paris, 1959), 213. The reference to merchants of Lyons is
in *Éphémérides*, 1770, 4:185.

73. *Éphémérides*, 1768, 12:114, and 8:205 (Baudeau); 1769, 10:145 (Assembly of Police); 1769, 2:207ff. (cheap food).

74. *Éphémérides*, 1771, 4:191–192: "Il est à croire que tant d'exemples d'ouvrages
publics faits, bien faits & sans grande dépense à prix d'argent, contribueront à hâter l'abolition générale des corvées, qui détruisent des sommes immenses, et ne font jamais rien de
solide" (following descriptions of projects at Langres, Bresse, and elsewhere). See also the
praise for the intendant Montyon's system of *ateliers de charité* in the Auvergne (1771,
2:164) and the memoir, "Police établie pour les ateliers de charité dans la Généralité de
Limoges," 1772, 2:195.

75. Ibid., 1770, 7:234ff. ("Opérations paternelles en France"), followed by the heading,
"Autres établissemens du même genre, mais dirigés vers des travaux encore plus utiles,"
indicating a preference for the road projects also established in the *généralité* of Tours.

76. Ibid., 1771, 11:166. Louis S. Greenbaum identifies this statement as an important
precedent for Du Pont's interest in hospital reform in the 1780s, in his "Health-Care and
Hospital-Building in Eighteenth-Century France: Reform Proposals of Du Pont de Nemours
and Condorcet," *SVEC* 152 (1976): 908.

77. Bloch, *Assistance et l'état*, 181. Turgot justified a request for royal aid to the Limousin in a letter of December 16, 1769, to the controller-general: *Oeuvres de Turgot et
documents le concernant*, ed. Gustave Schelle, 5 vols. (Paris, 1913–1923), 3:111–129. In a

letter to Du Pont of March 29, 1770 (ibid., 384), Turgot explained: "Pour que le commerce puisse prévenir entièrement les disettes, il faudrait que le peuple fût déjà riche et que le prix des denrées ne fût pas trop au dessus du marché général." On Turgot's belief that a new political culture would have to be molded by new institutions, see Betty Behrens, "Government and Society," chapter 8 in the *Cambridge Economic History of Europe,* vol. 5: *The Economic Organization of Early Modern Europe,* eds. E. E. Rich and C. H. Wilson (Cambridge, 1977), 602.

78. "Éloge de Gournay," Schelle, 1:601 and 613. See also the text of the edict suppressing corporations, February 1776, Schelle, 5:238–256, and the interpretation of William H. Sewell, Jr., *Work and Revolution in France: the Language of Labor from the Old Regime to 1848* (Cambridge, 1980), 72–77.

79. Schelle, 3:313–354: Turgot to Terray, December 2, 1770 (the *arrêt du conseil* of December 23 reimposed controls).

80. Schelle, 1:591. In education Turgot preferred to see performance encouraged by prizes for merit.

81. Turgot spoke of a people that "has perhaps become unbelieving as a result of having been deceived" (Schelle, 2:234). On Turgot's theory of the "net product" and the *classe disponible,* see Edgar Faure, "Turgot et la théorie du produit net," *RHES* 39 (1961), no. 3:274–286, and no. 4:417–441.

82. For Turgot's "Confession of Augsburg" against the idea of "legal despotism" in a letter to Du Pont, see Schelle, 3:486. For his banter on "the sect" in a letter of September 25, 1767, to Du Pont, see Schelle, 2:667.

83. Schelle, 2:542 and note (in text of *Réflexions sur la formation et la distribution des richesses*); Turgot to Du Pont, February 2, 1770, Schelle, 3:373: "L'endroit des *avances foncières,* en particulier, m'a fait bien mal au coeur; vous savez combien j'ai disputé avec l'abbé Baudeau sur cet article en votre présence; je puis avoir tort, mais chacun veut être soi, et non un autre." See also Louis Salleron, "Le produit net des physiocrates," in *François Quesnay et la physiocratie,* 1:148.

84. See p. 104.

85. Dakin, *Turgot,* 164; Edgar Faure, *La Disgrâce de Turgot* (Paris, 1961), chapter 5, "Vue générale de la gestion technique," and chapter 7, "La politique budgétaire." Turgot's efforts are placed in an institutional context by John Bosher, *French Finances, 1770–1795: From Business to Bureaucracy* (Cambridge, 1970), 142–165.

86. See p. 87 (advice of engineer). Accounts for the first quarter of 1772 include charges for twenty-seven burials, accompanied by a list of those who died in that period. A note by de Beaulieu of February 18, 1773, states that there were usually about one hundred inmates in the *dépôt* at Limoges, sometimes more, often far fewer (A.D. Haute-Vienne, C.366).

87. A.D. Haute-Vienne, C.365: "Mémoire sur la fourniture du tabac faite aux fols du dépôt de Limoges." Accounts show twelve livres paid the next year to a locksmith "pour avoir fait boucher les troux faits aux murs des loges, par les fous." The original receipt for tobacco given to six inmates was dated January 2, 1772.

88. A.D. Haute-Vienne, C.364 (observations on the accounting for receipts in 1770), and C.365, "État des sols par lieues donnés aux mendians élargis des dépôts de la G[énérali]té," for 1770, in amounts totaling 205 l. 4s. Many of the disbursements were to couples and families; the majority involved travel within a radius of about fifty miles. Schelle refers to Turgot's whimsical "library" in the second part of his biographical introduction to *Oeuvres de Turgot,* 2:71.

89. A.D. Haute-Vienne, C.366, and A.D. Seine-Maritime, C.1009. Schelle, 3:560, cites Turgot's marginal comment.

90. Turgot to Du Pont, October 24, 1773, Schelle, 3:627–629.

91. Turgot to Condorcet, June 8, 1773, Schelle, 3:633. Du Pont included letters from both in his correspondence with the margrave of Baden, published in Carl Knies, ed., *Carl Friedrichs von Baden brieflicher Verkehr mit Mirabeau und du Pont,* 2 vols. (Heidelberg, 1892). See also Turgot to Condorcet, July 16, 1771, Schelle, 3:529.

92. Knies, *Verkehr,* 2:100. The reference to the "old proverb" (an aphorism of canon law) is consistent with Turgot's praise of the Christian ideal of service to the poor in his "Discours sur les advantages que l'établissement du christianisme a procurés au genre humain, prononcé en latin à l'ouverture des Sorboniques par M. l'abbé Turgot, prieur de Sorbonne, le vendredi 3 juillet 1750," in Schelle, 1:202–204. The reference would be less likely to occur to Du Pont, who, in his edition of Turgot's writings, according to Schelle (1:31), deleted "tout ce qui, dans ce premier discours appartenait aux fonctions, au devoirs, à la position du prieur de Sorbonne."

93. Knies, *Verkehr,* 2:100–101. On the general contract with Manié, Rimberge et Cie, see p. 99.

94. Ibid. The entire passage on workshops is cited by Georges Weulersse, *La physiocratie à la fin du règne de Louis XV (1770–1774)* (Paris, 1959), 205. Du Pont had criticized the policy of confining beggars in workhouses in the *Éphémérides,* 1769, 4:212, while commenting on a prize-essay subject offered by the administrators of La Charité at Lyons on the best means of employing the poor confined in hospitals. See also above, note 75 (Rattier's workshop).

95. Knies, *Verkehr,* 2:105 (a lyrical glimpse of a liberal Physiocratic utopia).

96. Ibid., 2:107, and, for Du Pont's earlier letter on the reform of the *hôtel-Dieu,* 2:32. See also Greenbaum, "Health-Care," 908–912.

97. Abbé E. Lavaquery, *Le cardinal de Boisgelin, 1732–1804,* 2 vols., vol. 1: *Un prélat d'ancien régime* (Paris, 1920), 75; Dakin, *Turgot,* 9. Turgot refers to Boisgelin's presence in Limoges in a letter of June 5, 1770, to Du Pont, Schelle, 3:387.

98. A.N., 80AP 3, letters exchanged between Madame de Sauvigny and the abbé de Rousseau, October 6, 16, and 26, 1774. Auget de Montyon served as intendant of Aix from 1771 to 1773.

99. Faure, *Disgrâce de Turgot,* 68 (dismissal of Foullon).

100. Lavaquery, *Boisgelin,* 1:307. One source said Boisgelin spoke "comme Fénelon de la misère du peuple et des devoirs du Roi." See also Hermann Weber, "Das Sacre Ludwigs XVI vom 11 Juni 1775 und die Krise des Ancien Regime," in *Vom Ancien Régime zur französischen Revolution,* ed. Ernst Hinrichs et al. (Göttingen, 1978), 553 and note.

101. B.N. f.f. 8129, fol. 1. Bertier, in a retrospective memoir after a meeting late in 1775 entitled, "Mémoire sur la Mendicité—Par M. Bertier en résultat d'une conférence tenue à Fontainebleau," ibid., fol. 338–343, indicates that Turgot presided at the first meeting in October 1774. He states (fol. 339) that Turgot asked Brienne to draw up a new plan for "this essential part of administration" after that first session. It is possible that Turgot had asked Brienne to preside over this review earlier, without Bertier's knowledge.

102. Schelle comments on Daniel Trudaine and his son, Jean-Charles-Philibert (known as Trudaine de Montigny) in *Oeuvres de Turgot,* 2:64–65 and notes, and includes their correspondence with Turgot on the subject of *corvées,* 2:344 and 626. Schelle enumerates the attributions of Trudaine de Montigny and describes his role with respect to the grain trade, the *corvée,* and the guilds in Turgot's ministry (4:27). Compare Faure, *Disgrâce de Turgot,* 64, and Weulersse, "Les physiocrates sous le ministère de Turgot," *RHES* 13 (1925):317. Weulersse describes Trudaine as "un des plus solides appuis du nouveau contrôleur-général"; he helped draw up the decree on the grain trade of September 13, 1774.

103. A letter from Turgot to Le Noir, dated Versailles, November 19, 1774, in A.N. F^{15} 3590, indicates that Le Noir had been unable to attend the meeting on mendicity. Turgot sent him copies of the resulting letters to bishops and intendants, and invited Le Noir's

recommendations, along with any materials relating to rebuilding of the *hôtel-Dieu* of Paris. On Le Noir's replacement by Albert as *lieutenant de police* in December 1774, see Robert Darnton, "Le lieutenant de police J. P. Lenoir, la guerre des farines et l'approvisionnement de Paris à la veille de la Révolution," *RHMC* 16 (October–December 1969):611–624, especially 613–617. On Albert's promotion of *ateliers* in 1770, see Bloch, *Assistance et l'état,* 201–203. B.N. f.f. 8129, fol. 1, includes both Lenoir and Albert among those initially named to the commission.

104. B.N. f.f. 8129, fol. 119, "Projets et opérations depuis 1764 jusqu'à 1776."

105. Ibid., fol. 1.

106. Ibid., fol. 338v.

107. Ibid., fol. 119 and 339.

108. Ibid., fol. 339. Bertier referred to costs rising as high as 1.5 million livres in 1770, but declining thereafter by about 100,000 livres per year. In fact, the budget for the *dépôts* appears to have stabilized at about 1.2 million livres, the amount given in the table of expenditures for 1774 in Alfred Neymarck, *Turgot et ses doctrines,* 2 vols. (Paris, 1885), 2:423. The same annual figure is given in Necker's *Administration des finances,* 3 vols. bound as one (Paris, 1785), 2:338–339.

109. B.N. f.f. 8129, fol. 343. The letter is undated but is clearly the one referred to by Brienne in his report to the Estates of Languedoc of January 6, 1775, A.N., H.910. The letter states, "S.M. est en même temps occupée des moyens de remédier à la mendicité, et c'est ce que vous pouvez avoir vu par la lettre que j'ai eu l'honneur de vous écrire à ce sujet," no doubt referring to the circular addressed to all bishops on November 18 (see note 112, below).

110. The circular of November 16 is reproduced in Bloch, *Assistance et l'état,* 191, citing A.D. Marne, C.1940; other copies are in A.D. Indre-et-Loire, C.307, and A.D. Orne, C. 283. The copy of this letter and that of the November 18 circular to bishops sent to Le Noir are in A.N. F^{15} 3590.

111. The principles stated here coincide with those of Du Pont's letters to the Duke of Baden (cited p. 127), and with those of the abbé Baudeau (p. 47).

112. Bloch, *Assistance et l'état,* 191, omits part of the text at this point in the letter; as he notes, (p. 192n.), there is no central collection of the replies. A circular of April 12, 1775, reminded intendants who had not yet completed the reports that they were due (e.g., A.D. Indre-et-Loire, C.307, and A.D. Calvados, C.6776).

113. The sample table accompanying the letter (as in A.D. Seine-Maritime, C.1009) includes the following headings: "ville ou bourg; diocèse; paroisse; dénominations des différens établissemens de charité de toute nature; objets des éstablissements suivant les fondations ou donations; titres des fondations et revenus; date des titres; produite des rentes ou revenus de toute nature dont jouissent cesd. éstablissements; observations."

114. B.N. f.f. 8129, fol. 343v. This copy of the letter is addressed to Brienne from Turgot, although it is quite possible that Brienne drafted it. The copy addressed to the bishop of Fréjus is published in Schelle, 4:264.

115. Letters from two curés in the Dauphiné addressed to their bishop expressed the fear that Turgot's *enquête* was a prelude to the consolidation of traditional charitable funds to finance the new *"maison de bicestre,"* according to René Favier, "L'Église et l'Assistance en Dauphiné sous l'ancien régime: le vingt-quatrième des pauvres," *RHES* 31 (1984):448–464, especially 462. Several of the replies to Turgot's call for proposals and model projects are included in the second volume of the *Recueil,* B.N. f.f. 8130.

116. This circular to intendants of November 19, 1774, includes the telling phrase, "S.M. désireroit n'avoir plus à punir (même par le renfermement) que les vagabonds" (A.D. Indre-et-Loire, C.307, and A.D. Orne, C.283).

Chapter 7

1. *Arrêt du Conseil établissant la liberté du commerce des grains et des farines à l'intérieur du Royaume et la liberté de l'importation,* Versailles, September 13, 1774, reproduced in *Oeuvres de Turgot et documents le concernant avec biographie et notes,* ed. Gustave Schelle, 5 vols. (Paris, 1912–1923), 4:202–210 (especially 203).

2. Ibid., 209.

3. "Instruction aux curés" accompanying royal letter to archbishops and bishops, Versailles, May 9, 1775, in Schelle, 4:438.

4. Schelle, 4:46 (biography of Turgot) and 213 ("circulaire aux procureurs-généraux," September 19, 1774). The latter directive favored the provision of work as a remedy; in extremity bounties might be given to importers—no other form of intervention would be countenanced by His Majesty. See also letter to intendant of Caen, September 20, ibid., 349.

5. See p. 124 and note 77.

6. "Mémoire au roi sur les ateliers de charité à ouvrir à Paris," Schelle, 4:500. This and other memoirs reproduced by Schelle were sent to intendants with a circular of May 8, 1775 (ibid., 514). See the correspondence of Albert, Fargès, and d'Ormesson concerning ateliers in the spring of 1775 (de Crosne at Rouen, Cypierre at Orleans, and intendants of Moulins and Paris), in A.N. F.^{11} 1191 and printed *factum* with circular in A.D. Ille-et-Vilaine, C.1294.

7. Schelle, 4:416–418 (three letters to Turgot from the king, dated May 2 and 4, 1775). The *Chronique secrète* (September 14, 1774) had described "the two Bertier de Sauvigny" as being "résolus de ne rien abandonner de l'ancienne police des grains"—cited in Weulersse, "Les physiocrates sous le ministère de Turgot," *RHES,* 13 (1925):329. As a sign of the king's gratitude and confidence, Bertier was appointed superintendant of finance of the queen's household, and received a set of four tapestries, including one—reproduced as the frontispiece to this volume—on the occasion of the marriage of his oldest daughter Antoinette to the marquis de la Bourdonnaye in 1782. It was in 1776 that Bertier formally assumed his father's title as intendant of Paris, although he had functioned as such since his father's appointment as first president of the Maupeou court that replaced the parlement of Paris in 1771. See Guillaume de Bertier de Sauvigny, *Le comte Ferdinand de Bertier (1782–1864) et l'énigme de la congrégation* (Paris, 1948), 8, and Gustave Bord, *La conspiration révolutionnaire* (Paris, 1909), 205 and 210. For a sidelight on the sense of impending disfavor at the beginning of Turgot's ministry, see the correspondence between Mme de Sauvigny and the abbé Rousseau in A.N. 80AP 3.

8. Douglas Dakin, *Turgot and the Ancien Regime in France* (1939; New York, 1965), 236 and 241.

9. B.N. f.f. 8129, fol. 346v.

10. Ibid., fol. 346v. and 347. On December 3 Brienne thanked Bertier for providing documents that would allow Brienne to present his opinion with greater "knowledge and assurance."

11. Ibid., fol. 348; see also p. 113.

12. Brienne's memoir runs from B.N. f.f. 8129, fol. 245 to fol. 287; its contents are summarized by Camille Bloch, *L'assistance et l'état en France à la veille de la Révolution: généralités de Paris, Rouen, Alençon, Orléans, Soissons, Amiens (1764–1790)* (Paris, 1908), 185–190. The memoir provides the main argument for Bloch's contention that "Turgot posa avec une grande fermeté les bases d'un service public en faisant très large la part de l'État et ses représentants" (181). For another general commentary on Brienne's memoir and others in the *Recueil,* see Ira Wade, "Poverty in the Enlightenment," in *Europäische Aufklärung: Herbert Dieckmann zum 60sten Geburtstag,* eds. Hugo Friedrich and Fritz Schalk (Munich, 1976), 311–323.

13. B.N. f.f. 8129, fol. 245v. For Du Pont's memoir, see p. 127.

14. B.N. f.f. 8129, fol. 245v. Brienne's diagnosis of what Max Weber would call a "systems conflict" may be usefully compared with the ideas advanced in Ernst Hinrichs, "Justice versus Administration: Aspeckete des politischen Systemkonflikts in der Krise des Ancien Régime in Frankreich," in Hinrichs et al., eds., *Vom Ancien Régime zur Französischen Revolution: Forschungen und Perspektiven* (Göttingen, 1978), 125–150.

15. B.N. f.f. 8129, fol. 248.

16. Ibid., fol. 249.

17. Ibid., fol. 247.

18. Ibid., fol. 249v.–250. See also fol. 254v. on "being seen."

19. Ibid., fol. 249.

20. Ibid., fol. 246v.

21. Ibid., 260v. The remark on prisons occurs in the context of disciplinary provisions to be established in forced labor companies.

22. Ibid., fol. 253.

23. Ibid., fol. 254.

24. Ibid., fol. 255v. On Beccaria, see Peter Gay, *The Enlightenment: An Interpretation*, vol. 2: *The Science of Freedom* (New York, 1969), 44. See also Pierre Bouzat, "L'influence de Beccaria sur la culture juridique française," in *Secondo centenario della pubblicazione dell'opera Dei Delitte et della Pene di C. Beccaria* (Rome and Milan, 1964–1965), 33–48, especially 42.

25. Ibid., fol. 255v.

26. Ibid., fol. 256v.

27. Ibid., fol. 257v.–259.

28. Ibid., fol. 259–261. On the implied or explicit use of alchemical concepts in the context of rehabilitating beggars, see the discussion of work as "the philosopher's stone," pp. 240 and 243–244. For a description of an operation in which an amalgam is "digested" in a sealed vessel, then purged of "feces," washed, and distilled anew, see Richard S. Westfall, "Alchemy in Newton's Career," in *Reason, Experiment and Mysticism in the Scientific Revolution*, eds. M. L. Righini Bonelli and William R. Shea (New York, 1975), 208.

29. Ibid., fol. 259.

30. Ibid., fol. 260v.–261.

31. Ibid., fol. 265v.: "Je mets dans la classe des enfans trouvés, les enfans qui sont arrêtés mendians."

32. On Du Pont's proposals, see pp. 124 and 128, notes 76 and 96.

33. B.N. f.f. 8129, fol. 276.

34. Ibid., fol. 268 and 268v.

35. See the recent synthesis by Charles Coulston Gillispie, *Science and Polity in France at the End of the Old Regime* (Princeton, 1980); and Caroline C. Hannaway, "The Société Royale de Médecine and Epidemics in the Ancien Régime," *BHM* 46 (1972):257–273.

36. Ibid., fol. 270v.

37. Ibid., fol. 271.

38. Ibid., fol. 272v. See Du Pont's "Mémoire sur les municipalités," Schelle, 4:568–628, and Turgot's letter of September 23, 1775 (Schelle, 4:676), acknowledging Du Pont's manuscript with the remark that it was far more detailed than the broad "canvas" he had intended. On Turgot's intentions for municipal reform, see the discussions in Dakin, *Turgot*, 272–280; Faure, *Disgrâce de Turgot*, 356–362; William H. Sewell, Jr., *Work and Revolution in France: The Language of Labor from the Old Regime to 1848* (Cambridge, 1980), 127–131; and Gerald J. Cavanaugh, "Turgot: The Rejection of Enlightened Despotism," *FHS* 6:1 (Spring 1969):31–58.

39. B.N. f.f. 8129, fol. 277.

40. See the entire section, "Fonds pour la subsistance de la pauvreté," ibid., fol. 276–283. On the use of *régies,* see Dakin, *Turgot,* 164–166. For Loménie de Brienne's later role in founding a modern treasury, see J. F. Bosher, *French Finances, 1770–1795: From Business to Bureaucracy* (Cambridge, 1970), 196ff.

41. B.N. f.f. 8129, fol. 278v.

42. Ibid., fol. 274 (use of term "superogation") and fol. 281v., where the argument is made that the aim of "public charity" is like that of an individual's *charité bien entendue.*

43. Ibid., fol. 283v.–285.

44. Ibid., fol. 285. Brienne was aware that bureaus, or boards, were imperfect institutions, but found them preferable to the earlier forms of management that had "absorbed funds destined for public interests." Brienne himself would have preferred to see a systematic "municipal" organization, as noted earlier. Here he notes: "J'ai donc pensé que n'y ayant point d'administration municipale établie, on ne pouvoit donner de meilleurs agens à la charité publique que des bureaux."

45. Ibid., fol. 285v. On the next page he reiterated, "les opérations précédentes n'ont pas réussi faute d'ensemble."

46. In what follows, statements in support of these general impressions are drawn from about one-third of the intendances. For intendants' attitudes toward Turgot's proposed reform of the *corvées,* see the extract of Vignon's summary in Schelle, 4:538–547, and the discussion in Dakin, *Turgot,* 240. On the reformist attitudes of the intendants as a group, see Vivian Gruder, *The Royal Provincial Intendants: A Governing Elite in Eighteenth-Century France* (Ithaca, N.Y. 1968), 215.

47. Esmangart reacted strongly to the proposal to shut down the *dépôt* at Caen along with most others, following the meeting at Montigny. He cited the need for keeping an asylum for the dangerous insane, and suggested that Beaulieu, one of the largest *dépôts* in the kingdom, might serve all Normandy (to Turgot, November 28, 1775, A.D. Calvados, C.652). See also Robert M. Schwartz, *Policing the Poor in Eighteenth-Century France* (Chapel Hill, N.C., 1988), 180 and 199. Jullien reviews the substance of his correspondence with Turgot in a lengthy letter to the new controller-general, de Clugny, June 6, 1776, A.D. Orne, C.284.

48. Jullien to controller-general, August 2, 1776, A.D. Orne, C.284.

49. Caze de la Bove to Turgot, February 15, 1775, concerning the *dépôt,* A.N. H.556, and August 16, 1775, beginning, "Permettez que je vous parle encore des pauvres de Bretagne," A.N. H.565. For du Cluzel's belief in the priority of ateliers in the measures to be taken against mendicity, see his letter to Turgot, December 20, 1774, A.D. Indre-et-Loire, C.307, cited on p. 103.

50. Letter of March 12, 1775, A.D. Aisne, C.666.

51. Ibid. On the fiscal implications of large- and small-scale farming, cf. Turgot, "Mémoire au Conseil sur la surcharge des impositions," Schelle, 2:445–477, published with modifications to veil Turgot's authorship in the *Éphémérides du Citoyen,* 1767, vol. 5. Gabriel Ardant discusses these views in the context of "economic obstacles" to fiscal reform in a chapter entitled "Financial Policy and Infrastructure in Modern States and Nations," in *The Formation of National States in Western Europe,* ed. Charles Tilly (Princeton, 1975), 210.

52. Laverdy had reminded the intendant of Châlons-sur-Marne that it was improper to make beggars in confinement happier than "les autres habitants de la campagne qui outre la peine qu'ils se donnent ont encore l'inquiétude du lendemain." See p. 92.

53. See p. 122 and note 65.

54. Belbeuf to Bertier, June 14, 1775. De Crosne did not provide a formal rebuttal of Belbeuf's charges until November 24 (*minute* of letter sent); Turgot accepted de Crosne's explanations in a reply of December 11, 1775. See A.D. Seine-Maritime, C.1040.

55. De Crosne's letter of November 24. If de Crosne seems insensitive to the rights of inmates in this passage, it should be noted that he had helped to secure a retrial for Jean Calas, while serving on a special tribunal in 1765 (Vivian Gruder, *The Royal Provincial Intendants*, 84).

56. The change in de Crosne's text indicates at least a formal awareness of a possible conflict between police practice and general principles of liberty. It is natural for *hommes* to seek liberty; it is natural for *scélérats* to be detained against their will.

57. B.N. f.f. 8130, fol. 14–23v., "Extrait des Registres des délibérations prises par les Gens des trois Etats généraux de la Province de Languedoc assemblées par Mandement du Roy en la ville de Montpellier au mois de 9bre et xbre 1772," beginning with the proceedings of December 1, 1772, presided over by the archbishop of Narbonne.

58. Ibid., fol. 17: the administrators of The Hospital St. Eloy claimed that the real cost of caring for the sick transferred from the *dépôt* was 16s. per *journée* instead of the 10s. allowed.

59. Ibid., fol. 23v. The Commission on Public Works argued for more substantial aid to hospitals and setting sturdy beggars to work on *galères de terre* as needed in the province.

60. See p. 112 and note 20.

61. B.N. f.f. 8130, fol. 23v.–30: untitled memoir following proceedings of December 1772 and beginning with the words, "Les Etats ont applaudi à l'intention où étoit Sa Majesté d'arrêter la mendicité et se feront toujours un devoir de concourir à l'exécution de ses vues."

62. Ibid., fol. 24 and 25.

63. Ibid., fol. 25v. and 26v.

64. Ibid., fol. 26v.

65. Ibid., fol. 26v. and 29.

66. Ibid., fol. 27.

67. Ibid., fol. 27v.–28v. The memoir stressed the point that the Estates were more than willing to cooperate with the intendant in designating *ateliers* and providing funds for them.

68. Ibid., fol. 29. The reference to the *corvée* is on fol. 27v.

69. Ibid., fol. 28v.

70. Ibid., fol. 29.

71. Bertier's memoir, "Établissement des Compagnies d'Ouvriers Provinciaux," B.N. f.f. 8130, fol. 91–96, is followed by two memoirs similar in concept: a "Project d'Ordonnance pour les atteliers . . .," fol. 96–114, and a "Mémoire sur la suppression des Mendiants valides . . .," fol. 114–122. See also "Mémoire en faveur des Orphelins élevés dans les hôpitaux de Paris," fol. 2–11. The code of military discipline is outlined in the "Projet d'Ordonnance."

72. B.N. f.f. 8130, fol. 55–89v., relate primarily to the question whether the *hôtel-Dieu* of Paris should be transferred from its ancient site. For Turgot's involvement, see especially fol. 55, 59, and 61. See the excellent review of the question in Louis S. Greenbaum, "Jean-Sylvain Bailly, the Baron de Breteuil and the 'Four New Hospitals' of Paris," *Clio Medica* 8 (1973):261–284.

73. The proposal of the municipal officers of Reims was outlined in a letter of July 12, 1775 (A.D. Marne, C.2001). Turgot wrote in his own hand on December 25, 1775, to rule out the use of the *don gratuit* for the proposed project, but suggested that other funds be identified and asked for copies of the regulation for the *bureau d'aumône*. Turgot's close involvement in these proposals appears to have arisen from a verbal commitment made at the time of the *sacre* of Louis XVI, according to the letter of July 12. The *sacre* took place on June 11, 1775, in the Reims cathedral.

74. "Règlement pour l'aumône-générale de la ville de Bourg," B.N. f.f. 8130, fol. 39–43v., and "Mémoire des officiers municipaux de la ville de Carcassonne sur la mendicité," fol. 30–38v., ibid.

75. "Mémoire sur le moyens de remédier à la mendicité dans la ville et dans le Diocèse de Toulouse," ibid., fol. 125–146v.

76. Ibid., fol. 125: The categories of poor are defined in article 11 of a regulation of sixty-seven articles included in the memoir.

77. "Modèle des Pièces necessaires dans l'administration des pauvres," ibid., fol. 147–152v.

78. This information relating to Raynal's memoir is drawn from the account of Josselyne Guyader, "La répression de la mendicité et du vagabondage dans la ville de Toulouse depuis la déclaration de 1724 jusqu'à la Révolution de 1789" (diplôme d'études supérieures en droit, Toulouse, 1966), 273–278. Guyader cites A.D. Hérault, C.559, "Mémoire sur les moyens de bannir les mendiants et vagabonds de la province de Languedoc," dated May 20, 1775. Turgot's reply to the intendant of Montpellier is cited by Guyader, 275, from A.D. Hérault, C.570.

79. Schelle, 4:696; L'abbé Joseph-Alphonse de Véri, *Journal*, ed. De Witte, 2 vols. (Paris, 1928–1930), 1:363.

80. de Véri, *Journal*, 1:364–366.

81. B.N. f.f. 8129, fol. 313–314. The precise order of discussion at Montigny can only be surmised, with the help of a summary given in "Mémoire sur la mendicité—par M. Bertier en résultat d'une conférence tenue à Fontainebleau," ibid., fol. 338–343. This summary, by its own account (fol. 339v.), refers mainly to what transpired at Montigny, but an additional meeting was to have been held (fol. 342v.). This later meeting may have been held at Fontainebleau. See p. 154, note 109, for evidence of a further review of Brienne's memoir, with Bertier's participation.

82. Ibid., fol. 305. On sorcery and evolving concepts of proof in French law, see Robert Mandrou, *Magistrate et sorciers en France au XVIIe siècle, une analyse de psychologie historique* (Paris, 1968).

83. Ibid., fol. 306v.–309.

84. Ibid., fol. 311.

85. Ibid., fol. 304. Like Montesquieu, Brienne believed that the state had a responsibility to remove the causes of mendicity, or in the popular phrase, "not to make men poor." Boisgelin took the argument a step further, counting the state doubly at fault for punishing crimes it might have prevented. Beccaria undoubtedly contributed to the currency of this notion. See his comments on begging in *Dei Delitti e della pene,* ed. Franco Venturi (Turin, 1965), 79: "non si puo chiamare precisamente giusta (il che vuol dire necessaria) une pena di un delitto, finché la legge non ha adoperato il miglior possibilità nelle date circonstanze d'una nazione per prevenirlo." Schelle (2:67) notes that Turgot, with Malesherbes, d'Alembert, and others invited Beccaria to Paris. Beccaria visited together with Alessandro Verri in 1766, at the invitation of the *Encyclopédistes,* according to Jacques Godechot, "Beccaria et la France," *Atti del Convegno internazionale su Cesare Beccaria. Turin, 1964* (Turin, 1966), 69.

86. B.N. f.f. 8129, fol. 295.

87. Ibid., fol. 297v.

88. Ibid., fol. 300v.

89. Ibid., fol. 304.

90. Relations between Turgot and Bertier were strained especially by the *guerre des farines.* Evidence of animosity against the intendant of Paris may be gleaned from letters of Mme de Sauvigny in A.N. 80AP 3 (archives of the Bertier family). In particular, a letter of October 6, 1774, defends her son against an imputation of lacking concern for the unfortunate raised by Boisgelin. Boisgelin was having difficulty processing a complaint regarding a revised tax assessment on abbey property in the *généralité* of Paris and had suggested that

Bertier showed "special interest" for "M. de M." (possibly Montyon, previously intendant at Aix and a friend of Bertier).

91. B.N. n. acq. fr. 943, fol. 270–273v., beginning "Associé en 1767 à une commission composée de magistrats respectables. . . ." See earlier references to this memoir, p. 63 and note 56, and p. 71. The supposition that this memoir was presented at Montigny in October 1775 is based on a reference to Trudaine's critique of Brienne's memoir, and a mention of the harmful consequences of releasing beggars (presumably following Turgot's directives of 1774). Further, the context is an oral report to several persons (see the phrase, "those to whom I have the honor of reporting," and the remarks directing attention to sample forms). Finally, the recommendations fit with the discussion at Montigny and its outcome as reported in other identified documents.

92. Ibid., fol. 271v. Those who should have been locked up, according to Bertier, were the "gens absolumment sans aveu ou abandonnés à cause de leurs vices par leurs familles, les fols et tous les sujets dangereux."

93. Ibid., fol. 272. Pierre Grosclaude, *Malesherbes: témoin et interprète de son temps* (Paris, 1961), 348–349.

94. Ibid., fol. 272: "Ce fléau avoit disparu pendant quelque tems; depuis que l'on s'est relâché sur les captures, il s'est renouvellé."

95. Ibid., fol. 272v.–273.

96. Ibid., fol. 316v.–321. The text of this memoir was published, after a comparison with the text of the original manuscript in A.N. F.^{15} 138 (leaves numbered 235, 236, and 238), in Thomas Adams, "Turgot, mendicité et réforme hospitalière: l'apport d'un mémoire inédit," *Actes du 99ᵉ Congrès national des sociétés savantes (Besançon, 1974). Section d'histoire moderne et contemporaine*, vol. 2 (Paris, 1976), 343–357. The attribution of the memoir is based on the following points: (1) authorship is limited to a fairly small circle of those invited to read and respond to Brienne's memoir, which is reviewed in detail. (2) The stance of the author is that of a minister deciding policy, a stance confirmed by (3) the fact that the author introduces Malesherbes to present further arguments. This point in turn indicates (4) that the text is a transcript of an oral statement at a meeting, presumably at Montigny. (5) A reference to the difficulties in executing orders by the *maréchaussée*, "d'après l'expérience que j'en ai eu pendant que j'ai été intendant," identifies the author as a former intendant. A habit of discretion (see for example, Turgot to Du Pont, February 20, 1766, Schelle, 2:515) accounts for (6) the use of the anagram "Ducroc" in place of "Turgot," if mere playfulness is not sufficient explanation (compare Turgot's reference to Dr. "Nisaque" where Dr. "Quesnay" is intended (same letter to Du Pont, Schelle, 2:512). Finally, (7) there is no Ducroc among the corps of intendants of the period (cf. Gruder, *The Royal Provincial Intendants*), although one "Du Crocq de la Cour," a secretary of d'Alembert, was implicated in a maneuver to suppress a libel against de Vaines in the summer of 1775, adding a touch of irony to the disguise (Faure, *Disgrâce*, 364).

97. B.N. f.f. 8129, fol. 316v.

98. Ibid., fol. 317v.

99. Ibid., fol 318 and 318v.

100. Ibid., fol. 318v. Compare Beccaria, *An Essay on Crimes and Punishments: translated from the Italian of Marquis Beccaria: with the Commentary by Voltaire, translated from the French* (London, 1804), 156: "to what situation should we be reduced, if everything were to be forbidden that might possibly lead to a crime? We must be deprived of the use of our senses."

101. Ibid., fol. 318v.–319.

102. Ibid., fol. 319.

103. Ibid., fol. 319. Also, Turgot had argued the need for municipal administration in

the context of reforming the *corvée* as early as 1762 (Schelle, 2:203); see also Schelle, 4:582 and 605.

104. B.N. f.f. 8129, fol. 319–320v.

105. Ibid., fol. 320v. See also "Mémoire sur la Mendicité" (marginal note: "Résultat par M. Berthier"), dated October 21, 1775, ibid., fol. 322: "On s'est décidé en discutant cet objet [care of children] de faire venir de Bavière plusieurs femmes accoutumés à nourrir des enfants avec du lait de vache pour faire faire de nouveaux essais de cette méthode dans les terres et sous les yeux des administrateurs qui s'occupent de l'affaire de la Mendicité." Malesherbes had included a suggestion to this effect in the observations he wrote in the margin of Brienne's memoir, according to Grosclaude, *Malesherbes,* 374. The Faculté de Médecine inquired into these methods in 1775, according to A. Chamoux, "L'allaitement artificiel," *Annales de démographie historique,* 1973, 411–415, note 21.

106. B.N. f.f. 8129, fol. 320v.–321. The awkward, fragmentary style of this passage seems to suggest oral delivery, with a sweep of the hand to underline the rubrics mentioned. Since publishing the text of Turgot's memoir, I have decided that the reading *diminuer* is preferable to *terminer,* to give the translation "works of charity that will diminish" at the beginning of the paragraph. The word is not very legible in either manuscript, but *diminuer* matches Brienne's choice of words in the same context, ibid., fol. 281v. ("les autres [établissements en faveur des pauvres malades] qui doivent diminuer insensiblement").

107. A note added on a circular prepared for intendants shows that Brienne had sought out such examples. It states that the letters addressed to the intendants of Flanders and Artois should include a request for information on "administrations particulières sur la subsistance des pauvres," with details on regulations, funding, and use of resources. A similar request was to be added to the letters sent to the bishops of Arras and St. Omer, and the archbishop of Cambray. These notations follow the text of the circular to bishops dated November 18, 1774, B.N. f.f. 8129, fol. 345.

108. Grosclaude, *Malesherbes,* 346–348. The text of Malesherbes's observations on Brienne's memoir is in A.N. 177 Mi 158 (microfilm copy of A.N. AP 154), and includes the remark, "Les deux pouvoirs Royal et marital sont injustes par leur excès, sont contraires au droit naturel." See also Dakin, *Turgot,* 215, and Schelle, 5:464, on Bicêtre and the use of *lettres de cachet.*

109. B.N. f.f. 8129, fol. 338–343, "Mémoire sur la Mendicité—par M. Bertier en résultat d'une conférence tenue à Fontainebleau." The account of the meeting at Montigny suggests that further meetings may have been held:

> . . . on a trouvé qu'il étoit indispensable de changer l'ordre du travail de M. l'archevêque de Toulouse.
>
> On a pensé qu'il étoit indispensable d'offrir des ressources à la pauvreté avant de faire un crime de la mendicité.
>
> On s'est donc occupé dans les dernières conférences plus essentiellement de la partie du Mémoire de M. l'archevêque de Toulouse qui détermine la marche de l'administration. (fol. 340)

110. Ibid., fol. 343.

111. Schelle, 4:515–517; summarized in Bloch, *Assistance et l'état,* 193–194. Also found in A.D. Indre-et-Loire, C.307; A.D. Orne, C.284; and A.D. Ille-et-Vilaine, C.1295.

112. Turgot to intendant to Caen, January 15, 1776, Schelle, 5:426: "Il ne faut pas les faire escorter par la maréchaussée; ils sont destinés à devenir libres, il faut donc les essayer; s'ils s'écartent de leur route, et ne se rendent pas à leur destination, on les arrêtera et ils seront punis."

113. Schelle, 4:516 and 517. See p. 127.

114. Turgot to intendant of Caen, November 22, 1775, Schelle, 4:518. See also A.D. Indre-et-Loire, C.307, for a dossier of negotiations with contractors.

115. Schelle, 4:516; B.N. f.f. 8129, fol. 343.

116. Du Pont de Nemours, *Mémoires sur la vie et les ouvrages de M. Turgot Ministre d'État* (Philadelphia, 1782), 246.

117. B.N. f.f. 8129, fol. 319. Brienne's original phrase is at fol. 272v.

118. Ibid., fol. 321–325v., "Mémoire sur la Mendicité," with marginal note, "Résultat par M. Berthier" and in particular, fol. 323.

119. Ibid., fol. 320v. See also fol. 319 where Turgot remarks, "Voilá d'abord les atteliers publics dont la cessation des corvées va nécessiter l'établissement." Brienne's references to the *corvée,* free trade, corporations, and municipal administration correspond to the agenda for reform that Morellet addressed to Lord Shelburne in a letter of September 4, 1775 (Schelle, 4:693). See also Faure, *Disgrâce,* 340 (timing of Montigny retreat), and Schelle, 4:676 (Turgot to Du Pont).

120. Bloch, *Assistance et l'état,* 209. Brienne had recommended strict restrains on indebtedness by hospitals. B.N. f.f. 8129, fol. 278v.

121. Bloch, *Assistance et l'état,* 209–210. The growing influence of medical experts in administrative matters will be evident in the next chapter.

122. Faure, *Disgrâce,* 409–410, 449, and 518; Dakin, *Turgot,* 244–246 and 263–264. See the analysis in Herbert Lüthy, "Outlines of the 'Age of Louis XV,' " in his *Calvin to Rousseau: Tradition and Modernity in Socio-Political Thought from the Reformation to the French Revolution,* trans. Salvator Attanasio (New York, 1970), 147.

123. Bertier mentions the meeting in A.N. 80AP 81; this memoir is discussed on p. 166. See also the mention of pressure from the parlement to restore the *dépôts* in B.N. n. acq. fr. 2799, fol. 40.

124. Schelle, 5:474; doggerel translation from Thomas M. Adams, "An Approach to the Problem of Beggary in Eighteenth-Century France: the Dépôts de Mendicité" (Ph.D. diss., University of Wisconsin, 1972), 465; Turgot's reference to the *Sainte Hermandad* is in B.N. f.f. 8129, fol 317 (at Montigny).

125. Condorcet, *Vie de M. Turgot* (1786), in *Oeuvres,* ed. O'Connor and Arago (Paris, 1847), 5:140.

126. Montlinot, *État actuel du dépôt de Soissons, précædé d'un essai sur la mendicité* (Soissons, 1789, 19. Montilnot had spoken in even harsher terms of Turgot, by name, in the article *dépôt de mendicité* that he contributed to the *Encyclopédie méthodique. Economie politique et diplomatique,* vol. 2 in 1786:

> M. Turgot appeared, and by virtue of the word "liberty," which his disciples have so often abused, the *dépôts* were opened; about seven thousand individuals, with no refuge and no resource, spread out into the countryside and on the high roads; it was soon perceived that troops of them were multiplying in the kingdom: the former regulations were enforced anew; and without principles, without order, without provision for anything, all the beggars were shut away a second time.

Chapter 8

1. B.N. Joly de Fleury 1309, fol. 179–180. See references to work projects at Barcelonnette and Sassenage (pp. 241 and 246). Bertier referred to excesses committed by beggars in Provence as a result of Turgot's relaxation of arrests in a memoir entitled "Provence 1777 contribution à la dépense des mendiants," A.N. H.1417. The intendant of Soissons minimized the problem (cf. p. 143). The subdelegate of Bernay, in the *bocage normand,* reported serious incidents (A.D. Orne, C.284, letter to intendant, July 6, 1776). Du Cluzel at Tours reported incidents and welcomed Clugny's resumption of arrests (June 23, 1776, A.D. Indre-et-Loire, C.308).

2. B.N. Joly de Fleury 1309, fol. 179–180. The documents in B.N. n. acq. fr. 2799 appear to come from the same period and may also be related to the inquiry conducted by the parlement of Paris (see p. 166).

3. A.D. Indre-et-Loire, C.308, and A.D. Marne, C.2026.

4. A.D. Marne, C.2001, and A.D. Calvados, C.652.

5. Danger agreed to take over the last seven years of the contract (to 1783), A.D. Indre-et-Loire, C.308 (circular of July 9, 1776), and A.D. Orne, C.284. The instruction of June 27, 1776, on the pensioning of children is in A.D. Marne, C.2001, and A.D. Orne, C.284.

6. Circular from Clugny, July 29, 1776, in A.D. Orne, C.284, and A.D. Indre-et-Loire, C.308; The text is cited from no longer extant archives of the *intendance* of Orleans in Paultre, *De la répression de la mendicité et du vagabondage* (Paris, 1906), 411–412.

7. De Crosne to the controller-general, August 6, 1776, referring to letter of July 29, A.D. Seine-Maritime, C.1009.

8. Jullien to the controller-general, August 2, 1776, A.D. Orne, C.284. Bertier's lengthy reply of October 17, 1776, was authorized by Maurepas, since Clugny was mortally ill (A.D. Orne, C.285, among papers from 1777). Many other documents related to enforcing the Ordinance of Moulins are to be found in A.D. Orne, C.284, including a letter of Clugny, August 12, 1776, offering to authorize Jullien by *arrêt de conseil* to raise a poor tax by parish "sur tous les possédants fonds, sans aucune exception."

9. Deliberation of the bureau of the Hôpital Général de la Charité, September 14, 1787, referring to contract of August 9, 1776, A.D. Indre-et-Loire, C.315. Jullien entered into similar negotiations at Alençon, letter of August 2, 1776, A.D. Orne, C.284.

10. Cited in Paultre, *Répression*, 413–414. The king added that he wished to know how these establishments were provided for, and rejected the notion of levying a new tax in advance: "La création de nouveaux impôts me répugne; où seroit le bienfait pour le peuple, s'il y trouvoit une charge nouvelle?"

11. Bertier explains the two variants in the letter to the intendant of Brittany, cited below, note 17. A copy of the text, 'Ordonnance du Roi concernant les mendians du 30 juillet 1777,'' is in A.D. Ille-et-Vilaine, C.1294. See Bloch, *L'assistance et l'état en France à la veille de la Révolution: généralités de Paris, Rouen, Alençon, Orléans, Soissons, Amiens (1764–1790)* (Paris, 1908), 219, referring to the text of July 27 (printed copy in A.N. AD I 25). Bloch is skeptical of any personal initiative by the king in this matter.

12. Letter of Bertier, August 8, 1777, at Versailles, to intendant of Alençon, accompanying ordinance of July 30, 1777, A.D. Orne, C.285. Cf. A.D. Ille-et-Vilaine, C.1294. The title of director-general of finance was a compromise reflecting Necker's status as a foreigner. Since the death of Clugny de Nuis in October 1776, Necker had served officially as deputy to the controller-general, Taboureau de Réaux.

13. Bloch, *Assistance,* 210 and 226.

14. A.N. H.912. Necker asked Bertier to comment on article 7 of the *cahier* of the Estates of Languedoc (letter of August 28). Bertier replied on September 9 that the province could not be excused from the payment requested, in light of expansion of the *dépôt* and the issuance of a new ordinance; but since Taboureau had led the archbishop of Narbonne to believe the request would be reduced, the amount might be cut by ten thousand to a sum of fifty thousand. On November 6 Bertier acknowledged receiving from Necker a copy of the king's reply to the Estates. Necker may have conferred with Bertier at the latter's estate: Josseline Guyader refers to a letter from Necker dated November 16 at Sainte-Geneviève in her thesis, "La répression de la mendicité at du vagabondage dans la ville de Toulouse depuis la déclaration de 1724 jusqu' à la Révolution de 1789," typescript D.E.S. droit (Toulouse, 1966), 282–283. A.D. Orne, C.285, contains a letter of the same date from Bertier at Sainte-Geneviève.

15. Copies of Bertier's circular of October 20 in A.D. Aisne, C.711, and in A.D. Ille-et-Vilaine, C.1294.

16. "Copie de la lettre écrite à M. Bertier par M. l'intendant de la Rochelle le 21 novembre 1777," A.D. Ille-et-Vilaine, C.1294.

17. Bertier to Caze de la Bove, October 29, 1777, A.D. Ille-et-Vilaine, C.1294. Caze de la Bove had earlier raised sweeping objections to the ordinance of July, especially to its assumption that the invalid and unemployed had been suitably provided for. Bertier may have used the example of measures taken in the *généralité* of Paris in response to other intendants' objections to the ordinance of 1777. The text of a letter on alms bureaus addressed to the intendant of Châlons in 1777 by Bertier is cited by Paul Ardascheff, *Les intendants de province sous Louis XVI* (1909; Geneva, 1978), 337. The extract is identical to the letter received by Caze de la Bove.

18. Same letter of October 29. The printed letter to Bertier's subdelegates, accompanying the instruction on alms bureaus, stressed the important role of the subdelegates in carrying out past reforms. Case de la Bove wrote from Paris on November 1 to the intendants of La Rochelle, Poitiers, Tours, Orleans, and Caen indicating his compliance with the procedures of exchanging inmates as outlined by Bertier. In a later note of November 29, 1777, Caze de la Bove wrote his secretary, Petiet, from Paris to say that he was persuaded by the arguments of Montyon; although "M. Necker and M. Bertier would not adopt them for Paris . . . we can continue to do for our *généralités* as we have done in the past."

19. Bertier to Baudry, July 18 and 22, 1778, A.D. Yonne, C.196.

20. Bertier at Saint-Geneviéve to intendant of Alençon, November 16, 1777, with copy of memoir on the execution of the ordinance of July 30 in the province of Perche, A.D. Orne, C.285.

21. A.D. Aisne, C.711, and A.D. Ille-et-Vilaine, C.1294. The circular is cited indirectly by Bloch, *Assistance,* 222. Cf. Le Peletier's letter cited on p. 143.

22. Some examples of alms bureaus promoted in connection with the policy concerted by Necker and Bertier are cited in Bloch, *Assistance et l'état,* 223.

23. Le Peletier's inquiry is in A.D. Aisne, C.711, in a letter of October 30, 1777. He doubted that the number of beggars in his *généralité* would diminish, even though he used many of the same measures that Bertier had employed. Bertier sent him a printed brochure entitled *Ordre d'administration pour le soulagement des pauvres de la paroisse de Saint-Sulpice* (A.D. Aisne, C.666).

24. B.N. f.f. 8129, fol. 269v.–270.

25. Archbishop of Aix to M. Contaud, December 11, 1776, A.N. H.1417. In a later memoir Boisgelin referred to the ordinance of July 30, 1777, as "ambigue, insuffisante, et de difficile exécution" (Bibliothèque Mazarine, MS. 3433 (1691).

26. A.D. Ille-et-Vilaine, C.4937. See p. 143. In a letter drafted in reply to Amelot's notification of the July ordinance, Caze de la Bove went so far as to ask for a second *dépôt* at Quimper. At the same time he was sharply critical of the failure of royal policy with respect to providing *ateliers* and a resolution to the crisis of charitable finance (A.D. Ille-et-Vilaine, C.1294).

27. A.N. H.556. The opening lines of the memoir indicate that it was composed in 1777 in rebuttal to a challenge to the ordinance of July 30, 1777: "Le Parlement de Bretagne a formé des réclamations vives sur l'ordonnance de police du 30 juillet dernier [inscribed correction: "27 juillet 1777"]; ces réclamations ont donné lieu à un arrêté par lequel il a été nommé des commissaires. Ces commissaires ont dressé un memoire dont ils ont rendu compte à la chambre de vacations et dont copie a été adressée à M. Le Garde des Sceaux." The same memoir was used on later occasions.

28. Ibid. The last two points echo Montesquieu's *Spirit of the Laws.* cf. above, Chapter

6, note 31. See Caze de la Bove's insistent letters in A.N. H.565, and Bertier's discussion of the 50,000 livres that Necker had purportedly led the intendant to expect, in a letter to Necker of December 29, 1777.

29. See the definition of *caput mortuum* in Wolfgang Schneider, *Lexikon alchemistich-pharmazeutischer Symbole* (Weinheim, 1962), 35. See also the notion that the clinician's gaze is like the fire that allows 'the essential purity of phenomena" to be distinguished, leaving an inert *caput mortuum,* in Michel Foucault, *Naissance de la clinique* (Paris, 1972), 121. See also p. 139 and p. 240.

30. The coarse bran *(le gros son)* is removed from the grain used in making the bread for the *dépôts.*

31. A.N. X^{1B} 8971; speech by Louis Séguier, July 31, 1778; proceedings reproduced in part in H. Monin, *L'état de Paris en 1789, études et documents sur l'ancien régime* (Paris, 1889), 259–260.

32. A.N. 80AP 14. The central issue in the struggle between Bertier and the communities in which his properties lay focused on the collection of the seigneurial levy known as the *tierce* on allodial properties governed by the custom of Troyes, according to a richly informed study of the case by Mary Ann Quinn, "Pratiques et théories de la coutume: alliodité et conflits de droits dans la seigneurie de L'Isle-sous-Montréal au XVIIIe siècle," *Études rurales* 103–104 (July-December 1986):71–104.

33. A.N. 80AP 81. Some of the arguments are similar to those contained in the memoirs of 1778 already cited.

34. This outline of his accomplishments appears to have been used as a source for the anonymous *Notice biographique sur M. de Bertier, intendant de Paris* (Paris, 1847). Guillaume de Bertier de Sauvigny has suggested in conversation that this *Notice* was the work of Alfred Nettement, a legitimist sharply critical of Lamartine's paean to the Girondins, which also appeared in 1847.

35. A.D. Ille-et-Vilaine, C.4937.

36. Letter of July 7, 1780, A.D. Ille-et-Vilaine, C.1302.

37. Caze de la Bove to Joly de Fleury, March 13, 1782, A.N. H.556.

38. See especially intendant of Soissons to Terray, July 6, 1773, A.D. Aisne, C.704. Compare the letter of the subdelegate Alexandre at Rouen, August 16, 1768, A.D. Seine-Maritime, C.1008.

39. Clugny to intendant of Alençon, July 29, 1776, A.D. Orne, C.284; same text in A.D. Marne, C.2026.

40. Bertier to intendant of Alençon, May 29, 1777, A.D. Orne, C.285; same text to intendant of Caen, A.D. Calvados, C.653.

41. Documents cited in the *inventaire* of A.D. Loiret, C.886 (the departmental archives themselves were largely destroyed in World War II).

42. Necker to intendant of Tours, April 22, 1779, A.D. Indre-et-Loire, C.313. Necker's elimination of *caissiers* is referred to in Calonne's circular reinstating them in February 1784, A.D. Indre-et-Loire, C.313.

43. Joly de Fleury to intendant of Tours, June 22, 1781, A.D. Indre-et-Loire, C.313.

44. Memoranda prepared for the intendant in the same dossier spoke more sharply of "ces prétendus munitionnaires" and their profiteering: "on pourroit plustot dire qu'ils sont honteux de faire un pareil bénéfice qui n'auroit pû avoir lieu qu'en retranchant une partie de la subsistance et de l'entretien de ces malheureux." The new terms provided by Joly de Fleury might be expected to swell the number of beggars arrested voluntarily, according to these drafts.

45. Documents relating to Antoine-Basile Pierre de Rimberge, Jacques-Bernard Leroy, and their fellow contractors show that they obtained a six-month delay in their obligations in September 1784 that was renewed for another six months in March 1785, and a second

reprieve for a year as of September 1788. The first of these is described as "Lettre de surséance générale obtenue au Conseil d'État du Roi de 17 septembre 1784, signée le baron de Breteuil portant délai de six mois à compter du 28 du présent en faveur d'Antoine Bazile de Rimberge et autres munitionnaires des dépôts de mendicité. . . . (Administration générale des domaines, ville de Paris, Lettres de Chancellerie, A.D. Seine, D.C⁶ 28, fol. 115). In A.N. V⁷ 370 (Commissions extraordinaires du Conseil), there is a claim advanced by a Sieur Jean-Jacques Bellon, "Cydevant négociant à Lyon et entrepreneur de la fourniture des cotons à filer dans les dépôts de mendicité," against the general contractors concerning supplies to four *dépôts* under an agreement of October 6, 1776 (the dossier is dated December 26, 1789).

46. Joly de Fleury to intendant of Tours, June 22, 1781, A.D. Indre-et-Loirs, C. 313.

47. A.D. Marne, C.2030.

48. Memoir of January 14, 1784, reviewing Colombier's services in support of a request to fix his yearly compensation at 12,000 livres (probably prepared for Calonne by Chaumont de la Millière), A.N. F¹⁵ 2866. For a general introduction to Colombier's career, see Pierre Gallot-Lavallée, *Un hygiéniste au XVIIIᵉ siècle: Jean Colombier, rapporteur du conseil de santé des hôpitaux militaires, inspecteur général des hôpitaux et prisons du royaume (1736–1789)* (Paris, 1913). See also Paul Delaunay, *La vie médicale aux XVIᵉ, XVIIᵉ, et XVIIIᵉ siècles* (Paris, 1935), 262, 279, 283. The following account is adapted in part from Thomas M. Adams, "Medicine and Bureaucracy: Jean Colombier's Regulation for the French *Dépôts de Mendicité* (1785)," *BHM* 52 (1979):529–541, with the kind permission of the Johns Hopkins University Press.

49. On the hospital commission chaired by La Millière in 1777, see Bloch, *Assistance et l'état*, 227–233, and Louis S. Greenbaum, "Jacques Necker's *Enquête* of the Paris Hospital (1777)," *Consortium on Revolutionary Europe: Proceedings, 1984* (Athens, Ga., 1986), 26–40. For practices that would later be adopted in the *dépôts,* see Marcel Spivak, "L'hygiène des troupes à la fin de l'ancien régime," *Dix-huitième siècle* 9 (1977):115–122, especially 118; Rudolph Bruppacher, *Militärmedizin in der Aufklärung* (Zurich, 1967), 68; Jean Colombier, *Code de médecine militaire pour le service de terre,* 5 vols. (Paris, 1772), 2:91; *Ordonnance du Roi concernant les hôpitaux militaires et ceux de charité au compte de S.M. du 1ᵉʳ janvier 1780* (Paris, 1780), 116ff.

50. Antoine Laurent Lavoisier, *Oeuvres de Lavoisier,* 6 vols. (Paris, 1862–1893), 3:465–466 and 474; Denis I. Duveen and Herbert S. Klickstein, "Antoine Laurent Lavoisier's Contribution to Medicine and Public Health," *BHM* 29 (1955):164–179, especially 169; Louis S. Greenbaum, "The Humanitarianism of Antoine Laurent Lavoisier," *SVEC* 88 (1972):651–675. Duhamel du Monceau had articulated the expertise of engineers and architects on matters of hygiene in *Moyens de conserver la santé aux équipages des vaisseaux, avec la manière de purifier l'air des salles des hôpitaux, et une courte description de l'hôpital Saint-Louis à Paris* (Paris, 1759).

51. Colombier's first emoluments as inspector-general were authorized January 7, 1781 (A.N. F¹⁵ 2866). His office was in the Hôtel de la Force. See also Gallot-Lavallée, *Colombier,* 75.

52. A.N. F¹⁵ 2806: 45 livres for *robes des malades.*

53. Jean Colombier, *Description des épidémies qui ont régné depuis quelques années dans la généralité de Paris . . . publiée par ordre de M. l'intendant* (Paris, 1783), premier cahier, 96. For the emergence of these public health activities, see Caroline C. Hannaway, "The Société Royale de Médecine and Epidemics in the Ancien Régime," *BHM* 46 (1972):257–273; and Jean Meyer, "L'enquête de l'Académie de Médecine sur les épidémies, 1774–1794," *Études rurales* 34 (1969):7–69.

54. A.D. Aisne, C.714.

55. A.N. F¹⁵ 2806. A letter of Bertier to the intendant of Tours, May 30, 1785, A.D.

Indre-ét-Loire, C.313, announces that the controller-general has decided to provide various *dépôts* with "ventilators similar to those installed in the *dépôt* at St. Denis, in order to diminish the insalubrity of places that are too closed-in and cannot be sufficiently aired out." Payments were made to a Sieur Weulersse, "ingénieur de la marine du Roy," for installations at Tours. Doublet's article is cited at the end of this chapter.

56. A.N. F^{15} 2866 (travel expenses); A.D. Seine-Maritime, C.1035, letter of April 13 (reference to regulation at St. Denis); letter of May 10, 1783, from intendant, and reply of d'Ormesson, May 25, 1783, approving new contract but objecting to high cost of food in comparison with prices at *dépôt* of St. Denis. See also Marie-Odile Deschamps, "Le dépôt de mendicité de Rouen" (D.E.S. Faculté des Lettres, Caen, 1965), 69. Montlinot, inspector of the *dépôt* at Soissons, refers to Colombier's recommendations in a letter to the intendant of May 10, 1783, A.D. Aisne, C.749.

57. A.N. H.921 and 927 (*cahiers* of Languedoc, 1780–1782). See also Iain A. Cameron, *Crime and Repression in the Auvergne and the Guyenne, 1720–1790* (New York, 1981), 115.

58. A.D. Aisne, C.749, and A.D. Calvados, C.6776: d'Ormesson circular of May 25, 1783.

59. Letter of Joly de Fleury to Flesselles, January 4, 1783, A.D. Rhône, C.165. On Colombier's visit, see Jean-Pierre Gutton, *La société et les pauvres: l'exemple de la généralité de Lyon, 1534–1789* (Paris, 1971), 461.

60. *Règlement concernant le dépôt royal de mendicité de Lyon, lu et arrêté au Bureau d'Administration dudit Dépôt Royal de la Quarantaine, le 4 Décembre 1783* (Lyons, 1783): A.D. Rhône, C.175.

61. Ibid., title 11, article 32.

62. Ibid., title 11, articles 35–38.

63. A.N. F^{15} 2866.

64. Bertier to Gojart, July 10, 1784, A.N. F^4 1026.

65. A.D. Rhône, C.175. Calonne approved further building and the establishment of a manufacture at Lyons in a letter of May 23, 1784.

66. A.D. Rhône, C.165. De Flesselles had advised the administrators of the *dépôt* that the king had called him to the post of *conseiller d'état,* and thanked them for their cooperation, in a letter of August 18, 1784, A.D. Rhône, C.175. Terray replaced him at Lyons.

67. Colombier to Terray, March 4, 1785, A.D. Rhône, C.165.

68. Letter of the intendant of Caen to subdelegate, A.D. Calvados, C.718.

69. Letter to intendant from Calonne, followed by letter from Colombier, May 27, A.D. Somme, C.1624.

70. A.N. H.556, "Règlement concernant la constitution et la régime intérieur des dépôts de mendicité du Royaume," title 3, article 19 (further references by section only). The *lieutenant de police* of Paris, Lenoir, had forbidden the use of copper containers for keeping milk in order to prevent poisoning from verdigris, according to Alan Williams, "The Police and Public Welfare in Eighteenth-Century Paris," *Social Science Quarterly* 56:3 (December 1975):408. On experiments of the 1770s relating to disinfection, see Louis Bernard Guyton de Morveau, *A treatise on the means of purifying infected air, of preventing contagion, and arresting its progress* (London, 1802), especially 28 and 33.

71. Title 3, article 17.

72. Title 3, article 18. The draft of a letter to Bertier from Rouen May 10, 1783, offers testimony to Colombier's views on a minimal diet for beggars: "M. Colombier . . . m'a observé que les mendians qui sont accoutumés à manger de la viande lorsqu'ils sont en liberté dépérisoient, si on ne leur en donnoit pas quelquefois et il m'a assuré qu'il étoit indispensable de leur donner cette nourriture fortifiante et des légumes le soir au moins deux fois par semaine" (A.D. Seine-Maritime, C.1035). See also p. 172 and note 56.

73. On meat consumption, see Marcel Baudot, "L'alimentation carnée en France à la fin du premier empire," in *Actes du XCIII^e Congrès national des sociétés savantes, Tours, 1968. Section d'histoire moderne et contemporaine,* vol. 1: *L'alimentation et ses problèmes* (Paris, 1971):139–146; and Gabriel Désert, "La viande dans l'alimentation des bas-Normands au XIXe siècle," ibid., 147–169. Ordinary Parisians ate fish and meat in 1789, according to Robert Philippe, "Une opération pilote: l'étude du ravitaillement de Paris au temps de Lavoisier," *AESC*, 1961, 564–568. A more representative diet for eighteenth-century France is described in Émile Appolis, "L'alimentation des classes pauvres dans un diocèse languedocien au XVIIIe siècle," *Actes . . . Tours,* 55–58.

74. Title 3, articles 79–80. Inmates would receive one-half to two-thirds of the normal wage, depending on the product and its value.

75. Title 3, article 5: "Il y aura dans chaque dépôt une piscine pour laver et désinfecter les nouveaux renfermés avant de leur donner les vêtements et linges de la maison, une étuve pour détruire l'infection et la vermine des habits et linges appartenans aux renfermés, et de ceux de la maison qui seront dans le même cas."

76. Title 3, articles 6–16.

77. Title 3, articles 46–67. Articles pertaining to the regime of the infirmaries are reproduced in an appendix to Thomas M. Adams, "Niveau de vie et correction dans les dépôts de mendicité au XVIIIe siècle," *Bulletin de la Société française d'histoire des hôpitaux* 33 (1976):53–72.

78. Bannefroy, *Mémoire sur la mendicité par M. Bannefroy, ancien inspecteur des maisons de force et des dépôts de mendicité* (Paris, 1791), 26. Bannefroy appears on the accounts of St. Denis for visits in 1783 (A.N. F¹⁵ 2806).

79. Colombier, *Code de médecine militaire,* 2:91.

80. Title 1, article 3. Personnel listed in accounts for St. Denis as early as 1780 include an *inspecteur économique,* an *inspecteur de justice,* and an *inspecteur pour la sureté,* as well as doctors, surgeons, and an apothecary (A.N. F¹⁵ 2806).

81. The minister of the interior would later insist on the role of a trained *régisseur* in maintaining "l'ordre des écritures et de la comptabilité": letter of April 20, 1791, to the new administrators of the Orne (A.N. F¹⁵ 2800).

82. The *maîtresse infirmière* had the key to a separate cabinet for the linens of the infirmary. She would be responsible for having them washed and returned in a batch (3:44).

83. See Toby Gelfand, "A Clinical Ideal: Paris 1789," *BHM* 51 (1977):401, on "the clinic as written observation" and on Chambon's debt to Colombier.

84. Copies of the standard printed form are to be found in various departmental archives, e.g., A.D. Hérault, C.588; A.D. Cher, C.36; A.D. Seine-Maritime, C.1020. The inspector Montlinot at Soissons criticized the *régie* for requiring "geometrical exactitude" in the cost of grain used in a specific batch of bread: letter of January 20, 1788 (A.D. Aisne, C.733).

85. See the works by Foucault and Eisenstein cited above in the context of the first instructions for the *dépôts,* p. 81 and note 28.

86. A.N. F¹⁵ 2800. In a letter to the intendant of Caen, October 22, 1785, Calonne had insisted on having as overseers "des gens éprouvés et élevés dans le dépôt de Saint-Denis où la nouvelle régie est établie." A.D. Calvados, C.718. In granting a commission to a new *régisseur* at Grenoble August 19, 1790, La Millière insisted that this action was not to be taken as a precedent, "attendu que le Sr. Pasque n'a pas fait de surnumérariat au dépôt de Saint Denis suivant la règle établie à cet égard et qui jusqu'à présent a toujours été exactement suivie." A.N. F¹⁵ 2794. See also note 81 above.

87. A.N. F¹⁵ 2787. Accounts for 1786 at St. Denis include payments to three *surnuméraires.* Henrion de Bussy, later overseer at Riom (see below, note 94), is mentioned in the account for 1785 at St. Denis, A.N. F¹⁵ 2806.

88. Gallot-Lavallée, *Colombier,* 95. See Robert M. Schwartz, *Policing the Poor in*

Eighteenth-Century France (Chapel Hill, N.C., 1988) 176, on the number of *dépôts* placed under the management of a royal *régie* by 1789.

89. A.D. Seine-Maritime, C.1035, and A.D. Indre-et-Loire, C.313.

90. [Jean Colombier and François Doublet]. *Instruction sur la manière de gouverner les insensés et de travailler à leur guérison dans les asiles qui leur sont destinés* (Paris, 1785), 5, 33, 44. Cf. Gallot-Lavallée, *Colombier*, 65. The instruction is promised in title 3, article 67, of the general regulation of 1785 and in title 11, article 38, of the Lyons regulation of 1783. Michel Foucault interprets this instruction as an ambiguous compromise between old concepts of confinement and a new obligation of medical assistance, in *Folie et déraison: histoire de la folie à l'âge classique* (1961; Paris, 1971), 452. Payments to Mauduyt at St. Denis appear in A.N. F¹⁵ 2806. The papers of the Comité de Mendicité of the Constituante include Thouret's copy of a memoir by Mauduyt, "Sur l'utilité d'établir des traitements électriques dans les hôpitaux," A.N. F¹⁶ 936.

91. A.D. Indre-et-Loire, C.315, and A.D. Aisne, C.711. Colombier outlined a reporting role for hospitals in his *Code de médecine militaire,* 2:122. See also the "Plan de la correspondence des hôpitaux militaires et de charité du Royaume, où l'on reçoit des soldats malades," by the inspector of military hospitals, François Marie Clavell Richard de Hautesierck, *Recueil d'observations de médecine des hôpitaux militaires,* vol. 1 (Paris, 1766): xxiv. On the correspondence of military hospitals and its relationship to the Société Royale de Médecine, see Caroline C. Hannaway, *Public Welfare and the State in Eighteenth-Century France: The Société Royale de Médecine of Paris (1776–1793)* (Ph.D. diss., The Johns Hopkins University, 1974), 71 and 167.

92. On Dupichard, see p. 96. On Davan, see p. 171. La Hardrouyère appears in accounts for the *dépôt* at Rennes in 1785 (A.D. Ille-et-Vilaine, C.1301) and is active in the fight against epidemics, according to Jean-Pierre Goubert, *Malades et médecines en Bretagne, 1770–1790* (Paris, 1974), 232n.

93. François Doublet, *Observations faites dans le département des hôpitaux civils,* vol. 3 (Paris, 1787):73. A decade before, Le Pecq de la Clôture published observations on epidemics and hygiene dating from 1773 in the *dépôt* at Rouen and on the unhealthy quarter of Martainville, in which it was situated, in his *Collection d'observations sur les maladies et constitutions épidémiques* (Rouen, 1778), 117 and 942.

94. A.D. Puy-de-Dôme, C.1188.

95. Ibid. Colombier's strictures on the workshop in the *hôpital-général* at Riom are in a report of November 18, 1785, A.D. Puy-de-Dôme, C.1043.

96. Note of Montlinot to Favier on accounting for 1787, A.D. Aisne, C.733; A.D. Somme, C.1624. Accounts for the *dépôt* at Tours (A.D. Indre-et-Loire, C.316) record 116 deaths in 1787, compared with a yearly average of 30 in the old *dépôt*. See other related correspondence of La Millière and the intendant in A.D. Indre-et-Loire, C.313 and 315, and A.N. F¹⁵ 2793. La Millière announced in a letter of September 5, 1788 (C.315), that Colombier was to inspect the hospitals and prisons at Tours, Saumur, Angers, La Flèche, Le Mans, and Amboise, including the *dépôt* at Tours. See Raoul Mercier, *Le monde médical de Touraine pendant la Révolution* (Tours, 1936), 339–342.

97. Report of May 1789, A.N. F¹⁵ 2800. See also correspondence with intendant of Caen, who thought a contract would be more economical: A.D. Calvados, C.757.

98. In addition to reports already cited, see A.N. F¹⁵ 2810. Colombier criticizes faulty record-keeping at Limoges in a report of October 11, 1788, and acknowledges improvements March 18, 1789. A letter of the inspector Montlinot at Soissons discussing accounts for 1787 refers to the building of a large bath *(piscine)* and a "Fournaise ou four en tôle pour désinfecter," and requests "des corsets de force" for use in restraining an insane inmate (A.D. Aisne, C.733).

99. Charges of gambling, graft, and general disorder at the *dépôt* of Rennes are con-

tained in an undated memoir with papers from the late 1780s relating to the Estates: A.D. Ille-et-Vilaine, C.1299, 'Mémoire concernant le dépôt de mendicité connu sous le nom de maison de force établie à Rennes rue St. Hélier.'' Bertier promised that the *maréchaussée* would be given strict instructions not to allow inmates to barter their clothes in a letter to the intendant of Soissons, March 26, 1782, A.D. Aisne, C.714. The connection between discipline, routine, and maintenance standards is discussed in François Béguin, "La machine à guérir," the title essay in Michel Foucault et al., *Les machines à guérir: aux origines de l'hôpital moderne* (Paris, 1976), 55–69, and more broadly by Harvey Mitchell, "Rationality and Control in French Eighteenth-Century Medical Views of the Peasantry," *Comparative Studies of Society and History* 21:1 (January 1979):82–112.

100. Colombier to intendant of Châlons, January 30, 1788, A.N. F^{15} 2796; report on *dépôt* at Amiens, January 28, 1789, A.N. F^{15} 2808.

101. See especially Louis S. Greenbaum, "Scientists and Politicians: Hospital Reform in Paris on the Eve of the French Revolution," in *The Consortium on Revolutionary Europe, 1750–1850. Proceedings, 1973* (Gainesville, Fla., 1975), 168–191; and Greenbaum, "Science, Medicine, Religion: Three Views of Health Care in France on the Eve of the French Revolution," *Studies in Eighteenth-Century Culture,* vol. 10, ed. Harry C. Payne (Madison, Wis., 1981), 373–391. See also the seminal article of Harold T. Parker, "French Administrators and French Scientists during the Old Regime and the Early Years of the Revolution," in Richard Herr and H. T. Parker, eds., *Ideas in History: Essays Presented to Louis Gottschalk by his Former Students* (Durham, N.C., 1965); and the broad synthesis of Charles Coulston Gillispie, *Science and Polity in France at the End of the Old Regime* (Princeton, 1980).

102. *Encyclopédie méthodique. Médecine,* vol. 1, ed. Vicq d'Azyr (Paris, 1787), s.v. "Air," subheading, "Air des hôpitaux de terre et de mer," 569–575. Doublet's authorship is confirmed in *Dictionnaire des sciences médicales. Biographie médicale,* ed. Antoine J. L. Jourdan, 7 vols. (Paris, C.L.F. Panckoucke, 1820–1825), vol. 3 (1821), s.v. "Doublet, François," 518. For background and synthesis, see Richard Etlin, "L'air dans l'urbanisme des lumières," *Dix-huitième siècle* 9 (1977):123–134. See p. 171 and note 55.

103. In the period 1779–1783, the number of deaths each year had ranged from 322 to 481, according to registers of burials at the *dépôt*. The number ranged from 234 to 290 in the next five years, with the greatest improvement in 1784, according to J. Béaud and C. Bouchart, "Le dépôt de pauvres de Saint-Denis (1768–1792)," *A.D.H. 1974,* 127–143, especially 130.

Chapter 9

1. Camille Bloch, *L'assistance et l'état en France à la veille de la Révolution: généraltés de Paris, Rouen, Alençon, Orléans, Soissons, Amiens (1764–1790) (Paris, 1908),* 211–214; Daniel Roche, *Le siècle des lumières en province: académies et académiciens provinciaux, 1680–1789,* 2 vols. (Paris, 1978), 36, 57, 124, 164, 206, 375.

2. [Abbé Malvaux], ed., *Les moyens de détruire la Mendicité en France, en rendant les Mendians utiles à l'état sans les rendre malheureux; tirés des Mémoires qui ont concouru pour le Prix accordé en l'année 1777, par l'Académie des Sciences, Arts et Belles Lettres de Châlons-sur-Marne* (Châlons-sur-Marne, 1780), 3, 12, and 478–497.

3. Ibid., 124 and 478–497.

4. Ibid., 498–499.

5. Ibid., 61; manuscript memoir and related documents of the Société Royale d'Agriculture de Soissons, A.D. Aisne, D.21 and 22. The memoir was published in Montlinot's name as *Discours qui a remporté le prix de la Société royale d'agriculture de Soissons en l'année*

1779, sur cette question proposée par la même société: quels sont les moyens de détruire la mendicité, de rendre les Pauvres valides utiles et de les secourir dans la ville de Soissons (Soissons, 1779); it was also published under the same title at Lille that year.

6. Claude Bellanger et al., *Histoire générale de la presse française,* vol. 1: *Des origines à 1814* (Paris, 1969), 378–380; Louis Trénard, "L'influence de Voltaire à Lille," *SVEC* 58 (1967):1607–1634, and "La presse périodique en Flandre au 18ᵉ siècle," *Dix-huitième siècle, 1969,* 89–105, and *1970,* 77–101.

7. Suzanne Tucoo-Chala, *Charles-Joseph Panckoucke et la librairie française, 1736–1798* (Pau and Paris, 1977), 137 and passim (best source for Montlinot's association with Panckoucke). See also M. Braure, *Lille et la Flandre wallonne,* 2 vols. (Lille, 1932), 2:570. Full title of published memoir is given in note 5, above.

8. Malvaux, *Moyens,* 61–63.

9. Ibid., 63. I have compared the manuscript of the original memoir, side 21, in A.D. Aisne, D.21. Further comparisons noted were generally made from a close reading of this source on microfilm. The published version of the memoir consulted at the Bibliothèque Nationale appears to follow the manuscript, at least on major points.

10. Ibid., 85–86; side 10 of Montlinot's manuscript. The heading "Les hôpitaux étouffent les sentimens" is in Malvaux, 95.

11. Ibid., 49; manuscript, side 3.

12. Ibid., 50.

13. Ibid., 349.

14. Ibid., 277. Cf. Harvey Chisick, *The Limits of Reform in the Enlightenment: Attitudes toward the Education of the Lower Classes in Eighteenth-Century France* (Princeton, 1981), 141. Noting Montlinot's failure to promote literacy, Chisick overlooks the theme of civic autonomy.

15. Malvaux, *Moyens,* 218 and 223; manuscript, sides 29–33.

16. Ibid., 354.

17. In the following pages and elsewhere in this study, I have drawn on my previously published article, "Mendicity and Moral Alchemy: Work as Rehabilitation," *SVEC* 151 (1976):47–76. On the relationship between work and penalty in the Enlightenment, see Franco Venturi, "The Right to Punish," in his *Utopia and Reform in the Enlightenment* (Cambridge, 1971), especially 113.

18. Malvaux, *Moyens,* 412–416, 422, 435, 453.

19. Ibid., 411. Malvaux cites Lambert, director of apprentices at the *hôpital-général,* as the source for these ideas. Similar ideas occur throughout the work. On the evolution of ideas about work, I have found no published study to match the richness of Clinio Duetti, "Work Noble and Ignoble: An Introduction to the Modern Idea of Work" (Ph.D. diss., University of Wisconsin, 1954). See also the essay by Lucien Febvre, "Travail: évolution d'un mot et d'une idée," reprinted in the collection of his essays and reviews, *Pour une histoire à part entière* (Paris, 1962), 649–658.

20. Ibid., 419 *(aisance),* 372 (Duperron's reference to planned workshops at the *dépôt* of Moulins), and 361 (Duperron's suggestion for an enormous workshop at the château of Chambord, to be peopled by inmates from various *dépôts*). Among many references to memoirs by de la Balme, and by Decan *(lieutenant de police* at Meaux), see pp. 290, 456–457, and 475.

21. Manuscript, side 1.

22. *Discours* (Soissons, 1779), 3.

23. Manuscript, sides 15 and 16.

24. Manuscript, side 17.

25. Darline Levy, *The Ideas and Careers of Simon-Nicolas-Henri Linguet: A Study in Eighteenth-Century French Politics* (Urbana, Ill., 1980), 174 and 183.

26. Malvaux, *Moyens,* 64 and 207 (Blanchard), 348 (Pankouke). On p. 204, Malvaux cites Linguet's *Annales,* no. 12, concerning a description by Tainteneur ("Taintenier" in Malvaux) of poor-relief bureaus in the town of Ath. Montlinot's description of the failure of certain hospital enterprises in a town "not far away" (*Discours,* 16–17) parallels the account in François Joseph Tainteneur, *Traité sur la mendicité avec les projets de règlement propres à l'empêcher dans les villes et villages, dédié à messieurs les officiers de justice et de police, par un citoyen.* . . . (Tournai, 1774), 15. For a commentary on the local context of Montlinot's memoir, see also Louis Trénard, "Pauvreté, charité, assistance à Lille, 1708–1790," in *Assistance et assistés de 1610 à nos jours* (vol. 1 of *Actes du 97ᵉ Congrès des sociétés savantes, Nantes, 1972. Section d'histoire moderne et contemporaine*) (Paris, 1977), 473–498, especially 486.

27. Levy, *Linguet,* 74–75 and 104–105; also, by the same author, "Simon Linguet's Sociological System: An Exhortation to Patience and Invitation to Revolution," *SVEC* 70 (1970):219–293, especially 259.

28. Bloch, *Assistance et l'état,* 221. See also the brief summary of Montlinot's career in Camille Bloch and Alexandre Tuetey, eds., *Procès-verbaux et rapports du Comité de la Constituante, 1790–1791* (Paris, 1911), xviii.

29. A.D. Aisne, C.749. Noirfosse, *prévôt* of the *maréchaussée* at Soissons, had been one of the judges of Montlinot's winning essay (A.D. Aisne, D.22).

30. Jacques Necker, *De l'administration des finances de la France,* 3 vols. (1785), 3:116–117. See Le Peletier to Turgot, March 12, 1775 (A.D. Aisne, C.666): "L'aisance rendu au peuple que le régime de la prohibition tirannisoit fera disparaître insensiblement la mendicité dans le Royaume."

31. "Mémoire concernant la réduction à un seul dépôt les trois établissements existans dans la Généralité de Soissons pour le renfermement des mendiants désirée par M. Le Directeur Général des finances, suivant la lettre écrite par M. Bertier à l'intendant le 10 décembre 1780 avec le détail des moyens économiques que l'on juge possible d'employer pour diminuer les dépenses dudit renfermement," A.D. Aisne, C.749. See the exchange between the intendant and Terray in July 1773, A.D. Aisne, C.704, and the intendant's request for an inspector again in a letter of October 30, 1777, A.D. Aisne, C.711.

32. A.D. Aisne, C.749.

33. See p. 170, note 43.

34. Many of the notes to Favier are undated but most refer clearly to the business contained in papers that are dated. Some notes do not even refer to Favier; some give his complete title, "Mr. Favier, premier secrétaire de l'intendance" (A.D. Aisne, C.733); one begins "Mon cher premier" (A.D. Aisne, C.745). Typical of Montlinot's allusiveness is a long letter describing how he organized inmates to empty the cesspits of the *dépôt* in the dead of night, when funds for this urgent operation had been tied up. "*Mitte sapientiam et nihil dicas*" ("Be wise and say nothing"), he begins, citing the tag used by the memoir that came in second after his in the Soissons contest of 1779. "Fort bien," he continues, in a libertine vein, "il y aura cependant quelquefois des instans ou je vous dirai, *Domine labia mea aperies et mundo cor meum*" ("Lord, you will open my lips and my heart to the world"). A.D. Aisne, C.733.

35. *Compte Rendu au Roi, par M. Necker, Directeur général des Finances, au mois de Janvier 1781, imprimé par ordre de Sa Majesté* (original brochure in collection of the University of Kentucky), 101. For a much earlier example of published accounts, see the printed placard drawn up by the administrators of the Hôpital Général de la Charité of Tours in 1702, in A.D. Indre-et-Loire, C.305.

36. The four printed accounts from 1781 to 1785 are in A.D. Aisne, C.743, and are also available on microfilm, A.D. Aisne, 2 Mi 130. The first is entitled, *État actuel de la Maison de Travail de la Généralité de Soissons (1781);* the second, *État actuel du dépôt de mendicité*

ou de la maison du travail de la généralité de Soissons. Deuxième Compte. Année 1782; the third, *État actuel du dépôt de mendicité de la généralité de Soissons. Troisième Compte. Année 1783;* and the fourth, *État actuel du dépôt de mendicité de la généralité de Soissons. IV Compte. Années 1784 et 1785.* The fifth accounting, for the year 1786, was appended to his more broadly disseminated brochure, *État actuel du dépôt de Soissons, précédé d'un essai sur la mendicité* (Soissons, 1789). The variation in nomenclature will be explained in the context of the third account.

37. A.D. Aisne, C.749.

38. Ibid.; Montlinot wrote August 16, and the intendant replied August 28. The further exchange concerning the hospital took place in October and November. Bertier spelled out the understanding that 28,000 livres per annum would be available in three-month installments, with some delay in the transfer of funds authorized, in a letter of November 28, 1781.

39. *État actuel . . . 1781,* 20.

40. Ibid., 3–5. On sparing the poor from humiliation, see the published version of Montlinot's *Discours* of 1779, p. 55.

41. *État actuel . . . 1781,* p. 27.

42. Ibid., 12.

43. Ibid., 5–8 and 26–27.

44. Intendant to Joly de Fleury, April 10, 1782, A.D. Aisne, C.749.

45. *État actuel . . . 1782,* 5.

46. Ibid., 7. "Ces détails," adds Montlinot, "pourroient éclairer le ministre sur les moyens différens qu'il faudroit employer dans chaque lieu pour diminuer la mendicité."

47. Ibid., 13, 18, and 27.

48. Ibid., 34.

49. Ibid., 8–9 ("police") and 23–24 ("l'espoir des récompenses").

50. Ibid., 39.

51. Colombier's role is discussed above, chapter 8.

52. D'Ormesson's circular of May 25, 1783, beginning, "Quelques pays d'États, Monsieur, ayant adressé des réclamations . . . ," is in A.D. Aisne, C.749; A.D. Marne, C.2026; and elsewhere. Chamfort depicts Le Peletier gently reproving his son-in-law the controller-general for denigrating great authors, in *Maximes et pensées* (Paris, 1963), 209.

53. A.D. Indre-et-Loire, C.313 (Calonne reestablishes *caissiers,* February 1784). Calonne's complaint against Montlinot's favorable review of *Émile* is mentioned in Suzanne Tucoo-Chala, *Panckoucke,* 68.

54. A.D. Aisne, C.749.

55. Ibid. Calonne's opening sentences appear to be directed especially at the line in Montlinot's *État actuel . . . 1782,* 39, in which he states, "Celui qui aura pris la peine de parcourir ce compte, s'appercevra facilement que toute l'économie n'a consisté qu'à faire un bon emploi de ses fonds, et à rendre le sort du mendiant meilleur."

56. Ibid.

57. Ibid. The November 1, 1783, issue of the *Mercure de France* announced news from Fontainebleau of October 28: "M. le Peletier, Intendant de Soissons, désigné Prévôt des Marchands de la ville de Paris, nommé à la place de Conseiller d'état, vacante par la mort de M. de Boynes, [and another courtier] eurent l'honneur de faire le 18 de ce mois leur remerciment à Sa Majesté, et d'être présenté ensuite à la Famille Royale."

58. Same letter of May 20, 1784.

59. On the marquis de la Bourdonnaye de Blossac and his marriage to Bertier's oldest daughter Antoinette in 1782, see especially Guillaume de Bertier de Sauvigny, *Le Comte Ferdinand de Bertier, 1782–1864, et l'énigme de la Congrégation* (Paris, 1948), 8. A tapestry depicting the wedding party is owned by the Cincinnati Art Museum. Based on a *carton*

by Fragonard, it includes a nurse with a child and an obviously "domiciled" beggar! A photograph of the tapestry serves as the frontispiece to this volume.

60. *État actuel . . . 1783*, 2.

61. D'Agay to Blossac, December 21, 1784, A.D. Aisne, C.708. Cf. Blossac's reply to query from intendant of Châlons, December 22, 1785, A.D. Marne, C.2001. On Garat's reviews of Montlinot's published accounts, see the beginning of chapter 11.

62. *État actuel . . . 1783*, 45 ("Résultat").

63. Ibid., 5, 9, 11, and 13. Montlinot avoids using the phrase *le plaisir de consommer* and speaks (p. 25) of the goad of hunger in a mildly parodic vein: "C'est ce besoin impérieux qui compte le lion et soumet l'homme dans tous les états." But then he speaks of the "justice" of allowing the inmate the opportunity of working at every instant. There is no evidence that Montlinot adopted harsher methods than in the past to correspond to the chill in his rhetoric.

64. Foucault, *Surveiller et punir*, 219–229.

65. Ibid., 29.

66. Ibid., 20–22. See Foucault, *Surveiller et punir*, 202.

67. Ibid., 29–30.

68. A.D. Aisne, C.744: memoir beginning, "Je fais mille compliments a M. Favier, je lui adresse un mémoire de confiance pour lui seul concernant la comptabilité," dated "9 xb" [décembre 1784], with the note, presumably by Favier "R[épondu] 12 jan" [1785].

69. Ibid.; further undated memoir also in A.D. Aisne, C.744.

70. A.D. Aisne, C.744: note marked as received February 26, 1785.

71. A.D. Aisne, C.744: undated note with others from January and February 1785. Jacques Necker, *De l'administration des finances de la France*, 3 vols. (n.p., 1785), 3:111–122.

72. Necker, *Administration des finances*, 3:114.

73. Ibid., 111 and 113. Robert D. Harris, *Necker: Reform Statesman on the Ancien Régime* (Berkeley, 1979), 161, calls attention to Necker's formulation of the mediating role of government in this passage.

74. Necker, *Administration des finances*, 3:115–117.

75. Ibid., 119–122.

76. Ibid., 122. I have translated *aisance* as "prosperity."

77. A.D. Aisne, C.744 ("best of all possible *dépôts*") and C.745 (ill winds mentioned in note of March 21).

78. A.D. Aisne, C.744 (note of March 14 on the *"medico-chemico-burocratie"* of St. Denis) and C.745 ("État de travail—Avril 1785").

79. Tucoo-Chala, *Panckoucke*, 137, includes Montlinot in Panckoucke's "stable" of writers. On Panckoucke's conception of the work, see Robert Darnton, *The Business of Enlightenment: A Publishing History of the Encyclopedia, 1775–1800* (Cambridge, Mass., 1979), chapter 8, "The Ultimate Encyclopedia."

80. Montlinot, "dépôt de mendicité," *Encyclopédie méthodique. Dictionnaire d'économie politique et diplomatique*, vol. 2 (Liège, 1786), 71–80, especially 72.

81. Ibid., 73; cf. note 40 above.

82. Ibid., 75. The journalistic fascination with promoting an altruistic ethnic among the lower classes is well treated in Harvey Chisick, *The Limits of Reform in the Enlightenment: Attitudes toward the Education of the Lower Classes in Eighteenth-Century France* (Princeton, 1981), 225–238.

83. *"Dépôt de mendicité,"* 77–78.

84. *État actuel . . . 1784–1785*, 1, 18, and 20. This discussion is based on the text of the printed copy of this *État* in A.D. Marne, C.2001, which is accompanied by a letter to the intendant of Châlons from de Blossac, December 22, 1785.

85. Ibid., 19. Cf. Malvaux, *Moyens*, 462.

86. *État actuel . . . 1784–1785,* 7.

87. Ibid., 10 and 20–21.

88. Ibid., 4.

89. Ibid., 4 and 19.

90. Ibid., 5 and 10.

91. Ibid., 22. Montlinot had made a similar point in his prize-winning memoir (side 25 of manuscript).

Chapter 10

1. Jean Égret, *La pré-révolution française (1787–1788)* (Paris, 1962), 21, 47, and 144; Marcel Marion, *Histoire financière de la France depuis 1715. Tome 1: 1715–1789* (Paris, 1914), 402; Vivian Gruder, "Paths to Political Consciousness: The Assembly of Notables of 1787 and the 'Pre-Revolution' in France," *FHS* 13:3 (Spring 1984):323–355.

2. *Compte rendu au Roi au mois de mars 1788 et publié par ses ordres* (Paris, 1788), 124; J. F. Bosher, *French Finances, 1770–1795: From Business to Bureaucracy* (Cambridge, 1970), 139 and 209. Annual accounts of the *dépôt* at St. Denis include payments for the feeding of the *pionniers* every year from 1781 to 1786, rising steadily in amount to 44,389 libres in 1786 (A.N., F^{15} 2806).

3. *Compte rendu,* 124; see A.N. H.1663 for payments to *caissiers.*

4. J. F. Bosher, *French Finances,* 141; A.N. F^{15} 2791.

5. See pp. 180–181.

6. A.D. Aisne, C.733; A.D. Seine-Maritime, C.1020. Of the circulars we have identified in the departmental archives, this is the first to be signed by La Millière.

7. F^{15} 2810.

8. A.D. Aisne, C.710; A.D. Indre-et-Loire, C.315.

9. A.D. Calvados, C.657.

10. Ibid.

11. On this subject, see letters in departmental archives such as that of April 1, 1789, in A.D. Indre-et-Loire, C.315, and various reports and letters from Bourges, Poitiers, and elsewhere continuing into 1790 in F^{16} 965.

12. F^{15} 2811. See especially La Millière to de Crosne, July 3, 1789, threatening to withhold payment for ninety-five arrests.

13. *Mercure de France,* November 13, 1784. The quotation from the Assembly of Notables is in the Bertier de Sauvigny papers, A.N. 80 AP 46, "Mémoire présenté au Roi, par Mgr. le Comte d'Artois, M. le prince de Condé, Mr. le duc de Bourbon, M. le duc d'Enghien et M. le prince de Conti." I have outlined Bertier's self-image as a reformer in "A Reconsideration of Bertier de Sauvigny, Last *Intendant* of Paris," in *Proceedings of the Fourth Annual Meeting of the Western Society for French History, 11–13 November, 1976, Reno, Nevada,* ed. Joyce Duncan Falk (Santa Barbara, 1977), 230–238. The best exposition of the contradictions in Bertier's role is provided by Henri Dinet, "Les peurs du Beauvaisis et du Valois, juillet 1789," in *Mémoires de la Fédération des sociétés historiques et archéologiques de Paris et de l'Île-de-France* 23–24 (1972):199–392, especially the first chapter, "Le rôle de l'intendant de Paris," 203–225.

14. *Procès-verbal des séances de l'assemblée provinciale de l'Isle de France, tenues à Melun, en novembre et décembre 1787; précédé de l'édit de création, des divers règlements faits par Sa Majesté, du procès-verbal de l'Assemblée préliminaire, etc.* (Sens, 1788), xii–xiv.

15. Ibid., xii, 6–12.

16. Ibid., xiii–xiv.

17. Ibid., xiv and 173.

18. Ibid., 208ff.; 210 *(règlement).*

19. Ibid., 282–293.

20. Ibid., 217.

21. Ibid., 218 and 284.

22. Antoine Lavoisier, *Oeuvres*, vol. 6 (1893):251. "Mémoires présentés à l'assemblée provinciale de l'Orléanais," no. 2, "Ateliers de charité et mendicité."

23. *Procès-verbal des séances de l'assemblée provinciale d'Auvergne, tenue à Clermont-Ferrand, août et novembre 1787* (Bibliothèque Nationale, Lk[15].13), 2:375. On the political impact of the provincial assemblies, see Rolf Reichardt, "Die Revolutionäre Wirkung der Reform der Provinzialwaltung in Frankreich, 1787–1791," in Ernst Hinrichs et al., eds., *Vom Ancien Regime zur Französischen Revolution: Forschungen und Perspectiven* (Göttingen, 1978), 66–124, especially 78–79. See also Prosper Boissonnade, *L'assemblée provinciale du Poitou et la question de la mendicité* (Paris, 1904), and, among the many speeches made in the assemblies and published at the time, Delachaize, *Discours prononcé à l'assemblée des États, en 1787 . . . sur la mendicité* (Dijon, 1787).

24. Report of the *commission intermédiaire* to the Estates of Rennes, 1788, A.D. Ille-et-Vilaine, C.4937.

25. Beatrice Fry Hyslop, *French Nationalism in 1789 according to the General Cahiers* (New York, 1968), 138–140.

26. Ferdinand Dreyfus, *Un philanthrope d'autrefois: La Rochefoucauld-Liancourt, 1777–1827* (Paris, 1903), 51 and 63; 35–39 (charity workshops). A letter to the intendant Blossac at Soissons from Lazowski follows up on an earlier discussion about the cotton manufacture at Liancourt and the possibility of employing women from the *dépôt* in it (A.D. Aisne, C.744; undated, ca. 1785).

27. René Mantel, "La Rochefoucauld-Liancourt: un novateur français dans la pratique agricole du xviiie siècle," in *Études d'histoire économique rurales au XVIIIe siècle*, with a preface by Robert Besnier (Paris, 1965), 151–206, especially 161.

28. Charles-L. Chassin, ed., *Les élections et les cahiers de Paris en 1789, documents recueillis, mis en ordre et annotés par Ch.-L. Chassin*, 4 vols. (Paris, 1888–1889), 262, 264, and passim; Michel Mollat, ed., *Histoire de l'Île-de-France et de Paris* (Toulouse, 1971), 359–362.

29. See the bibliographical note on Lambert in Camille Bloch and Alexandre Tuetey, eds., *Procès verbaux et rapports du Comité de mendicité de la Constituante, 1790–1791* (Paris, 1911), xvii.

30. *Précis de vues générales en faveur de ceux qui n'ont rien pour les mettre sous la sauvegarde de la bienfaisance publique et de la constitution de l'état* (Lons-le-Saunier, n.d.). Lambert includes his "Lettre à Messieurs des Assemblées Provinciales, des Assemblés d'états de la prochaine Assemblée des des États-Généraux, et à tous les Citoyens humains et sensibles," dated January 22, 1789. He also cites as an epigraph the following advice from the memoirs of the academy of Châlons: "Allez au devant du Pauvre, faites-lui trouver dans sa maison du travail, le nécessaire; et vous n'aurez plus besoin, ni de lois, ni de chaînes, pour réprimer la mendicité."

31. Ibid., 5.

32. *Cahier des pauvres* (Paris, 1789), 5 and 15. Internal evidence situates the brochure between publication of the *Précis* and the meeting of the Estates-General.

33. Ibid., 7.

34. *Supplique à l'assemblée de MM. les électeurs du tiers-état de Paris, pour l'intérêt commun des riches et des pauvres* (n.p., n.d.), 4. The brochure was addressed to the electors of Paris as the Estates-General was meeting.

35. Ibid., 6 and 15–16. The comments of Necker to which Lambert refers are to be

found in Georges Lefebvre and Anne Terroine, eds., *Recueil de documents relatifs aux séances des États-Généraux, mai-juin, 1789,* 2 vols. (Paris, 1953–1962), 1:338: "Quel bien ne pourront donc pas faire des États Provinciaux? quels services ne pourront-ils pas rendre à l'humanité souffrante, s'ils inspirent au Roi de la confiance dans leur zèle et leur activité, et s'ils encouragent Sa Majesté à les associer à la plus précieuse et la plus douce des fonctions de l'autorité souveraine, la défense et la protection des malheureux?"

36. Guillaume de Bertier de Sauvigny, *Le comte Ferdinand de Bertier (1782–1864) et l'énigme de la Congrégation* (Paris, 1948), 12. Bertier's descendant responds to Michelet's portrayal of an intendant in panic by reconstructing his last days. The mention of "twenty" proscriptions is in B. J. B. Buchez and P. C. Roux, *Histoire parlementaire de la Révolution française, ou journal des assemblées nationales depuis 1789 jusqu'en 1815,* 40 vols. (Paris, 1838), 2:149.

37. Bertier, *Le comte Ferdinand de Bertier,* 13–17. The intendant's role in the rural panics of the Île-de-France is treated by Henri Dinet in the article cited above (note 13), but there are only passing mentions of the killing of Bertier and Foullon in George Lefebvre, *The Coming of the French Revolution,* tr. R. R. Palmer (Princeton, 1967), 118–119, and in his seminal work on revolutionary mass psychology, *The Great Fear of 1789* (New York, 1973), 62. George Rude, *The Crowd in the French Revolution* (New York, 1959), 56, mentions the killings only as an instance of popular vengeance. Steven L. Kaplan, *The Famine Plot Persuasion in Eighteenth-Century France,* Transactions of the American Philosophical Society, vol. 72, part 3, 1982 (Philadelphia, 1982), 56–57, mentions the fact that Leprévost de Beaumont linked the names of Foullon and Bertier with a famine conspiracy in testimony he gave after their deaths. Buchez and Roux, *Histoire parlementaire,* 2:460–474, reasserted these allegations. Gustave Bord, *Histoire du blé en France: Le pacte de famine, histoire, légende* (Paris, 1887), 36–46, explains the transactions that gave rise to the belief in Bertier's involvement.

38. *Pennsylvania Gazette,* September 30, 1789, and preceding numbers. On Breteuil's search for a finance minister to succeed Necker, see Jacques Godechot, *The Taking of the Bastille, July 14, 1789* (New York, 1970), 186. On Bertier's ties with the queen's household, see Gustave Bord, *La conspiration révolutionnaire de 1789, les complices, les victimes* (Paris, 1909), 211. For Bertier's objections to Necker's subsistance measures, see his letter to Necker of May 18, 1789, in A.N. 80AP 81.

39. In addition to accounts by Bertier and Bord, see that of Bertrand de Molleville, *Histoire de la Révolution en France* (Paris, year IX [1801]), 2:81.

40. Buchez and Roux, *Histoire parlementaire,* 2:148–149; J. Destrem, "Document sur le mouvement populaire du 14 juillet et sur le meurtre de Foulon et Berthier," *Revue critique d'histoire et de littérature* 2 (1883):273–280, especially 277.

41. Barnave's speech is reproduced in *Archives parlementaires* 8:266. An engraving that depicts the parading of Foulon's and Bertier's heads around the Halle au Bleds on July 22, 1789, is reproduced in Howard C. Rice, Jr., *Thomas Jefferson's Paris* (Princeton, 1976), 120. On the institutional repercussions of the killings, see J. M. Thompson, *The French Revolution* (New York, 1966), 70. On the ironic treatment of the concept of "pure" noble blood in revolutionary writings, see Antoine De Baecque, "Le discours anti-noble (1787–1792): Aux origines d'un slogan: 'Le peuple contre les gros,' " *RHMC,* 36 (1989):3–28, esp. 4 and 18.

42. The deposition of July 23, 1789, identifying the two corpses is signed by Pierre Racle, aged 35, "secrétaire particulier de M. Bertier"; Jean-Pierre Jullien, aged 72, "valet de chambre"; and Philibert Juillet, aged 39, "portier de l'intendant de Paris": A.N. Y.11285. On the "lettres circulaires dites de Saint-Jean de Jerusalem," see Alexandre Tuetey, ed., *L'assistance publique à Paris pendant la Révolution,* 5 vols. (Paris, 1895–1897), 2:325: a

letter of the acting minister of the interior to administrators of the department of Paris, February 7, 1793.

43. A.N. Y.11285, "Scellé après décès de M. Bertier Intendant de Paris, 21 juillet 1789," and estimation of real property in A.N. Y.5197, December 22, 1790.

44. A.N. Y.11285, "Scellé après décès"; *Extraits des lettres trouvées dans les porte-feuilles de M. B., Intendant de Paris, pris la nuit du 16 juillet dans sa voiture* (brochure), including a letter of the 5th, "M. le Comte de . . . demande de partager les fonds dans la vente de grains, faite par le gouvernement," and another notation following a letter of July 11: "Intention d'établir un camp à St. Denis. De couper les récoltes à verd; sauf indemnité."

45. Lefebvre, *Great Fear*, 144. The text ascribes this report of July 26 to the then deceased intendant; it is likely in any case that such a report would have come from the subdelegate of the intendant at Clermont or nearby.

46. A.N. Y.11285, "Scellé après décès."

47. *Dialogue entre M. de Launay, Flesselles, Foulon et Berthier, aux enfers,* brochure (n.p., n.d.), 5. For ease of reference, Bibliothèque Nationale call-numbers for this and several items that follow are provided in the bibliography.

48. *Convoi, service et enterrement, des très-hauts, très-puissants seigneurs Foulon, Président, et Berthier de Sauvigny, Intendant de Paris, morts subitement en place de Grève, et enterrés à . . . leur paroisse,* brochure (n.p., n.d.), 4 and 8.

49. *Les enragés aux enfers, ou nouveau dialogue des morts,* brochure (n.p., 1789), 28. Did the title perhaps alude to the fact that experiments in the treatment of rabies victims were conducted at St. Denis? Of the other pamphlets inspired by the killing of Bertier, the one entitled *Les tyrans anéantis* (n.p., n.d.) contains the most lurid concatenation of "execrable exploits" being prepared by "this sanguinary intendant." After the pillage and ruin of Paris, "la montagne de Montmartre applanie devoit servir de tombeau à ceux même qui y travaillaient pour subsister." This phantasmagoria reflects a recurrent message in the pamphlets, namely, that Bertier's projects for the poor were designed for their destruction and his profit.

50. See the accounting for the *dépôt* of St. Denis in A.N. F^{15} 2806.

51. Buchez and Roux, *Histoire parlementaire,* 2:156; *Lettre de M*** à son ami, habitant de Perpignan. Récit des faits relatifs à la mort de MM. Foulon et Berthier, à la démission et à la seconde proclamation de M. le Marquis de La Fayette* brochure, (n.p., n.d.) 10; *Extrait des lettres trouvées dans le portefeuille de M. Berthier, intendant de Paris, pris dans la nuit du 16 juillet, dans sa voiture (n.p., n.d.); Les enragés aux enfers, ou nouveau dialogue des morts,* brochure (n.p., 1789), 12, 18, 22, and 25.

52. The mock epitaph translates roughly as, "Foulon and Bertier are buried at these sites/They both died with no last rites." *Épitaphes des sieurs Foulon et Berthier, affichés et publiés au Palais-Royal: ou Oraison Funèbre, suivie du récit historique de leur mort par M. l'abbé A.L.L.,* brochure published by Volland, rue du Hurepoix, n° 25 (n.d.). The pamphlet begins with an epigraph from the *Aeneid,* book 2.

53. J. Béaud and G. Bouchard, "Le dépôt de pauvres de St. Denis," *Annales de démographie historique* (1974), 130. There is an uncanny rhetorical similarity between the pamphlets that appeared at Bertier's death and Montlinot's letters to Favier from Soissons. However, other enemies of Bertier were equally likely to have been involved in engineering his proscription. One of the deputies who represented the communities of L'Isle-sous-Montréal in their resistance to Bertier's seigneurial claims was named Labbé; see Mary Ann Quinn, "Pratique et théories de la coutume: allodialité et conflits de droits dans la seigneurie de l'Isle-sous-Montréal au XVIIIe siècle," *Études rurales* 103–104 (1986): 90. Gustave Bord, *Conspiration révolutionnaire,* 214, noted that a clerk fired by Bertier in 1777, Poultier

d'Elmotte, was reponsible for charges leveled against Bertier in *La Bastille dévoilée* ed. Charpentier, 3 vols. (Paris, 1789), and in Louis Prudhomme's journal, *Révolutions de Paris* (Paris, 1790).

54. These details are drawn from letters cited elsewhere in this chapter and the preceding, particularly from A.D. Aisne, C.745 (letter of June 1785).

55. Separate note accompanying letter just cited.

56. See above, chapter 9.

57. A.D. Aisne, C.733; C.710: November 8, 1787, to Blossac, referring to a proposal regarding transfers; December 23, 1787, on the use of the château of Villers-Cotterets. On the exile of the duc d'Orléans on November 20, 1787, see Egret, *Pré-révolution,* 191.

58. A.D. Aisne, C.710.

59. Ibid.

60. Ibid. Montlinot's note to Favier bears the note that it was received August 25. Bertier's reply to Blossac of September 1 refers to a letter of the 9th [of August]. Blossac had spoken of "circonstances où toutes les parties de l'administration sont éclairées." Montlinot had said of Bertier, "nous allons l'éclairer encore une seconde fois par le raport du dernier convoi."

61. Ibid. Montlinot's note to Favier containing the reference to "the trial" is undated but refers undoubtedly to Bertier's letter of September 1. News of the recall of Necker had been celebrated in Paris from August 25 on (Égret, *Pré-révolution,* 317). In a letter requesting that Blossac speak to both La Millière and Necker about the cost of bread rations (November 30, 1788), Montlinot wrote, "La chose publique me touche comme citoyen et sans approuver tout, je cherche à faire le bien de ma manière." Montlinot's seventy-page pamphlet of early 1789 was entitled *État actuel du dépôt de Soissons, précédé d'un essai sur la mendicité V. Compte. Année 1786* (Soissons, 1789). It was printed by Ponce Courtois, the printer to the king, and bore the royal fleur-de-lys on its title page.

62. *État actuel* (1789), 1, 7–9, 19, 24.

63. Ibid., 10–11. Jeffry Kaplow cited these passages in *The Names of Kings: The Parisian Laboring Poor in the Eighteenth Century* (New York, 1972), 131.

64. *État actuel,* (1789), 1, 12–13, and 31–48. He counted 208 "dangerous" inmates.

65. Ibid., 14–15. Montlinot also favored mutual-aid associations among workers, citing the statutes of one such *confrérie* at Lille (12 and 53–54).

66. Ibid., 15–17. Some of the revolutionary *cahiers* suggested a retirement allowance or tax concessions for aged workers, according to Jacques Godechot, *Les institutions de la France sous la Révolution et l'Empire* (Paris, 1951), 179.

67. Ibid., 2, 5, and 11.

68. Abbé Malvaux, ed., *Les moyens de détruire la Mendicité en France, en rendant les Mendians utiles à l'état sans les rendre malheureux; tirés des Mémoires qui ont concouru pour le Prix accordé en l'année 1777, par l'Académie des Sciences, Arts et Belles Lettres de Châlons-sur-Marne* (Châlons-sur-Marne, 1780), 501. The text, identified merely as "Pensées de J. J. Rousseau," is found in Jean-Jacques Rousseau, *Émile, ou de l'éducation,* ed. F. and P. Richard (1762; Paris, 1964), 226. In various writings, Rousseau blamed society for degrading the poor. In a paper delivered at the meeting of the American Historical Association in December 1988, William J. Olejniczak commented on Rousseau's defense of the vagabond in *La Nouvelle Héloïse.* Particularly noteworthy in this context is Mme de Wolmar's question, "Croyez-vous dégrader un pauvre de sa qualité d'homme en lui donnant le nom méprisant de gueux?": Jean-Jacques Rousseau, *Julie ou La Nouvelle Héloïse* (1761; Paris, 1967), 407.

69. Malvaux, 502.

Chapter 11

1. Michel Foucault refers to the Société Royale de Médecine and the Comité de Mendicité in *Naissance de la clinique* (1963; Paris, 1972), 29–31 and 31, and wrote of the tendency of closed institutions "to add to their specific internal function a role of external surveillance" in *Surveiller et punir: naissance de la prison* (Paris, 1975), 213. On clinical practice, medicine, and "the sciences of man," see Gilles-Gaston Granger, *Formal Thought and the Sciences of Man* (Boston, 1983), 152; Sergio Moravia, "Philosophie et médecine en France à la fin du XVIIIe siècle," *SVEC* 89 (1972):1089–1151; and George Gusdorf, *Introduction aux sciences humaines: essai critique sur leurs origines et leur développement* (Paris, 1960), 113–134.

2. *Mercure de France. Journal de Politique,* January 31, 1784, 222–228 (Montlinot's account for 1782), especially 227. Garat reviewed Montlinot's account for 1783 in the *Mercure* of November 20, 1784, 115–135. The article "Garat (Dominique-Joseph)," in Hoefer, ed., *Biographie générale* (Paris, 1857), notes that Panckoucke invited Garat to write articles for the *Encyclopédie méthodique* and the *Mercure de France.*

3. *Mercure de France,* November 20, 1784, 129. On Garat, see Eugène Goyheneche, *Le pays basque* (Pau, 19779), 369 and 381; and Emmet Kennedy, *Destutt de Tracy and the Origins of "Ideology": A Philosophe in an Age of Revolution* (Philadelphia, 1978), 32 and 40. On early methods of statistical "conjecture" from medical observation, see George Rosen, "Problems in the Application of Statistical Analysis to Questions of Health, 1700–1800," *BHM* 29 (1955):27–45. Garat discusses Montlinot's conjectures and revisions in his review of November 1784, p. 116.

4. On Colbert's collection of statistics, see James E. King, *Science and Rationalism in the Government of Louis XIV (1661–1684* (Baltimore, 1949), chapters 5 and 6. See also Louis Trénard, "Les intendants et leurs enquêtes (d'après des travaux récentes)," *Information historique* 38 (January–February 1976):11–23; Bertrand Gille, *Les sources statistiques de l'histoire de France: des enquetes du xviie siècle à 1870* (Paris, 1964), especially 38 and 60 (Orry's map). On the limits of the intendants' power to gather and use data, see Robert Mandrou, *La France au xviie et xviiie siècles* (Paris, 1967), 210.

5. Circular from Boullongne to intendant, September 3, 1749, A.D. Indre-et-Loire, C.305.

6. A.N. H.371.

7. Bertier to intendant of Caen, August 31, 1774, A.D. Calvados, C.650: "il peut être intéressant pour l'administration de se réserver les moyens de pouvoir par les calculs au moins d'approximation apprécier les profits ou les pertes des entrepreneurs." On Terray's use of data, see Chapter 5.

8. See above, chapters 6–7, and Edgar Faure, "Les bases expérimentales et doctrinales de la politique économique de Turgot," *Revue historique de droit français et étranger,* 4e série, 39 (1961):255–295 and 382–447.

9. See lists of beggars dating from 1775, including "État des mendiants du dépôt d'Alençon qu'il convient d'y retenir," A.D. Orne, C.284. For a modern discussion of "academic," "clinical," and "strategic" uses of data, see Kathleen A. Archibald, "Alternative Orientations to Social Science Utilization," *Social Science Information* 9:2 (1970):7–34. On the interdependence of bureaucratic tools and reforms, see L. J. Hume, *Bentham and Bureaucracy* (Cambridge, 1981), 49.

10. Jean Colombier mentions attempts to treat rabies at St. Denis in 1781 in his *Description des Epidémies qui ont régué depuis quelques années dans la généralité de Paris* (Paris, 1783), 37; see also Jean Théodorides, "Quelques aspects de la rage au 18e siècle," *Clio Medica,* 11:2 (1976):95–109. The pharmacy established at Alfort was to supply that of the *dépôt* at St. Denis, according to accounts of 1783 in A.N. F^{15} 2806. On Colombier's role there, see Paul Delaunay, *La vie médicale aux XVIe, XVIIe, et XVIIIe siècle* (Paris, 1935),

271. On links between human and veterinary medicine, see Caroline C. Hannaway, "Veterinary Medicine and Rural Health Care in Pre-revolutionary France," *BHM* 51 (1977):431–437. On twelve-year-olds to be brought to St. Denis, see Bertier to Lenoir, July 22, 1783, A.N. F^{15} 2811.

11. See Doublet's account of St. Denis, above, at the end of chapter 8. Tables analyzing mortality at the *dépôt* of Beaulieu at Caen from March 1768 to January 1778 as a percentage of *journées* are in A.D. Calvados, C.678. Similar lists for Tours, 1770–1782, are in A.D. Indre-et-Loire, C.313.

12. See pp. 189 and 255–228; the most pertinent letters of Montlinot are in A.D. Aisne, C.710; his article on the *dépôts* in the *Encyclopédie méthodique* contains the remark: "J'ai trop de fois mis la main sur leurs plaies." For a similar rhetorical concoction, see Louis-Sébastien Mercier, *Tableau de Paris,* 6 vols. (Amsterdam, 1782), for example, "Au plus pauvre le besace" (1:39). See also Jean Fabre, "L'article 'Peuple' de l'*Encyclopédie* et le couple Coyer-Jaucourt," in Jean-Robert Armogathe et al., *Images du peuple au XVIIIe siècle. Colloque, Aix-en-Provence 1969* (Paris, 1973), 11–24.

13. *Encyclopédie méthodique. Médecine,* vol. 1 (1787), A.V. "Agriculture," 391–393. Compare the observations on poverty and poor health in the *généralité* of Tours in 1773, A.D. Indre-et-Loire, C.341; Jean-Pierre Peter, "Malades et maladies à la fin du XVIIIe siècle," in J.-P. Desaive et al., *Médecine, climat et épidémies à la fin du XVIIIe siècle* (Paris, 1972), 166; François Lebrun, "Une grande épidémie en France au XVIIIe siècle," in A. Armengaud et al., *Sur la population francaise au XVIIIe siècle: hommage à Marcel Reinhard* (Paris, 1973), 403–415; and the section entitled, "Vie matérielle et hygiène des 'pauvres malades'," in Jean-Pierre Goubert, *Malades et médecins en Bretagne, 1770–1790* (Paris, 1974), 184–228. See also Louis Greenbaum, "The Humanitarianism of Antoine Laurent Lavoisier," *SVEC* 88 (1972):651–675, especially 666; and the critical analysis of the "pessimism" of Hallé and other doctors in Daniel Roche, *The People of Paris: An Essay in Popular Culture in the 18th Century* (Berkeley, 1987), 47–51.

14. Antoine-François Fourcroy suggested that the Société Royale de Médecine include data on the maladies of artisans in their survey of epidemics, writing in his foreword to a new translation of Bernardino Ramazzini, *Essai sur les maladies des artisans, traduit du latin de Ramazzini, avec des notes et des additions; par M. de Fourcroy* (Paris, 1777), li. For mordant commentary on efforts to improve the quality of air in urban and institutional settings, see Louis-Sébastien Mercier, *Tableau de Paris,* 4 vols. (Amsterdam, 1782), 1:126, "L'air vicié." For a historical perspective on contemporary observation, see J. Rousset, "Essai de pathologie urbaine. Les causes de morbidité et de mortalité à Lyon aux XVIIe et XVIIIe siècles," *Cahiers d'histoire* 8 (1963):71–105; and Arlette Farge, "Work-Related Diseases of Artisans in Eighteenth-Century France," in *Medicine and Society in France. Selections from the Annales. Economies. Sociétés. Civilisations,* vol. 6, ed. Robert Forster and Orest Ranum (Baltimore, 1980), 89–103.

15. A.D. Ille-et-Vilaine, C.3796, memoir approved in committee December 25, 1786, prior to reading in Estates assembled. On the Estates' treatment of this matter, see C. 3184. Noting that 137 inmates had died in a space of eleven and a half months in an institution generally holding six hundred inmates, the Commission on Finances compared the much lower rates of the Hôpital Saint-Yves. Factors tending to produce a lower mortality rate at the hospital receiving sick patients included: better rations and care; short hospital stays; many patients' returning home to die; and the fact that half of them were under twenty-nine years of age. See Yves Pottier, "La population de l'Hôpital Saint-Yves de Rennes dans la Iere moitié du 18ème siècle (1710–1750)" (mémoire de maîtrise, University of Haute-Bretagne, 1974), 89.

16. *Mercure de France,* November 20, 1784, p. 132. Montlinot wrote in *État actuel*

(1781), 2: "Le grand art d'un Administrateur éclairé est de tendre une main bienfaisante aux malheureux que l'on punit." See also above, Chapter 9, and Hippocrates, "Le Pronostic," in E. Littré's translation, *Oeuvres complètes* (1840; Amsterdam, 1961), 2:111: "Le meilleur médecin me paroît être celui qui sait connoître d'avance. Pénétrant et exposant, au préalable, près des malades, le présent, le passé et l'avenir de leurs maladies, expliquant ce qu'ils omettent, il gagnera leur confiance; et, convaincu de la supériorité de ses lumières, ils n'hésiteront pas à se remettre à ses soins." Of course the themes of Hippocratic medicine were adjusted to the state of scientific knowledge in the eighteenth century; see the excellent discussion in Martin S. Staum, *Cabanis: Enlightenment and Medical Philosophy in the French Revolution* (Princeton, 1980), 49–55.

17. Bannefroy, *Mémoire sur la mendicité* (Paris, 1791), 34—inspired perhaps by volcanic imagery of Louis-Michel Musquinet de la Pagne, *Bicêtre réformé: Établissement d'une maison de discipline* (Paris, 1784), 18–19. Barère speaks of mendicity as "une dénonciation vivante contre le gouvernement" and as "la lèpre des monarchies" in his *Premier Rapport fait au nom du comité de salut public, sur les moyens d'extirper la mendicité dans les campagnes, & sur les secours que doit accorder la République aux citoyens indigents; par Barère. Séance du 22 Floréal* (B.N., Le[38] 791). The statement that "la mendicité est le thermomètre des gouvernements" is in *Réflexions sur la mendicité; ses causes, et les moyens de la détruire en France, par M. de Montaignac, Lieutenant de Vaissaux* (Paris, 1790), 4 (copy in A.N. F[15] 138). I am grateful to Prof. Edward Gargan for bringing to my attention the report by Barère and several other key texts of the Revolutionary assemblies.

18. See the excellent introduction to Camille Bloch and Alexandre Tuetey, eds., *Procès-verbaux et rapports du Comité de mendicité de la Constituante (1790–1791)* (Paris, 1911), especially xiii–xix. La Millière advised Brayer, subdelegate-general of the intendance of Soissons (Blossac had resigned on news of his father-in-law's death), that "le premier Ministre des finances . . . a désiré que M. Montlinot s'occupât d'un travail qui l'empêchera de se rendre à Soissons de quelque tems," in a letter of January 21, 1790, A.D. Aisne, C.710.

19. "Quatrième rapport du Comité de Mendicité: Secours à donner à la classe indigente dans les différentes âges et dans les différentes circonstances de la vie, par M. de Larochefoucauld-Liancourt," in Bloch and Tuetey, *Procès-verbaux*, 383–464, especially 388. Caze de la Bove's letter is in A.N. H. 565. Henry Sée, "Les conceptions économiques et sociales du Comité de Mendicité de la Constituante," *AHRF* (1926), 330–337, is useful. Richard B. Du Boff, "Economic Thought in Revolutionary France, 1789–1792: The Question of Poverty and Unemployment," *FHS* 4:4 (1966):434–451, emphasizes the influence of English writings.

20. 'Quatrième rapport," 383–464, especially 388.

21. Ibid., 389. See also p. 395 on the local knowledge of medical officers, to be gathered into "une grande masse de faits, qui constituant la véritable science de la médecine, pourront lui faire quelques pas de plus, et rendront ses soins plus utiles à l'humanité." For the geographical dimension of this ordering of useful knowledge, see Sergio Moravia, "Philosophie et géographie à la fin du XVIIIe siècle," *SVEC* 57 (1967):937–1011.

22. Before the new *départements* had been created, Montlinot had recommended that a local network of *comités de bienfaisance* be established; their responsibilities were to include care of foundlings and the *régime intérieur* of *dépôts de mendicité*, in his *Observations sur les enfans-trouvés de la généralité de Soissons* (Paris, 1790), 37–39.

23. Montlinot's work on foundlings is cited in the preceding note; Liancourt's discussion of children and the aged is in Bloch and Tuetey, *Procès-verbaux*, 459. The letter of November 1, 1790, to the Academy of Sciences, requesting an opinion on Duvillard's calculations, is in ibid., 167 (minutes of sessions). On Duvillard's contribution to the Comité de Mendicité, see also Keith Michael Baker, *Condorcet: From Natural Philosophy to Social Mathe-*

matics (Chicago, 1975), 280. On Laplace, see Victor Hilts, "Statistics and Social Science," in *Foundations of Scientific Method: The Nineteenth Century,* eds. Ronald N. Giere and Richard S. Westfall (Bloomington, Ind., 1973), 206–237, especially 209.

24. *Procès-verbaux,* 437–453; B.N. f.f. 8129, fol. 131 (Laverdy commission on question of domicile).

25. *Procès-verbaux,* 466–468 ("Fixation de la proportion du nombre des pauvres par rapport à la population") and 478–498 ("Pièces justificatives"). The partial returns and tables used by the committee are in A.N. F^{15} 1861, including "Observations sur le tableau de la population et des branches de la classe indigente."

26. *Procès-verbaux,* 71 (Thouret), 481–482 (Montlinot), and 484 (Thouret).

27. Ibid., 485–487. The committee used the work of Angot des Rotours, *Notice des principaux règlemens publiés en Angleterre concernant les pauvres à laquelle on a joint quelques Réflexions, qui peuvent la rendre utile aux assemblées provinciales* (London and Paris, 1788). Cf. Bloch, *L'assistance et l'état en France à la veille de la Révolution: généralités de Paris, Rouen, Alençon, Orléans, Soissons, Amiens (1764–1790) (Paris, 1908),* 389, and *Procès-verbaux,* xxxviii.

28. *Procès-verbaux,* 476–477.

29. In addition to the general assessment by Alan Forrest, *The French Revolution and the Poor* (New York, 1981), see Olwen Hufton, "Women in Revolution, 1789–1796," in Douglas Johnson, ed., *French Society and the Revolution* (Cambridge, 1976), 148–166. There are also two excellent local studies: Colin Jones, *Charity and Bienfaisance: The Treatment of the Poor in the Montpellier Region, 1740–1815* (Cambridge, 1982), chapters 8 and 9, 159–200; and Marc Bouloiseau, "Assistance publique: secours ou aumône? l'exemple de Saumur (1792–1799)," in *Actes du 97ᵉ Congrès national des sociétés savantes,* 1:531–543.

30. Abbé Malvaux, ed., *Les moyens de détruire la mendicité,* 323. Jeffry Kaplow, *The Names of Kings: The Parisian Laboring Poor in the Eighteenth Century* (New York, 1972), 130, alludes to Malvaux's image of the "philosopher's stone." Mircea Eliade, *Forgerons et alchimistes* (Paris, 1956), 203, notes that the qualities of the philosopher's stone imply "la liberté de changer le monde, de le 'sauver.' " For Bertier's use of a term common in alchemy, see p. 165 and note 29.

31. Feodor Dostoevsky, *Crime and Punishment,* ed. George Gibian (New York, 1975), 217 and 223. Cf. the comments on "human artifice" and work in Hannah Arendt, *The Human Condition* (Chicago, 1958), 139.

32. Pierre Samuel Du Pont de Nemours, *Idées sur les secours à donner aux pauvres malades dans une grande ville* (Philadelphia and Paris, 1786), 15. See Louis S. Greenbaum, "Health-Care and Hospital-Building in Eighteenth-Century France: Reform Proposals of Du Pont de Nemours and Condorcet," *SVEC* 152 (1976):895–930.

33. See pp. 89 and 92. According to the summary of expenses in B.N. f.f. 8129, fol. 330, only 5,638 livres were spent in all 88 *dépôts* for the provision of work to the end of 1768, in a total budget of over 1.2 million. The next year the sum rose to 37,029; but in 1770, a year in which the *dépôts* offered little more than stop-gap relief, expenditure fell again to 10,061.

34. A memoir read to the Estates of Brittany on December 25, 1786, complained that small producers of "futaines, bazins et autres ouvrages semblables en cotton" near Guérande and Dinan had suffered from the competition of Cabanes' protected workshops in the *dépôt* at Rennes: "pour tirer des gens de la mendicité on y en a précipité d'autres." The same dossier contains a complaint signed in 1780 by fifteen weavers of Rennes and outlying areas against competition from the cheap, shoddy slave labor of the *dépôt* (A.D. Ille-et-Vilaine, C.3796).

35. According to an "Extrait du mémoire contenant le détail des opérations et du travail établi dans les divers dépôts confiés à la compagnie générale," in B.N. f.f. 8129, fol. 332–

333, spinning occupied inmates in 25 of the 32 *dépôts* governed under their contract. Cotton was spun in 18 of these. Facilities varied from "un atelier très considérable" at Caen to those at Saintes, where "les renfermés sont fort à l'étroit, les femmes pouvant à peine y trouver place pour filer dans leur chambre," and 7 *dépôts* where no work was done at all. Work at 13 *dépôts* included clothmaking (weaving).

36. For a discussion of the relationships between factory organization and penal arrangements, see Georg Rusche and Otto Kirchheimer, *Punishment and Social Structure* (New York, 1939), 41–52; Thorsten Sellin, *Pioneering in Penology: The Amsterdam Houses of Correction in the Sixteenth and Seventeenth Centuries* (Philadelphia, 1944); and the seminal essay of Max Adler, *Fabrik and Zuchthaus* (Leipzig, 1924). More generally, see also Catharina Lis and Hugo Soly, *Poverty and Capitalism in Pre-Industrial Europe* (Atlantic Highland, N.J., 1979), 124–129; and C. W. Cole, *French Mercantilist Doctrines before Colbert* (New York, 1931), 172.

37. See "Résultat des travaux publics établis en 1768 pour le soulagement et la subsistance des pauvres," and other documents in A.N. F^{11} 1191. See also Shelby T. McCloy, *Government Assistance in Eighteenth-Century France* (Durham, N.C., 1946), 284.

38. On the seasonal release of inmates, see Terray's circulars of June 24, 1772, and May 10, 1774, in A.D. Marne, C.2026. He cites the practice of the Hôpital de la Charité of Lyons in pensioning children in a letter of December 26, 1769, and recommends d'Audiffret's project at Barcelonnette in another of September 4, 1771, ibid. De Premion, subdelegate at Nantes, expressed his suspicions in a letter of September 24, 1771 (A.D. Ille-et-Vilaine, C.1295). D'Audiffret offered to take two hundred children of both sexes, aged ten to fifteen, in a silk manufacture. The children would work for six years and receive a pension of forty livres for four years and a new suit of clothes on completing their term of service. On hearing that her child would be sent there, the mother of an inmate appeared before the *dépôt* at Tours in tears, fearing he would never return (A.D. Indre-et-Loire, C.304). See also above, Chapter 4, note 56 (children and the insane).

39. The use of hand mills was encouraged by Terray's predecessor, d'Invau, who offered to send the intendant of Tours a model machine from Paris or Orleans, where they had been used in *dépôts* (letter of November 11, 1769, A.D. Indre-et-Loire, C.307). Condorcet's remark was addressed to the secretary of the academy of Châlons, and was published in Malvaux, ed. *Moyens de détruire la mendicité en France,* 392 (in the chapter entitled, "Travaux des invalides").

40. Charles-Louis de Secondat, baron de la Brède et de Montesquieu, *De l'esprit des lois* (1748), XV:8, "Inutilité de l'esclavage parmi nous," in *Oeuvres,* ed. Caillois, 2 vols. (Paris, 1949), 2:496.

41. Olwen Hufton, *The Poor of Eighteenth-Century France 1750–1789* (Oxford, 1974), 183–184.

42. B.N. f.f. 8129, fol. 311.

43. Ibid., fol. 299.

44. Memoir by Boisgelin in Bibliothèque Mazarine Mss. 3433 (1691A); Malesherbes, "Réflexions ultérieures sur la sûreté de Paris et les moyens de séquestrer les mauvais sujets de la société," in A.N. 177 Mi 158 (154 AP).

45. B.N. f.f. 8130, fol. 91v. The projected ordinance to provide military discipline in companies incorporating free workers and chain gangs in addition to sentenced beggars and regular soldiers follows at fol. 96ff.

46. B.N. f.f. 8129v. (Brienne). Steven L. Kaplan, "Réflexions sur la police du monde du travail, 1700–1815," *Revue historique* 529 (January–March 1979): 17–77, notes that the word *contenir* is "la grande métaphore de la mission policière" (p. 18).

47. Letter of Trudaine, Paris, December 6, 1749, to Perronet, Archives des Ponts et Chaussées, Mss. 764. Forwarding a proposal to employ sturdy beggars and vagabonds, he

noted: "je pense que l'on peut prendre de telles measures que le travail qui seroit donné à ces pauvres pour les occuper, loin d'être onéreux aux entrepreneurs, pourroit leur procurer quelque avantage."

48. B.N. f.f. 8129, fol. 311v.

49. Archives du Ministère de la Guerre, Mss. 1769 (60), unsigned and undated memoir tentatively identified ca. 1773 in the context of accompanying correspondence between Bertier and Monteynard.

50. Ibid., undated, unsigned memoir, assigned to Bertier, ca. 1774, on the basis of substance, style, and continuity of argument in context of dossier; it is not clear whether it was intended for Monteynard, the comte de Muy, or another.

51. See André Corvisier, *L'armée française de la fin du XVIIᵉ siècle au ministère Choiseul: le soldat* (Paris, 1964), 2:984.

52. See above, chapter 7.

53. Malvaux, *Moyens,* 463 and 499.

54. Ibid., 51; 419; 462 and 470–472.

55. Ibid., 460, 462, and 466.

56. Ibid., 462. Projects for island colonies are outlined in A.D. Ille-et-Vilaine, C.1289 and C.1294.

57. Bibliothèque de l'Arsènal, Mss. 12,673–12,682, papers of Pierre-François de Rivière du Puget, "ci-devant major du corps des pionniers, nommé lieutenant de Roi à la Bastille le 27 novembre 1785." The work of the *pionniers,* or "provincial companies," is mentioned in J. R. Perronet, *Description du projet du canal de Bourgogne par Dijon,* 2 vols. (Paris, 1782–1783), 2:73. The presence of companies of *pionniers* in Corsica is confirmed in Louis Villat, *La Corse de 1768 à 1789,* 2 vols. (Besançon, 1925), 2:223 and notes. For Montlinot's comment, see p. 210.

58. Letter from Besanval on revolt at St. Denis, ibid., Mss. 12,674. On du Puget, see *Cataloque des manuscrits de la Bibliothèque de l'Arsénal,* vol. 9: *Table générale des archives de la Bastille, A–L. par Frantz Funck-Brentano, sous-bibliothéquaire à la bibliothèque de l'Arsénal* (Paris, 1894), s.v. "du Puget": "Il était parmi les défenseurs de la Bastille le 14 juillet 1789 et parvint à s'échapper; il mourut le 20 septembre 1807." Du Puget is listed as inspector of security at St. Denis in A.N. F¹⁵ 2806. See also the discussion in J. Chagniot, "Le problème du maintien de l'ordre à Paris au XVIIIᵉ siècle," *Bulletin de la Société d'histoire moderne,* 1974, no. 8:32–39.

59. Arsénal Mss. 6,814, fol. 19–25: "Projet pour ne plus rompre, brûler, pendre, etc." Du Puget envisaged four thousand uniformed workers under strict military discipline in forty companies.

60. A.N. H.927: observations of Bertier alongside letter from Saint-Priest, intendant of Languedoc, in support of objections from Estates of the province, ca. 1780. It was probably Bertier who drafted the letter from Necker to Cypierre cited by Bloch, *Assistance et l'état,* 175 (February 3, 1780; A.D. Loiret, *inventaire,* C.7; archives since destroyed):

> . . . qu'il serait peut-être dangéreux de trop bien traiter les mendiants dans le dépôt parce que, accoutumés à y trouver une nourriture meilleure que celle qu'ils auraient chez eux, que leur procurerait le travail, et ne ressentant pas assez les effets de la coercition que leur a fait mériter la vie errante et vagabonde, il serait à craindre qu'en leur rendant la liberté, ils ne reprissent avec plus de hardiesse qu'auparavant l'usage de mendier.

61. See p. 168.

62. Regulation of 1785, title 2, articles 44 and 46.

63. See the involvement of doctors in complaints against violence by a concierge in the *dépôt* at Amiens, in lengthy extracts of letters reproduced in the printed *inventaire* of the C. Series of A.D. Somme, C.1625 (1786–1787).

64. A.N. F^{15} 231: "La machine fustigatoire doit être supprimée. Elle est l'objet de la terreur des renfermés, et en a excité plusieurs à des révoltes." Report from tour of inspection in 1789.

65. Title 3, articles 79 and 80.

66. See above, chapter 8, notes 59 and 95.

67. A.N. F^{15} 2794. The file includes a printed brochure dated August 20, 1790, "Mémoire sur la Maison de Charité, servant de Manufacture de Blondes, établie à Sassenage, présenté à MM. du Directoire du Département de l'Isère, par Antoine-Henri Ducoin," and a memoir signed by Colombier on June 18, 1788, insisting that further funding would have to draw on allocations for foundlings. See also Kathryn Norberg, *Rich and Poor in Grenoble, 1600–1814* (Berkeley, 1985), 218.

68. Title 2, article 15.

69. Bannefroy, *Mémoire sur la mendicité* (Paris, 1791), 35.

70. *Mercure de France,* November 20, 1784, 132.

71. A.D. Ille-et-Vilaine, L.1157, "Rapport sur le dépôt de mendicité établi à Rennes"; 1F 1828 (fonds Guillet), memoir of Cabanes to Necker and letters of Bertrand de Molleville to La Millière October 23 and November 27, 1789; and L.1152, La Millière to intendant du Faure de Rochefort, December 9, 1789. On the shift from virtue to avarice as a motive for frugality, see Franco Venturi, *Utopia and Reform in the Enlightenment* (Cambridge, 1971), 83.

72. Bloch and Tuetey, eds., *Procès-verbaux,* 703–713; Yvonne Forado-Cunéo, "Les ateliers de charité à Paris pendant la Révolution française," *La Révolution française* 86 (1933): 317, and 87 (1934): 29–61 and 103–123. The surge of provincials returning from Paris is reflected in the arrests recorded by the *maréchaussée* of the Touraine, according to Jean-Pierre Surrault, "Mendiants et vagabonds en Touraine à la fin du XVIIIe siècle—étude sociale" (mémoire de maîtrise, Tours, 1970), 85.

73. Bloch and Tuetey, eds., *Procès-verbaux,* xxvii, 190, and 228. Confirmation of Montlinot's key role in preparing the sixth report comes from Jacques Tenon's notes on the committee's consultation with the Committee on the Constitution (B.N. n. acq. 22747, p. 53): "Liancourt, Thouret et Montlinot se sont occupés sérieusement des objets qui composent ce rapport. C'est à ces trois citoyens qu'on doit ce travail dont l'exécution intéresse la société."

74. *Procès-verbaux,* 511–534, "Sixième rapport du Comité de Mendicité sur la répression de la mendicité," especially 512–513.

75. Liancourt refers to article 22 of the decree accompanying his third report as *la pierre angulaire* of the committee's reforms in the discussion before the Assembly reported in *Archives parlementaires* 22:592. After some debate, the Assembly adjourned discussion "jusqu'à ce qu'elle ait statué sur les bases générales de l'impôt."

76. Bloch and Tuetey, eds., *Procès-verbaux,* 513.

77. Ibid., 518 and 522. Cf. Malvaux, ed., *Les moyens de détruire la mendicité,* 462: "La justice le mieux ordonné, est celle qui détruit les crimes et conserve les hommes: en traitant les criminels avec plus de douceur, on les forcera en quelque sorte à devenir honnêtes gens."

78. *Procès-verbaux,* 523. Cf. the memoir of the Estates of Brittany in 1786, cited above, Chapter 11, note 15: "Ces 137 morts sont 137 témoins irrécusables des plaintes qui se font entendre."

79. *Procès-verbaux,* 524–525.

80. Ibid., 526; A.D. Aisne, C. 747 (cleaning cesspit); Dora B. Weiner, "Health and Mental Health in the Thought of Phillippe Pinel: The Emergence of Psychiatry during the French Revolution," in *Healing and History: Essays for George Rosen,* ed. Charles E. Rosenberg (New York, 1979), 59–85.

81. *Procès-verbaux,* 528–529.

82. Ibid., 532. See also pp. 4, 63, and 89 relating to a report of June 18, 1790, on *pioniers* in Corsica, and pp. 97 and 130 on a memoir relating to the island of Boulam based on a statement from Montmorin, read in the session of September 13, 1790.

83. *Archives parlementaires,* 26:314 (session of May 22, 1791) and text of report, 319–345. See also Gordon Wright, *Between the Guillotine and Liberty: Two Centuries of the Crime Problem in France* (New York, 1983), 27–33; and Antoinette Wills, *Crime and Punishment in Revolutionary Paris* (Westport, Conn., 1981), 40 (arguments of Duport).

84. *Archives parlementaires* 26:323.

85. Ibid. 26:331. Cf. Michel Foucault, *Histoire de la folie,* 505: "le fou doit revenir à sa conscience de sujet libre et responsable," and 465, on the connection between the status of the citizen and the ability to judge insanity.

86. *Archives parlementaires* 26:331. See above, chapter 7, note 85, for Brienne. For Lavoisier, see *Oeuvres,* 3:477 (1780 report on prisons).

87. Ibid. On the abandonment of a penitential view of work in favor of work as a means to well-being, see Bernard Groethuysen, *The Bourgeois: Catholics versus Capitalism in 18th Century France* (New York, 1968), 171–173. An instance of the revolutionary grievance that citizens are "laborieux, mais réduits à la plus grande misère" is cited in Régine Robin, *La société française en 1789: Sémur-en-Auxois* (Paris, 1970), 427–428. On the newly focused rejection of *misère* see Harry C. Payne, *"Pauvreté, misère,* and the aims of Enlightened Economies, *SVEC* 154 (1976): 1581–1592, and the discussion above, in Chapter 9.

88. J. B. Duvergier, ed., *Collection complète des lois, decrets, ordonnances, règlements, avis du Conseil d'État depuis 1788,* 3:132ff. (July 19–22, 1791), especially 139. See note 75 above on the rejection of the "cornerstone" proposed by Liancourt. Wills, *Crime and Punishment in Revolutionary Paris,* 41, notes that Le Peletier de Saint-Fargeau's emphasis on rehabilitation yielded to the Assembly's concern for the protection of society.

Epilogue and Conclusion

1. A.N. F^{15} 2807.

2. Ibid. For a brief introduction to the reshaping of criminal law and the prison system during the Revolution, see Gordon Wright, *Between the Guillotine and Liberty: Two Centuries of the Crime Problem in France* (New York, 1983), 24–33. The law to which the minister refers is in J. B. Duvergier, 3:132ff.

3. Ibid. (Rouen); F^{15} 2801 (Riom); F^{15} 2797 (Nancy); F^{15} 2787 (Bourges). For a discussion of similar political tensions in hospital administrations, see Alan Forrest, *The French Revolution and the Poor* (New York, 1981), 44.

4. F^{15} 2806. Colombier had suggested providing pensions for *régisseurs,* in the context of dismissing an incompetent at Châlons (F^{15} 2796; letter of January 30, 1788). According to a calculation of probabilities, he noted, there would never be more than three or four persons drawing these modest benefits.

5. F^{15} 2806.

6. Ibid. A discussion of commercial use appears in Archives de la Seine, 4 AZ 1012. The penury of the *dépôts* is attested in almost any file one consults for the Revolutionary decade, before and after Thermidor. On the period following Thermidor, see the general remarks in Alan Forrest, *The French Revolution and the Poor* (New York, 1981), 56ff., and the brilliant article of Colin Jones, "Picking Up the Pieces: The Politics and the Personnel of Social Welfare from the Convention to the Consulate," in Gwynne Lewis and Colin

Lucas, eds., *Beyond the Terror: Essays in French Social and Regional History* (Cambridge, 1982), 53–91.

7. Louis Passy, *Frochot, préfet de la Seine: Histoire administrative (1789–1815)* (Evreux, 1867), 294 and 300–308; Duvergier, *Lois,* 16:323, "Décret sur l'extirpation de la mendicité" (July 5, 1808); Alban de Villeneuve-Bargemont, *Économie politique chrétienne, ou recherches sur la nature et les causes du paupérisme en France et en Europe, et sur les moyens de le soulager et de le prévenir* (Brussels, 1837), 377; David Higgs, "Politics and Charity at Toulouse, 1750–1850," in *French Government and Society, 1500–1850,* ed. J. F. Bosher (London, 1973), 191–207, especially 203 and 206. On the extension of the *dépôts* beyond France under Napoleon, see especially Stuart Woolf, "The Treatment of the Poor in Napoleonic Tuscany, 1808–14," in Woolf, *The Poor in Western Europe in the Eighteenth and Nineteenth Centuries* (New York, 1986), 76–117 and the essays following. Funds budgeted for *départements* (Ain to Zuydersee) pursuant to the decree of 1808 are listed in A.N. F^4 361.

8. Laîné, *Rapport au Roi sur la situation des hospices, des enfants trouvés, des aliénés, de la mendicité, des prisons* [Paris], 1818), 20–42. Guillaume de Bertier de Sauvigny, *Le comte Ferdinand de Bertier 1782–1864, et l'énigme de la Congrégation* (Paris, 1948), 238 and 255; Roberte Pautreau, "La survivance du système du renfermement des pauvres au XIXe siècle: le dépôt de mendicité de Saint-Maixent," in *Actes du 97e Congrès national des sociétés savantes,* 1:205–211; Maurice Rochaix, *Essai sur l'évolution des questions hospitalières de la fin de l'ancien régime à nos jours* (Saintes, 1959), 173.

9. William Coleman, *Death Is a Social Disease: Public Health and Political Economy in Early Industrial France* (Madison, Wis. 1982), 122, 237 and *passim.* See the editorial remarks in *Oeuvres de Turgot,* eds. Eugène Daire and Hippolyte Dussard, 2 vols. (Paris, 1844), 2:46, and the comments of Gustave d'Hugues, *Essai sur l'administration de Turgot dans la généralité de Limoges* (Paris, 1859), 235.

10. Theodore Zeldin, *France 1848–1945,* vol. 1: *Ambition, Love and Politics* (Oxford, 1973), 665–671; John H. Weiss, "Origins of the French Welfare State: Poor Relief in the Third Republic, 1871–1914," *FHS* 13:1 (Spring 1983): 47–78.

11. Joseph Viple, *La répression pénale de la mendicité* (Paris, 1905), 107.

12. Fernand Dubief, *La question du vagabondage* (Paris, 1911), 258, reports that one-third of all *départements* have some institution answering to the name of *dépôt,* but describes them as "maisons de repos à l'usage des gueux les plus habiles à se faire protéger."

13. Ferdinand-Dreyfus, *L'assistance sous la Législative et la Convention (1791–1795)* (1905; Geneva, 1978), 28: "À défaut du mot, l'idée de solidarité se trouve affirmé sous la forme d'équivalence et de mutualité des services sociaux" (a propos of a 1792 report of the Comité de Secours Publics), and 168 (Jaurès).

14. See above, chapters 7 (Turgot) 11 (comité de Mendicité). The works of the great archivist Alexandre Tuetey and of Léon Cahen, the biographer of Condorcet, also contributed to the historical study of welfare institutions, ideas, and policies.

15. Patricia O'Brien, *The Promise of Punishment: Prisons in Nineteenth-Century France* (Princeton, 1982), 54; Pierre-Jean-George Cabanis, "Observations sur les hôpitaux," in *Oeuvres complètes,* 5 vols. (Paris, 1823–1825), 2:315–362, especially 313, "infirmeries du crime," and "Quelques principes et quelques vues sur les secours publics," ibid., 2:185–306, especially 249 on prisons as "maisons du traitement pour le vice." See also Martin S. Staum, *Cabanis: Enlightenment and Medical Philosophy in the French Revolution* (Princeton, 1980), 222, and chapter 11 above.

16. O'Brien, *Promise of Punishment,* 152; Michel Foucault, *Folie et déraison: histoire de la folie à l'âge classique* (1961; Paris, 1971), 505–506; Michelle Perrot, "The Three Ages of Industrial Discipline in Nineteenth-Century France," in John M. Merriman, ed.,

Consciousness and Class Experience in Nineteenth-Century Europe (New York, 1979), 149–168.

17. On the vicissitudes of prison standards, see Gordon Wright, *Between the Guillotine and Liberty*, 68 (return to punitive concept of prison labor in 1832 and curtailment of the *cantine*), and 132 (conditions in 1870s). The experience of the *dépôts* is strongly in evidence in the recommendations and model regulation contained in François Doublet, *Mémoire sur la nécessité d'établir une réforme dans les prisons et sur les moyens de l'opérer suivi de la conclusion d'un rapport sur l'état actuel des prisons de Paris* (Paris, 1791), 44, 53, and 79.

18. L. R. Villermé, "Prisons," in *Encyclopédie méthodique,* 163:2 ("Médecine," 13:2) (Paris, 1830), 651–669, especially 168. Compare above, Chapter 11, note 11.

19. Montlinot's observations on stature, noted by Garat, contribute to a field later known as "auxiological epidemiology." See J. M. Tanner, *A History of the Study of Human Growth* Cambridge, 1981), chapters 6 and 7, especially 142ff.

20. Compare discussion above in chapters 8 and 11 with Coleman, *Death is a Social Disease,* chapter 5, "Number in Medicine," 124–148; and Erwin H. Acknerknecht, "Hygiene in France, 1815–1848," *BHM* 22 (1948): 117–155. The legacy of Deparcieux from the eighteenth century to the nineteenth is one element of intellectual continuity noted by Louis Chevalier in *Laboring Classes and Dangerous Classes in Paris during the First Half of the Nineteenth Century* (Princeton, 1981), 47 and 331. See also Michel Foucault, "La politique de la santé au XVIIIe siècle," in Foucault et al., *Les machines à guérir: aux origines de l'hôpital moderne* (Paris, 1976), 11–22.

21. On Parent-Duchâtelet and prostitution, see Chevalier, *Laboring Classes,* 48. Compare Erica-Marie Bénabou, " 'La maladie antisociale': le 'danger vénérien' à Paris au XVIIIe siècle," in *La France d'Ancien Régime: études réunis en l'honneur de Pierre Goubert,* 2 vols. (Toulouse, 1984), 1:47–54, on new attitudes of the medical profession toward treatment of venereal disease in the eighteenth century.

22. Jacques Tenon, *Mémoires sur les hôpitaux de Paris* (Paris, 1788), 187 (Lavoisier's data) and 399; Antoine-Laurent Lavoisier, "Mémoire sur le degré de force que doit avoir le bouillon, sur sa pésanteur spécifique et sur la quantité gélatineuse solide qu'il contient," in *Oeuvres,* 6 vols. (Paris, 1893), 3:563. On Tenon, see especially Louis Greenbaum, " 'Measure of Civilization.' The Hospital Thought of Jacques Tenon on the Eve of the French Revolution," *BHM* 44 (1975): 43–56. On the scientific design of hospital beds, see Françoise Boinet, *Le lit d'hôpital en France, étude historique* (Paris, 1945), 34–35.

23. "Rapport fait à l'Académie royale des sciences, le 17 mars 1780, par MM. Duhamel de Monceau, de Montigny, Le Roy, Tenon, Tillet et Lavoisier," in Lavoisier, *Oeuvres,* 3:465–485, especially 477. The report refers to memoirs by Colombier on the state of the prisons (465–466).

24. See pertinent comments of Daniel Roche in "Personnel culturel et représentation politique de la fin de l'ancien régime aux premières années de la Révolution," in Ernest Hinrichs et al., *Vom Ancien Régime zur Französischen Revolution: Forschungen und Perspectiven* (Göttingen, 1978), 502.

25. On the deputy Delecloy's denunciation of Liancourt's work, see Colin Jones, "Picking up the Pieces," 60.

26. Coleman, *Death is a Social Disease,* 122, 237, and passim; Maurice Rochaix, *Essai sur l'évolution des questions hospitalières de la fin de l'ancien régime à nos jours* (Saintes, 1959), 145. On the postponement of Condorcet's dream for a central statistical office that would serve an activist social science, see Keith Baker, *Condorcet: From Natural Philosophy to Social Mathematics* (Chicago, 1975), 372.

27. On this point, see George Klosko, "Montesquieu's Science of Politics: Absolute Values and Ethical Relativism in l'*Esprit des lois,*" *SVEC* 189 (1980): 153–177. Klosko adds a most useful reformulation to a rich and varied literature. It is remarkable that in

Montesquieu à Marseille (Lausanne, 1784), a play dramatizing the character of Montesquieu and his ideas, Louis-Sébastien Mercier centers the action on a symbolic act of anonymous charity: Montesquieu ransoms an honest merchant who is the captive of pirates. In the play, the abbé de Guasco tells Montesquieu: "Vous êtes le premier qui avez publié cette vérité lumineuse, que la servitude, en aucun sens, ne peut être légitime ni utile; c'est dans l'histoire, surtout, que cette grande vérité est empriente" (p. 109).

28. Montesquieu, *Cahiers (1716–1755)* (Paris, 1941), 112. Compare Montlinot, p. 203. For another striking formulation of this paradox, see Rousseau's remarks on household management in *La Nouvelle Héloïse,* cited by Sarah C. Maza, *Servants and Masters in Eighteenth-Century France: The Uses of Loyalty* (Princeton, N.J., 1983), 301: "The very art of the master lies in concealing that coercion under a veil of pleasure, so that servants will imagine that they actually want to do things which are in fact forced upon them."

29. Jean Lecuir, "Criminalité et "moralité': Montyon, statisticien du parlement de Paris," *RHMC* 21 (July–September 1974): 445–493, especially 466–467 and 490; Michelle Perrot, "Premières mesures des faits sociaux: les débuts de la statistique criminelle en France (1780–1830)," in François Bédarida, ed., *Pour une histoire de la statistique,* vol. 1: *Contributions* (Paris, n.d. [ca. 1980]), 125–135.

30. On the notion of *cas fortuit,* see Turgot's usage, see p. 152; and André Laingui, *La responsabilité pénale dans l'ancien droit (XVI*e*–XVIII*e *siècle)* (Paris, 1970), 71, citing Muyart de Vouglans: "on appelle proprement crime commis par cas fortuit celui qui n'a point été prévu et ne pouvait raisonnablement l'être, suivant l'ordre des choses."

31. *Mémoire sur les établissements publics de bienfaisance, de travail et de correction, considérés sous le rapports politiques et commerciaux, présentés au Comité de Secours publics de la Convention Nationale, le 28 brumaire, l'an 2 de la République une et indivisible. Par Jacques Dillon, Citoyen français, artiste hydraulicien & mécanicien, imprimé en vertu d'un décret de la Convention Nationale, sur le rapport du même comité* (Paris, n.d.), title page. From the same work of Voltaire, Dillon also cites the dictum, "Forcez les hommes au travail, vous les rendrez honnêtes gens," and adds that of Rousseau, from the *Social Contract,* "Il n'y a point de méchant qu'on ne puisse rendre bon à quelque chose."

32. See the definition of *bienfaisance publique* in Liancourt's fourth report, Camille Bloch and Alexandre Tuetey, ed., *Procès-verbaux et rapports du Comité de mendicité de la Constituante (1790–1791)* (Paris, 1911), 385.

Bibliography

The following list of archival sources actually consulted for this study provides a fairly comprehensive guide to what is available in Paris and a sampling of the much larger body of documentation available in the *départements*. The listing of books and articles includes only a selection of the most generally significant titles. Further bibliography on specific topics is to be found in chapter notes. Additional references may be found in my dissertation, "An Approach to the Problem of Beggary: The *dépôts de mendicité* in Eighteenth-Century France" (Ph.D. diss., University of Wisconsin, 1972).

Manuscripts and Archives

Libraries in Paris

Bibliothèque Nationale (B.N.)—Cabinet des Manuscrits

fonds français (f.f.)
6801 Dépenses pour les établissements de charité, 1714–1790
8129–8130 Recueil sur la mendicité fait sur l'ordre de Turgot (two bound volumes)

nouvelles acquisitions françaises (n. acq. fr.)
943 Memoirs on mendicity collected by Lefebvre d'Amécourt, *conseiller au Parlement de Paris* (all appear to have been obtained from Bertier de Sauvigny)
2799 Memoirs on mendicity, relating especially to 1777
22046; 22136; 22747 Papers of Jacques Tenon, relating especially to the work of the Comité de Mendicité of the Constituent Assembly
23616–23617 Assembly of Notables, 1787

Joly de Fleury MSS
1307–1309 Mendicity

Archives de l'Assistance Publique à Paris
Papers of Auget de Montyon, carton 8 (administration) and carton 16 (including "mendicité")
Papers of Ballainvilliers: "Mémoire sur le Languedoc," vol. 3, "Hôpitaux," manuscript volume (1788)

Archives de l'École des Ponts et Chaussées
  764 (1835). Organisation et suppression de la corvée. Emploi des mendiants, des déserteurs, etc.

Archives du Ministère de la Guerre (Vincennes)
  1765 (55) milices et régiments provinciaux, 1688–1773
  1769 (60) mémoires, projets d'ordonnances, lettres de Bertier, intendant de la généralité de Paris, au sujet de la création des compagnies d'ouvriers notamment dans ladite généralité, 1772–1774

Bibliothèque de l'Arsénal
  6,814, fol. 19–25: "Projet pour ne plus rompre, brûler, pendre, etc."
  12,673–12,682 papers of Pierre-François de Rivière du Puget (relating to companies of *pionniers*)

Bibliothèque Mazarine
  3433 (1691A) Boisgelin de Cucé, archevêque d'Aix; administration de la Provence

Archives Nationales (A.N.)

Section Ancienne: Ancien Régime
H—Administrations locales
  133–135 (Burgundy; 371; 373; 374; 392; 393; 414; 556; 565 (Brittany); 892; 910; 912; 921; 927; 939 (Languedoc); 1235; 1236 (Provence); 1417 (Burgundy and Provence); 1501–1502 (Sociétés d'agriculture); 1535; 1537 (Provence); 2105 (Généralité de Paris. Travaux de charité)
K—Monuments historiques
  683 (Laverdy to the *élus* of Burgundy); 911
0—Maison du Roi
  590–591; 3705 (arrests at Versailles; transfers to St. Denis)
V^7—Conseil
  370. Commission extraordinaire, December 26, 1789
X—Parlement de Paris
  X^{1B} 8971. Conseil secret; deliberations of July 24 and 31, 1778.
Y—Châtelet de Paris et Prévôté de l'Île-de-France
  5197 (inventaire après décès: enumeration of Bertier's effects and property at the time of his death)
  11285 (scellé après décès de M. Bertier intendant de Paris)

Section Moderne: après 1789 (including related files from Old Regime)
F^4—Comptabilité générale
  360 (bound volume; funds budgeted for *dépôts*, 1768)
  361 (initial funding of *dépôts* under Napoleonic decree of 1808, listed by *département*, Ain to Zuydersee)
  1026 Dépenses occasionées par l'opération de la destruction de la mendicité et du vagabondage. 1770–1791
F^{11}—Subsistances
  1191 Ateliers de charité
F^{12}—Commerce
  1563 Enquête Champigny, 1806; cotton manufacturing (note on this dossier kindly communicated by Prof. Serge Chassagne)
F^{15}—Hospices et secours
  101; 138; 231; 977; 1861; 2783–2801; 2804; 2806–2811, 2866; 3590, 3591

F^{16}—Prisons
936; 965; 977

Fonds Particuliers
AD I 25B (published ordinances)
AP—Private Archives
80 AP Bertier de Sauvigny papers (consulted with kind permission of Comte Henri de
Bertier de Sauvigny) 80 AP 3; 12–14; 19; 46–47; 81
154 AP II Fonds Lamoignon (microfilm reference 177 Mi)
107 Ministry of Malesherbes (first)—memoirs (177 Mi 158)
175 (includes printed memoir relating to affairs of Reculé de Basmarein, one of general
contractors for *dépôts*) 177 Mi 216

Archives Départementales (A.D.)   •

The accidents of history have destroyed the greater part of the central files of the *contrôle-
général* and almost all the records of the *intendance* of Paris and of Bertier's bureaus. For
that reason, a comparative reading of the files of the provincial intendants, contained in the
C. series of the *Archives départementales,* provides the best means for reconstructing the
correspondence between Paris and the provinces relating to the "operation of mendicity."
After the Revolution breaks out, the story may generally be pursued in the modern series
"L." The listing of departmental archives below includes mention of the seat of the *intendance.* (A few useful documents pertain to other "subdelegations" of an *intendance.*)

Aisne (Soissons)
Old Series
C.666–667; 701; 704–705; 707–711; 714; 716; 733, 743–745; 747; 749; 1023
D.20–21 (Société Royale d'Agriculture de Soissons, 1779)
New Series
L.1555–1556
Calvados (Caen)
C.614; 647–650; 652; 654; 656–661; 677–678; 702; 716; 718–719; 722; 757; 763; 6774;
6776
Charente-Maritime (La Rochelle)
C.216 (medical topography, 1789)
Cher (Bourges)
C.36 (régie économique)
Doubs (Besançon)
C.1582 (carton 1115); 1647 (1161); 1673 (1186)
Finistère (Rennes; subdelegation of Quimper)
E.1502 (municipal deliberations of Quimper)
Haute-Vienne (Limoges)
C.362; 364–366
Hérault (Montpellier)
C.588 (régie économique)
Ille-et-Vilaine (Rennes)
Old Series
8B 69–70 (*maréchaussée, 1777*)
C.1288; 1294–1305; 1309–1311; 3184; 3796; 3838; 3840; 3796; 4043; 4937

New Series
L. 1152; 1157

Special Collection
1F 1828 (fonds Guillet; papers relating to Cabanes contract, *dépôt* at Rennes; papers of
Bertrand de Molleville)

Indre-et-Loire (Tours)
C.286 (inspection of prisons); 302–311; 313–316; 339–345 (census data); 405 (epidemics)

Loire-Atlantique (Rennes; subdelegation of Nantes)
C.450–459 (registers of Estates of Brittany); 663 (Nantes; mendicity)
E. 72–73 (Le Sanitat, *hôpital-général* at Nantes)

Marne (Châlons-sur-Marne)
C.2000–2001; 2026; 2030
1J 38–41 (1777 contest on mendicity; Archives de la Société d'Agriculture, Commerce,
Sciences et Arts de la Marne, consulted on microfilm, Archives Nationales, 357 Mi
1–9)

Orne (Alençon)
C.283–285

Puy-de-Dôme (Riom)
C.1043; 1085; 1090; 1188

Rhône (Lyons)
C.165; 175

Seine (Paris)
2AZ 172 (District of St. Denis during Revolution)
4AZ 16 (letter of Lafayette, July 22, 1789, on capture of Bertier)
4AZ 1012 (a few letters concerning the *dépôt* at St. Denis/"Franciade" during the Revolution)
D.C^6 27 (fol. 212); 28 (fol. 115) and 29 (fol. 49)
Lettres de chancellerie relating to Rimberge and general contractors of *dépôts* (Administration générale des domaines, ville de Paris).

Seine-Maritime (Rouen)
C.1008–1009; 1020; 1035; 1040

Somme (Amiens)
C.1624

Yonne (Paris; subdelegation of Sens)
196

Municipal Archives and Libraries

Bibliothèque municipale de Besançon
Archives communales
GG 436 Maison de force, dite du Bon Pasteur et Hôpital des mendiants de Bellevaux
GG 446 Extinction de la mendicité. Aumône-générale, 1693–1770
Collection Droz (parlement of Besançon), vol. 65 and 68
MS 1781 (memoirs on mendicity; d'Auxiron collection)

Centre Régional Hospitalier et Universitaire (Besançon)
Aumône-générale
Deliberations, XIX (Registre)

Mémoires historiques sur l'Aumône-générale et établissements annexes faites en 1781 par l'avocat Ignace Joseph Bichat, l'un des directeurs de l'aumône (box 99)

Printed Sources

Books and Journals (first printing before 1850)

Bannefroy. *Mémoire sur la mendicité par M. Bannefroy, ancien inspecteur des maisons de force et des dépôts de mendicité du royaume.* Paris, 1791.

Baudeau, l'abbé Nicolas. *Idées d'un citoyen sur les besoins, les droits, et les devoirs des vrais pauvres.* Amsterdam, 1765.

Beccaria, Cesare. *Dei Delitta e della pene. Con una raccolta di lettere e documenti relativi alla nascita dell'opera e alla sua fortuna nell'Europa de Settecento,* ed. Franco Venturi. Turin, 1965.

Colombier, Jean. *Code de médecine militaire pour le service de terre.* 5 vols. Paris, 1772.

———. *Description des épidémies qui ont régné dupuis quelques années dans la généralité de Paris. . . . Publié par ordre de M. l'intendant.* Paris, 1783.

Colombier, Jean, and François Doublet. *Instruction sur la manière de gouverner les insensés et de travailler à leur guérison dans les asiles qui leur sont destinés.* Paris, 1785.

Delachaize. *Discours prononcé à l'assemblée des États en 1787, sur la mendicité.* Dijon, 1787.

Doublet, François. *Observations faites dans le département des hôpitaux civils,* vol. 3. Paris. 1787. Copy at B.N., 8° Td^{34} .592. Series ran 1785–1788, but not all volumes appear to be extant.

Dupin, Claude. *Oeconomiques.* 1745. 2 vols. Paris, 1913.

Knies, Carl, ed. *Carl Friedrichs von Baden brieflicher Verkehr mit Mirabeau und du Pont.* 2 vols. Heidelberg, 1892.

Leclerc de Montlinot, l'abbé Charles Antoine-Joseph. *Discours qui a remporté le prix de la Société royale d'agriculture de Soissons en l'année 1779. Question: quels sont les moyens de détruire la mendicité, de rendre les pauvres valides utiles et de les secourir dans la ville de Soissons.* Soissons, 1779.

———. *État actuel de la Maison de Travail de la Généralité de Soissons (1781).* Lacks publication information. Copy in A.D. Aisne, C.743.

———. *État actuel du dépôt de mendicité ou de la maison de travail de la généralité de Soissons. Deuxième Compte. Année 1782.* Lacks publication information. Copy in A.D. Aisne, C.743.

———. *État actuel du dépôt de mendicité de la généralité de Soissons. troisième compte. année 1783.* Lacks publication information. Copy in A.D. Aisne, C.743.

———. *État actuel du dépôt de mendicité de la généralité de Soissons. IV Compte. Années 1784 et 1785.* Lacks publication information. Copy in A.D. Marne, C.2001.

———. *État actuel du dépôt de mendicité de Soissons, précédé d'un essai sur la mendicité V. Compte. Année 1786.* Soissons, 1789.

———. *Observations sur les enfans-trouvés de la généralité de Soissons.* Paris, 1790.

Lenoir, Jean Charles Pierre. *Détail sur quelques établissements de la ville de Paris demandé par S.M. la Reine de Hongrie à M. Lenoir, lieutenant général de police.* Paris, 1780.

Le Trosne, Guillaume François. *Mémoire sur les vagabonds et sur les mendiants.* Soissons and Paris, 1764.

Malvaux, l'abbé, ed. *Les moyens de détruire la Mendicité en France, en rendant les Mendians utiles à l'état sans les rendre malheureux; tirés des Mémoires qui ont concouru pour le prix accordé en l'année 1777, par l'Académie des Sciences, Arts et Belles Lettres de Châlons-sur-Marne.* New ed. Châlons-sur-Marne, 1780.

Mercier, Louis-Sébastien. *Tableau de Paris*. 1781. 5 vols. (Preface refers to 4 vols.; fifth is lacking.) Amsterdam, 1782.

Montlinot. See "Leclerc de Montlinot."

Necker, M. Jacques. *De l'Administration des finances de la France*. 3 vols. Place of publication lacking. 1785.

Saint-Pierre, Charles Irénée Castel de, abbé de Tiron. *Les Rêves d'un homme de Bien, qui peuvent être réalisés, ou les vues utiles et pratiques de M. l'Abbé de Saint-Pierre, choisie dans ce grand nombre de projets singuliers, dont le bien publique étoit le principe*. Paris, 1775.

Turgot, Anne Robert Jacques, baron de l'Aulne. *Oeuvres de Turgot et documents le concernant, avec biographie et notes, par Gustave Schelle*. 5 vols. Paris, 1912–1923.

Turmeau de la Morandière. *Police sur les mendians, les vagabonds, les joueurs de profession, les intrigants, les filles prostitués, les domestiques hors de maison dupuis longtems, et les gens sans aveu*. Paris, 1764.

Journals

Annales politiques, civiles et littéraires du dix-huitième siècle, ed. S. N. H. Linguet

Éphémérides du citoyen, ou Bibliothèque raisonnée des sciences morales et politiques

Journal oeconomique

Mercure de France

Dictionaries and Encyclopedias

Dictionnaire des Sciences Médicales. Biographie Médicale, ed. Antoine J. L. Jourdan. 7 vols. Paris: C. L. F. Pancoucke, 1820–1825.

Encyclopédie, ou Dictionnaire raisonné des sciences, des arts et des métiers par une societé de gens de lettres, ed. Diderot and d'Alembert. 28 vols. Paris, 1751–1772.

Encyclopédie méthodique par ordre des matières par une société de gens de lettres, de savans et d'artistes. Paris, 1782–1832. 166½ vols. of text, plus supplements and illustrations. Published in the form of multivolume topical encyclopedias, including "Économie politique et diplomatique," "Jurisprudence," and "Médecine."

Official Publications, Printed Collections of Documents, and Selected Reference Works

Almanach Royal. Paris, 1699 and years following.

Archives parlementaires de 1787 à 1860: recueil complet des débats législatifs et politiques des chambres francaises. Paris, 1879– . 1st series, 1787–1794. 2nd series, 1814–1839.

Bloch, Camille. *Inventaire sommaire des volumes de la collection Joly de Fleury concernant l'assistance et la mendicité*. Paris, 1908.

Bloch, Camille, and Alexandre Tuetey, eds. *Procès-verbaux et rapports du Comité de mendicité de la Constituante*. Paris, 1911.

Boislisle, A.M. de, ed. *Mémoires des Intendants sur l'État des généralités dressés pour l'instruction du Duc de Bourgogne*. Vol. 1. *Mémoire de la Généralité de Paris*. Paris, 1881.

Candille, Marcel, and Françoise Levy. *Bibliographie d'histoire des hôpitaux*. Paris, 1957–. Cumulative bibliography extracted from *Revue de l'Assistance publique à Paris*, continued in the *Bulletin de la Société française d'histoire des hôpitaux*.

Compte rendu au Roi au mois de mars 1788 et publié par ses ordres. Paris, 1788.

Dollinger, Philippe, and Philippe Wolff. *Bibliographie des villes de France.* Paris, 1967.

Duvergier, J. B., editor. *Collection complète des lois, décrets, ordonnances, règlemens, . . . de 1788 à 1824.* 69 vols. Paris, 1824–1869.

Funck-Brentano, Frantz, ed. *Catalogue des manuscrits de la Bibliothèque de l'Arsénal.* Vol. 9. *Table générale des Archives de la Bastille, A–K.* Paris, 1894.

Garçon, Émile. *Code pénal annoté.* Vol. 1. *Articles 1–294.* new ed. revised by Marcel Rousselet, Maurice Patin, and Marc Ancel. Paris, 1952.

Hecht, Jacqueline, and Claude Levy, eds. *Économie et population, les doctrines françaises avant 1800: bibliographie générale commentée.* Institut National d'Études Démographiques, cahier no. 21. Paris, 1954.

Isambert, Jourdan and Decrusy. *Recueil général des anciennes lois françaises, depuis l'an 420 jusqu'à la Révolution de 1789.* Paris, 1822–1827.

Marion, Marcel. *Dictionnaire des institutions de la France aux XVIIe et XVIIIe siècles.* 1923. Paris, 1968.

Martin-Doisy. *Dictionnaire d'économie charitable.* 4 vols. Paris, 1857.

Molinier, Auguste. *Inventaire sommaire de la collection Joly de Fleury.* Paris, 1881.

Monin, Hippolyte. *L'état de Paris en 1789.* Paris, 1889.

Prévost and Roman d'Amat, eds. *Dictionnaire de biographie française.* Vol. 6. Paris, 1954. Includes articles "Bertier de Sauvigny" and "Bourgeois de Boynes."

Pamphlets Relating to Bertier de Sauvigny in the Bibliothèque Nationale (catalog references cited)

L'audience des enfers, dialogue entre de Launay, de Flesselles, de Sauvigny et Foulon. Lb³⁹ 7453.

Convoi, service et enterrement des très hauts, très puissants seigneurs Foulon, président, et Berthier de Sauvigny, intendant de Paris. 1789. Lb³⁹ 2035.

Dialogue entre M. de Launay, Flesselles, Foulon et Berthier aux enfers. Paris. Lb³⁹ 2041.

Les enragés aux enfers, ou nouveau dialogue des morts. 1789. Lb³⁹ 2040.

Épitaphes des sieurs Foulon et Berthier. Affichée et publiée au Palais-Royal, ou Oraison funèbre suivi du récit historique de leur mort. Paris. Lb³⁹ 7452.

Extraits des lettres trouvées dans le portefueille de M. Berthier, intendant de Paris, pris dans la nuit du 16 juillet, dans sa voiture. Lb³⁹ 1984.

Lettre de M^xxx à son ami, habitant de Perpignan. Récit des faits relatifs à la mort de MM Foulon et Berthier, à la démission et à la seconde proclamation de M. le M^ns de La Fayette. LB³⁹ 7541.

La mort tragique de l'Intendant de Paris. Lb³⁹ 2032.

Les quatre têtes, ou la trahison punie. Paris. Lb³⁹ 7454.

Les quatre traitres aux enfers: dialogue. Paris, 1789. Lb³⁹ 2039.

Les tyrans anéantis, ou Foulon, ex-controlleur-général des finances, et l'intendant de Paris, punis par la nation. Lb³⁹ 2033.

Secondary Works

Books

Actes du 97e Congrès national des sociétés savantes. Nantes. 1972. Section d'histoire moderne et contemporaine. Vol. 1. *Assistance et assistés de 1616 à nos jours.* Paris, 1977.

Beaurepaire, Charles de. *Recherches sur la répression de la mendicité dans l'ancienne gé-néralité de Rouen*. Rouen, 1887.

Bertier de Sauvigny, Le Père Guillaume de. *Le comte Ferdinand de Bertier, 1782–1864, et l'énigme de la Congrégation*. Paris 1948.

Bloch, Camille. *L'assistance et l'état en France à la veille de la Révolution: généralités de Paris, Rouen, Alençon, Orléans, Soissons, Amiens (1764–1790)*. Paris, 1908.

Bolotte, Marcel. *Les hôpitaux et l'assistance dans la province de Bourgogne au dernier siècle de l'Ancien Régime*. Dijon, 1968.

Bouloiseau, Marc, et al. *Contributions à l'histoire démographique de la Révolution française*. Memoires et documents, XIV. Paris, 1962.

Braudel, Fernand, and Ernest Labrousse, eds. *Histoire économique et sociale de la France*. Vol. 2. Ernest Labrousse, Pierre Léon, Pierre Goubert, Jean Bouvier, Charles Car-rière, Paul Harsin. *Des derniers temps de l'âge seigneurial aux préludes de l'âge industriel (1660–1789)*. Paris, 1970.

Cameron, Iain A. *Crime and Repression in the Auvergne and the Guyenne, 1720–1790*. New York, 1981.

Carillion, Cathérine. "À Bicêtre: mendiants 1755–1770 et bons pauvres 1746–1789." Mém-oire de maîtrise, University of Paris I, 1973. Consulted with kind permission of the author.

Chisick, Harvey. *The Limits of Reform in the Enlightenment: Attitudes toward the Education of the Lower Classes in Eighteenth-Century France*. Princeton, 1981.

Deschamps, Marie-Odile. "Le dépôt de mendicité de Rouen (1764, an V)." Mémoire pour le D.E.S. d'histoire, Caen, 1964–1965. Consulted at Bibliothèque de l'Assistance Publique, Paris.

Deyon, Pierre. *Le temps des prisons. Essai sur l'histoire de la délinquance et les origines du système pénitentiaire*. Paris, 1975.

Duby, Georges, ed. *Histoire de la France rurale*. 3 vols. Paris, 1975.

Duetti, Clinio. "Work Noble and Ignoble: An Introduction to the History of the Modern Idea of Work." Ph.D. diss., University of Wisconsin, 1954.

Dumas, F. *La généralité de Tours au XVIIIᵉ siècle. L'administration de l'indendant du Cluzel (1766–1783)*. Paris, 1894.

Fairchilds, Cissie. *Poverty and Charity in Aix-en-Provence, 1640–1789*. Baltimore, 1976.

Ferdinand Dreyfus. *Un philanthrope d'autrefois: La Rochefoucault-Liancourt, 1747–1827*. Paris, 1903.

Forrest, Alan. *The French Revolution and the Poor*. New York, 1981.

Foucault, Michel. *Folie et déraison: histoire de la folie à l'âge classique*. 1961. Paris, 1972.

———, *Surveiller et punir: naissance de la prison*. Paris, 1975.

Gallot-Lavallée, Pierre. *Un hygiéniste au XVIIIᵉ siècle. Jean Colombier, rapporteur du Con-seil de santé des hôpitaux militaires, inspecteur général des hôpitaux et prisons du royaume (1736–1789)*. Paris, 1913.

Gay, Peter. *The Enlightenment: An Interpretation*. 2 vols. New York, 1966–1969.

Goubert, Jean Pierre. *Malades et médecins en Bretagne, 1770–1790*. Paris, 1974.

Gutton, Jean-Pierre. *L'état et la mendicité dans la première moitié du XVIIIᵉ siècle: Au-vergne, Beaujolais, Forez, Lyonnais*. Centre d'études foréziennes. Lyons, 1973.

———. *La société et les pauvres. L'exemple de la généralité de Lyon, 1534–1789*. Paris, 1971.

Guyader, Josseline. "La répression de la mendicité et du vagabondage dans la ville de Tou-louse depuis la déclaration de 1724 jusqu'à la Révolution de 1789." D.E.S. droit, Toulouse, 1966. Consulted at Bibliothèque de l'Assistance Publique, Paris.

Harouel, Jean-Louis. *Les ateliers de charité dans la province de la Haute-Guyenne*. Paris, 1969.

Harris, Robert D. *Necker, Reform Statesman of the Ancien Régime.* Berkeley, 1979.

Hufton, Olwen. *The Poor of Eighteenth-Century France, 1750–1789.* Oxford, 1974.

Jones, Colin. *Charity and Bienfaisance: The Treatment of the Poor in the Montpellier Region, 1740–1815.* New York, 1983.

Kaplan, Steven L. *Bread, Politics and Political Economy in the Reign of Louis XV.* 2 vols. The Hague, 1976.

Kaplow, Jeffry. *The Names of Kings: The Parisian Laboring Poor in the Eighteenth Century.* New York, 1972.

Lallemand, Léon. *Histoire de la charité.* 4 vols. Paris, 1902–1912.

Lebrun, François. *Les hommes et la mort en Anjou aux 17ᵉ et 18ᵉ siècles—essai de démographie et de psychologie historiques.* Paris, 1971.

Lefebvre, Georges. *La Grande Peur de 1789.* Paris, 1932.

Levy, Darline Gay. *The Ideas and Careers of Simon-Nicolas-Henri Linguet: A Study in Eighteenth-Century French Politics.* Urbana, Ill., 1980.

Lis, Catharina, and Hugo Soly. *Poverty and Capitalism in Pre-Industrial Europe.* Atlantic Highlands, N.J., 1979.

McCloy, Shelby T. *Government Assistance in Eighteenth-Century France.* Durham, N.C., 1946.

Mandrou, Robert. *La France aux XVIIᵉ et XVIIIᵉ siècles.* Paris, 1967.

Les marginaux et les exclus dans l'histoire, articles by M. Baulant et al., introduced by B. Vincent. Cahiers Jussieu, 5. Paris, 1979.

Norberg, Kathryn. *Rich and Poor in Grenoble, 1600–1814.* Berkeley, 1985.

Patureau, Nicole. "L'hôpital-général de la charité de Tours (1656–1802)." Thesis, École des Chartes, Paris, 1967. Consulted at Archives Départementales de l'Indre-et-Loire.

Paultre, Christian. *De la répression de la mendicité et du vagabondage.* Paris, 1906.

Payne, Harry C. *The Philosophes and the People.* New Haven, 1976.

Perrot, Jean-Claude. *Genèse d'une ville moderne: Caen au XVIIIᵉ siècle.* Paris, 1975.

Perrot, Michelle, ed. *L'impossible prison.* Paris, 1980.

Poitrineau, Abel. *La vie rurale en Basse-Auvergne au XVIIIᵉ siècle (1726–1789).* Paris, 1965.

Poussou, Jean-Pierre. *Bordeaux et le Sud-Ouest au XVIIIᵉ siècle: croissance économique et attraction urbaine.* Paris, 1983.

Roche, Daniel. *The People of Paris: An Essay in Popular Culture in the 18th Century.* Berkeley, 1987.

Rosen, George. *From Medical Police to Social Medicine. Essays in the History of Health Care.* New York, 1974.

Rusche, Georg, and Otto Kirchheimer. *Punishment and Social Structure.* New York, 1939.

Schwartz, Robert M. *Policing the Poor in Eighteenth-Century France.* Chapel Hill, N.C., 1988.

Sellin, Johan Thorsten. *Pioneering in Penology: The Amsterdam Houses of Correction in the Sixteenth and Seventeenth Centuries.* Philadelphia, 1944.

Sewell, William H. *Work and Revolution in France: The Language of Labor from the Old Regime to 1848.* New York, 1980.

Surreault, Jean-Pierre. "Mendiants et vagabonds en Touraine à la fin du XVIIIᵉ siècle—étude sociale." Mémoire de maîtrise, Tours, 1970. Consulted with kind permission of author at Archives Départementales de l'Indre-et-Loire.

Weulersse, Georges. *Le mouvement physiocratique en France (de 1756 à 1770).* 2 vols. Paris, 1910.

Williams, Alan. *The Police of Paris, 1718–1789.* Baton Rouge, 1979.

Articles

Abbiatéci, André. "Les incendiaires dans la France du XVIIIe siècle: essai de typologie criminelle." *AESC* 25:1 (1970):229–248.

Béaud, J., and G. Bouchart, "Le dépôt des pauvres de Saint–Denis (1768–1792). *ADH*, 1974, 127–143.

Bordes, Maurice. "Les intendants éclairés de la fin de l'Ancien Régime." *RHES* 39:1 (1961): 57–83.

Bosher, J.F. "The French Crisis of 1770." *History,* February 1972, 17–30.

Boucheron, Véronique. "La montée du flot des errants de 1760 à 1789 dans la généralité d'Alençon." Introduction by P. Chaunu. *Annales de Normandie* 21:1 (March 1971): 55–86.

Candille, Marcel. "Commentaire autour du chapitre de l' "Esprit des lois" relatif aux hôpitaux." *Revue de l'Assistance publique à Paris* 22 (1953): 316–323.

Castan, Nicole. "La justice expéditive." *AESC* 31 (1976): 331–361.

Chaunu, Pierre, François Billacois, and Roger Chartier. "Rapports sociaux et répression dans la société d'Ancien Régime." *AESC* 24:4 (1969): 895–918.

Combes-Monier, J. "Population mouvante et criminalité à Versailles à la fin de l'Ancien Régime." In A. Armengaud et al., *Sur la population française au XVIIIe et au XIXe siècles: hommage à Marcel Reinhard,* Société de démographie historique, 135–159. Paris, 1973.

Crépillon, Paul. "Un gibier des prévôts: mendiants et vagabonds au XVIIIe siècle entre la Vire et la Dives. 1720–1789." *Annales de Normandie* 17:3 (October 1967): 223–252.

Daumard, Adeline. "Une référence pour l'étude des sociétés urbaines en France aux XVIIIe et XIXe siècles: projet de code socio-professionel." *RHMC* (July–September 1963): 185–210.

Davis, Natalie Zemon. "Poor Relief, Humanism and Heresy: The Case of Lyon." In *Society and Culture in Early Modern France: Eight Essays by Natalie Zemon Davis,* 17–64. Stanford, 1975.

Depauw, Jacques. "Pauvres, pauvres mendiants, mendiants valides ou vagabonds? Les hésitations de la législation royal." *RHMC,* July–September 1974, 401–418.

Dérouet, B. "Une démographie différentielle: les populations rurales d'Ancien Régime." *AESC* 35:1 (January–February 1980): 3–41.

Deschamps, Marie-Odile. "Le dépôt de mendicité de Rouen (1768–1820)." *Bulletin d'histoire économique et sociale de la Révolution française,* 1977, 81–93.

Égret, Jean. "Malesherbes, premier président de la cour des aides (1750–1775)." *RHMC,* April–June 1956, 97–119.

Farge, Arlette. "Le mendiant, un marginal? (les résistances aux archers de l'hôpital dans le Paris du XVIIIe siècle)." In *Les marginaux et les exclus dans l'histoire,* introduction by Bernard Vincent, Cahiers Jussieu (University of Paris VII), no. 5, 313–329. Paris, 1979.

Faure, Edgar. "Les bases expérimentales et doctrinales de la politique économique de Turgot." *Revue historique de droit français et étranger,* 4th series, 39 (1961): 255–295 and 382–447.

Febvre, Lucien. "Pour l'histoire d'un sentiment: le besoin de sécurité." *AESC* 11 (1956): 244–247.

———. "Travail—évolution d'un mot et d'une idée." In *Pour une histoire à part entière,* 649–658. Paris, 1962.

Forrest, Alan. "The Condition of the Poor in Revolutionary Bordeaux." In Douglas Johnson, ed., *French Society and the Revolution,* 217–247. Cambridge, 1976.

Furet, François. "Pour une définition des classes inférieures à l'époque moderne." *AESC* 18 (1963): 459–474.

Geremek, Bronislaw. "Criminalité, vagabondage, paupérisme: la marginalité à l'aube des temps modernes." *RHMC*, July–September 1974, 337–375.

Godechot, Jacques. "Beccaria et la France." In *Atti del Convegno internazionale su Cesare Beccaria. Turin, 1964,* 67–83. Turin, 1966.

Goubert, Pierre. "Le monde des errants, mendiants et vagabonds à Paris et autour de Paris au 18ᵉ siècle." *Clio parmi les hommes. Recueil d'articles.* Paris, 1976.

———. "Sociétés rurales françaises du XVIIIᵉ siècle: vingt paysanneries contrastées. Quelques problèmes." In Fernand Braudel et al., *Conjoncture économique: structures sociales: hommage à Ernest Labrousse,* 375–387. Paris, 1974.

Greenbaum, Louis. "Health-Care and Hospital-Building in Eighteenth-Century France: Reform Proposals of Du Pont de Nemours and Condorcet." *SVEC* 92 (1976): 895–930.

———. "The Humanitarianism of Antoine Laurent Lavoisier." *SVEC* 88 (1972): 651–675.

———. "Jacques Necker's *Enquête* of the Paris Hospital (1777)." *The Consortium on Revolutionary Europe, 1750–1850 Proceedings, 1984,* 26–40. Athens, Ga., 1986.

———. "Science, Medicine, Religion: Three Views of Health Care in France on the Eve of the French Revolution." *Studies in Eighteenth-Century Culture* 10 (1981): 373–391.

———. "Scientists and Politicians: Hospital Reform in Paris on the Eve of the French Revolution." *The Consortium on Revolutionary Europe, 1750–1850. Proceedings, 1973,* 168–191. Gainesville, Fla., 1975.

Gruder, Vivian R. "Paths to Political Consciousness: The Assembly of Notables of 1787 and the 'Pre-Revolution' in France." *FHS* 13:3 (Spring 1984): 323–355.

Guéguen, P.-E. "La mendicité au pays de Vannes dans la 2ᵉ moitié du XVIIIᵉ siècle." *Bulletin de la Société polymathique du Morbihan,* 1970 (1969), 105–134.

Gutton, Jean-Pierre. "Les mendiants dans la société parisienne au début du XVIIIᵉ siècle." *Cahiers d'histoire* 13 (1968): 131–141.

Hannaway, Caroline C. "The Société Royale de Médecine and Epidemics in the Ancien Régime." *BHM* 51 (1977): 431–437.

Higgs, David. "Politics and Charity at Toulouse, 1750–1850." In J. F. Bosher, ed., *French Government and Society, 1500–1850,* 191–207. London, 1973.

Hufton, Olwen. "Begging, Vagrancy, Vagabondage and the Law: An Aspect of the Problem of Poverty in Eighteenth-Century France." *European Studies Review* 2:2 (April 1972): 97–123.

———. "Toward an Understanding of the Poor in Eighteenth-Century France." In J. F. Bosher, ed., *French Government and Society, 1500–1850,* 145–165. London, 1973.

———. "Women and the Family Economy in Eighteenth-Century France." *FHS* 9:1 (Spring 1975): 1–22.

Jones, Colin. "Picking Up the Pieces: The Politics and the Personnel of Social Welfare from the Convention to the Consulate." In Gwynne Lewis and Colin Lucas, eds., *Beyond the Terror: Essays in French Regional and Social History, 1794–1815,* 53–91. Cambridge, 1983.

Kaplan, Steven. "Réflexions sur la police du monde de travail, 1700–1815." *RH* 529 (January–March 1979): 17–77.

Kaplow, Jeffry. "The Culture of Poverty in Paris on the Eve of the Revolution." *International Review of Social History* 12:2 (1967): 277–291.

———. "Sur la population flottante de Paris à la fin de l'ancien régime." *AHRF* 39 (1967): 1–14.

Le Bour'his, Fr. "Jean Chouan au dépôt de mendicité de Rennes." *Bulletin et mémoires de la Société archéologique d'Ille-et-Vilaine* 67 (1944): 135–152.

Lebrun, François. "Les crises démographiques en France aux XVIIe et XVIIIe siècles."
    AESC 35:2 (March–April 1980): 205–233.
Le Roy Ladurie, Emmanuel. "Pour un modéle de l'économie rurale française au XVIIIe
    siècle." *Cahiers d'histoire* 19:1 (1974): 5–27.
Liris, Robert. "Mendicité et vagabondage en Basse-Auvergne à la fin du XVIIIe siècle."
    Revue d'auvergne 79:2 (1965): 65–78.
Mandrou, Robert. "Un problème de diététique à l'Hôtel-Dieu de Paris, à la veille de la
    Révolution." *Actes du 93e Congrès des sociétés savantes, Tours, 1968. Section
    d'histoire moderne*, 1:125–137. Paris 1971.
Martin, D. "La maréchaussée d'Auvergne face aux autorités administratives et judiciaires au
    XVIIIe siècle." *Cahiers d'histoire* 18 (1973): 337–349.
Meuvret, Jean. "Les crises de subsistances et la démographie de la France d'Ancien Régime."
    Population 1:4 (1946): 643–650.
Mitchell, Harvey. "Politics in the Service of Knowledge: The Debate over the Administration
    of Medicine and Welfare in the Late Eighteenth Century." *Social History* 6 (1981):
    185–207.
Moravia, Sergio. "Philosophie et médecine en France à la fin du XVIIIe siècle." *SVEC* 89
    (1972): 1089–1151.
Morineau, Michel. "Budgets popularies en France au XVIIIe siècle, I." *RHES* 50:2 (1972):
    203–237.
Neveu, Hughes. "L'alimentation du XVIe au XVIIIe siècle: essai de mise au point." *RHES*
    51:3 (1973): 336–379.
Norberg, Kathryn. "Educating the Poor: Charity Schools and Charitable Attitudes: Grenoble,
    1600–1789." *Proceedings of the Western Society for French History* 8 (1980): 181–
    190.
Olejniczak, William J. "Recasting the Disordered Poor: The *dépôt de mendicité* at Châlons-
    sur-Marne during the Decade before the Revolution." *The Consortium on Revolutionary
    Europe, 1750–1850. Proceedings, 1984*, 16–25. Athens, Ga., 1986.
Parker, Harold T. "French Administrators and French Scientists during the Old Regime and
    the Early Years of the Revolution." In Richard Herr and H. T. Parker, eds., *Ideas
    in History: Essays Presented to Louis Gottschalk by his Former Students*, 85–109.
    Durham, N.C., 1965.
Payne, Harry C. "*Pauvreté, Misère*, and the Aims of Enlightened Economics." *SVEC* 154
    (1976): 1581–1592.
Perrot, Michelle. "The Three Ages of Industrial Discipline in Nineteenth-Century France."
    In John M. Merriman, ed., *Consciousness and Class Experience in Nineteenth-Century
    Europe*, 149–168. New York, 1979.
Peter, Jean-Pierre. "Malades et maladies à la fin du XVIIIe siècle." In J.-P. Desaive et al.,
    Médecins, climat et épidémies à la fin du XVIIIe siècle, 135–170. Paris, 1972.
Poitrineau, Abel. "Aspects de l'émigration temporaire et saisonnière en Auvergne à la fin
    du XVIIIe siècle et au début du XIXe siècle." *RHMC*, 1962, 5–50.
Poussou, Jean-Pierre. "Les mouvement migratoires en France et à partir de la France de la
    fin du XVe siècle au début du XIXe siècles: approches pour une synthèse." *ADH*,
    1970, 11–78.
Quétel, Claude. "Lettres de cachet et correctionnaires dans la généralité de Caen au XVIIIe
    siècle." *Annales de Normandie* 28:2 (1978): 127–159.
Raeff, Marc. "The Well-Ordered Police State and the Development of Modernity in
    Seventeenth- and Eighteenth-Century Europe: An Attempt at a Comparative Approach."
    American Historical Review 80:5 (December 1975): 1221–1243.
Ricci, Giovanni. "Naissance du pauvre honteux: entre l'histoire des idées et l'histoire sociale."
    AESC 38:1 (January–February 1983): 158–177.

Roche, Daniel. "A Pauper Capital: Some Reflections on the Parisian Poor in the Seventeenth and Eighteenth Centuries." *French History* 1:2 (October 1987): 182–209.

———. "La diffusion des lumières. Un exemple: l'Académie de Châlons-sur-Marne." *AESC,* 1964, 887–922.

Romon, Christian. "Le monde des pauvres à Paris au XVIIIᵉ siècle." *AESC* 37 (1982): 729–763.

Rousset, Dr. J. "Essai de pathologie urbaine. Les causes de morbidité et de mortalité à Lyon aux XVIIᵉ et XVIIIᵉ siècles." *Cahiers d'histoire,* 1963, 71–105.

Sée, Henri. "La population et la vie économique de Rennes vers le milieu du VIIIᵉ siècle d'après les rôles de la capitation." *Mémoires de la Société d'histoire de Bretagne* 4 (1923): 89–136.

Trénard, Louis. "Pauvreté, charité, assistance à Lille, 1708–1790." *Actes du 97ᵉ Congrès national des sociétés savantes. Nantes, 1972. Section d'histoire moderne et contemporaine.* Vol. 1: *Assistance et assistés de 1610 à nos jours,* 473–498. Paris, 1977.

Villemon, Marie-José. "À partir des sources hospitalières: l'alimentation du pauvre de l'Hôpital général de Caen au début du XVIIIᵉ siècle." *Annales de Normandie* 21:3 (1971): 235–260.

Vovelle, Michel. "De la mendicité au brigandage. Les errants en Beauce sous la Révolution française." *Actes du 86ᵉ Congrès national des sociétés savantes (Montpellier, 1961). Section d'histoire moderne et contemporaine,* 483–512. Paris, 1962.

———. "Le prolétariat flottant à Marseille sous la Révolution française." *ADH,* 1968, 111–138.

Weiner, Dora B. "Le droit de l'homme à la santé: une belle idée devant l'Assemblée Constituante, 1790–1791." *Clio Médica* 5 (1970): 209–223.

Weulersse, Léon. "Les physiocrates sous le ministère de Turgot." *RHES* 13 (1925): 314–337.

Index

49, 66; plans for, at Sens, 53; draft edict
of 1765 draws upon, 59, 60; Bertier
comments upon, 63, 67; cited as
precedent, 76, 110, 111; at Besançon,
108; and finance for mendicity in
Provence, 117; ordinances of 1777
reaffirm, 161. *See also* Three deniers per
livre of the *taille*
Declaration of February 5, 1731, on
maréchaussée, 64
Declaration of 1750, 32, 41, 54; Bertier
cites, 66; and professional beggars, 73;
Laverdy cites, 76; de Fleury cites, 110
Declaration of August 3, 1764 concerning
vagabonds and shiftless persons, 5, 49;
Journal Oeconomique comments upon,
46; Baudeau criticizes, 48; registered by
parlement of Paris, 49; and intendants,
50, 52; royal aid promised in, 51, 114;
and authorization for *dépôts*, 57; prisons
and, 61; "strict execution" of, 66–68;
and *arrêt du conseil* of 1767, 68, 73;
"renewed" according to Choiseul, 74;
explained by Laverdy, 75; seen as act of
rigor, 119; Turgot's instructions on, 133;
Brienne on, 137; Trudaine on, 149;
ordinances of 1777 and, 161
Declaration of the Rights of Man, 258
Delinquents: government as therapist and
educator of, viii; Montlinot on, 202,
210, 228. *See also* Beggars; Crime;
Rehabilitation
Demography: and economic conditions, 9;
and family structures, 13; and estimating
incidence of poverty, 239; data and, 257
Deparcieux, Antoine II, 236
Depont, Jean-Samuel (intendant at
Moulins), 106
Dépôts de mendicité: and social policy; vii,
72; institutional precedents for, 30–32,
42; *Résultat* gives signal for establishing,
50, 52; de Fleury insists on need for, 62;
Bertier reports to Turgot on, 63, 71,
131, 151; conceived as "supplement to
hospitals," 67–68, 76, 88; initial budget
for, 69, 83; instructions for establishing,
72; numbers of inmates in, 80;
management of, 80–86; layout of, 85;
policy review of (1769), 85–86;
concentration of network, 90; stocks of,
used for relief, 104; Brienne and, 135–

36; confinement in, condemned, 137;
Turgot closes all but five, 154–55, 180;
Turgot reopens eleven, 157; policy of
transfers among, 162; Necker curtails
network of, 169, 193; Colombier and,
171; d'Ormesson affirms utility of, 172;
Regulation of 1785 and, 175–80;
Châlons essayists on, 190; Montlinot
and, 194; Necker discusses, 203–4;
article in *Encyclopédie Méthodique* on,
206; provincial assemblies and, 215–17;
Estates General and, 218–20;
Revolutionary mass psychology and,
220–24; Montlinot favors retaining, 228;
and empirical social observation, 232–
33; and social medicine, 234; work and
rehabilitation in, 240–41, 244–47; as
observatory and laboratory, 247, 255;
Comité de Mendicité condemns record
of, 248; finds favor in nineteenth
century, 254; as "total institution," 255;
Tenon mentions, 256; harsh lessons of,
258. *See also places of individual*
dépôt
Desbrières, *régisseur* (overseer) of *dépôt* at
Rouen, 252
Deserters from army, 76
Detention. *See* Terms of detention
Diamond Necklace Affair, 225
Diderot, 35, 206
Diet: for inmates in poor health, 81, 85; as
provided by 1785 regulation, 176; of
poor, debilitating, 230. *See also* Food
Dillon, Arthur Richard de (archbishop of
Narbonne), 56, 113, 131, 133
Directory, Revolutionary government of,
253
Disability: as cause of begging, 8, 11, 17,
19, 22; request for information on
inmates with, 85; hand-mills provide
work in case of, 95, 241; feigned (see
"*Piètre*"), *See also* Infirm beggars;
Insane; Invalids
Discipline: Le Trosne on, 40; Bertier on,
80; De Prémion on, 89; in general
contract, 99; at Soissons, 109, 201;
almsbureaus provide framework for,
147; for *pionniers*, 151, 243; *concierges*
and, 169; *régie* reinforces, 180; Turgot
rules out military, for *pionniers*, 243–
44; regulated, 246; and respect for

Esmangart, Charles François Hyacinthe
(intendant of Caen), favors *dépôt* at
Beaulieu, 142
Estates, provincial: challenge to *dépôts*
from, 107, 110–18, 164, 172. See also
Pays d'états
Estates of Brittany, 244; hear report on
mendicity (1786), 14; and funds for
dépôts, 113, 115; condemn *dépôts,* 116;
intendant and, 143; demand public
accountability for *dépôts,* 168; denounce
''Bastilles for the people,'' 217–18;
denounce exploitation of inmates, 236,
245, 247
Estates of Burgundy asked to contribute
funds for *dépôts,* 111
Estates of Languedoc, 136; preserve
municipal forms, 43; debate *dépôts,* 107;
fund *dépôts* conditionally, 112;
responsible for ''economic''
administration of *dépôts,* 113; elicit
assurances from Turgot, 118, 131;
Brienne's views shaped in, 145–46;
Bertier and Necker respond to, 162;
object to *dépôts,* 172; block use of funds
outside of province, 213; and discussion
of workshops, 245
Estates of Provence: reject funding of
dépôts, 116; claim payments from 1724,
117; argue ''municipal'' measures
suffice, 164; Bertier cites claim of, 165–
66
Estates-General of 1789, 222, 227; called,
217; *cahiers* of, and *dépôts,* 218; attack
upon, feared, 223
Exercise, 87
Experiment: Bertier proposes, 67; Laverdy
and, 86; data and, 233
Exploitation: of worker, 202, 219, 236; of
poor by rich, 209. *See also* Contract,
general, for provisioning of *dépôts;*
Earnings of inmates

Family, 71; economy of, 8, 11; police
support discipline of, 20–21. *See also*
Children; Father, authority of; Women
Famine plot: mentality of, 221–22; in
revolutionary pamphlets, 223
Father, authority of, 154
Faure, Edgar (historian), 156

Favier (first secretary of intendant of
Soissons), 194, 203, 205–6; 224–27
Faye, Sieur (doctor at Limoges), 126
Femmes et filles de mauvaise vie (women
and girls of ill repute), 20, 88, 214. *See
also* Venereal disease; Women
Fénélon, François de Salignac de La
Mothe, 33, 234
Fevers, 210
Feydeau de Marville, Claude Henri
(councillor of state), 45, 46
Finance. *See* Accounts; Alms bureaus;
Assistance, public; Nation; Parish
responsibility for relief; Poor tax; Royal
domain; Royal treasury, commitments by
Laverdy from; Three deniers per livre of
the taille; Uniformity
Financial accounting for *dépôts:* intendant
and, 82; Bertier and, 83, 84, 85;
monthly and quarterly, 85; overseer and,
177
Flanders: charitable reforms of Charles V
in, 28; Declaration of 1750 in, 32;
charitable measures in, 124; Malesherbes
cites, 154; Montlinot also cites, 189;
traditions of social policy in, 193;
Calonne in parlement of, 199
Flesselles, Jacques de: as intendant of
Brittany, 55, 113; as intendant of Lyons,
172; as *prévôt des marchands,* 222
Fleury, de. *See* Joly de Fleury
Floating population, 9
Fondations. See Endowments; Foundations
Fontainebleau, 159
Fontette, Jean-François Orceau de
(intendant of Caen), 52, 142
Food: Dupichard on, 96; in report to
Academy of Sciences, 171; in *régie
économique,* 177; Montlinot supplies
''healthy and very common,'' 201. *See
also* Diet; Provisioning; Rations for
inmates
Forbonnais. *See* Véron de Forbonnais,
François
Forms, standard: 78; printed, for surety
bonds, 71, 79; and *maréchaussée,* 76,
78; for management records, 81, 85; for
alms bureaus of Toulouse, 147–48
Foucault, Michel: and ''the Great
Confinement,'' 29; and the *''réseau
d'écritures''* (network of writing), 80;

Montlinot and the "disciplinary" model of, 202; on clinical observation, 232

Foullon, Joseph François (father-in-law of L.-B.-F. de Bertier de Sauvigny): and Turgot, 129; slain, 220; in pamphlets, 222–24

Foundations: critique of charitable, 33; de Fleury proposes reform of, 50; Bertier says *dépôts* not permanent, 108; Boullongne oversees, 130. *See also* Endowments

Foundlings and orphans: in Brienne's memoir, 139; as wards of state, 142; to be fed with goat's milk, 153, 157; Necker on feeding of, 195; at *dépôt* of Soissons, 195; to become citizens, 219; Necker has Montlinot survey, 238

Franche-Comté, 45

Franciade, District of, and *dépôt* of St. Denis, 253

Fraternity, 254

Fraude pieuse: pleasure of consumption as, 198; government and, 257

Freedom: rehabilitation and denial of, 79; and *pionniers,* 155; to consume, 201; spheres of, limited, 203; public assistance and, 257, 258

Free industry, workshops for poor compete with, 204, 240. *See also* Work projects outside of *dépôts*

Free market: utilitarian view of, 125; public assistance and, 126; as basis for Turgot's reforms, 134; produces new "slave class" according to Linguet, 192; workshops at Soissons as microcosm of, 208; and surveillance, 233

Free men and women: inmates at Soissons paid as if, 198; can perform all labor, 242; people believe themselves, 257

Free trade in grain, 39, 123–25,129; limits to efficacy of, 135; as remedy for mendicity, 143. See also *Laisser-faire;* Physiocrats

French Revolution, 9, 27

Fresnais, subdelegate at Rennes, 86, 88, 89, 120, 168

Galiani, abbé Ferdinando, 81, 123, 190

Galleys: released convict from, 25; penalty before 1764, 30, 38, 40; Le Trosne recommends as penalty for men, not

women, 41; subdelegate of Guise favors, 43; as penalty in Declaration of 1764, 49, 108; as penalty in draft edict of 1765, 59–62; Bertier on sentences to, 71, 79; *dépôt* as alternative to, 75, 76; too severe as penalty for beggars, 146; rejected by parlement as penalty, 150; deaths of vagabonds in, 206; forced labor and, 242. *See also* Vagabonds

Gallois de la Tour, Charles Jean-Baptiste des (intendant of Provence), 117, 118

Gambling, 184, 191

Gangs or bands of beggars, 10, 60, 151

Garat, Dominique-Joseph: reviews Montlinot's published accounts, 232, 236, 247; as minister of interior, 253

Gardes françaises, 245, 253

Gellée de Prémion (subdelegate of Nantes): critical of charitable endowments, 54; and *dépôt* at Nantes, 87–89; and workshop at Tours, 98; on abuses in arrests, 120

General Assembly of Police, 123–24

Gens sans aveu, 18. *See also* Vagabonds

Girls, 207

Gojard, Achille-Joseph (*premier commis* of controller-general), 173

Gournay, Vincent de, 124

Government: role in assuring well-being, viii; faults of, cause mendicity, 149; "interpreter and depository of social harmony" (Necker), 204. *See also* Administration

Grains: provisions of, 99; milling of, 124; shortages of, 134, Terray and, 233. *See also* Subsistence

Grand Bureau des Pauvres (Paris), 29

Granier (nineteenth-century inspector of prisons), 254

Great Fear of 1789, 10, 220

Grégoire, Henri (abbé), 223

Grenoble, 254; Colombier visits, 174, 246. *See also* Sassenage, work project at

Guérin, Jean, on confinement, 30, 34

Guerre des farines (1775), 135

Guichetiers (turnkeys), 84

Guignard de Saint-Priest, Jean Emmanuel de (intendant of Languedoc), 148; and Estates, 56, 118, 172; and finance of *dépôts,* 112, 114, 213